Parallel Processing for Computer Vision and Display

Parallel Processing for Computer Vision and Display

Edited by
P.M. Dew
Department of Computer Studies, University of Leeds
R.A. Earnshaw
University Computing Service, University of Leeds
T.R. Heywood
IBM UK Scientific Centre, Winchester

ADDISON-WESLEY PUBLISHING COMPANY

Wokingham, England • Reading, Massachusetts • Menlo Park, California
New York • Don Mills, Ontario • Amsterdam • Bonn
Sydney • Singapore • Tokyo • Madrid • San Juan

Cover designed by Crayon Design of Henley-on-Thames with illustration by Charlie Brown.
Cover printed by The Riverside Printing Co. (Reading) Ltd.
Text designed by Lesley Stewart.
Typeset by Colset Private Limited, Singapore.
Printed and bound in Great Britain by The Bath Press, Avon.

First printed 1989.

British Library Cataloguing in Publication Data

Parallel processing for computer vision and
display.
1. Computer systems. Graphic displays.
Applications of parallel-processor systems.
I. Dew, P.M. II. Earnshaw, R.A. (Rae A.)
III. Heywood, T.R.
006.6

ISBN 0-201-41605-0

Library of Congress Cataloging in Publication Data

Parallel processing for computer vision and display / edited by P.M.
Dew, R.A. Earnshaw, T.R. Heywood.
p. cm.
Papers presented at the International Conference on Computer
Vision and Display, held at University of Leeds on 12-15 January
1988.
Bibliography: p.
ISBN 0-201-41605-0
1. Computer vision–Congresses. 2. Parallel processing
(Electronic computers)–Congresses. I. Dew, P. M. II. Earnshaw,
Rae A., 1944- . III. Heywood, T. R. (Tom R.) IV. International
Conference on Computer Vision and Display (1988 : University of
Leeds)
TA1632.P38 1989
006.3′7–dc19 88-36982
CIP

Preface

Introduction

The widespread availability of high performance computers has led to an increased awareness of the importance of visualization techniques particularly in engineering and science [1]. However, many visualization tasks involve processing large amounts of data or manipulating complex computer models of 3D objects. For example, in the field of computer aided engineering it is often necessary to display and edit solid objects (see Plate 1) which can take many minutes even on the fastest serial processors. Another example of a computationally intensive problem, this time from computer vision, is the recognition of objects in a 3D scene from a stereo image pair. To perform visualization tasks of this type in real and reasonable time it is necessary to exploit the advances in parallel processing that have taken place over the last decade. This book uniquely provides a collection of papers from leading visualization researchers with a common interest in the application and exploitation of parallel processing techniques.

The last decade has seen the emergence of processor arrays and networks as practical computing engines for many of the low level tasks in computer vision and graphics. This has resulted in a number of special-purpose architectures such as the Pixel Plane machines (see the contribution of *Fuchs et al.*). As the issues have become better understood more general-purpose, programmable SIMD array computers have emerged, such as the AMT DAP series and Thinking Machines' Connection Machine (see the contributions by *Smallbone* and *Crow et al.* in this book). These machines exploit **fine grain** parallelism using the SIMD model of computation. They consist of a large array of simple 1-bit processors where each processor executes the same instruction at each cycle. For example, the AMT DAP is currently available as a 32×32 or 64×64 array of processors and much larger arrays are planned for the future. In contrast, processor networks constructed from programmable microprocessors such as the INMOS transputer exploit **coarse grain** parallelism. They are a subclass of the general class of MIMD machines [2]. Applications for both SIMD and MIMD processor networks/arrays are discussed in the book. As a general conclusion, it would appear that the fine grain SIMD processor arrays are well suited to the low level image processing and image generation computations. This is because the computations are very regular and involve mainly integer arithmetic. On the other hand, the coarse grain MIMD processor array networks are more suited to the higher level computations involving geometric models such as ray tracing and image reconstruction algorithms. These computations are highly dependent on the data and normally require floating-point arithmetic. An interesting solution that is emerging is to consider a hybrid architecture that supports both the SIMD and MIMD paradigms. This is discussed in a number of chapters in this book.

The book provides a state-of-the-art survey of the application of processor network architectures to problems in Computer Vision and Display. Much work still needs to be done to develop a sound understanding of parallel algorithms and architectures for visualization problems. A promising new highly parallel architecture for pattern recognition is neural networks [3]. This is beyond the scope of this book. An active and important research topic is the development of methodology for the design of parallel programs that can be mapped onto a variety of parallel computers. This will lead the way to the development of parallel software architectures that will provide the visualization researchers with powerful environments to exploit the new opportunities afforded by parallel computing. The program 'Apply' (see the contribution by *Deutch et al.*) is an example of what can be achieved for a very specific application class, namely the local image-to-image computations. At the other extreme, many computer scientists believe that functional and object-oriented languages provide a general-purpose interface from which application specific interfaces can be developed.

Research into the application of parallel processing techniques to visualization problems is gaining momentum as the availability of parallel computers becomes more widespread. The editors believe that the contributions in this book provide a valuable pointer to the research issues in this area.

About the book

The book has been divided into five sections. The first section contains a collection of papers concerned with the **theory and practice of processor networks**. The contributions reflect important parallel processing research which is of relevance to the subject of this book. For example, *Kung and Lam* discuss the problems of developing a linear systolic array compiler for the CMU Warp machine. *Eker and Tucker* illustrate how the emerging theory for the specification and verification of synchronous algorithms can be applied to the Pixel Plane architectures. The remaining papers in this section propose new architectures, analyse algorithms for a processor network and discuss applications not covered elsewhere in the book.

The second section discusses **parallel architectures for vision and image processing**. It describes recent research aimed at constructing the next generation of fine-grain SIMD processor array architectures that exploit Ultra Large Scale Integration (ULSI) and Wafer Scale Integration (WSI). For example, *Krikelis and Lea* discuss associative string architectures that promise more cost effective machines than the traditional SIMD processor array. Other topics include benchmarking for the CMU Warp machine (*Deutch et al.*) and exploring the dual SIMD and MIMD paradigms (*Page*).

Recent work in devising **parallel algorithms for higher level computer vision and image processing computation** is discussed in the next section. The subject is still in its infancy. Contributions include descriptions of parallel algorithms for labelling, segmentation and pattern recognition.

Section 4 is concerned with **high performance techniques for image synthesis**. The papers included in this section are mainly, though not exclusively, concerned with rendering polygonal models using conventional graphical techniques. This area has seen a rapid growth in the last few years and a comprehensive account of the research issues is provided. *Fuchs et al.* discuss the next generation of the Pixel Plane architecture which will widen its applicability to more sophisticated modelling techniques such as constructive solid geometry. The Pixel Plane architectures exploit spatial parallelism. In contrast, *Grimsdale* reports on recent work to build a highly pipelined VLSI architecture for the classical 3D graphics pipeline. *Theoharis and Page* and *Cheng* also make contributions to this subject. *Crow* and *Smallbone* take a different approach and report on the use of the Connection Machine and AMT DAP respectively for image synthesis. Finally, the problems of developing a graphics library on a multiprocessor workstation are discussed by *Tanner et al.* and *Felger et al.*

The final section reports on recent research to apply **parallel processing techniques to the visualization of 3D models**. It is mainly concerned with improving the performance of high quality image-rendering techniques for 3D solid models and for reconstructing 3D models. *Kunii et al.* describe techniques for partitioning the computations into tasks which can be implemented on a coarse-grain processor network. *Kedem and Ellis* report on the current status of the Ray-Casting Machine which is a customized VLSI architecture for rendering solid objects modelled using constructive solid geometry. The contribution by *Barton* describes his early experiences in developing graphics applications on a transputer array. This is followed by a comprehensive set of papers on parallel algorithms for ray tracing, many of which have been implemented on a transputer-based machine. Finally, the problems involved in developing parallel algorithms for image reconstruction are discussed.

Audience

This book is suitable as a reference book for visualization scientists, computer scientists and professionals interested in finding out about parallel processing techniques for image processing and reconstruction, computer vision, computer graphics and geometrical modelling. It is also suitable as a supporting textbook for a course on advanced computer graphics, computer vision and parallel processing.

Acknowledgements

This book contains a selection of papers that were initially presented at the International Conference on Computer Vision and Display, held at the University of Leeds on 12–15 January 1988. The conference attracted over 50 contributions from the USA, UK and 10 other countries, and was attended by approximately 250 researchers in the field. The authors would like to thank their industrial and academic cosponsors of the conference: IBM UK Laboratories Ltd, British

Computer Society, Computer Graphics Society and Eurographics. They also thank the School of Computer Studies, Department of Mechanical Engineering, University Computing Service and the Centre for Theoretical Computer Science at Leeds University for their support and encouragement. Particular thanks are due to Mr D. Hutchinson, Professor A. de Pennington and Professor M. Wells.

A large number of people helped with the conference and special thanks are due to: Dr Michael Wozny for providing an interesting and stimulating after-dinner speech; Mrs Frances Johnson and Mr Brian Booker in the Commercial Office of Leeds University for handling the secretarial arrangements for the conference and exhibition; Dr David Morris, Mr John Davy and Mr Nick Holliman for organizing the conference demonstrations; Mr Han Wang, Mr Chris Davis and Mr Martin Hepworth for providing the audio/visual technical support; Ms Kate Perry and Mrs Judith Thursby for secretarial support with the academic programme and production of this book.

We thank all those who refereed papers for the conference and this book, and especially thank the following colleagues at the University of Leeds and elsewhere for all their help and support: Dr R.D. Boyle, Dr K.W. Brodlie, Mr C. Chan, Dr T.J. Fountain, Mr N.S. Holliman, Mrs L.J. Manning, Dr K. McEvoy, Dr W.R. Moore, Dr D.T. Morris, Miss C.A. Pogue, Dr G. Oliver, Mr J.H. Race, Dr M.B. Sandler and Dr. R. Thomas.

Peter M. Dew
Rae A. Earnshaw
Tom R. Heywood

20 February 1989

[1] Visualisation in Scientific Computing – A Synopsis. From a report by the National Science Foundation Advisory Panel on Graphics, Image Processing and Workstations. *IEEE Computer Graphics and Applications*, **7**(7), July 1987, 61–70

[2] Hwang K. and Briggs F.A. (1984). *Computer Architecture and Parallel Processing*. Maidenhead: McGraw-Hill

[3] Anderson J.A. and Rosenfeld E. (1988). *Neurocomputing: Foundation of Research*. Cambridge MA: MIT Press

Contents

Section I

Processor Networks: Theory and Practice

1 · An approach to automatic generation of linear systolic array programs

H.T. Kung
M. Lam

Carnegie Mellon University

The process of developing applications on a parallel computer consists of two main steps: allocation of the computation across the processors, and implementation of the allocation decision. While the former step is usually quite simple and intuitive, but may require insight into the specific application, the latter step is often error prone and time consuming. This chapter outlines an approach to automatic generation of efficient linear systolic array programs, using the users' advice on allocation of computation.

1.1 Introduction

Recently, various parallel machines supporting different computation models have been built; among them are the Hypercube, the transputer, the Connection Machine and the Warp systolic array. However, the use of parallel machines is not widespread and the potential computation power of these machines has not been fully exploited. One of the barriers in the use of parallel machines is the difficulty in developing parallel applications. This chapter proposes an approach to automating the task of programming fine-grain parallel machines.

The target machine model for this chapter is the linear systolic array. The Warp systolic array [1] is an example of such a machine. The linear systolic array is chosen because of its simple structure as seen by a user, and our extensive application experience with Warp. We show that efficient parallel programs for many applications that operate on data matrices can be generated automatically. The technique described here exploits the parallelism within the loops of a program. Information necessary to support this technique can be derived from sequential programs, using global flow analysis techniques similar to those used in vectorizing compilers. The technique can be used with other programming languages, as long as the same information can be made available.

We partition the code compilation problem into two phases: allocation of computation across the array, and the actual implementation of the allocation scheme. In the course of using the Warp machine, we have discovered several simple yet powerful allocation schemes. In this chapter, we describe these allocation schemes and the considerations required to make allocation decisions. Our experience in developing applications on Warp indicates that while the allocation step is usually quite simple and intuitive, the implementation step is error prone and time consuming. We show here that once the allocation decisions are made, either by an earlier phase in the compiler or by the user, the steps of implementing these allocation schemes can be automated.

Our basic approach is as follows. Processors, or cells, in a systolic array, can only operate on their own local data. It is the algorithm designer's responsibility to map the data space of the computation (which we call the **global** data space) onto the **local** data space of the cells. The designer manages data caching at program design time. If sharing of data is necessary, 'cache coherency' is maintained by explicit cell communication. In our approach, this data caching is implemented at compile time.

Two levels of abstraction are used in the generation of parallel programs. The first abstraction is that each cell can transfer data between its own local data space and the global data space via COPY operations. Within this abstraction, called the COPY abstraction, code optimizations to reduce the latency of the computation and the data transfer between cells are performed. In the second abstraction, machine features to implement data movements are visible. COPY operations are implemented using the set of machine primitives available. Using this approach, regular computation, such as innermost loops in scientific computation, can be mapped into efficient fine-grained parallel code; inherently sequential, data-dependent code will simply be mapped onto just one cell.

The technique is different from other systolic array synthesis tools. Previously, automatic synthesis has been demonstrated to be possible for regular recurrences such as matrix multiplication [2, 3, 4, 5]. The main concern was in mapping specific algorithms onto a regular layout of simple, identical hardware components. The target machine model was custom hardware implementation using VLSI technology. The computation performed by each cell was regular, repetitive and data-independent. The problem of generating code for a *linear, programmable* systolic array is significantly different. The allocation of computation to processors is much simpler; however, the synthesis technique must handle complex, irregular computations and allow for the complex cell timing of a programmable processor. The technique proposed here has a greater scope of applicability than previous techniques; in particular, all sequential programs can be mapped onto the array, although inherently sequential code segments will be executed slowly owing to the absence of parallelism in the computation.

Our approach is closer to Cytron's DOACROSS compilation technique [6]. In the DOACROSS technique, iterations of a loop are spread across the processors of a shared memory multiprocessor. Here, we spread the iterations across processors with partitioned memory. The compile-time data-caching problem is specific to the processor array architecture.

In the following, we first walk through the compilation process. Two program examples are used to illustrate the entire process. A summary describing the general procedure and discussing the strengths and weaknesses of the approach follows.

1.2 Overview of compilation steps

The compilation process is structured as follows:

(1) Allocate computation across cells in the array.
(2) Translate the single-cell program to a multi-cell program.
(3) Optimize the multi-cell program using the COPY abstraction.
(4) Generate individual cell programs using machine primitives.

Step 1 is the allocation phase, whereas the other three steps constitute the implementation phase.

1.2.1 Allocation

We illustrate the allocation phase with our first program example: polynomial evaluation. Suppose we wish to evaluate the polynomial:

$$C_0x^m + C_1x^{m-1} + \ldots + C_m$$

for $x_0, x_1, \ldots, x_{n-1}$. By Horner's rule, the polynomial can be reformulated from a sum of product terms into an alternating sequence of multiplications and additions:

$$((C_0x + C_1)x + \ldots + C_{m-1})x + C_m$$

A sequential program based on Horner's rule for evaluating a polynomial of degree $m = 99$ for $n = 1000$ data points is shown in Figure 1.1. This computation can be mapped onto a parallel implementation by distributing the evaluations of the polynomial to different cells. This mapping can be succinctly represented by annotating the loops with allocation decisions (enclosed in curly braces). When we specify {across 0:9} on a loop, we mean that the iterations are evenly divided between cell 0 to cell 9, with cell 0 taking the first set of iterations, and 9 taking the last.

```
for i := 0 to 999 do begin {across 0:9}
   y[i] := 0.0;
end;

for j := 0 to 99 do begin
   for i := 0 to 999 do begin {across 0:9}
      y[i] := y[i] * x[i] + c[j];
   end;
end;
```

Figure 1.1
Polynomial evaluation program with allocation annotations.

1.2.2 Single- to multi-cell program

After the computation has been allocated across the array, we proceed to transform this single-cell program into a multi-cell program. A naive, inefficient multi-cell program is first generated in a straightforward manner. The inefficient multi-cell program for polynomial evaluation is shown in Figure 1.2.

Figure 1.2
Inefficient multi-cell program for polynomial evaluation.

```
ON cell := 0 to 9 do begin
   for i := 0 to 99 do begin
      y[i] := 0.0;
   end;
   COPY (y[0:99], $y[cell*100:cell*100+99]);
end;

for j := 0 to 99 do begin
   ON cell := 0 to 9 do begin
      COPY ($y[cell*100:cell*100+99], y[0:99]);
      COPY ($x[cell*100:cell*100+99], x[0:99]);
      COPY ($c[j], c[j]);
      for i := 0 to 99 do begin
         y[i] := y[i] * x[i] + c[j];
      end;
      COPY (y[0:99], $y[cell*100:cell*100+99]);
   end;
end;
```

We introduce a new construct here: the ON construct. For example, the statement:

```
ON cell := 0 to 9 do begin
...
end;
```

means that the body within the construct is first executed on cell 0, followed by cell 1, and up to cell 9. The semantics, called the **sequential semantics**, is that the computations on the cells are performed sequentially. At any one time, only one cell is active; the order of execution is the same as the original program. The only difference is that the computation must be done on different cells. This strict order of sequential execution will be relaxed below.

Each cell can operate only on local data; data communication with other cells is specified through the COPY operations. The COPY primitive enables the cell to transfer values of global variables in the original program to the cell's local variables, and to update global variables with the values of the local variables. In the multi-cell program, all global variables are distinguished by an initial dollar sign ($) in their names.

More precisely, the steps to mapping a single- to multi-cell program are:

(1) Copy all necessary global variables accessed in the cell code into local variables at the beginning of the cell code segment.

(2) If the cell code updates any of the global variables, the newest value is copied back at the end of the cell code segment.

It is obvious that the multi-cell program, under the sequential semantics, is equivalent to the original program in the sense that these two programs carry out the same computation. However, as pointed out above, the sequential semantics means that only one cell can be active at any one time. In the following, we introduce another set of semantics, called **parallel semantics**, for the multi-cell program. The program under the parallel semantics is equivalent to the program under the sequential semantics, but the parallel semantics allows the cells to execute in parallel.

The executions of two cell programs need to be synchronized only if one program uses results from the other. Since data communication between cell programs are through the COPY operations, this data dependency relation can be derived from the COPY operations in the program (or from the original information, on which the insertion of COPY operations was based). The parallel semantics is that the computation on the cells are performed in parallel as long as the data dependency, as defined by the COPY operations (under the sequential semantics), is maintained.

With the parallel semantics, we see that all cell programs in the multi-cell program in Figure 1.2 can execute in parallel, since each program updates a disjoint subset of global variables. For the rest of the paper, only the parallel semantics will be used.

1.2.3 Multi-cell program optimizations

The naive multi-cell programs generated in the previous step are, in general, extremely inefficient, and must be optimized. There are two major optimization criteria: minimizing communication and maximizing throughput.

Minimizing communication

Optimizations of multi-cell programs rely on data dependency information extracted from the original program. A formal discussion on data flow analysis and data dependency representation is outside the scope of this paper. In the following, we only describe the optimizations in an informal manner, specifying the condition in which an optimization can be applied and the optimization itself.

Consider the program in Figure 1.2. We observe that a cell copies the value of the global variable $x into its local space in each iteration of the second nested loop. As $x remains constant throughout the loop, the same values are copied every iteration. The communication can be reduced by simply initializing the local variables with the global variable values before the loop starts.

Next, we observe that the values copied out to $y at the end of each iteration in the second nested loop are only to be brought back in and overwritten by the same

Figure 1.3
Multi-cell polynomial evaluation program after applying two optimizations.

```
ON cell := 0 to 9 do begin
    for i := 0 to 99 do begin
       y[i] := 0.0;
    end;
    COPY (y[0:99], $y[cell*100:cell*100+99]);
end;

ON cell := 0 to 9 do begin
    COPY ($x[cell*100:cell*100+99], x[0:99]);
    COPY ($y[cell*100:cell*100+99], y[0:99]);
end;

for j := 0 to 99 do begin
   ON cell := 0 to 9 do begin
       COPY ($c[j], c[j]);
       for i := 0 to 99 do begin
          y[i] := y[i] * x[i] + c[j];
       end;
   end;
end;

ON cell := 0 to 9 do begin
    COPY (y[0:99], $y[cell*100:cell*100+99]);
end;
```

cell in the next iteration. Therefore, we can simply omit the execution of the COPY primitive at the end of all but the last iteration, and the COPY primitive executed at the beginning of all but the first iteration. The results of applying the two optimizations are shown in Figure 1.3.

The latter optimization described can be applied a second time to eliminate the redundant pair of copies between the first and second nested loops. The final multi-cell program is shown in Figure 1.4.

Maximizing throughput

To illustrate the optimization of maximizing throughput, we use the second program example of this paper: solution of elliptic partial differential equations using Successive Over-Relaxation (SOR). Consider the following equation:

$$\frac{\partial^2 u}{\partial x^2} + \frac{\partial^2 u}{\partial y^2} = f(x,y)$$

The system is solved by repeatedly combining the current values of u using the following recurrence:

```
On cell := 0 to 9 do begin
    for i := 0 to 99 do begin
        y[i] := 0.0;
    end;
end;

ON cell := 0 to 9 do begin
    COPY ($x[cell*100:cell*100+99], x[0:99]);
end;

for j := 0 to 99 do begin
    ON cell := 0 to 9 do begin
        COPY ($c[j], c[j]);
        for i := 0 to 99 do begin
            y[i] := y[i] * x[i] + c[j];
        end;
    end;
end;

ON cell := 0 to 9 do begin
    COPY (y[0:99], $y[cell*100:cell*100+99]);
end;
```

Figure 1.4
Multi-cell polynomial evaluation program after all optimizations.

$$u'_{i,j} = (1 - \omega)u_{i,j} + \omega \frac{f_{i,j} + u_{i,j-1} + u_{i,j+1} + u_{i+1,j} + u_{i-1,j}}{4}$$

Figure 1.5 shows a sequential program that executes ten relaxations for 100 × 100 unknowns. The allocation scheme used in the implementation on Warp is to allocate a relaxation to each cell. This allocation decision can be simply expressed, as shown in the figure.

The naive multi-cell program is shown in Figure 1.6(a). There is little concurrency in this program. The computation of each cell starts by copying the $u array into the local data space, and finishes by updating the $u array. A cell therefore cannot start until the previous cell is finished. The lack of concurrency is due to the large grain size in data communication. We can improve the throughput by having a cell compute and output data as it receives data. In general, we want to input as late as possible, and output as soon as possible. To achieve this, it is necessary to break up array variables into subarrays, and handle these subarrays independently. Figures 1.6(b) and (c) show the application of the optimizations starting with the outermost control construct and working inwards.

1.2.4 Generation of individual cell programs

From a multi-cell program, we generate individual cell programs. Each cell program consists of only the code executed on the cell, and the control constructs in which the

Figure 1.5
Program of SOR.

```
for p := 0 to 9 do begin {across 0:9}
   for i := 0 to 99 do begin
      for j := 0 to 99 do begin
         u[i, j] := g(f[i, j],u[i, j],u[i-1, j],u[i, j-1],u[i, j+1],u[i+1, j]);
      end;
   end;
end;
```

code is nested. The implementation of the COPY primitive and the 'global' variables is machine dependent, and generally efficiency can be traded off for ease of implementation. For example, an easy implementation calls for allocating all global variables to a 'master' cell, which has the most up-to-date values at all times. Every COPY primitive is translated into an input and output on the master and on the cell involved. Or, in a more efficient implementation, global data can reside on different cells, at different times, and data may be transferred between any pairs of cells. In the SOR example above, the recognition that the data consumed by a cell is produced by the preceding cell leads to routeing the data directly between neighboring cells. This implementation is especially efficient on Warp, since the machine has dedicated hardware queues capable of performing flow control

Figure 1.6
Optimizing the multi-cell SOR program.

(a)

```
ON cell := 0 to 9 do begin
   COPY ($u[0:99,0:99], u[0:99,0:99]);
   COPY ($f[0:99,0:99], f[0:99,0:99]);
   for i := 1 to 98 do begin
      for j := 1 to 98 do begin
         u[i,j] := g(f[i,j],u[i,j],u[i-1,j],u[i,j-1],u[i,j+1],u[i+1,j]);
      end;
   end;
   COPY (u[0:99,0:99], $u[0:99,0:99]);
end;
```

(b)

```
On cell := 0 to 9 do begin
   COPY ($u[0:1,0:99], u[0:1,0:99]);
   for i := 1 to 98 do begin
      COPY ($u[i+1,0:99], u[i+1,0:99]);
      COPY ($f[i,0:99], f[i,0:99]);
      for j := 1 to 98 do begin
         u[i, j] := g(f[i,j],u[i,j],u[i-1,j],u[i,j-1],u[i,j+1],u[i+1,j]);
      end;
      COPY (u[i,0:99], $u[i,0:99]);
   end;
end;
```

(c)

```
On cell := 0 to 9 do begin
    COPY ($u[0:1,0:99], u[0:1,0:99]);
    for i := 1 to 98 do begin
        COPY ($u[i+1,0:1], u[i+1,0:1]);
        for j := 1 to 98 do begin
            COPY ($u[i+1,j+1], u[i+1,j+1]);
            COPY ($f[i,j], f[i,j])
            u[i, j] := g(f[i,j],u[i,j],u[i-1,j],u[i,j-1],u[i,j+1],u[i+1,j]);
            COPY (u[i,j], $u[i,j]);
        end;
    end;
end;
```

between each pair of cells. The cell programs written in the Warp programming language, W2 [7], are shown in Figure 1.7.

```
cellprogram SOR (cellid : 0 : 9)
begin

    for i := 0 to 1 do begin
        for j := 0 to 99 do begin
            receive (L, X, u[i,j]);
        end;
    end;
    for j := 0 to 99 do begin
        send (R, X, u[0,j]);
    end;
    for i := 1 to 98 do begin
        receive (L, X, u[i+1, 0];
        receive (L, X, u[i+1, 1];
        send (R, X, u[i,0]);
        for j := 1 to 98 do begin
            receive (L, X, u[i+1,j+1]);
            receive (L, Y, f[i,j]);
            send (R, Y, f[i,j]);
            u[i,j] := g(f[i,j],u[i,j],u[i-1,j],u[i,j-1],u[i,j+1],u[i+1,j]);
            send (R, X, u[i,j]);
        end;
        send (R, X, u[i,99]);
    end;
    for j := 0 to 99 do begin
        send (R, X, u[99,j]);
    end;
end;
```

Figure 1.7
Warp cell programs for SOR.

1.3 Summary of the approach

1.3.1 Allocation

The proposed approach is driven by our observation that many numerical programs can be efficiently parallelized with simple allocation schemes, which map sequential code segments to different cells. Iterative statements are given special attention because most of the computation time is spent inside innermost loops. A loop statement is not treated as an atomic object; iterations of a loop can be spread across different cells. Allocation of a loop takes the following form:

```
across l:u by s
```

It means that the iterations are distributed between cell l to cell u with swathe size s. If there are more swathes than cells, the distribution is wrapped around. If the swathe size is not specified, it simply means that the iterations are spread evenly across the range of cells.

There are several useful and general heuristics in allocation. The primary concern is to maximize concurrency between cell programs. Therefore, we want to spread the computation along the nesting level that allows the cells to start computing as soon as possible. That is, we want to minimize the **initiation interval** between the computations of the cells. For example, if there is a loop in which there is no data dependency between iterations, it is often a good idea to spread that loop across the cells. Each cell is simply loaded with the data that it requires, and it can then execute independently and concurrently with other cells.

We have addressed only the allocation of computation in this paper, and shown how the computation allocation decisions can be implemented. In general, we can allocate either data or computation. These two types of allocation are often interrelated in the sense that decision in one leads to a decision in the other. Also, there are other secondary performance criteria that must be considered, such as the memory requirement, and the latency of the computation if the number of iterations in the program is small.

1.3.2 Single- to multi-cell programs

The proposed mapping from a single- to multi-cell program is straightforward, relying on no specialized knowledge or specific data access pattern in the program. As we have shown, those sections of code that are amenable to parallel execution can then be optimized later to result in efficient parallel code. This approach allows us to compile entire applications where scalar code is intermixed with parallel code. Previous systolic array synthesis techniques can map perfectly nested loops with regular data dependencies onto systolic arrays of dimensions and sizes fitting the computation perfectly. The examples in this chapter suggest that our approach can also deliver similarly efficient code for these programs. The strength of the approach is in handling the other cases. It can model resident data on the cells better, generate efficient code for a sequence of loops, and handle scalar code within a program more gracefully.

1.3.3 Multi-cell program optimization

There are two major optimization criteria: minimizing communication and maximizing throughput. First, the transformation rules in minimizing communication can be succinctly represented as:

(1) COPY (v1,v2); COPY (v1,v2) ==> COPY (v1,v2)

(2) COPY (v1,v2); COPY (v2,v3) ==> COPY (v1,v3)
provided v2 is not used again.

(3) COPY (v1,v1) ==> nil

Rule 1 states that if the same COPY operations are repeated, and that the source variable is not updated by any intervening COPY operations, then one of them can be removed. This rule is applied to remove the copying of the $x variable in the loop of the polynomial evaluation example. Rule 2 states that if data is copied into a variable so that it can be copied to a third variable, then the intermediate copy can be eliminated if it is not used elsewhere. Rule 3 states that if the source and destination variable of a COPY operation are identical, then the operation can be eliminated. The combination of Rules 2 and 3 is applied in the polynomial evaluation example by copying the $y variable only once before and once after the second loop.

In both optimizations to reduce communication and increase throughput, it may be necessary to partition the manipulation of a data array into operations on smaller subarrays. This decomposition is useful in reducing communication because different parts of an array may have different properties. For example, if part of the array to be copied into the local space is resident on the cells already, we can eliminate part of the data traffic. Similarly, if part of an array is not used immediately, we can delay its input to increase parallelism in the computation. The use of this optimization is shown in the SOR example. The basic mechanisms to implement these optimizations are similar.

1.3.4 Generating individual cell programs

The COPY operations in an optimized multi-cell program need to be implemented within the constraints of the given machine architecture. A key issue is to decide where global variables should be allocated. Some simple heuristics can be used, such as allocating a global variable to the cell which accesses the variable most frequently. After all the global variables have been allocated, code for individual cells to synchronize their accesses to the global variables can be generated. Cells may also need to be synchronized in order to preserve the data dependency in the multi-cell program. On the Warp architecture, synchronization is done through the input data queues of each cell. Synchronization and data movements between non-adjacent cells must be routed explicitly by all cells in between. In the follow-on VLSI implementation of Warp – the iWarp – hardware support is provided to route data and enforce synchronization between two arbitrary cells automatically.

Conclusions

Improved support of program development is absolutely necessary before benefits of parallel computing can be realized in many applications. We outline an approach to achieving automatic parallel code generation for linear systolic arrays. One important result is that we have identified a useful level of abstraction in describing a parallel program: sequential programs with advice on allocation of computation. The commonly-used allocation schemes are simple and can be expressed easily. The allocation decisions can be derived automatically or easily supplied by a user who desires a better control over the allocation process.

The second phase of the compilation process carries out the mundane and error-prone process of generating individual cell programs. Our experience with developing applications on Warp indicates that such a tool would greatly accelerate the implementation of applications on the machine. Our initial investigation suggests that the optimizations required to implement the allocation decisions efficiently are viable. The state-of-the-art compiler technology already allows us to implement some of the proposed optimizations on some of the simpler problems. Since the scheme of mapping single-cell code to multi-cell code and to individual cells code is rather straightforward, implementation of a compiler that generates code for all sequential programs, and efficient code for special cases, is within reach. Such a compiler would provide a framework for the development of more sophisticated optimizations, while supporting the development of new applications on parallel machines.

Acknowledgements

The research was supported in part by Defense Advanced Research Projects Agency (DOD) monitored by the Space and Naval Warfare Systems Command under Contract N00039-87-C-0251, and in part by the Office of Naval Research under Contracts N00014-87-K-0385 and N00014-87-K-0533.

References

1. Annaratone M., Arnould E., Gross T. *et al.* (1987). The Warp Computer: architecture, implementation and performance. *IEEE Transactions on Computers*, **C-36**(12), 1523–38
2. Chen M. (1983). *Space-Time Algorithms: Semantics and Methodology.* Technical Report 5090:TR:83, California Institute of Technology
3. Delosme J.-M. and Ipsen I.C.F. (1986). Design methodology for systolic arrays. In *Proc. SPIE Sym.*, pp. 245–59. San Diego CA, August 1986
4. Fortes J.A.B. and Moldovan D.I. (1985). Parallelism detection and transformation techniques useful for VLSI algorithms. *Journal of Parallel and Distributed Computing*, **2**(3), 277–301
5. Quinton P. (1984). Automatic synthesis of systolic arrays from uniform recurrent equations. In *Proc. 11th Annual Symposium on Computer Architecture*, pp. 208–14. Ann Arbor MI, June 1984

6. Cytron R.G. (1984). Compile-time scheduling and optimization for asynchronous machines. *PhD Thesis*, University of Illinois at Urbana-Champaign
7. Gross T. and Lam M. (1986). Compilation for a high-performance systolic array. In *Proc. of the SIGPLAN 86 Symposium on Compiler Construction*, 27–38. ACM SIGPLAN, June 1986

S.M. Eker
J.V. Tucker

University of Leeds

2· Specification and verification of synchronous concurrent algorithms: a case study of the Pixel Planes architecture

We describe some simple mathematical tools for the formal specification and verification of synchronous hardware, and illustrate their use in a case study of the Pixel Planes architecture. The tools are based on the theory of recursive functions on many-sorted algebras and are independent of particular specification languages. To verify Pixel Planes we introduce a new technique for verifying the composition of synchronous networks. A detailed top-down verification of the architecture is presented.

2.1 Introduction

A **synchronous concurrent algorithm** is an algorithm based on a network of modules and channels, computing and communicating data in parallel, and synchronized by a global clock. Synchronous algorithms process infinite streams of input data and return infinite streams of output data. Examples of synchronous concurrent algorithms include systolic algorithms (Kung, 1982); neural nets (McCulloch and Pitts, 1943; Minsky, 1967); cellular automata (Codd, 1968; Soulie *et al.*, 1987) and clearly much clocked digital hardware.

In this chapter, we will consider this informal general concept of a synchronous concurrent algorithm and, by means of a detailed case study of some graphics hardware, show how to:

(1) specify formally the architecture and behaviour of a synchronous concurrent algorithm, and

(2) verify that the algorithm correctly meets its specifications.

In particular, we will examine the top-down specification and bottom-up verification of algorithms. The case study is based upon a part of the Pixel Planes architecture of Fuchs and Poulton: see Fuchs and Poulton (1981); Fuchs *et al.* (1982); Fuchs *et al.* (1985); Poulton *et al.* (1985); and Weste and Eshraghian (1985).

The techniques used are general and can be applied to a wide range of examples; they have been applied to rasterization algorithms and architectures in Eker and Tucker (1988), for instance. They are based on a mathematical theory of synchronous concurrent computation due to Tucker and Thompson: see Thompson and Tucker (1985, 1988a, 1988b), Hobley *et al.* (1988), and the comprehensive account in Thompson (1987).

This mathematical theory is based on the observation that a synchronous concurrent algorithm of interest has a simple and elegant formalization by means of **simultaneous primitive recursive functions over abstract algebras**. The basic idea is as follows. Given a synchronous concurrent algorithm, the data sets, clock and functions that specify the component modules of the algorithm are combined to form a many-sorted algebra A. This A defines an abstract data type over which the algorithm is constructed. The algorithm is then defined by simultaneous primitive recursive functions over the algebra A augmented with infinite streams. The mathematical theory leads to formal systems of use to several formal machine-oriented approaches to hardware specification and verification, including higher-order logic as in Hanna and Daeche (1986) and Gordon (1988); for other approaches see the collections Milne and Subrahmanyam (1986) and Birtwhistle and Subrahmanyam (1988). It also leads to a new approach, based on many-sorted logic. The simultaneous recursive functions over many-sorted algebras, their representability in many-sorted logic and use in program verification were first studied in Tucker and Zucker (1988) (work of 1979).

In addition to hardware verification, there is also complementary work on software tools in Martin and Tucker (1987); specification theory in Harman and Tucker (1987, 1988a, 1988b); and architectures and their compilation theory in Meinke (1988).

The structure of this chapter is as follows. In Section 2.2, we describe a general model of synchronous concurrent computation informally, and we explain the structure of a basic part of Pixel Planes. In Section 2.3, the simultaneous primitive recursive functions on an abstract data type are defined in order to formalize the synchronous concurrent algorithms. In addition, we introduce simple user specifications for the input-output (I/O) behaviour of certain architectures.

In Section 2.4, we introduce sequential and parallel composition operators on user specifications and on the synchronous concurrent algorithms that implement them. We give **soundness theorems** that state that operations on algorithms correspond with operations on specifications. This is a fairly involved piece of general theory that is necessary for top-down design and bottom-up verification. The material of Sections 2.3 and 2.4 is directly relevant to several approaches to formal verification of hardware.

In Section 2.5, we begin the study of Pixel Planes by defining a data type specification and a user specification for the **linear expression evaluator** (LEE). This specification is decomposed into simpler specifications based on a single generic module. This generic module is implemented in Section 2.6.

In Section 2.7, we perform the verification by proving that the generic module implementation algorithm correctly meets its specification and, by applying our soundness theorems, we deduce that the compiled architecture, obtained by substituting the algorithm for the generic module, correctly meets its specification.

The prerequisites of this chapter are the elements of data type theory, logic and, of course, parallel computation in hardware.

2.2 Informal description of synchronous algorithms and Pixel Planes

In this section, we introduce the idea of a synchronous concurrent algorithm and give an informal description of the Pixel Planes linear expression evaluator as a synchronous algorithm.

2.2.1 Intuition

Consider a synchronous algorithm as a network of **sources**, **modules** and **channels** computing and communicating data, as depicted in Figure 2.1. For simplicity, we will assume that all the data is drawn from a single set A. The network has a global discrete clock $\mathbf{T} = \{0, 1, \ldots\}$ to synchronize computations and the flow of data between modules. There are c sources labelled $s_1, \ldots, s_c$, and k modules labelled $m_1, \ldots, m_k$. The sources perform no computation; they are simply input ports where fresh data arrives at each clock cycle. Each module m_i has $p(i)$ inputs and a single output as depicted in Figure 2.2. The action of a module m_i is specified by a function:

$$f_i : A^{p(i)} \to A$$

If the diagram in Figure 2.1 is to be a **graph** then edges may not branch. Thus where the output of a module is required as an input to several other modules, extra output channels that copy the value must be added to the module. (There are a number of conventions available to handle this point.) Results are read out from a subset of the modules $m_{\alpha(1)}, \ldots, m_{\alpha(d)}$ which may be termed output models or **sinks**.

The interconnections between the sources and modules are represented by a pair of partial functions:

$$\gamma : \mathbf{N}_k \times \mathbf{N} \to \{S, M\}$$

and:

$$\beta : \mathbf{N}_k \times \mathbf{N} \to \mathbf{N}$$

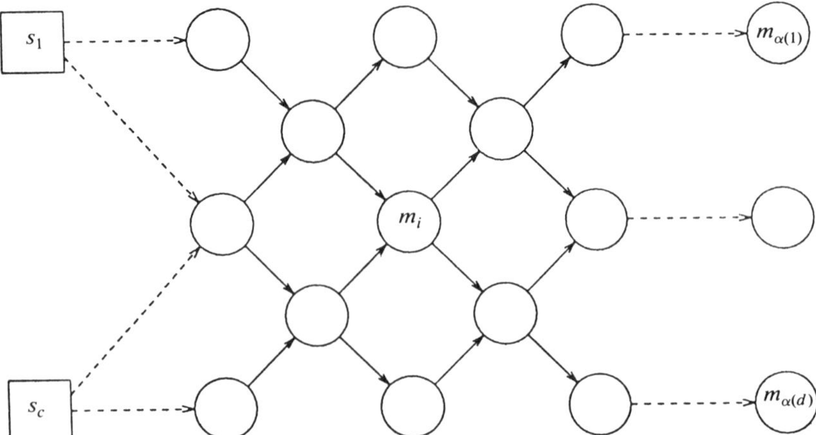

Figure 2.1
A synchronous algorithm as a network.

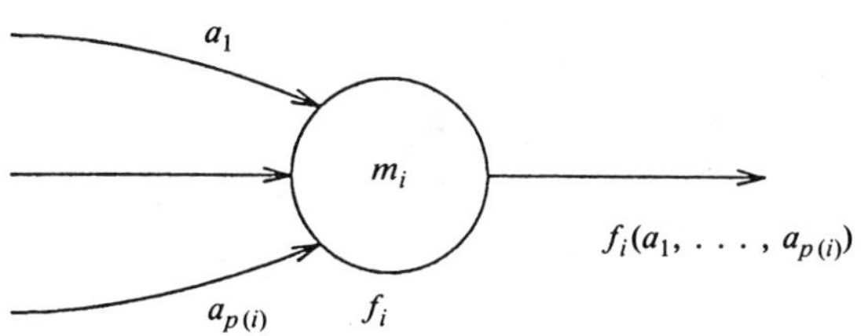

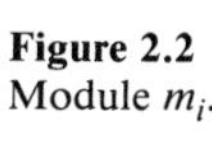
Figure 2.2
Module m_i.

where $\mathbf{N}_k = \{1, 2, \ldots, k\}$. Intuitively, $\gamma(i, j) = S$ indicates that the jth input to module m_i comes from a source whereas $\gamma(i, j) = M$ indicates that it comes from another module. The index of the source or module in question is given by $\beta(i, j)$.

To ensure that our networks are well defined, we impose the following conditions on γ and β:

$$\forall i \forall j[(1 \leqslant i \leqslant k) \wedge (1 \leqslant j \leqslant p(i)) \rightarrow \beta(i, j)\downarrow] \tag{2.1}$$

$$\forall i \forall j[(1 \leqslant i \leqslant k) \wedge (1 \leqslant j \leqslant p(i)) \rightarrow \gamma(i, j)\downarrow] \tag{2.2}$$

$$\forall i \forall j[(\gamma(i, j) = S) \rightarrow (1 \leqslant \beta(i, j) \leqslant c)] \tag{2.3}$$

$$\forall i \forall j[(\gamma(i, j) = M) \rightarrow (1 \leqslant \beta(i, j) \leqslant k)] \tag{2.4}$$

Here the notation $\beta(i, j)\downarrow$ means that $\beta(i, j)$ is defined on the specified arguments i, j given in the expression. The first two conditions ensure that β and γ are defined for every input of every module. The latter two conditions ensure that the sources or modules named by β and γ actually exist.

We will assume that each module is initialized with a well-defined output assigned to its output channel. Thus the initial state of the network is an element $b \in A^k$ and we will use the notation b_i to denote the initial value of the output of module m_i for $i = 1, \ldots, k$.

In terms of our intuitive picture, new data are available at each source, and new results at each sink, at every tick of the global clock $\mathbf{T}$. Thus the algorithm processes infinite sequences or streams of data. A stream $a(0), a(1), \ldots$ of data from A is represented by a map $a: \mathbf{T} \rightarrow A$ and the set of streams of data is represented by the set $[\mathbf{T} \rightarrow A]$ of all such maps. Thus we will specify the I/O behaviour of an architecture, initialized by b, by a mapping:

$$V_b: [\mathbf{T} \rightarrow A^c] \rightarrow [\mathbf{T} \rightarrow A^d]$$

that maps streams of data into streams of data. We call V_b a **stream transformer** and the **I/O specification** of the algorithm.

2.2.2 Representing stream algorithms

We represent each module m_i by a **value function** v_i: $\mathbf{T} \times [\mathbf{T} \rightarrow A^c] \times A^k \rightarrow A$. Intuitively, $v_i(t, a, b)$ represents the output of module m_i at time t, when the network is initialized with values b and is computing on the input stream a. The function v_i is specified as follows:

$$v_i(0, a, b) = b_i$$

$$v_i(t + 1, a, b) = f_i(arg_1, \ldots, arg_{p(i)})$$

where for $j = 1, \ldots, p(i)$:

$$arg_j = \begin{cases} a_{\beta(i,j)}(t) & \text{if } \gamma(i, j) = S \\ v_{\beta(i,j)}(t, a, b) & \text{if } \gamma(i, j) = M \end{cases}$$

We can now write down the I/O specification of the algorithm V_b when initialized with values b and executed on input stream a as:

$$V_b(a)(t) = (v_{\alpha(1)}(t, a, b), \ldots, v_{\alpha(d)}(t, a, b))$$

where $\alpha(1), \ldots, \alpha(d)$ are the labels of the sinks.

2.2.3 Conventions

Looking at the synchronous network depicted in Figure 2.1, a number of conventions are involved in this informal notation that are motivated by the formalization, by means of the value functions above. In particular, channels do not branch and modules only have a single distinct output value. Where the output of a module is required in several places, we need separate channels which carry duplicate outputs of the module in question. In the Pixel Planes example later on, we will find it convenient to draw networks with more than one distinct output value and branching channels (such networks are no longer graphs). When we formalize these networks as shown above, we deal with this pictorial convention in the following way: modules with more than one distinct output are split into separate single output modules, one for each output, and each module takes all the inputs of the original (see the translation in Figure 2.3); branching channels are replaced by a set of non-branching channels, one for each of the branches of the original (see the translation in Figure 2.4).

2.2.4 Informal description of Pixel Planes' linear expression evaluator

In this section, we discuss one example of a synchronous algorithm which we will analyse later using the formal tools described in the next section. This algorithm is the **linear expression evaluator** (LEE) section of the Pixel Planes architecture which

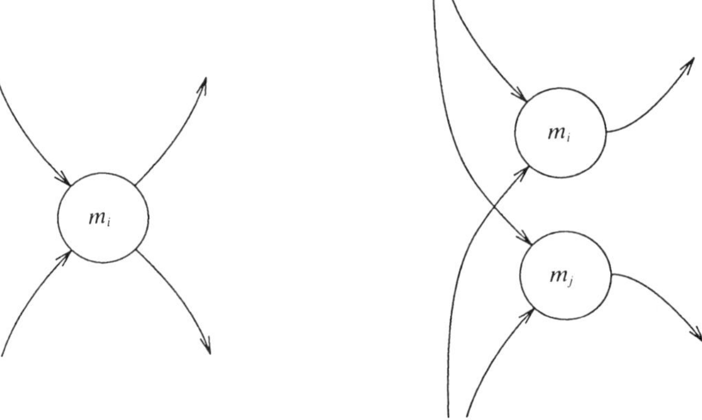

Figure 2.3
Splitting modules with more than one output.

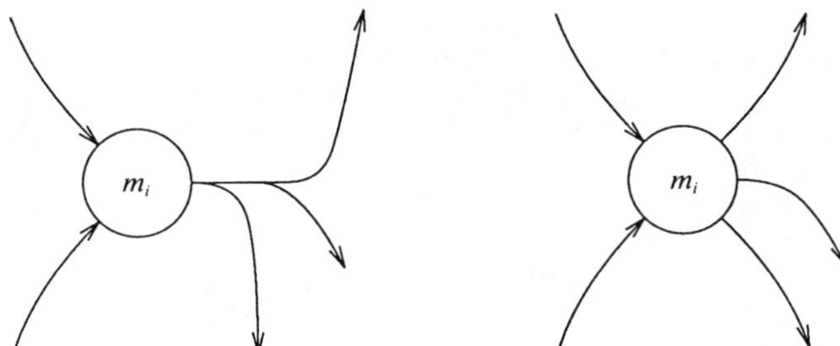

Figure 2.4
Replacing branching channels.

is a graphics engine described in Fuchs and Poulton (1981) and Fuchs *et al.* (1982). Further extensions are described in Fuchs *et al.* (1985) and implementation details are given in Poulton *et al.* (1985). A view of current experimental and commercial VLSI graphics systems, including Pixel Planes, is given in Fuchs (1988). We shall examine the algorithm in its 'pure' form without the modifications (such as super trees) required to implement it in current VLSI technology.

The Pixel Planes LEE has the task of taking an input stream:

$$(a(0), b(0), c(0)), (a(1), b(1), c(1)), \ldots$$

of triples of numbers, and generating in parallel for each point (x, y) on a discrete $n \times m$ grid, the stream:

$$a(0)x + b(0)y + c(0), a(1)x + b(1)y + c(1), \ldots$$

of values of the linear expression $ax + by + c$. This is shown diagrammatically in Figure 2.5. At this top level of description it is enough to assume that input and output data are numbers (such as integers or reals); in more specific accounts, including the original paper, the input and output data are bit representations.

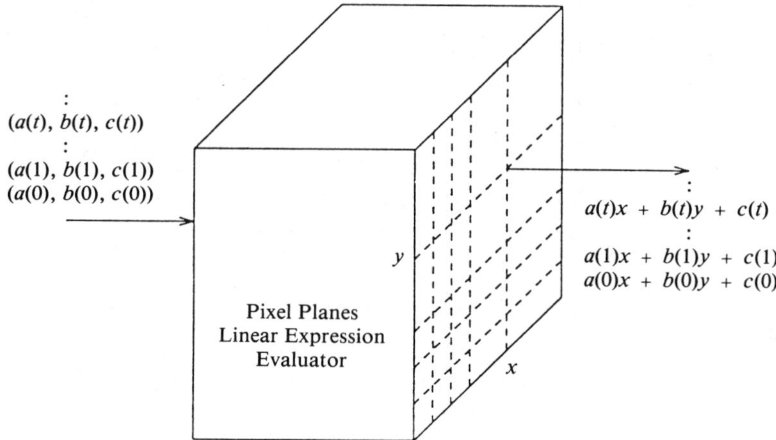

Figure 2.5
Pixel Planes LEE.

The architecture that implements this specification consists of 1D LEE modules which evaluate $v + uz$ on an input (u, v) for each value of z. Note that the 2D expression $ax + by + c$ is evaluated as $(c + ax) + by$. The way the 1D LEE modules are connected together to perform this is shown in Figure 2.6, with the 1D LEE modules represented by triangles. Each output of the first 1D LEE module, which computes the $ax + c$ terms in parallel for each value of x, is connected to a 1D LEE module, which adds the by term in parallel for each value of y.

The internal structure of the 1D LEE module is shown in Figure 2.7. To understand how it works, we will make a digression and consider a 3-bit serial–parallel multiplier. This is shown in Figure 2.8 and consists of three Carry-Save Adders (CSA) with and-gates (&). We assume that there is a one cycle delay on each of the CSA outputs in order to make the design synchronous. The device computes $A \times B + C$, where $A = A_2A_1A_0$ and $C = C_2C_1C_0$ arrive sequentially and $B = B_2B_1B_0$ is present on the inputs throughout the computation. The output is generated sequentially.

The usual way of explaining how this circuit works is to say that the first two clock cycles initialize the circuit so that the value C is read into the register formed by the CSAs. At each successive cycle, we consider that a copy of B is added to the register contents if the current bit of A is 1 and the register contents are shifted right one place, any carry bits being held over until the next addition. Hence, all the partial products of the bits of A and B are computed in turn and added together with the carry bits produced at the correct relative positions in the output word.

We notice that if a particular bit of B is zero, the corresponding CSA is unused so we can modify the design using multiplexors (MUX) and delays (Δ) to obtain the equivalent circuit shown in Figure 2.9.

Suppose we now view the way it works as follows. Each CSA is considered in isolation as a serial adder, computing the sum of its input from the left and the A sequence of bits. Because of the leading zeros on the A input, the output of the first

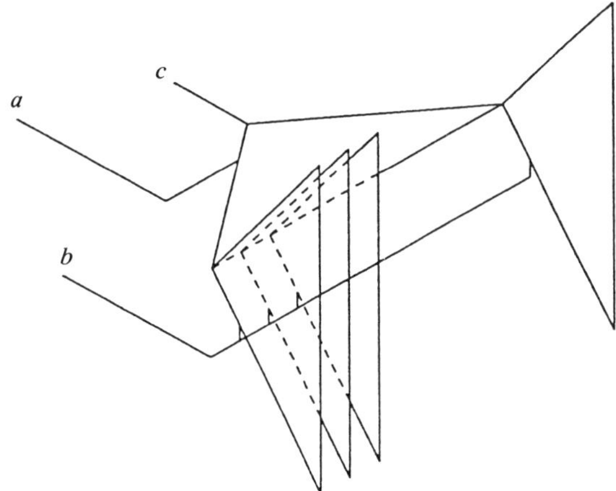

Figure 2.6
Connection of 1D LEE modules.

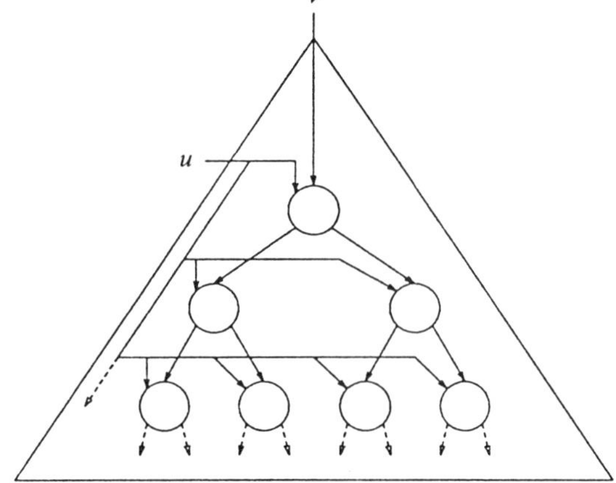

Figure 2.7
Internal structure of 1D LEE module.

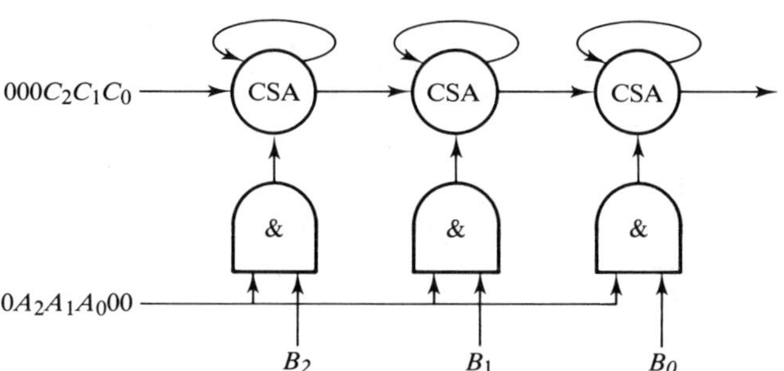

Figure 2.8
Three-bit serial–parallel multiplier.

adder is actually $C + 2^2 \times A$. If the input to the second adder is D, then its output will be $D + 2^1 \times A$ because of the relative delays between the A and D inputs. For the same reason, if the input to the final adder is E then its output will be $E + 2^0 \times A$. Now whether the output of each adder or its delayed left input is propagated to the next stage is controlled by the bits of B which are fed into the multiplexors. We can then view this process as classical binary multiplication.

The crucial idea behind the 1D LEE module is that instead of propagating *either* the added *or* unadded result of each stage, according to the particular value of B present on the inputs, we propagate both to take care of all values of B. This means that at each stage we have two ways to continue the computation, and this naturally gives rise to a binary tree structure. If we consider the design shown in Figure 2.7, we see that the u input corresponds to A and the v input corresponds to C in Figure 2.9. The B input of Figure 2.9 of course disappears, since we have a device that generates an output for each possible value of B simultaneously. The circle components of Figure 2.7 are, as we shall see, just CSAs with an extra 'unadded' output. The unadded result is passed through the left output and the added result is passed through the right one. In order to be initialized correctly, the stored bits in the tree modules must be initialized to zero and the u argument must be preceded by a sequence of zero bits of length one less than the height of the tree.

The structure of the tree nodes is shown in Figure 2.10. The left output is simply the top input delayed by one clock cycle. The right output is formed by adding the two inputs, together with the carry bit saved from the previous addition.

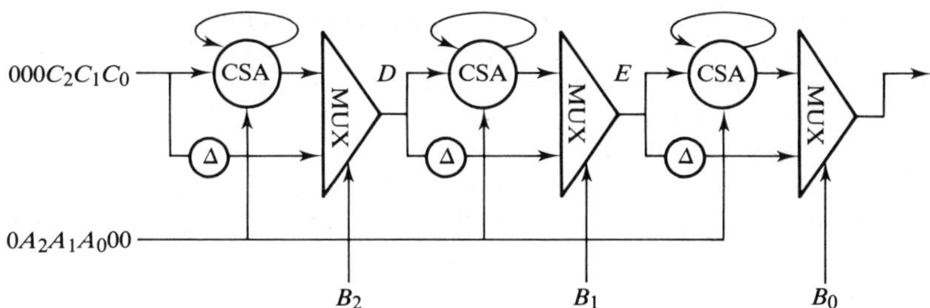

Figure 2.9
Modified circuit using multiplexors and delays.

Figure 2.10
Tree nodes structure.

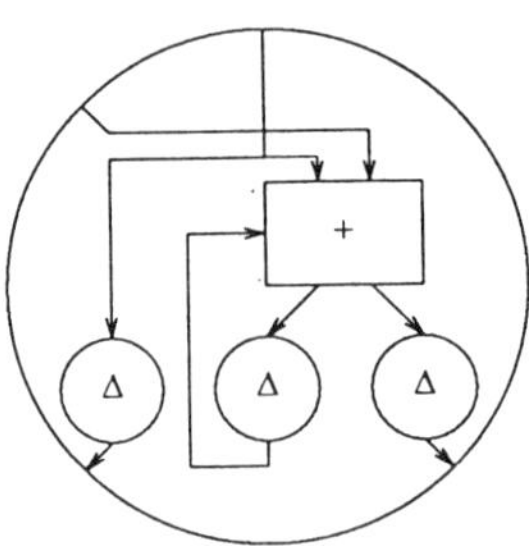

2.2.5 Levels of abstraction

To specify formally a synchronous algorithm, we first need to specify an algebra which defines data and the operations which may be performed on data by the modules. In the case of the general synchronous algorithm described in Section 2.2.1, this algebra is made from the single data set A, clock **T** and booleans **B** equipped with the functions:

$$f_i\colon A^{p(i)} \to A$$

specifying the actions of the modules m_i for $i = 1, \ldots, k$ and some simple functions such as the clock tick $t + 1$. (For the equations of Section 2.2.2 that define the algorithm to be constructed from this algebra, we must also add the streams $[\mathbf{T} \to A]$ with the operation of stream evaluation to form an algebra $\underline{A}$.) The algebra defines what details of the algorithm will be highlighted and what details will be abstracted away, that is, the level of abstraction of the algorithm.

For example, with the Pixel Planes LEE, we could, at the lowest level, choose an algebra of bits and bit streams and appropriate bit operations. In this case, the inner workings of the tree nodes will be visible, together with details such as the trailing zeros on the multiplicand, and the formal specification will correspond closely to the real world implementation of the architecture.

Alternatively, at a higher level, we could choose an algebra of integers and integer operations such as addition and multiplication, in which case such bit level representation detail will disappear from the specification, and the problem of the feedback loop within the tree nodes will disappear, simplifying correctness proofs. The price paid for this abstraction is that explicit multiplication modules and extra delays must be included in the specified architecture, since the implicit multiplication by powers of two by delaying the bit stream is no longer present.

At the highest level, we could choose an algebra of integers where the simultaneous evaluation of the polynomial in the manner of the 1D LEE modules is itself a primitive operation. This abstracts away the internal tree structure of the LEE module and only the connections between them are then visible.

For our specification and correctness proof in later sections, the structure we choose is a more general version of the second option: we work with a class of algebras axiomatized by just the properties required to prove the architecture correct.

2.3 Formal definition of synchronous algorithms

In this section, we show how the informal method of defining synchronous algorithms presented in Section 2.2 may be formalized in an algorithmic language, and we also define user specifications. This formal approach to the definition is necessary because:

(1) We require a machine-representable and executable formalization, and

(2) We need to compute not on a single structure but on a class of algebras.

This class is the semantics of the abstract data type defined by the data and the component modules. It can be the class of *all* algebras that conform to a set of axioms which specify the data type: this will be the case for the LEE architecture that computes on all rings or semi-rings, for example. Or it can be the class of all isomorphic copies of a particular algebra: this is often the case when computing over the integers.

2.3.1 Abstract data types and primitive recursive functions

To represent and analyse synchronous algorithms formally, we need to define a formal algorithmic description language that allows us to represent the functions v_i and the equations seen in Section 2.2.2. The language we will use is based on generalizing the simultaneous primitive recursive functions on **N** to an abstract data type A.

Recall from Section 2.2.1 that the data processed by the algorithm comes from a set A and that the component modules compute a set of functions $f_1, \ldots, f_k$ on A. Together, these define the level of abstraction of the algorithm which can be formalized by an **abstract data type**: we create an algebra with domain A and basic operations $f_1, \ldots, f_k$; and consider it unique only up to isomorphism, see ADJ (1978) and Ehrig and Mahr (1985).

A synchronous concurrent algorithm will now be defined by its value functions $v_1, \ldots, v_k$ on the abstract data type A, augmented with time $\mathbf{T} = \{0, 1, \ldots\}$ and the booleans $\mathbf{B} = \{tt, ff\}$ and suitable operations on these two sets. First, let A denote the three-sorted algebra obtained from the data set and the functional specifications of the modules together with the clock **T**, consisting of $\{0, 1, \ldots\}$ with constant 0 and operation $succ(t) = t + 1$; and the booleans **B**, consisting of $\{tt, ff\}$ with constants tt and ff, and operations $\wedge$ (and) $\neg$ (not). The class of functions used to formally represent the $v_1, \ldots, v_k$ is the class $PR(A)$ of *simultaneous primitive recursive functions on an algebra A* which are defined as follows.

Let D and R be any Cartesian products of the three domains of the algebra A.

(1) *Constants*: for each constant c^A of A, the function $f(a) = c^A$, where $a = (a_1, \ldots, a_n) \in D$, is in $PR(A)$.

(2) *Primitive operations*: for each operation σ^A of A, the function $f(a) = \sigma^A(a)$, where $a = (a_1, \ldots, a_n) \in D$, is in $PR(A)$.

(3) *Projections*: for each $n > 0$ and each i such that $n \geqslant i > 0$, the function $f(a) = a_i$, where $a = (a_1, \ldots, a_n) \in D$, is in $PR(A)$.

(4) *Definition by cases*: for each domain A_s of A, the function:

$$f(b, a_1, a_2) = \begin{cases} a_1 \text{ if } b = tt \\ a_2 \text{ if } b = ff \end{cases}$$

where $b \in \mathbf{B}$ and $a_1, a_2 \in A_s$, is in $PR(A)$.

(5) *Vectorization*: for each $n > 0$ and each sequence of functions $f_1, \ldots, f_n$ in $PR(A)$ sharing the same domain D, the function $f(a) = (f_1(a), \ldots, f_n(a))$ is in $PR(A)$.

(6) *Composition*: for each function g in $PR(A)$ with range D and each function h in $PR(A)$ with domain D, the function $f(a) = h(g(a))$ is in $PR(A)$.

(7) *Primitive recursion*: for each function $g: D \to R$ in $PR(A)$ and each function $h: \mathbf{T} \times D \times R \to R$, in $PR(A)$, the function f defined by:

$$f(0, a) = g(a)$$

$$f(t + 1, a) = h(t, a, f(t, a))$$

is in $PR(A)$.

We will now define an algorithmic language *PR* whose semantics is based on this class of functions.

2.3.2 Abstract syntax of *PR*

We define the abstract syntax of *PR* to be the collection of $PR(\Sigma)$ of **function terms** or **programs** over any many-sorted signature Σ. Each Σ consists of a set $S = \{s_1, \ldots, s_n\}$ of sort names, and a family of disjoint sets:

$$\Sigma = \langle \Sigma_{w,s}: w \in S^*, s \in S \rangle$$

Here each set $\Sigma_{w,s}$ contains constant names, in the case where w is λ the empty string, or function names otherwise. For our purposes, we will assume that S contains at least T (to name $\mathbf{T}$), B (to name $\mathbf{B}$) and that the appropriate sets $\Sigma_{w,s}$ contain the names of the usual operations on these sorts. Given $\Sigma = \langle S, \Sigma \rangle$ we define the family of sets $PR_{u,v}(\Sigma)$ of function programs of type $u \to v$ inductively as follows:

(1) *Constants*: for all $w \in S^+$, for all $s \in S$, for all $c \in \Sigma_{\lambda,s}$:

$$c^w \in PR_{w,s}(\Sigma)$$

(2) *Primitive operations*: for all $w \in S^+$, for all $s \in S$, for all $\sigma \in \Sigma_{w,s}$:

$$\sigma \in PR_{w,s}(\Sigma)$$

(3) *Projections*: for all $w \in S^+$ such that $w = s_1 \ldots s_n$, for all $i \in 1, \ldots, n$:

$$U_i^w \in PR_{w,s_i}(\Sigma)$$

(4) *Definition by cases*: for all $s \in S$:

$$DC_s \in PR_{Bss,s}(\Sigma)$$

(5) *Vectorization*: for all $u \in S^+$, for all $v \in S^+$ such that $v = s_1 \ldots s_n$, for each vector $(\alpha_1, \ldots, \alpha_n)$ with $\alpha_j \in PR_{u,s_j}(\Sigma)$ for $n \geqslant j \geqslant 1$:

$$vec(\alpha_1, \ldots, \alpha_n) \in PR_{u,v}(\Sigma)$$

(6) *Composition*: for all $u, v, w \in S^+$, for all $\alpha \in PR_{w,v}(\Sigma)$, for all $\beta \in PR_{u,w}(\Sigma)$:

$$comp(\alpha, \beta) \in PR_{u,v}(\Sigma)$$

(7) *Primitive recursion*: for all $u, v \in S^+$, for all $\alpha \in PR_{u,v}(\Sigma)$, for all $\beta \in PR_{Nuv,v}(\Sigma)$:

$$prim(\alpha, \beta) \in PR_{Nu,v}(\Sigma)$$

We can now define the set $PR(\Sigma)$ of all syntactically correct PR function terms or programs by:

$$PR(\Sigma) = \bigcup_{u,v \in S^+} PR_{u,v}(\Sigma)$$

2.3.3 Semantics of *PR*

The semantics of $PR(\Sigma)$ is defined over a many-sorted algebra A which models Σ. The algebra A comprises a family of sets $Carr(A) = \langle A_s : s \in S \rangle$ indexed by S and a collection of mappings $Ops(A)$. We introduce the notation A^w, where $w \in S^*$, $w = s_1 \ldots s_n$ to stand for the Cartesian product $A_{s_1} \times \ldots A_{s_n}$. Then for all $w \in S^*, s \in S$, for each $\sigma \in \Sigma_{w,s}$ there exists $\sigma^A \in Ops(A)$ such that $\sigma^A : A^w \to A_s$; σ^A is called the interpretation of σ in A. In symbols:

$$A = \langle Carr(A), Ops(A) \rangle$$

We will assume that $A_N = \{0, 1, \ldots,\}$ has basic operations 0, $n + 1$ (that is it is isomorphic to Presburger arithmetic); and that $A_B = \{tt, ff\}$ together with its basic operations is the standard interpretation **B** of the booleans.

The semantics of $PR(\Sigma)$ can now be defined by a map:

$$[\![\ ]\!]_A : PR(\Sigma) \to PR(A)$$

where $PR(A)$ is the collection of functions computable by $PR(\Sigma)$ expressions interpreted over the algebra A. In general, if $\alpha \in PR_{u,v}(\Sigma)$ then $[\![\alpha]\!]_A : A^u \to A^v$. We define the semantics by induction on the syntactic structure of program:

(1) *Constants*:

$$[\![c^w]\!]_A : A^w \to A_s \quad \text{where } c \in \Sigma_{\lambda,s}$$

$$[\![c^w]\!]_A(a) = c^A$$

(2) *Primitive operations*:

$$[\![\sigma]\!]_A : A^w \to A_s \quad \text{where } \sigma \in \Sigma_{w,s}$$

$$[\![\sigma]\!]_A(a) = \sigma^A(a)$$

(3) *Projections*:

$$[\![U_i^w]\!]_A : A^w \to A_{s_i} \quad \text{where } w = s_1, \ldots, s_n$$

$$[\![U_i^w]\!]_A(a_1, \ldots, a_n) = a_i$$

(4) *Definition by cases*:

$$[\![DC_s]\!]_A : \mathbf{B} \times A_s \times A_s \to A_s$$

$$[\![DC_s]\!]_A(b, a_1, a_2) = \begin{cases} a_1 \text{ if } b = tt \\ a_2 \text{ if } b = ff \end{cases}$$

(5) *Vectorization*:

$$[\![vec(\alpha_1, \ldots, \alpha_n)]\!]_A: A^u \to A^v \quad \text{where } vec(\alpha_1, \ldots, \alpha_n) \in PR_{u,v}(\Sigma)$$

$$[\![vec(\alpha_1, \ldots, \alpha_n)]\!]_A(a) = ([\![\alpha_1]\!]_A(a), \ldots, [\![\alpha_n]\!]_A(a))$$

(6) *Composition*:

$$[\![comp(\alpha, \beta)]\!]_A: A^u \to A^v \quad \text{where } comp(\alpha, \beta) \in PR_{u,v}(\Sigma)$$

$$[\![comp(\alpha, \beta)]\!]_A(a) = [\![\alpha]\!]_A([\![\beta]\!]_A(a))$$

(7) *Primitive recursion*:

$$[\![prim(\alpha, \beta)]\!]_A: \mathbf{N} \times A^u \to A^v \quad \text{where } prim(\alpha, \beta) \in PR_{Nu,v}(\Sigma)$$

$$[\![prim(\alpha, \beta)]\!]_A(0, a) = [\![\alpha]\!]_A(a)$$

$$[\![prim(\alpha, \beta)]\!]_A(n + 1, a) = [\![\beta]\!]_A(n, a, [\![prim(\alpha, \beta)]\!]_A(n, a))$$

In the case of primitive recursion, a proof is required to justify the existence of the function. This is easy to supply using induction over n (Tucker and Zucker, 1988).

We can now give a formal definition of $PR(A)$:

$$PR(A) = \{[\![\alpha]\!]_A: \alpha \in PR(\Sigma)\}$$

2.3.4 Stream signatures and algebras

The class of functions $PR(A)$ does not include the stream functions used in Section 2.2.2. In order to use PR to specify algorithms, we must extend the abstract data type to include streams. We define the notion of a stream signature and its corresponding algebra. Given a signature $\Sigma = \langle S, \Sigma \rangle$, we define the stream signature $\underline{\Sigma}$ to be $\langle \underline{S}, \underline{\Sigma} \rangle$ where:

$$\underline{S} = S \cup \{T \to s : s \in S\}$$

$$\underline{\Sigma} = \Sigma \cup \{eval_s : s \in S\}$$

The corresponding algebra $\underline{A}$ is A augmented by additional carriers $[\mathbf{T} \to A_s]$ named by $T \to s$ and additional operations $eval_s^{\underline{A}}$ named by $eval_s$ where:

$$eval_s^{\underline{A}}: [\mathbf{T} \to A_s] \times \mathbf{T} \to A_s$$

$$eval_s^{\underline{A}}(\underline{a}, t) = \underline{a}(t)$$

Because $\underline{\Sigma}$ and $\underline{A}$ are standard, $PR(\Sigma)$ and $PR(\underline{A})$ are defined automatically from the general account in Section 2.3.3 above. Now it is easy to check that a synchronous concurrent algorithm is programmable by functions:

$$v_1, \ldots, v_k \text{ in } PR(\underline{A})$$

as defined in Section 2.2.1.

2.3.5 User specifications

In order to be able to prove a given algorithm correct, we need a formal specification of the task which the algorithm is supposed to perform, that is, a **user**

specification which defines the task in terms of outputs required at particular times. Formally, a user specification is a stream transformation of the form:

$$S: [\mathbf{T} \to D] \to [\mathbf{T} \to R \cup \{u\}]$$

where D and R are Cartesian products over the abstract data type A, and u is a special undefined element. Furthermore, for many purposes, including the graphics hardware we are examining here, it is sufficient to assume that the applicative form of S is a vector polynomial over $\underline{A}^u$, the algebra $\underline{A}$ with an unspecified element adjoined to each data set, and hence is a member of $PR(A^u)$. Hence, the algorithm definition and the user specification of the task it performs are written in the same language, over slightly different data types. Often the specification will have a simple structure which can be clearly seen to match our informal intuitive idea of the task, but it will be written in terms of complicated or expensive operations. The algorithm, on the other hand, will be a larger and more complicated function program written in terms of simpler cheaper module operations.

An I/O specification i: $[\mathbf{T} \to X] \to [\mathbf{T} \to Y]$ of an algorithm is said to *directly satisfy* or *directly meet* a user specification S: $[\mathbf{T} \to X] \to [\mathbf{T} \to Y \cup \{u\}]$ if, and only if, for all input streams $\underline{x}$ and $t \geqslant 0$, either:

$$S(\underline{x})(t) = u \quad \text{or} \quad I(\underline{x})(t) = S(\underline{x})(t)$$

There are occasions when the definition of correctness of an algorithm with respect to a specification is more complicated. For example, correctness can involve the scheduling or translation of I/O streams: see Hobley *et al.* (1988) and Meinke (1988).

2.3.6 Simpler user specifications

We define a class of user specifications which we will call **simple user specifications**. These are user specifications that may be written in the following form:

$$S(\underline{x})(t) = \begin{cases} u & \text{if } t' = t - d < 0 \\ s(\underline{x}(t')) & \text{otherwise} \end{cases}$$

where $t' = t - d$ for some $d \geqslant 0$ and s is a polynomial over A of the appropriate functionality. Intuitively, specifications of this kind specify a device which has an initial period of d clock cycles when its output is undefined, and after this the output is the result of applying function s pointwise to the input stream, delayed by d clock cycles. User specifications of this form are closed under a modified form of function composition, and restricted vectorization which will be defined in Section 2.4.

2.3.7 Literature

The primitive recursive functions on the natural numbers first appeared in Dedekind (1888); a basic reference for their theory is Peter (1967). A different definition of the primitive recursive functions in an abstract setting can be found in Engeler (1968). Independently, the simultaneous primitive recursive functions on a many-sorted algebra are included in the study of partial recursive functions on such an algebra in Tucker and Zucker (1988) (work of 1979). The functions were first applied to synchronous concurrent computation (in the case of implementing functions

$f: A^n \rightarrow A^m$ rather than stream transformations) in Thompson and Tucker (1985). This section is based on further collaborative work with B.C. Thompson: see Thompson and Tucker (1988a) and Hobley *et al.* (1988). A comprehensive account of the functions and their use in designing synchronous concurrent algorithms is Thompson (1987). User specifications and their classification are considered in detail in Harman and Tucker (1987) and further applied in Harman and Tucker (1988a, 1988b).

The functional language *PR* is well suited to the specification and verification of synchronous algorithms. A complementary alternative account of synchronous algorithms is possible using a von Neumann language suited to simulation and testing. This language is based on abstract data types, functional routines and concurrent assignments: see Thompson and Tucker (1988b). In Thompson (1987), it is proved to be computationally equivalent with *PR* (with respect to the correctness and performance of implementing functions). An account of the practical development of this second language, into which *PR* will be compiled, is given in Martin and Tucker (1987). A third equivalent approach is to model formally the network architectures using graph theory. This account is suited to the formal study of architectures and layout: see Meinke (1988).

2.4 Constructors for specifications and networks

In order to do the top-down specification and bottom-up verification of architectures, we need ways of decomposing user specifications and equivalent ways of combining simple networks and their I/O specifications. We also need theorems that say that if we decompose a large user specification into simpler ones, and design synchronous networks whose I/O specifications can be proven to satisfy the simpler user specifications, then we can combine these networks to form a large network whose I/O specification meets the large user specification.

There are many possible choices of sets of constructors for combining networks and specifications (Sheeran, 1985, 1986). They offer various trade-offs between theoretical elegance, intuitive interpretations and straightforward representation at the level of module and channel interconnections. We require only simple constructors for Pixel Planes so we do not consider cases where feedback paths occur at the level of interconnections between networks.

The constructors we choose for I/O specifications are normal function composition and vectorization, together with selection operators to do the 'plumbing'. For user specifications and synchronous networks (or rather their formalization as systems of simultaneous primitive recursive equations), we define equivalent constructors.

2.4.1 Composition of user specifications

Let F and G be the following simple user specifications:

$$F: [\mathbf{T} \rightarrow W] \rightarrow [\mathbf{T} \rightarrow X \cup \{u\}]$$

$$F(\underline{w})(t) = \begin{cases} u & \text{if } t_1 = t - d_1 < 0 \\ f(\underline{w}(t_1)) & \text{otherwise} \end{cases}$$

where $t = t - d_1$, and:

$$G\colon [\mathbf{T} \to X] \to [\mathbf{T} \to Y \cup \{u\}]$$

$$G(\underline{x})(t) = \begin{cases} u & \text{if } t_2 = t - d_2 < 0 \\ g(\underline{x}(t_2)) & \text{otherwise} \end{cases}$$

where $t = t - d_2$. Then we define the **user specification composition** $G * F$ of G and F as follows:

$$(G * F)\colon [\mathbf{T} \to W] \to [\mathbf{T} \to Y \cup \{u\}]$$

$$(G * F)(\underline{w})(t) = \begin{cases} u & \text{if } t_3 = t - d_3 < 0 \\ g(f(\underline{w}(t_3))) & \text{otherwise} \end{cases}$$

where $t_3 = t - d_3$ and $d_3 = d_1 + d_2$.

Lemma 2.1

Suppose that a and b are I/O specifications that satisfy user specifications F and G as defined above respectively. Then $b \cdot a$ satisfies $G * F$.

Proof

We consider two cases.

(1) $t < d_1 + d_2$

$$(G * F)(\underline{w})(t) = u$$

So the lemma holds trivially.

(2) $t \geqslant d_1 + d_2$ Now since b satisfies G and $t \geqslant d_2$ (as $d_1 \geqslant 0$):

$$(b \cdot a)(\underline{w})(t) = b(a(\underline{w}))(t) = G(a(\underline{w}))(t) = g(a(\underline{w})(t - d_2))$$

But since a satisfies F and $t - d_2 \geqslant d_1$:

$$\begin{aligned} g(a(\underline{w})(t - d_2)) &= g(F(\underline{w})(t - d_2)) = g(f(\underline{w})(t - d_2 - d_1)) \\ &= g(f(\underline{w})(t - d_3)) = (G * F)(\underline{w})(t) \end{aligned}$$

2.4.2 Vectorization of user specifications

Let F and G be the following simple user specifications with common delay d:

$$F\colon [\mathbf{T} \to W] \to [\mathbf{T} \to X \cup \{u\}]$$

$$F(\underline{w})(t) = \begin{cases} u & \text{if } t' = t - d < 0 \\ f(\underline{w}(t')) & \text{otherwise} \end{cases}$$

$$G\colon [\mathbf{T} \to W] \to [\mathbf{T} \to Y \cup \{u\}]$$

$$G(\underline{w})(t) = \begin{cases} u & \text{if } t' = t - d < 0 \\ g(\underline{w}(t')) & \text{otherwise} \end{cases}$$

Then we define the **user specification vectorization** $\langle F, G\rangle$ of F and G as follows:

$$\langle F, G\rangle\colon [\mathbf{T} \to W] \to [\mathbf{T} \to (X \times Y) \cup \{u\}]$$

$$\langle F, G\rangle(\underline{w})(t) = \begin{cases} u & \text{if } t' = t - d < 0 \\ (f(\underline{w}(t')), g(\underline{w}(t'))) & \text{otherwise} \end{cases}$$

where $t' = t - d$.

LEMMA 2.2
Suppose that a and b are I/O specifications that satisfy user specifications F and G as defined above respectively. Then (a, b) satisfies $\langle F, G\rangle$.

Proof
We consider two cases.

(1) $t < d$

$$\langle F, G\rangle(\underline{w})(t) = u$$

So the lemma holds trivially.

(2) $t \geqslant d$ Now since a satisfies F and b satisfies G:

$$\begin{aligned}(a, b)(\underline{w})(t) &= (F, G)(\underline{w})(t) = (F(\underline{w})(t), G(\underline{w})(t)) \\ &= (f(\underline{w}(t - d)), g(\underline{w}(t - d))) = \langle F, G\rangle(\underline{w})(t)\end{aligned}$$

2.4.3 User specification selection operators

In order to do the 'plumbing' of input and output when user specifications are combined, we define the following subclass of simple user specifications. For $\phi_i \in \{1, \ldots, n\}$:

$$USEL^n_m[\phi_1, \ldots, \phi_m]: [\mathbf{T} \to A^n] \to [\mathbf{T} \to A^m \cup \{u\}]$$

is defined by:

$$USEL^n_m[\phi_1, \ldots, \phi_m](\underline{a}_1, \ldots, \underline{a}_n)(t) = \begin{cases} u & \text{if } t < 0 \\ (\underline{a}_{\phi_1}(t), \ldots, \underline{a}_{\phi_m}(t)) & \text{otherwise} \end{cases}$$

Here the delay d is 0 so $t - d = t$. Each such user specification selection function is satisfied by a selection function:

$$SEL^n_m[\phi_1, \ldots, \phi_m]: [\mathbf{T} \to A^n] \to [\mathbf{T} \to A^m]$$

where $\phi_i \in \{1, \ldots, n\}$ and:

$$SEL^n_m[\phi_1, \ldots, \phi_m](\underline{a}_1, \ldots, \underline{a}_n)(t) = (\underline{a}_{\phi_1}(t), \ldots, \underline{a}_{\phi_m}(t))$$

2.4.4 Composition of networks

Let N and N' be networks of the form given in Section 2.2.1. We consider the construction of a network N'' from N and N' that represents computation with N' followed by computation with N. We will use the notation of Section 2.2.1, with objects referring to N' and N'' distinguished by affixing a prime ('), and double prime (") respectively. If $c = d'$ (where c is the number of sources in N and d' is the number of sinks in N', then we define the composition of N and N' as:

$$N \# N' = N''$$

where N'' is defined as follows: network N'' consists of $k'' = k + k'$ modules m''_i, and $c'' = c'$ sources s''_i. Modules $m''_{\alpha''(1)}, \ldots, m''_{\alpha''(d'')}$ are sinks, where $d'' = d$ and $\alpha''(i) = \alpha(i) + k'$. Each module m''_i has $p''(i)$ inputs where:

$$p''(i) = \begin{cases} p'(i) & \text{if } i \leqslant k' \\ p(i - k') & \text{otherwise} \end{cases}$$

The action of each module m''_i is specified by a function:

$$f''_i\colon A^{p''(i)} \to A$$

where:

$$f''_i(a) = \begin{cases} f'_i(a) & \text{if } i \leqslant k' \\ f_{i-k}(a) & \text{otherwise} \end{cases}$$

The partial functions γ'' and β'' which specify the module and source interconnections are defined by:

$$\gamma''\colon \mathbf{N}_{k''} \times \mathbf{N} \to \{S, M\}$$

$$\beta''\colon \mathbf{N}_{k''} \times \mathbf{N} \to \mathbf{N}$$

$$\gamma''(i, j) = \begin{cases} \gamma'(i, j) & \text{if } i \leqslant k' \\ M & \text{if } i > k' \text{ and } \gamma(i - k', j)\downarrow \end{cases}$$

$$\beta''(i, j) = \begin{cases} \beta'(i, j) & \text{if } i \leqslant k' \\ \alpha'(\beta(i - k', j)) & \text{if } i > k' \text{ and } \gamma(i - k', j) = S \\ \beta(i - k', j) + k' & \text{otherwise} \end{cases}$$

The network N'' can now be formalized as a system of simultaneous primitive recursive equations and its I/O specification derived as in Section 2.2.2.

SOUNDNESS LEMMA 2.3
Let N and N' be networks and let $N'' = N \# N'$. Let V_b, $V'_{b'}$ and $V''_{b''}$ be the stream transformers derived from N, N' and N'' respectively and let $b'' = (b', b)$. Then:

$$V_b \cdot V'_{b'} = V''_{b''}$$

2.4.5 Vectorization of networks

Let N and N' be networks of the form given in Section 2.2.1. We consider the construction of a network N'' from N and N' that represents computation with N and N' in parallel. Again we will use the notation of Section 2.2.1. If $c = c'$ (where c and c' are the number of sources of N and N' respectively), then we define the vectorization of N and N' as:

$$\{N, N'\} = N''$$

where N'' is the following network: network N'' consists of $k'' = k + k'$ modules m''_i and $c'' = c$ sources s''_i. Modules $m''_{\alpha''(1)}, \ldots, m''_{\alpha''(d'')}$ are sinks where $d'' = d + d'$ and:

$$\alpha''(i) = \begin{cases} \alpha(i) & \text{if } i \leqslant d \\ \alpha'(i - d) + k & \text{otherwise} \end{cases}$$

Each module m''_i has $p''(i)$ inputs where:

$$p''(i) = \begin{cases} p(i) & \text{if } i \leqslant k \\ p'(i - k) & \text{otherwise} \end{cases}$$

The action of each module m''_i is specified by a function:

$$f''_i: A^{p''(i)} \to A$$

where:

$$f''_i(a) = \begin{cases} f_i(a) & \text{if } i \leqslant k \\ f'_{i-k}(a) & \text{otherwise} \end{cases}$$

The partial functions γ'' and β'' which specify the module and source interconnections are defined by:

$$\gamma'': \mathbf{N}_{k''} \times \mathbf{N} \to \{S, M\}$$

$$\beta'': \mathbf{N}_{k''} \times \mathbf{N} \to \mathbf{N}$$

$$\gamma''(i, j) = \begin{cases} \gamma(i, j) & \text{if } i \leqslant k \\ \gamma'(i, j) & \text{otherwise} \end{cases}$$

$$\beta''(i, j) = \begin{cases} \beta(i, j) & \text{if } i \leqslant k \\ \beta'(i - k, j) & \text{if } i > k \text{ and } \gamma'(i - k, j) = S \\ \beta'(i - k, j) + k & \text{otherwise} \end{cases}$$

The network N'' can now be formalized as a system of simultaneous primitive recursive equations and its I/O specification derived as in Section 2.2.2.

SOUNDNESS LEMMA 2.4
Let N and N' be networks, where $c = c'$ and let $N'' = \{N, N'\}$. Let V_b, $V'_{b'}$ and $V''_{b''}$ be the stream transformers derived from N, N' and N'' respectively and let $b'' = (b, b')$. Then:

$$(V_b, V'_{b'}) = V''_{b''}$$

2.4.6 Network plumbing

Ideally, we would like to give a direct interpretation:

$$NSEL^q_r[\phi_1, \ldots, \phi_r]$$

which would be a network corresponding to:

$$SEL^q_r[\phi_1, \ldots, \phi_r]$$

Unfortunately, the selection operator corresponds to rerouteing channels at network level and so we define network selection operators by their effect when combined with normal networks. In this chapter, we will only consider the single case which we will need for the Pixel Planes example, but others are possible.

Let N be a network of the form given in Section 2.2.1. We consider the construction of a network N' that represents N with its sources rerouted by a network section operator. Again we will use the notation of Section 2.2.1. If $c = r$, then we define:

$$N \,\#\, NSEL^q_r[\phi_1, \ldots, \phi_r] = N'$$

where N' is the following network: network N' consists of $k' = k$ modules m'_i and $c' = q$ sources s'_i. Modules $m'_{\alpha'(1)}, \ldots, m'_{\alpha'(d')}$ are sinks where $d' = d$ and $\alpha'(i) = \alpha(i)$. Each module m'_i has $p'(i)$ inputs where $p'(i) = p(i)$. The action of each module m'_i is specified by a function:

$$f'_i: A^{p'(i)} \to A$$

where:

$$f'_i(a) = f_i(a)$$

The partial functions γ' and β' which specify the module and source interconnections are defined by:

$$\gamma': \mathbf{N}_{k'} \times \mathbf{N} \to \{S, M\}$$

$$\beta': \mathbf{N}_{k'} \times \mathbf{N} \to \mathbf{N}$$

$$\gamma'(i, j) = \gamma(i, j)$$

$$\beta'(i, j) = \begin{cases} \phi_{\beta(i,j)} & \text{if } \gamma(i, j) = S \\ \beta(i, j) & \text{otherwise} \end{cases}$$

The network N'' can now be formalized as a system of simultaneous primitive recursive equations and its I/O specification derived as in Section 2.2.2.

SOUNDNESS LEMMA 2.5
Let N be a network, where $c = r$ and let:

$$N' = N \# NSEL^q_r[\phi_1, \ldots, \phi_r]$$

Let V_b and $V'_{b'}$ be the stream transformers derived from N and N' respectively and let $b' = b$. Then:

$$V'_{b'} = V_b \cdot SEL^q_r[\phi_1, \ldots, \phi_r]$$

2.5 User specification of the Pixel Planes LEE

In this section, we give the overall strategy for the specification and verification of the Pixel Planes example using the machinery introduced in the previous three sections. We will also formulate a user specification of the Pixel Planes LEE over a class of suitable abstract structures and decompose this in terms of simpler user specifications. The class of abstract structures we use is defined by axioms that are chosen to be just the properties required for the correctness proof, so that when an appropriate concrete structure, such as the integers $\mathbf{Z}$, is selected from the class, the formal user specification meets our formal definition of what the LEE should do on that data.

2.5.1 Top-down strategy

A diagrammatic representation of the specification and proof strategies is shown in Figure 2.11. We start with the top level user specification which is essentially a vector polynomial over $\underline{A}^u$ for any A satisfying certain axioms. Our goal is to arrive at the complete network, which is a set of simultaneous primitive recursive functions over A and whose I/O specification can be shown to satisfy this user specification.

The first step is to express the top level user specification as a combination of a number of simpler lower level user specifications. In the Pixel Planes example, this is done by noticing that the 2D linear expression $c + xa + yb$ can be evaluated as $(c + xa) + yb$ by using 1D expressions. The simpler user specifications are

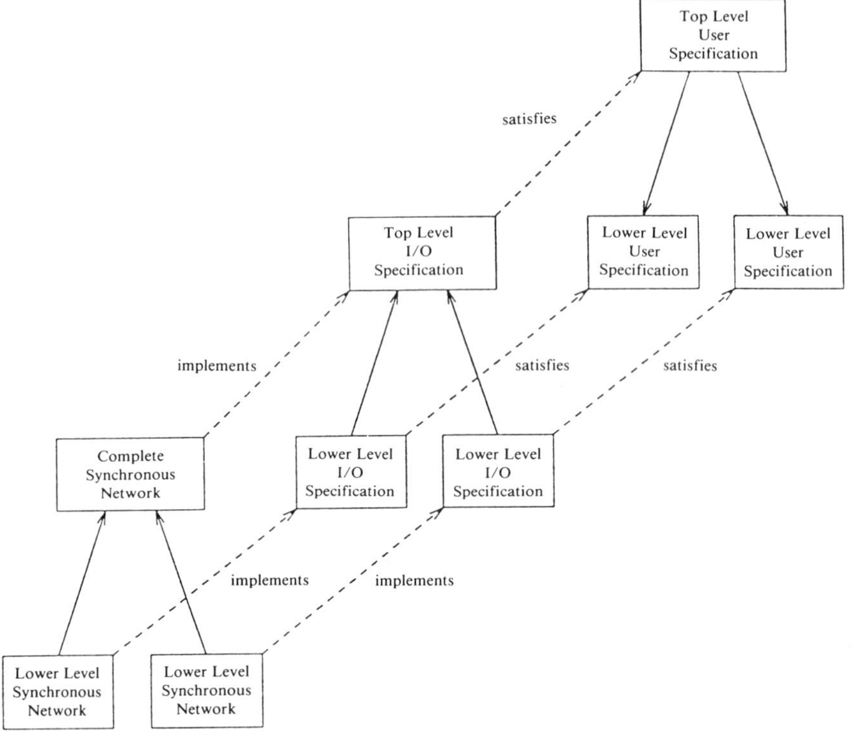

Figure 2.11
Specification and proof strategies.

combined using the user specification constructors (composition, vectorization and selection operators) defined in Section 2.4. The correctness of the way that this is done is proved by substituting in the definitions of Section 2.4 and rearranging to get back to the original top level user specification.

We next propose synchronous networks to implement the component synchronous specifications. For each network an I/O specification is defined in Section 2.2.2 in terms of the output of each sink of the network. This is not a suitable form for proving that it satisfies the corresponding user specification, so we give closed forms (that is, expressions that do not depend on the outputs of other modules) for the outputs of each module. Obtaining these closed forms (which is done by guesswork) and proving that they are correct (which is done by induction on time) is the hardest part of the verification process.

We now have an I/O specification which has a similar form to the user specification that it is supposed to satisfy. The satisfaction proof is done by making suitable substitutions for certain undefined delay parameters in the user specification and showing that the user specification and I/O specification agree whenever the output of the user specification is not u. In this way, the undefined delay parameters of the user specifications become defined by the chosen implementation.

Now, because we have I/O specification constructors (standard composition, vectorization and selection operators), which correspond with the user specification constructors used to decompose the top level user specification, we can build a corresponding top level implementation specification from the lower level I/O specifications. Furthermore, by Lemmas 2.1 and 2.2, this top level I/O specification will satisfy the top level user specification.

Finally, we need to give the complete synchronous network which implements this I/O specification. This will consist of the lower level synchronous networks combined in a manner corresponding to the way the lower level I/O specifications were combined to obtain the top level implementation specification. Here we have a problem, in that there is no object in our definition of synchronous networks that can correspond with a selection operator in the I/O specification formalism. We get around this problem by creating a new class of 'honorary' networks – the network selection operators which are defined by (and only then have nice intuitive interpretations) the effect they have when combined with normal networks. In this paper, we only consider one way of combining network selection operators and other networks, which we will need for the Pixel Planes example, but others are possible and have consistent semantics.

We can now construct the complete synchronous network by combining the lower level networks in a manner corresponding to the way the lower level I/O specifications were combined to form the top level I/O specification. By Lemmas 2.3, 2.4 and 2.5 we know that this design will implement the top level I/O specification.

2.5.2 Abstract arithmetic

We consider the evaluation of the linear expressions $c + xa + yb$ at grid point (x, y) for $x \in \mathbf{Z}_n$, $y \in \mathbf{Z}_m$ in an abstract way. Let R be a set equipped with the operations:

$$+_R : R^2 \to R \quad \text{and} \quad \times_R : R^2 \to R$$

and constant $0_R \in R$, and which satisfies the following properties: for $a, b, c \in R$:

$$(a +_R b) +_R c = a +_R (b +_R c) \tag{2.1}$$

$$a +_R 0_R = a \tag{2.2}$$

$$0_R \times_R a = 0_R \tag{2.3}$$

$$(a +_R b) \times_R c = (a \times_R c) +_R (b \times_R c) \tag{2.4}$$

These axioms will be sufficient to verify the Pixel Planes LEE architecture. Notice that these properties are simpler than those of a *commutative ring* or *semi-ring* which are true of most examples of structures on which we evaluate linear expressions.

In addition, we choose some $\alpha \in R$ and define an operation $r_\alpha : \mathbf{N} \to R$ which we will use to map the x and y coordinates of the grid into elements of R, in order that we may evaluate the above linear expression using operations on R. Intuitively, the natural choice is $\alpha = 1$ if R has a 1 (a multiplicative identity), however our proofs will be valid for any choice of α. We define:

$$r_\alpha(0) = 0_R$$

$$r_\alpha(a + 1) = r_\alpha(a) +_R \alpha$$

Thus, $r_\alpha(0) = 0_R$, $r_\alpha(1) = 0_R +_R \alpha$, $r_\alpha(2) = 0_R +_R \alpha +_R \alpha$, and so on; and in the case where $R = \mathbf{Z}$ and $\alpha = 1$, $r_\alpha(a) = a$. We choose the dimensions of the LEE to be $n \times m$ and assume without loss of generality that $n \geqslant m$.

We can now define the many sorted algebra with which we will work:

$$A = \langle \mathbf{T}, \mathbf{N}, \mathbf{B}, R \mid 0_\mathbf{T}, t+1, 0_\mathbf{N}, a+1, a+b, tt, ff, \wedge, \neg, 0_R, \alpha, \\ r_\alpha(1), \ldots, r_\alpha(2^n - 1), +_R, \times_R \rangle$$

Here $\mathbf{T}$ is a clock, $\mathbf{N}$ and $\mathbf{B}$ together with their usual constants and operations are the standard models of the natural numbers and the booleans. To simplify the notation we will, in future, drop the subscript from the symbols $0_\mathbf{T}$, $0_\mathbf{N}$, 0_R, $+_R$ and $\times_R$ where the meaning is clear from the context.

Lemma 2.6

r_α is a homomorphism on $\mathbf{N} = \langle \mathbf{N}, 0_\mathbf{N}, a+b \rangle$ to $R = \langle R, 0_R, +_R \rangle$

Proof

We prove that $r_\alpha(a+b) = r_\alpha(a) + r_\alpha(b)$ for any $a, b \in \mathbf{N}$ by induction on b. Consider the basis case:

$$r_\alpha(a+0) = r_\alpha(a)$$

$$r_\alpha(a) + r_\alpha(0) = r_\alpha(a) + 0 = r_\alpha(a)$$

Now consider the induction step. Suppose $r_\alpha(a+b) = r_\alpha(a) + r_\alpha(b)$, then:

$$\begin{aligned} r_\alpha(a+(b+1)) &= r_\alpha((a+b)+1) \\ &= r_\alpha(a+b) + \alpha \quad \text{(by definition)} \\ r_\alpha(a) + r_\alpha(b+1) &= r_\alpha(a) + (r_\alpha(b) + \alpha) \quad \text{(by definition)} \\ &= (r_\alpha(a) + r_\alpha(b)) + \alpha \quad \text{(using property 2.1)} \\ &= r_\alpha(a+b) + \alpha \quad \text{(by induction hypothesis)} \end{aligned}$$

2.5.3 Top level user specification

At the top level we have the user specification for the complete LEE as depicted in Figure 2.5. Formally, this is a function:

$$LE: [\mathbf{T} \to R]^3 \to [\mathbf{T} \to R \cup \{u\}]^{2^n \times 2^m}$$

with $2^n \times 2^m$ coordinate functions:

$$LE_{ij}: [\mathbf{T} \to R]^3 \to [\mathbf{T} \to R \cup \{u\}]$$

where $2^n > i \geqslant 0$ and $2^m > j \geqslant 0$, and LE_{ij} gives the output stream at position i, j on the grid. We define LE in terms of the grid coordinate functions:

$$LE_{ij}(\underline{a}, \underline{b}, \underline{c})(t) = \begin{cases} u & \text{if } t_1 = t - d_1 < 0 \\ \underline{c}(t_1) + r_\alpha(i) \times \underline{a}(t_1) + r_\alpha(j) \times \underline{b}(t_1) & \text{otherwise} \end{cases}$$

where $t_1 = t - d_1$ for some constant d_1.

2.5.4 Intermediate level user specifications

We now split the top level user specification into two simpler user specifications, one for the first 1D LEE module and delay unit and one for the remaining n 1D LEE modules.

First intermediate level user specification

This user specification LD is for the first LEE module which inputs the streams $\underline{a}$ and $\underline{c}$ and for a delay unit which keeps the stream $\underline{b}$ in step:

$$LD: [\mathbf{T} \to R]^3 \to [\mathbf{T} \to R \cup \{u\}]^{2^n} \times [\mathbf{T} \to R \cup \{u\}]$$

with $2^n + 1$ coordinate functions:

$$LD_i: [\mathbf{T} \to R]^3 \to [\mathbf{T} \to R \cup \{u\}]$$

$$LD_i(\underline{a}, \underline{b}, \underline{c})(t) = \begin{cases} u & \text{if } t_2 = t - d_2 < 0 \\ \underline{b}(t_2) & \text{if otherwise } i = 2^n \\ \underline{c}(t_2) + r_\alpha(i) \times \underline{a}(t_2) & \text{otherwise} \end{cases}$$

where $t_2 = t - d_2$ for some constant d_2.

Second intermediate level user specification

This user specification LL is for the array of n 1D LEE modules that generate the output for the complete architecture:

$$LL: [\mathbf{T} \to R]^{2^n} \times [\mathbf{T} \to R] \to [\mathbf{T} \to R \cup \{u\}]^{2^n \times 2^m}$$

with $2^n \times 2^m$ coordinate functions:

$$LL_{ij}: [\mathbf{T} \to R]^{2^n} \times [\mathbf{T} \to R] \to [\mathbf{T} \to R \cup \{u\}]$$

$$LL_{ij}(\underline{v}_0, \underline{v}_1, \ldots, \underline{v}_{(2^n-1)}, \underline{b})(t) = \begin{cases} u & \text{if } t_3 = t - d_3 < 0 \\ \underline{v}_i(t_3) + r_\alpha(j) \times \underline{b}(t_3) & \text{otherwise} \end{cases}$$

where $t_3 = t - d_3$ for some constant d_3.

Combining the intermediate level user specifications

By putting $d_1 = d_2 + d_3$, the user specifications LD and LL may be combined using the user specification composition constructor defined in Section 2.4.1 to give the top level user specification LE.

$$LD * LL = LE$$

This may be checked by substituting in the definition of '*' and rearranging.

2.5.5 Low level user specifications

We now give the user specifications of the generic 1D LEE module and the generic delay module and show how these specifications may be combined using the user specification constructors of Section 2.4 to give the intermediate user specifications *LD* and *LL*.

Generic LEE module

The user specification of the generic LEE module of size l is a function:

$$L^l\colon [\mathbf{T} \to R]^2 \to [\mathbf{T} \to R \cup \{u\}]^{2^l}$$

with 2^l coordinate functions:

$$L_i^l\colon [\mathbf{T} \to R]^2 \to [\mathbf{T} \to R \cup \{u\}]$$

where $2^l > i \geq 0$.

$$L_i^l(\underline{v}, \underline{w})(t) = \begin{cases} u & \text{if } t_4 = t - d_4(l) < 0 \\ \underline{w}(t_4) + r_\alpha(i) \times \underline{v}(t_4) & \text{otherwise} \end{cases}$$

where $t_4 = t - d_4(l)$ for some monotonic function $d_4\colon \mathbf{N} \to \mathbf{T}$. Notice that d_4 has to be a function rather than a constant as this is a generic specification and the delay may depend on the parameter l. Of course for any particular instantiation of the generic specification, $d_4(l)$ will be a constant as is required by our definition of a simple user specification.

Generic delay module

The user specification of the generic delay of length l clock cycles is a function:

$$D^l\colon [\mathbf{T} \to R] \to [\mathbf{T} \to R].$$

$$D^l(\underline{v})(t) = \begin{cases} u & \text{if } t_5 = t - l < 0 \\ \underline{v}(t_5) & \text{otherwise} \end{cases}$$

where $t_5 = t - l$.

Combining the low level user specifications

By putting $d_2 = d_4(n)$ and $d_3 = d_4(m)$, the user specifications L^l and D^l may be combined using the user specification constructors defined in Section 2.4 to give the intermediate level user specifications *LD* and *LL*:

$$LD = \langle L^n * USEL_2^3[1, 3], D^{d_4(n)} * USEL_1^3[2]\rangle$$

$$LL = \langle L^m * USEL_2^{2^n+1}[2^n + 1, 1], L^m * USEL_2^{2^n+1}[2^n + 1, 2], \ldots, L^m * USEL_2^{2^n+1}[2^n + 1, 2^n]\rangle$$

These may be checked by substituting in the definition of '*', '⟨⟩' and '$USEL_r^q[\phi_1, \ldots, \phi_r]$' and rearranging. We can now substitute these results in the earlier result giving LE in terms of LD and LL, to get an expression for LE in terms of L^l and D^l, with $d_1 = d_4(n) + d_4(m)$:

$$\begin{aligned} LE = {} & \langle L^m * USEL_2^{2^n+1}[2^n + 1, 1], L^m * USEL_2^{2^n+1}[2^n + 1, 2], \ldots, \\ & L^m * USEL_2^{2^n+1}[2^n + 1, 2^n]\rangle * \langle L^n * USEL_2^3[1, 3], \\ & D^{d_4(n)} * USEL_1^3[2]\rangle \end{aligned}$$

2.6 Implementation of the Pixel Planes LEE

We have shown that the top level user specification LE can be written as a combination of simpler user specifications L^l and D^l. We now give implementations for these user specifications. The implementation for the generic LEE module L^l is shown in Figure 2.12. Informally, this consists of a binary tree of adders of height l, together with a processor performing multiplication by a constant, together with some one cycle delays to sort out the timing at each level. Formally, this implementation is specified by a system of simultaneous primitive recursive equations which we obtain by assigning a function to each processor, using the method described in Section 2.2. To make the implementation simpler, we assume that the output of every module is initialized to $0 \in R$ so that the initialization state b disappears from the description.

2.6.1 Tree implementation of generic LEE module

The processors $Q_1, Q_2, \ldots, Q_{l-1}$ are merely one cycle delays and are represented by functions $q_1, q_2, \ldots, q_{l-1}$. For $1 \leqslant i < l$:

$$q_i: \mathbf{T} \times [\mathbf{T} \to R]^2 \to R$$

$$q_i(0, \underline{v}, \underline{w}) = 0$$

For $i = 1$:

$$q_1(t + 1, \underline{v}, \underline{w}) = \underline{v}(t)$$

For $1 < i < l$:

$$q_i(t + 1, \underline{v}, \underline{w}) = q_{i-1}(t, \underline{v}, \underline{w})$$

The processors $M_1, M_2, \ldots, M_l$ perform multiplication by constants in the ring, corresponding to powers of two. They are represented by functions $m_1, m_2, \ldots, m_l$. For $1 \leqslant i \leqslant l$:

$$m_i: \mathbf{T} \times [\mathbf{T} \to R]^2 \to R$$

$$m_i(0, \underline{v}, \underline{w}) = 0$$

$$m_1(t + 1, \underline{v}, \underline{w}) = r_\alpha(2^{n-1}) \times \underline{v}(t)$$

For $1 < i \leqslant l$:

$$m_i(t + 1, \underline{v}, \underline{w}) = r_\alpha(2^{n-i}) \times q_{i-1}(t, \underline{v}, \underline{w})$$

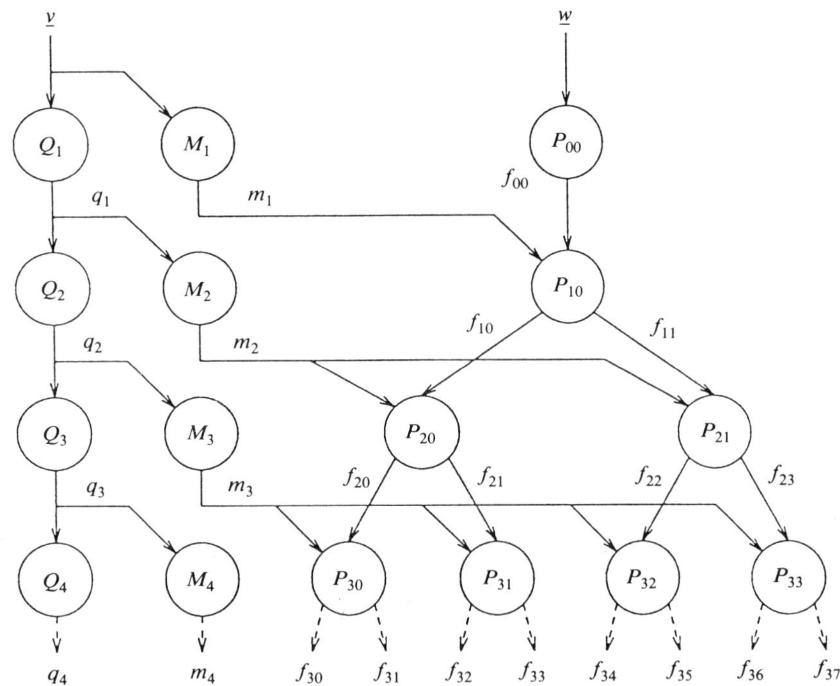

Figure 2.12
Implementation for the generic LEE module.

The processor P_{00} is just a one cycle delay needed to balance the timing. For notational convenience, we represent it by a function:

$$f_{00}: \mathbf{T} \times [\mathbf{T} \to R]^2 \to R$$

defined by:

$$f_{00}(0, \underline{v}, \underline{w}) = 0$$

$$f_{00}(t + 1, \underline{v}, \underline{w}) = \underline{w}(t)$$

The processors P_{ij} at level i and position j, for $1 \leqslant i \leqslant l$, $0 \leqslant j < 2^{i-1}$, form the actual nodes of the tree. Each processor P_{ij} is really a pair of processors (recall our conventions of Section 2.2.3) which are represented by functions:

$$f_{i\,2j}, f_{i\,2j+1}: \mathbf{T} \times [\mathbf{T} \to R]^2 \to R$$

For $1 \leqslant i \leqslant l$, $0 \leqslant j < 2^i$:

$$f_{ij}(0, \underline{v}, \underline{w}) = 0$$

$$f_{ij}(t + 1, \underline{v}, \underline{w}) = \begin{cases} f_{i-1\,j/2}(t, \underline{v}, \underline{w}) & \text{if } j \text{ is even} \\ f_{i-1(j-1)/2}(t, \underline{v}, \underline{w}) + m_i(t, \underline{v}, \underline{w}) & \text{otherwise} \end{cases}$$

The stream transformer defined by this system is:

$$T^l: [\mathbf{T} \to R]^2 \to [\mathbf{T} \to R]^{2^l}$$

with 2^l coordinate functions:

$$T^l_i: [\mathbf{T} \to R]^2 \to [\mathbf{T} \to R]$$

where $0 \leqslant i < 2^l$.

$$T^l(\underline{v}, \underline{w})(t) = (f_{l0}(t, \underline{v}, \underline{w}), f_{l1}(t, \underline{v}, \underline{w}), \ldots, f_{l2^l-1}(t, \underline{v}, \underline{w}))$$

2.6.2 Implementation of the generic delay module

The implementation for the generic delay module, D^l consists of a linear array $H_1, \ldots, H_l$ of l one clock cycle delays, which we represent by functions:

$$h_i: \mathbf{T} \times [\mathbf{T} \to R] \to R$$

where $1 \leqslant i \leqslant l$. For $1 \leqslant i \leqslant l$:

$$h_i(0, \underline{v}) = 0$$

For $i = 1$:

$$h_i(t + 1, \underline{v}) = \underline{v}(t)$$

For $1 < i \leqslant l$:

$$h_i(t + 1, \underline{v}) = h_{i-1}(t, \underline{v})$$

The stream transformer defined by this system is:

$$A^l: [\mathbf{T} \to R] \to [\mathbf{T} \to R]$$

$$A^l(\underline{v})(t) = h_l(t, \underline{v})$$

2.6.3 Complete implementation

We now combine the I/O specifications obtained from the above implementations, using standard function composition, vectorization and the selection operators defined in Section 2.4.3, to get the top level I/O specification I. This construction mirrors the way that the top level user specification LE was decomposed into the simpler user specifications L^l and D^l:

$$I: [\mathbf{T} \to R]^3 \to [\mathbf{T} \to R]^{2^n \times 2^m}$$

$$I = (T^m \cdot SEL_2^{2^n+1}[2^n + 1, 1], T^m \cdot SEL_2^{2^n+1}[2^n + 1, 2], \ldots, T^m \cdot SEL_2^{2^n+1}[2^n + 1, 2^n] \cdot (T^n \cdot SEL_2^3[1, 3], A^{d_4(n)} \cdot SEL_1^3[2])$$

We can be sure that a complete implementation (that is, a set of simultaneous primitive recursive equations with I/O specification I) actually exists, by application of Lemmas 2.3, 2.4 and 2.5.

2.7 Verification of the Pixel Planes LEE

We want to prove that I/O specification I satisfies user specification LE. By Lemmas 2.1 and 2.2 in Section 2.4 about combining user specifications, this problem reduces to showing that the I/O specification of the generic LEE module T^l meets its user specification L^l, and that the I/O specification of the generic delay A^l meets its user specification D^l.

2.7.1 Correctness of the generic tree

We need to show that the I/O specification T^l, defined by the simultaneous primitive recursive equations of the implementation, meets the user specification L^l, that is, for all $\underline{v}$, $\underline{w}$ and $t = 0, 1, 2, \ldots$

$$L^l(\underline{v}, \underline{w})(t) = u \quad \text{or} \quad T^l(\underline{v}, \underline{w})(t) = L^l(\underline{v}, \underline{w})(t) \tag{2.5}$$

We prove this by using the following lemma about the values of the f_{ij} functions that represent the processors in the implementation.

Lemma 2.7
For $0 \leqslant i \leqslant l, 0 \leqslant j < 2^i$:

$$f_{ij}(t, \underline{v}, \underline{w}) = \underline{w}(t - i - 1) + r_\alpha(2^{l-i} j) \times \underline{v}(t - i - 1)$$

Thus putting $d_4(l) = l + 1$ we get that for $t \geqslant d_4(l)$ and $0 \leqslant j < 2^l$:

$$\begin{aligned} T^l{}_j(\underline{v}, \underline{w})(t) &= f_{lj}(t, \underline{v}, \underline{w}) \\ &= \underline{w}(t - l - 1) + r_\alpha(j) \times \underline{v}(t - l - 1) \\ &= \underline{w}(t - d_4(l)) + r_\alpha(j) \times \underline{v}(t - d_4(l)) \\ &= L^l{}_j(\underline{v}, \underline{w})(t) \end{aligned}$$

Hence for $t \geqslant d_4(l)$, $T^l(\underline{v}, \underline{w})(t) = L^l(\underline{v}, \underline{w})(t)$. From the definition, $L^l(\underline{v}, \underline{w}) = u$ when $t < d_4(l)$, so (2.5) holds. In order to prove Lemma 2.7, we need the following lemma about the values of the m_i functions which represent the multiplication processors.

Lemma 2.8
For $1 \leqslant i \leqslant l$:

$$m_i(t, \underline{v}, \underline{w}) = r_\alpha(2^{l-i}) \times \underline{v}(t - i)$$

Proof of Lemma 2.7
By induction on i: consider the basis, $i = 0$. By definition:

$$f_{00}(t, \underline{v}, \underline{w}) = \underline{w}(t - 1)$$

and for $i, j = 0$ the right side of the equation is:

$$\begin{aligned} \underline{w}(t - (i + 1)) + r_\alpha(2^{l-i}j) \times \underline{v}(t - (i + 1)) &= \underline{w}(t - 1) + r_\alpha(0) \times \underline{v}(t - 1) \\ &= \underline{w}(t - 1) + 0 \times \underline{v}(t - 1) \\ &= \underline{w}(t - 1) + 0 \text{ (by property of } R \text{ in Equation 2.3)} \\ &= \underline{w}(t - 1) \text{ (by property of } R \text{ in Equation 2.2)} \end{aligned}$$

Consider the induction step where:

$$f_{i+1j}(t, \underline{v}, \underline{w}) = \begin{cases} f_{ij/2}(t - 1, \underline{v}, \underline{w}) & \text{if } j \text{ is even} \\ f_{i(j-1)/2}(t - 1, \underline{v}, \underline{w}) + m_{i+1}(t - 1, \underline{v}, \underline{w}) & \text{otherwise} \end{cases}$$

We now consider the two cases:

(1) j is even.

$$\begin{aligned} f_{i+1j}(t, \underline{v}, \underline{w}) &= f_{ij/2}(t - 1, \underline{v}, \underline{w}) \\ &= \underline{w}((t - 1) - i - 1) + r_\alpha(2^{l-i}j/2) \times \\ &\quad \underline{v}((t - 1) - i - 1) \quad \text{(by induction hypothesis)} \\ &= \underline{w}(t - (i + 1) - 1) + r_\alpha(2^{l-(i+1)}j) \times \\ &\quad \underline{v}(t - (i + 1) - 1) \end{aligned}$$

(2) j is odd.

$$\begin{aligned} f_{i+1j}(t, \underline{v}, \underline{w}) &= f_{i(j-1)/2}(t - 1, \underline{v}, \underline{w}) + m_{i+1}(t - 1, \underline{v}, \underline{w}) \\ &= \underline{w}((t - 1) - i - 1) + r_\alpha(2^{l-i}(j - 1)/2) \times \underline{v}((t - 1) - i - 1) + r_\alpha(2^{l-(i+1)}) \times \underline{v}((t - 1) - i - 1) \quad \text{(by induction hypothesis and above lemma)} \\ &= \underline{w}(t - (i + 1) - 1) + r_\alpha(2^{l-(i+1)}j - 2^{l-(i+1)}) \times \underline{v}(t - (i + 1) - 1) + r_\alpha(2^{l-(i+1)}) \times \underline{v}(t - (i + 1) - 1) \\ &= \underline{w}(t - (i + 1) - 1) + (r_\alpha(2^{l-(i+1)}j - 2^{l-(i+1)}) + r_\alpha(2^{l-(i+1)})) \times \underline{v}(t - (i + 1) - 1) \quad \text{(by property 2.4)} \\ &= \underline{w}(t - (i + 1) - 1) + r_\alpha(2^{l-(i+1)}j) \times \underline{v}(t - (i + 1) - 1) \quad \text{(by Lemma 2.6)} \end{aligned}$$

Now in order to prove Lemma 2.8 we need the following lemma about the values of the q_i functions which represent one cycle delays.

LEMMA 2.9
For $1 \leqslant i < l$:

$$q_i(t, \underline{v}, \underline{w}) = \underline{v}(t - i)$$

Proof of Lemma 2.8
By cases:

(1) $i = 1$

$$m_1(t, \underline{v}, \underline{w}) = r_\alpha(2^{l-1}) \times \underline{v}(t - 1) \quad \text{(from definition)}$$

(2) $i > 1$

$$\begin{aligned} m_i(t, \underline{v}, \underline{w}) &= r_\alpha(2^{l-i}) \times q_{i-1}(t - 1, \underline{v}, \underline{w}) \\ &= r_\alpha(2^{l-i}) \times \underline{v}(t - 1 - (i - 1)) \quad \text{(by above lemma)} \\ &= r_\alpha(2^{l-i}) \times \underline{v}(t - i) \end{aligned}$$

Proof of Lemma 2.9
By induction on i: the basis is trivial.

$$q_1(t, \underline{v}, \underline{w}) = \underline{v}(t - 1) \quad \text{(from definition)}$$

Consider the induction step:

$$\begin{aligned} q_{i+1}(t, \underline{v}, \underline{w}) &= q_i(t - 1, \underline{v}, \underline{w}) \\ &= \underline{v}((t - 1) - i) \quad \text{(by induction hypothesis)} \\ &= \underline{v}(t - (i + 1)) \end{aligned}$$

2.7.2 Correctness of the generic delay

We need to show that the I/O specification of the generic delay A^l meets its user specification D^l, that is, for $t = 0, 1, 2, \ldots$

$$D^l(\underline{v})(t) = u \quad \text{or} \quad A^l(\underline{v})(t) = D^l(\underline{v})(t) \tag{2.6}$$

We prove this by using the following lemma about the values of the h_i functions that represent the one cycle delays which make up the delay unit.

LEMMA 2.10
For $1 \leqslant i \leqslant l$:

$$h_i(t, \underline{v}) = \underline{v}(t - i)$$

Now for $t \geqslant l$:

$$A^l(\underline{v})(t) = h_l(t, \underline{v}) = \underline{v}(t - l) = D^l(\underline{v})(t)$$

From the definition, $D^l(\underline{v})(t) = u$ when $t < l$ so (Equation 2.6) holds.

Proof of Lemma 2.10
By induction on i: the basis is trivial.

$$h_1(t, \underline{v}) = \underline{v}(t - 1) \quad \text{(from the definition)}$$

Consider the induction step:

$$\begin{aligned} h_{i+1}(t, \underline{v}) &= h_i(t - 1, \underline{v}) \\ &= \underline{v}((t - 1) - i) \quad \text{(by induction hypothesis)} \\ &= \underline{v}(t - (i + 1)) \end{aligned}$$

2.7.3 Correctness of the complete implementation

We need to show that our top level I/O specification:

$$I: [\mathbf{T} \to R]^3 \to [\mathbf{T} \to R]^{2^n \times 2^m}$$

$$\begin{aligned} I = {} & (T^m \cdot SEL_2^{2^n+1}[2^n + 1, 1], T^m \cdot SEL_2^{2^n+1}[2^n + 1, 2], \ldots, \\ & T^m \cdot SEL_2^{2^n+1}[2^n + 1, 2^n]) \cdot (T^n \cdot SEL_2^3[1, 3], A^{d_4(n)} \cdot SEL_1^3[2]) \end{aligned}$$

meets our initial user specification:

$$LE: [\mathbf{T} \to R]^3 \to [\mathbf{T} \to R \cup \{u\}]^{2^n \times 2^m}$$

with $2^n \times 2^m$ coordinate functions:

$$LE_{ij}: [\mathbf{T} \to R]^3 \to [\mathbf{T} \to R \cup \{u\}]$$

$$LE_{ij}(\underline{a}, \underline{b}, \underline{c})(t) = \begin{cases} u & \text{if } t_1 = t - d_1 < 0 \\ \underline{c}(t_1) + r_\alpha(i) \times \underline{a}(t_1) + r_\alpha(j) \times \underline{b}(t_1) & \text{otherwise} \end{cases}$$

where $t_1 = t - d_1$ for some constant d_1. We have shown in Section 2.5 that by putting $d_1 = d_4(n) + d_4(m)$:

$$\begin{aligned} LE = {} & \langle L^m * USEL_2^{2^n+1}[2^n + 1, 1], L^m * USEL_2^{2^n+1}[2^n + 1, 2], \ldots, \\ & L^m * USEL_2^{2^n+1}[2^n + 1, 2^n]\rangle * \langle L^n * USEL_2^3[1, 3], D^{d_4(n)} * \\ & USEL_1^3[2]\rangle \end{aligned}$$

These expressions for I and LE have the same form. We have proved above that T^l satisfies L^l and A^l satisfies D^l. From Section 2.4.3 we know that each I/O specification of the form:

$$SEL_r^q[\phi_1, \ldots, \phi_r]$$

satisfies a user specification of the form:

$$USEL_r^q[\phi_1, \ldots, \phi_r]$$

Thus each term of the above expression for I not involving composition or vectorization satisfies the corresponding term in the above expression for LE. Finally, by Lemmas 2.1 and 2.2, we know that satisfaction is preserved by composition . and vectorization ( ) on implementations with respect to user specification composition * and vectorization ⟨ ⟩ on user specifications and thus that I satisfies LE.

Timing

From the decomposition of the user specification LE, we know that $d_1 = d_4(n) + d_4(m)$. This is a consequence of composing 1D LEEs of size m with one of size n. From the proof that the implementation of the generic LEE module meets its specification, we know that $d_4(l) = l + 1$. Hence the actual delay through the complete implementation is $d_1 = n + m + 2$.

Acknowledgements

S.M. Eker acknowledges the financial support of Mullards Ltd. J.V. Tucker acknowledges the financial support of the Science and Engineering Research Council through grants GR/C/96548 under the Alvey Programme (VLSI Arch 005) and GR/D/90345.

We thank N.A. Harman, K.M. Hobley, A.R. Martin, K. Meinke and B.C. Thompson for useful discussions and criticisms of the material in this paper.

References

Birtwhistle G. and Subrahmanyam P.A. (1988). *VLSI Specification, Verification and Synthesis*. Kluwer: Dordrecht

Codd E.F. (1968). *Cellular Automata*. New York: Academic Press

Dedekind, R. (1888). *Was sind und was sollen die Zahlen?* Braunschweig

Ehrig H. and Mahr B. (1985). *Fundamentals of Algebraic Specifications 1 – Equations and Initial Semantics*. EATCS Monograph Series Vol 6. Berlin: Springer–Verlag

Eker S.M. and Tucker J.V. (1988). Specification, Derivation and Verification of Concurrent Line Drawing Algorithms and Architectures. In *Theoretical Foundations of Computer Graphics and CAD* (Earnshaw R.A., ed.), pp. 449–516. Springer–Verlag

Engeler E. (1968). *Formal Languages, Automata and Structures*. Chicago: Markham Publishing Company

Fuchs H. and Poulton J. (1981). Pixel-planes: A VLSI-orientated design for a raster graphics engine. *VLSI Design*, **2**(3), 20–8

Fuchs H., Poulton J., Paeth A., and Bell A. (1982). Developing pixel planes, a smart memory-based raster graphics system. In *Proceedings of the 1982 MIT*

Conference on Advanced Research in VLSI, pp. 137–46. Dedham MA: Artech House

Fuchs H., Goldfeather J., Hultquist J.P. *et al.* (1985). Fast spheres, shadows, textures, transparencies, and image enhancements in pixel-planes. *Computer Graphics*, **19**(3)

Fuchs H. (1988). An introduction to pixel-planes and other VLSI-intensive graphics systems. In *Theoretical Foundations of Computer Graphics and CAD* (Earnshaw R.A., ed.), pp. 675–88. Berlin: Springer–Verlag

Gordon M. (1988). HOL: A proof generating system for higher-order logic. In *VLSI Specification, Verification and Synthesis* (Birtwhistle G. and Subrahmanyam P.A., eds), pp. 73–128. Kluwer: Dordrecht

Hanna F.K. and Daeche N. (1986). Specification and verification user higher-order logic: a case study. In *Formal aspects of VSLI* (Milne G.J. and Subrahmanyam P.A., eds), pp. 179–213. Amsterdam: North–Holland

Harman N.A. and Tucker J.V. (1987). *The Formal Specification of a Digital Correlator I: User Specification*. Centre for Theoretical Computer Science Report 9.87, University of Leeds

Harman N.A. and Tucker J.V. (1988a). *Clocks, Retimings and the Formal Specification of a UART*. Centre for Theoretical Computer Science Report 15.88, University of Leeds

Harman N.A. and Tucker J.V. (1988b). *Formal Specification and the Design of Verifiable Computers*. Centre for Theoretical Computer Science Report 19.88, University of Leeds

Hobley, K.M., Thompson B.C. and Tucker J.V. (1988). *Specification and Verification of Synchronous Concurrent Algorithms: A Case Study of a Convolution Algorithm*. Centre for Theoretical Computer Science Report 14.88, University of Leeds

Kung H.T. (1982). Why systolic architectures? *Computer*, **15**(1), 37–46

Martin A.R. and Tucker J.V. (1987). The concurrent assignment representation of synchronous systems. In *Parallel Architectures and Languages Europe Vol II: Parallel Languages* (de Bakker J.W., Nijman A.J. and Treleaven P.C. eds), pp. 369–86. Heidelberg: Springer–Verlag

McCulloch W.S. and Pitts W. (1943). A logical calculus of the ideas immanent in nervous activity, *Bulletin of Mathematical Biophysics*, **2**(5), 115–33

Meinke K. (1988). A graph-theoretic model of synchronous concurrent algorithms. *PhD Thesis*, University of Leeds

Milne G.J. and Subrahmanyam P.A. (1986). *Formal Aspects of VLSI Design*. Amsterdam: North-Holland

Minsky M. (1967). *Computation: finite and infinite machines*. Englewood Cliffs: Prentice-Hall

Peter R. (1967). *Recursive Functions*. New York: Academic Press

Poulton J., Fuchs H., Austin J.D. *et al.* (1985). PIXEL-PLANES: Building a VLSI-Based Graphic System. In *Chapel Hill Conference on VLSI* (Fuchs H., ed.), pp. 35–60. Rockville MA: Computer Science Press

Sheeran M. (1985). Designing regular array structures using higher order functions. In *Proc. of the International Conference on Functional Programming Languages and Computer Architecture*, LNCS 201. Berlin: Springer–Verlag

Sheeran M. (1986). Design and verification of regular synchronous circuits. *Proc. Pt. E, IEE*, **133**(5), 295–304

Soulie F. Fogelman, Robert Y. and Tchuente M. (1987). *Automata Networks in Computer Science: Theory and Applications*. Manchester: Manchester University Press

Thompson B.C. and Tucker J.V. (1985). Theoretical considerations in algorithm design. In *Fundamental algorithms for computer graphics* (Earnshaw R.A., ed.), pp. 855–78. Berlin: Springer–Verlag

Thompson B.C. (1987). A mathematical theory of synchronous concurrent algorithms. *PhD Thesis*, University of Leeds

Thompson B.C. and Tucker J.V. (1988a). *Synchronous Concurrent Algorithms*. Centre for Theoretical Computer Science, University of Leeds

Thompson B.C. and Tucker J.V. (1988b). *A Parallel Deterministic Language and Its Application to Synchronous Concurrent Algorithms*. Centre for Theoretical Computer Science Report 18.88, University of Leeds

Tucker J.V. and Zucker J.I. (1988). *Program Correctness over Abstract Data Types, with Error State Semantics*. Amsterdam: North-Holland

Weste N. and Eshraghian C. (1985). *Principles of CMOS VLSI Design*. Reading MA: Addison-Wesley

ADJ (Goguen J.A., Thatcher J.W., Wagner E.G. and Wright J.B.) (1978). An initial algebra approach to the specification, correctness and implementation of abstract data types. In *Current trends in programming methodology: IV Data Structuring* (Yeh R.T., ed.), pp. 80–149. Englewood Cliffs: Prentice-Hall

W. Luk
G. Jones

University of Oxford

3 · Parametrized retiming of regular computational arrays

Retiming concerns the performance optimization of a digital system by the appropriate distribution of delay elements. The mathematical description of regular computational arrays using combinators enables the development of algebraic theorems which capture the retiming of such circuits parametrically. This simplifies the rapid production of such architectures and the exploration of various design choices.

3.1 Introduction

Many graphics and image processing algorithms have a uniform structure which facilitates their implementation using a regular array of processors. Custom hardware provides the fastest implementation with minimal area and power, but it may not be cost effective since the limited applicability of these circuits increases the design cost for each chip [1]. For this reason, our research has been concentrated on developing systematic design methods and the associated tools for reducing the design cost of regular array architectures.

How can such methods and tools lower the cost of designs without sacrificing performance? It is perhaps instructive to look at the evolution of semi-custom design. While early approaches involved customizing the interconnection of pre-fabricated circuits, the current trend is towards employing **parametrized** cell libraries for increased flexibility, packing density and performance. The main attraction of parametrization is **reusability**: the gross structure of a design is pre-defined while detailed arrangements can be altered according to some parameters to suit a particular situation. The applicability of the support tools depends on two factors – the generality of the predefined structures, and the parameters that can be varied to produce different designs.

The strength of regular architectures is that a relatively small number of pre-defined structures appears to be sufficient to capture the main design idioms. These structures are known as **combinators** in our framework, and they correspond to common patterns of computation that can be laid out efficiently on a 2D surface.

What are the parameters relevant to the generation of regular computational arrays? For a particular interconnection pattern, obvious parameters include the array size and the building blocks making up the array. For clocked circuits (on which this chapter will concentrate), it will be shown that an important parameter is the *degree of pipelining*, the variation of which may result in trade-offs in many aspects of performance. This will be demonstrated in a subsequent example on convolver design. First, let us introduce the notation for describing regular arrays and the notation of retiming for such circuits.

3.2 Notation

Our notation is based on the work of Sheeran and Jones [2]. A circuit is described by a (binary) relation f defined by $x f y \stackrel{\text{def}}{=} P(x,y)$ where x,y, representing the interface signals, belong to $dom(f)$ and $rng(f)$ (domain and range of f) respectively, and P is a predicate describing the intended behaviour. The design process can then be seen as finding an appropriate expression for f that relates the interface signals x,y according to the specification P.

We follow common mathematical notation as much as possible: for instance, the converse f^{-1} of a relation f is defined by $x(f^{-1})y \stackrel{\text{def}}{=} y f x$, and the identity relation id is given by $x\ id\ y \stackrel{\text{def}}{=} x = y$. A **function** is a relation with the property that each possible value in its domain has a unique value in its range. We write $(f\,x)$ to represent the value of f for the argument x: $y = f\,x \stackrel{\text{def}}{=} x\,f\,y$. The arguments of a function can themselves be functions or relations; a higher-order function is a function that takes one or more relations as arguments or returns a relation as result. An example of a higher-order function is **relational composition**: $x(f;\,g)z \stackrel{\text{def}}{=} \exists y.(x\,f\,y) \wedge (y\,g\,z)$.

If there is a need to distinguish infix operators from relations the former will be underlined to avoid confusion, so $y = a\,\underline{f}\,b \stackrel{\text{def}}{=} y = f\langle a,b\rangle \equiv \langle a,b\rangle f\,y$. For instance, $\langle a,b\rangle\ add\ y \equiv y = a\ \underline{add}\ b \equiv y = a + b$.

A tuple, such as $\langle a,b\rangle$, is an ordered collection of elements. The empty tuple is denoted by $\langle\rangle$. Tuples are formed by constructors *append left* (app_L) and *append right* (app_R), which respectively append an element to the left and to the right of a tuple:

$$a\ \underline{app_L}\langle b,c,d\rangle = \langle a,b,c\rangle\ \underline{app_R}\ d = \langle a,b,c,d\rangle$$

We shall also use the abbreviation $app_{LR} \stackrel{\text{def}}{=} app_L;\, app_R^{-1}$ and $app_{RL} \stackrel{\text{def}}{=} app_R;\, app_L^{-1}$.

A tuple with subscript i denotes its ith element (i starts from zero), so x_0 is the first element of tuple x. $x_{i,j}$ is defined to be $(x_i)_j$. The number of elements in x is written as $\#x$. The function el is used to extract a specific component of a tuple: given $1 \leqslant n \leqslant \#x$, $el_n\,x \stackrel{\text{def}}{=} x_{n-1}$. Another useful function is **group**, which groups together segments of a tuple to form a tuple with a specified number of components:

$$x\,(group_n)y \stackrel{\text{def}}{=} \forall i,j\colon 0 \leqslant i < n,\ 0 \leqslant j < m.y_{i,j} = x_{mi+j} \qquad \text{where } m \times n = \#x.$$

For instance, $group_3\,\langle x_0, x_1, x_2, x_3, x_4, x_5\rangle = \langle\langle x_0, x_1\rangle, \langle x_2, x_3\rangle, \langle x_4, x_5\rangle\rangle$.

For a rectangular circuit with ports on every side, the following convention is used to partition the interface signals into domain and range: signals for the west or north side are allocated to the domain, and for the south or east side to the range. If there are two or more signals in the domain (or range), the signals are represented as tuples with the position of a particular signal corresponding to its relative position,

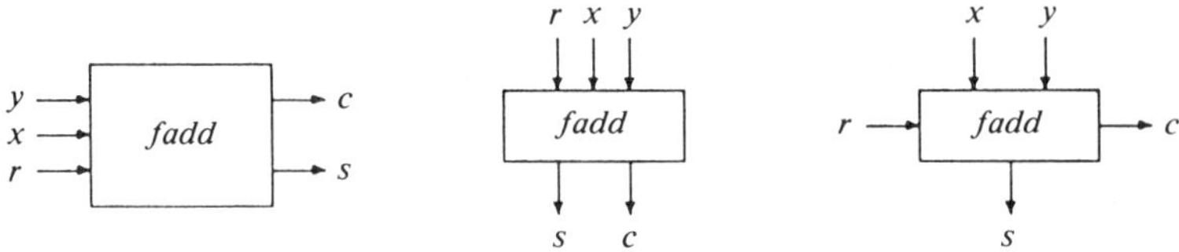

Figure 3.1 Alternative implementations of *fadd*.

and the tuple structure – the grouping of signals – reflecting the logical organization of adjacent signals. For example, a full adder, specified by:

$$\langle r, \langle x,y\rangle\rangle \; fadd \; \langle s,c\rangle \overset{\text{def}}{=} r + x + y = 2 \times c + s$$

where $r, x, y, s, c \in \{0, 1\}$, can be laid out by the configurations in Figure 3.1, depending on context. Inputs and outputs of a circuit are not indicated in the corresponding expression; they are labelled in the diagrams for clarity.

3.3 Combinators

Combinators are higher-order functions that capture common patterns of computation as parameterized expressions. These patterns can represent behaviour, in which case the behaviour of a composite device is expressed in terms of the behaviour of its components; or they can represent the spatial organization of a circuit, in which case they describe the wiring together of components to form the composite device. Let us now look at combinators that have been found useful for describing regular array designs.

3.3.1 Binary combinators

When two components are wired together, it is important to know where the connections are. Two common cases can be distinguished:

- **Sequential composition** This is just relational composition. It corresponds to connecting together two adjacent components by coupling the range of one component to the domain of the other:

  $$x(f;\, g)z \overset{\text{def}}{=} \exists y.(x \, f \, y) \wedge (y \, g \, z)$$

  Notice that component interconnection corresponds to conjunction of predicates and unobservable signals are represented by existentially quantified variables.
- **Parallel composition** This describes two adjacent circuits operating independently on the components of a pair of signals:

  $$\langle x, y\rangle(f \parallel g)\langle x', y'\rangle \overset{\text{def}}{=} (x \, f \, x') \wedge (y \, g \, y')$$

All our descriptions can be expressed using only sequential and parallel composition together with the appropriate tuple manipulation. For convenience, we also have the combinators *beside* and *above*, which correspond to joining together two components with connections on every side of their boundaries (Figure 3.2):

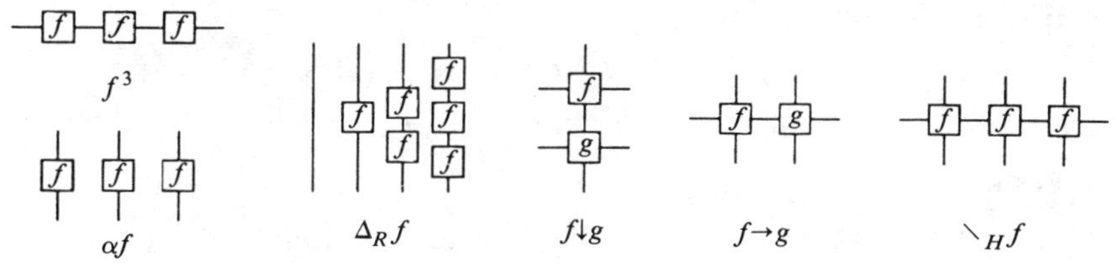

f^3 αf $\Delta_R f$ $f \downarrow g$ $f \rightarrow g$ $\searrow_H f$

Figure 3.2
Pictures of some combinators.

$$\langle a, \langle b, c\rangle\rangle(f \rightarrow g)\langle\langle p, q\rangle, r\rangle \stackrel{\text{def}}{=} \exists s.\langle a, b\rangle f\langle p, s\rangle \wedge \langle s, c\rangle g\langle q, r\rangle$$

$$\langle\langle a, b\rangle, c\rangle(f \downarrow g)\langle p, \langle q, r\rangle\rangle \stackrel{\text{def}}{=} \exists s.\langle b, c\rangle f\langle s, r\rangle \wedge \langle a, s\rangle g\langle p, q\rangle$$

Since *above* is a reflected version of *beside*, we only need to work out the properties of one of them; the result, suitably adjusted, will apply to the other.

Beside and *above* can also be expressed in terms of sequential and parallel composition:

$$f \rightarrow g = app_{LR};\ \mathsf{fst}\, f;\ app_{RL};\ \mathsf{snd}\, g;\ app_{LR},$$

$$f \downarrow g = app_{RL};\ \mathsf{snd}\, f;\ app_{LR};\ \mathsf{fst}\, g;\ app_{RL},$$

where:

$$\mathsf{fst}\, f \stackrel{\text{def}}{=} f \parallel id \quad \text{(apply to first)}$$

$$\mathsf{snd}\, f \stackrel{\text{def}}{=} id \parallel f \quad \text{(apply to second)}$$

3.3.2 Homogeneous combinators

We now use the binary combinators introduced in the previous section to define combinators for describing repetitive structures. The resulting combinators are called **homogeneous combinators**, since the components that are wired together are identical (Figure 3.2); the extension of this notation to cover networks with heterogeneous components is discussed in [3]. We adopt the convention that prefix combinators have a higher precedence than infix ones, and sequential composition has the least precedence. The bracketed superscripts are size parameters, often omitted when they can be deduced from the size of signals.

- **Pipe**

$$f^0 \stackrel{\text{def}}{=} id$$

$$f^{N+1} \stackrel{\text{def}}{=} f^N; f$$

- **Map**

$$x(\alpha^{(0)} f)y \stackrel{\text{def}}{=} x = y = \langle\rangle$$

$$app_L;\ \alpha^{(N+1)} f \stackrel{\text{def}}{=} f \parallel (\alpha^{(N)} f);\ app_L$$

- **Left and Right triangle** The base case for these combinators is similar to that for map. The induction case is given by:

$$app_R;\ \Delta_L^{(N+1)} f \stackrel{\text{def}}{=} \mathsf{fst}(\alpha^{(N)} f;\ \Delta_L^{(N)} f);\ app_R$$

$$app_L;\ \Delta_R^{(N+1)} f \stackrel{\text{def}}{=} \mathsf{snd}(\alpha^{(N)} f;\ \Delta_R^{(N)} f);\ app_L$$

- **Horizontal array**

$$\langle x0, x1\rangle(\setminus_H^{(0)} f)\langle y0, y1\rangle \stackrel{\text{def}}{=} (x0 = y1) \wedge (x1 = y0 = \langle\rangle)$$

$$\textsf{snd}\ app_R;\ \setminus_H^{(N+1)} f \stackrel{\text{def}}{=} (\setminus_H^{(N)} f) \rightarrow f;\ \textsf{fst}\ app_R$$

- **Vertical array**

$$\langle x0, x1\rangle(\setminus_V^{(0)} f)\langle y0, y1\rangle \stackrel{\text{def}}{=} (x0 = y1 = \langle\rangle) \wedge (x1 = y0)$$

$$\textsf{fst}\ app_L;\ \setminus_V^{(N+1)} f \stackrel{\text{def}}{=} (\setminus_V^{(N)} f) \downarrow f;\ \textsf{snd}\ app_L$$

- **Rectangular array**

$$\setminus^{(M,N)} f \stackrel{\text{def}}{=} \setminus_V^{(M)}(\setminus_H^{(N)} f)$$

Other useful structures, such as tree-shaped circuits, can also be parametrized in a similar manner [3].

3.4 Streams

For systems with sequential elements, we use streams – infinite tuples with the innermost subscript representing time – to describe and reason about them. A stream operator relates a single stream in its domain to a single stream in its range. Square brackets will be used to indicate the interleaving of a tuple of streams to form a stream of tuples, so that $[[x,y], z]_t = \langle\langle x_t, y_t\rangle, z_t\rangle$. A stream operator will be denoted by capitalizing the first letter of the corresponding static operator; thus $[x, y]\ Add\ z \stackrel{\text{def}}{=} \forall t . z_t = x_t\ \underline{add}\ y_t = x_t + y_t$. The same symbols are used for both stream and static combinators – no confusion should arise since stream combinators will be confined to stream components and static combinators will be confined to static components.

A delay D is defined by $xDy \stackrel{\text{def}}{=} \forall t . y_t = x_{t-1}$. x_ts with $t < 0$ can be regarded as undefined values or values defined by initialization. An *anti-delay* D^{-1} is such that $D; D^{-1} = D^{-1}; D = Id$. A latch is modelled by a delay with data flowing from domain to range, or by an anti-delay with data flowing from range to domain. From its definition, D can be used on all types of signals, so that for example $D; \alpha F = \alpha D; \alpha F = \alpha(D; F)$.

We shall use the symbols

$\rightarrowtail$ and $\downarrow$

to represent delays for horizontal and vertical dataflows respectively, so for example:

$\rightarrowtail\rightarrowtail\rightarrowtail\rightarrowtail\rightarrowtail$

is the picture for D^5. Similarly

$\leftarrowtail$ and $\uparrow$

represent respectively anti-delays for horizontal and vertical dataflows.

3.5 Retiming

Retiming is a technique that can be used to achieve pipelining – the simultaneous invocation of successive stages of a computation – by relocating latches [4]. The aim

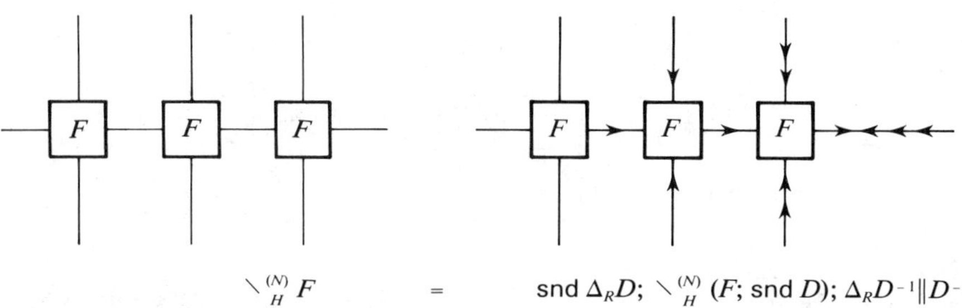

Figure 3.3
A theorem for retiming horizontal array ($N = 3$).

is to reduce the length of long combinational paths so that a faster clock can be used. For systems with no primitives possessing a measure of absolute time, delaying every domain signal and anti-delaying every range signal (or vice versa) will not alter the observable behaviour: $D; F; D^{-1} = D^{-1}; F; D = F$. With this condition **retiming theorems** for our combinations can be derived, such as:

$$F^N = (F; D)^N; D^{-N} \tag{3.1}$$

$$\setminus_H^{(N)} F = \text{snd } \Delta_R D; \setminus_H^{(N)}(F; \text{snd } D); \Delta_R D^{-1} \parallel D^{-N} \tag{3.2}$$

$$\setminus_V^{(M)} F = \text{fst } \Delta_L D; \setminus_V^{(M)}(F; \text{fst } D); D^{-M} \parallel \Delta_L D^{-1} \tag{3.3}$$

$$\setminus^{(M,N)} F = \Delta_R D^{-1} \parallel (D^{-M}; \Delta_R D^{-1}); \setminus^{(M,N)}(\text{snd } D; F; \text{snd } D^{-1}); \Delta_R D \parallel (D^N; \Delta_R D) \tag{3.4}$$

Take Equation 3.2 as an example. It states that one can distribute delays within a horizontal array as long as the appropriate triangles and pipes of delays and anti-delays are introduced (Figure 3.3). Theorems like this can be proved by induction [3].

Both latency (the number of clock cycles elapsed before the first output appears) and data skewing information may be extracted from retiming theorems. As an example, consider a horizontal array of N identical circuits F, each of which has inputs in its domain and outputs in its range. Sequentially composing both sides of Equation 3.2 with D^N yields:

$$\setminus_H^{(N)} F; D^N = \text{snd } \Delta_R D; \setminus_H^{(N)}(F; \text{snd } D); \text{fst } (D; \Delta_L D)$$

since $\Delta_R^{(N)} D; \Delta_L^{(N)} D = D^{N-1}$. This shows that the retimed array $\setminus_H(F; \text{snd } D)$ has its latency extended by N clock cycles, and requires data skews represented by $\Delta_R D$ and $D; \Delta_L D$ for the appropriate domain and range signals respectively.

Delays and anti-delays, together with combinators like Δ_R, provide a simple means of characterizing the boundary conditions – the latency and data-skews – for pipelined circuits. When subsystems are put together, data-skews between adjacent circuits should be matched to minimize the number of latches required for skewing. On completing the design one must ensure that all delays and anti-delays within the network can be implemented by latches: data must flow from domain to range for delays and vice versa for anti-delays.

3.6 Graphical interpretation of retiming theorems

The retiming theorems essentially perform a housekeeping role: if delays are added to a circuit, then the same number of anti-delays must be added at the appropriate

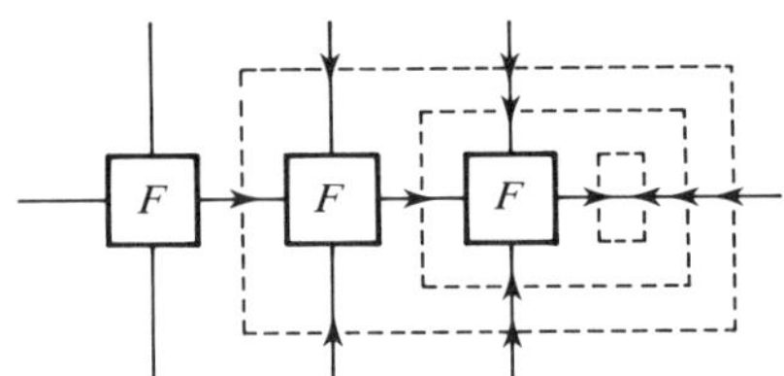

Figure 3.4
Contours for retiming a horizontal array.

locations to preserve its behaviour. There is a simple graphical method that provides the intuition behind the concise equations, using contours to isolate particular parts of the system. At the contours, delays are introduced on each domain signal and the same number of anti-delays are introduced on each range signal, or vice versa. This ensures that the number of delays is equal to that of anti-delays. Notice that a contour simply identifies the locations of instances of a specific component and its converse: in general, one may need to label a contour with the component to which it associates. The application of this method for retiming a horizontal array is shown in Figure 3.4; a retiming theorem thus corresponds to a family of contours on the circuit diagram.

Graphical methods similar to this have been proposed independently; an example is the 'cut theorem' of Kung and Lam [5]. They can be applied to any synchronous circuits, not just regular ones. We emphasize in our graphical interpretation that the retiming contours should be *closed* curves to maintain correct sequencing for all input and output signals. For a circuit with three or more dimensions, the contours become surfaces or hypersurfaces.

Pictures complement textual descriptions by providing a means of visualizing the retiming transformations. They may also provide inspiration for novel retiming strategies. Algebraic theorems, on the other hand, are applicable to entire families of circuits, and are more tractable for formal manipulations.

3.7 Controlling pipelining

Although pipelining can increase the throughput of a system, it may also increase its latency and the amount of area and power for latches, both within the array and at its periphery for data-skewing. A recent study [6] shows that the area overhead for some fabricated designs can be as much as 60 to 70%. Moreover, the increase in throughput may not be linear with respect to the number of pipelined stages for the following reasons.

First, some other components in the system, other than the regular processor array, may contain the critical path. This may be the case as more function blocks can be integrated on chip with the reduction of feature size. The speed of the processor array is then limited by the available I/O bandwidth.

Second, the throughput may be limited by clock skew and by propagation delay and settling time of registers. This becomes more significant as technologies become faster, since the delay of combinational components is reduced more than the propagation delay of interconnections and routeings. The effect is especially severe for large chips. Additional clock buffering may alleviate the problem, but this requires extra design efforts, increases area and power overheads, and makes the design more sensitive to process variations [6].

It is therefore crucial to be able to incorporate the appropriate degree of pipelining in a processor array. In many cases, it may be better to pipeline a network only partially by placing latches between groups of cells instead of between every single cell.

Grouping cells in different ways can also be described succinctly in our notation. For instance, a horizontal array with NK components, $\setminus_H^{(NK)} f$, can be regarded as a horizontal array of N horizontal arrays each of which has K components: $\setminus_H^{(N)}(\setminus_H^{(K)} f)$. It can be shown that the relationship between these two descriptions is given by

$$\setminus_H^{(NK)} f = \mathsf{snd}\ group_N;\ \setminus_H^{(N)}(\setminus_H^{(K)} f);\ \mathsf{fst}\ group_N^{-1}$$

Similar relationships exist for other combinators.

If components are grouped together to form clusters before retiming theorems are applied, then the size of the clusters becomes a parameter controlling the degree of pipelining: the larger the number of components in the cluster, the lower the degree of pipelining. As an example, retiming theorems for arrays of circuit clusters corresponding to Equations 3.1–3.4 are given by:

$$F^{NK} = (F^K; D)^N; D^{-N} \tag{3.5}$$

$$\setminus_H^{(N)}(\setminus_H^{(K)} F) = \mathsf{snd}\ \Delta_R D;\ \setminus_H^{(N)}(\setminus_H^{(K)} F;\ \mathsf{snd}\ D);\ \Delta_R D^{-1} \parallel D^{-N} \tag{3.6}$$

$$\setminus_V^{(M)}(\setminus_V^{(K)} F) = \mathsf{fst}\ \Delta_L D;\ \setminus_V^{(M)}(\setminus_V^{(K)} F;\ \mathsf{fst}\ D);\ D^{-M} \parallel \Delta_L D^{-1} \tag{3.7}$$

$$\begin{aligned}\setminus^{(M,N)}(\setminus^{(P,Q)} F) = {} & \Delta_R D^{-1} \parallel (\Delta_R D^{-1}; D^{-M});\ \setminus^{(M,N)}(\mathsf{snd}\ D;\ \setminus^{(P,Q)} F;\\ & \mathsf{snd}\ D^{-1})\ \Delta_R D \parallel (\Delta_R D; D^N)\end{aligned} \tag{3.8}$$

An instance of Equation 3.6 is shown in Figure 3.5.

For rectangular arrays, a more even distribution of latches can be obtained by pipelining 'through' the clusters rather than 'around' the clusters. Given that lead $\langle P, Q\rangle$ represents a square array of Ps with its leading diagonal replaced by Qs:

$$x(\mathsf{lead}^{(0)}\langle P, Q\rangle)y \stackrel{\text{def}}{=} \forall t.x_t = y_t = \langle\langle\ \rangle, \langle\ \rangle\rangle$$

$$\begin{aligned}App_L \parallel App_R;\ \mathsf{lead}^{(N+1)}\langle P, Q\rangle \stackrel{\text{def}}{=} {} & ((\mathsf{lead}^{(N)}\langle P, Q\rangle) \downarrow (\setminus_H^{(N)} P)) \rightarrow\\ & ((\setminus_V^{(N)} P) \downarrow Q);\ App_R \parallel App_L\end{aligned}$$

it can be shown that

$$\begin{aligned}\setminus^{(M,N)}(\setminus^{(K,K)} F) = {} & \Delta_R D^{-1} \parallel (\Delta_R D^{-1}; D^{-M});\ \setminus^{(M,N)}(\mathsf{lead}^{(K)}\\ & \langle F,\ \mathsf{snd}\ D;\ F;\ \mathsf{snd}\ D^{-1}\rangle)\ \Delta_R D \parallel (\Delta_R D; D^N)\end{aligned} \tag{3.9}$$

In contrast to Equation 3.8 which corresponds to pipelining 'around' the clusters, Equation 3.9 corresponds to pipelining 'through' the clusters by decomposing a rectangular array into square arrays latched along their leading diagonals. This may result in a more even distribution of latches, implying better performance.

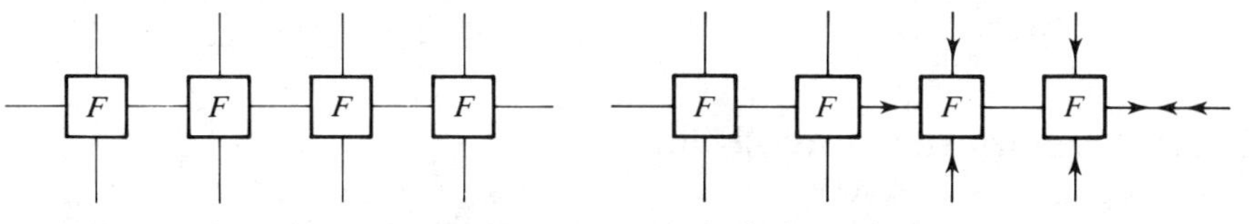

Figure 3.5
A theorem for retiming horizontal array by clusters ($N = K = 2$).

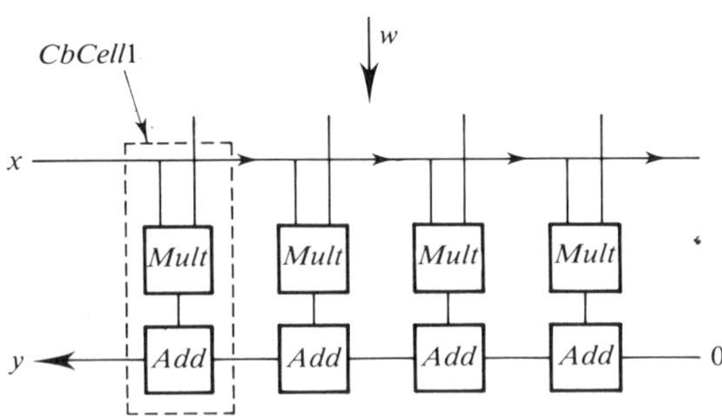

Figure 3.6
Design *Cb*1 ($N = 4$).

3.8 Slowdown

A technique related to retiming is **slowdown** [4]. Sometimes more delays or anti-delays are needed to pipeline a circuit fully. They may be introduced by making an n-**slow** system which corresponds to replacing every delay in the circuit by n delays, and similarly for anti-delays. However, only one out of n adjacent processors is active at any time for a particular computation. Slowdown can also be reasoned about in our framework [3].

Slowdown can be implemented in a number of ways. Several independent computations can be interleaved so that useful work is performed on every cycle. Alternatively, a special clocking scheme can be devised such that the appropriate processors are activated on different clock phases.

3.9 Design measurements

A realistic design approach has to include methods to assess design trade-offs so that an appropriate design can be selected for a particular application. Once a design is captured by combinators, it is usually straightforward to calculate quantities that are useful for performance estimation. For instance, both circuit area and power dissipation depend on the number of components on chip. An expression such as $\alpha(\Delta_R D); \Delta_R(\alpha D)$ provides a formula for computing the number of Ds: if there are N inputs clustered in groups of K, then $\alpha(\Delta_R D)$ indicates that there are N / K triangles with $K(K - 1) / 2$ elements each, and $\Delta_R(\alpha D)$ indicates that there is a single triangle with $N((N / K) - 1) / 2K$ blocks of K elements each, so the total number of Ds is $N(K^2 - 2K + N) / 2K$. Other measures, such as minimum clock period and latency, can also be obtained.

Measurements like these provide a basis for comparing different designs. To illustrate this some simple measurements of two convolver designs will be included in the next section.

3.10 Circuits for convolution

In this section, we describe a few convolver designs that demonstrate the techniques outlined in the previous sections. A circuit for one-dimensional adaptive convolution can be specified as follows: given the data stream x, and the coefficient stream $\langle w_0 \ldots w_{N-1} \rangle$, compute the result stream y given by:

$$\forall t . y_t = \sum_{0 \leqslant n < N} w_{t,n} \times x_{t-n}$$

The first $N - 1$ elements of y contain values of x that are either undefined or defined by initialization.

*Cb*1 is an 'obvious' word-level implementation involving counterflowing data streams as shown in Figure 3.6.

$$Cb1 \stackrel{\text{def}}{=} \searrow_H^{(N)} CbCellw; El_2 \quad \text{where} \quad CbCellw \stackrel{\text{def}}{=} CbCell1; \text{snd } D; El_2^{-1}$$

$$\text{and} \quad \langle\langle y', x\rangle, w\rangle \; cbCell1 \; \langle y, x'\rangle \stackrel{\text{def}}{=} (x' = x) \wedge (y' = w \times x + y)$$

This can in fact be systematically *derived* from the specification [3], although the derivation cannot be included here because of space limitation.

If the coefficients w are only one bit wide, the multiplication becomes a boolean *and* operation and the addition can be implemented by a full adder, so a cell for the bit-level implementation of *Cb*1 can be specified as:

$$\langle\langle y', x\rangle, \langle c, w\rangle\rangle \; cbCellc \; \langle\langle c', w'\rangle, \langle y, x'\rangle\rangle \stackrel{\text{def}}{=} (w' = w) \wedge (x' = x) \wedge (\exists u . \langle w, x\rangle \; and \; u \wedge \langle c, \langle u, y\rangle\rangle \; fadd \; \langle y', c'\rangle)$$

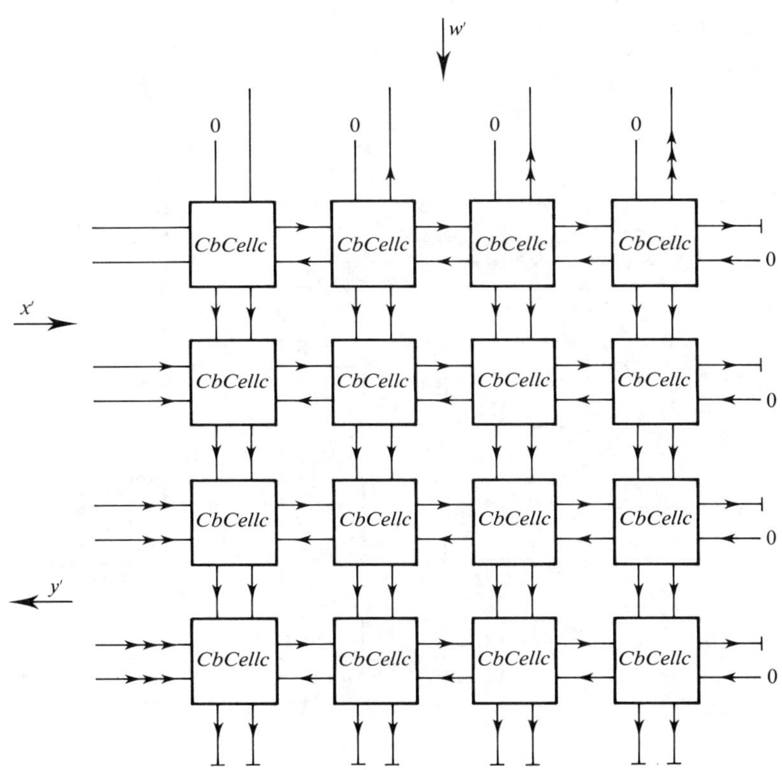

Figure 3.7
Design *Cbb*2
($M = N = 4$).

If M full adders are used to implement each *Add* cell, a bit-level array corresponding to *Cb*1 is $Cbb1 \stackrel{\text{def}}{=} \backslash^{(M,N)}\ CbCellb$, where $CbCellb \stackrel{\text{def}}{=} CbCellc;$ snd(snd D). Informally, this corresponds to decomposing each *CbCellw* of *Cb*1 into a column of M *CbCellb*s for *Cbb*1 and interleaving the x, y streams accordingly. This step can also be formally derived using techniques of **data refinement** [3].

To pipeline *Cbb*1 fully, we slow it down by two and use Equations 3.2 and 3.3 to obtain *Cbb*2 (Figure 3.7), where:

$$Cbb2 \stackrel{\text{def}}{=} \backslash^{(M,N)}\ (CbCellc;\ D \parallel (D^{-1} \parallel D))$$

This solution was described by McCabe *et al.* [7] and a rigorous development was provided by Sheeran [8]. Note that in Figure 3.7, w', x' and y' are bit-level inputs and output for *Cbb*2 which correspond respectively to the word-level inputs and output w, x and y for *Cb*1. One can in fact derive a mathematical formula relating the word-level and the bit-level quantities [3].

Another way of pipelining *Cbb*1 is to use Equation 3.9 to obtain *Cbb*3 (Figure 3.8):

$$Cbb3 \stackrel{\text{def}}{=} \backslash^{(P,Q)}(\text{lead}^{(K)}\ \langle CbCellb,\ CbCellb' \rangle)$$
$$\text{where } K > 1,\ P \times K = M \text{ and } Q \times K = N$$

$$CbCellb' \stackrel{\text{def}}{=} \text{snd } D;\ (CbCellc;\ \text{snd (snd } D));\ \text{snd } D^{-1}$$
$$= \text{snd } D;\ CbCellc;\ \text{snd(fst } D^{-1})$$

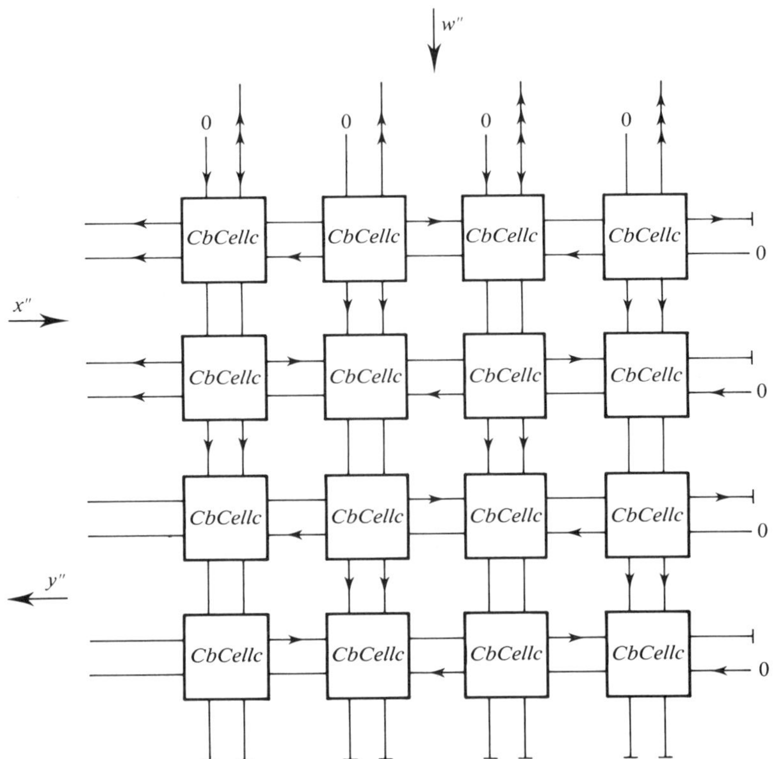

Figure 3.8
Design *Cbb*3
($M = N = 4$, $K = 2$).

since snd(snd D); snd D^{-1} = snd(snd D); snd(fst D^{-1}; snd D^{-1}) = snd(fst D^{-1}).

*Cbb*3 is an array pipelined 'through' $K \times K$ clusters of *CbCellb*s, such that:

$$\setminus^{(P,Q)}(\setminus^{(K,K)}\ CbCellb) = \Delta_R D^{-1} \parallel (D^{-P}; \Delta_R D-1);\ Cbb3;$$
$$\Delta_R D \parallel (D^Q; \Delta_R D)$$

Some characteristics of convolvers *Cbb*2 and *Cbb*3 are summarized in Table 3.1. N refers to the number of stages of convolution (the width of the coefficient stream), M refers to the number of *CbCellc* cells in each stage, and T_C refers to the combinational delay of cell *CbCellc*.

Perhaps the most obvious trade-off arises from varying the degree of pipelining. As remarked in Section 3.7, a more fully pipelined network may attain a higher throughput at the expense of greater overheads of latches both in the array and for skewing. It can be seen from Table 3.1 that pipelining by groups of K by K cells increases the minimum clock period by a factor of K while halving the latency. The number of skewing latches tends to decrease by a factor of K (if $M, N \gg K$), and the total number of latches in the array (excluding that for skewing) tends to a quarter of that for the fully pipelined array. The actual percentage decrease in area and power will also depend on the ratio of area and power for a latch to that for a combinational element. There will be a reduction in the area and power requirement for clock drivers as well. Furthermore, the benefits of pipelining may decrease at higher speed as the set up and hold time for a latch becomes significant.

Throughout it has been assumed that all latches are driven by a single clock. This means that a slowed down array such as the fully pipelined convolver *Cbb*2 interleaves two distinct computations. It would also be possible to drive successive stages of latches by alternate phases of a two-phase clock, with outputs occurring at every half-cycle. In this way, starting with twice the number of delays and anti-delays, the circuits can still be reasoned about by our method, the delays and anti-delays being implemented by half latches. The trade-off analysis is similar – for instance, it can be shown that in the above comparison of bit-level convolvers the saving in the number of skewing latches is the same as before while the saving in the number of latches in the array tends to a half instead of a quarter. The minimum clock period for the fully pipelined circuit is two cell delays, and K times that for the array pipelined by groups of K by K cells.

The retiming theorems preserve the regularity of a circuit. As cells are clustered into bigger groups, the granularity of regularity increases accordingly.

Table 3.1 Comparing *Cbb*2 and *Cbb*3.

Design	*Min. Clock period*	*Latency (cycles)*	*Slow down by 2*	*Number of skewing latches*	*Number of latches in array*
*Cbb*2	T_C	$2(N-1)$	Yes	$\frac{N(N-1)}{2} + M(M-1)$	$4MN$
*Cbb*3 ($K > 1$)	KT_C	$N-1$	No	$\frac{N(N-K)}{2K} + \frac{M(M-K)}{K}$	$\frac{MN(K+2)}{K}$

Within each cluster, the cells are still uniformly arranged, and a cluster is usually symmetric along one of the main diagonals. On the other hand, one may consider the tradeoffs involved in combining adjacent combinational circuits inside a cluster. This optimization may be worthwhile if the unit is repeated a large number of times in the array.

Other factors, such as the number of input and output lines, testability and fault tolerance, should also be taken into account. For instance, it has been suggested that a unidirectional array is more fault tolerant [4]. The choice of implementation may also be influenced by technology-dependent considerations.

Conclusion

A framework for designing and analyzing regular computational arrays based on the notion of parameterized retiming has been presented. An implementation is improved by applying successive correctness-preserving transformations. The application of the retiming theorems is made simpler by associating the transformation to the drawing of appropriate contours. The trade-off resulting from alternative pipelining strategies is discussed.

The parameterization of retiming facilitates the mechanization of incorporating pipelining in regular structures. Simulators, floorplanners and transformation assistants have been prototyped; besides providing the capability of rapidly generating regular array chips or modules, they would also allow the designer to explore many design options to select the most appropriate architecture for a particular application.

Acknowledgement

We are grateful to Andrew McCabe for his comments on comparing convolver designs, and to an anonymous referee for commenting on an earlier draft. This work has been undertaken as part of the UK Alvey Programme (Project ARCH 013) whose support is gratefully acknowledged. The first author also expresses his gratitude to St. Edmund Hall, Oxford for a Brockhues Senior Scholarship.

References

1. Kung H.T. (1982). Why systolic architectures? *IEEE Computer,* **15**(1), 37–46
2. Sheeran M. and Jones G. (1987). Relations + higher order functions = hardware descriptions. In *Proc. CompEuro 87* (Proebster W.E. and Reiner H., eds), pp. 303–6. Hamburg, May 1987
3. Luk W. (1988). Parameterised design of regular processor arrays. *D. Phil. Thesis*, Oxford University
4. Leiserson C.E., Rose F.M. and Saxe J.B. (1983). Optimizing synchronous circuitry by retiming. In *Third Caltech Conference on Very Large Scale Integration* (Bryant R., ed.), pp. 87–116. Rockville MA: Computer Science Press
5. Kung H.T. and Lam M.S. (1984). Wafer-scale integration and two-level pipelined implementations of systolic arrays. *J. Parallel and Distributed Computing,* **1**, 32–63

6. Hatamian M. and Cash G.L. (1987). Parallel bit-level pipelined VLSI designs for high-speed signal processing. *Proc. IEEE,* **75**(9), 1192–202
7. McCabe M.M., McCabe A.P.H., Arambepola B., Robinson I.N. and Cory A.G. (1982). New algorithms and architectures for VLSI. *GEC J. of Science and technology,* **48**(2), 68–75
8. Sheeran M. 'Retiming and slowdown in Ruby'. In *Design for behavioural verification* (Milne G., ed.). To be published by North-Holland.

C.S. Jeong
D.T. Lee

Northwestern
University, Evanston

4 · Parallel convex hull algorithms in 2D and 3D on mesh-connected computers†

Given a set of n points, the convex hull of S, $CH(S)$, is the intersection of all convex sets containing S. The convex hull $CH(S)$ is a convex polygon in 2D and a convex polyhedron in 3D. In this chapter, efficient parallel convex hull algorithms in 2D and 3D on a Mesh-Connected Computer (MCC) are presented. The algorithms for computing convex hulls of n points in 2D and 3D take $O(\sqrt{n})$ time on a $\sqrt{n} \times \sqrt{n}$ MCC, which is asymptotically optimal. The previous result on MCC [1] for convex hull problem in 2D has the same time complexity. However, that algorithm required $\log n$ iterations for the computation of tangent lines between two convex hulls and hence it took $O(\log^3 n)$ time on a Cube-Connected Cycle (CCC) or Perfect Shuffle Computer (PSC). The algorithm used here directly computes the tangent lines in one iteration in $O(\sqrt{n})$ time on MCC, thus requiring only $O(\log^2 n)$ time if implemented on CCC and PSC. Also, this algorithm refines and simplifies the algorithm in [2] with fewer data broadcasting operations. For convex hull problem in 3D, the $O(\sqrt{n}\log n)$ time complexity of Lu's algorithm [3] is reduced to $O(\sqrt{n})$ by using planar point location [4] and efficient data routeing schemes.

4.1 Introduction

A Mesh-Connected Computer (MCC) is a SIMD-type computer, where n Processing Elements (PEs) indexed from 0 to $n - 1$ are arranged in a 2D $\sqrt{n} \times \sqrt{n}$ array and synchronized under one control unit. In an MCC, each processor has a constant number of storage registers and is connected to its four neighbors if they exist. The MCCs are used for a wide variety of problems such as sorting, graph theoretic problems, image processing, pattern recognition, computational geometry, etc. In this chapter, it is shown that convex hull problems for n points in 2D and 3D can be solved in $O(\sqrt{n})$ time on a $\sqrt{n} \times \sqrt{n}$ MCC with one point per PE.

Miller and Stout described an $O(\sqrt{n})$ convex hull algorithm in 2D on a $\sqrt{n} \times \sqrt{n}$ MCC. Their algorithm has the same time complexity on MCC as the algorithm presented in this chapter. However, it required $O(\log n)$ iterations for the computation of tangent lines between two convex hulls, which resulted in a large

† Supported in part by the National Science Foundation under Grants DCR 8420814.

number of data movements between PEs. The number of data movements is reduced by directly computing tangent lines in one iteration and hence the algorithm now presented for convex hull in 2D can be directly implemented in $O(\log^2 n)$ time on other SIMD-type computers such as Perfect Shuffle Computer (PSC) [5] and Cube-Connected Cycles (CCCs) [6], while Miller and Stout's algorithm requires $O(\log^3 n)$ time. The algorithm also refines the $O(\log^2 n)$ algorithm by Chow [2], by using fewer data movements. Recently, an $O(\log n)$ convex hull algorithm on Shared Memory Model (SMM) was proposed by Aggarwal *et al.* [7] and Atallah and Goodrich [8]. But their merge method (due to Overmars and Van Leeuwen [9]), used on SMM, cannot be directly implemented on MCC. For the convex hull in 3D, Lu presented an $O(\sqrt{n}\log n)$ algorithm which is used for computing Voronoi diagrams. The algorithm is speeded up by eliminating the $\log n$ factor to achieve an $O(\sqrt{n})$ running time. The time complexity of this algorithm is optimal to within a constant factor, since a non-trivial data movement on an MCC requires $\Omega(\sqrt{n})$ time.

In the following discussions, MCC is indexed in shuffled row – major order and divided into two sections of equal size, called left and right blocks, each of which is recursively divided into equal sections. The well-known operations such as sorting, Random Access Read (RAR) and Random Access Write (RAW) [10, 11, 12] are used throughout this paper. All the above operations take $O(\sqrt{n})$ on a $\sqrt{n} \times \sqrt{n}$ MCC, and $O(\log^2 n)$ time on CCC and PSC. The following basic operations which take $O(\sqrt{n})$ on a $\sqrt{n} \times \sqrt{n}$ MCC, and $O(\log n)$ time on CCC and PSC [2, 6, 12, 13] are used:

(1) **MERGE:** Two sorted lists are merged, producing a combined sorted list.

(2) **BROADCASTING:** Data in a special PE is sent to all the other PEs.

(3) **CONCENTRATION**: Selected data are moved to consecutive PEs, preserving the original order.

(4) **SELECTED BROADCASTING**: Given a selected subset $\{a_1, a_2, \ldots, a_m\}$ of an array A, such that each PE of index $I(a_i)$ stores a_i and the destination PE index $H(a_i)$ with $I(a_1) < I(a_2) < \ldots < I(a_m)$ and $H(a_1) < H(a_2) < \ldots < H(a_m)$, each a_i is sent to every PE with index from $H(a_i)$ to $H(a_{i+1}) - 1$ by SELECTED BROADCASTING. (We assume that $H(a_{m+1}) = n$.)

(5) **PRECEDE**: Given two sorted lists $A = (a_1, a_2, \ldots, a_n)$ and $B = (b_1, b_2, \ldots, b_m)$, we define the predecessor of a_i as the greatest element b_j in B previous to a_i in the sorted list of A and B, that is, $b_j \leqslant a_i < b_{j+1}$. If there is no such b_j, we assume its predecessor is the greatest element b_m in B. The PRECEDE operation computes, for each element a_i in A, its predecessor in B. This can be done by sending each b_j to every PE containing a_i such that $b_j \leqslant a_i < b_{j+1}$, using SELECTED BROADCASTING after merging A and B.

4.2 Convex hull in 2D

The convex hull of S, $CH(S)$, is the intersection of all convex sets containing S. In the plane, the convex hull $CH(S)$ is a convex polygon. In this section, a parallel algorithm to determine the convex hull of a finite set of points in 2D, is presented.

4.2.1 Basic properties

A convex polygon is represented by its vertices. In the following discussion, we assume that all the vertices of a convex polygon are distinct, and that no three consecutive vertices are collinear. Let us consider the properties of two non-intersecting convex polygons P and Q such that the y values of vertices in P are greater than those in Q (Figure 4.1a). There are two tangent lines, left and right, between P and Q such that all the vertices of P and Q lie on the right and left sides of left and right tangent lines respectively when those tangent lines are directed from bottom up.

We define $pred(p)$ and $suc(p)$ of a vertex p in the convex hull as the previous and next vertex to p when the vertices of the convex hull are ordered in counter-clockwise order. We associate each vertex p of convex hull with a range of angles $\underline{R}(p) = [Amin(p), Amax(p)]$, where $Amin(p)$ is the angle determined by the line directed from p to $pred(p)$ with p as the origin, and $Amax(p)$ is the angle determined by the line directed from the $suc(p)$ to p with p as origin. $Amin(p)$ is equal to

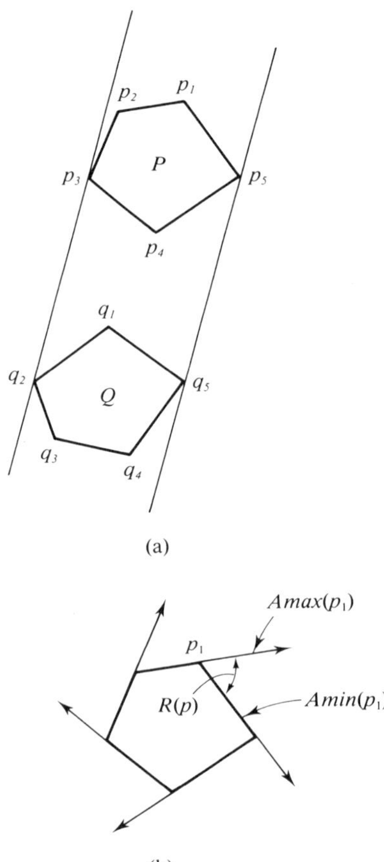

Figure 4.1
Convex hulls P and Q.
(a) P and Q.
(b) $R(P)$.

Amax(*pred*(*p*)) and *Amax*(*p*) is equal to *Amin*(*suc*(*p*)) (Figure 4.1b). *Amin*(*p*) and *Amax*(*p*) are in the range from 0 to 2π. Actually, $R(p)$ represents the range of angles where the slope of a tangent line may lie if it passes through p. (We define *Amin* and *Amax* as angles for explanatory purposes. In the real implementation, we can avoid the computation of angles by making use of the vectors to represent *Amin* and *Amax*.) Two points p_l and q_l (p_r and q_r) in P and Q respectively are called left supporting vertices (right supporting vertices) if the left tangent (right tangent) line passes through those points. For simplicity, we assume that there is only one tangent line between one pair of points.

LEMMA 4.1
For p in P and q in Q, p and q are supporting vertices if, and only if, the intersection of $R(p)$ and $R(q)$ is non-empty and the slope of the line joining p and q lies in that intersection.

Proof
Immediate.

COROLLARY 4.1
Given $R(p)$ and $R(q)$ for p in P and q in Q, we can determine in O(1) time whether there exists a tangent line between p and q.

For any two vertices a and b, we shall use $a \leqslant b$ to denote $Amin(a) \leqslant Amin(b)$. For p in P and q in Q, we define the set M as follows. (See Figure 4.2.)

(a)

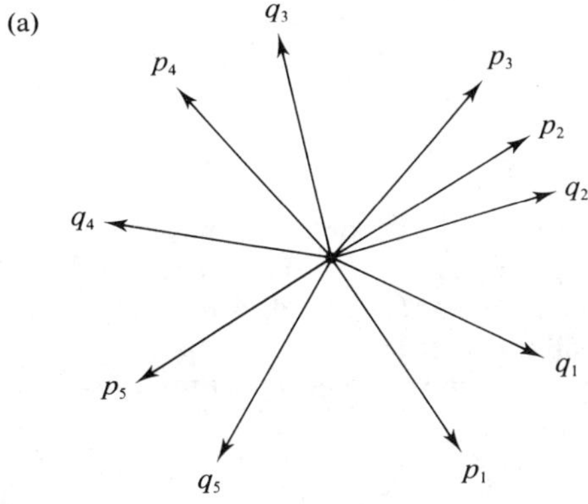

(b)

PE	0	1	2	3	4	5	6	7	8	9
v	q_2	p_2	p_3	q_3	p_4	q_4	p_5	q_5	p_1	q_1

(c)

$M_{p1} = \{(p_1, q_1), (p_1, q_2)\}$ $\quad M_{q1} = \phi$
$M_{p2} = \phi$ $\quad M_{q2} = \{(p_2, q_2), (p_3, q_2)\}$
$M_{p3} = \{(p_3, q_3)\}$ $\quad M_{q3} = \{(p_4, q_3)\}$
$M_{p4} = \{(p_4, q_4)\}$ $\quad M_{q4} = \{(p_5, q_4)\}$
$M_{p5} = \{(p_5, q_5)\}$ $\quad M_{q5} = \{(p_1, q_5)\}$

Figure 4.2
Computation of M.
(a) *Amin* of each vertex.
(b) Vertices of P and Q sorted by *Amin*.
(c) M_1 and M_2.

$$M_1 = \cup M_p \text{ where } M_p = \{(p,q) \mid p \leqslant q < suc(p)\} \quad \text{if } p < suc(p)$$
$$= \{(p,q) \mid p \leqslant q \text{ or } q < suc(p)\} \quad \text{otherwise}$$
$$M_2 = \cup M_q \text{ where } M_q = \{(p,q) \mid q \leqslant p < suc(q)\} \quad \text{if } q < suc(q)$$
$$= \{(p,q) \mid q \leqslant p \text{ or } p < suc(q)\} \quad \text{otherwise}$$
$$M = M_1 \cup M_2$$

Figure 4.2c shows an example of M for the convex hull in Figure 4.1. Note that M is the set of pair of vertices (p,q) such that the intersection of $R(p)$ and $R(q)$ is not empty.

Lemma 4.2
The pairs (p_l, q_l) and (p_r, q_r) determined by left and right supporting vertices respectively are in M.

Proof
First, we shall show (p_l, q_l) is in M. If $p_l \leqslant q_l$, then (p_l, q_l) is in M_1 since by Lemma 4.1 $q_l < suc(p_l)$. If $q_l \leqslant p_l$, (p_l, q_l) is in M_2 since $p_l < suc(q_l)$ by Lemma 4.1. Similarly, we can prove (p_r, q_r) is in M.

From Corollary 4.1 and Lemma 4.2, it follows that given the set M and $R(r)$ for each vertex r in M, left and right supporting vertices can be determined in O(1) time.

4.2.2 Algorithm

In this section, we shall consider the problem of merging two convex hulls P and Q in the left and right blocks of $\sqrt{n} \times \sqrt{n}$ MCC respectively. Briefly, it is done as follows: we first compute the set M, and then after finding left and right supporting vertices in M, discard all the internal vertices that do not belong to the new convex hull. A detailed description of the parallel algorithm for merging two convex hulls in 2D follows. (See Figure 4.3.)

PE		0	1	2	3	4	5	6	7	8	9
		p_2	p_3	p_4	p_5	p_1	q_2	q_3	q_4	q_5	q_1
Step	(1)	q_2	p_2	p_3	q_3	p_4	q_4	p_5	q_5	p_1	q_1
	(2a)	p_1			p_3		p_4		p_5		p_1
	(2b)		q_2	q_2		q_3		q_4		q_5	
	(2c)			(p_3, q_2)					(p_5, q_5)		
	(4)	q_2	p_2	p_3	q_3	*	q_4	p_5	q_5	p_1	*

* denotes the deleted elements.

Figure 4.3
Example for algorithm MERGE-CONVEX2.

Algorithm MERGE-CONVEX2

Input: two convex polygons P and Q in the left and right blocks of $\sqrt{n} \times \sqrt{n}$ MCC respectively, one vertex per PE with its R value. The vertices of P and Q are sorted by *Amin* value respectively and the y values of vertices in P are greater than those in Q.

Output: a new convex polygon C containing $P \cup Q$ with each vertex p having $R(p)$ such that the vertices of C are sorted by *Amin* value.

(1) Sort all the vertices in P and Q by *Amin* value by using MERGE operation.

(2) Find the left and right supporting vertices as follows.
Comment Note that given two lists P and Q sorted by *Amin* value, if (p,q) is in M_1, p is the predecessor of q, that is, the greatest element of P previous to q in the sorted list $S(= P \cup Q)$ if it exists; otherwise the greatest element in P. Similarly, if (p,q) is in M_2, q is the predecessor of p.
  (a) Find every pair of vertices in M_1 by computing, for each vertex v in Q, its predecessor in P by PRECEDE operation. After this step, every PE containing q in Q stores the pair (p,q) in M_1.
  (b) Find every pair of vertices in M_2 by computing, for each vertex in P, its predecessor in Q by PRECEDE operation. After this step, every PE containing p in P stores the pair (p,q) in M_2.
  (c) Determine, for each pair (p,q), whether p and q are supporting vertices, and if they are, decide if they are left or right supporting vertices.

(3) Send p_l and p_r (respectively q_l and q_r) to all the PEs which contain vertices in P(respectively Q).

(4) Discard every internal vertex p in P such that $Amin(p_l) < Amin(p) < Amin(p_r)$ if $Amin(p_l) < Amin(p_r)$, and $Amin(p_l) < Amin(p)$ or $Amin(p) < Amin(p_r)$ otherwise. Discard every internal vertex q in Q such that $Amin(q_r) < Amin(q) < Amin(q_l)$ if $Amin(q_r) < Amin(q_l)$, and $Amin(q_r) < Amin(q)$ or $Amin(q) < Amin(q_l)$ otherwise.

(5) Update *Amin* values of q_l and p_r, and *Amax* values of p_l and q_r. *Amax* and *Amin* of p_l and q_l respectively, are determined by the line connecting p_l and q_l. Similarly, *Amax* and *Amin* of q_r and p_r respectively, are determined by the line connecting q_r and p_r.

(6) Place the remaining convex hull vertices that are sorted by *Amin* values in the consecutive PEs starting from PE(0) by CONCENTRATE operation.

LEMMA 4.3
The algorithm MERGE-CONVEX2 can be executed in $O(\sqrt{n})$ time on a $\sqrt{n} \times \sqrt{n}$ MCC, where $|P| + |Q| \leqslant n$.

Proof
The correctness of the algorithm follows from Corollary 4.1 and Lemma 4.2. As for the time complexity, steps (1), (2) and (3) take $O(\sqrt{n})$ time on MCC, and $O(\log n)$ on PSC and CCC for MERGE, PRECEDE and BROADCASTING respectively. Steps (4) and (5) take constant time and (6) takes $O(\sqrt{n})$ time on MCC, and $O(\log n)$ on PSC and CCC for CONCENTRATION. Therefore, the overall time complexity is $O(\sqrt{n})$ on MCC for merging two convex hulls P and Q.

THEOREM 4.1
Given a set S of n planar points, the convex hull for S can be computed in $O(\sqrt{n})$ time on an $\sqrt{n} \times \sqrt{n}$ MCC.

Proof
We use the divide-and-conquer strategy. First, sort points by their y values and then find two convex hulls P and Q recursively. The final convex hull is obtained by merging P and Q using the algorithm MERGE-CONVEX2. Therefore, the time complexity can be written as $T(n) = T(n / 2) + M(n)$, where $M(n)$ is the merge time. Since $M(n)$ is $O(\sqrt{n})$ on MCC by Lemma 4.3, the theorem follows.

4.3 Convex hulls in 3D

The convex hull in 3D plays an important role in a host of applications such as computer graphics, design automation, and operations research [6]. Preparata and Hong [14] presented an $O(n\log n)$ sequential algorithm for convex hull problems in 3D. For parallel processing, Chow [2] gave an $O(\log^4 n)$ parallel algorithm on CCC and Lu [3] obtained $O(\sqrt{n}\log n)$ parallel algorithms on a $\sqrt{n} \times \sqrt{n}$ MCC by applying Chow's idea directly onto MCC. In this section, we shall show that the convex hull of a set of n points in 3D can be computed on $O(\sqrt{n})$ time on a $\sqrt{n} \times \sqrt{n}$ MCC.

4.3.1 Preliminaries

Consider two non-intersecting convex polyhedra P and Q such that the y values of vertices in P are greater than those of vertices in Q (Figure 4.4). A convex polyhedron is represented by a set of faces determined by three points. A face of P or Q is called **external** if it belongs to the new convex hull of $P \cup Q$ and **internal** otherwise. The merging of P and Q can be executed as follows: we first determine for each face of P and Q that it is external, remove from P and Q the **internal** faces, and then add **supporting** faces that are tangent to P and Q along two circuits C_P and

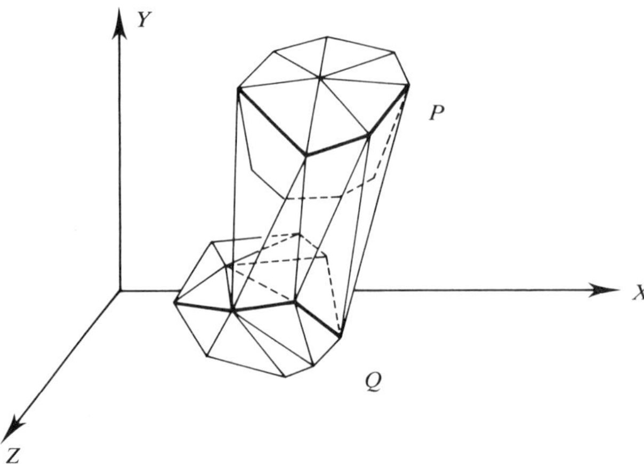

Figure 4.4
Two convex polyhedra P and Q.

C_Q in P and Q respectively. Note that C_P and C_Q consist of edges, each of which is shared by internal and external faces. In this section, we shall describe how to decide for each face if it is external or not.

Let H_{iP} denote the halfspace that contains P and is bounded by face F_i.

Lemma 4.4
Face F_i of P is external if Q lies in H_{iP}.

Let $n_i = (a_i, b_i, c_i)$ be a normal vector of F_i directed outward from inside P. There are two supporting planes which are parallel to F_i and contain Q in between. Of those two, let PL_i be the supporting planes which first hit Q when we move the plane parallel to F_i in the direction opposite to n_i from infinity. We define, for each face F_i of P, its associated face F_{ij} of Q such that PL_i make the smallest angle with F_{ij} among all the faces of Q, where the angle formed by faces F_i and F_j with unit normal vectors (a_i, b_i, c_i) and (a_j, b_j, c_j) respectively is $\cos^{-1}(a_i, b_i, c_i) \cdot (a_j, b_j, c_j) = \cos^{-1}(a_i a_j + b_i b_j + c_i c_j)$.

Lemma 4.5
Q lies in H_{iP} if, and only if, F_{ij} of Q associated with F_i of P is in H_{iP}.

Proof
Clearly, F_{ij} is in H_{iP} if Q lies in the halfspace H_{iP}. Next, we want to show that Q is in H_{iP} if F_{ij} is in H_{iP}. We shall prove it by showing that PL_i is in H_{iP} if F_{ij} is in H_{iP}, since Q is in H_{iP} if PL_i is in H_{iP}. Suppose PL_i is not in H_{iP}. Let v_i be a vertex of Q that supports PL_i. We can easily see that F_{ij} shares with PL_i the vertex v_i, since F_{ij} makes the smallest angle with PL_i. Therefore, F_{ij} is not in H_{iP}, making a contradiction.

From Lemmas 4.4 and 4.5, we have the following result.

Lemma 4.6
A face F_i of P is external if, and only if, its associated face F_{ij} of Q is in H_{iP}.

Therefore, given a face F_{ij} of Q associated with F_i of P, we can determine in O(1) time whether or not F_i is external. We define similarly, for each face of Q, its associated face of P.

Now, we discuss how to find, for each face F_i of P, F_{ij} of Q. Let N_Q be a set of points on the surface of the unit sphere, where each point represents a unit normal vector of a face of Q. Since the distance between two points (a_i, b_i, c_i) and (a_j, b_j, c_j) is $2(1 - a_i a_j + b_i b_j + c_i c_j)$, the angle that face F_i forms with face F_j decreases as the distance between points (a_i, b_i, c_i) and (a_j, b_j, c_j) decreases. Therefore, we have the following lemma.

Lemma 4.7
For each face F_i of P with normal vector $n_i = (a_i, b_i, c_i)$, its associated face F_{ij} of Q has a normal vector $n_{ij} = (a_j, b_j, c_j)$ such that the point (a_i, b_i, c_i) is nearest to the point (a_j, b_j, c_j) among all the points in N_Q.

Based on Lemma 4.7, we can find, for each face F_i of P, F_{ij} of Q as follows: we first construct a spherical Voronoi diagram for N_Q. A spherical Voronoi diagram for N_Q is a partition of the surface of the unit sphere into regions, where each region for a point in N_Q is the locus of points on the surface of the sphere which are closer to that point than to any other point in N_Q. Brown [15] presents an algorithm for constructing the spherical Voronoi diagram of a set of points on the surface of a sphere by intersecting halfspaces. For each point p_i in N_Q, there is a plane L_i tangent to the sphere at point p_i. Let H_i be the halfspace bounded by L_i which contains the entire sphere. The intersection of the halfspaces, H_is, for all the points p in N_Q forms a convex polyhedron C. The intersection of L_i and L_j is an edge of C if, and only if, F_i and F_j in Q are adjacent. The spherical Voronoi diagram is now obtained by a simple projection of the edges of C to the surface of the sphere. Next we find, for each face F_i of P, its associated face F_{ij} by performing point locations in the spherical Voronoi diagram.

4.3.2 Parallel algorithm in 3D

The following algorithm merges two convex polyhedra in the left and right blocks of MCC, producing the new combined convex polyhedron.

Algorithm MERGE-CONVEX3

Input: two convex polyhedra P and Q such that the y values of vertices of P are greater than those of vertices of Q. Each PE containing a face also stores its three adjacent faces that share a common edge.

Output: a new convex polyhedron containing $P \cup Q$.

(1) Determine for each face of P and Q whether or not it is external. We consider only faces of P since the other case is similar.
   (a) Construct the spherical Voronoi diagram $V(N_Q)$ for a set N_Q of points each of which represents a normal vector of a face in Q. Since each PE containing a face also stores three adjacent faces associated with it, the edges of the convex polyhedron C can be generated in O(1) time, and the edges of the spherical Voronoi diagram can be computed in O(1) time by projecting each edge of C onto the sphere.
   (b) Find, for each face F_i of P with normal vector $n_i = (a_i, b_i, c_i)$, its associated face F_{ij} of Q with normal vector $n_{ij} = (a_j, b_j, c_j)$ such that n_i is nearest to n_{ij}. This can be done in $O(\sqrt{n})$ time by executing planar point location for n_i in Vor_Q[4].
   (c) Determine, for each face F_i, whether or not F_{ij} is in H_{iP}. If it is, F_i is external; otherwise it is internal. This step takes constant time.

(2) Construct the circuit C_P as follows: first, check for each external face F_i of P, whether its adjacent face F_j is internal or not by RAR from the PE containing F_j, and if it is, then the edge shared by F_i and F_j is in C_P. Similarly, we find the circuit C_Q. Step (2) takes $O(\sqrt{n})$ time for RAR.

(3) Construct faces which are tangent to P and Q along the circuits C_P and C_Q.
   (a) Order the edges and vertices in C_P and C_Q respectively in counter-clockwise order when observed from the direction of negative infinity of y-axis.
   Comment Let $E_P = \{e_0, e_1, \ldots, e_a\}$ and $V_P = \{v_0, v_1, \ldots, v_a\}$ be the edge and vertex sets of C_P, and $E_Q = \{e'_0, e'_1, \ldots, e'_b\}$ and $V_Q = \{v'_0, v'_1, \ldots, v'_b\}$ be the edge and vertex sets of C_Q respectively, such that

$e_i = (v_i, v_{i+1})$, $0 \leqslant i < a$, $e'_i = (v'_i, v_{i+1})$, $0 \leqslant i' < b$, $e_a = (v_a, v_0)$, $e'_b = (v'_b, v'_0)$, and e_0 makes the tangent face with v'_0. Each tangent face is determined, in general, by an edge e_i in E_P and a vertex v'_{ti} in V_Q such that $A(e_i, v'_{ti})$ is maximum among all $A(e_i, v_k)$ for v_k of V_Q, where $A(e_i, v_k)$ denotes the interior angle formed by the face determined by e_i and v_k and the external face associated with e_i. The vertex v'_{ti} of V_Q is referred to as the **critical vertex** of edge e_i of E_P. Similarly, an edge of E_Q and its critical vertex of V_P determine a tangent face. Step (3a) can be implemented as follows: we only consider the ordering of C_P, since the other case is symmetric. Let F_e be the set of external faces associated with edges of E_P, and let N_e be the set of points, each of which represents a normal vector of each face of F_e. Consider the unit sphere R centered at the origin, with H plane as a supporting plane on the bottom and with each point of N_e on the surface. We find, for each point p of N_e, the line l_p which is the intersection between H and the plane tangent to the sphere R at the point p. Those lines for all points in N_e form a convex CH on H and each convex hull edge corresponding to l_p is associated with the edge of C_P in the external face with normal vector p. After selecting any edge of C_P as e_0, we can find its critical vertex v'_0 of C_Q after sending e_0 to all PEs containing vertices of V_Q by BROADCASTING operation. Then, we obtain E_P and V_P by sorting each edge e_i of C_P according to the corresponding convex hull edge of CH on H as in a 2D case.

(b) Determine, for each edge e_i in E_P(respectively E_Q), its critical vertex v'_{ti} in V_Q(respectively V_P) such that the angle $A(e_i, v'_{ti})$ is the maximum among all $A(e_i, v_k)$ for v_k in V_Q (respectively V_P). This step can be executed in two phases:

(i) Let $E'_P = \{e_0, e_m, e_{2m}, \ldots\}$ be the set of every mth elements in E_P, and $E'_Q = \{e'_0, e'_m, e'_{2m}, \ldots\}$ be the set of every mth elements in E_Q, where $m = \sqrt{n}$. In the first phase, we find for each edge in E'_P(respectively E'_Q), its critical vertex in V_Q(respectively V_P). (We will describe only how to find, for each edge in E'_P, its critical vertex in V_Q since the other case is symmetric.) This can be done as follows: suppose each element in E'_P is stored in the first column of MCC. First, copy each edge in E'_P along each row and find, for every edge e_i in each column c_i, a vertex v_i of V_Q that makes the largest internal angle among those vertices of V_Q in column c_i by shifting the vertices of V_Q in each column up and down $m - 1$ times. Then, by shifting v_i in each column along row to the left $m - 1$ times, we can find, for e_i of E_P in each row, a vertex of V_Q which makes the largest internal angle among those v_is.

Comment After the first phase, the circuit C_P (respectively C_Q) is divided into a set of subcircuits by edges in E'_P (E'_Q) and critical vertices of edges in E'_Q (E'_P), and each subcircuit of C_P is associated with a unique subcircuit of C_Q such that tangent faces are determined by edges and vertices in those two subcircuits. (See Figure 4.5.) Note that the length of each subcircuit is less than m.

(ii) In the second phase, we want to find, for each edge in the

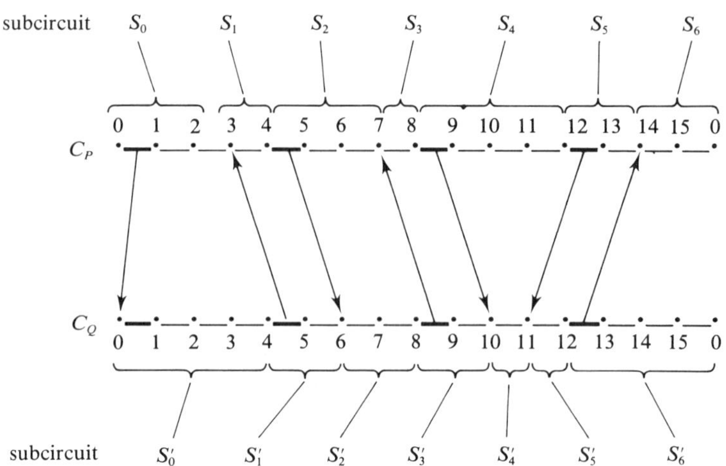

Figure 4.5
Two circuits C_P and C_Q.

subcircuit of C_P (respectively C_Q) its critical vertex in the corresponding subcircuit of C_Q(respectively C_P). (For simplicity, we only consider the case of mapping each subcircuit S_i of C_P to the corresponding subcircuit S'_i of C_Q when the length of S_i is smaller than that of S'_i; the other case is similar.) This can be done as follows: first, the indices A_i and A'_i of PEs containing the first element respectively in subcircuits S_i and S'_i are sent to all the PEs containing elements in S_i by SELECTED BROADCASTING. Each element e_i of S_i in the PE with index k is mapped to the PE with index $A'_i + (k - A_i)$ by RAW, where $(k - A_i)$ is the local rank of e_i in S_i. We compare each element in S_i and S'_i with all the other elements respectively in S'_i and S_i, moving the mapped elements of S'_i respectively to the next and previous PEs consecutively at most m times. (At this time, an MCC is treated just like a linearly-connected computer using snake-like order.)

Lemma 4.8
The algorithm MERGE-CONVEX3 can be executed in $O(\sqrt{n})$ time on a $\sqrt{n} \times \sqrt{n}$ MCC, where $|P| + |Q| \leqslant n$.

Proof
It follows from the properties described in the previous section and comments in the algorithm.

The convex hull in 3D can be computed similarly as in 2D using the divide-and-conquer strategy. Therefore, we have the following theorem.

Theorem 4.2
Given a set S of n points in 3D, the convex hull for S can be computed in $O(\sqrt{n})$ time on a $\sqrt{n} \times \sqrt{n}$ MCC.

Conclusion

In this chapter, we have presented $O(\sqrt{n})$ parallel algorithms for convex hulls in 2D and 3D. The tangent lines for two disjoint convex hulls in 2D have been computed in one iteration by keeping track of the range of angles where they can lie, and hence the parallel algorithm for computing the convex hull on MCC can be directly implemented in $O(\log^2 n)$ time on other SIMD-type computers, such as PSC and CCC.

For convex hulls in 3D, we reduce $O(\sqrt{n}\log n)$ time complexity of Lu's algorithm to $O(\sqrt{n})$ by performing $O(\sqrt{n})$ planar point location algorithm in the spherical Voronoi diagram, to determine the external and internal faces, and by executing efficient data routeing schemes to find the tangent faces between two disjoint convex polyhedra in the merge step.

References and further reading

1. Miller R. and Stout Q.F. (1986). *Mesh Computer Algorithms for Computational Geometry*. Technical Report, 86–18, State University of New York At Buffalo
2. Chow A.L. (1980). Parallel algorithms for geometric problems. *PhD dissertation*, University of Illinois
3. Lu M. (1986). Construction of the Voronoi diagram on a mesh connected computer. In *Proc. of 1986 Int. Conf. on Parallel Processing*, pp. 806–11. Chicago IL
4. Jeong C.S. and Lee D.T. (1987). Parallel geometric algorithms on mesh-connected-computers. In *Proc. 1987 Fall Joint Comp. Conf.*, Dallas TX
5. Stone H. (1971). Parallel processing with the perfect shuffle. *IEEE Trans. on Comput.*, **C-20**, 153–61
6. Preparata F.P. and Vuillemin J. (1979). The cube-connected-cycles: a versatile network for parallel computation. In *Proc. IEEE Sym. on Foundations of Computer Science*, pp. 140–7
7. Aggarwal A., Chazelle B., Guibas L. *et al.* (1988). Computational Geometry. *Algorithmica,* **3**(3), 293–327
8. Atallah M.J. and Goodrich M.T. (1986). *Efficient Plane Sweeping in Parallel.* Computer Science Technical Report CSD-TR-563, Purdue University
9. Overmars M.H. and van Leeuwen J. (1981). Maintenance of configurations in the plane. *J. Comp. and Syst. Sci.* 23, 166–204
10. Hirschberg D.S. and Kumar M. (1983). An efficient implementation of Batcher's odd–even merge algorithm and its application in parallel sorting schemes. *IEEE Trans. on Comput.,* **C-32**, 254–64
11. Nassimi D. and Sahni S. (1979). Bitonic sort on a mesh-connected computer. *IEEE Trans. on Comput.,* **C-28**, 2–7
12. Nassimi D. and Sahni S. (1981). Data broadcasting in SIMD computers. *IEEE Trans. on Comput.,* **C-30**(2), 101–6
13. Thompson C.D. and Kung H.T. (1977). Sorting on a mesh-connected parallel computer. *Comm. ACM,* **20**, 263–71
14. Preparata F.P. and Hong S.J. (1977). Convex hulls of finite sets of points in two and three dimensions. *Comm. ACM,* **20**(2), 87–93

15. Brown K.Q. (1979). Voronoi diagrams from convex hulls. *Information Processing Letters,* **9**, 223–328
16. Lee D.T. and Preparata F.P. (1984). Computational geometry – a survey. *IEEE Trans. on Comput.,* **C-33**(12), 872–1101
17. Miller R. and Stout Q.F. (1984). Computational geometry on a mesh connected computer. *Proc. of 1984 Int. Conf. on Parallel Processing*, 66–73
18. Nassimi D. and Sahni S. (1980). An optimal routing algorithm for mesh-connected parallel computer. *J. of ACM*, **27**(1), 6–29

5 Toward connection autonomy of fine-grain SIMD parallel architecture

M. Maresca†
H. Li

DIST, University of Genova
IBM T.J. Watson Research Center

Fine-grain Single Instruction stream – Multiple Data stream (SIMD) parallel architectures have been shown to be extremely suitable for low-level vision, graphics display and image processing, mainly because of the massive data parallelism. It is, however, desirable to increase the autonomy of the SIMD architecture for further efficiency. For example, with address autonomy, each processor can fetch data from memory locations different from the other processors. At the extreme, there can be autonomy at the operation level so that each processor executes different but cooperative algorithms. Because of the quantity (tens of thousands) and the simplicity (for example, bit-serial) of the processors in fine-grain SIMD systems, these autonomies may be too expensive to justify their benefits. Nevertheless, one type of autonomy, connection autonomy, is extremely beneficial and is economic in VLSI implementation. We investigate connection autonomy for fine-grain SIMD parallel architecture by showing a model for connection autonomy, the utilization of connection autonomy and its VLSI implementation. We show that, by adding 20% silicon area over each processor, connection autonomy can deliver orders of magnitude of performance improvement over the same network without connection autonomy.

5.1 Introduction

Fine-grain parallel computers consist of a large number (tens of thousands) of simple Processing Elements (PEs) connected by an Interconnection Network (IN). Due to the quantity of PEs, the model of computation is usually SIMD. A central controller broadcasts a stream of instructions to all the PEs to control both the PE operations and the interconnection network [1, 2].

Fine-grain PEs are relatively simple compared with today's microcomputers. Each PE contains a few registers and a one-bit ALU; therefore it can be very slow in carrying out a complex algorithm. However, since each PE only has to carry out a small fraction of the algorithm, the overall performance can be great if communication among PEs does not degrade the computation. For this reason, the most important issue in designing a fine-grain parallel computer is the design of the interconnection network.

† Work done at IBM Research on leave from DIST, University of Genova

In fine-grain parallel computers the interconnection network is usually directly connected [3], because the large number of PEs makes the indirect connection (for example, multistage) undesirable. The topology of the directly connected INs is implemented by physical links directly interconnecting the PEs. Two issues are very important in IN design.

The first issue is concerned with matching the application task graph to the network topology. When the application is well known, one can choose a particular topology for the best performance. For example **mesh-connected computers** [4,5,6] are popular for image processing. On the contrary, when the application environments are not known, topology with small diameter is favored. A modern and popular choice is the hypercube topology [7] which offers flexible and efficient embedding of many task graphs, but at the expense of high wiring complexity. In this regard we have shown in [8, 9, 10] that connection autonomy can offer the same flexibility and efficiency in embedding many task graphs at much lower wiring complexity. This was accomplished through a synergy of the network topology and the packaging technology, which is the theme of this chapter.

The synergy is related to the second issue, the engineering of the network, which is the main theme of this chapter. Implementing a network with a high degree of connectivity (for example, a hypercube) in today's 2D packages (for example, VLSI chips or printed circuit boards) is like unfolding a clump of paper. The pairs of processors that are logically close can be physically distant, which leads to less efficient implementation than it appears because of the mismatching between the network topology and the 2D package. We will show how the engineering of a network with connection autonomy takes advantage of the package.

Our approach is as follows. Section 5.2 describes the basic idea of connection autonomy. In Section 5.3 we apply the idea of connection autonomy to the 2D torus topology; we also describe the characteristics of such a network, called Polymorphic-Torus. Section 5.4 deals with a VLSI implementation of the Polymorphic-Torus. The benefit of connection autonomy demonstrated via its implementation is discussed in Section 5.5.

5.2 Connection autonomy

Autonomy is a deviation from and an extension of the SIMD computational model which demands the identical behavior of all processing elements via the broadcast instruction issued by a central controller. The instruction in general contains three main fields. The first is the 'operation' field which drives the ALUs, the loading of the storage units (registers and memories), the operand selection, and all the data movements and manipulations. The second is the 'address' field which controls the simultaneous access for all the PEs to their own memory at the same address, to fetch or store data. The third is the 'connection' field which controls the network topology as well as the data movements in the network.

Autonomy can be provided at all three levels. **Operation autonomy** allows each PE to behave independently from the others in ALU operations as well as data manipulation. This is a movement towards an MIMD computational model. Considering the large number of PEs in a SIMD system, such autonomy is quite expensive because the controller must be replicated at each PE. Compared with the simplicity of each PE (that is, bit-serial), the cost of the replicated controller is very high. The high cost offsets the justification for the level of autonomy.

Address autonomy allows each PE to fetch or store operands from different memory locations under SIMD control [11]. This is usually implemented by providing an 'address offset' mechanism to every PE and is useful in using 1D arrays to solve problems with 2D data structures (for example, region) [11]. Generally, for a multidimensional mesh, address autonomy is useful when the data structure of the problem is one dimension higher than the network topology. The cost can be high if address autonomy is applied to bit-serial PE.

As we will show, the addition of **connection autonomy** to a SIMD system with bit-serial PEs can be implemented with relatively low cost, but it offers significant performance improvement. The idea is to equip each PE with a switch which is able to interconnect the physical links according to the specification from the instruction. The flavor of connection autonomy comes in the sense that the connection field of the instruction is interpreted differently by each PE. The synthesis of different connection at each local switch allows the efficient matching to a task graph not known presumptively.

More precisely, connection autonomy can be implemented by placing a 'Connection Control Register' (CCR) in each PE. The CCR determines the behavior of the local switch; hence collectively all CCRs determine the global topology. The CCR can be viewed as an extension of the 'connection' field of the instruction. However, the important enhancement is that the locally generated CCR leads to different connection behavior under SIMD control.

Connection autonomy can be applied to any topology; however, the most advantageous application is to a 2D torus due to its optimum match to 2D package. As shown in [8, 9], the resulting network, called Polymorphic-Torus has an optimal flux-time product for many vision algorithms among all members of the torus family. The flux-time product indicates the performance of an algorithm on an interconnection network. It depends both on the time complexity of the algorithm and on the topology of the interconnection network. The Polymorphic-Torus architecture is discussed next.

5.3 Polymorphic-Torus architecture

5.3.1 Applying connection autonomy to a 2D torus

The Polymorphic-Torus consists of a Physical NETwork (PNET) and a programmable Internal NETwork (INET) at each node of the PNET. The PNET is global while the INET is local. In a Polymorphic-Torus consisting of $N = n \times n$ processors, the PNET is an $n \times n$ mesh with its boundary connected in either torus mode or spiral mode (Figure 5.1). A processor P(i,j) is situated at the mesh junction with coordinate (i,j) and is equipped with four ports (or physical links) N(i,j), E(i,j), W(i,j) and S(i,j). These four ports connect themselves to both PNET and INET, and are the interface between the PNET and the INET. Except for the selection of 'torus' or 'spiral' mode, the PNET is a hard-wired, fixed, non-programmable network.

In contrast, the INET is totally programmable. At the (i,j) junction of the PNET, there resides an INET(i,j) which is a complete graph of four ports (N(i,j),

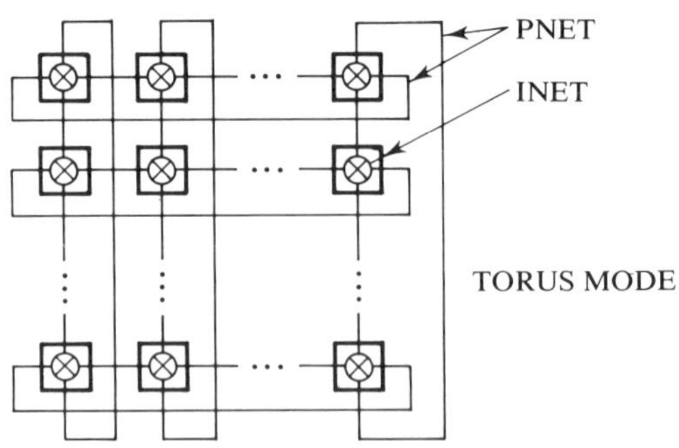

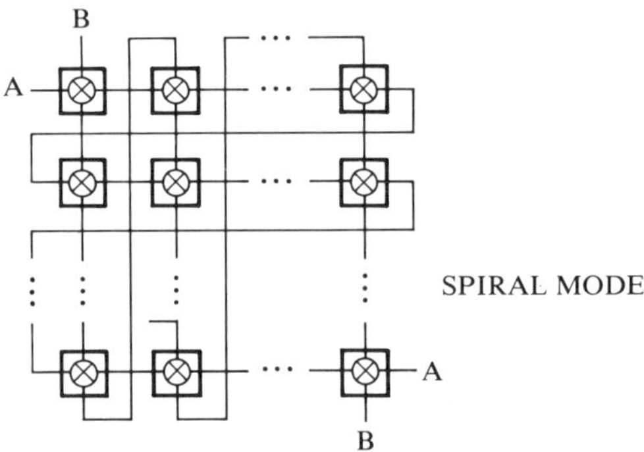

Figure 5.1
Composite physical and internal network in the Polymorphic-Torus. The Polymorphic-Torus can be reconfigured by programming the INETs.

E(i,j), W(i,j) and S(i,j)). By 'complete', we mean that each port can be connected to every other port. In the matrix representation in Figure 5.2, a 1 in the entry (port(s), port(t)) of the matrix means that port(s) and port(t) are connected where port(s) and port(t) can be N(i,j), E(i,j), W(i,j) or S(i,j). The insertion of 1 into the matrix is controlled by program, furthermore, each INET can be programmed differently. By default, the diagonal entries of the matrix are all 1. Note that only the upper or lower triangle of the matrix is needed to express the connection.

The processor connection of the Polymorphic-Torus is programmable by inserting an 'INET control pattern' into the entries of the matrix. Subject to the INET control pattern local to each processor, a pair of ports can be connected (for example, N connected to S and E connected to W), a triplet of ports can be connected (for example, N connected to both E and W) or all four ports are connected together. By synthesizing a concerted set of INET control patterns according to processor identification (pid), one can derive out of the Polymorphic-Torus a network matching the task graph. It is the synthesis of the INET control pattern that gives connection autonomy to the SIMD system. A switch function, the SHORTPORT, is needed to support connection autonomy. This is discussed next.

$$
\begin{array}{c} \\ N \\ E \\ W \\ S \end{array}
\begin{array}{c} \begin{array}{cccc} N & E & W & S \end{array} \\
\left(\begin{array}{cccc} I & X & X & X \\ & I & X & X \\ & & I & X \\ & & & I \end{array}\right) \end{array}
$$

$$
X = \begin{cases} \text{I CONNECTED} \\ \text{O NON-CONNECTED} \end{cases}
$$

Figure 5.2
Matrix representation of the INET connections. Each PE autonomously controls its own INET.

5.3.2 A switch function to support connection autonomy

The SHORTPORT function is a textual notation for the INET control pattern. The format is SHORTPORT (pid condition) {g1}, {g2}; where pid is the processor identification, which indicates that the SHORTPORT function is local and dependent on the position of the INET. The parameters g1 and g2 are group of ports that are connected (or 'short-circuited'). For example, {E, W} can be in the same group or three ports can be in the same group (for example, {N, E, W}). In the extreme case, all four ports can be in the same group (for example, {N, E, W, S}).

The effect of the SHORTPORT is to equate the logical level of the ports. For example, SHORTPORT {E, W}; will make the signals on port E and port W be at the same logical level so that they are in effect short-circuited, a phenomenon from which the switch function receives its name. The short-circuit phenomenon is an efficient mechanism for communication between two processors that are far apart physically in the PNET. Such a long-distance communication can be done by SHORTPORT along with two other traditional communication protocols: SEND (value, port) and RECEIVE (port); the former sends a 'value' to the prescribed port while the latter receives a 'value' from the prescribed port.

For example, the communication between P(1) and P(N) in a row of N processors can be established by the following commands simultaneously executed:

```
SEND (if pid == 1, value, E);
RECEIVE (if pid == N, W);
SHORTPORT (if pid != 1 && pid != N) {E,W};
```

Under the command, P(1) sends 'value' to port E, then the signal 'value' ripples through P(2), P(3), . . ., P(N − 1) because of their port E and port W are all short-circuited. Finally, 'value' arrives at port W of P(N) and is received by P(N). The above example shows that the distance between two processors can be shortened by connection autonomy. In other words, connection autonomy decreases the diameter of the PNET. Utilization of this property leads to efficient task graph embedding [8, 10].

5.4 A VLSI implementation

There are certain costs associated with connection autonomy:

(1) the extra silicon area required to implement the INET in each PE and
(2) the propagation delay introduced by the INET in each PE.

These costs are investigated in detail in this section via a VLSI chip implementation of the 2D Polymorphic-Torus called the Yorktown Ultra Parallel Polymorphic Image Engine (YUPPIE). These costs fully characterize the engineering of an interconnection network with connection autonomy.

The YUPPIE chip contains 16 nodes, arranged in a 4 × 4 mesh. Each node is made up of the following blocks:

- PE It consists of a one-bit ALU equipped with carry–save logic, a one-bit accumulator and a CCR selecting the INET functions.
- INET It is a switch that allows connection of the accumulator register to one of the four I/O ports (NEWS), as well as short-circuiting two of them, either horizontally (East with West) or vertically (North with South). The selection of the INET switch function is controlled by the CCR. The current YUPPIE INET implements only the SHORTPORT switching functions that are most frequently found in computer vision algorithms. The emulation of more complex interconnection schemes can be done in several steps.
- Data memory (DM) It is a one-bit RAM memory addressed by the single instruction incoming from the program controller. All the DMs receive the same address. The YUPPIE chip contains 4K bits of DM, arranged as 16 columns (one for each PE) of 256 bits. In order to make the system expandable, the chip is also provided with 16 other connections (one for each PE) to an external memory. In this way, the DM can be seen as a large continuous address space partially mapped into the chip and partially outside.

The layout of the YUPPIE chip is shown in Figure 5.3. The lower half of the picture shows the 16 nodes. They are physically arranged as a stack of 16 rows each of which contains the PE block and the INET block. An area on the right side of the rows is the INET and the mesh interconnection. Controls are generated by random logic for instruction decoding and timing generation, as shown in the figure. Control lines flow vertically through the processor array on a dedicated metal layer, feeding all 16 PEs. The upper half of the chip is the on-chip DM, built as an array of 256 words of 16 bits.

The chip has been fabricated in 2μ CMOS technology, with one level of polysilicon and two levels of metal. It has 68 pins and contains about 50 000 active devices. The die size is 5.0 mm × 6.5 mm (excluding I/O pads) and the area is divided as follows:

- 24% for the DM block,
- 38% for the PE block and
- 12% for the INET block.

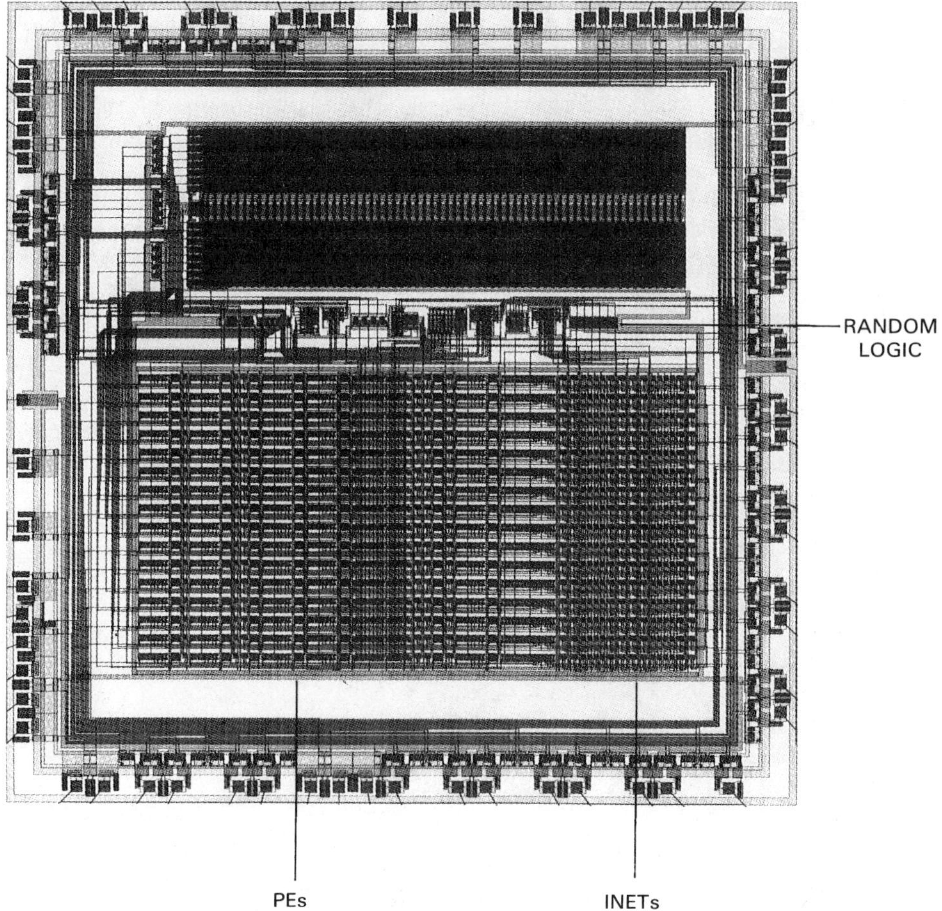

Figure 5.3
The YUPPIE chip. The INET section occupies about 20% of processors and memory.

5.5 Cost and performance of connection autonomy

In this section, we characterize cost and performance of connection autonomy by evaluating:

- the silicon area required to implement the INET with respect to a regular bit-serial PE and
- the propagation delay through a chain of short-circuited PEs, as a function of the number of INETs to be crossed.

According to the YUPPIE chip design, the cost of connection autonomy in terms of silicon area is fairly low. The whole Polymorphic-Torus network, consisting of the INETs and the mesh wires, takes roughly one-third of the PE area (12:38) or half of the memory (12:24). Actually, if we consider a complete PE as made up of the data path and the memory, the Polymorphic-Torus network adds less than one-fifth (that is, 12:(38 + 24)) extra silicon area. By adding 20% overhead to each processor (that is, ALU plus memory), the INET control leads to a significant reduction of the network diameter, which in turn allows us to reduce the complexity of many vision algorithms.

On the other hand, the INET propagation delay is closed related to the performance of the Polymorphic-Torus network. Their relationship can be represented by the function $t = f(d)$, that gives the number of clock cycles required to perform communication between a pair of PEs at distance d. Figure 5.4 shows the complexity of embedding a tree on a Polymorphic-Torus, compared against three other types of network: the tree, the hypercube and the mesh. The mesh is the least efficient, due to its nearest-neighbor connections, and requires the execution of d steps to cross d intermediate nodes. The hypercube complexity (via packet switching) is $\log^2 d$, since crossing each level of the tree requires the execution of $\log d$ steps. The tree network is optimum (complexity $\log d$), due to its direct matching with the algorithm graph. The tree embedding complexity for the Polymorphic-Torus is a function of several parameters that represent the propagation delays of the INETs. The formula will be given later in this section.

The impact of the INET propagation delay is worth further explanation. To accommodate the INET delay, a non-symmetrical variable-length clocking strategy is adopted. The length of the clock is dependent on the length of the short-circuited path that a signal must travel while communicating. This clocking technique

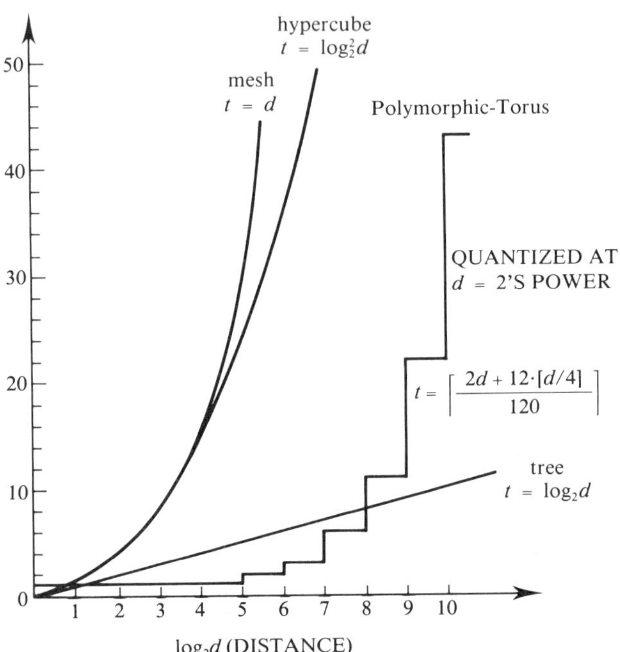

Figure 5.4
Tree embedding complexity. The curves show the number of cycles required to embed a tree in mesh, hypercube, tree and Polymorphic-Torus.

guarantees that a datum arrives at the receiving processor in time, regardless of the physical distance between a communicating pair of processors. Furthermore, the variable-length clocking scheme is an effective mechanism to resolve the clock-skew problem in a large SIMD system.

According to the measurements from the YUPPIE chip, we can write the propagation delay (in units of machine cycles) as a function of the length of the short-circuited path (in units of the number of short-circuited processors). The following equation represents that function:

$$t = \left\lceil \frac{u \times d + 2 \times v \times \left\lceil \frac{d}{w} \right\rceil}{c} \right\rceil$$

where:

t is the propagation delay (in normalized machine cycles),
d is the distance between a pair of communicating processors,
u is the propagation delay per INET,
v is the delay per chip-crossing,
w is the square root of the number of processors per chip, and
c is the machine cycle time.

In the YUPPIE chip $c = 120$ ns, $w = 4$ (16 processors per chip), $u = 2$ and $v = 6$ at 50 pF.

The first measurement of the performance of connection autonomy can be obtained by comparing the complexity curves for the mesh and the Polymorphic-Torus. The tree embedding for the mesh is of $O(\sqrt{N})$ complexity while that of the Polymorphic-Torus is of $O(\log^s \sqrt{N})$ where $1 < s < 2$ and N is the total number of processors in the system. The added 20% silicon overhead to implement connection autonomy leads to orders of magnitude performance improvements for large N in this case. This comparison indicates the tremendous benefit of a network with connection autonomy over the network of the same topology without connection autonomy.

Another performance measurement of connection autonomy can be obtained by comparing the complexity of the curves for the Polymorphic-Torus and the hypercube, both of which grow as $O(\log^s \sqrt{N})$ but the raised power (s) for the Polymorphic-Torus is smaller than that of the hypercube for $N < 2^{24}$ [8,9,10]. This indicates that, with connection autonomy, a low-dimension network can perform better than a high-dimension network without connection autonomy. The significance here is that connection autonomy provides an alternative to high-degree connection for achieving higher performance. Considering the VLSI pin restriction, connection autonomy is a superior solution.

Summary and concluding remarks

The constraints of identical behavior of all processors in a SIMD system can be relaxed by applying autonomy at different levels for performance enhancement. We have investigated connection autonomy in this chapter. Connection autonomy can be applied to any network topology by inserting a switch at each processor and by controlling each local switch from conditions generated locally. Different network topologies can be created by properly driving the local switches, in order to match the application task graphs efficiently.

Although connection autonomy is applicable to all network topologies, its most advantageous application is to a 2D torus as has been studied in [8, 9]. The resulting architecture, called the Polymorphic-Torus, emphasizes the packaging issue of interconnection network design.

The cost of connection autonomy in terms of silicon area and in terms of the propagation delay in each local switch was investigated in detail by a VLSI implementation of the Polymorphic-Torus, called YUPPIE. We found that, by adding 20% silicon area over each processor, connection autonomy can deliver orders of magnitude of performance improvement over the same network without connection autonomy in a tree embedding problem. Furthermore, according to the parameters extracted by the YUPPIE design, the Polymorphic-Torus performs better than the hypercube in the tree embedding problem when the number of PEs does not exceed 2^{24}, a size beyond the reach of today's practical engineering implementation. Performance improvement offered by connection autonomy for other problems can be found in [8, 10].

References

1. Enslow P.H. (1977). Multiprocessor organisation - a survey. *ACM Computing Surveys,* **9**(1), 103–29
2. Flynn M.J. Very high speed computing systems. *Proc. IEEE,* **54**(12), 1901–9
3. Uhr L. (1984). *Algorithm Structured Computer Arrays and Networks.* New York: Academic Press
4. Danielsson P.E. and Levialdi S. (1981). Computer architectures for pictorial information systems. *IEEE Computer,* **14**(11), 53–67
5. Reeves A.P. (1984). Parallel computer architectures for image processing. *Computer Vision Graphics and Image Processing,* **25**(1), 68–88
6. Rosenfeld A. (1983). Parallel image processing using cellular arrays. *IEEE Computer,* **16**(1), 14–20
7. Seitz C.L. (1985). The Cosmic Cube. *Comm. ACM,* **28**(1), 22–33
8. Li H. and Maresca M. (1987). *Polymorphic-Torus Network for Supercomputing.* Technical Report IBM RC 12568
9. Li H. and Maresca M. (1987). Polymorphic-Torus Network. In *Proc. Int. Conf. on Parallel Processing*, pp. 411–14. St. Charles IL, Aug. 1987
10. Li H. and Maresca M. (1987). Polymorphic-Torus: A new architecture for vision computation. In *Proc. Workshop on CAPAMI*, pp. 176–83. Seattle WA, Oct. 1987
11. Fountain T.J. (1987). *Processor Array Design.* London: Academic Press

Section 2

Parallel Architectures for Vision and Image Processing

6· Graphics + Vision = SIMD + MIMD (A novel dual-paradigm approach)

I. Page

University of Oxford

Many computer applications are amenable to huge increases in execution speed through the deployment of parallel processing. Two of the most powerful paradigms of parallel processing which have so far seen extensive use are the MIMD and SIMD models. These models are often considered as suitable implementation vehicles for control-parallel algorithms and data-parallel algorithms, respectively. However, many applications, particularly in the areas of computer graphics and vision, use a number of algorithms at different stages where some of the algorithms are naturally control parallel and others data parallel. The algorithms of early vision and those late in the graphics pipeline typically deal with large rectangular arrays of pixels, and they extensively exploit spatial coherence in the data. Such algorithms are best considered as data parallel and a SIMD computational environment may well be the most cost effective for high-speed execution. The algorithms in higher-level vision and those close to the display data-structures in graphics are probably best considered as control parallel and best suited to a MIMD environment, although progress in developing parallel algorithms has so far been slower in these areas.

In order to provide an environment in which highly complex vision and graphics algorithms can run at high speed, we have constructed a computing engine (the Disputer) which encompasses both a data-parallel computing paradigm in a 256-processor SIMD array, and also a control-parallel paradigm in a MIMD network of transputers. The two parallel machines are closely coupled and the entire system is controlled by a single program in the occam 2 parallel-processing language. This system allows us to investigate dual paradigm algorithms and we report some of the early results from using this novel parallel processor for applications in both graphics and vision.

This is an updated version of Page (1988) and reports on recent changes to the Disputer hardware and some more results on applications software.

6.1 Introduction

6.1.1 The SIMD parallel processing paradigm

The processes of image formation in computer graphics and of scene analysis in computer vision are two sides of the same coin, whose currency is computational geometry (Faux and Pratt, 1982). Image-rendering algorithms at the end of the graphics pipeline and the spatial-filtering and edge-detection algorithms of early vision, all work in a domain of 2D arrays of picture elements (pixels). Such local support operations are very well supported on a 2D array of simple processors, simultaneously executing the same program on the spatially distributed data in the pixel arrays. This **Single Instruction stream, Multiple Data stream** (SIMD) or **data-parallel** model of computation has been revisited many times since an early proposal (Unger, 1958) for a spatially distributed processor. The first design of a SIMD computing engine was the Solomon computer (Slotnick, 1960), followed by a partial implementation of Illiac IV (Falk, 1976). More recently there have been a number of such machines built such as the DAP (Reddaway, 1973; Parkinson, 1983), CLIP (Duff, 1976), MPP (Batcher, 1980), DisArray (Page, 1983a, 1983b) and the Connection Machine (Hillis, 1985).

Such locally-based computations can be very powerful, and algorithms which determine *global state from local interactions* are now a common research theme. Some important recent examples of this approach are structure from motion (Ullman, 1979), surface interpolation (Grimson, 1981), optic flow (Horn and Schunk, 1981), shape from shading (Ikeuchi and Horn, 1981), stereo (Marr and Poggio, 1982) and image restoration (Geman and Geman, 1984). These locally-based computations are usually very well supported by SIMD processors and the kernel operations of the algorithms can often best be thought of in terms of generic operations over 2D bitmaps, the archetypical operation being **RasterOp**.

RasterOp (Newman, 1979), also known as Bit Block Transfer (BitBlt), is a primitive operation originally defined for use in raster graphics, which operates over 2D arrays of bits. More recently, it has been extended to arrays of scalar and colour-valued pixels (Van Den Bos, 1987; Guttag, 1986). In its simplest form, RasterOp takes two similarly-sized rectangular image portions, source and destination, and performs:

```
destination := destination OP source
```

where OP is one of a predefined set of functions mapping pairs of pixels into single pixels. Hardware support for this operation has been a big factor in increasing the performance of a number of workstations, starting with the Xerox Alto (Thacker *et al.*, 1979). Square array SIMD processors can be extremely efficient at supporting the RasterOp function and the DisArray processor (Page, 1983a, 1983b) was built to demonstrate and investigate this fact. There are a huge number of examples of the application of RasterOp in raster graphics, including linear image transformations (Goldberg and Robson, 1983), parallel line drawing (Gupta, 1982) and incremental polygon rendering (Theoharis and Page, 1987).

In fact, the ubiquity of RasterOp even outside its originally-intended domain is shown by the fact that it is critically involved in the implementation of the following vision algorithms at the MIT AI Laboratory:

- Canny's optimal edge finder (Canny, 1983).
- Hildreth's motion analysis algorithm (Hildreth, 1985).
- Marr-Poggio-Grimson (MPG) stereo (Grimson, 1985).
- Terzopoulos' multilevel surface reconstruction algorithm (Terzopoulos, 1982).

6.1.2 The MIMD parallel processing paradigm

For the algorithms earlier in the graphics pipeline and for many intermediate-level and high-level vision problems, the algorithms typically need much longer range (and unpredictable) support in the data, with computation being centred on a relatively small number of non-rectangular **regions of interest**. The SIMD paradigm would usually be very inefficient in such circumstances, since data-dependent conditional branching is almost always required. As there can only be one control stream under the SIMD regime, this effectively means that the whole array can only deal with one region of interest at any one time. Clearly, if such regions are very much smaller than the size of the array, as is often likely to be the case, then the bulk of the processing elements can contribute nothing useful to the computation. Although we can be more profligate with hardware than we have been in the past, there will always be big payoffs for those that heed the basic nature of the algorithms and run them on appropriate hardware. It is wiser therefore to take a pragmatic attitude to the zealots who claim that low utilization factors of hardware are not of much significance any longer!

Although it is harder to justify the following claim, it seems more reasonable to use the **Multiple Instruction stream, Multiple Data stream** (MIMD) or **control-parallel**, or **task-oriented** model of computation for this type of algorithm. The justification is weaker than that presented for SIMD processing in early vision, since there has been relatively little work to date on the parallelization of higher-level vision algorithms, so we know relatively little about the support architectures required.

6.2 The Disputer (the best of both worlds?)

Through becoming more involved in the development of vision algorithms, it became clear that a single computational paradigm would be ineffective across all levels of a comprehensive vision system. Current work in the robotics group at Oxford concentrates on the problems of predominantly vision-directed autonomously guided vehicles (Brady *et al.*, 1988) where the range of problems is *even greater* than in vision. We were thus motivated to build an engine which supported both MIMD and SIMD computational paradigms. Earlier work had resulted in a SIMD machine for graphics applications (Page, 1983a, 1983b). The initial motivation for building this **Dis**play **Array** (DisArray) system was to execute the RasterOp (Newman and Sproull, 1979) primitive in parallel at high speed. DisArray uses an array of 16 × 16 special-purpose, single-bit processing elements and is, in fact, a reasonably general-purpose SIMD machine, similar in some ways to the AMT (previously ICL) Distributed Array Processor (DAP) (Reddaway, 1973).

So as to realize quickly our goal of a dual-paradigm parallel processor to investigate dual-paradigm approaches to algorithm design, we replaced the original control unit of DisArray with a purpose-designed controller (Winder, 1986) based on a T800 floating-point transputer (INMOS, 1988). Naturally, the synthesis of the DisArray and a transputer system simply had to be called the **Disputer**. The new transputer-based controller is somewhat slower than the original microprogrammable (AMD 29116-based), purpose-designed controller, but it has the significant benefit of a much better software development environment.

The transputer is a powerful component in building general-purpose MIMD computing systems. The built-in serial communications links, the clean, mathematically-specified model of communication and the occam language (INMOS, 1988), make it relatively easy to build MIMD systems and to program complex parallel algorithms. Although there are currently more difficulties in the way of someone wanting to use transputers than there ought to be, it is a sheer delight to be able to build an asynchronous multiprocessor system where the communications simply *work*. The INMOS links are rather slow when compared with the nearest-neighbour bandwidths of a SIMD processor, but they are extremely well designed and easily yield rock-solid communications to the systems designer. This is in very sharp contrast to the difficulties usually encountered when designing such hardware from the ground up (or even when building systems at the board level with *reputedly* compatible boards on a *reputedly* standard bus!). In fact, we believe that the links rather than the transputers are the really important innovation that INMOS has made and that they ought to be trading more heavily on that fact.

The MIMD computational resource of the Disputer is provided by a dedicated array of ten T414 transputers each with 1 Mbyte of dynamic RAM and with two INMOS C004 crossbar switches which allow almost arbitrary networks of transputers to be set up almost instantaneously and entirely under software control. There is a further dedicated resource of 30 memoryless T414s in a fixed 5×6 configuration, though these have had little use since we added the 1 Mbyte transputers. We can further extend the system at any time, by connecting to a further forty 1 Mbyte T414 transputers which can be reconfigured by patching cables (but never are). Since all of the *programmable* processors are transputers, the whole system is programmed in occam 2 and a complete SIMD/MIMD application is thus a single occam program. This arrangement allows us to investigate those computationally-intensive applications which can benefit from two parallel computation paradigms, both well supported in hardware. At the moment, it seems that the class of such applications may in fact be quite wide, possibly much wider than the vision and graphics areas with which we are currently concerned.

6.3 The architecture of the Disputer

6.3.1 DisArray

The DisArray processor consists of an array of 256 single-bit Processing Elements (PEs) in a 2D (16×16) arrangement. Figure 6.1 shows the internal architecture of each PE of the DisArray processor. Each PE has bidirectional data links to its four nearest neighbour PEs. Row-based and column-based broadcast lines transmit data, addressing and control information to the PEs from the controller. In addition, a video shift register is threaded through all of the PEs, and this supports real-time display of a 512×512, 16-colour bitmap from some part of the distributed array memory. A proposed redesign of the video board will upgrade the screen resolution and allow real-time video input as well.

Each PE has a $256K \times 1$-bit memory, implemented by a single dynamic RAM, giving a total array memory size of 8 Mbyte. This is enough to hold a number

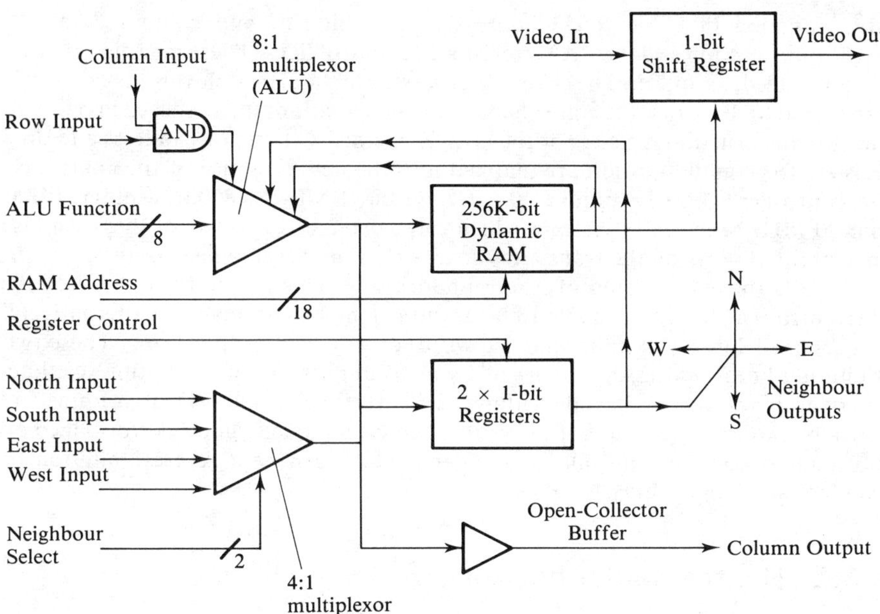

Figure 6.1
The internal architecture of the processing elements.

of images and related data during execution of some of the more data-intensive algorithms, and it can even hold a significant number of consecutive images for image sequence analysis. All processors in the array execute the same (globally broadcast) instruction at the same time. The array has a hardware low-level scheduler which arbitrates between requests from the controller for such computational cycles and from the refresh controller for video refresh cycles.

The T800 controller generates instructions for the SIMD array according to the algorithm being executed and places these instructions directly into the microinstruction register of the array. Synchronization is achieved by polling on the part of the T800, which allows some measure of parallelism between the controller and the array operations.

The array instructions are generally of the form:

Memory__Plane [addr] := **Func** (Memory__Plane [addr], Register__Plane, RowData **AND** ColumnData)

where **Func** is an arbitrary three-operand Boolean function. The operation takes place between two 256-bit square words, called **planes** (one in array memory and one in a specified register) and a further **mask** plane. The mask plane is generated by **AND**ing together at each PE a 16-bit value which is broadcast row-wise through the array and another 16-bit value broadcast column-wise. The addr field refers to one of the 256K planes in the array memory.

The microinstruction for the array processor consists primarily of the eight

ALU function bits, the RAM address, the 16-bit row and column data, the neighbour selection and the RAM/register file control lines. These microinstruction bits are copied, as appropriate, to every processor in the array. Having given a single instruction to the array, the controller and array operations then proceed in parallel. The microinstruction register for the array, together with various address and data registers for communication are mapped into the address space of the controller. The controller is based around a 20 MHz, 32-bit, 1 Mbyte T800 transputer. It has four 20 MHz serial line interfaces which can be connected to any of the otherwise uncommitted ports on the transputer array or on the development system.

Due to the provision of a novel addressing scheme, the basic word of the SIMD array can be regarded as a 16 × 16-bit patch of some image, or alternatively, as a 256 × 1-bit row (scanline aligned word) or a 64 × 4-bit pixel row. These two additional linear addressing modes allow us to implement many existing scanline-based graphics and vision algorithms very effectively. The 2D algorithms are typically harder to develop but offer the promise of equally good performance on short, fat objects and on tall, thin objects which can be a severe limitation of scanline-based algorithms.

6.3.2 The transputer network

The transputer network is based on a Transtech motherboard system with up to 16 plug-in modules (see Figure 6.2) each containing one 20 MHz T414 and 1 Mbyte dynamic RAM. Currently we have 10 such modules, but should soon have a full complement. The motherboard also hosts two INMOS C004 crossbar switches which allow almost arbitrary networks to be set up under software control. In a slightly earlier incarnation of the Disputer, we found that physically replugging

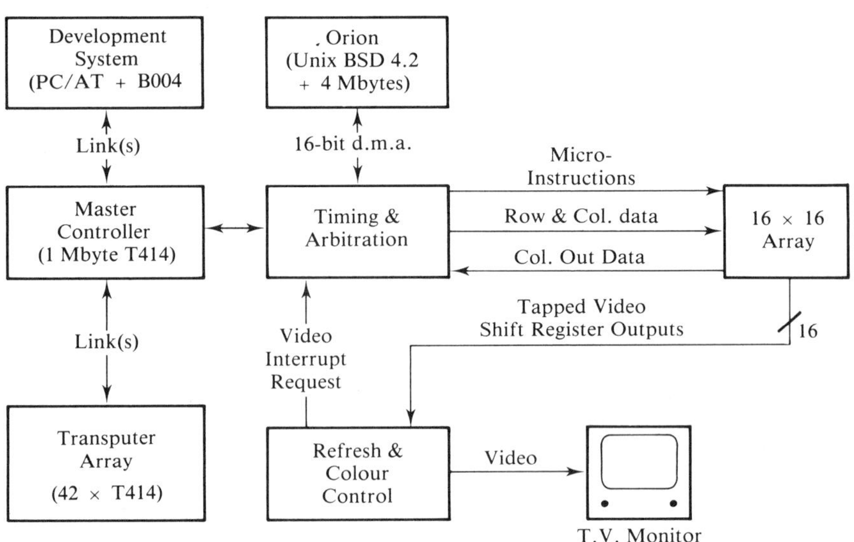

Figure 6.2
The major modules in the Disputer system.

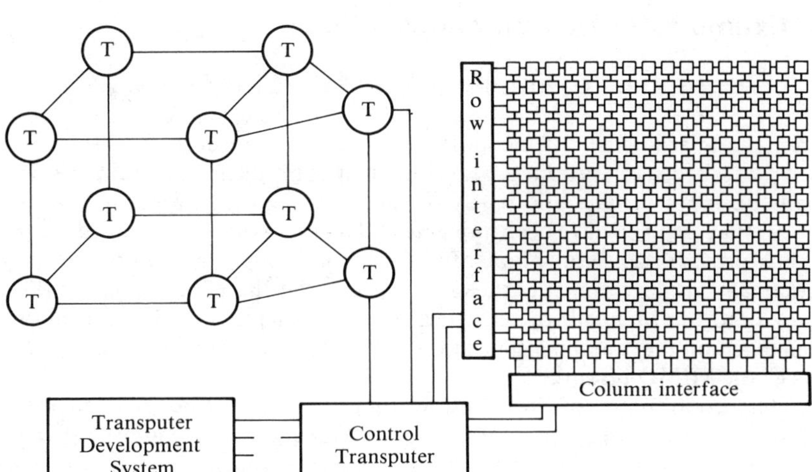

Figure 6.3
An overview of the Disputer architecture

links certainly allowed experimentation with various architectures, but it was virtually impossible to have more than one person working on the system when they required different configurations. The result was that the system stayed for long periods in a particular configuration, and when it changed, it hardly ever reverted to its previous form. This is clearly not an acceptable way of working in a research environment, and we expect the crossbar switches to be of great value. The top left corner of Figure 6.3 shows just one possible configuration of the network.

There is an obvious problem with this architecture in the nature of the connection between the SIMD control transputer and the MIMD network. With a maximum bandwidth of 4 × 20 Mbits/s between the two systems, there will inevitably be a communications bottleneck here for some applications. There is two-fold justification for this state of affairs; firstly, it was expedient to do it this way (within the timescale of an MSc. summer project!), and secondly, we had little idea what structure would be appropriate for *any* dual-paradigm system, so we wanted to keep it simple until we have some measure of experience in the construction of algorithms and applications.

6.3.3 The host/development system

At present, all of the software for the Disputer is written in occam 2, and software development is carried out on a 2 Mbyte T414 transputer hosted in an IBM PC/AT. The PC acts as a terminal and filestore to the development transputer and we run the INMOS Transputer Development System (TDS2) software. The development system also acts as a host to the Disputer system, with communication being supported by either a single transputer link, or two of them in parallel. We intend to move the development environment from the PC/AT onto a networked Sun workstation in the near future.

6.4 Examples of Disputer applications

6.4.1 A graphics example: a Mandelbrot browser

Our first dual-paradigm implementation was of a Mandelbrot set browser. This was chosen partly because it produces beautiful pictures (Peitgen and Saupe, 1988) from virtually no input of data and partly because it is the only program, that we are aware of, that seems to have been implemented on every other machine in the world, and thus provides a useful point of comparison! This application uses a small program on the development transputer to provide the coordinates of the next window onto the Mandelbrot set which is to be evaluated. This application was implemented on the initial configuration of the Disputer which had 42 memoryless T414s as the MIMD resource.

The coordinates of the window to be evaluated are generated by the development system transputer, either from a dialogue with the user or at random, and are then passed to the control transputer. This transputer splits the window space into 1024 **work packets**, each one corresponding to a half scanline subwindow. The transputer network is configured as a linear pipeline of 42 processors in this application, and the control transputer sends the work packets sequentially down the pipeline. Each transputer in the pipeline takes a work packet from the pipeline and evaluates the Mandelbrot set at each pixel position along the half scanline subwindow specified in the work packet. When finished, each transputer sends a run-coded representation of the pixels calculated for that subwindow back down the pipeline to the control transputer and picks up another work packet from the pipeline. Figure 6.4 shows the gross process architecture of the program, which is that of the **processor farm** model of parallelism (May, 1986).

A buffer process which keeps one work packet 'in hand' is essential to ensure that the processors are always kept busy. This is because waiting for the round trip from a result packet being sent off to the controller, to a new work packet arriving back at the now free transputer, can be quite long. However, the buffering scheme itself has a small problem, in that towards the end of evaluation of a complete window, some processors are idle whilst others still have an unevaluated work packet buffered. This problem can be partly or wholly overcome by a number of strategies; for instance, a reasonable heuristic is that no processor should buffer a work packet when there are fewer remaining in the controller than there are processors in the pipeline.

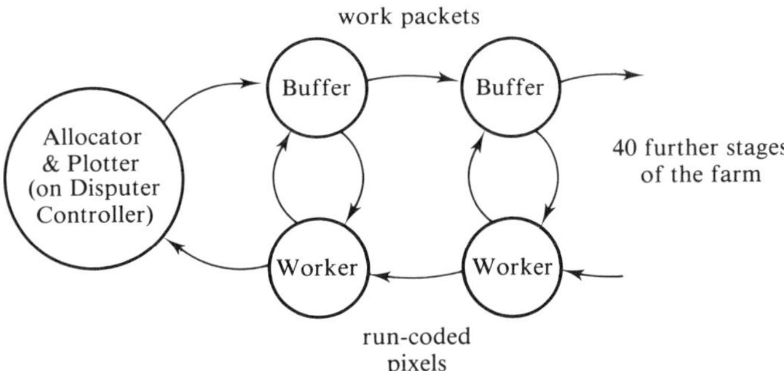

Figure 6.4
The Mandelbrot processor farm.

The control transputer receives the run-coded result packets and uses the SIMD processor to render the pixels. Using DisArray's linear addressing mode, two table lookups and one write operation are all that are required to render up to 64 4-bit pixels in a row. This takes only three SIMD instructions (currently about 500 ns each). In this application, the 42 transputers are the bottleneck and the fast rendering capability of DisArray is a little superfluous. The performance of the system is such that with a generous iteration limit of 250 on the Mandelbrot equation, an 'average' 512 × 512 image is computed and displayed in around three seconds. The worst-case (completely 'black') image takes about 25 seconds.

6.4.2 A simulation example: Newtonian particles

A dual-paradigm program has been written to simulate the interaction of a number of ideal, circular Newtonian particles in the plane (Winder, 1988a). Each particle has a mass and a velocity vector in the plane. The particles interact, through perfectly elastic collisions, with each other and with a rectangular bounding box, thus preserving the total energy of the system.

The interaction computations are mapped onto a rectangular array of transputers, with each transputer being responsible for the interactions within a sub-rectangle of the bounding box. The mapping is defined by splitting the object space into a set of rectangles with exactly the same topology as the array of transputers. These *basic* rectangles are then *extended* so that they overlap each other by a fixed amount. The purpose of the overlap is to provide a 'guard band' around the primary region of interest of each transputer, so that interactions across the boundaries of the basic rectangles will not be missed. This means that most parts of the object space are 'covered' by only one transputer, but some parts are covered by two, and some by four transputers. The size of the guard bands is critical, since it effectively determines the maximum velocity that any particle can have under a fixed time-step regime. Thus, each transputer, at each time step, only has to look at the possible interactions within its extended rectangle, which it can do without communicating with any other processor.

The algorithm proceeds by calculating the new position of each particle according to its velocity vector and then looking at the possible interactions and determining any collisions that actually occur. With n particles in the extended rectangles, there are factorial (n)-possible collisions, and determining these is naturally the bottleneck in the process. Any collisions are resolved by the laws of elastic collision. We conveniently forget about multiple collisions (as they are hard), although we do preserve the number of particles and total system energy. At the end of each time step, the transputers enter a dialogue with their neighbours to inform them of any particles which will have come into their extended rectangles during the current time step. Each transputer then forgets about any particle which has gone outside its own extended rectangle. The step is completed by each transputer informing the controller of the current identity, velocity and position of each of the particles in its basic rectangle. This communication is done by sending the data column-wise up through the array and then along the top row to the corner transputer which is linked to the control transputer.

The control transputer then creates the corresponding picture using SIMD RasterOp operations to plot the circles (64 SIMD read/modify/write cycles for a

16-pixel diameter circle). The picture plotting is done according to a double-buffered regime, so that the user never sees an incomplete picture. The particles are colour coded according to either their identity or their kinetic energy. On a single transputer, we can support about 200 particles with a 25 frames/s animation rate. In this case, the single transputer is the control transputer, so it is doing the SIMD control as well. We cannot yet give useful performance figures for the multiple transputer implementation, because it has not yet been ported to the new transputer network. The original implementation was on the 6×7 array of bare T414 transputers, and the lack of memory severely distorted the algorithm. Given the nature of the algorithm, however, we can expect a nearly linear speedup when we eventually port the program.

6.4.3 A vision example: low-pass filtering and edge detection

A simple early vision system can consist of a low-pass filtering, or smoothing, operation followed by edge detection. We have implemented such a system on the Disputer. The part of the program presented here runs entirely on the SIMD machine and performs a repeated convolution with a 3×3 discrete approximation of a Gaussian kernel to form a low-pass filtered version of the original image. The convolution kernel was chosen for ease of implementation, in that the postscaling division is by a power of 2. The central limit theorem ensures that only a very few applications of this kernel result in a good approximation to convolution with a true Gaussian (Burt, 1981). With n applications of the 3×3 convolution, the result is equivalent to convolving with a $2n + 1 \times 2n + 1$ sized kernel. This size represents the 'scale' of the filtering operation and is clearly related to the highest spatial frequencies that remain in the image.

Subsequently, edges can be located by looking for zero-crossings of the first spatial derivatives of the filtered image. Typically, edges will be detected at various scales, that is, with varying amounts of prefiltering. This is because the original image has a great deal of high spatial frequency information which results in a huge number of edges being located, each with very good spatial resolution. At larger scales, the higher frequencies have been removed, which means that many fewer edges are detected and, with any luck, these might correspond to the edges of gross objects in the scene. However, this prefiltering/edge detection mechanism *inevitably* results in poor location of the resulting edges at larger scales (Blake and Zisserman, 1987). For this reason, it is usual to combine the results from various scales to get a useful set of edges from the larger scales, but with their spatial determination improved by combination with the smaller scale results.

On the Disputer, the convolution uses bit-serial arithmetic, performed over sets of 256 n-bit integers. Each set of 256 n-bit numbers is stored as a set of n planes in array memory. Figure 6.5(a) shows n memory planes standing, in a columnar arrangement, on top of plane 0, which contains the 256 least significant bits (lsb) of such a set. Figure 6.5(b) shows the kernel and Figure 6.5(c) shows how the convolution operation is achieved. A plane-sized set of columnar numbers representing a 16×16 patch of pixels from the input image is multiplied by 16. This operation is made very simple by the choice of the small integers in the kernel, so that multiplication by a power of two involves only an address offset calculation and implies no data movement at all. Eight other sets of 256 pixel values, each offset from the first

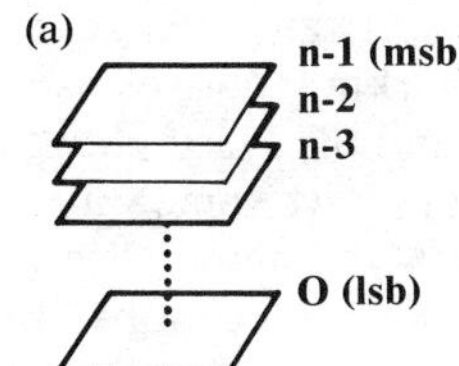

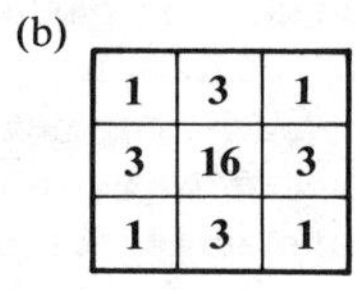

1	3	1
3	16	3
1	3	1

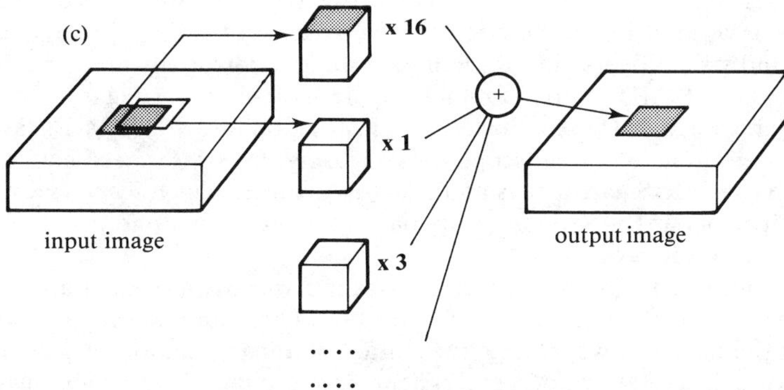

Figure 6.5
(a) 16 × 16 columnar numbers. (b) Gaussian kernel. (c) The steps of the Gaussian convolution.

by one pixel in the eight compass directions respectively, are similarly extracted from the input image, using the RasterOp primitive, and then multiplied by the corresponding constants from the kernel. The multiplication by 3 is, of course, achieved by multiplying by 1 and 2 separately (both virtually cost-free) and adding the results. All the partial products are added bit-serially into a running total and placed in the output image, with a final division by 32 to rescale appropriately. The edge finding is currently very crude, being based on a Sobel operator (Ballard and Brown, 1982). The essence of operators like the Sobel is that they are also convolutions, so they can be implemented exactly like the Gaussian convolution above. As some of the elements in the kernel of this type of edge detector are often zero, there are obvious optimizations that can be made to the algorithm.

A convolution on a 256 × 256 image involves repeating this operation 256 times to cover the whole image and this takes about 120 ms, which is fast compared with a conventional sequential processor, but is really quite slow when contrasted with the (interpolated) speed of say a DAP. The reason is simply that DisArray is showing its origins here, in that, being designed to support only the RasterOp function, it has no direct support for arithmetic operations and must inefficiently manufacture them from two-operand logical operations.

6.4.4 Future applications

At present we are only just starting to mount vision algorithms on the Disputer which, as stated above, was originally built for computer graphics applications. We are currently developing some more interesting software than described here, and this will be reported later. In particular, we are working towards parallel implementations of the Canny edge finder (Canny, 1985) and the Fleck phantom edge finder (Fleck, 1987) in the SIMD engine and hope soon to have some simple intermediate-level vision demonstrations running in the MIMD engine. We are also slowly developing a **virtual machine** for graphics and vision applications, the eventual goal being the simplification of graphics and vision applications software.

Summary

Early results from the Disputer have been extremely encouraging. We have found that there is a good match between the hardware and a number of interesting graphics and vision algorithms. Although small and potentially quite inexpensive, our system has a SIMD computational bandwidth of about 0.5 Gigabits per second and an aggregate MIMD execution (RISC) instruction rate of 200 MIPs (assuming 10 transputers). There is great scope for increasing the SIMD speed considerably, using perhaps CMOS gate arrays and static RAM technology. The system is relatively straightforward to program, since only a single occam program is constructed to control all of the processors.

We are developing a superset of occam 2 which will enable us to express algorithms in a single language which uses both computational paradigms effectively. At the moment, we manage the storage and manipulation of planar SIMD objects by the side effects of occam 2 assignments into the DisArray instruction and data registers. Storage management of the array store currently has to be done at run-time in the controller. All of this is tedious and unaesthetic, but it is acceptable in the short term since there is only a relatively small amount of such code and it can usually be hidden away in library procedures. Our extensions to occam 2 will involve integrating planar objects, columnar numbers and suitable arithmetic and logical operators into the language.

Algorithms for computer graphics and those being developed by the machine vision community, have a great deal in common; this is most evident in the data-parallel algorithms. The degree of commonality is such that it warrants the development of a virtual machine for graphics and vision, and we are actively working on this. It should provide an interface between applications programs and the highly-parallel hardware which implements the kernel algorithms. It is the intention that the virtual machine is not heavily oriented towards any particular hardware model; rather, it should be implementable in a number of different ways on different types of parallel hardware.

Both the graphics and vision research communities urgently need hands-on access to parallel computing workstations with image input and output facilities, and the Disputer is a prototype of such a machine. Experience has shown that sometimes promising lines of research are not followed up, simply because inadequate computing resources result in algorithms that run at an unacceptably low speed. The only foreseeable route ahead for real-time vision is to learn to exploit the massive parallelism that is now being offered by VLSI technology. Luckily, there appears to be a good match between what is becoming available in hardware and what may be needed by the software. As always, the real problem will lie in the understanding of the algorithms and languages.

Acknowledgements

I particularly want to thank the Science and Engineering Research Council, INMOS Ltd, IBM (UK) Ltd, Sigmex Ltd and International Computers Ltd for their financial support of this work and Phil Winder for his heroic works in building the Disputer controller and developing a software library.

References

Ballard D. and Brown C.M. (1982). *Computer Vision.* Englewood Cliffs NJ: Prentice Hall

Batcher K. (1980). The design of a massively parallel processor. *IEEE Trans. on Computing,* **C-29**(9), 836–40

Blake A. and Zisserman A. (1987). *Visual Reconstruction.* Cambridge MA: MIT Press

Brady J.M., Cameron S., Durrant-Whyte H., Fleck M., Forsyth D., and Page I. (1988). In Progress toward a system that can acquire pallets and clean warehouses. *Proc. 4th Int. Symp. Robotics Research* (Bolles and Roth eds). Cambridge MA: MIT Press

Burt F.P. (1981). Fast Filter Transforms for Image Processing, *Computer Graphics and Image Processing,* **16**(1), 20–51

Canny J.F. (1985). Finding edges and lines in images. *PhD Thesis,* MIT AI Laboratory

Duff M.J. (1976). CLIP 4. A Large Scale Integrated Circuit Array Parallel Processor. In *3rd Joint Int. Conf. on Pattern Recognition*, Coronado CA

Falk H. (1976). Reaching for the Gigaflop. *IEEE Spectrum,* **13**(10), 65–9

Faux I.D. and Pratt M.J. (1982). *Computational Geometry for Design and Manufacture.* Ellis Horwood

Fleck M. (1988). Representing space for practical reasoning. *Image and Vision Computing,* **6**(2), 75–86

Geman S. and Geman D. (1984). Stochastic relaxation, Gibbs distributions and the Bayesian restoration of images. *IEEE Trans. PAMI,* **PAMI-6**(6)

Goldberg A. and Robson D. (1983). *Smalltalk-80. The Language and its Implementation.* Reading MA: Addison-Wesley

Grimson W.E.L. (1981). *From Images to Surfaces.* Cambridge MA: MIT Press

Grimson W.E.L. (1985). Experiments with an edge-based stereo algorithm. *IEEE Trans. PAMI*

Gupta S. (1982). Architectures and algorithms for parallel updates for raster scan displays. *PhD Thesis,* Carnegie Mellon University

Guttag K. *et al.* (1986). Requirements for a VLSI graphics processor. *IEEE Computer Graphics and Applications,* **6**(1), 32–47

Hildreth E.C. (1985). *The Measurement of Visual Motion.* Cambridge MA: MIT Press

Hillis W.D. (1985). *The Connection Machine.* Cambridge MA: MIT Press

Horn B.K.P. and Schunk B.G. (1981). Determining optical flow. *Artificial Intelligence,* **17**(1–3), 185–203

Ikeuchi K. and Horn B.K.P. (1981). Numerical shape from shading and occluding boundaries. In *Computer Vision* (Brady J.M., ed.). North Holland

INMOS Ltd (1988). *Communicating Process Architecture.* London: Prentice Hall

Marr D. and Poggio T. (1982). Stereo. In *Computer Vision* (Ballard D.H. and Brown C.M., eds.). Englewood Cliffs NJ: Prentice-Hall

May D. (1986). *Communicating Process Computers.* Technical Note 27, INMOS Ltd

Newman W.M. and Sproull R.F. (1979). *Principles of Interactive Computer Graphics* 2nd edn. Tokyo: McGraw-Hill

Page I. (1983a). DisArray: A 16 × 16 rasterop processor. In *Eurographics '83*, Zagreb

Page I. (1983b). DisArray: A graphics-oriented fifth generation workstation. In *Proc. Nicograph '83*, Tokyo

Page I. (1988). The Disputer: A dual paradigm parallel processor for graphics and vision. In *Parallel Architectures and Computer Vision* (Page I. ed.). Oxford: Oxford University Press

Parkinson D. (1983). The Distributed Array Processor (DAP). *Computer Physics Communications,* **28**(4), 325–36

Peitgen H.O. and Saupe D., eds (1988). *The Science of Fractal Images.* Berlin: Springer-Verlag

Reddaway S.F. (1973). DAP – A Distributed Array Processor. In *1st Annual Sym. on Computer Architecture*, Gainsville FL

Slotnick D.L., Borck W.C., McReynolds R.C. (1960). The SOLOMON computer. In *Proc. AFIPS Conference*

Terzopoulos D. (1982). *Multilevel Reconstruction of Visual Surfaces: Variational Principles and Finite Element Representations.* AIM-671 Artificial Intelligence Laboratory, MIT

Thacker C.P., McCreight E.M., Lampson B.W., Sproull R.F., and Boggs D.R. (1979). *Alto: A Personal. Computer.* Palo Alto CA. Xerox Palo Alto Research Center

Theoharis T. and Page I. (1987). Parallel polygon rendering with pre-computed surface patches. In *Proc. Eurographics '87*

Theoharis T. and Page I. (1988). Parallel incremental polygon rendering on a SIMD processor array. In *Proc. Int. Conf. Parallel Processing for Computer Vision and Display*, Leeds

Ullman S. (1979). *The Interpretation of Visual Motion.* Cambridge MA: MIT Press

Unger S.H. (1958). A computer oriented towards spatial problems. In *Proc. IRE*, 46, 1744–50

Van Den Bos J. (1987). Raster Calc: Calculus for Operations on Graphics Colour Rasters. *Computer Graphics Forum,* **6**(3)

Winder P. (1986). Transputer upgrade for the DisArray graphics processor. *MSc Thesis*, Programming Research Group, Oxford University

Winder P. (1988a). *Bouncing Balls on the Disputer.* Internal Report, Programming Research Group, Oxford University

Winder P. (1988b). Parallel processing with the Disputer. In *Proc. 8th occam User Group*, Sheffield, March 1988

7 · Low-level vision tasks using parallel string architectures

A. Krikelis†
R.M. Lea

Brunel University

In this chapter, the implementation of low-level computer vision tasks on a fine-grain associative string SIMD structure, which has highly efficient VLSI implementation, is presented. A detailed description of a VLSI ASP implementation, called SCAPE, is presented initially. The SCAPE specification is used for the explanation and evaluation of the low-level vision algorithms. The main part of this chapter consists of the description and analysis of local operations (convolution-like) and of the histogramming algorithm. Novel algorithmic techniques are motivated and described, and simulation timings are presented and discussed. The conclusion is that it is possible to exploit the massive parallelism available, while avoiding many of the communication overheads usually associated with the string architectures, by careful algorithm design and careful mapping of the image data structures to the architecture.

7.1 Introduction

The field of image processing has developed considerably during the last decade, with growing applications in various fields. Industrial production, medicine, space exploration, robotics and the discovery of natural resources are but a few examples of such areas. An important goal for researchers in this field is to construct computer-based vision systems that receive an image or a sequence of images from a sensory device, and output an interpretation of this input in real time (approximately 33 ms per image).

With recent advances in Very Large Scale Integration (VLSI) circuitry, it is feasible now to embed a number of processing and memory elements within a single silicon device (chip) in a cost-effective manner. This has led to a surge in research aimed at developing new computer organizations that meet the large computational and design requirements of image-processing tasks by exploiting the new technology. Various kinds of special parallel machines for image processing have been proposed and some have been implemented; examples are described in [1, 2, 3, 4, 5 and 6].

† A. Krikelis is now with Aspex Microsystems Ltd, Brunel University.

The organization of some of the proposed machines is based on a very large number of very small Processing Elements (PEs). Such machines will be referred to as fine-grain, highly parallel or bit-serial machines. In such architectures, different schemes are used to interconnect the PEs. For example, the PEs can be connected together in the form of a linear string, 2D mesh or they can be placed at the nodes of a tree. If all the PEs simultaneously execute the same instruction on their own data, the machine is said to be operating in Single Instruction stream on Multiple Data stream (SIMD) mode [7]. On the other hand, if the PEs execute different instruction streams concurrently on different data streams, then the machine is said to be operating in Multiple Instruction streams on Multiple Data streams (MIMD) mode.

This chapter describes how fine-grain, linear, 1D (string) structured SIMD computer architectures, which have favourable characteristics for efficient VLSI implementation, can be used for the rapid execution of image-processing tasks. The algorithms described in this work incorporate novel approaches to reduce the effects of image data mapping generally associated with linear 1D architectures.

7.2 The SCAPE chip

The Single Chip Array Processing Element (SCAPE) chip [8, 9, 10] is a practical VLSI implementation of the Associative String Processor (ASP) [11, 12], which has been optimized for numerical computation. The SCAPE chip is a versatile addition to the bit-serial SIMD class of parallel-processing VLSI chip architectures. It integrates a string of 256 identical PEs, each comprising of 37 bits of content-addressable memory (32-bit data register and 5-bit activity register), a 1-bit full adder and logic for communication with other PEs. SCAPE chips can be linked together to configure a chain, increasing linearly the processing power of the system; the chip interconnection strategy is transparent. In addition to a single chain of linked SCAPE chips, multiple channels of linked SCAPE chips can support computational configurations such as:

(1) Single Instruction control of Multiple SIMDs (SIMSIMD)

(2) Multiple Instruction control of Multiple SIMDs (MIMSIMD)

All SCAPE chips in a SCAPE chain or SCAPE channel are controlled by the SCAPE chain controller, which comprises the standard bit-slice microprocessor components of typical high-speed microprogram controllers. The chain controller also buffers data transmitted between the SCAPE chain and the host environment.

The SCAPE chip floorplan is shown in Figure 7.1. It comprises four major functional blocks, configured in an array of 'exactly butting' quadratures. The function of each block is described below:

(1) Every one of the four Associative Memory Array (AMA) blocks comprises 64 AMA-rows (word-rows) of content-addressable memory, each formatted as a 32-bit data field and a 5-bit activity field.

(2) Each of the two Bit Control Logic (BCL) blocks is composed of 37 similar bit-column controllers in support of bit-serial operations on programmable declared serial fields or bit-parallel operations on byte or 32-bit word fields. The BCL comprises a serial field partition register to support programmable partition of the AMA data field into up to three serial data fields; pointer and

AMA	WCL	WCL	AMA
BCL	MOGL		BCL
AMA	WCL	WCL	AMA

Figure 7.1
SCAPE chip floorplan.

marker registers, identified with each serial field, enable or inhibit associated bit-planes of the AMA for bit-serial processing. Additionally, the Data Interpretation Logic (DIL) allows bit-masking of AMA bit-columns during search and write operations, tertiary mode.

(3) Every one of the four Word Control Logic (WCL) modules includes 64 similar local PEs. Closely integrated with the local AMA block, each module provides manipulation of the match vector, temporary storage, bit-arithmetic functions and inter-APE communication. Each WCL block incorporates:
   (a) A match network for mapping multiple AMA match vectors into a single overall match vector. The match network determines which AMA registers have matched a content search.
   (b) An adder block which supports bit-arithmetic functions; each local PE has a 1-bit full adder to support bit-serial addition and subtraction operations.
   (c) A TR12 block which incorporates two 64-bit tag registers TR1 and TR2 to hold the 'result vectors' of search operations. TR1 also provides a synchronous data channel for shifting of the 'result vector'.
   (d) An alternate network which distributes into TR1 and TR2 alternately, the matching elements for pairing and divide-and-conquer algorithms.
   (e) An activation network which provides a data-dependent asynchronous channel for the support of activation mappings between staticized 'result vectors' and the PEs selected for subsequent read or write operations.

(4) The inter-APE communication network of the SCAPE chip consists of the serial communication channels implied in the alternate, TR12 and activation networks; these channels are multiplexed onto the single-bit ports (namely, left link port and right link port) of the SCAPE chip interface.

(5) The Micro-Order Generation Logic (MOGL), during SCAPE operations, issues dynamic micro-orders to the BCL and WCL functional blocks, derived from the static micro-orders and operation code of each microinstruction

and the current time slot issued by a timing generator. Input-output (I/O) multiplexing (to minimize pincount and package dimensions) and internal clock generation are also performed in the MOGL.

7.2.1 SCAPE chip operations

The SCAPE chip can operate in any one of the following three modes: bit-serial, byte-parallel and word-parallel. In all three modes, the SCAPE chip executes Associative Processing Instructions (APIs). Each API is divided into four basic phases: **content-search, clear, activate, read/write**.

(1) **content-search** During the content-search phase, serial, byte or word search data and activity bits on the chip pins are routed to the AMA interface through the appropriate routeing channels of the BCL. The subsequent associative search operation produces memory bit-planes (namely, match vectors) which pass into the corresponding processing module of the WCL, where they are either stored as a single overall match vector into the tag registers TR1 and/or TR2, or they undergo control-specified processing (for example, addition/subtraction) and then are stored into the tag register TR1.

(2) **clear** During the clear phase, memory bit-planes, identified by a combination of the control parameters and data stored in the BCL block, are cleared (zeros are written in the corresponding locations).

(3) **activation** During the activation phase, the activation network is employed to provide an activation mapping, according to the control parameters, between 'result vectors' in TR12 and the SCAPE PEs. Such activation mappings are:
   (a) Activate SCAPE PEs tagged in TR1.
   (b) Activate SCAPE PEs not tagged in TR1.
   (c) Activate neighbours of those SCAPE PEs which are tagged in TR1.
   (d) Activate SCAPE PEs tagged in TR1 and that are the nearest to one end of the AMA substring in which they occur.
   (e) Activate SCAPE PEs tagged by those tags in TR2 which are the nearest to each tag in TR1 within the same AMA substring.
   (f) Activate SCAPE PEs between all tags in TR1 and one end of the AMA substring in which they occur.
   (g) Activate SCAPE PEs between all tags in TR1 and the nearest tag in TR2 within the same AMA substring.
   (h) Activate SCAPE PEs in TR1 after the contents of TR1 have been shifted a number of APEs within the same AMA substring.

(4) **read/write** The SCAPE read phase employs the BCL to provide channels for the routeing of data (namely byte or word) from activated SCAPE PEs to the SCAPE pins. The SCAPE write phase also employs the BCL to route serial, byte or word data and activity bits from the chip external interface into the local associative store of all activated PEs.

In addition, the SCAPE chip supports microinstructions for control of the bit-serial mode: for example, declaration microinstruction for programmable partitioning of the content-addressable memory of each PE into up to three different serial fields;

index and reset microinstructions for the control of pointers and markers.

The SCAPE chip is designed to operate with two 10 MHz clock inputs, with 25 ns phase difference between them, to allow the MOGL to subdivide each 100 ns clock period into four 25 ns time-slots. The operation of the MOGL is fully pipelined with the function of the main processing logic with a quarter-clock cycle latency. In operation, the MOGL allocates time-slots to specific dynamic micro-order selections. The operation codes have been optimized for performing, in digital signal and image processing, often-used sequences; for example, the addition of two bits and the writing of the sum back into a memory location is performed in one clock cycle (100 ns).

7.2.2 SCAPE chip software

SCAPE application programs can be written entirely in a block-structured high-level language; present SCAPE applications are expressed using Modula-2. The application programs include calls to external precompiled blocks of code, known as SCAPE procedures. These blocks of code can also be written in a high-level language, not necessarily the same as the host application program, using a set of built-in SCAPE 'APE activation functions' and 'active APE procedures' [13], which correspond to the classes of APIs executable by the SCAPE chip; the definitions of the functions and procedures have been optimized to provide capabilities of exploiting parallelism beyond the level foreseen by the present SCAPE chip applications. In operation, selected blocks of SCAPE code are stored as micro-programs in the SCAPE chain controller, with the application program calling the appropriate sequence of blocks.

Table 7.1 summarizes the SCAPE chip characteristics. Tables 7.2 and 7.3 are indicative of the performance of a single SCAPE chip. The system performance increases linearly with the number of SCAPE chips in it; for example, Table 7.3 is indicative of the performance of a system with 16 cascaded SCAPE chips.

Table 7.1 SCAPE chip characteristics.

Number of PEs	256
Memory per PE	32 (data) + 5 (activity)
Programmable	High-level language interface
Chip size	8.5 mm × 8.8 mm
Number of transistors	145K (approx)
Process technology	2 μm CMOS (2-layer metal)
I/O	TTL compatible
Number of pins	68
Cycle time	100 ns
Power dissipation	980 mW (maximum)

Table 7.2 Single SCAPE chip performance (MOPS)†.

	8-bit operands	*16-bit operands*
Addition/subtraction	250.000	125.000
Scalar-vector multiplication	37.500	6.500
Vector-vector multiplication	23.750	4.375

† 1 MOP is 10^6 operations per second

Table 7.3 16-SCAPE chip system performance (GOPS)†.

	8-bit operands	*16-bit operands*
Addition/subtraction	4.00	2.00
Scalar-vector multiplication	0.60	0.10
Vector-vector multiplication	0.38	0.07

† 1 GOP is 10^9 operations per second

7.3 Image representation on SCAPE

The majority of image-processing algorithms designed for parallel processor arrays assume that the array operates in the pixel parallel mode: a PE is assigned to each image pixel. Digital images typically contain 10^4 to 10^6 pixels. Having a physical array of the image size presents several problems, mainly by being very large in size and cost ineffective (despite the advantages offered by semiconductor technology, for example, VLSI). Therefore, parallel image-processing architectures have to cope with the situation where the array processor has many fewer PEs than there are pixels in a typical image. Hence, consideration must be given as to how these 'oversized' images are mapped onto the array.

Array processors with many bits of memory per PE alleviate the problem to some extent, by using the concept of virtual PEs. This is accomplished by actually storing more than one pixel per PE and operating only on the pixel data when it is actually required. The main obstacle of such image-processing techniques is that each PE of the array has a primary and a secondary storage device associated with it, mainly due to the limited number of memory cells which can be accommodated on the same physical device. The primary memory is the storage located on the same physical media (for example, silicon area) as the logic of the PE; the secondary memory consists of memory cells resident on a different physical device to the one where the logic of the PE is. The access time of the secondary memory is slower, in comparison with the primary memory, due to the need of accessing 'off-chip' devices. Additional, external interface, chip pins are required for communication with the secondary storage devices; in the best of the cases an additional interface line is required per PE. Because of the external interface, parallel architectures using virtual PE techniques do not fully benefit from the advantages offered by semiconductor technology; VLSI technology favours the architectures with constant interface.

A SCAPE-based image-processing system has a limited number of memory cells per PE (32 data bits and 5 activity bits); in addition, there is no provision for an individual PE to interface with external memory. Therefore, for grey-level image-processing applications, it is rather difficult to implement virtual PEs on the SCAPE chain. If eight bits are devoted for the pixel information of the input image, only a small number of memory cells (24 data bits and 5 activity bits) remain available to be used as workspace.

The obvious choice for performing image processing with a SCAPE system, when the image size is larger than the size of the SCAPE chain, is to repeat the load–process–unload sequence of operations on subimages of the input image until the whole image is processed. Each subimage is called an **image patch**. The image patch is defined as a subset, $n \times m$ pixels, of the input image. A SCAPE image patch must contain, in the best case, as many image pixels as there are PEs available in the SCAPE chain.

The image patches are defined using the **scanline** approach to image representation. Scanline approaches to image representation make use of strings. According to these approaches, each scanline (row) of an image (array) is treated as a 1D signal converted to a string of values. A problem that arises from this method of image description, is relating information from one scanline to the next (namely, for local image operations), on the basis of its string representation. Computationally expensive communication is necessary to compute a line-to-line relationship, whereas it is normally easier to compute on a 2D array structure. In order to avoid the communication problems arising from the concatenation of entire scanlines in the SCAPE chain, the SCAPE image patches contain only part of the scanline. In that way, the severe communication (very long communications) obstacle is somewhat cut down. Therefore, an entire scanline is contained in a number of adjacent image patches. Figure 7.2 depicts three possible ways of defining an image patch.

Each image patch is loaded into the SCAPE chain by concatenating patch scanlines. Hence, if p(m, n) is a pixel corresponding to mth line and nth column of the patch, then Figure 7.3 depicts the way that the patch containing this pixel is distributed in the SCAPE chain. The size of the image patch is selected on the base that will give an optimal ratio between computation and communication portions of the processing time for a given image. The aim is to maximize this ratio, and therefore minimize the communication percentage. This can be achieved if the patch size,

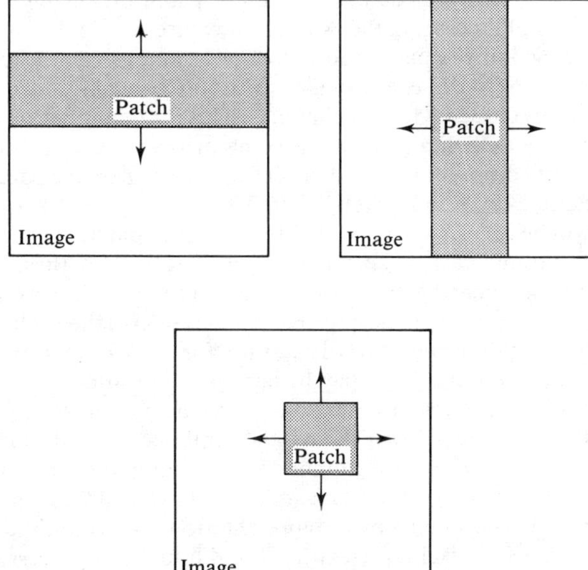

Figure 7.2
Image patch definition.

$P_{1,1}$	$P_{1,2}$	$P_{1,3}$	$P_{1,4}$	$P_{1,5}$
$P_{2,1}$	$P_{2,2}$	$P_{2,3}$	$P_{2,4}$	$P_{2,5}$
$P_{3,1}$	$P_{3,2}$	$P_{3,3}$	$P_{3,4}$	$P_{3,5}$
$P_{4,1}$	$P_{4,2}$	$P_{4,3}$	$P_{4,4}$	$P_{4,5}$
$P_{5,1}$	$P_{5,2}$	$P_{5,3}$	$P_{5,4}$	$P_{5,5}$

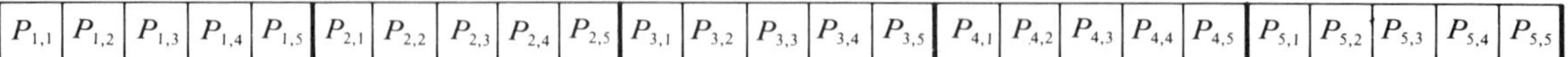

Mapping Images onto the ASP chain

Concatenation of image lines

One pixel per APE

Figure 7.3 Patch distribution onto the ASP chain.

in the scanline direction, is kept small; but that could lead to an increased number of the load–process–unload sequence of operations, which might eventually increase the overall image processing time.

More than one image patch might be processed simultaneously on a SCAPE chain, depending on the relation between the operating patch size and the number of PEs available in the SCAPE chain. The patches are concatenated in the SCAPE chain; the first scanline of the following image patch follows the last scanline of the previous image patch. The computational techniques applied to the SCAPE chain are identical for either case: single-patch or multi-patch processing, which shows how parallelism is exploited using the ASP architecture.

A disadvantage of the patch-processing techniques is that a number of the available PEs in the SCAPE chain make no useful contribution during image-processing algorithms based on local techniques. This is a combination of the nature of the local techniques (which require all the pixels in a defined neighbouring area to be present during the computation), and the definition of an image patch where only part of image scanlines exist in a patch. Therefore, if $p \times q$ is the size of the local operator, there will be $(p - 1) \times (q - 1)$ PEs per image patch, which will perform no useful computational task. The image pixels assigned to these PEs may be envisaged as occupying 'guard strips' around the image patch. The pixels included in these strips have to be repeated in the adjacent patches, where they will be processed, together with the neighbouring pixels necessary for the computations. Detailed discussion on selecting the optimum patch shape can be found in [14].

Earlier in this section, it was mentioned that the main reason for not implementing virtual PEs with the SCAPE chain is the combination of the limited amount of memory available per PE and the number of bits required to represent the grey-level information of each image pixel. Image segmentation and higher-level, image-processing algorithms use binary pixel representation, where only a single bit is sufficient to represent the pixel information. In addition, the processing of binary images is dominated by logical operations which do not demand as much workspace as the arithmetic operations dominant at the low-level image processing. If binary representation is used, then virtual PEs can be implemented in the SCAPE chain. In that case, individual SCAPE PEs contain information sampled from identical locations of different image patches. With that representation, up to 32 pixels can reside in each SCAPE PE. Although the processing time remains the same when virtual PEs are used, because the processing will be sequential, the performance of the SCAPE chain is considerably enhanced because the I/O time, a significant percentage of the overall processing time, is reduced, and in many occasions minimized; for example, a 256 × 256 binary image needs to be loaded and unloaded once on a 16-chip SCAPE chain.

7.4 SCAPE-based image convolution

Raw images often contain high frequency noise. This can be induced by limitations of the imaging system, by errors in image digitization, and even by failures in storage media when images are held for later processing. Noise can also be a part of the actual image in the form of texture or specular reflection. The presence of high frequency noise can impair other image-processing and analysis operations. Thus, it is often desirable to first apply a low-pass filter to an image in order to smooth out the noise. The 2D convolution operation is typical of those used to accomplish this. Its function results in a weighted average of each pixel with its neighbours. For example, given the value of each pixel, $p(x,y)$, the 2D convolution computes the following quantity for each pixel:

$$P(x,y) = \sum_{i=-n}^{n} \sum_{j=-n}^{n} W_{i,j} * p(x - i, y - j)$$

This is called a convolution of radius n, where the $W_{i,j}$ terms are constants representing the function with which the image is being convolved. It is essentially a blurring step that filters out noise with spatial frequency less than n.

The implementation of a discrete 2D convolution is based on a mask of multipliers. Figure 7.4 depicts a 3 × 3 mask that each pixel applies to its local neighbourhood, forming the sum of the pairwise products of the pixel's neighbours with their corresponding mask values. Typically, the sum is then scaled in some manner, and the resulting value is used to update the original pixel value. On a parallel processor, the application of the mask can be performed simultaneously by all of the

$W_{1,1}$	$W_{1,2}$	$W_{1,3}$
$W_{2,1}$	$W_{2,2}$	$W_{2,3}$
$W_{3,1}$	$W_{3,2}$	$W_{3,3}$

Figure 7.4
3 × 3 convolution window/mask.

cells on the grid, as can the update operation. Thus, the algorithm for the convolution can be described as the actions of a single pixel, with the understanding that each action is performed simultaneously by all of the pixels.

There are several ways of approaching the problem of calculating the sum of neighbouring pairwise products. The first is that each pixel 'requests' from its neighbouring pixels the information it needs to calculate the sum. In practice, this involves moving data from each pixel in the neighbourhood into the 'central' pixel, where the multiplication-accumulation function is applied and the result is stored for the subsequent phase of the convolution. The problem with this is that the data must, in the cases of all but the two nearest neighbours (on a two-way connected ASP structure), pass through other cells before it reaches the central pixel. For example, when the applied convolution mask is 5×5, data from the outer ring of pixels must pass through an average of $2 \times M$ pixels, where M is the patch width used, before reaching the centre pixel. Because movement of data takes time, especially when the movement is performed in a bit-serial manner, this 'passing through' is rather inefficient.

The solution is to have the data interacting with the intermediate pixels on the way through to the centre. Such a solution takes advantage of the fact that the intermediate pixels will either also need to know the transferred data information in order to compute the convolution function of their neighbourhoods if the pixel information is transferred, or need to transfer their contribution to the centre pixel if information contributing to the convolution sum is transferred. An appropriate metaphor of portraying the former case, a distributing-information-based convolution, is the situation where several items must be delivered to several different destinations along the same route. Instead of transferring one item at a time, when it is requested, ensuing multiple trips, it will be more effective if all the items are distributed in a single trip along the full length of the route, delivering each item to its appropriate destination. Such a distribution strategy is conditional on each destination having the capability (storage facilities) of preserving the item for as long as it is required. A suitable analogy for describing the latter case, which can be described as collecting-information-based convolution, is when passengers want to travel to the same destination from different spots along the same route where only one coach at a time can travel. Instead of having different nonstop coaches travelling, one from each spot, arriving one at a time at the destination, it will be more practical to employ a single coach, originating its trip from the remotest spot on the route, collecting passengers, if its capacity allows, from each appropriate spot on its route towards its final destination.

The distance that data information has to travel, in both convolution techniques described above, is identical. However, it is the *amount* of the information, since it is transferred bit-serially, which will influence the decision on which technique should be used. The distributing-information-based convolution transfers pixel information, with maximum 8-bit precision. The collecting-information-based convolution transfers information related to the convolution sum, which for the case of m-bit pixels, n-bit convolution weights and $M \times N$ convolution mask, can be anything between $m + n$ to $m + n + \log_2 * M * N$-bit long. It is clear then that the distributing-information-based convolution is more efficient.

The ASP architecture with its global inter-APE communication network is

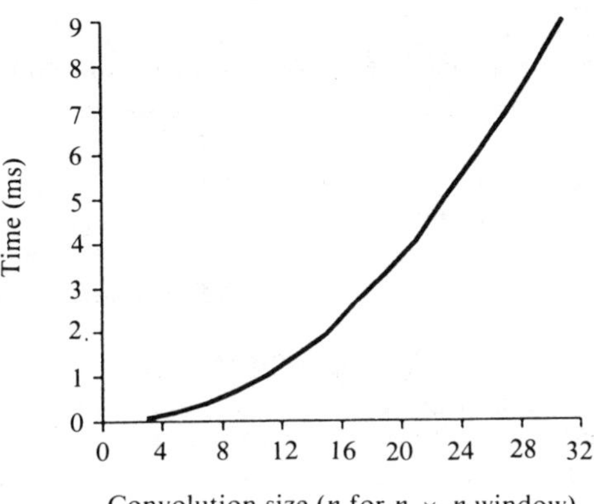

Figure 7.5
SCAPE convolution performance.

capable of supporting, very effectively, the information transfer required by the convolution algorithm. However, it is the limited capacity of the data register of each SCAPE (a particular ASP implementation) PE that influences the choice of the convolution technique. A scalar-vector-based algorithm, with the convolution weights being the scalars, is used for the multiply-accumulate steps of the convolution, because it guarantees faster execution and no PE memory is allocated for the convolution mask's coefficients.

In the case of the distributing-information-based convolution technique, using 8-bit pixels, each pixel has to cover all its neighbourhood covered by the convolution mask when the pixel is the 'central' pixel of the mask. That implies that the pixel must travel in both directions (that is, to its left and to its right) on the linear structure of the ASP architecture. Pixel information on the inter-APE communication network must be temporarily stored in the PEs which will use the information. The pixel can be stored in a virgin field of the data register or can overwrite already existing information in the data register. If the former option is followed, then the available workspace per PE will be reduced, thus forcing the algorithm to use the data register of the neighbouring PE. Such concatenation of the data registers of PEs will halve the number of available 'effective' (namely, one pixel per effective PE) SCAPE PEs on the SCAPE and also will double the distance between 'effective' PEs. As a consequence of that, the execution speed of the convolution algorithm will, at least, be halved. Therefore, it is better to overwrite information already existing in the data register of the PE. The most likely information to be deleted is the pixel information, since that information already exists somewhere else in the SCAPE chain. To preserve information located at the edges of the SCAPE chain, it is appropriate to link together the two ends of the SCAPE chain, LinkL and LinkR, so that the information is circulated. Information transfer is accomplished using the synchronous mode of the inter-APE communication network (that is, the shift register is employed) in the SCAPE chain, since information from all pixels is transferred simultaneously.

The following program describes the distributing-information-based convolution algorithm for an $M \times N$ convolution mask:

```
MultiplyAccumulate;
(*calculates the influence of each pixel on the convolution sum of the
mask centred on itself*)
FOR LoopControl := 1 TO TRUNC(M*N/2) DO
        MoveEachPixelLeft;
        MultiplyAccumulate
END; (* FOR *)
(*calculates the contribution of each pixel to its left neighbourhood in
M * N/2 steps*)
FOR LoopControl := 1 TO TRUNC(M*N/2) DO
        MoveEachPixelRight;
        MultiplyAccumulate
END; (* FOR *)
(*calculates the contribution of each pixel to its right neighbourhood in
M * N/2 steps*)
ScaleResult;
UpdatePixel;
(*scales the result down to the required number of bits and updates the
original pixel value with the new one. The scaling technique followed is based
on keeping the number of the most significant bits of the result required for
the final pixel value and adding the leading bit of the least significant part of
the result. Negative results produce updated pixel values of zero*)
```

Figure 7.5 depicts overall convolution performance for SCAPE-based, systems.

7.5 SCAPE-based image histogramming

A grey-level histogram of a grey-scale image is a function that gives the frequency of occurrence in the image of each possible grey level. The grey level at each image point is quantized from 0 to m (typically m is equal to 255). The value of the histogram at a specific grey level p is the number of image points with grey level equal to p. The histogram of an image can be useful in many ways. It can be used to select a threshold value (or values) for segmenting an image into a foreground–background image, or it can be used to guide the filtering of an image [15]. Other applications include image enhancement and image encoding [16].

A SCAPE-based implementation of the image histogramming algorithm makes use of the following parallel counting technique. The technique is based on the divide-and-conquer method, which SCAPE can implement directly by using the alternate network in WCL, which can provide statistics in $\log_2 * N + 1$ steps instead of the N steps required by the sequential method. According to the divide-and-conquer algorithm, all the selected PEs are alternately tagged in the SCAPE tag registers TR1 and TR2. Next, using the asynchronous communication channel in the SCAPE inter-APE communication network (namely, activate link option) the tags are paired together; for example, a TR1 tag is paired with the subsequent TR2 tag on its left. The aim of pairing the tags is to detect if there is an odd or even number of selected PEs at this particular stage of the algorithm. If the number is odd, there will be a tag which cannot be paired; therefore a ‘1’ can be set in the result bit. If the number is even, then all the tags have been paired together, therefore a ‘0’ will be set in the corresponding bit of the result. The building of the result starts from the least significant bit moving towards the most significant bit. Next, half of the selected PEs are discarded (namely, the ones tagged in TR2) and the algorithm is repeated in the next stage with the remaining PEs. The stages are repeated until all PEs have been discarded as a result of the algorithm stages. As mentioned above, the algorithm is completed in $\log_2 * N + 1$ stages where N is the number of the items to be counted. The algorithm requires $\log_2 * N + 1$ steps and not $\log_2 * N$ steps as many would have thought, because in order to represent the number N, $\log_2 * N + 1$ bits are required; for example, the number 256 in binary form is represented as 100000000.

The SCAPE-based image histogramming technique exploits the image I/O phase to dump the histogramming results, hence avoiding the extra operational cycles for result disposal. With this histogramming technique, all the possible bins are computed before the results are dumped. Each SCAPE chip in the chain collects grey-level statistics regarding the patch pixels stored in it. The results are stored one per PE. In this configuration, each SCAPE chip can store information for up to 256 grey levels (8-bit pixels have 256 grey levels). During the patch I/O phase, the bins from each chip are transferred into outside buffers where the histogramming computation is completed. This histogramming technique, for a single image patch, is described by the following program:

```
Load Image Patch; (*one pixel per SCAPE PE*)
FOR Bin := BinMin TO BinMax DO
        COUNT (Bin);
        StoreBin;
END (*for*)
Dump Image Patch; (*and histogramming results*)
```

The histogramming algorithm is schematically depicted in Figure 7.6.

Table 7.4 shows the evaluation of the histogramming algorithm for image sizes 256×256 and 512×512 and SCAPE chain sizes of 16, 32 and 64 SCAPE chips. The image I/O time is included and 256 bins (all possible grey levels for an 8-bit pixel) are computed.

One of the main reasons for the ease of developing histogramming algorithms on linear 1D parallel architectures, compared to other highly-parallel architectures, is the ability to perform global scalar-vector operations. 2D architectures, the majority of which can only support bit-serial scalar-vector operations (the global broadcast is done bit serially), use other slow and memory-consuming ($2^n - 1$ bits per pixel for n-bit pixel images) bit-serial techniques to compute the histogramming algorithm.

Table 7.4 Image histogramming, SCAPE system performance (ms).

	16 chip chain	*32 chip chain*	*64 chip chain*
256×256	6.66	3.33	1.67
512×512	26.62	13.31	6.66

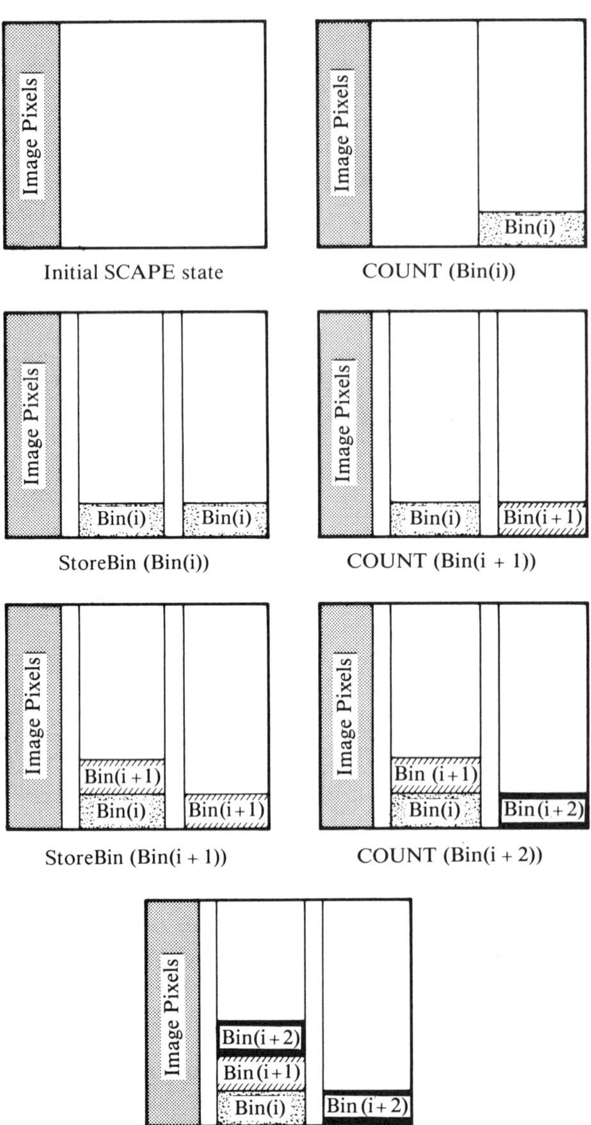

Figure 7.6
SCAPE-based image histogramming.

Conclusions

In this chapter, the implementation of low-level computer vision tasks on a fine-grain associative string SIMD structure (the ASP), was demonstrated. The ASP architecture offers a great degree of parallelism due to the distributed nature of its processing power. Probably the greatest assets of the ASP structure are the characteristics which enable exploitation of VLSI technology. The characteristics, compact structure and external interface independent of the number of PEs in the system, allow the implementation of ASP VLSI devices (for example, SCAPE) integrating a large number (256) of fine-grain PEs on a single VLSI device. One of the main disadvantages of applying string architectures on computer-vision problems is the unapparent mapping of the structure onto the perceived image data structure. A method of mapping images onto string architectures was proposed. The method deals with the problem of supporting local operations on linear structures. Simply concatenating image lines creates a severe communication problem. To resolve that problem, the method divides the image into patches; patch lines are then concatenated. Multiple patches can be processed simultaneously on the same string.

This chapter has demonstrated the feasibility of using fine-grain string-structure SIMD machines for high-speed execution of low-level computer vision tasks by discussing the implementation of image convolution and histogramming. The principal novelties of the algorithms can be summarized as:

(1) The use of scalar-vector operations on the image data (for example, scalar-vector multiplication for the convolution algorithm and the scalar-vector comparison for the histogramming algorithm), and

(2) The distribution of pixel information to its neighbourhood during the image convolution algorithm. The distribution strategy reduces the communication overhead due to the interaction of neighbouring pixels.

Acknowledgements

The authors acknowledge the contributions of the members of the ASP and Computer Architecture groups at Brunel University.

References

1. Duff M.J.B. (1978). Review of the CLIP Image Processing System. In *Proceedings of AFIPS Conference,* **47**, 1055–60. Arlington VA: AFIPS Press
2. Reddaway S.F. (1983). DAP and its applications to image processing. In *IEE Electronics Division Colloquium on VLSI modules for image processing*, London, December 1983
3. Batcher, K.E. (1980). Design of a massively parallel processor. *IEEE Transactions on Computers,* **C-29**(9), 48–56
4. Lougheed R.M., McCubbrey D.L. and Sterneberg S.R. (1980). Cytocomputer: architectures for parallel image processing. In *Proceedings of the Workshop on Picture Data Description and Management*, Pacific Grove CA
5. Hillis W.D. (1985). *The Connection Machine*. Cambridge MA: MIT Press
6. Reeves A.P. (1984). Parallel Computer Architectures for Image Processing. *Computer Graphics and Image Processing,* **25**(1), 68–88
7. Flynn M.J. (1972). Some computer organizations and their effectiveness. *IEEE Transaction on Computers,* **21**(9), 948–60
8. Lea R.M. (1982). *SCAPE: a Single-Chip Array Processing Element, Original specification*. Internal Report, Computer Architecture Group, Brunel University
9. Lea R.M. (1986). SCAPE: a single-chip array processing element for signal and image processing. *IEE Proc., Pt. E,* **133**(3), 145–51

10. Jalowiecki I.P. and Lea R.M. (1987). A 256-element associative parallel processor. In *Proc. Int. Solid State Circuits Conf.*, pp. 196–7. New York, February 1987
11. Lea R.M. (1986). VLSI and WSI associative string processors for cost-effective parallel processing. *The Computer Journal,* **29**(6), 486–94
12. Lea R.M. (1986). VLSI and WSI associative string processors for structured data processing. *IEE Proc., Pt. E,* **133**(3), 153–62
13. Aspex Microsystems Ltd. (1986). *SCAPE Programming Language – Users' Reference Manual*. Brunel University: Aspex Microsystems Ltd.
14. Krikelis A. (1987). *Computer Vision with Fine-grain Parallel One-dimensional Structured Computer Architectures*. Uxbridge: Brunel University
15. Rosenfeld A. and Kak A.C. (1976). *Digital Picture Processing*. New York: Academic Press
16. Gonzalez R.C. and Wintz P. (1977). *Digital Image Processing*. Reading MA: Addison-Wesley

8· Performance of Warp on the DARPA image understanding architecture benchmarks

J. Deutch
P.C. Maulik
R. Mosur
H. Printz
H. Ribas
J. Senko
P.S. Tseng
J.A. Webb
I-C. Wu

Carnegie Mellon University

Warp was a participant in the DARPA Image Understanding Architecture Workshop Benchmark Study, which compared the performances of a variety of architectures for image processing on image-processing tasks from low- and mid-level vision. We present algorithms and performance figures resulting from this study. These algorithms and performance figures can be used as a benchmark of the Warp machine, and also as a guide to programming Warp.

8.1 Introduction

The DARPA Image Understanding Architecture Workshop Benchmark Study was conceived for these reasons:

- To arrive at an initial understanding of the general strengths and weaknesses for Image Understanding (IU) of the architectures represented.
- To project needs for future development of architectures to support IU.
- To promote communication and collaboration between various groups within the CS community, which are expected to contribute to development of real-time IU systems.

The benchmarks chosen represented common image-processing operations from low- and middle-level vision, but did not include high-level image-processing operations, such as recognition; these operations were felt to be too ill defined at present to evaluate machine architectures properly. Warp was one of the participants in the study. This is a summary of our results, which reflects the performance on Warp on this level of vision, and can also serve as a guide for programming Warp in this area.

The precise definitions of each of the tasks are given ahead of the section in which they are discussed. In what follows, we first describe the current Warp status, and then describe the work on each of the algorithms. The Warp architecture or programming environment are not reviewed here, since complete reviews are available elsewhere [1, 2, 3, 4, 5].

8.2 Warp status

There are three operating Warp machines at Carnegie Mellon University. Two of them are prototypes. One was built by General Electric Radar Systems Department (Syracuse) and the other by Honeywell Marine Systems Department (Seattle). Both consist of a linear array of ten cells, each giving 10 MFLOPS, for a total of 100 MFLOPS, and operate in an identical software environment. These machines are referred to as **WW Warp**, since they are of wirewrap construction. The machines are fed data by MC68020 processors, called the 'external host', and the whole system is controlled from a Sun 3/160.

The third machine is a production machine, one of several being constructed by General Electric Corporation. The production machines are built from printed-circuit boards, and are called **PC Warp**. The baseline power of these machines is also 100 MFLOPS, although they can easily be expanded to 160 MFLOPS simply by adding more cells. (The array can be expanded still further, but this requires a special repeater board and a second rack.) The PC Warp is changed in several ways from the WW Warp: cell data and program memories are larger, there is on-cell address generation, and there is a large register overflow file to provide a second memory for scalars. Some of these improvements imply an increased speed on some of the benchmarks, as will be noted. For example, because of on-cell address generation, the cell is able to tolerate an arbitrary skew in computation, which makes it possible to overlap input, computation and output in many algorithms. Also, improved processor boards in the external host allow improved Input/Output (I/O) rates between Warp and the host through DMA, removing the host I/O bottleneck in many cases. Finally, since each cell has more local control, it is possible to make Warp computation more data dependent, by allowing data-dependent I/O between cells, as well as heterogeneous computation (different programs on different cells).

Carnegie Mellon and Intel Corporation are developing the 'integrated' version of Warp, called **iWarp**. In this machine, each cell of Warp will be implemented on a single chip. The clock rate will be increased so that each chip will support at least 16 MFLOPS computation, as opposed to 10 MFLOPS in WW and PC Warp. In the baseline machine, the cells will be organized into a linear array of 72 cells, giving a total computation of 1.152 GFLOPS. In the following analysis, it has been assumed that each iWarp cell can do everything a PC Warp cell can, with an increase of 1.6 in speed (this is a design goal). When I/O bottlenecks have led to a maximum performance time on a benchmark, this has been noted.

All the benchmarks listed below as being implemented on Warp are written in W2, the Warp programming language. W2 is a procedural language, on about the same level as C or Pascal. Arrays and scalars are supported, as are for loops, and if statements. The programmers are aware that they are programming a parallel machine, since each program is duplicated to all cells and then executed locally (with local sequencing) on each cell.

8.3 Vision programming on Warp

We have studied vision programming at various levels on Warp for some time now, and developed and documented several different models [6, 7]. In this section, we briefly review the various models of Warp programming, for reference in later sections.

All the programs here use the cells in a **homogeneous** programming model: that is, all cells execute the same program, although the program counters on the different cells can differ, and each has its own local data memory. This is a restriction imposed by the hardware of WW Warp. Programs on PC Warp need not follow this restriction.

8.3.1 Input partitioning

In this model, which is used for local operations like convolutions, the image is divided into a number of portions by column, and each of the ten cells takes one-tenth of the image. Thus, in 512 × 512 image processing, cell 0 takes columns 0–51 of the image, cell 1 takes columns 52–103, and so on (a border is added to the image to take care of images whose width is not a multiple of ten). The image is divided in this way because it makes it possible to process a row of the image at a time, and because the host need only send the image in raster order, which is important, because the host tends to be a bottleneck in many algorithms.

8.3.2 Output partitioning

This model is used for algorithms in which the operation to be performed is global, so that any output can depend on any input, but can still be computed independently. In this model, each cell sees the complete input image, and processes it to produce part of the output. Generally, the output data set produced by a cell is stored in the cell's local memory until the complete input image is processed. The Hough transform is implemented in this way.

8.3.3 Pipelining

In this model, which is the classic type of 'systolic' algorithm, the algorithm is divided into regular steps, and each cell performs one step. This method can be used when the algorithm is regular. (Because the cell code must be homogeneous, this method is of less use on the WW Warp machine than it usually is in systolic machines.) When this method can be used, it is generally more efficient in terms of input and output overlap with computation and local memory use than either of the two models above.

8.4 Laplacian

> **Laplacian.** Convolve the image with an 11 × 11 sampled 'Laplacian' operator [8]. (Results within 5 pixels of the image border can be ignored.)

The Laplacian given [8] is symmetric, but not separable. (Separable filters can be computed more efficiently, in general, than non-separable filters.) In this section, we describe a series of optimizations we applied to the Laplacian filter in the Warp implementation, which led to an efficient implementation. These optimizations can be applied to any symmetric filter, and will lead to efficient implementations on many different computer architectures. Since most filters use masks with an odd number of rows and columns, the rest of this discussion will deal with this case. Let the size of the mask be represented by $N = 2M + 1$.

In order to see where the optimizations come from, we first notice that an unoptimized $N \times N$ convolution takes N^2 multiplications and $N^2 - 1$ additions per pixel. A separable convolution of the same size would take only $2N$ multiplications and $2(N - 1)$ additions.

One way to compute the Laplacian is as a series of column convolutions. Each column takes N multiplications and $N - 1$ additions, and then $N - 1$ additions are required to add all of the partial sums. The total number of multiplications is $N \times N = N^2$, and the number of additions is $N \times (N - 1) + (N - 1) = N^2 - 1$.

Due to symmetry, we can add the pairs of corresponding pixels within a column before multiplying them by the weights. Each of the N columns contains M pixels that can be added in this way, and one pixel in the middle which is not part of a pair. We call this column of $M + 1$ pixels a 'folded' column. After the multiplication, the pixels in each folded column must be added, and then all the columns must be added as before. This saves multiplications, but not additions: the number of multiplications is $N(M + 1) = (N^2 + N)/2$, while the additions sum to $N \times M + N \times M + (N - 1) = N^2 - 1$.

Now note that calculations for a given pixel can share partial results with neighboring calculations in the same row. As we shift the convolution window one step from the left to the right, we can retain all but one of the folded columns from the previous convolution, and sum just one new folded column. The rest of the algorithm is unchanged. Multiplications are unaffected, but additions are reduced almost by half, to $M + N \times M + (N - 1) = (N^2 + 3N - 3)/2$.

Finally, we notice that the column convolutions are not done with N unique column weights, but rather with $M + 1$ unique weights. As we shift the window to the right, we can compute and store the convolution of the new column with all $M + 1$ column weights. Then, as we shift the window up to N pixels to the right, we will only have to add the appropriate convolved column sums. Thus, again, nearly half of the multiplications and additions can be saved. Thus, for each pixel, only $M + 1$ partial weighted column sums need be generated, and then $N - 1$ additions are required to add the proper partial sums together. The number of multiplications is then $(M + 1) \times (M + 1) = ((N + 1)/2)^2$, while the additions come to $(M + 1) \times M + M + (N - 1) = M^2 + 4 \times M$.

An algorithm based on the above model was implemented using input partitioning on the WW Warp, and gave a runtime of 432 ms. The same algorithm was compiled for the PC Warp, and gave a runtime of 350 ms. The change was due to overlap of I/O with computation in PC Warp, which is not possible for this algorithm on the WW Warp. On iWarp, assuming a straightforward speedup arising from a 72-cell array with a 16 MHz clock, the time will be 30 ms.

8.5 Zero-crossings detection

> **Zero-crossings detection.** Detect **zero-crossings** of the output of the operation, that is, pixels at which the output is positive but which have neighbors where the output is negative.

Zero crossing was implemented using the input partitioning model. A three by three window was taken around each pixel. If any elements of the window were negative, but the central pixel was positive, a zero crossing was declared and a '1' was output, otherwise '0' was output. This computation was performed by transforming each 9-element window into a 9-bit integer, with which a table lookup was performed. Input and output were represented as 8-bit pixels. Execution time on the WW Warp was 172 ms; on the PC Warp the time will be approximately 92 ms, due to overlap of I/O with computation. On iWarp, the time will be limited by I/O bandwidth to the array to at least 7.8 ms.

In many cases, it is desirable to perform the Laplacian and zero-crossing computations in sequence, without saving the results of the Laplacian. In this case, on iWarp, the computation can be done more quickly than by performing each individually. We estimate that such a computation will take 31 ms, fast enough for video-rate image processing.

8.6 Border following

> **Border following.** Output sequences of the coordinates of pixels that lie on the borders of regions where the Laplacian is positive. (On **border following** see [9, Section 11.2.2].)

The algorithm is mapped in two steps. First, each Warp cell performs the border-following technique on part of the image. Then, these partial results are combined within the array to produce the complete border trace for the image. The full algorithm is:

- Each cell sends its bottom row to its successor.
- Starting with the bottom row, on the left, each cell inspects the pixels on this row. If the pixel is turned on, the cell begins to trace this connected component. As it traces the component, it builds a list of its pixels to the next cell. As it visits pixels, it turns them off, so they will not be visited on scans of higher rows.
- Either this component extends to the cell's top row, or it does not. If not, then the list of pixels eventually terminates within the cell's strip; the cell queues the whole list of pixels for output to the next cell, marking the component as complete. But if the component extends to the top row, it may join with a component of the preceding cell. The cell checks its copy of the previous cell's last row to see if this is a possibility. If not, again the list may be passed to the next cell. But if it is, the cell stacks the list it has built so far, and begins processing another component, bottom to top.

This completes the parallel phase of the computation.

Each cell now has two lists of borders: those ready for output, and those that must be merged with borders in preceding cells. The cells now run the following merge phase: each cell tries to do two things:

(1) empty its ready-for-output queue, and

(2) move all the components on its stack to this queue.

Operation (1) happens asynchronously, depending upon the next cell's input queue. Operation (2) is performed as follows: eventually, the preceding cell will emit a list of the components touching the stacked component. When this happens, the component may be unstacked, the stacked pixels attached to the proper end of the list received from the previous component (note that this may involve attaching lists to both ends), and pass the now completed list at least, complete in its path through the given cell and its predecessor to the ready-for-output queue.

This algorithm must terminate, since the first cell never has any stacked components. Hence, it will eventually flush all the components on its output queue to the second cell, giving the second cell all the information it needs to move all its stacked components to its output queue. By iterating this argument, it follows that each cell must eventually clear its stack and then its output queue.

Finally, we must provide a time estimate for this algorithm. The first step is essentially a connected-components computation. This will take no longer than the parallel step of a UNION-FIND-based connected-components program below. For PC Warp, with 10 cells, this is 73 ms; for iWarp, with 72 cells, this is 6.3 ms. These estimates were obtained by dividing the uniprocessor time of the Hughes HBA [10] implementation of a pure UNION-FIND algorithm by the number of cells, and again by suitable numbers to correct for processor speed.

The second step is a serial merge (in the worst case). We estimate this step will take about 1.02 s for PC Warp, and 690 ms for iWarp. These estimates are based on our experience with similar merge steps for the connected-components algorithm, and the I/O bandwidth of each machine. Hence our estimates are:

PC Warp: 1.1 s
iWarp: 690 ms

8.7 Connected-components labelling

Connected-component labelling. Here the input is a 1-bit digital image of size 512 × 512 pixels. The output is a 512 × 512 array of non-negative integers in which:

(1) Pixels that were 0s in the input image have value 0.

(2) Pixels that were 1s in the input image have positive values; two such pixels have the same value if, and only if, they belong to the same connected component of 1s in the input image. (On connected-component labelling see [9, Section 11.3.1].)

In this section, we present our parallel-sequential-systolic algorithm for this computation, and discuss a modification to make the last phase parallel. We then give estimates of its execution time on WW Warp, PC Warp and iWarp. Section 8.7.1 gives the algorithm. Section 8.7.2 discusses the implementation, covering both our existing C simulation and our planned Warp implementations; here we give the actual execution time of the simulations and the estimated execution times for the Warp implementation, and discuss the constraints imposed by the Warp architecture.

8.7.1 Sketch of the algorithm

Vocabulary and notation

The input to the algorithm is a $N \times N$ array (512×512 in this case) of binary pixels. A 1-valued pixel is called **significant**; all others are **insignificant**. We label the rows and columns consecutively from 0 to $N - 1$, starting in the upper left-hand corner. The **4-neighbors** of a pixel are the pixels that lie immediately above, below, left and right of it; its **8-neighbors** are the eight pixels that surround it. Two significant pixels x and y lie in the same **connected 4-component (connected 8-component)** of the image if there is a sequence of significant pixels $p_0, \ldots, p_n$ with $p_0 = x$, $p_n = y$, and p_{i-1} a 4-neighbor (8-neighbor) of p_i for each $i = 1, \ldots, N$. The algorithm we present here computes connected 4-components. It is straightforward to modify it to compute connected 8-components; the timing estimates we present later are for the connected 8-component version.

Our algorithm executes on a linear systolic array of K processing cells, numbered consecutively from 0 to $K - 1$. Each cell processes a set of adjacent rows of the image, called a **slice**. We assume that K divides N, and that the slices are of uniform size N / K rows. The 0th cell processes the first N / K rows of the image, called slice 0, and so on. When data flows from cell i to cell $i + 1$, we will say it crosses the $i, i + 1$ **boundary**, or simply, an **intercell boundary**. A cell's **label space** is the set of all labels that it may assign to any pixel; cell i's label space is denoted L_i. We choose suitable bounds on the label spaces so that they are guaranteed disjoint.

The algorithm

The algorithm proceeds in three phases: parallel, sequential and parallel. The present algorithm is based on the algorithm due to Kung and Webb [11].

In the first parallel phase, each cell computes labels for its slice of the image, using an efficient algorithm [12].

In the sequential phase, computation proceeds serially over each $i - 1, i$ boundary, for $i = 1, \ldots, K$. The ith stage of this computation effectively passes information about the connectivity of slices 0 through $i - 1$ to slice i. The actual computation consists of scanning the $i - 1, i$ boundary to construct two maps, which record connectivity information, then applying the second of these maps along the bottom row of slice i to propagate this information downward. Note that after this phase finishes, lower-numbered slices still lack information about higher-numbered slices. We perform this computation in K serial steps because of the limited interconnection topology of Warp.

In the final parallel phase, the maps generated in the last phase are first resolved sequentially, then the labels generated in the last phase are remapped and pumped out of the array.

8.7.2 Implementation details

In this section we discuss two implementations of this algorithm, and we discuss the Warp implementation on each of WW Warp, PC Warp, and iWarp.

Table 8.1 Estimated WW Warp timings.

Phase	*Time (ms)*	*Time (ms)*
Initial Parallel Phase	2450	2400
Sequential Phase	840	840
Final Parallel Phase	2290	2300
Total		5600

We have not yet completed a Warp implementation. In this section, we discuss the implementation for the WW Warp architecture, and give execution time estimates for the planned PC Warp and iWarp implementations. All our estimates are for the parallel–sequential–parallel version of the algorithm, computing connected 8-components.

WW Warp

Our implementation for the WW Warp divides the computational burden between the linear systolic array and the cluster processors. The initial and final labellings are done by the systolic array; the sequential step is done by the cluster processors. This permits us to use algorithms with fast amortized time in the sequential step. After the initial labelling, we would like to retain the initial results in cell memory, transmitting only each cell's boundary rows to the external host for generating the necessary maps. Unfortunately, the WW Warp cell memory is not large enough to hold a labelled slice, and barely large enough to hold the intermediate result required by the initial marking algorithm. This forces us to send the entire contents of each cell's slice to the external host as the labels are generated, then pump these slices back through the array for the final labelling.

We have written, but not yet debugged, all the code for the cell array. We have accurate estimates of the running time of this code, provided by the compiler. We have also estimated the running time of the sequential phase. We derived this estimate from the sequential phase running time of a C implementation, allowing for a slight speedup of the cluster processors over the VAX, and also for the extra work (computing the λ_i) done in this phase by the parallel–sequential–parallel algorithm. The resulting estimate appears in Table 8.1.

PC Warp and iWarp architectures

In this section, we derive estimated execution times for these architectures. There are three key differences between the design of these cells and those of the WW Warp. The first is that each cell has enough memory to maintain a full slice of labels. This means that we do not need to pump the intermediate labels to an external memory. The second is that the cells are not bound by the synchronization constraints of the WW machine. This means that the sequential phase computation can be performed on the cell array. This saves time because we no longer have to do I/O to the cluster processors for this phase, and because the cells run 2.8 times faster than the cluster processors. The third is that each of these machines is more powerful than the WW Warp. Both the PC Warp and the iWarp can do arithmetic directly on integers; this

Table 8.2 Estimated PC Warp timings.

Phase	*Time (ms)*	*Time (ms)*
Initial Parallel Phase	760	760
Sequential Phase	130	130
Final Parallel Phase	89	89
Total		980

Table 8.3 Estimated iWarp timings.

Phase	*Time (ms)*	*Time (ms)*
Initial Parallel Phase	224	224
Sequential Phase	200	200
Final Parallel Phase	42	42
Total		470

speeds up any integer arithmetic computation by a factor of 3. Furthermore, the iWarp cells run 1.6 times faster than the Warp and PC Warp cells.

The only other salient difference between PC Warp and iWarp, for our purposes, is that the iWarp contains 72 cells. Thus, we can potentially attain more parallelism on iWarp. However, because the time taken in the merge phase varies linearly with the number of cells, while the time taken in each parallel phase varies inversely with this number, it is not necessarily best to use the greatest possible number of processors. If the execution time of the algorithm as a function of the number of cells is $T(K) = A / K + BK$, then the best time will be obtained with $K = \sqrt{A / B}$. In the case of iWarp, we have $A \approx 4.994$, $B \approx .008\,12$, so the best K is 25. The estimate below for iWarp execution time was made using this value. The resulting estimates appear in Tables 8.2 and 8.3.

8.8 Hough transform

> **Hough transform.** The input is a 1-bit digital image of size 512×512. Assume that the origin (0,0) image is at the lower left-hand corner of the image, with the x-axis along the bottom row. The output is a 180×512 array of non-negative integers constructed as follows: for each pixel (x,y) having value 1 in the input image, and each i, $0 < i < 180$, add 1 to the output image in position (i,j), where j is the perpendicular distance (rounded to the nearest integer) from (0,0) to the line through (x,y) making angle i-degrees with the x-axis (measured counterclockwise). (This output is a type of Hough transform; if the input image has many collinear '1's, they will give rise to a high-valued peak in the output image. On Hough transforms see [9, Section 10.3.3].)

The Hough transform algorithm has been previously described [11]. Briefly, each of the ten cells gets one-tenth of the Hough array, partitioned by angle. The input image flows through the Warp array, and each cell increments its portion of the Hough array for all image pixels which are '1'. Once the image has been processed, the Hough array is concatenated and output to Warp's external host.

For the particular parameters of this benchmark, which uses an array of 180×512 data, this requires each cell to store $18 \times 512 = 9K$ words of data. This will not fit on the WW Warp, which has a memory of 4K words/cell. But on PC Warp, each cell will have a memory of 32K words, so that the Hough array fits easily. On iWarp 60 cells are used (60 being the largest number less than 72 which evenly divides 180), so that each cell needs to store only $3 \times 512 = 1536$ bytes of data.

In order to derive estimates, we implemented a Hough transform program (with a smaller number of angles than in the benchmark) and ran it on the WW machine. The algorithm does not change for more angles, so the estimates given by this method are accurate for the PC Warp with the benchmark parameters.

By derivation from this program, the time per pixel with value '1' is 13 microseconds. Assuming 10% of the image is one, on PC Warp the benchmark will execute in 340 ms. On iWarp, the estimated execution time is 60 ms. These times scale linearly with the number of '1's in the image.

8.9 Convex hull

> **Convex hull.** The input is a set S of 1000 real coordinate pairs, defining a set of 1000 points in the plane, selected at random, with each coordinate in the range [0,1000]. The output is an ordered list of the pairs that lie on the boundary of the convex hull of S, in sequence around the boundary. (On convex hulls see [13, Chapters 3–4].)

R.A. Jarvis's [14] algorithm was used. This algorithm works as follows:

- Sort the points according to (x,y)-coordinate. The first point is a convex hull point. Call it A_0.
- Let $i = 0$. Repeat the following until $A_{i+1} = A_0$:
  - For each point B in the set, do the following:
    - Calculate the angle from the vector $A_i - A_{i-1}$ to the vector $B - A_i$. (If $i = 0$ we take the second vector to be $(-1,0)$.)
    - The point with smallest angle is a convex hull point. Call it A_{i+1}.

This algorithm obviously has time complexity $O(KN)$, where K is the number of convex hull points, and N is the number of points in the set. The time-consuming step in the algorithm is the scan through the set of points to find the next convex hull point.

We implemented the above algorithm on the WW Warp, using C code to program the cluster processors and W2 to program the Warp array. In our implementation, the Warp array performs the inner loop in the algorithm, which finds a new convex hull point by calculation of the angle with all points. This is done in parallel on all cells, by partitioning the set of data points across the array and finding the best point in each cell's dataset individually, then finding the best point of the cell's points. The cluster processors repeatedly accept the new point from the Warp array and pass in this new convex hull point for the next step of the computation.

To test this algorithm, we generated a 1000 node random graph, which had 13 hull points. The measured time on the WW Warp was 6.76 ms, with the same execution time on PC Warp. The time for this algorithm scales linearly with the number of hull points.

Assuming a 16 MHz clock time and 72 cells in iWarp, each point location will take 26 μs, based on an operation count from the Warp implementation. Loading the initial array to the cells will take 250 μs, for a total time of 590 μs for our sample problem.

8.10 Voronoi diagram

> **Geometrical constructions.** The input is a set *S* of 1000 real coordinate pairs, defining a set of 1000 points in the plane, selected at random, with each coordinate in the range [0,1000]. The output is the Voronoi diagram of *S*, defined by the set of coordinates of its vertices, the set of pairs of vertices that are joined by edges, and the set of rays emanating from vertices and not terminating at another vertex. (On Voronoi diagrams see [13, Section 5.5].)

We consider the computation of the Voronoi diagram of a set of 1000 real points [15]. The algorithm is:

(1) The coordinates of the points are sorted, divided equally among the cells, so that each cell has 100 points. The sorting is done systolically on the Warp array, using a heapsort algorithm in which each cell builds a heap of 100 points as the data values stream in, passing the rest of the data on to the next cell.

(2) Each cell computes the Delauney triangulation of 100 points using a standard sequential algorithm.

(3) Cells 1, 3, 7 and 9 receive the Delauney triangulation of their left neighbors. The two Delauney triangulations are then merged to form a single Delauney triangulation in these receiving cells. At the end of this stage we have four Delauney triangulations of 200 points each, and two Delauney triangulations of 100 points each in cells 4 and 5. Six cells will be idle during this step.

(4) The 200 point triangulations are merged to form 400 point triangulations. At the end of this step we have two triangulations of 400 points each and two triangulations of 100 points each. Eight cells are idle during this step. The mergings are carried out in the third and eighth cells.

(5) The 400 point and 100 point triangulations are merged to form 500 point triangulations in cells 4 and 6. At the end of this step there are two triangulations of 500 points each. Eight cells are idle during this step.

(6) The two 500 point triangulations are merged to give the Delauney triangulation of 1000 points. This operation is carried out in the fifth cell. Nine cells are idle.

(7) The dual of the Delauney triangulation thus obtained will give the Voronoi diagram.

Table 8.4 Operation counts for Voronoi diagram.

Step	*Assignments*	*Array references*	*Comparisons*	*Arithmetic operations*	*Logical operations*
2	86 897	192 695	60 149	71 572	36 290
3	89 529	198 309	60 209	74 221	36 343
4	91 754	202 898	60 264	76 401	36 388
5	94 504	208 420	60 326	79 030	36 441
6	97 313	214 221	60 394	81 733	36 502

Table 8.4 gives operation counts for each of the steps in the Voronoi diagram algorithm above. These counts were obtained through a C program which computed the Voronoi diagram.

iWarp will have 72 cells instead of 10. Since the time for intermediate data transfers is small, we ignore any changes in that and assume linear speedup in the Delauney triangulation computation. Since the computation of addresses for the array references appears to be the critical path, we considered this as the bottleneck in the computation. (PC Warp and iWarp will have parallel address computation engines in each cell.) Each array reference takes 300 ns on PC Warp (100 ns for the address computation and 200 ns for the memory access) and 100 ns on the baseline iWarp. The total computation time therefore comes to 64 ms on PC Warp and 8.9 ms on iWarp. The initial sort step requires 24 ms on PC Warp and 10 ms on iWarp. The number of floating-point data transfers internal to the computation is 3600 (400 in Step 3, 800 in Step 4, 400 in Step 5 and 2000 in Step 6). This will take 800 μs on PC Warp and 63 μs on iWarp.

Since the Voronoi diagram computation is taking the dual of the Delauney triangulation, this can be done in parallel, in pipelined mode (concurrent I/O and computation in a cell), so that the total time of computation will be around the total time for I/O which is around 200 ms on PC Warp and 120 ms on iWarp. The conversion to Voronoi diagram will be part of a pipeline at the end of which Voronoi diagram edges will be transmitted to the host. Hence, time for transmission to the host will be included in this.

The total times for the computation are, on PC Warp, 64 ms + 24 ms + 800 μs + 200 ms = 290 ms, while on iWarp the time is 8.9 ms + 10 ms + 63 μs + 120 ms = 140 ms.

8.11 Minimum spanning tree

> **Geometrical constructions.** The input is a set *S* of 1000 real coordinate pairs, defining a set of 1000 points in the plane, selected at random, with each coordinate in the range [0,1000]. The output is the minimal spanning tree of *S*, defined by the set of pairs of points of *S* that are joined by edges of the tree. (On minimal spanning trees see [13, Section 6.1].)

We use Shamos's algorithm [13], in which we have only to examine edges in the Delauney triangulation to find an incremental edge in the minimum spanning tree.

In the worst case, 1000 vertices can correspond to 3000 edges, implying an average of three edges per vertex. This means that we have to make a maximum of two comparisons to find the edge of minimum length out of a vertex. Since there are 1000 vertices, we have to make only 2000 comparisons per stage of the algorithm and, since there are $\log(N)$ stages, we have to make 20 000 comparisons in all. Also, as part of the initialization step, we have to compute the lengths of all the 3000 edges, which will involve 6000 floating-point multiplications and 3000 floating-point additions. We also have to prepare a data structure which will give the out-degree of a particular vertex. This will involve 2 comparisons per edge, for a maximum of 6000 comparisons in all. We assume that the minimum spanning tree will be computed. We also assume that a floating-point multiplication takes 5 μs and a floating-point addition takes 2.5 μs, and each comparison takes 1 μs. Adding up the respective times the total comes to about 65 ms. This time is the worst case since the Delauney triangulation of 1000 points will typically contain much less than 3000 edges.

8.12 Visibility

> **Visibility.** The input is a set of 1000 triples of triples of real coordinates $((r,s,t),(u,v,w),(x,y,z))$, defining 1000 opaque triangles in 3D space, selected at random with each coordinate in the range [0,1000]. The output is a list of vertices of the triangles that are visible from (0,0,0).

An input partitioning method is used. Each vertex is simply tested to see if it is obscured by any of the triangles. This is done by taking the four planes defined by the triangle vertices, and the origin and any two of them, and testing to see if the vertex point lies in the interior of the region defined by the three planes including the origin, but on the far side of the triangle. The mapping onto Warp is to broadcast the set of triangle points to all cells, and then to send to each of the ten cells one-tenth of the vertex set, with each cell testing its portion to see if it is visible. The execution time on the WW Warp is 825 ms (however, the WW Warp cannot hold the entire dataset due to memory limitations – this time is a compiler-estimated execution time). Some improvement (probably a factor of two to three) is expected on PC Warp, since the algorithm will be able to stop testing a vertex when it is found that a vertex is definitely not obscured by a particular triangle. On iWarp, we estimate a speedup of about 10, giving an execution time of 40 ms.

8.13 Graph matching

> **Graph matching.** The input is a graph G having 100 vertices, each joined by an edge to 10 other vertices selected at random, and another graph H having 30 vertices, each joined by an edge to three other vertices selected at random. The output is a list of the occurrences of (an isomorphic image of) H as a subgraph of G. As a variation on this task, suppose the vertices (and edges) of G and H have real-valued labels in some bounded range; then the output is that occurrence (if any) of H as a subgraph of G for which the sum of the absolute differences between corresponding pairs of labels is a minimum.

This problem includes two subproblems. The first is to find isomorphic embeddings of the smaller graph in the larger one. Finding one such embedding (or determining the existence of one) is known to be NP-complete [16]. Finding all isomorphisms actually grows exponentially. For example, in one set of randomly-generated data, we found about 10^{16} solutions. Because there are too many solutions, at present no existing machine can produce all the solutions in one year.

The second problem is to find the one isomorphism to the graph with the least differences between the corresponding edge and vertex costs. The complexity of the second problem is obviously between finding one and finding all. This problem has not been completed because there were too many solutions to the first problem.

Our parallel algorithm is based on Ullmann's refinement procedure [17] which can prune the search tree by eliminating mappings that are infeasible because of connectivity requirements. The method eliminates mappings as early as possible. In addition, we developed a more powerful method to cut the search tree as early as possible. The new method uses graph analysis and makes use of some special features of the graph.

We implemented the problem on the Warp host, which is a Sun workstation. Running on a set of randomly-generated data for over one hour, we obtained 1 188 174 solutions, giving 267 solutions/s or about 3.75 ms/solution. At this point, by counting the branching factors of the tree above the portion we had processed, we estimated that we had found only about $1.2 \times 10^{-9}\%$ of the solutions, leading to our estimate of 10^{16} solutions for this example.

In the Warp implementation, we parallelize the exploration of the search tree. This is easy to do because the search tree is so large that we can easily assign each subtree to a processor. By straightforward extrapolation of cycle time, we estimate the solution rate in PC Warp to be 2700 solutions/s. Similarly, we estimate the solution rate in iWarp to be 19 000 solutions/s.

8.14 Minimum-cost path

> **Minimum-cost path.** The input is a graph G having 1000 vertices, each joined by an edge to 100 other vertices selected at random, and where each edge has a non-negative real-valued weight in some bounded range. Given two vertices P, Q of G, the problem is to find a path from P to Q along which the sum of the weights is minimum. (Dynamic programming may be used, if desired.)

The algorithm used here is the best-known sequential algorithm, Dijkstra's Single Source Single Destination [18] (SSSD). The algorithm works by repeatedly 'expanding' nodes (adding all their neighbors to a list) then finding the next node to expand by choosing the closest unexpanded node to the destination.

The lack of a while loop on the WW Warp results in a significant loss of performance, compared to PC Warp and iWarp. PC Warp and iWarp have very similar mappings:

WW Warp

The WW Warp cannot execute a loop a data-dependent number of times, so the outer loop of SSSD must be mapped into the cluster processors. In this case, the Warp array is used for expanding nodes, and for calculating which node should be expanded next. Node expansion is done by feeding from the cluster processor the descendants of the node to be expanded, and by calculating the distance to the goal of each of these nodes. The computation is extremely simple, and I/O bound on the Warp array. Each node expansion involves the transfer of 200 words of data, which takes 200 × 1.2 μs = 240 μs, since the transfer of a single word takes 1.2 μs.

To find the next node to be expanded, the entire set of nodes must be scanned, and the node nearest the goal is selected. On the WW Warp this means 1000 nodes must be scanned. Again, the computation is I/O bound, so that the execution time is 1000 × 1.2 μs = 1.2 ms. In the worst case, 1000 nodes must be expanded, for a total time of 1000 × (1.2 ms + 240 μs) = 1.44 s. This number scales linearly with the number of nodes that must be expanded to find the goal.

PC Warp

In PC Warp it is possible to map the outer loop of SSSD into the Warp array, giving a much better time. Node expansion is done by prestoring at each cell the costs, giving each cell 100 data. Node expanding is done in parallel in all cells. In the worst case, the slowest cell will have to expand 100 nodes, so that the time for one node expansion is 100 × 0.25 μs = 25 μs.

The global minimum is calculated in parallel in all cells, and then the minimum among cells is found in one pass through the array. Finding the minimum on each cell takes 0.4 μs × 100 = 40 μs. Finding the minimum among cells takes 0.4 μs × 10 = 4 μs. The total time for one node expansion is therefore 69 μs. In the worst case, when 1000 nodes are expanded, the time is 69 ms. This time scales linearly with the number of nodes that must be expanded to find the goal.

iWarp

Following the same algorithm-partitioning method as for PC Warp, we use 72 cells instead of 10. Now each cell need store only 14 data. The faster cycle time of iWarp gives a 10 μs time for one node expansion, 7 μs to find the global minimum in each cell, and 8 μs to find the global minimum across cells. (The minimum across cells is done sequentially from cell to cell, so it takes longer on longer arrays.) The total time for one node expansion on iWarp is 25 μs. In the worst case, the total time for the solution will be 25 ms. This number scales linearly with the number of nodes that must be expanded to find the goal.

8.15 Warp benchmarks summary

In Table 8.5 we summarize Warp's performance on the IU architecture benchmarks. With each time, we give its source – from an actual run of WW Warp, from

Table 8.5 Warp benchmark summary.

Algorithm	*WW Warp*	*PC Warp*	*iWarp*
Laplacian	430 ms actual run	350 ms compiled code	7.8 ms
Zero crossing	170 ms actual run	50 ms estimate	7.8 ms
Border following	N/A	1.1 s estimate	690 ms
Connected components	5.6 s compiled code	980 ms estimate	470 ms
Hough transform	N/A	340 ms compiled code	60 ms
Convex hull	9 ms actual run	9 ms compiled code	3.2 ms
Voronoi diagram	N/A	290 ms estimate	140 ms
Minimal spanning tree	N/A	160 ms estimate	43 ms
Visibility	830 ms compiled code	400 ms estimate	40 ms
Graph matching	N/A	1800 soln/s estimate	19 000 soln/s
Minimum-cost path	1.4 s estimate	69 ms estimate	25 ms

compiled code, or by an estimate (all iWarp times are estimated). The times from an actual run are, of course, the most reliable – they are observed times, from an actual run on our WW Warp at Carnegie Mellon, and include I/O. Times marked 'compiled code' are just as reliable; the W2 compiler for Warp produces a time estimate, which gives the actual execution time for the algorithm on Warp (we have modified these times as appropriate when the Warp array is not the bottleneck in the execution time of the algorithm). Finally, 'estimate' indicates a time which is not based on compiled code, but on some other method, which may not be as reliable. The source of the time is given in the relevant section. We have tried to be as accurate as possible in these estimates, and have tried to err on the side of caution.

Acknowledgments

The research was supported in part by Defense Advanced Research Projects Agency (DOD), monitored by the Air Force Avionics Laboratory under Contract F33615-81-K-1539, and Naval Electronic Systems Command under Contract N00039-85-C-0134, in part by the US Army Engineer Topographic Laboratories under Contract DACA76-85-C-0002, and in part by the Office of Naval Research under Contracts N00014-80-C-0236, NR 048-659, and N00014-85-K-0152, NR SDRJ-007.

Bibliography

1. Annaratone M., Arnould E., Cohn R. *et al.* (1987). Warp architecture: from prototype to production. In *Proceedings of the 1987 National Computer Conference*. AFIPS, 1987
2. Annaratone M., Arnould E., Gross T. *et al.* (1986). Warp architecture and implementation. In *Conference Proceedings of the 13th Annual International Symposium on Computer Architecture*, pp. 346–56
3. Annaratone M., Arnould E., Cohn R. *et al.* (1987). Architecture of Warp. In *COMPCON Spring '87*, pp. 264–7. IEEE Computer Society
4. Bruegge B., Chang C., Cohn R. *et al.* (1987). The Warp programming environment. In *Proceedings of the 1987 National Computer Conference*. AFIPS, 1987
5. Bruegge B., Chang C., Cohn R. *et al.* (1987). Programming Warp. In *COMPCON Spring '87*, pp. 268–71. IEEE Computer Society
6. Gross T., Kung H.T., Lam M. and Webb J. (1985). Warp as a machine for low-level vision. In *Proceedings of 1985 IEEE International Conference on Robotics and Automation*, pp. 790–800
7. Kung H.T. and Webb J.A. (1986). Mapping image processing operations onto a linear systolic machine. *Distributed Computing*, **1**(4), 246–57
8. Haralick R.M. (1984). Digital step edges from zero crossings of second directional derivatives. *IEEE Transactions on Pattern Analysis and Machine Intelligence*, 6:58–68
9. Rosenfeld A. and Kak A.C. (1982). *Digital Picture Processing*. New York: Academic Press
10. Wallace R.S. and Howard M.D. HBA vision architecture: built and benchmarked. In *Computer Architectures for Pattern Analysis and Machine Intelligence*. Seattle WA: IEEE Computer Society
11. Kung H.T. and Webb J.A. (1985). Global operations on the CMU Warp machine. In *Proceedings of 1985 AIAA Computers in Aerospace V Conference*, pp. 209–18. American Institute of Aeronautics and Astronautics
12. Schwartz J., Sharir M. and Siegel A. (1985). *An efficient algorithm for finding connected components in a binary image*. Technical Report 154, New York University Department of Computer Science
13. Preparata F.P. and Shamos M.I. (1985). *Computational Geometry – An Introduction*. New York: Springer
14. Jarvis R.A. (1973). On the identification of the convex hull of a finite set of points in the plane. *Information Processing Letters*, 2, 18–21
15. Guibas L.J. and Stolfi J. (1985). Primitives for the manipulation of general subdivisions and the computation of Voronoi diagrams. *ACM Transactions on Graphics* 4
16. Garey M.R. and Johnson D.S. (1979). *Computers and Intractibility: A guide to the theory of NP-completeness*. W.H. Freeman
17. Ullman J.R. (1976). An algorithm for subgraph isomorphism. *Journal of the ACM*, **23**(1), 31–42
18. Dijkstra E. (1959). A note on two problems in connexion with graphs. *Numerische Mathematik*, 1, 269–71

J.A. Trotter
W.R. Moore

University of Oxford

9 · MESH: an architecture for image processing

This chapter describes a SIMD 2D array architecture for computer vision. The machine, called MESH, is designed to execute low- and intermediate-level vision algorithms and be implemented using VLSI. One major problem on large systems with this method of implementation is that faults are bound to occur due to defects on the silicon, so the MESH system is designed with the technology constraints of large chips in mind. MESH uses a novel combination of hardware fault tolerance with inherent robustness in vision algorithms to overcome these faults and provide a working image-processing system.

9.1 Introduction

The increasing interest in computer vision in both industry and universities has led to a growth in the amount of research being done in this area. New and more complex algorithms are being developed, giving better results but requiring immense amounts of processing power. To overcome this computational deficit and support practical implementations, faster and more cost-effective ways of processing must be found. The vision system may be split up into a number of stages each having distinct hardware requirements. The low and intermediate levels, the first parts of the vision chain, are inherently parallel and are most suited to a Single Instruction stream, Multiple Data stream **(SIMD) architecture**. Thus a cost-effective, parallel, image-processing unit is required.

This paper describes MESH, a **2D array** architecture for low- and intermediate-level image processing which could be used as a building block in bigger image-processing or computer vision systems. The proposed architecture is being designed with the constraints of large Integrated Circuits (ICs) in mind and is therefore concerned with fault tolerance and other implementation aspects. Fault tolerance is the subject of the initial study as described in this chapter. In this way, we aim to provide an efficient and cost-effective unit for intermediate- and low-level computer vision.

9.2 Requirements of the hardware system

To provide the computational speed necessary for real-time image processing some parallelism must be provided. Low-level vision processing is based on identical operations executed on all the data. An effective machine for these types of algorithms is a parallel SIMD machine. A 2D array of processors is likely to be an effective architecture since it reflects the topology of the vision problem (Duff, 1983; Offen, 1985). The image is mapped into the processor array. The SIMD controller broadcasts its instructions to all the processors in the array. All the processors then carry out the same instruction on their data. The quick and efficient execution of image-processing instructions is paramount and to help this some generic operations may be supported by hardware.

9.3 The software system

Vision processing uses a variety of algorithms which can be classified into high, intermediate and low levels (Ballard and Brown, 1982). Low- and intermediate-level algorithms include edge finding, filtering and thinning, etc. Often, the image given to these algorithms is noisy or blurred, a few pixels may be wrong, but the algorithms can still operate on the image satisfactorily. The fact that algorithms do not need perfect data shows that they are inherently robust and a system using these algorithms may also be able to cope with hardware faults.

9.4 2D array architecture

Because low and intermediate algorithms are based on local nearest-neighbour operations and all pixels have the same instruction executed on them, the 2D SIMD array is an appropriate architecture.

An efficient way of implementing a large 2D array of processors is by using **Ultra Large Scale Integration** (ULSI) or **Wafer Scale Integration** (WSI). These technologies can provide the means to put down a large array on silicon, but when designing for them, certain constraints are imposed by the fabrication process. One of the biggest problems on large chips is that defects are always present; they may occur during fabrication, in the starting material, wafer testing, mounting and during the lifetime of the IC. Fault tolerance is necessary to counter the effects of the faults in these large circuits and obtain reasonable yield and reliability.

9.4.1 Previous approaches

Typical approaches which have been proposed for fault tolerance of 2D arrays are:

- **Row/column redundancy.** In this approach, spare rows and/or columns are used. Rows or columns with faulty cells (even with a single faulty cell) are replaced by the fault-free spares which would otherwise be inactive. This scheme is the most popular one for adding redundancy to memory chips. The row/column approach has also been used in 2D arrays (Bentley and Jesshope, 1986). In general, approaches based on this type of redundancy have simple hardware and require no extra software at run time.

- **Restructurable VLSI.** The Restructurable VLSI (RVLSI) approach to fault tolerance is based on laser cutting and welding technology. The RVLSI research, which is aimed at implementing systems with complexities approaching a million gates, is being conducted at MIT Lincoln Laboratory (Raffel, 1986). The approach is targeted at modular architectures that can be arranged as an array of cells embedded in a regular interconnection matrix. A laser is used to form interconnections between two levels of metal and the same laser can be used to disconnect a wire link by removing the metal on either level. A 16-point × 16-bit Fast Fourier Transform (FFT) 2D array has been implemented (Rhodes, 1986).
- **Triple Modular Redundancy (TMR).** The TMR is a masking redundancy approach where a unit is triplicated and a voter scheme is used to poll the outputs and mask the faulty ones. The TMR approach was implemented by Trilogy in ECL technology (Peltzer, 1983). In the implementation, triplicated modules were separated on the wafer so they were less sensitive to clustered defects. However, delays were introduced as a consequence of the long lines required to communicate the three modules with their voter circuit.
- **Switching technologies for 2D arrays.** The switching fault-tolerant approach uses standby switches to bypass faulty modules and reconfigure a 2D array onto a faulty grid. The Configurable Highly Parallel (CHiP) processor (Hedlund and Snyder, 1982) is essentially a 2D array but the inclusion of extensive switching between cells allows it to be configured in a variety of architectures (such as trees, linear arrays, etc.). Switching strategies may be optimized for mapping 2D arrays, and more efficient solutions are possible (Moore and Mahat, 1985; Sami and Stefanelli, 1983; Evans *et al.*, 1986). These approaches use complicated switching networks that increase the hardware overhead and the through-switch delay.

The objective of all these approaches is to try and construct perfect arrays from the processors available. They tend to make use of a relatively low proportion of the working processors (a low 'harvest') for two reasons. Firstly, even with quite sophisticated reconfiguration switches, some good processors will have to be sacrificed to preserve regular interconnections and secondly, an excess of spare processors is needed to be sure that there are enough to configure the target array size. In configuring a perfect array, the data paths have to be routed around faulty areas introducing many switches and/or long lines into the path. This means there is a hardware overhead and increase in complexity involved for the extra lines and reconfiguration logic. The extra switches and long lines introduce significant delays that become worse as the number of faults increases.

The 2D SIMD array is a good architecture for the problems considered, although a number of major aspects associated with fabrication have to be taken into account.

9.5 The MESH system

The MESH system tries to overcome some of the problems described above. It is fundamentally a 2D SIMD array which uses a novel fault-tolerant strategy to enhance yield and improve reliability. The strategy is aimed at trying to obtain a high harvest of working processors with a low hardware overhead.

9.5.1 MESH operation

The operation of MESH consists of a number of stages. On power-up, the processors are tested and the faulty ones identified. The array is then reconfigured, and once this has been done the array can be used for computation. This consists of mapping the data into the array, processing it and then mapping the data back out.

The key to the fault-tolerant strategy is the hardware reconfiguration to eliminate the defective processors, in combination with data reconfiguration to redistribute the problem over all the working processors. After the faulty processors have been identified, the hardware fault tolerance comes into operation. The approach used is very simple: faulty processors' horizontal and vertical neighbours are connected together, effectively removing the faulty processor from the array. This introduces voids in the array where the faulty processors are, but data can still pass through these areas. In the event of a cluster of faults, many processors in the same area could be lost and significantly large areas of the problem space may now not be covered (see Figure 9.1). A non-faulty array would take its data from the pixels of the image using a one-to-one mapping to the processors. If any of the processors were faulty, then the corresponding part of the image would be lost. In MESH, the data is reconfigured to avoid this problem, that is, the data that would have been lost is now taken by another processing element. The aim of the reconfiguration is to produce a more even distribution of working processors over the image. The effect is that the processors surrounding a defect appear to change their positions with respect to the image. This can be thought of as moving the conceptual positions of the processors. After data reconfiguration, the processors have taken up their new conceptual positions, as shown in Figure 9.2. Now both the

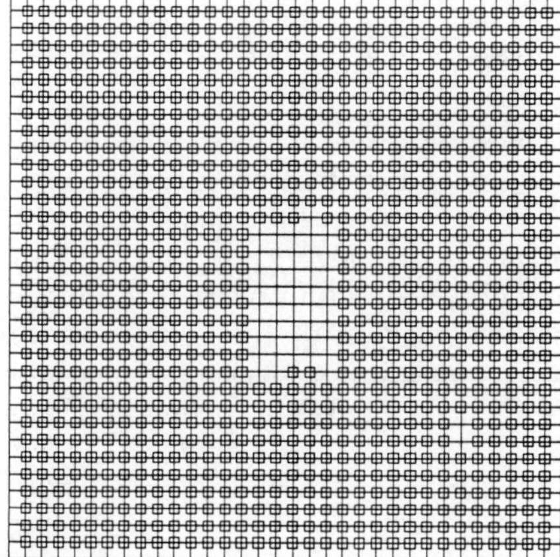

Figure 9.1
MESH array with defective processors not shown.

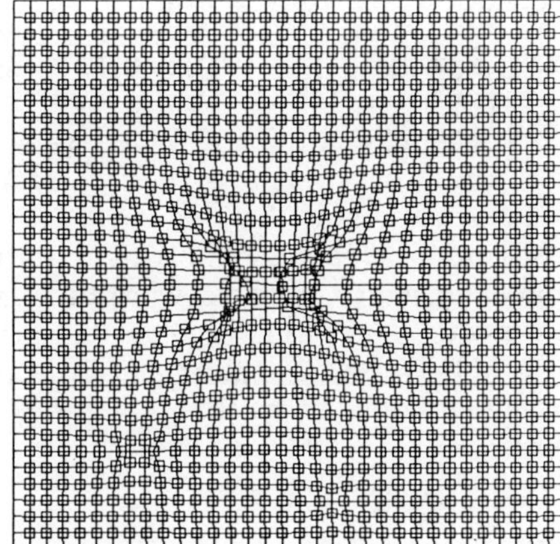

Figure 9.2
MESH array after reconfiguration.

locality of the processors and their connections have been maintained, MESH still acts like a nearest-neighbour 2D array, as is shown later.

The image can now be mapped into the array. Because the conceptual processor positions have now changed, a normal one-to-one pixel-to-processor mapping is no longer valid. Instead, the input image has to be mapped onto the processor array using some algorithm that takes into account the data reconfiguration. Once the image is in the array, image processing can be carried out in the normal way and when this is complete the image can be mapped back out. Thus the reconfigured processor positions are mapped onto the perfect pixel grid.

Thus MESH uses very simple hardware reconfiguration which it combines with data reconfiguration to provide the overall system fault tolerance. It uses the inherent robustness in many vision algorithms to provide a working image-processing system.

9.5.2 MESH advantages and problems

The MESH system overcomes many of the problems associated with other 2D array systems. It uses a very simple fault-tolerance strategy with the minimum of hardware overhead. 2D connectivity is maintained over the array and this, coupled with the robust nature of many algorithms, means that image-processing operations still remain valid. The method of reconfiguration used means that all the working processors are used, that is, the system has a 100% harvest. The system operates at constant speed and trades the granularity of the solution as more processors fail. A low communication bandwidth is used to reduce the interprocessor communications and hence the reconfiguration hardware overhead.

The MESH system assumes that some self test is available and that the lines that bypass the processors in the event of defects are highly reliable. MESH combines hardware tolerance with algorithmic robustness to provide a system that works on imperfect hardware.

9.5.3 Data reconfiguration algorithm

Data reconfiguration is necessary to cover the problem space with a more even distribution of processors. The data reconfiguration moves the conceptual positions of the processors so that they cover a slightly different area of the image and so the distribution of processors is more even. Our current algorithm works on the minimum energy principle. The positions of a processor's four nearest neighbours are averaged and this becomes the new virtual position of the processor: this algorithm is applied iteratively until the processor positions settle. The result of this reconfiguration can be seen in Figure 9.2; the squares mark the virtual processor positions.

The equations are:

```
Xpos := [ Xpos(N) + Xpos(E) + Xpos(S) + Xpos(W) ] / 4
Ypos := [ Ypos(N) + Ypos(E) + Ypos(S) + Ypos(W) ] / 4
```

Where Xpos is the X position of the processor in question and Xpos(N) is the X position of its nearest working neighbour to the north etc.

Other data reconfiguration algorithms are possible, such as moving processors only to discrete positions, or using a different type of algorithm, such as evenly distributing a line of processors across the problem space. Such algorithms may yield better results for different image operations and will be investigated in due course. The above algorithm is the one that has been used so far and appears to be quite effective.

9.5.4 Data input mapping

Because there is no longer a one-to-one correspondence of pixels to processors, the input data now has to be mapped onto the array of processors. The input mapping can introduce errors since it must average or estimate in some way. A number of algorithms are possible, but the one we use at the moment is that processors take the value of the pixel they are nearest to. Other possibilities include taking an average over the pixels which the processor covers.

Figure 9.3 shows the result of mapping a triangle into the array. Even though the array is severely distorted, the image has mapped in successfully.

9.5.5 The processing stage

Once the image is in the MESH system, normal image-processing algorithms can be executed. The one that has been implemented so far is a Sobel edge operator. Because locality and connections are maintained, the MESH system remains a valid processor for the algorithm. The result of the edge operator can be seen in Figure 9.4. Even though the edge was through a very defective part of the array, the algorithm still operated successfully and detected the edge, introducing only a few erroneous pixels.

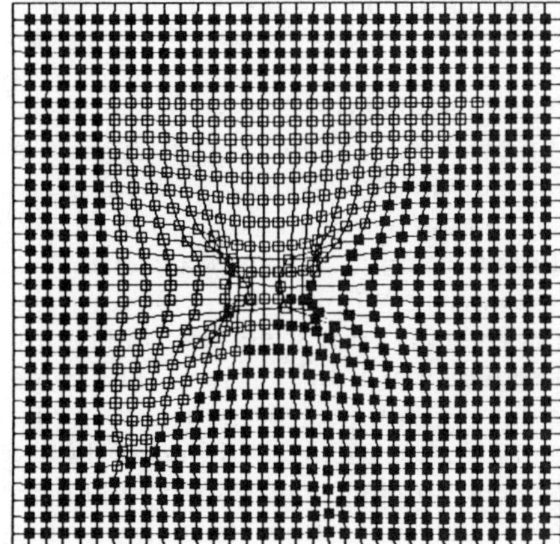

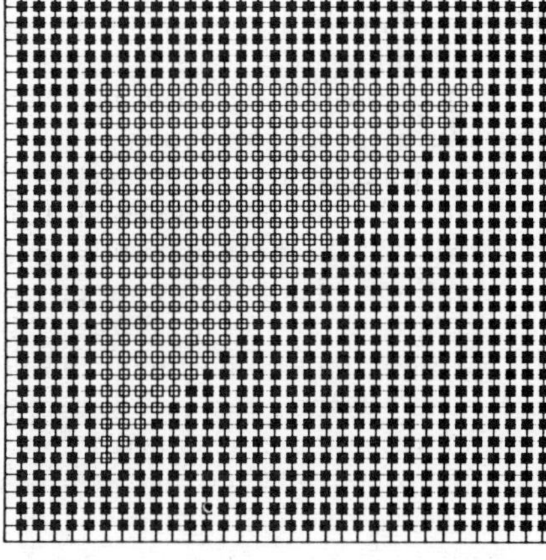

Figure 9.3
Defective and perfect MESH array with a triangle mapped in.

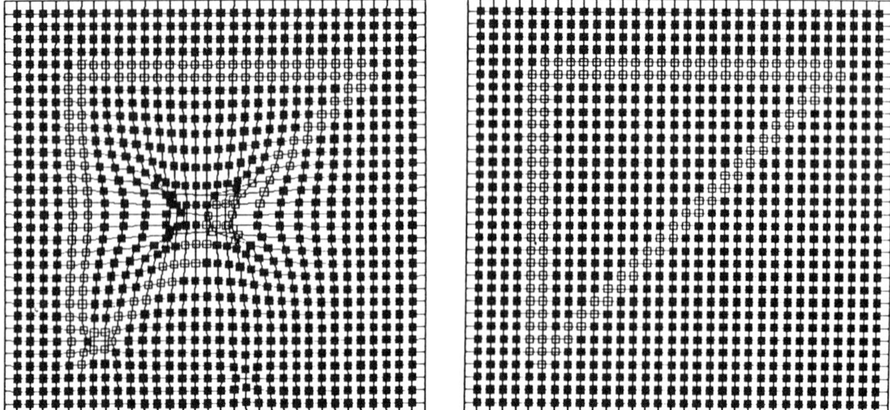

Figure 9.4
MESH arrays after a Sobel edge detector has been executed.

9.5.6 Outputting the image

The output map is the reverse of the input map; the data is mapped from the processors to the pixel grid. Again, a number of algorithms are possible and the one used at the moment is to take a weighted average of the processors contributing to a pixel value; the weight being proportional to the pixel's distance from the processor. The image is then mapped out of the array so it can be displayed (see Figure 9.5). Of course, the data may not need to be mapped out if a subsequent system is able to interrogate MESH directly. This may avoid any errors associated with the output mapping algorithm.

9.6 Experimental results

A simulation of the MESH system, written in C, was used to investigate the data reconfiguration algorithms and the input and output mappings. The program that MESH executes is included in the simulation, so image-processing algorithms can be executed on MESH.

A number of examples have been used to test the MESH system. To try to assess the input and output mappings, a line and an edge were mapped in and out to observe the inaccuracies introduced by the mappings and the lower granularity areas of MESH. The lines and edges were mapped in and out with a high degree of success indicating that the input and output maps do not introduce a significant error.

A Sobel edge operator was programmed into the MESH system. On an array with no defects, the system performed like a normal 2D array processor, indicating that the input and output maps did not introduce a significant error. The same experiment was then tried on a system where defects were present in the array. The array was reconfigured and then the Sobel operator was executed in the normal way. The results obtained from this experiment were encouraging. The system had maintained the line even though it was through a severe distortion. This shows that

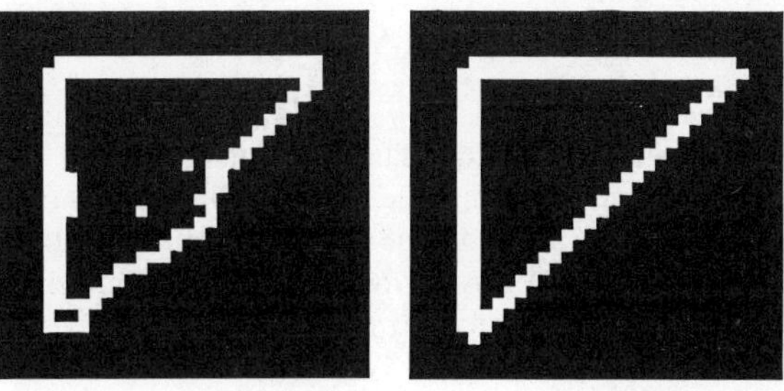

Figure 9.5
The output from a defective and perfect MESH.

algorithms can be executed on defective hardware and still retain a good performance.

The input and output mappings of data for MESH do introduce some errors. If any processors are defective, some averaging is bound to occur and the MESH system loses granularity. The mapping of data into and out of MESH also introduces a time overhead for the input and output of data.

Conclusion

The development of the MESH system is ongoing work at Oxford University. MESH is being designed with the constraints of ULSI/WSI in mind, and by considering the system as a whole, a cost-effective image-processing unit is realizable.

To overcome defects introduced by fabrication, the MESH system uses an effective combination of hardware fault tolerance with the inherent robustness of vision algorithms. This combination allows parallel image-processing algorithms to be executed on the machine.

The MESH system has been simulated and shown to work for basic image-processing algorithms. The Sobel edge detector worked successfully operating on an image, even though the simulated hardware had many defects. In the future, grey-level images will be used with this and other algorithms, and results from these investigations will be assessed.

This architecture may also be used to solve minimum energy problems such as surface reconstruction (Blake and Zisserman, 1987). The processors can all calculate a value of a position on the surface. If there are fewer processors in an area then the surface will be calculated with less resolution. The same machine may also be used for finite element analysis since some algorithms have similar robust properties and so can run using the MESH system.

MESH provides a novel 2D array architecture for image processing. The architecture combines hardware and software tolerance to provide a robust parallel image-processing system.

Acknowledgements

The authors wish to thank José Delgado-Frias for his help and SERC for funding the work.

References

Ballard D.H. and Brown C.H. (1982). *Computer Vision*. London: Prentice-Hall

Bentley L. and Jesshope C.R. (1986). The implementation of a two dimensional redundancy scheme in a wafer scale high-speed disk memory. In *Wafer Scale Integration* (Jesshope C.R. and Moore W.R., eds). Bristol: Adam Hilger

Blake A. and Zisserman A. (1987). *Visual Reconstruction*. Cambridge MA: MIT Press

Duff M.J.B. (1983). *Computing Structures for Image Processing*. London: Academic Press

Evans R.A., McCanny J.V. and Wood K.W. (1986). Wafer scale integration based on self-organization. In *Wafer Scale Integration* (Jesshope C.R. and Moore W.R., eds). Bristol: Adam Hilger

Hedlund K.S. and Snyder L. (1982). Wafer scale integration of Configurable Highly Parallel (CHiP) processor. In *Proc. Int. Conf. on Parallel Processing*, pp. 262–4. Ohio State University, August 1982

Moore W.R. and Mahat R. (1985). Fault-tolerant communications for wafer scale integration of a processor array. *Microelectronics and Reliability,* **25**(February), 291–4

Offen R.J., ed. (1985). *VLSI for Image Processing*. London: Collins

Peltzer D.L. (1983). Wafer-scale integration: the limits of VLSI? *VLSI Design,* **4**(May), 43–7

Raffel J. (1986). The RVLSI approach to wafer scale integration. In *Wafer Scale Integration* (Jesshope C.R. and Moore W.R., eds). Bristol: Adam Hilger

Rhodes F.M. (1986). Applications of the RVLIS to signal processing. In *Wafer Scale Integration* (Jesshope C.R. and Moore W.R., eds). Bristol: Adam Hilger

Sami M.G. and Stefanelli R. (1983). Reconfigurable architectures for VLSI processing arrays. *Proc. IEEE,* **74**(5), 565–77

10· Performance of the OSMMA image processing system

A.A. Naqvi
M.B. Sandler

King's College
London

OSMMA is a flexible multiprocessor architecture based on the 'overlapped shared memory' processor interconnection scheme. An image-processing system based on this architecture has been designed using fast digital signal processors. The basic module of the system consists of a 2-PE board with associated program and data memory. The single module is capable of real-time processing of 128 × 128 8-bit pixel images. The full system is made up by plugging the required number of such modules into a backplane. The modules are controlled and loaded with program/image data via a PC memory-map interface. Results of the performance of a single module are presented for some low-level image-processing algorithms.

10.1 Introduction

The Overlapped Shared Memory Multiprocessor Architecture (OSMMA) image-processing system forms the low-level, computationally intensive part of a 3-level machine vision system. It is based on a new memory organization and processor interconnection scheme. Most MIMD multiple-processor image-processing systems presently developed or designed [1] use either the globally shared memory or distributed memory architectures with some interconnection network among the Processing Elements (PEs) employed. Multiple processors in image-processing systems need to share common data, and efficient architectures must allow for the common data to be accessible to all PEs requiring it, with the least possible overheads.

In globally shared memory architectures, all common data is placed in a common memory, accessible by all the system PEs with suitable arbitration and access protocols. However, the major drawbacks with such systems are the memory bandwidth bottleneck and the mean delay between memory accesses for individual PEs to the common memory. These factors contribute significantly to determining the overall system efficiency and the number of PEs that reasonably can be used. On the other hand, in distributed memory systems each PE has access to its 'local' data memory but can communicate to other PEs' memory via an interconnection network. Although overall memory access is greatly increased, these systems involve significant hardware and software overheads in communication.

The **Overlapped Shared Memory** (OSM) scheme [2] is neither a globally shared nor entirely distributed memory architecture. Rather, it is an arrangement that retains the merits of both. It provides for a memory bandwidth directly proportional to the number of PEs employed and allows limited sharing of memory, while greatly reducing contention. It is also flexible for expansion and involves no significant interconnection and arbitration overheads.

The architecture has been implemented using fast digital signal processors (Texas Instruments' TMS32020s). Since the design methodology employs the sharing of any data memory between two processors only, the performance of the system in terms of memory access, contention and message passing can be reasonably predicted from the performance results of a 2-PE prototype. The prototype is capable of processing 128 × 128 8-bit pixel images at real-time speeds (that is, one image frame in about 40 ms). Results are presented for sample algorithms, including an edge-detecting operator. The full 8-PE OSMMA system is formed by plugging such 2-PE modules into a backplane.

The image processing hardware is interfaced to a PC host for program/data loading and control.

An overview of the overlapped shared memory architecture is presented in the next section, followed by details of the 2-PE implementation and performance results. Section 10.4 describes an 8-PE version of the above implementation along with projected performance.

10.2 Overview of the OSM architecture

This architecture is based on the concept of image parallelism, that is, distributing the image data into image segments to be processed concurrently by an equal number of PEs. These image segments are loaded into the 'local' data memories of individual PEs. However, the 'local' memory of each PE is also accessible by the adjacent PEs (either in full or a portion thereof) thus providing the vital near-neighbour interconnection (see Figure 10.1a).

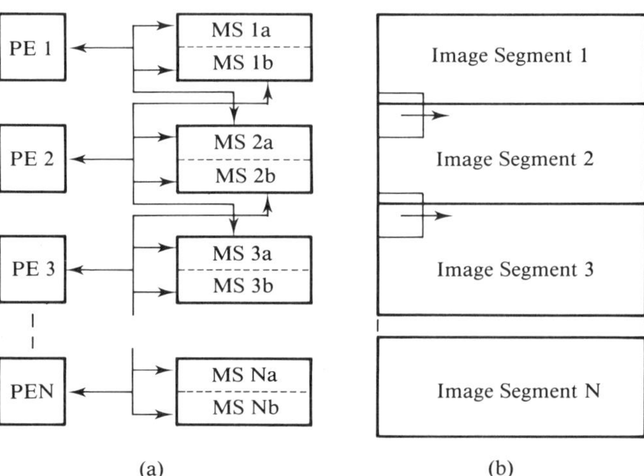

Figure 10.1
Mapping image processing algorithms on an OSM array.

If the memories of individual PEs are viewed as an array of Memory Segments (MSs) of an image memory, it is clear from the above that each MS is shared by a set of adjacent PEs and different MSs will, in general, not be shared by all the same PEs. Furthermore, a MS may be divided into subsegments and the PEs sharing it may share different subsegments rather than the entire segment. This reduces the number of PEs sharing any memory region and hence the contention, while allowing two PEs to access different areas of a shared memory simultaneously.

In effect, it can be seen that the PEs share overlapped regions of memory, hence the name 'overlapped shared memories'. The OSM architecture is more suitable for low-level image processing, as most of the inter-PE communication involved is amongst near neighbours. The implementation design described in the next section is based on such applications in particular. It is to be noted that, by virtue of the memory overlap, the 'local' memory of individual PEs is, in effect, extended into that of the neighbours' memory. Therefore a PE accesses adjacent PEs' memory just as its own, thereby achieving fast inter-PE communication at a rate equal to its memory bandwidth, with no overheads.

Implementation of an image-processing algorithm like a 3 × 3 window Laplacian operator on an image would proceed as follows (see Figure 10.1b):

(1) The image data is partitioned into strips and distributed equally into the local data memories of an equal number of PEs.

(2) These strips are processed simultaneously by the PEs, from top left to bottom right, and on each strip of the image a PE, having access to adjacent strips also, performs the convolution.

(3) The result of the convolution (that is, processed data) is stored in a separate memory area to avoid erasing the original image data as it may be required for use by other PEs.

It is to be noted that near-neighbour access here is not restricted to performing mere 3 × 3 window operations, as on SIMD image-processing arrays (for example, CLIP4, DAP), rather, the size of the window convolution that can be performed is restricted only by the extent of overlap between adjacent PEs' memories. This in turn depends on the size of the image and the number of PEs involved. Thus, for the implementation described in the next section, a 65 × 65 window convolution could also be performed with no additional communication overheads. However, if the same image is processed by twice the number of PEs, the maximum window size is reduced to 33 × 33.

The arrangement of memories in an overlapped manner is similar to the concept of reduced/restricted shared memories presented in [3–5]. The difference between these and OSMs is that in the latter the entire MS or module is not shared by PEs linked to it. OSM can therefore be viewed as an extension of the former concept to reduce further the problem of shared memory contention.

These overlapped regions of the memory, apart from holding common data, may be used for message passing between adjacent PEs in the first instance and among arbitrarily distant processors via intermediary PEs. This aspect is exploited in implementing the histogramming algorithm described in the next section. However, since overlapped memories are part of a PE's 'local' data memories, no overheads are involved in communicating with immediately adjacent PEs as the data may be placed into these virtual communication memories while it is processed.

An arbitration mechanism is provided to avoid adjacent PEs accessing the common overlapped memories simultaneously. However, since only two PEs will ever contend for any memory subsegment, the probability of contention is low. Also, for some regular and deterministic image-processing algorithms, like having the PEs processing data from top left to bottom right as explained in the previous example, contention can be totally avoided.

10.3 Performance of the 2-PE OSMMA prototype

10.3.1 Introduction

A 2-PE version of the OSMMA image-processing system has been implemented using fast digital signal processors. It is capable of performing image-processing algorithms in real time (under 40 ms), for 128 × 128 8-bit pixel images. The single board system is interfaced to a PC-AT and the system's memories are mapped onto the PC's. The following sections describe the hardware of the system, program development, PC interface protocol and performance results of sample image-processing algorithms implemented on the system.

10.3.2 Hardware

A block diagram of the system hardware is depicted in Figure 10.2. Each 16 kbyte image memory for the 128 × 128 image is divided into two 8 kbyte MSs to form the 'local' memories of the two PEs. Each MS is divided into two 4 kbyte subsegments, one of which acts as the OSM region described in the OSM architecture above. Two separate image memories implemented in the same OSM format are provided to hold the raw and processed data. However, the role of the raw and processed data

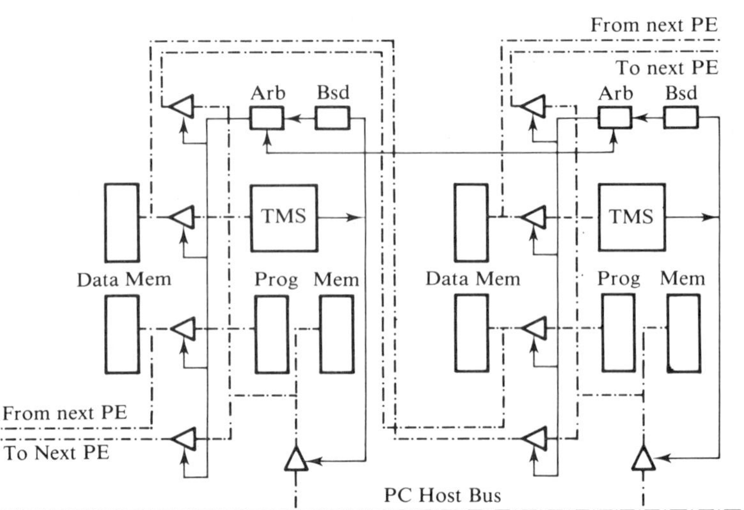

Figure 10.2
2-PE OSMMA module.

memories may be interchanged for further processing. This simply involves swapping memory address in the software.

The processors used are the TMS32020 version of Texas Instruments' digital signal processors which have a Harvard architecture and special features for fast implementation of image-processing algorithms [6, 7]. The processor can support program and data memories of 64 kwords each. There is provision for DMA protocol which is used by the host PC for program and data loading.

The memories are accessed via buffers enabled by a combination of the memory decode and arbitration logic. To reduce the number of buffers, the raw and processed image memories have common buffers. Each processor has its own program memory. All memory is implemented as fast static RAM so that the processors operate at the maximum speed of 200 ns instruction cycle time without wait states. Both processors are provided with common external clocks and their internal clocks are synchronized. A single logic chip acts as the arbitrator between the processors and when contention for access to a common subsegment occurs, one of the PEs is put into a wait state while the other proceeds normally.

10.3.3 Program development and control

All control and program software for the system is written on the PC host and debugged using the simulation package of the TMS32020. Although, for the moment, all programs have been written in TMS assembler, a Pascal compiler for the DSP chip is also available. Program and data for the image-processing hardware is loaded into its memories, which also appear in the PC's memory map. The host sends a DMA request to each PE and upon receiving the acknowledge, the address and data lines of the PE come into control of the host.

When both PEs are ready to proceed, the host simultaneously signals both processors to start processing. Upon completion of a particular task, a PE signals the host and then goes into a 'wait until interrupt' state. The host monitors the state of all attached PEs and decides further action accordingly. A common clock synchronization signal is provided by the host to all system processors in conjunction with the common external clock. Although clock synchronization among the PEs is essential, program synchronization is not critical. The PEs need not be executing the same instruction simultaneously. This is in contrast to the well-known SIMD form of parallel processing. The TMS32020s have a built-in mechanism for clock synchronization.

10.3.4 Interprocessor communication

As mentioned in Section 10.2, the OSM regions can be used as communication memories. Any one of the adjacent processors places data to be communicated to the other processor in the common overlapped region/subsegment and signals the other processor when it has done so. Upon receiving this signal the other processor begins using this data. This aspect is made clearer by considering the following implementation of the image-histogramming algorithm.

Once the image data is placed in the respective data memories of the two PEs, the calculation of the histogram bins for each half of the image begins simultaneously in the two processors. When completed, one of the PEs puts its histogram values into a common memory region of the processed data memory. Meanwhile, the other processor waits for a signal from the first processor that it has placed the values into the common memory. Upon receiving this, it adds its histogram bin values to the values calculated by the other processor. The TMS32020 has dedicated signalling pins for such communications, namely the XF and BIO pins.

10.3.5 Results of sample algorithm implementations

A number of low-level image-processing algorithms have been implemented on the OSMMA system. One of the major results of the performance is that, as predicted, given hardware and software synchronization, memory contention between the processors is totally avoided. Individual PEs perform their tasks on image segments just as they would in a stand-alone system without any multiprocessor overheads. This is strictly true for thresholding, averaging and the Sobel, Roberts and Laplacian edge-detecting algorithms. For the histogramming algorithm, where results are to be added, one processor has to wait at the end of its processing for the results of the other before the final result is obtained.

Table 10.1 Algorithm timings.

No.	*Algorithm*	*t1 = Time for 2 PEs (ms)*	*t2 = Time for 1 PE (ms)*	*t2 / t1*
1	Threshold	18.17	36.05	1.98
2	Histogram	13.95	26.62	1.96
3	8 pt Ave.	36.91	73.23	1.98
4	Laplacian(8)	41.70	82.76	1.98
5	Sobel masks	62.50	120.37	1.93

Table 10.1 shows the timing for various algorithms implemented on the system for 128 × 128 8-bit pixel images. Timings for similar implementation on a single TMS32020 are also shown for comparison.

10.4 Design of/extension to an 8/32-PE system

The 2-PE prototype system described above is, in fact, a single module of the full 8-PE system designed for OSMMA. Containing four such modules, the full system will be capable of processing 256 × 256 8-bit pixel images at the same speeds as the 2-PE module processes 128 × 128 ones. Here the 64 kByte image data is divided into eight strips of 8 kByte data processed by an equal number of PEs. The four modules plug into a backplane that carries the PC host's busses and also links adjacent modules. As is clear from Figure 10.2, the modules are linked together as a chain like resistors in series. The last and first processors may also be linked to form a ring interconnection topology.

The nature of the OSM architecture is such that simply by plugging modules into the backplane the system size can be increased. No hardware changes are required as the system size increases, and it is only the software or the overall control by the host that is to be modified. The host is to divide and distribute image data according to the number of PEs attached, and load programs into the system accordingly.

It can be visualized from the performance of the 2-PE prototype that on the 8-PE system algorithms like thresholding and edge detecting will perform as efficiently, while algorithms like the histogramming, that involve passing of results from one processor to another, will incur a small overhead. In such a case, results have to be passed in sequence from top and bottom to the central processors where they are accumulated to obtain final results.

Continuing the above argument, the OSMMA system could be extended to a 32-PE version for processing 512 × 512 images. The same arguments about performance would hold as for the 8-PE system. The maximum window size on the system would, however, be reduced to 17 × 17, which is still reasonable for most applications.

It may be emphasized here, again, that due to the restricted shared memory architecture of the OSMMA system, where sharing of any MS is restricted to 2 PEs only, irrespective of the number of PEs in the system, memory contention can be totally avoided for regular low-level vision algorithms.

For algorithms that involve memory contention, the architecture supports a simple and efficient arbitration mechanism, maintaining overheads to the barest minimum. In such a situation, one of the contending PEs is allowed to proceed normally while the other is held in a wait state for one machine cycle only (which is half the off-chip-memory cycle) before it too is allowed access. Henceforth, the instruction execution of the two PEs is offset by one machine cycle until another contention arises.

Conclusions

A new shared-memory multiprocessor architecture has been implemented, and the conformity of performance with theoretical claims regarding memory access and contention proves the advantage of this technique over conventional shared-memory image-processing system designs. The use of off-the-shelf processors for the implementation has been instrumental in early realization of the design and has kept the cost considerably low. Performance timings may be slashed to almost half by replacing the TMS32020 chips with their pin-compatible TMS320C25 ones which are twice as fast.

As the design is not dependent on any particular processor chip, it could be implemented with other/future more powerful chips to improve overall performance. Although only a 2-PE system has been implemented, as argued in Section 10.3, the design would be significantly advantageous for higher PE systems especially for low-level image processing. OSMMA is to form the preprocessing part of a multilevel vision system and will be linked to an array of transputers. This work will be reported separately.

References

1. Edwards M.D. (1985). A review of MIMD architectures for image processing. In *Image Processing System Architectures* (Kittler J. and Duff M.J.B. eds.), pp. 85–99. London: Academic Press
2. Naqvi A.A. and Sandler M.B. (1987). A low-cost multiprocessor architecture for real-time image processing. *IEE colloquium digest*, 1987/14, pp. 6/1–5
3. Handler W., Maehle E. and Wirl K. (1985). DIRMU multiprocessor configuration. In *Proc. IEEE Int. Conf. on Parallel Processing 1985*, pp. 652–6. Penn State University PA
4. Teng P., Hwang K. and Kumar K. (1985). A VLSI-based multiprocessor architecture for implementing parallel algorithms. In *Proc. IEEE Int. Conf. on Parallel Processing 1985*, pp. 657–64. Penn State University PA
5. Danielsson P. and Ericsson T. (1982). *Suggestions for an Image Processing Array*. Internal report LiTH–ISY–I–0507, Dept. of Elect. Engg. Linkoping University
6. Ngan K.N., Kassim A.A. and Singh H.S. (1987). Parallel image processing system based on the TMS32010 digital signal processor. In *IEE proc. -E.* **134**(2), pp. 119–24
7. Naqvi A.A. and Sandler M.B. (1987). Image processing with multiple DSPs. *IEE colloquium digest*, 1987/41, pp. 7/1–4

11· A dynamically reconfigurable multimodal architecture for image processing

I.R. Greenshields

University of Connecticut

This chapter describes a dynamically reconfigurable architecture amenable to imaging operations which are either parallel (in the 2- or 3D pixel sense) or sequential (in the sense of MIMD non-paralizable processes). It also describes both the architectural design and the VLSI implementation, and touches on certain aspects of the removal of unwanted symmetries in the system.

11.1 Introduction

Considerable attention has been focussed recently on the application of highly-parallel architectures to image processing (see [1–10] for representative samples), as well as hierarchical (pyramidal) [11–15] or algorithm specific (such as the systolic systems [16–20]). Each of these architectures meets a perceived requirement in imaging, and each (justifiably) can lay claim to satisfying their particular niche in one elegant way or another. Nevertheless, it remains true that generalized image processing is a discipline in which various types of algorithmic structure are appropriate, and similar mixed-structure processes are evidenced in computer graphics. Thus, while the Whitted ray-tracing paradigm [21–4] cries out for MIMD super-parallelism of the processor-per-pixel type, interactive CAD–CAM is inherently sequential (and consequently wasteful of a highly-parallel system). Similarly, while no one would argue the ability of a highly-parallel tightly-coupled machine's ability to evaluate and subsequently equalize an image's histogram, the validity of developing an optimal parallel algorithm (other than the usual vectorization implicit in any repetitive loop) is open to debate. Other tasks are simply not paralizable in the usual sense of the word; immediate (and unfortunately non-pathological) examples include the determination of connectivity, topological genus or shape. Unfortunately, machines optimized to parallel computation are rarely well suited to fast, general, sequential computation; the converse is so obvious that it need not be stated.

A utopian (but completely unattainable) solution to the conflicting requirements of fast, per-pixel parallelism against equally fast (and possibly concurrent) sequentialism might be the collecting of $n \times n$ minisupercomputers tightly coupled via a shared (image, graphics) memory, each capable of producing the required MIMD concurrent sequentialism when purely parallel tasks are not required. This chapter adopts a somewhat more pragmatic approach. Here, we accept that many highly-parallel tasks in imaging and graphics need not necessarily be performed on a processor element of great complexity, while (equivalently) many of the concurrent processes associated with imaging and graphics usually do require processor architectures of greater scalar accuracy and throughput. Thus, a classical per-pixel convolution of complexity $O(n^2)$ (such as an edge-detecting filter on an anti-aliasing operation), usually computed today through some $O(n \log n)$ transform, can be computed readily in linear time on a fully parallel architecture whose individual Processing Elements (PEs) are essentially rudimentary. Conversely, a maximum-likelihood classification or a quarternion-based rotation, while potentially paralizable, requires a PE architecture of considerably greater sophistication, requiring (for example) real arithmetic and (perhaps) hardware floating-point multiplication and division. Approaching this duality by means of conventional multimicroprocessor architectures is not a feasible solution. In the first place, while the single microprocessor is (usually) overdesigned for elementary per-pixel operations (a bearable 'problem' if the price/performance ratio per-pixel operation is acceptable), they are most definitively unsuited for massive sequential throughput. Secondly, they are not particularly amenable to massive fast parallelism of the SIMD type (a common occurrence in imaging and graphics), since they are difficult to synchronize (not being driven in common 'broadcast' mode). Finally, and most importantly, they are architecturally static; if the machines do not come with floating-point hardware of required accuracy, nothing (short of purchasing a new system) can easily rectify that. Similarly, if the image grows from 1024×1024 to 2048×2048, nothing other than a substantial loss of speed and a repartitioning of the problem can solve that.

The architecture described here is motivated by an attempt to rectify at least some of the inherent SIMD/MIMD dichotomy encountered in imaging and graphics. It takes as its basic premise the fact that most (not all, acceptably) SIMD operations applied to images can be evaluated on primitive PE structures, while those processes more naturally MIMD will require somewhat more complex PEs. Similarly, it accepts that the parallelism can be extended to other image sizes (and topologies) provided the user is willing to tolerate a concomitant reduction in PE capability. In other words, the architecture trades off individual PE complexity for parallelism.

11.2 Architectural model and definitions

The architectural model described here is motivated by the following considerations:

- The requirement for per-pixel SIMD parallelism.
- The requirement for a per-pixel parallel environment with user-definable interconnection topologies.
- The requirement for a multiple sequential environment (MIMD-type parallelism).
- The ability to extend the architecture (in the sense defined below), so that

processes requiring greater computational throughput of a specific nature can be traded off against degrees of parallelism.

- The ability to partition the entire system into subsystems satisfying each of the areas described above, any number of which can be contained within the whole.

As a motivation for the more abstracted discussion to follow, consider the following (fairly typical) manipulation of some $n \times n$ grey-level image:

(1) Evaluate image histogram.

(2) Equalize histogram.

(3) Remap image to equalized version.

(4) Edge-detect by Laplacian convolution.

(5) Region-classify image based on previously evaluated edges.

(6) Compute area of classified regions.

Now consider the following (broad) structural breakdown of the above steps:

(1) Sequential (single processor, elementary architecture, computing over single image memory).

(2) As above (1).

(3) Parallel-per-pixel processing, elementary pixel processor structures.

(4) As above (3).

(5) MIMD parallelism (each independent processor being started on a different region boundary).

(6) As above (5).

(The author concedes other structural interpretations of the above.)

Simplistic as the example is, it nonetheless encapsulates the basic architectural requirements motivating this chapter. The conceptual model is of a single machine alternately configuring itself between a fully parallel, SIMD-type processor whose individual PEs are of minimum complexity, and a group of MIMD processors of greater individual complexity acting in parallel over regions of the image (not necessarily distinct), possibly evaluating quite different functions.

The keyword in the above is 'configuring'. Clearly, this architecture will be of the **Dynamically Reconfigurable** (DR) type. Dynamic reconfiguration has been around for some time now, with most such architectural models operating on very high levels of reconfigurability (see [25–30]). By this, we mean that the scope and granularity of the reconfigurability are at a conceptually high level, so that those primitive elements involved in the reconfiguration are at the level (say) of a bit-sliced microprocessor. (Thus, a DR system whose granularity is *physically* high (logically low) might be attempting to reconfigure elements that are basic logic gates; see [31] for a pedantic discussion of this.)

The basic architectural model is illustrated in Figure 11.1. As usual, the model is divided by functional categorization into the control, data and configuration paths. Our primary concern is with the reconfiguration of the data path, which can be defined, in an elementary sense, to consist of a set of identical primitive PEs which can be cascaded together to form systems of processors of varying word lengths, under the control of one or many distinct control units. Because images and

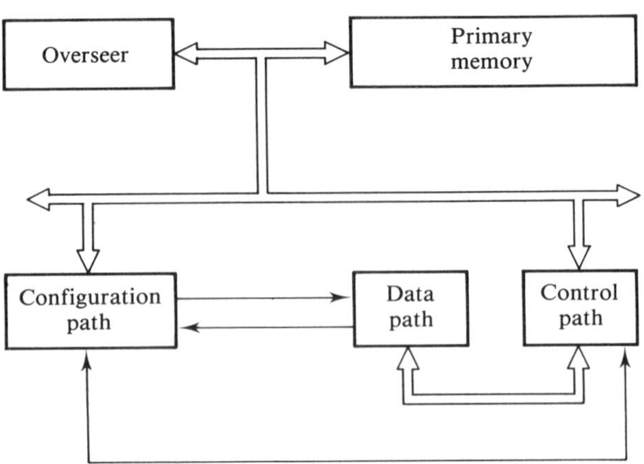

Figure 11.1
Basic architectural model.

pixel-mapped graphic images are usually construed to be 2D arrays, it is convenient to consider the data path as an array of PEs (as shown in Figure 11.1); however, this 'topology' is an artifact of the connection strategy imposed upon the data path (so the temptation to think 'array processor' should be subdued). In the model discussed here, the data path is considered to be the only site of reconfiguration, since reconfiguration of other sites (such as the control path) can lead to systemic difficulties (as are discussed in [31]). The control path consists of the source or sources of control signals driving the data path; in this model, it can be considered conveniently as a collection of microcontrollers and associated firmware, along with such control registers as are required. In the event that the data path is configured into an environment, such that each subprocessor in the data path is under the common control of one controller from the control path, then we will refer to the configuration as a **pure SIMD configuration**, no matter how each subprocessor may differ in structure from the others in the configuration. Figure 11.2 illustrates such a configuration.

Conversely, if the data path is subdivided into subprocessors in such a way as to associate each subprocessor with a different controller in the control path, the situation can be considered as a **pure MIMD configuration**. Obviously, it follows that the data path can be configured in such a way as to permit a group of subprocessors to be under the common control of one controller, while other subprocessors are associated with other controllers so that apparent SIMD behavior is occurring under an MIMD environment. Such a configuration is referred to as a **hybrid configuration**, and is illustrated in Figure 11.3.

The configuration path consists of all of the logic required to realize and sustain the configurations. The role of the configuration path will therefore include setting up and locking inter-PE configuration links, maintaining such multiprocessor status as is needed and directing the flow of control signals to the subprocessors of the data path from the required controller in the control path. Clearly, much of the configuration path is physically embedded in both the data and control paths in terms of signal multiplexors (in whatever physical realization). Although it might seem that the physical structure of the configuration path is in fact of paramount importance to the contents of this chapter, it actually transpires that the

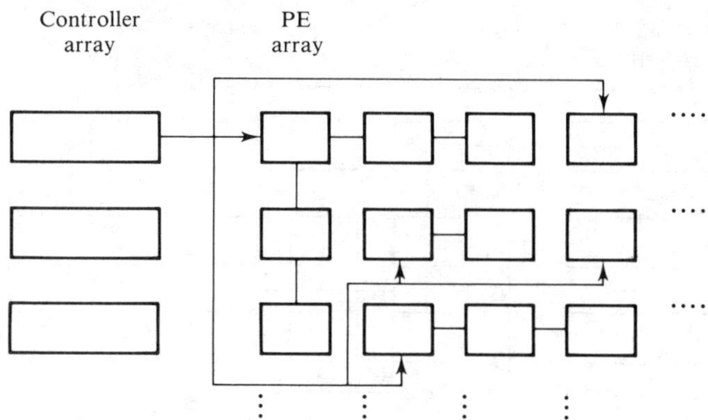

Figure 11.2
Pure SIMD configuration.

design of the configuration path is (for its most part) rather prosaic; for a detailed discussion of the construction of one such path we refer the reader to [30].

No discussion is made here as to the disposition of either the memory subsystem or the I/O subsystem. Since an architecture of this nature is likely to require some form of overall control (as indicated in Figure 11.1), we assume implicitly that the general overseer will field all I/O requests. Similarly, we assume that general program memory is held in the overseer; local memory for the data path is discussed below.

11.3 The data path

Clearly, the heart of the architecture is the data path, which consists of a group (an $n \times n$ array) of PEs so designed as to be cascadable into collections of PEs, referred to as subprocessors of a given configuration. Matters are considerably simplified if each PE is identical to every other PE, a situation we will refer to as **homogeneous**. When the data path is inhomogeneous (and there may be advantages to be accrued from such an approach), the formal symmetry-reduction problem (touched upon in Section 11.6) becomes somewhat more complex, as does the architecture of the configuration path. For our purposes, each PE should be powerful enough to perform some of the most common pixel-primitive operations, since it is likely that the purely parallel SIMD array-processing configuration will assign a PE to each pixel. The basic nature of the PE is dictated by this requirement; if each pixel is to be considered as 1 bit wide (as in binary images), then clearly the PE can be designed to be of extreme simplicity, capable itself of no more than the usual covering set of Boolean operations. If full true-color graphics is a major consideration, then it may be that each PE should be 24 bits wide, and capable of such 'primitive' operations as ray-surface intersection tests (and hence be fully equipped with floating point). Some form of subjective compromise is clearly called for here, and we choose a PE structure of moderate internal complexity and data width, modelled after the bit-slice microprocessors in common manufacture. The data path will hence be constructed, from a homogeneous $n \times n$ array of 4-bit-wide PEs, each of which is equipped with k 4-bit-wide registers and a normal 16-function ALU. In order that

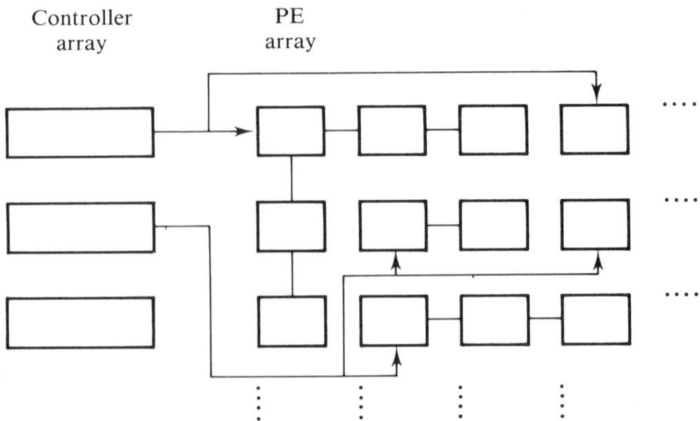

Figure 11.3
Hybrid configuration.

these PEs be cascadable, certain arithmetic and shift signals must be available from the PE. A usual set might include the common carry-out, carry-in, zero flag, overflow flag and shift left and right data lines. Typical PE interconnection points are illustrated in Figure 11.4.

Arranging for the PEs to communicate with each other in such a fashion as to generate the subprocessors, requires linking PEs up with each other so that required signals are sunk or sourced by PEs in a manner which guarantees a subprocessor of width $m \times 4$, where m is the number of PEs cascaded together. It is demonstrably wasteful to have every PE capable of receiving signals from, or sourcing signals to, every other PE, primarily because there are a finite number of configurations that the data path can enter. It therefore does not matter that a data path of four PEs is configured into three subprocessors (one 8-bit-wide subprocessor and two 4-bit-wide subprocessors) with PEs 1 and 2 cascaded to form the 8-bit subprocessor, or PEs 1 and 3 cascaded to form the subprocessor. What matters is the final configuration; provided all attainable configurations are reachable by the data path, full interelement communications may not only not be required, but will be exceedingly

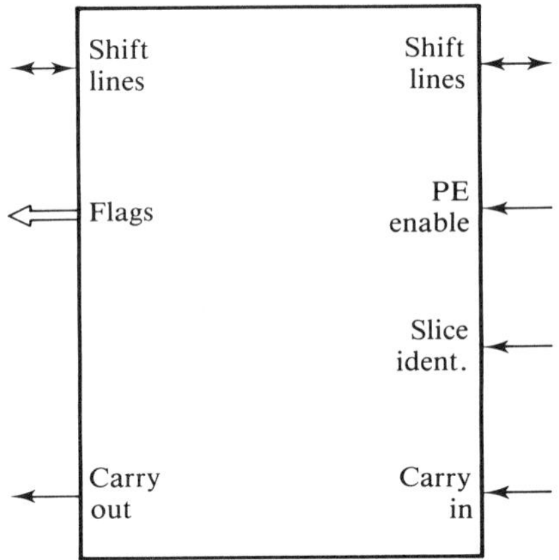

Figure 11.4
Typical PE.

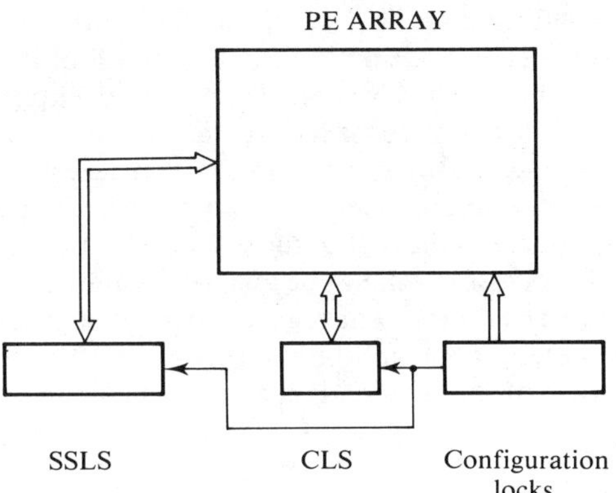

Figure 11.5
General architecture, data path.

wasteful of logic and space. This problem (the symmetry-reduction problem) transpires to be somewhat complex, and is discussed below (see Section 11.6).

Clearly, the duty of the configuration path is to arrange and lock the interelement signals so as to achieve the various configurations. Signal control is effected at the signal sinks of each PE, either by usual multiplexing or by tristate deletion. Each PE is therefore designed with the required **signal source select logic** to facilitate the sourcing of signals into the device. The predominant task of the configuration path is to control this logic.

If faster arithmetic than that provided by a carry-propagate method is required, a **Carry-Lookahead Subsystem** (CLS) is needed. The design of the CLS is necessarily complex, since it must take into consideration lookahead signals emanating from processors of quite different widths. Standard carry-generate devices can be employed here, and a certain degree of control over the signal sources must be effected by the configuration path. Again, we refer the reader to [30] for a more detailed discussion of such a system. A more finicky problem arises in the manipulation of subprocessor status signals (overflow, negative/zero flags etc.). These must be directed (under the control of the configuration path) to a special subunit of the data path referred to as the **Status and Shift Linkage Subsystem** (SSLS). Controller access to this status is then governed by the configuration path, so that conditional branching can be performed meaningfully. Central to the SSLS is the **Status Coordination Block** (SCB), which manipulates incoming subprocessor status and allows a multiprocessor configuration to elect branching on such conditions as 'branch on ⟨condition⟩, ⟨subprocessor⟩', 'branch on ⟨condition⟩ in any subprocessor' or 'branch on ⟨condition⟩ in all subprocessors'. Again, we refer the reader to [30] for structural details. Access to primary memory by subprocessors is the most complex part of the data path, and as in almost all DR systems, there is (as yet) no totally satisfactory method of achieving this. The solution proposed here simply defers the problem to the control path (see Section 11.4 below), in that all data and code transactions from memory are left to the individual controller associated with the subprocessor. Since controllers are required to broadcast control signals to the PEs, the easiest method of implanting data into a PE (or receiving data back from a PE) is to use the instruction lines arriving at the PE and extend their dimension to include a data field which can be written to by the controller or read by controller. However, the simplest implementation of this method implies that data arrives at a subprocessor in 4-bit (PE data width) packages, and must be subsequently realigned in the subprocessor to derive the data width of the subprocessor. This is a time/space trade-off; if faster data access to/from controllers is mandatory, then the signal interconnect problem (and hence the complexity of the configuration path) increases – the cost of the system goes up. Although there can be no guarantee that subprocessors will not be memory bound, it is a not unreasonable assumption that the local subprocessor registers will serve as a local data cache for each subprocessor, thereby reducing the total memory communication overhead. The overall architecture of the data path is given in Figure 11.5.

11.4 The control path and overseer

In essence, the control path consists of a collection of *n* equivalent microcontrollers, each consisting of a microsequencer, next-address logic, control firmware and overseer–memory interface. (The problem of sharing control firmware is too messy to warrant the use of a single copy of control firmware.) Each controller is assigned to one or more subprocessors by the overseer, which also affects the configuration path so that the data path is configured as required and the association of control signals from a controller is made in accordance with the configuration desired. Once a configuration has been determined and all required signal links are made, the overseer points each controller to the macrocode (process) associated with that controller in memory, and initiates the process in the controller. In this design, primary memory is shared between all controllers (and the overseer), so a usual shared-memory protocol is required to prevent memory contention problems. The process of overseer–control path–data path interaction is essentially straightforward, and can be summarized as follows:

(1) The overall task (including configuration-related information) is made available to the overseer.
(2) Upon process execution, the overseer selects the configuration required (including controller-to-subprocessor definitions) and sets the configuration path to generate this configuration.
(3) Each controller is pointed to its local process in primary memory and initiated.
(4) Once started, a controller fetches instructions and data from primary memory. These are subsequently decoded by the controller into the associated microlevel commands needed to drive the subprocessor(s) with which it is associated in the data path; these microlevel commands are broadcast simultaneously to each subprocessor.
(5) Upon process termination, each controller flags the overseer and awaits further initiation.

Three clear problems arise in this environment: access to the overseer and primary memory; access to subprocessor status; and correct routing of control and data to the subprocessors. Since the first problem reduces to a well-known multiprocessor problem, we omit it from further discussion. The remaining two are of immediate relevance to this architecture.

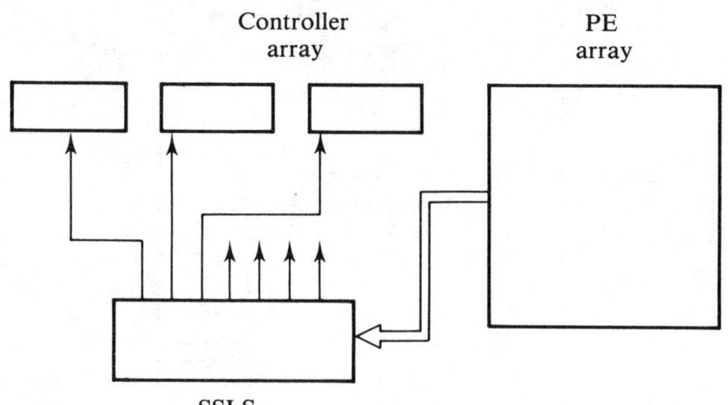

Figure 11.6
Control path, data path and SSLS.

We have mentioned the existence of the SSLS above, and reiterate that its primary duty with respect to the data path is to collect and hold status from each of the currently defined subprocessors. The larger problem is in fact in this collection, not in the subsequent transfer of data from the SSLS to the controllers, simply because the number of controllers is fixed and the number of status lines required by each controller is also fixed. Figure 11.6 illustrates the relationship between the controllers and the SSLS.

Since a controller need only view a small number of status lines from the SSLS, each controller is provided with individual access to the SSLS by these lines. The actual determination of *which* status signals are sent to the controller is under the control of the SCB within the SSLS (and this is in turn determined by the configuration path). Each controller communicates to the SSLS the type of status it expects to see from the SSLS (that is, status from all subprocessors associated with the controller ANDed (corresponding to a 'if all subprocessors have condition ⟨condition⟩ true' request), status from all subprocessors ORed ('if any subprocessor has condition ⟨condition⟩ true') or status from subprocessor *k*). Again, the mechanics of this process are described in [30].

Determination of the source of control and data signals by a subprocessor (PE) is in fact made at the PE itself; once the configuration path has locked the current configuration, each PE chooses its controller by multiplexing out the unwanted lines.

11.5 PE design

The majority of the PE requirements have been discussed above in Sections 11.3 and 11.4; Figure 11.7 presents a schematic of a PE as it might appear in this architecture.

11.6 Symmetry considerations

It is clear from the above discussion that an enormous amount of space and logic is devoted to routing signals and selecting them as they enter or emerge from the data path, the control path or the configuration path. An inappropriate design method

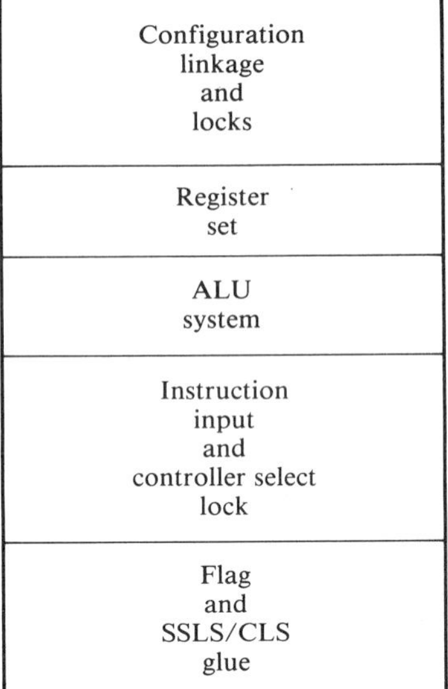

Figure 11.7
PE design.

might lead one to assume that all possible connections from all possible PEs to every other PE, and all possible controllers to every PE, is the only approach that can be taken in an architecture of this nature. In fact, this is not so; we have already alluded to the fact that such a choice is erroneous, based on considerations of symmetry. Since this topic is complicated (and long), we deal only with the important observations here, referring the reader to [32] for a fuller exposition of the subject.

Consider a data path consisting of three homogeneous PEs (labelled P_1, P_2 and P_3) and two controllers (labelled C_1 and C_2). Trivially, there are eight ways of combining the PEs so that eight 'different' configurations of the data path exist. Using parentheses to indicate subprocessors, these are:

$(P_1\ P_2\ P_3)$

$(P_1\ P_2)\ (P_3)$

$(P_1\ P_3)\ (P_2)$

$(P_2\ P_1)\ (P_3)$

$(P_2\ P_3)\ (P_1)$

$(P_3\ P_1)\ (P_2)$

$(P_3\ P_2)\ (P_1)$

$(P_1)\ (P_2)\ (P_3)$

Equally clear is the fact that, of these eight, only three combinations are, in fact, important: $((x\ y\ z), (x\ y)(z), (x)(y)(z))$ where x is (say) P_1, y is P_2 and z is P_3, every other combination being simply a permutation of one of these configurations. When two configurations are equivalent (except for the labelling of the processors), we say that the configurations are **symmetric**. Configurations which are not symmetric (that is, cannot be equated to each other by simple permutation of the PE labelling) are **antisymmetric**. If a system has n PEs, then the total number of configurations (including symmetric configurations) that the data path can reach is given by the Bell number B(n) (which is defined in terms of Stirling numbers of the second kind); B(n) grows combinatorially large very quickly (as might be expected), so that a data path with 15 PEs has (about) 1.38×10^9 total configurations. When only the antisymmetric configurations are counted (this is given by the coefficient of x^n in the expansion of the generating function $G(x) = (1 - x)^{-1}(1 - x^2)^{-1}(1 - x^3)^{-1},\ldots,$), this number is reduced to (about 9.47×10^2. As a measure of the effect of symmetry, one can postulate (reasonably) that the total cost of a DR system will vary directly with the number of configurations that the system can attain. Hence, if the **state reduction ratio** is defined as the ratio of antisymmetric configurations to total configurations (including symmetric configurations), then for a system of 15 PEs, the state reduction ratio is in the order of 6.8×10^{-7}.

This simple combinatorial analysis becomes considerably more complicated when the association of controllers to subprocessors is included. Consider the antisymmetric configurations given above for the 3-PE system ((x y z), (x y) (z), (x) (y) (z)). Denoting the controller associated with a subprocessor in angle brackets after the subprocessor (so that (x y z) $\langle C_1 \rangle$ means that controller C_1 is controlling the subprocessor (x y z)), then one could make the associations:

$(x\ y\ z)\langle C_1\rangle$

$(x\ y\ z)\langle C_2\rangle$

$(x\ y)\langle C_1\rangle(z)\langle C_1\rangle$

$(x\ y)\langle C_1\rangle(z)\langle C_2\rangle$

$(x\ y)\langle C_2\rangle(z)\langle C_1\rangle$

$(x\ y)\langle C_2\rangle(z)\langle C_2\rangle$

$(x)\langle C_1\rangle(y)\langle C_1\rangle(z)\langle C_1\rangle$

$(x)\langle C_1\rangle(y)\langle C_1\rangle(z)\langle C_2\rangle$

$(x)\langle C_1\rangle(y)\langle C_2\rangle(z)\langle C_2\rangle$

$(x)\langle C_2\rangle(y)\langle C_2\rangle(z)\langle C_2\rangle$

(among others). Unfortunately, the situation here becomes analytically unsolvable (in the sense of the elementary derivation of a numerical result from a closed equation). The problem lies in the need to recognize indistinguishable subprocessors in a configuration; such subprocessors, when present, must necessarily be enumerated (in terms of the number of antisymmetric associations of controllers to subprocessors) using a variant of Burnside–Polya enumeration (see [32]). Expressed simply, the problem is equivalent (in a limited sense) to enumerating necklaces whose beads can be any of m (the number of controllers) colors. Without going into the details of the analysis, we can state that for the 3-PE 2-controller system discussed above there are, in fact, only ten antisymmetric configurations (including controller assignment) that can occur; again, we refer the reader to [32] for technical details of the combinatorial analysis.

The impact of this kind of analysis is in the design of the communication paths connecting PEs to each other and to the controller body; once antisymmetry is established, the goal is to design into the system *only* those paths absolutely required for reconfigurability.

Conclusion

This chapter has discussed some of the salient design features of a dynamically reconfigurable, multimodal (supporting both SIMD and MIMD operations) architecture with specific regard to image processing.

Acknowledgments

The author wishes to express his thanks to the Computer Applications and Research Center, University of Connecticut, for their support of this work.

References

1. Fountain T.J. (1981). Towards CLIP 6 – an extra dimension. In *Proc. of the 1981 IEEE Workshop on Computer Architecture for Pattern Analysis and Image Data Base Management*, pp. 25–30, Hot Springs VA
2. Agarwal D.P. and Jain R. (1981). A multiprocessor system for dynamic scene analysis. In *Proc. of the 1981 IEEE Workshop on Computer Architecture for Pattern Analysis and Image Data Base Management*, pp. 96–103, Hot Springs VA
3. Cheng H.D. *et al.* (1985). Space-time domain expansion approach to VLSI and its application to hierarchical scene matching, *IEEE PAMI,* **7**(3), 306–19
4. Antonsonn D. *et al.* (1981). PICAP – a system approach to image processing. In *Proc. of the 1981 IEEE Workshop on Computer Architecture for Pattern Analysis and Image Data Base Management*, pp. 35–42, Hot Springs VA
5. Agrawal D.P. and Pathak G.C. (1984). Design of a VLSI based multicomputer for dynamic scene analysis. In *VLSI for Pattern Recognition and Image Processing* (Fu K.S., ed.), pp. 195–208. Tokyo: Springer-Verlag
6. Preston K. *et al* (1979). Basics of cellular logic with some applications of medical image processing. In *Proc. IEEE,* **67**(5), 826–56
7. Tsai W.H. *et al.* (1981). Architecture of a multi-microprocessor system for parallel processing of image sequences. In *Proc. of the 1981 IEEE Workshop on Computer Architecture for Pattern Analysis and Image Data Base Management*, pp. 104–10, Hot Springs VA
8. Kushner T. *et al.* (1981). Image processing on ZMOB. In *Proc. of the 1981 IEEE Workshop on Computer Architecture for Pattern Analysis and Image Data Base Management*, pp. 88–95. Hot Springs VA
9. Greenshields I.R. (1981). A matrix memory system for binary image preprocessing. In *Proc. of the 1981 IEEE Workshop on Computer Architecture for Pattern Analysis and Image Data Base Management*, pp. 154–7, Hot Springs VA
10. Sternberg S.R. (1981). Architectures for neighborhood processing. In *PRIP-81*, pp. 374–80, Dallas TX
11. Uhr L. (1981). Converging pyramids of arrays. In *Proc. of the 1981 IEEE*

Workshop on Computer Architecture for Pattern Analysis and Image Data Base Management, pp. 31–4, Hot Springs VA

12. Hanson A.R. and Riseman E.M. (1974). *Pre-processing Cones: a computational structure for scene analysis*. COINS Tech. Report, 74–C7, University of Massachussetts
13. Uhr L. and Douglass R. (1979). A parallel-serial recognition cone system for perception. *Pattern Recognition*, **11**, 29–40
14. Uhr L. *et al.* (1981). A 2-layered SIMD/MIMD parallel–pyramidal Array/Net. In *Proc. of the 1981 IEEE Workshop on Computer Architecture for Pattern Analysis and Image Data Base Management*, pp. 209–16, Hot Springs VA
15. Tanimoto S. and Klinger A. (1980). *Structured Computer Vision*. New York: Academic Press
16. Kung H.T. and Song S.W. (1981). A systolic 2-D convolution chip. In *Proc. of the 1981 IEEE Workshop on Computer Architecture for Pattern Analysis and Image Data Base Management*, pp. 159–60, Hot Springs VA
17. Kung H.T. (1982). Why systolic architectures?, *IEEE Computer*, **15**, 37–46
18. Kung H.T. and Picard R.L. (1984). One dimensional systolic arrays for multidimensional convolution. In *VLSI for Pattern Recognition and Image Processing* (Fu K.S., ed.), pp. 9–24. Tokyo: Springer-Verlag
19. Yen D.W.L. and Kulkarni A.V. (1982). Systolic processing and an implementation for signal and image processing. *IEEE TC*, **C-31**, 1000–9
20. Kung H.T. *et al.* (1983). Two level pipelined systolic array for multidimensional convolution. *Image and Vision Computing*, **1**, 30–6
21. Whitted T. (1980). An improved illumination model for shaded display. *CACM*, **23**(6), pp. 343–9
22. Roth S.D. (1982). Ray casting for modeling solids. *Computer Graphics and Image Processing*, **18**(2), 109–44
23. Harrington S. (1987). *Computer Graphics – A Programming Approach*. New York: McGraw-Hill
24. Horn B.K.P. (1986). *Robot Vision*, pp. 202–77. Cambridge MA: MIT Press
25. Kartashev S.I. and Kartashev S.P. (1977). Designing LSI modular computers and systems. In *Proc. IEEE Int. Symp. on Mini and Micro Computers*, pp. 1–9, Montreal, 1977
26. Kartashev S.I. and Kartashev S.P. (1980). Problems of designing supersystems with dynamic architectures. *IEEE TC*, **C-29**, 1114–32
27. Kartashev S.I. and Kartashev S.P. (1977). A multicomputer system with software reconfiguration of the architecture. In *Proc. 1977 SIGMETRICS*, pp. 271–86, WA
28. Scott M.A. (1981). A dynamically reconfigurable microprocessor architecture. *PhD Thesis*, University of Toronto
29. Scott M.A. and Smith K.C. (1980). A dynamically reconfigurable microprocessor architecture. In *Proc. IEEE Int. Conf. on Circuits and Computers*, pp. 504–7, New York
30. Greenshields I.R. (1982). Dynamically reconfigurable vector slice processor. *Proc. IEE, Pt. E*, **129**(5), 207–15
31. Greenshields I.R. (1983). *Systemic Aspects in Massively Dynamically Reconfigurable Multiprocessor Systems*. IPL–Tech. Report 83–005, University of Connecticut
32. Greenshields I.R. Antisymmetry in Massively Dynamically Reconfigurable Multiprocessor Systems. To appear.

Section 3

Parallel Algorithms for Vision and Image Processing

12 · A fast parallel algorithm for labeling connected components in image arrays†

W. Lim
A. Agrawal
L. Nekludova

MIT AI Laboratory,
Thinking Machines
Corporation

A fast parallel algorithm for labeling connected components in a 2D array of pixels is discussed. The algorithm has a time complexity of O(log N) for the exclusive-read-exclusive-write model of parallel computation and where the time to access to any memory location in any processor is constant. The algorithm is implemented on a Connection Machine by mapping the 2D array of values into a 2D array of processors. On this machine, time complexity is measured in terms of router cycles, that is, message transmissions through the routing network. Initially, each processor is assigned a unique label or id. The label of a region is the largest processor label of the processors in the region. Processors on region boundaries are connected as rings by using pointers. The boundary label, that is, the largest processor label of the processors, in the boundary of each boundary is computed. The processors on all the boundaries in the region are linked together into a long one and its label is computed. The label for this long boundary is the label of the region. This label is then propagated to all the interior processors in the region.

12.1 Introduction

In vision applications [1, 2], image arrays are frequently segmented into regions according to, say, color or intensity level. The pixels in a region might also share some properties, like the difference between their intensity values is below (or above) a certain threshold. Such regions are used for many image-understanding tasks. For example, the regions might be assigned semantic labels depending on their color and adjacency relationships. Thus, blue regions near the top boundary of a color picture of an outdoor scene might be assigned the label 'sky' and white patches surrounded by 'sky' regions might be labeled 'cloud'. In aerial and satellite images, blue regions might be assigned a label like 'water', 'lake', or 'ocean'. Before such semantic labels can be assigned, the regions have to be identified and merged when necessary. The identification step involves assigning a number (or label) to each pixel of the region. These labels are unique for each region.

The task of labeling such regions can be abstracted to a special case of the problem formally known as **labeling connected components**, that is, the problem of assigning labels to connected nodes in a graph. There is an O(log N) algorithm [3]

† This research is done at Thinking Machines Corporation, Cambridge MA.

that assumes a model of parallel computation, which allows more than one processor to write to the same memory location in another processor at the same time. For practical machines, such an algorithm is actually $O(\log^2 N)$ which is the same as that of an earlier algorithm [4] developed by Hirschberg, Chandra, and Sarwate. It turns out that algorithms with better best-case performances are possible. In [5], where time is measured in terms of the number of message-sending steps, a best-case behavior of $O(\log N)$ is possible. The worst-case performance of $O(\log^2 N)$ can be avoided by either preprocessing the image to fatten narrow regions so that all regions are at least two pixels wide (thus the smallest region is a 2×2 array), or by mapping each pixel to four processors resulting in an array of processors that is four times as large as the image array. The algorithm has been implemented on a Connection Machine [6] in which interprocessor memory access is restricted to exclusive read and exclusive write.

The emphasis in this chapter is on the structures and techniques used in implementing the algorithm. Formal proofs of the correctness are discussed in [7]. All terms used in the chapter are defined in Section 12.2. A technique that is used repeatedly in the algorithm for finding the maximum (or minimum) of numbers in a ring of processors is described in Section 12.3. Section 12.4 describes the algorithm. A brief history of the algorithm is given in the conclusion.

12.2 Terminology

The terms used here are adaptations of those used in [1, 8, 9]. The machine is a SIMD machine configured as a 2D array of N processors, where N is the number of array elements. Processors can communicate concurrently but a processor cannot send to, or receive messages from, more than one processor at any given time. Each processor is given a unique number called its **id**. The numbering is done in a left to right, top to bottom fashion. Thus, the processor at the top-left corner of the array has the smallest id (0) and the one at the bottom-right corner has the largest $(N - 1)$.

Each array element is stored in the processor at the corresponding position in the machine. The value held in each processor is termed its **color**. This term is particularly apt when the 2D array is thought of as an array of colors with each distinct value being represented by a different color. The processor with column index x and row index y is referred to as the processor $P(x,y)$. Two processors $P(x_1,y_1)$ and $P(x_2,y_2)$ are said to be **neighbors** in the **four-connected** sense if their row or column indices (but not both) differ by one, that is:

$$|x_1 - x_2| + |y_1 - y_2| = 1$$

They are neighbors in the **eight-connected** sense if one or both of their row and column indices differ by one, that is:

$$1 \leqslant |x_1 - x_2| + |y_1 - y_2| \leqslant 2$$

Unless otherwise stated, the term neighbors is used to mean neighbors in the four-connected sense.

Two neighbors are said to be **adjacent** if they have the same color. If a path of adjacent processors exists between a pair of processors, the pair is said to be **connected**. A **component** is a set of connected processors and a **connected component** or **region** is a maximal set of connected processors. Consider the situation where the processors at the physical boundary of the array are neighbors to imaginary processors that are outside the array and are not connected to the processors in the array. Suppose further that the processors not in the region R are thought of as components having a uniform but different color. Connected components of processors not in R are termed **holes**. A **boundary processor** is a processor with any of its eight-connected neighbors having a different color, that is, at least one of its eight-connected neighbors is in a hole. Thus, processors at the physical boundary of the grid of processors are boundary processors by this definition. A **boundary** of the region R is a set of boundary processors that are neighbors of the processors in the same hole. A processor of the physical array that is not a boundary processor is termed an **interior** processor.

A **chain** is a singly linked sequence of processors. If the processors at the start and the end of a chain are linked to each other, then the chain is referred to as a **ring**. A ring of boundary processors around a hole is termed a **boundary ring**. Note that since a boundary processor can be 'touching' more than one hole, it can be part of more than one boundary ring. For the four-connected case, there can be, at most, four such rings going through a boundary processor.

For any set of processors, the processor with the largest id is called the **principal processor**. (The algorithm described in this paper also works when the smallest id is used as the boundary/region label.) Given any set of processors, its **label** is the id of the principal processor in that set. The label is termed a **boundary label** or **region label** if the set is a boundary or region, respectively.

12.3 Distance doubling

A key point to note is that using a technique called **distance doubling** it takes $O(\log N)$ time to find the maximum or minimum of a number contained in each of the processors in a ring. (This segment of the algorithm was developed independently of Wyllie's work [10].) The main feature here is that at each iteration, each processor communicates with another processor at a distance double that of the previous iteration. This is illustrated in Figure 12.1 for a ring of eight processors. Each processor is represented as a pair (d, v) where d contains the id of a destination processor and v holds a value. The processor ids are shown in Figure 12.1a. In Figure 12.1b, the arrows point to the processors identified by the values of d. For the rest of Figure 12.1 (c to e), the current value of v is written inside each processor. Table 12.1 shows how the maximum value is computed (see (b) to (e) of Figure 12.1).

Each processor starts off by setting v to the value of the number it is holding and d to the id of its immediate neighbor in the clockwise direction. Let $d(P)$ and $v(P)$ be the d and v values of the processor P. Then the following distance-doubling algorithm is executed:

```
repeat logN times
    forall processors in the ring
        v(P) ← max(v(d(P)), v(P))
        d(P) ← d(d(P))
    endforall
endrepeat
```

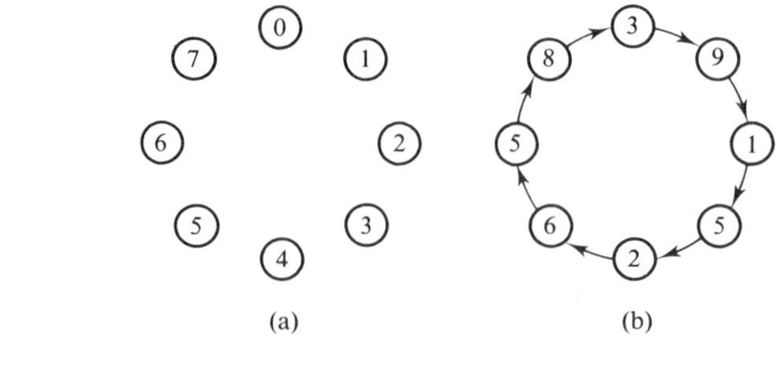

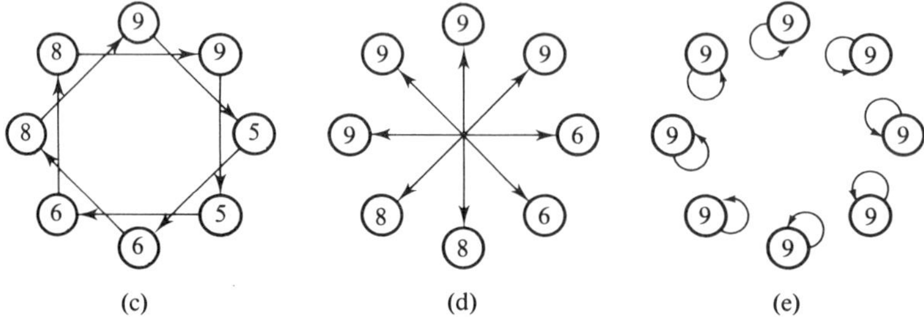

Figure 12.1
Hopping around a ring of processors by distance doubling.
(a) Processor id.
(b) (p, v) at initialization.
(c) After first hop.
(d) After second hop.
(e) After third hop.

At step (or hop) i ($0 \leqslant i < \log N$), d contains the id of the processor at distance 2^i away and v is the maximum of the v values of $2^i + 1$ processors (including itself) that are within distance 2^i in the direction of the hop. Thus at the end of O(log N) hops, v contains the maximum of the v values in all the n processors in the ring.

The rings are built using a data structure called a **pointer**. Each processor has a total of four pointers, one for each of the four cardinal directions – north, east, south and west. When used for connecting boundary processors in a ring, these pointers are termed **boundary pointers**. Each pointer has three fields: the **unused flag**, the **direction field** and the **destination address**. The labels and pointers are updated by each processor with the current label and pointer values for the specified direction field of the destination processor using the active pointer in the reading processor. The unused flag indicates whether the pointer is used (or active). Associated with each of the four pointers, is a label for holding the label of the boundary on which the processor is.

In the figures, a pointer is represented by a dot and an arrow. The dot is placed next to the edge of the cell in the respective direction and the arrow points to where the pointer is pointing.

Table 12.1 (d, v) values at each iteration.

Iteration	*(d, v) for processors*							
	0	*1*	*2*	*3*	*4*	*5*	*6*	*7*
Initial	(1,3)	(2,9)	(3,1)	(4,5)	(5,2)	(6,6)	(7,5)	(0,8)
0	(2,9)	(3,9)	(4,5)	(5,5)	(6,6)	(7,6)	(0,8)	(1,8)
1	(4,9)	(5,9)	(6,6)	(7,6)	(0,8)	(1,8)	(2,9)	(3,9)
2	(0,9)	(1,9)	(2,9)	(3,9)	(4,9)	(5,9)	(6,9)	(7,9)

12.4 The algorithm

The algorithm involves five steps:

(1) Initialization – set up boundary rings.
(2) Determine the boundary label for each boundary ring.
(3) Merge the boundary rings to form a longer ring passing through each boundary processor in the region by swapping pointers.
(4) Propagate the largest boundary ring label to all boundary processors in the region. This label becomes the region label.
(5) Propagate the region label to all interior processors in the region.

The first step takes constant time while the remaining four steps take O(log N) time. Each of the steps are described in the following sections.

12.4.1 Initialization

The initialization step takes constant time. Each processor is classified to be either a boundary or an interior processor according to whether or not it has an eight-connected neighbor of a different color.

To illustrate how the pointers for the boundary processor are set up, numbers are assigned to the eight directions in a counterclockwise direction as shown in Figure 12.2. The pointers for the boundary processor are set up by the following algorithm where *neighbor(D)* is the neighbor in the direction D, *pointer(P, D)* is the D pointer of processor P, *own* means the processor itself and $P \circ D$ is the pointer value (with the unused flag set to active) with the destination address set to P and the direction field set to D.

```
forall D ∈ 0, 2, 4, 6 do
    if not connected to neighbor(D)
    then
        if connected to neighbor((D + 2) mod 8)
        then
            pointer(own, D) ← neighbor((D + 2) mod 8) ∘ D
        else
            pointer(own, D) ← own ∘ ((D + 2) mod 8)
        endif
    else
        if not same color as neighbor((D + 1) mod 8)
            and connected to neighbor((D + 2) mod 8)
        then
            pointer(own,(D + 2) mod 8) ← (neighbor((D + 2)
                                              mod 8) ∘ D
        endif
    endif
endforall
```

1	0	7
2		6
3	4	5

Figure 12.2
Assignment of numbers to the eight directions.

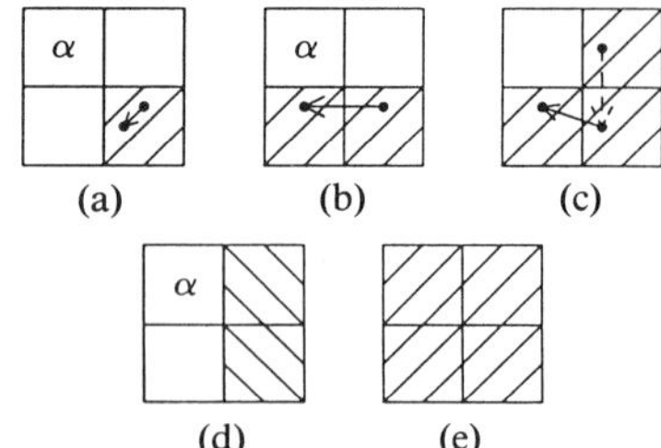

Figure 12.3
Pointer arrangement for various cases.

To illustrate how the above works, consider the case where $D = 0$. Figure 12.3 shows the pointer arrangement for the processor at the lower-right corner of the 2×2 array of processors. The other three processors are the neighbors in the 0, 1 and 2 directions. Each cell in the array is either blank, shaded or marked with the symbol α indicating that it can either be blank or shaded. With the lower-right cell shaded, the eight cases to consider are broken down into the five groups shown in Figure 12.3 (a to e). In Figure 12.3a the D pointer points to the processor's own $(D + 2)$ mode $8(= 2)$ pointer. There are two cases of (a), that is, when the corner processor $(D = 1)$ is blank and when it is shaded. For Figure 12.3b, the D pointer points to the D pointer of the neighbor in the $(D + 2)$ mod 8 direction. There are two cases for this group. In Figure 12.3c, the $(D + 2)$ mod 8 pointer points to the D pointer of the neighbor in direction $(D + 2)$ mod 8. The dashed arrow shows how the pointer of the neighbor in the D direction is set up. In (d) and (e), the D pointer is not used. There is only one possibility for both (c) and (e) while there are two possibilities for (d).

Figure 12.4 shows how the pointers are set up to form boundaries for a 5×5 array with the cells at positions (1,1), (1,3), (3,1) and (3,3) shaded and where the position of the top-left corner is (0,0) and that of the bottom-right corner is (4,4). Figure 12.4a shows the boundary rings for the array. There are five boundary rings in the unshaded region and one boundary ring for each of the shaded regions. The pointers are set up by the method described above and are shown in (b). Note that the number of boundary rings going through a processor can range from one (for example, the shaded processors) to four (the processor at the center).

12.4.2 Determining the boundary label

Using the pointers set up above, rings of boundary processors are built. Initially, each boundary processor uses its own id as the boundary label. (For a processor at position (x, y), $0 \leqslant x \leqslant X_{max}$, $0 \leqslant y \leqslant Y_{max}$, and where $y = 0$ at the top row and $x = 0$ at the leftmost column, its id is given by $x + y * (X_{max} + 1)$.) The principal processor in each boundary is found by distance doubling. After $O(\log N)$ iterations, all boundary processors would have found their boundary label. In the case of Figure 12.4, each of the nine boundary rings will have a label. The principal processors are marked by small solid squares in Figure 12.4c. Two of the boundaries in the unshaded region have the same principal processor, that is, the one at the lower-right corner of the array.

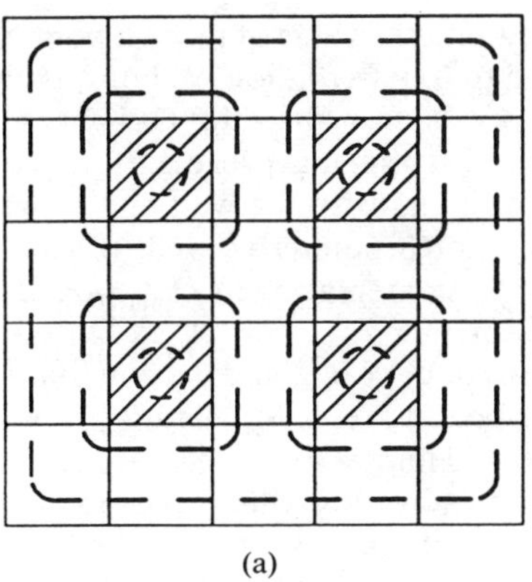

(a)

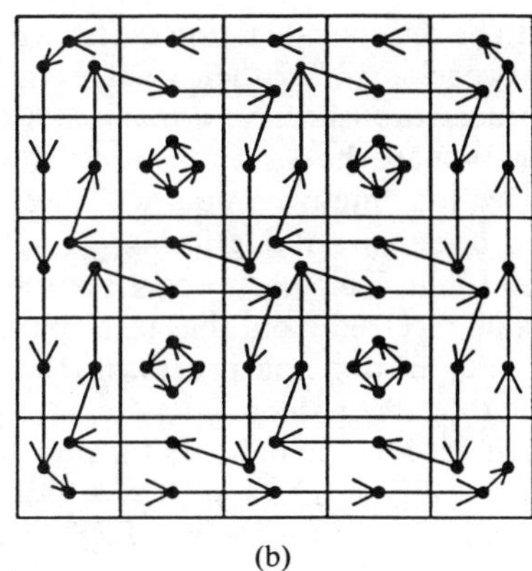

(b)

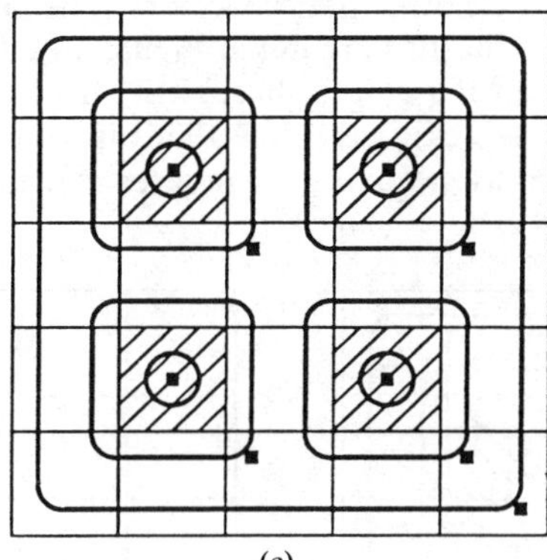

(c)

Figure 12.4
(a) Boundary rings.
(b) Pointer set up.
(c) Principal processors.

12.4.3 Merging boundaries

The boundary rings are merged by swapping pointers between the principal processor of an inner boundary (for brevity, this processor is referred to as a principal processor) and a processor on the boundary to its east. To do this, each principal processor propagates (via a chain of interior processors) its address and its pointer in the boundary ring, eastwards where possible. To form the ring for swapping pointers, every processor sets up its pointers as if it is a boundary processor that is not connected to its north and south neighbors, while leaving its adjacency relationship with its east and west neighbors the same. This will make all interior processors act as label 'propagators' and confine distance doubling to within east-west rings. Furthermore, every principal processor will pretend that it is also not connected to its west neighbor. The effect of this is that all principal processors become the east end of an east-west ring. All boundary processors which are not of the same color as their north-east and/or east neighbors will set their pointers as if they are not connected to their north, east and south neighbors. Some of these processors will become the west end for the east-west rings. The v value for each principal processor is set to be the concatenation of its own address and the value of its west pointer. All other processors have their v values initialized to 0. After O(log N) hops, the west-end processors will have a maximum of the v values in the ring. Only those processors that are the east ends of east-west rings with principal processors, and have a non-zero maximum v value, will swap their pointers with the west-end processor. This is done by sending its D_{swap} (= 0 if the north pointer is used, otherwise 6) pointer to the principal processor at the west end and replacing its D_{swap} pointer with the value received from that principal processor.

Let the principal processor P be on the boundary B_{own} and the boundary to its east be B_{east}. With the pointers set up as described above, if B_{own} and B_{east} both pass through P, then the pointers for direction $D = 0$ and $D = 2$ are swapped. This is shown in Figure 12.5a with the dashed lines indicating where the pointers are swapped. The figure shows merging of the five boundary rings in the unshaded region into one long boundary ring. The pointer arrangement for the east-west rings involving the principal processors are shown in Figure 12.5b. For this case, the east-west rings are self loops in the principal processors. The pointers that are swapped are represented by the dark dashed arrows in Figure 12.5c.

If the two boundaries do not pass through P, then their pointers are swapped by distance doubling through east-west rings. This is shown in Figure 12.6a where two boundaries are merged by swapping the pointer at the ends of the dashed lines.

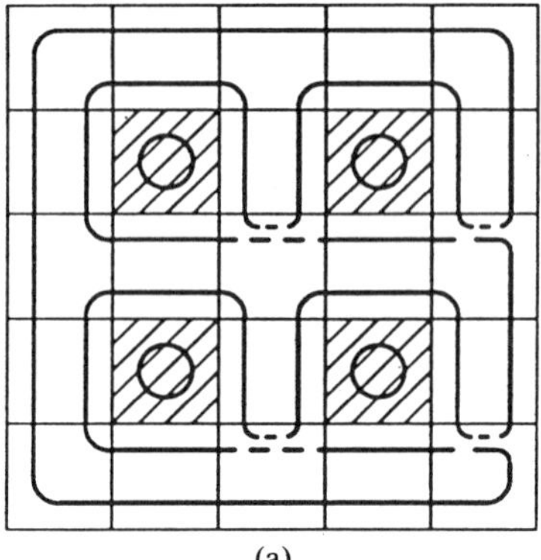

(a)

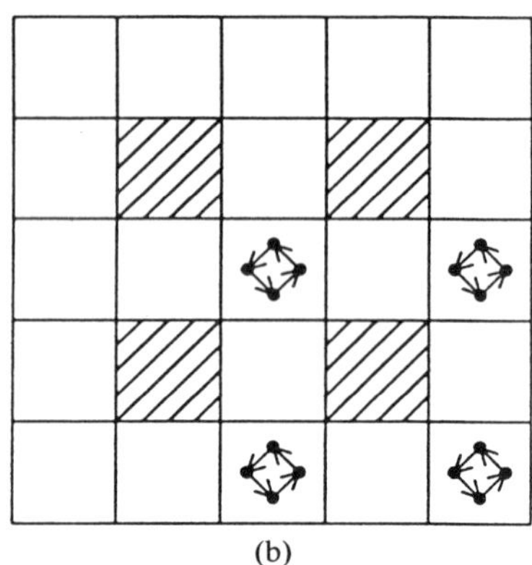

(b)

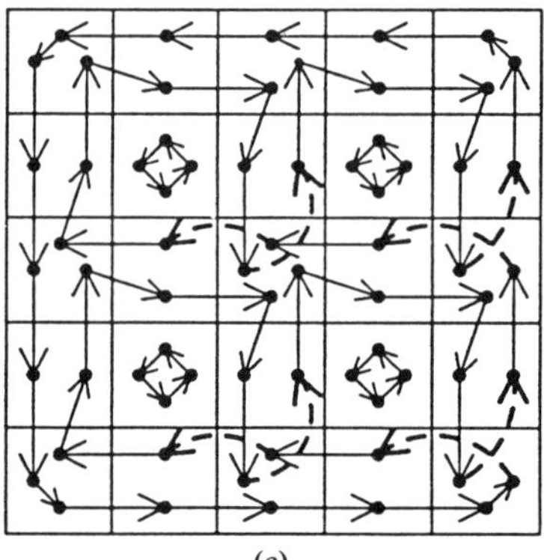

(c)

Figure 12.5
Swapping boundary pointers for a 5 × 5 array.
(a) Merging of rings.
(b) East-west rings.
(c) Pointer arrangement after swapping.

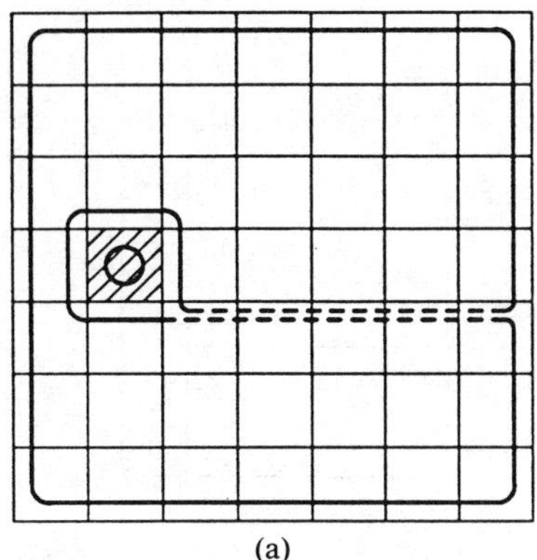
(a)

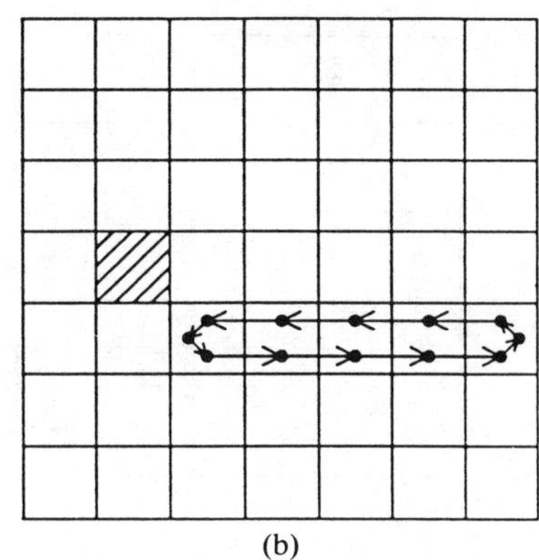
(b)

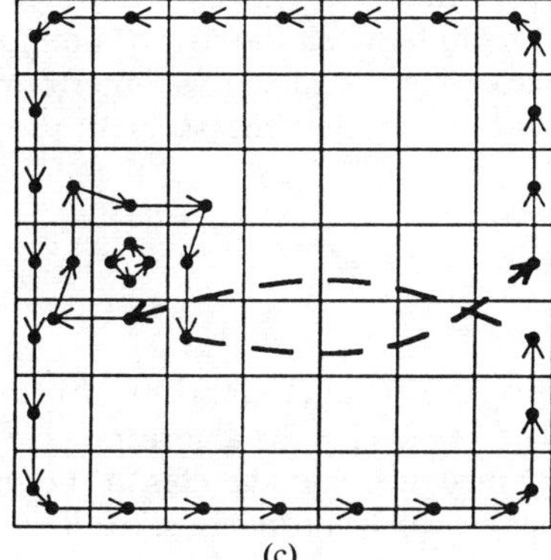
(c)

Figure 12.6
Swapping boundary pointers for a 7 × 7 array.
(a) Merging of two boundaries.
(b) An east-west ring.
(c) Pointer arrangement after swapping.

Figure 12.6b shows how the pointers are set up for an east-west ring. The pointer arrangement after pointer swapping is shown in (c) with dark dashed arrows representing the swapped pointers. The two boundary rings of the unshaded region are merged into one longer ring.

12.4.4 Determining the region label

The effect of swapping pointers between boundary rings is to merge them into one long boundary with its principal processor being the principal processor of the region. Note that during the boundary-merging step, the principal processor of the region cannot be the east end of an east-west ring that is longer than one, since being on the outermost boundary of the region, it does not have any boundary (belonging to the same region) to its east.

12.4.5 Propagating the region label to interior processors

The last step of the algorithm involves propagating the region label from the boundary processors to all the interior processors in the region. Since every interior

24	24	24	24	24
24	6	24	8	24
24	24	24	24	24
24	16	24	18	24
24	24	24	24	24

(a)

48	48	48	48	48	48	48
48	48	48	48	48	48	48
48	48	48	48	48	48	48
48	22	48	48	48	48	48
48	48	48	48	48	48	48
48	48	48	48	48	48	48
48	48	48	48	48	48	48

(b)

Figure 12.7
The region labels.
(a) 5 × 5 array.
(b) 7 × 7 array.

processor is on the same row of, and between a pair of boundary processors, the region label can be propagated to any interior processor by distance doubling along the row of interior processors in between the pair of boundary processors. Thus in O(log N) time, the region label is propagated to all interior processors of the region. Figure 12.7 shows the region labels of the processors for the 5 × 5 and 7 × 7 arrays discussed earlier.

Concluding remarks

We have described an O(log N) parallel algorithm for labeling connected components in image arrays. The key idea in the algorithm is to label all the boundaries first by distance doubling. Since the region label is the boundary label of the outermost boundary, the region label can be propagated to all the processors in the region after merging the boundaries and propagating the region label to all the boundary processors, again by distance doubling. The region label is further propagated to the interior processors by distance doubling from the boundary processors.

A prototypical version of an earlier version of the algorithm [5] was implemented on a Connection Machine and it had been recoded in *Lisp. That code took about 5 man-months to develop. Work on that algorithm began in the Summer of 1985. The code is being modified (in a straightforward fashion) to implement the algorithm described here. The elimination of the O($\log^2 N$) behavior has been indirectly discussed in [5] but is directly handled in a similar, though independently developed, algorithm by A. Agrawal and L. Nekludova.

Acknowledgments

The algorithm has gone through many refinements driven in part by the criticisms of Mike Drumheller, Ahbiram Ranade and Steve Omohundro. They have been helpful in pointing out the weaknesses of early versions of the algorithm. The authors would also like to thank Charles Leiserson and Guy Blelloch for their criticisms and suggestions. Furthermore, this work would not have been possible without the support and encouragement of Guy Steele and Allen Waxman. As a note, the algorithm has been successfully tested on the Connection Machine (that is, models CM1 and CM2).

References

1. Ballard D.H. and Brown C.M. (1982). *Computer Vision*. Englewood Cliffs, NJ: Prentice-Hall
2. Binford T.O. (1982). Survey of model-based image analysis systems. *The International J. of Robotics Research,* **1**(1), 18–64
3. Shiloach Y. and Vishkin U. (1982). An O(log *n*) parallel connectivity algorithm. *J. of Algorithms,* **3**(1), 57–67
4. Hirschberg D.S., Chandra A.K. and Sarwate D.V. (1979). Computing connected components on parallel computers. *Comm. ACM,* **22**(8), 461–4
5. Lim W.Y-P. (1986). *Fast Algorithms for Labeling Connected Components in 2-D Arrays*. Technical Report NA86-1, Thinking Machines Corporation, Cambridge MA
6. Hillis W.D. (1985). *The Connection Machine*. Cambridge MA: MIT Press
7. Agrawal A., Nekludova L. and Lim W. (1987). *A Parallel O(log N) Algorithm for Finding Connected Components in Planar Images*. Technical Report NA87-1, Thinking Machines Corporation, Cambridge MA
8. Rosenfeld A. and Kak A.C. (1976). *Digital Picture Processing*. New York: Academic Press
9. Stout Q.F. (1983). Topological matching. In *Proc. 15th Annual ACM Sym. on the Theory of Computing*, pp. 24–31
10. Wyllie J.C. (1979). *The Complexity of Parallel Computations*. Technical Report TR 79-387, Cornell University NY

G.N. Khan
D.F. Gillies

Imperial College of Science and Technology

13 · A highly parallel shaded image segmentation method

A parallel algorithm has been devised and implemented for segmenting shaded images. The method begins by building a quadtree from the original image. This is done recursively by averaging the pixel intensities in each square group of four to produce a lower resolution image. The tree is then searched for the largest coherent area of the desired properties. Finally, region merging is used to extract the required segment. The method has been successfully applied to detection of the darkest region in a variety of images. Its inherent parallelism makes it suitable for real-time applications.

13.1 Introduction

Segmentation of images can be defined as the process of isolating regions of interest. Most of these regions depict known objects in the scene, which are to be recognized, and which are defined by the values of one or more properties such as grey level, colour, texture etc. Many techniques have been proposed to accomplish the task of segmentation, but all of them are based on detecting either discontinuities or similarities in some property values in neighbouring parts of the image. The first of these approaches, based on the concept of discontinuity, works by detecting boundaries between homogeneous regions of some property. Such techniques are generally called **edge detection**. The second utilizes the concept of similarity by extracting homogeneous regions in the image, instead of boundaries between different regions.

Segmentation by edge detection is carried out in a way that is analogous to biological visual systems and assumes that most of the image information is embedded in the boundaries between different regions. Such techniques are well known for their limitations which are:

(1) Edge detection by differentiation is prone to high frequency noise.

(2) Closed boundaries of regions are difficult to find in practice, and require extensive tracking of edge segments.

(3) Homogeneous regions with smooth changes at the boundaries may not be detected.

(4) Extracted regions need to be reprocessed to obtain their properties (for example, average grey level or maximum and minimum intensities of the region).

We are presenting a new technique which is based on the concept of similarity for extracting a region in the image. In the specific application that was studied, our task was to track the lowest intensity region of an image, in real time and in the presence of noise. This task was a special case of tracking a region of given properties. Edge-detection techniques proved hard to use due to their poor performance in the presence of high frequency noise. Region growing techniques, based on similarity, are inherently sequential, which makes them less applicable for real-time image analysis. Consequently, a quadtree structure has been used in the algorithm for region representation and extraction. The introduction of quadtrees for region extraction has led to a highly parallel implementation of the algorithm.

13.2 Region extraction techniques: an overview

In region extraction, the image is divided into regions on the basis of its properties. Zucker (1976) has written an excellent survey on different region extraction techniques. We can categorize these techniques as follows.

13.2.1 Region merging

Merging starts with a region showing uniformity of one or more properties. In the worst case, this region can be a single pixel. An attempt is made to enlarge the region by searching for the similar properties in neighbouring regions, one at a time. The whole process is sequential and the resulting region's shape may depend on the starting point and direction of search.

Different forms of this basic method have been successfully applied. For example, Muerle and Allen (1968) used a three stage approach for region merging: firstly, the entire picture is segmented into blocks of ($2 \times 2, 4 \times 4$ etc.); secondly, a statistical measure is determined for each of these regions, and finally, the regional neighbour search method is used to merge the blocks of similar statistics. Brice and Fennema (1970) used so-called **atomic** regions of constant grey level to start with, then these atomic regions were merged by applying successively heuristics of **phagocyte** and **weakness**. Pavlidis (1972) presented an algorithm which divides the image into 1D thin strips. These strips are then approximated by finding the best partition of each strip into segments. Merging is then performed on these segments with similar approximations.

A parallel technique for region merging has been reported by Gambotto and Monga (1985). There are three basic steps in their algorithm which are iterative. The same operations can be performed on any region of the image in parallel. Firstly, the pixels are merged with their neighbouring pixels to form regions. Secondly, pixels are merged into regions, and finally, regions are merged into regions. The merging criteria is re-evaluated in every iteration.

13.2.2 Region splitting

This is the opposite approach to merging for segmentation. Splitting starts with the whole image which is considered as one region. It is then divided successively into smaller regions until each smaller region satisfies the similarity criterion.

Like merging, splitting has been used successfully as the basis of several algorithms. For example, Robertson, Fu and Swain (1973) developed an algorithm for partitioning multispectral images recursively. Their criterion for region uniformity, known as **G-Regularity**, is based on the mean vector of grey levels. The algorithm continues to subdivide blocks until a subregion is found whose mean grey level does not differ from that of its parents. Klinger and Dyer (1975) used regular decomposition for segmenting chrosmos pictures which have a lot of empty space. Partitioning of these pictures into two types of blocks resulted in significant data reduction, since only rough processing was needed for background blocks.

13.2.3 Region splitting and merging

It is clear from the previous two sections that a third class of segmentation algorithm can be devised by allowing splitting and merging in combination. Starting from any given partition of the image, these algorithms work by merging the adjacent regions, if the result will satisfy the uniformity criteria, or splitting a single region if it is not homogeneous enough. The process is continued until there are no regions to merge or split.

The first algorithm to develop the principle of split and merge was due to Horwitz and Pavlidis (1974, 1976). For an $N \times N$ image (where $N = 2^{Ik}$ for some integer Ik), a segmentation tree is constructed, whose nodes correspond to a square image region and whose leaves represent single pixels. The nodes of the tree are defined recursively. For example, a node b at level l (where $0 \leqslant l \leqslant Ik$) which is located at (x,y), having size $S = N / (2^l)$ will have four successors with sides of length $S / 2$ and located at (x,y), $(x + S / 2,y)$, $(x,y + S / 2)$ and $(x + S / 2, y + S / 2)$. The root node of the segmentation tree is at level zero and located at. (1,1). Each node also has attached to it an associated value which is the maximum (M_k) and minimum (m_k) brightness functions of the corresponding block. The algorithm begins with an arbitrarily chosen **cutset** of the nodes, which is subsequently refined by splitting and merging. The cutset is stored in five arrays $(x_k, y_k, S_k, M_k, m_k)$ of size N^2.

Merging of four nodes is done by removing them from the cutset and replacing them with the single node. Theoretically, this process can continue until there is no node left in cutset except the root. Similarly, splitting can proceed until the cutset consists of $4^{Ik} = N^2$ leaf nodes only. The constraints of a *pyramidal data structure* are relaxed by a grouping process which follows split and merge. This leaves the tree structure and examines unrelated blocks found in the final cutset. Segmentation is further improved by combining small regions with their neighbours and by merging similar regions of different sizes.

Other systems have employed split and merge. Burt, Hong and Rosenfeld (1980) employed an overlapped pyramid defined by 4×4 block averaging. Each block has four parents on the level above it. This mean that blocks overlap by 50% on all four sides. Pietikainen, Rosenfeld and Walter (1982) have suggested two methods for splitting and linking this overlapped pyramid.

13.3 Quadtrees: data structure for region extraction

Region-based segmentation techniques which employ a systematic 2D data structure can be more efficient and cost effective than those considered above. With the introduction of cheap VLSI memories, it is less important to save space in the data structure selected. The most important feature is the facility for computationally efficient operations and ease of access to arbitrary regions. The most important operations on regions are searching for suitable regions starting from the entire image, and finding the neighbouring regions of any size and at any level. We have found that these operations are best supported by quadtrees. The root of the tree gives the entire image and any required region can be tracked from the root in a few steps.

There are two major approaches for representing 2D data. The first specifies the boundaries of a region. Run length code is the simplest of this class, where the blocks are each $1 \times m$ rectangles (Rutovitz, 1968). The more general representation is known as **Medial Axis Transform** (MAT) (Blum, 1967; Rosenfeld and Pfaltz, 1966) whose blocks are specified by their centres and radii. The alternative method of representation is based on the organization of the interior of a region. Quadtrees belong to this second class and are categorized as a collection of maximal blocks which partition a given region.

Quadtrees do not strictly follow the maximal block representation. Their blocks are disjoint and have a standard size and location depending on the level of the tree. This provides a systematic way of representing squared regions in the image. The quadtree technique for image representation is based on the successive subdivision of the image into quadrants. It is represented in the memory by a tree of outdegree four, where the root node represents the whole image of $2^N \times 2^N$ pixels. The four sons of the root node represent the quadrants, and the terminal nodes correspond to pixels.

Work has already been done to convert between the quadtree representation and other representations such as chain codes (Dyer, Rosenfeld and Samet, 1980; Samet, 1980a), rasters (Samet, 1981, 1984), binary arrays (Samet, 1980b) and MAT (Samet, 1983, 1985). Samet (1982), Shneier (1981a, 1981b) and Samet and Shaffer (1984) have also introduced different search algorithms required for image processing using quadtrees. We have followed the established notations and have implemented some region-based neighbour search algorithms using the C programming language on a Sun workstation. Quadtrees have also been used successfully for representing binary images, different operations on binary images (Oliver and Wiseman, 1983a, 1983b), shape approximation (Ranade, Rosenfeld and Samet, 1982), threshold selection (Wu, Hong and Rosenfeld, 1982) and grey-scale image representation (Kunii, Fujishiro and Mao, 1986).

13.4 Detection of lowest intensity region

We now introduce an algorithm which uses quadtrees for detecting any homogeneous region in an image. The algorithm has three distinct steps:

(1) An image pyramid based on a quadtree is constructed by starting from the pixel level and averaging the pixels in each square group of four to produce

an image of half the resolution. The process is repeated until the root is reached.

(2) The tree is searched from the root downwards. The four sons of any given node are examined and the one having an average grey level closest to the region sought is selected. Its grey level is then compared with that of its father. If their difference is not within the given tolerance, the search continues from the selected son, otherwise it is terminated.

(3) When the tree search has been completed, neighbouring areas of the extracted region are examined and attached to the region if they are within a given tolerance. This process continues for all the newly attached regions until there is no neighbour left within the given tolerance. Normally, this search is performed on those nodes of the tree which are at the same level, and regions of equal area are connected, but for tracing accurate boundaries of the regions, the same process can be performed at lower levels of the pyramid.

13.4.1 Parallel implementation of the algorithm

The most objectionable feature of the region extraction techniques is their sequential nature. Our contribution in this algorithm is the adaptation of region extraction to parallelism by utilizing the quadtree's structure. Each node of the tree structure corresponds to a square region in the image and contains three types of field:

(1) The average grey level of the corresponding region.

(2) The relation of the node to the decomposition of its father, which can be NW, NE, SW and SE.

(3) Four links (pointers) for its sons and one to its father.

The quadtree is a well-organized structure, and for a given node we can find its corresponding position in the image, using the path from the root along with the level of the node in the tree, both of which can be obtained from our data structure. The pointer to the father is provided for finding the neighbouring nodes at any level and walking upward in the tree structure. The algorithm for constructing a quadtree from binary image (Samet, 1981) was modified for building the quadtree from a 512×512 image array of 256 grey levels. Neighbour-finding techniques developed by Samet (1981) have also been implemented with some modification and used for examining the neighbouring nodes for region merging.

We have implemented the algorithm for four processors but it can be extended to 16 or 256 processors. One pyramid corresponding to each image quadrant is constructed and then the best fitting area in each quadrant of the image is detected. An arbitrator at the end links the four pyramids to form a single quadtree pyramid for the entire image. It also looks for the best region extracted from four quadrants, and it may be required to combine some of the extracted regions, if they satisfy the merging criteria. Boundaries for the extracted region may also be smoothed at this stage.

13.4.2 Results

The method was employed to extract the darkest region in a variety of different images drawn from various sources. Two sample pictures are shown in Figures 13.1a and 13.1b. These were digitized using 256 levels, and the lighting was arranged to produce a full range of shades for test and demonstration purposes. Figures 13.2a and 13.2b show the area detected for a typical search and merging criterion, and Figures 13.3a, 13.3b and 13.3c illustrate the effect of further relaxation of the merging criterion up to ± 3 grey levels.

13.4.3 Extension to general-purpose segmentation

The method presented in the previous section was developed to detect one region only (for our application, the darkest), from an image. However, the technique is so general that it can be modified easily for general-purpose segmentation. The procedures developed for constructing the image pyramid, and techniques for neighbour finding in quadtrees may be used in the following, modified method for general-purpose segmentation:

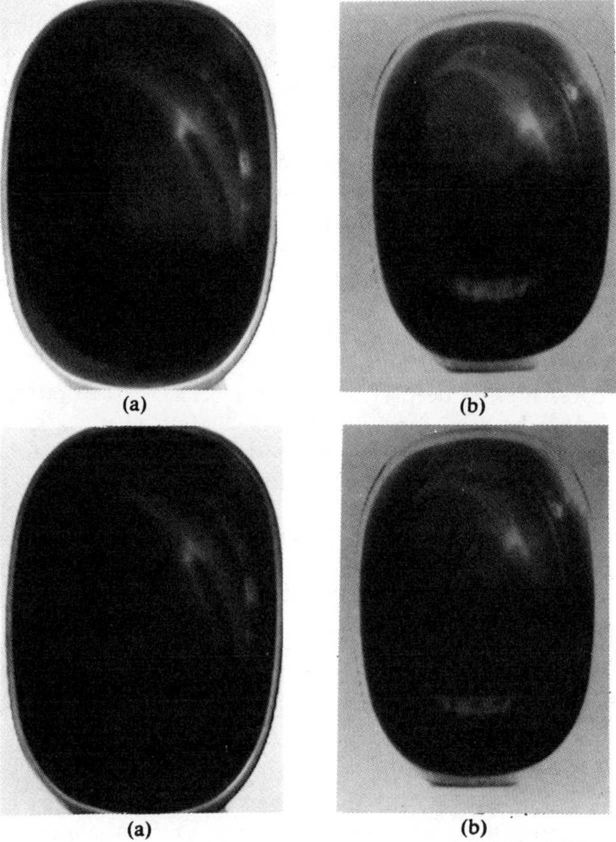

Figure 13.1
Images digitized using 256 levels.

Figure 13.2
Area detected for a typical search and merging criterion.

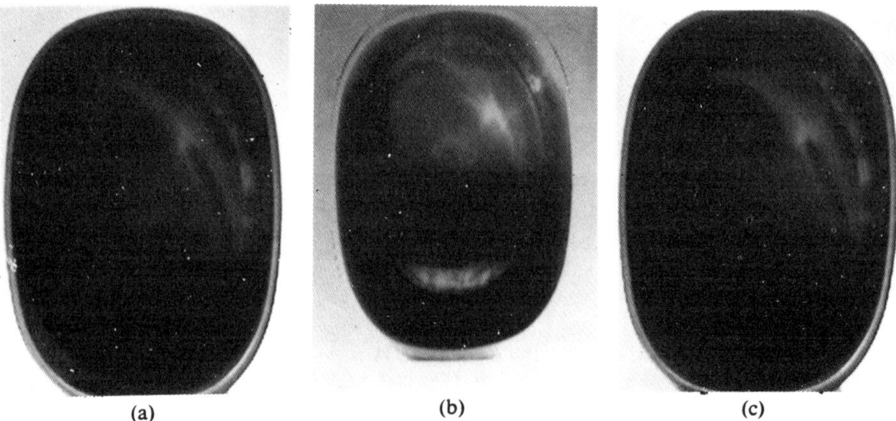

(a) (b) (c)

Figure 13.3
Further relaxation of the merging criterion up to ±3 grey levels.

(1) Extract the most promising region in terms of given properties, as described in our algorithm.

(2) Remove the pixels belonging to the extracted region from the structure of quadtree. This can be accomplished by isolating the nodes which correspond to the regions detected.

(3) Find the next most promising region in the modified pyramid.

(4) Continue the above process until all the pixels of the image have been isolated from the pyramid.

The modified algorithm can also be implemented on four or more processors. We can extract regions from each image quadrant in parallel and the arbitrator can merge the similar extracted regions afterwards if required.

13.5 Applications

If we can have a domain of application where the world is illuminated mainly by a single light source at the same point as the observation camera, then the darkest area in the image represents the deepest point in the scene. Detection of the darkest region can therefore be used for automatic navigation in pipes and ducts for a variety of instrumental purposes. The same method could also be applied in warehouses and buildings with appropriate lighting and for robot guidance in an automated factory environment.

In our biomedical application, the extraction of the darkest area during on-line image analysis plays an important role. The need for parallel implementation of a region extraction method has arisen because the image analysis has to be performed in less than one second.

Concluding remarks

We started with the objective of extracting a single region of given properties for an on-line machine vision system. Although edge-detection techniques can be implemented in a highly parallel way, they were found to be less suitable for this task.

Therefore we set out for a region-based segmentation technique and developed a region extraction method based on a quadtree pyramid.

In comparison with earlier work, our method has proved superior, since the Horwitz and Pavlidis's method of split-and-merge does not make use of the whole pyramid structure. They start from an arbitrary partition and sometimes a large number of iterations may be required to achieve a segmentation. Moreover, their method uses an adjacency graph structure for merging to achieve good segmentation results. The conversion from the pyramid structure, after performing splitting, to this new structure makes their technique unsuitable for parallel implementation. Burt, Hong and Rosenfeld extended the pyramid structure to an overlapped pyramid defined by 4 × 4 block averaging instead of 2 × 2. Each node in this structure has four inner children and twelve outer children while each child has three more parents in addition to the usual father. A similar system has been used by Pietikainen, Rosenfeld and Walter who performed different experiments and compared them with Pavlidis's split-and-merge process. They indicated that their hybrid process gives better results, specifically in texture classification, but they have not utilized the outer twelve children in the splitting process. We have found their method, using the overlapped pyramid structure, inefficient and uneconomical for extracting single regions because the overlapped structure needs more careful management procedures than quadtrees. Moreover, the construction of overlapped pyramid and other search operations are expensive in terms of computational cost and memory requirement.

It has been found that the method which uses only the pyramid structure for region-based segmentation has the advantage of being implementable in parallel. The method presented here employs only the pyramid structure based on quadtrees. Moreover, the efficient construction of quadtrees along with other image-processing operations have been well developed, and this has helped us in implementing the method successfully and efficiently for real-time image analysis.

Acknowledgements

The authors are indebted to the Ministry of Education, Government of Pakistan, parent department of Gul Khan, for enabling him to conduct this research at Imperial College.

References

Blum H. (1967). A transformation for extracting new descriptors of shape. In *Models for the Perception of speech and Visual Form* (Wathen-Dunn W., ed.), pp. 362–80. Cambridge MA: MIT Press

Brice C.R. and Fennema C.R. (1970). Scene analysis using regions. *Artificial Intelligence,* **1**(3), 205–26

Burt P., Hong T.H. and Rosenfeld A. (1980). *Segmentation and estimation of image region properties through co-operative hierarchical computation.* TR-297, Computer Vision Laboratory, University of Maryland MD

Dyer C.R., Rosenfeld A. and Samet H. (1980). Region representation: boundary codes from quadtrees. *Commun. Ass. Comput. Mach.,* **23**(3), 171–9

Gambotto J.P and Monga O. (1985). A parallel and hierarchical algorithm for region growing. In *Proc. IEEE CS. Conf. CVPR*, pp. 649–52. San Francisco CA

Horwitz S.L. and Pavlidis T. (1974). Picture segmentation by a directed split-and-merge procedure. In *Proc. Int. Joint Conf. Pattern Recognition*, pp. 424–33. Copenhagen

Horwitz S.L. and Pavlidis T. (1976). Picture segmentation by a tree traversal algorithm. *J. Ass. Comput. Mach.,* **23**(2), 368–88

Klinger A. and Dyer C.R. (1976). Experiments on picture representation using regular decomposition. *Computer Graphics and Image Processing,* **5**(1), 68–105

Kunni T.L., Fujishiro I. and Mao X. (1986). G-quadtree: A hierarchical representation of gray-scale digital images. *The Visual Computer,* **2**(4), 219–26

Muerle J.L. and Allen D.C. (1968). Experimental evaluation of techniques for automatic segmentation of objects in a complex scene. In *Pictorial Pattern Recognition* (Cheng G.C. *et al.*, eds), pp. 3–13. Washington: Thompson

Oliver M.A. and Wiseman N.E. (1983a). Operations on quadtree-encoded images. *Computer Journal,* **26**(1), 83–91

Oliver M.A. and Wiseman N.E. (1983b). Operations on quadtree leaves and related image areas. *Computer Journal,* **26**(4), 375–80

Pavlidis T. (1972). Segmentation of pictures and maps through functional approximation. *Computer Graphics and Image Processing,* **1**(4), 360–72

Pavlidis T. (1977). *Structural Pattern Recognition*. New York: Springer

Pietikainen M., Rosenfeld A. and Walter I. (1982). Split-and-link algorithms for image segmentation. *Pattern Recognition,* **15**(4), 287–98

Ranade S., Rosenfeld A. and Samet H. (1982). Shape approximation using quadtrees. *Pattern Recognition,* **15**(1), 31–40

Robertson T.V., Fu K.S. and Swain P.H. (1973). *Multispectral image partitioning*. Technical Report TR-EE73-26, Purdue University IN

Rosenfeld A. and Pfaltz J.L. (1966). Sequential operations in digital image processing. *J. Ass. Comput. Mach.,* **13**(4), 471–94

Rutovitz D. (1968). Data structures for operations on digital images. In *Pictorial Pattern Recognition* (Cheng G.C. *et al.*, eds), pp. 105–33. Washington: Thompson

Samet H. (1980a). Region representation: quadtrees from binary codes. *Commun. Ass. Comput. Mach.,* **23**(3), 163–70

Samet H. (1980b). Region representation: quadtrees from binary arrays. *Computer Graphics & Image Processing,* **13**(1), 88–93

Samet H. (1981). An algorithm for converting rasters to quadtrees. *IEEE Trans. Pattern Anal. & Mach. Intell.,* **PAMI:3**(1), 93–5

Samet H. (1982). Neighbour finding techniques for images represented by quadtrees. *Computer Graphics & Image Processing,* **18**(1), 37–57

Samet H. (1983). A quadtree medial axis transform. *Commun. Ass. Comput. Mach.,* **26**(9), 680–93

Samet H. (1984). Algorithm for the conversion of quadtrees to rasters. *Computer Graphics & Image Processing,* **26**(1), 1–16

Samet H. (1985). Reconstruction of quadtrees from quadtree medial axis transform. *Computer Vision, Graphics & Image Processing,* **29**(2), 311–28

Samet H. and Shaffer C.A. (1984). *A model for the analysis of neighbour finding in pointer-based quadtrees*. TR-1432, University of Maryland MD

Shneier M. (1981a). Calculations of geometric properties using quadtrees. *Computer Graphics & Image Processing,* **16**(3), 296–302

Shneier M. (1981b). Path-length distances for quadtrees. *Inf. Sci.,* **23**(1), 49–67

Wu A.Y., Hong T.H. and Rosenfeld A. (1982). Threshold selection using quadtrees. *IEEE Trans. Pattern Anal. & Mach. Intell.,* **PAMI-4**(1), 90–4

Zucker S.W. (1976). Region growing: childhood and adolescence. *Computer Graphics & Image Processing,* **5**(3), 382–99

B.M. McMillin
L.M. Ni

Michigan State University

14 · A reliable parallel algorithm for relaxation labeling

A relaxation labeling procedure such as that proposed by Hummel and Zucker can be used for scene analysis to resolve ambiguities in the interpretation of an image. Parallel computation on Distributed Multiprocessor Systems (DMPs) reduces the computation time. However, arbitrary failures in the DMP may cause undetectable subtleties in the final result. For large problems involving many objects, even parallel computation may require a great deal of time and thus increase the probability of error. This chapter presents a parallel probabilistic relaxation algorithm that utilizes reliable fault detection in the form of a constraint predicate to ensure algorithm correctness, without resorting to explicit system replication. This predicate serves a dual purpose of constraining processor errors within acceptable limits and providing a basis to detect faulty processors that deviate from these limits. The execution time penalty for this reliability is shown to be only a linear function of the fault-free cost of an unreliable solution versus an exponentially growing run time for the solution without reliability techniques.

14.1 Introduction

To describe the problem of relaxation labeling, we quote from the excellent paper by Hummel and Zucker (1984):

> 'Relaxation labeling processes are a class of mechanisms that were originally developed to deal with ambiguity and noise in vision systems. The general framework, however, has far broader potential applications and implications. The structure of relaxation labeling is motivated by two basic concerns: 1) the decomposition of a complex computation into a network of simple "myopic," or local, computations; and 2) the requisite use of context in resolving ambiguities . . .'

Parallelization of relaxation labeling for implementation on a multiprocessor system is advantageous for large problems, that is, problems that would otherwise take a long time on a conventional SISD computer (Hwang and Briggs, 1984). A large problem is characterized by a large number of objects. Indeed, some applications of relaxation labeling can include objects the size of pixels in a 512 × 512 image or 2^{18} objects (Stockman, private communication). Relaxation labeling lends itself easily to implementation as a data parallel algorithm (Hillis and Steele, 1986). The algorithm requires only local computations and data exchanges. Thus, good speedup may be obtained by parallelization.

The class of DMPs will be considered as target implementation machines (Ni *et al.*, 1987). A DMP is a loosely coupled multiprocessor system with distributed memory that uses message passing for interprocess communication. Application of this type of system yields a promising approach to allow hundreds and even thousands of processors to cooperate on the solution of a single problem. The communication delay between these homogeneous processors is relatively small, but not negligible. Examples of such machines are the Connection Machine (SIMD type with up to 65K processors) (Hillis, 1985), Intel's iPSC (up to 128 processors) (Grunwald and Reed, 1986), Ncube's Hypercube (up to 1024 processors) (Hayes *et al.*, 1986), and FPS's T series (up to 16K processors) (Gustafson *et al.*, 1986). Mapping of an algorithm to these machines requires definition of a problem topology and a decomposition of the algorithm into multiple communicating/cooperating subproblems. Each of these subproblems is assigned to a processor in the machine and the problem graph is mapped onto the machine interconnection architecture (Ni *et al.*, 1987).

Faulty processors within a multiprocessor may behave in many fashions. Two common fault classes are the **fail-stop** (Schlichting and Schneider, 1983; Toy, 1978) and the **Byzantine** (Lamport *et al.*, 1982) classes. A fail-stop processor, whenever it commits an error, will stop autonomously. Thus, if a receiving processor does not receive a message when expected, it can assume that the sender is faulty, that is, a fail-stop processor will never produce a result that is incorrect due to a hardware error. This model is limited in practice. Processor hardware must be sufficiently reliable to detect internal failures before they propagate out in the form of erroneous messages. By contrast, a Byzantine processor exhibits no such guaranteed behavior. Byzantine processors are assumed to take on a malicious intelligence – they essentially do the worst possible thing at the worst possible time to attempt to thwart algorithm correctness. Faulty senders under Byzantine failure conditions may withhold a value, send the wrong value, or send it at the wrong time. Thus no assumptions are made concerning the internal or external behavior of a faulty processor. Algorithms tolerant of Byzantine behavior can be proven correct by the use of this adversary model of processor behavior (McMillin and Ni, 1987).

This chapter focuses on the development of a reliable parallel algorithm tolerant of Byzantine faults on DMPs. The properties of the intermediate results of the computation are checked for faulty/nonfaulty behavior. The checking is performed in a distributed local manner which is made tolerant of Byzantine faults through the use of Byzantine Agreement (Lamport *et al.*, 1982). The major contribution of this chapter is the development of a constraint predicate that is tolerant of Byzantine faults for the relaxation labeling application. Application-oriented constraint predicates of this type were introduced by the authors in (McMillin and Ni, 1987). The idea of vector Byzantine Agreement is employed to reduce the complexity of the solution.

The remainder of this chapter is organized into five parts. Section 14.2 gives a parallelized version of Hummel and Zucker's relaxation algorithm. Section 14.3 gives an analytical motivation for this research. Section 14.4 gives a short introduction to the Byzantine Agreement problem and the requisite vector Byzantine Agreement algorithm AGREE. Section 14.5 presents the basis for design of a constraint predicate and gives the predicate for this problem integrated into the relaxation algorithm. The resulting algorithm is analyzed in Section 14.6.

14.2 Parallelized weighted relaxation labeling

The weighted relaxation labeling algorithm using the variational inequality method given by Hummel and Zucker yields a straightforward parallelization. The notation and algorithms are presented here for completeness. The basic idea is that given an initial feasible solution, attempt to maximize an objective function by taking small steps in the tangent direction which maximizes the directional derivative of the objective function. When the directional derivative becomes negative or zero, the objective function is at a local maximum and the procedure stops. Throughout this chapter, n is the number of objects and will be denoted with indices i and j, and m is the number of possible labels and will be denoted with λ and λ'. An objective function is defined as:

$$q_i(\lambda) = \sum_{\lambda=1}^{m} p_i(\lambda)s_i(\lambda),\ 1 \leqslant i \leqslant n \qquad \textbf{(14.1)}$$

where the support function $s_i(\lambda)$ is:

$$s_i(\lambda) = \sum_{j=1}^{n} \sum_{\lambda'=1}^{m} r_{ij}(\lambda, \lambda')p_j(\lambda') \qquad \textbf{(14.2)}$$

The compatibility matrix $R_{n \times n} = [r_{ij}(\lambda, \lambda')]$ is the relative compatibility of label λ at object i with label λ' at object j.

The weight vector $\vec{p}_i$ with components $p_i(\lambda)$ is the relative weighting for label λ at object i and is constrained by:

$$\sum_{\lambda=1}^{m} p_i(\lambda) = 1,\ 0 \leqslant p_i(\lambda) \leqslant 1,\ 1 \leqslant \lambda \leqslant m \qquad \textbf{(14.3)}$$

The weight vector $\vec{p}_i$ is constrained to be a consistent solution for each object i providing:

$$\sum_{\lambda=1}^{m} p_i(\lambda)s_i(\lambda) \geqslant \sum_{\lambda=1}^{m} v_i(\lambda)s_i(\lambda) \qquad \textbf{(14.4)}$$

for all labelings $\vec{v}_i$ satisfying Equation 14.3.

14.2.1 Non fault tolerant parallel relaxation algorithm

Parallelization of the algorithm is accomplished through assignment of each of the n objects to one of the n processors in the multiprocessor system. The ith processor is denoted by P_i. Each processor runs the same copy of the algorithm on different data, hence the term 'data parallel algorithm'. Each processor P_i has a copy of the entries relevant to it, of the compatibility coefficient matrix $R_{n \times n}$.

The **neighbors** of a processor in the problem domain of relaxation labeling

```
Initialize:
  (1) Start with a consistent initial labeling assignment p⃗⁰ k ← 0
      loop
(2a)     send p⃗_i^k to all N neighbors P_j
(2b)     receive p⃗_j^k from all N neighbors P_j
      /* nearest neighbor updating */
(2c)     s_i(λ) = Σ_j^N Σ_λ'^m r_ij(λ,λ')p_j(λ')
      /* find a feasible gradient direction */
 (3)     u⃗^k = projection-operator(p⃗^k, s⃗^k)
 (4)     if (u⃗^k = 0) break;
 (5)     p⃗^{k+1} ← p⃗^k + h u⃗^k
      /* where h is some small positive value */
      /* that keeps p⃗^{k+1} consistent
 (6)     k ← k + 1
         pool
```

Figure 14.1
Algorithm RL_{NR}, relaxation labeling with no added reliability.

$$s_i(\lambda) = \sum_{j}^{N} \sum_{\lambda'}^{m} r_{ij}(\lambda,\lambda')p_j(\lambda')$$

are those that have non-zero compatibility coefficients. Thus, each processor P_i has only the non-zero column elements j of row i in $R_{n \times n}$. The average number of non-zero entries per row is given by N. Communication with the neighbors in the physical machine is accomplished through **message passing**. Thus to implement a fast solution, the problem should be mapped such that the neighbors in the problem space correspond to the neighbors in the physical processor or, at the very least, processors that are the shortest distance away. In general, this is a known NP-hard problem in partition/mapping (Ni *et al.*, 1987). In this case, if the local non-zero compatibilities form a mesh problem topology, then the achievement of an optimal mapping is easy.

In the algorithm (Figure 14.1), the index i indicates the local object (processor), and the index j ranges over the neighbors. For example, $\vec{p}_j^{\,k}$ indicates the kth iteration value of $\vec{p}$ held by processor P_j. Each processor P_i executes the following algorithm $1 \leqslant i \leqslant n$. It is assumed here that the mapping is ideal, that is, each processor has a direct connection to its neighbors. This assumption is not critical and it simplifies complexity analysis.

14.2.2 Projection operator computation

Computation of the updating direction vector is presented in (Mohammed *et al.*, 1983). It is formulated as a linear optimization problem subject to quadratic constraints. We repeat the formal problem specification here.

Let IR^m be m-dimensional real space and let IK be the convex set defined by:

$$IK = \left\{ \vec{p} \in IR^m \mid \sum_{\lambda=1}^{m} p(\lambda) = 1,\ p(\lambda) \geqslant 0,\ 1 \leqslant \lambda \leqslant m \right\}$$

Figure 14.2
Algorithm *projection-operator*.

projection-operator $(\vec{p}, \vec{s})$
(1) $D \leftarrow \{\lambda \mid p(\lambda) = 0\}$
(2) $S_k \leftarrow \{\ \}$
loop
(3) $t_k \leftarrow \frac{i}{n - |S_k|} \sum_{\lambda \in S_k} s(\lambda);$
(4) $S_{k+1} \leftarrow \left\{\lambda \in D \mid s(\lambda) < t_k\right\};$
(5) **if** $(S_{k+1} = S_k)$ **break;**
(6) $k \leftarrow k + 1$
pool
(7) $u(\lambda) \leftarrow \begin{cases} 0 & \text{if } \lambda \in S_k \\ s(\lambda) - t_k & \text{otherwise} \end{cases}$
(8) $\vec{p} \leftarrow \begin{cases} 0 & \text{if } \vec{u} = 0 \\ \frac{\vec{u}}{\|\vec{u}\|} & \text{otherwise} \end{cases}$

For any vector $\vec{p} \in IK$, the tangent set $T_{\vec{p}}$ is:

$$T_{\vec{p}} = \left\{\vec{v} \in IR^m \mid \sum_{\lambda=1}^{m} v(\lambda) = 0,\ v(\lambda) \geqslant 0 \textit{ whenever } p(\lambda) = 0\right\}$$

The set of feasible directions to move at point $\vec{p}$ is:

$$F_{\vec{p}} = T_{\vec{p}} \cap \left\{ \vec{v} \in IR^m \mid \|\vec{v}\| \leqslant 1 \right\}$$

The subproblem to be solved by the projection operator algorithm is 'Given a current feasible weighting vector $\vec{p}$ and a current arbitrary direction $\vec{s} \in IR^m$, find $\vec{u} \in F_{\vec{p}}$ such that $\vec{s} \cdot \vec{u} \geqslant \vec{s} \cdot \vec{v}$ for all $\vec{v} \in F_{\vec{p}}$' (see Figure 14.2).

Note here that the vector $\vec{u}$ is normalized only locally. Since it is stated in the original paper that normalization over the entire problem is not a requirement for convergence, the local normalization makes the parallel algorithm possible.

14.2.3 Performance evaluation

Speedup can be defined as the ratio of the sequential complexity vs parallel complexity. For each processor, P_i, the complexity of the *projection-operator* routine is $O(m^2)$. All other steps for one iteration are $O(m)$ with the exception of the calculation of $\vec{s}_i$ which is $O(Nm)$. Thus, the complexity of a parallel iteration is $O(Nm + m^2 + c)$, where c is the communication time for message interchange among the neighbors. If a single processor works on all of the calculations, then an iteration is $O(Nm + m^2)$. Thus the speedup obtained by parallelization is the ratio:

$$O\left[\frac{n(m^2 + Nm)}{m^2 + Nm + c}\right]$$

If n is large, the speedup is significant.

14.3 Motivation and reliability analysis

Reliable parallel processing requires additional time to perform the various bounds checking and message interchanges associated with the constraint predicate. For small problems, this overhead may not be necessary. If the system has a high reliability and the problem incurs no more than a short execution time, the probability of an error occurring during the execution may be very small. In this case, it may be best to 'take your chances' and run the job with no fault tolerance. However, long run times with large numbers of processors may not be able to finish before an error occurs. The time between errors is called the Mean Time To Failure (MTTF). If the problem run time is long with respect to the MTTF, then reliability techniques are indicated. Furthermore, when an error occurs, the problem must be restarted from the beginning. Thus, if the MTTF is very small, the job may never complete.

Reliability modeling can provide a basis for quantification of these concepts. We must make some assumptions about the type of problem and solution being attempted (see Table 14.1).

Table 14.1 Model Assumptions.

Serial Reliability	Nearest neighbor iterative problem – All processors must function
iid Exponential	Processor failures are independent, identical exponentially distributed with parameter μ

14.3.1 Failure model

As noted in the assumptions, processor reliabilities are given by the random variable X and are iid exponential with parameter μ. The probability distribution function of X is given by:

$$f(t|\mu) = \frac{1}{\mu} e^{\frac{-t}{\mu}}, t > 0 \tag{14.5}$$

The probability that an individual processor fails at some time later than T is given by:

$$1 - F(T) = \int_T^\infty f(t|\mu)\mathrm{d}t = e^{\frac{-T}{\mu}} \tag{14.6}$$

The system reliability is given by the random variables $X_1, X_2, \ldots, X_n$. Since we have serial reliability, the system fails when one component fails. This is given by the random variable Y:

$$Y = min\{X_1, X_2, \ldots, X_n\} \tag{14.7}$$

Let the cdf of Y be $G(t)$. Since the X_is are independent:

$$1 - G(t) = \prod_{i=1}^{n} (1 - F(t)) = e^{\frac{-n}{\mu} t} \tag{14.8}$$

Thus $1 - G(t)$ is an exponential with parameter $\frac{\mu}{n}$.

14.3.2 Expected run time

The expected run time of a non-fault-tolerant system is constructed as follows. If the system does not fail before time T, then the job runs in time T. If the system fails before T, then the job must be restarted and the expected run time is the time spent before the failure plus another expected run time. The expected run time $E(R)$ is given by:

$$E(R) = TP_r[Y > T] + (E(R) + E(Z))P_r[Y < T] \tag{14.9}$$

where $E(Z)$ is the conditional MTTF given that the system has failed before T time units. Z is given by $P_r[Y = t \mid Y < T]$ for $0 < t < T$:

$$P_r[Y = t \mid Y < T] = \frac{P_r[Y = t, Y < T]}{P_r[Y < T]} = \frac{g(t)}{G(T)} \tag{14.10}$$

Since $g(t)$ is given by $\frac{n}{\mu} e^{\frac{-n}{\mu} t}$, we have:

$$E(Z) = \int_0^T \frac{n}{\mu} t \frac{e^{\frac{-n}{\mu} t}}{1 - e^{\frac{-n}{\mu} T}} dt = \frac{\mu}{n} - \frac{T}{e^{\frac{n}{\mu} T} - 1} \tag{14.11}$$

Solving Equation 14.9 for $E(R)$ and using the value for $E(Z)$ obtained in Equation 14.11 we obtain:

$$E(R) = T - E(Z) + E(Z)e^{\frac{n}{\mu} T} \tag{14.12}$$

14.3.3 Discussion

The $E(Z)$ is actually optimistic since it is assumed that when a processor fails, the system halts. In Section 14.4 it is shown that this is not always the case for Byzantine fault cases. If it cannot be determined that processor has failed until the end of the computation, then $E(Z)$ is replaced by the larger value of T. The general shape of Equation 14.12 is given in Figure 14.3 for fixed values of $n = 32\ 768$ and $\mu = 5000$ hours.

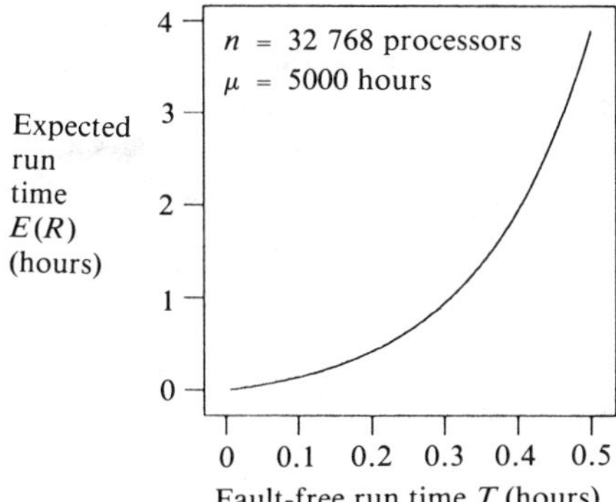

Figure 14.3
Expected run time for algorithm RL_{NR}.

The abscissa shows the time for a solution with no fault tolerance, that encounters no errors. The ordinate is the expected run time given the reliability of an individual processor and the number of processors involved in the solution. Since this is a serial reliability model, a single processor failure causes a job restart. We will use this result again in Section 14.6 to compare the reliable solution cost with the unreliable case.

14.4 Byzantine Agreement and fault-tolerance considerations

As shown in the previous section, large systems have a low reliability and thus some fault tolerance must be built in either at the system or application level to achieve reliability. In a distributed multiprocessor, since the only method of communication is message passing, it would seem that a Byzantine faulty processor can remain undetected as long as it continues to send messages. However, faulty processors can be detected through examination of their messages in the context of the system. It is with this goal in mind that the following two techniques represent possible approaches in detecting faulty processors.

(1) *Use an acceptance criterion.* Any non-faulty receiver of a message checks to see that some property of the message meets some predefined standard. Note that the message may be incorrect in format or content. In either case, the acceptance criterion rejects the processor as faulty if the standard is not met. However, if the sending processor broadcasts its value to many receivers over point-to-point links, it may send correct values to some and incorrect values to others. Thus, some processors will flag the sender as faulty and others will believe it to be non-faulty, resulting in an inconsistent diagnosis of the system.

(2) *Allow a consistent state to be reached by the non-faulty processors on any broadcast value.* The receivers of a value from a single sender compare the information they receive to attempt to determine the sender's validity. This is done by interchanging messages among receivers. These messages must be interchanged in a judicious manner to overcome the effects of faulty

messages introduced by faulty processors. Otherwise a faulty receiver may cause a non-faulty sender to appear faulty. The best that can be achieved is a procedure which can mask out the effects of faulty processors and achieve a consistent state among all non-faulty processors. However, the agreed message values, though consistent, may be incorrect if the sender is faulty.

Neither (1) or (2) alone can provide reliable parallel solutions although the coupling of these two techniques can produce reliable fault detection.

14.4.1 Byzantine Agreement

Problem (2) is the **Byzantine Generals problem** (Lamport *et al.*, 1982). While Byzantine Generals solution algorithms mask faults, they alone have a drawback in the solution of the fault-detection problem. If the sender is non-faulty and a receiver is faulty and thus relays the wrong values, processors may erroneously flag the sender as faulty when, in reality, some other processor is faulty. The Byzantine Generals solution cannot implicitly locate the faulty processor. It can only guarantee that a consistent state of the system can be produced for each processor. Thus, we must appeal to (1) above to provide the necessary fault coverage. Each processor applies an acceptance test to its set of processor values obtained in (2). Since by virtue of (2), each processor has the same 'view' of all processors' local values in the system. Thus the acceptance test run on this view by each non-faulty processor will produce the same set of faulty processors as a test result.

Our solution of the fault detection problem then requires that, based upon a proper constraint predicate, identification of a particular processor can be achieved, based upon its value with respect to other processors' values. A procedure for accomplishing this agreement simultaneously among a group of processors called a **fault group** is described in detail in (McMillin and Ni, 1987). Here, only a general overview of the procedure will be given.

Agreement over a set of values must achieve the **Vector Interactive Consistency** (VIC) conditions.

Vector interactive consistency conditions

VIC1 Any two non-faulty processors in a fault group obtain common values for all processors in the agreement.

VIC2 If a processor P_k is non-faulty and wishes to communicate a value v_k to the other members of the fault group, then at the end of the agreement, each other non-faulty processor receives P_k's intended value.

The above conditions may seem the same; however, they are not. Condition VIC1 states that any two non-faulty processors obtain the same copies of the local values of all the processors in the agreement. However, these values may or may not be equal to the local value v_i that a particular processor P_i actually holds. Condition VIC2 states that all non-faulty processors agree on the same value as a particular processor P_k's local value v_k if the particular processor is non-faulty.

The following algorithm is an English description of the formal algorithm *Agree* (Figure 14.4) presented in (McMillin and Ni, 1987). In *Agree*, the maximum

Figure 14.4
Algorithm *Agree*

Algorithm *Agree*(T)

(1) Broadcast T to the $n - 1$ other processors in the agreement group.

(2) Receive $(n - 1)T_j$s from the same $n - 1$ processors.

(3) Recursively call *Agree* to broadcast the received $T1$ until sufficient copies have been exchanged to mask the effects of t faulty processors.

(4) Return the set of agreed-upon $T1_j$s · $T1_j$ represents the agreed-upon data structure of processor P_j.

number of tolerable faults per fault group is t. The number of processors in the fault group is N. Note that this is not the number of processors in the system and further note that it is no coincidence that this is the same value of the average number of non-zero compatibility coefficients per object. T is a data structure holding the information to be agreed upon. Processors and communication are assumed to be synchronous.

Proof of correctness

THEOREM 14.1
Agree(T) achieves vectored interactive consistency VIC1 and VIC 2 for $N > 3t$ with $N > 3$, $t = 0,1,\ldots$

The proof is by induction and is given in (McMillin and Ni, 1987). In general, the algorithm *Agree* requires $O(n^{t+1})$ space and computation complexity and a communication complexity of $(n - 1)(t + 1)$ messages in $t + 1$ rounds of information exchange (McMillin and Ni, 1987).

14.4.2 Example of algorithm *Agree*

Agree is similar to the recursive algorithm given in (Lamport *et al.*, 1982) with the exception that all participants are both transmitters and receivers. A 4-processor agreement tolerant of one fault ($N = 4$ and $t = 1$) will require two rounds of information interchange. In the first round, each processor's local value is broadcast in step (1) and received in step (2). These received values are then agreed upon in step (3). A majority vote is taken to achieve a consistent agreement. At termination all processors that are non-faulty have the same 'view' of the other processors' values.

14.5 Constraint predicate

The design of the constraint predicate is equivalent to the design of a test. This method is made elegant by the following observation:

Since we test the intermediate results for correctness with respect to the algorithm, the end solution is correct if the intermediate results are correct. If processor errors occur that do not affect the solution, then they are not errors.

For application-oriented reliability, this method is clearly superior to component exercising or other offline tests. The test set consists only of what is necessary to ensure correctness for the current application.

A second property of the constraint predicate is its Block Box vs Glass Box approach to testing. Nothing need be assumed about the internal behavior of the processor. All that matters is the result of the computation. This is consistent with the Byzantine model of faults.

We introduce D as a formalism to represent a class of computable predicates which can be applied to the result of algorithm *Agree*.

THEOREM 14.2

Predicate $D_i \in D$ computes a decision $d \in \{\text{yes, no}\}$ if for any two results $T1_k$ and $T1_l$ from algorithm *Agree* in any two correct processors P_k and P_l, $D_i(T1_k)$ and $D_i(T1_l)$ return the same decision d.

Proof

By vector interactive consistency and Theorem 14.1, all non-faulty processors P_k and P_l hold the same $T1$ such that $T1_k = T1_l = T1$. By definition of D, D_i returns the same decision d in each non-faulty processor.

Theorem 14.2 is critical to the entire scheme. It simply states that any two processors that are correct, given the same agreed-upon values, reach the same conclusion. Thus any neighboring processors working on the same portion of the problem, can come to a common decision regarding their immediate neighbors, and thus report the same conclusion of error or no error. Furthermore, since each correct processor has obtained and verified the same data from some processor P_i, the solution of the problem can proceed correctly in the presence of maskable errors.

14.5.1 Predicate development

Intermediate values of the computation must be checked for validity. But one must ask what kind of properties are there to check?

Suppose that the problem is to compute the area of a plane figure. Clearly area cannot be negative, so any internal result that led to a negative area would certainly be in error. But it is easy to see that this test is not of much use, since the erroring processor is free to produce any positive value of area. Thus this predicate would only catch certain obvious errors. Byzantine processor errors are far more subtle.

A further constraint on a predicate is that it should not have to replicate the entire computation just to check an intermediate result, for that is just NMR. Thus, there are certain problem classes that lend themselves to good predicates. One might be tempted to consider nearest-neighbor problems such as 2D convolution (Fang *et al.*, 1986). Neighbors exchange values to compute the final result. However, there are really no properties that can be checked unless some presumptive knowledge is available concerning the image. Thus total replication is again necessary.

Convergent iterative problems might have a possibility since convergence can be tested for. However, for example, in a non-parallel implementation of Newton's method for finding the roots of a polynomial, there are no processors available to check intermediate results. Thus explicit replication is again necessary.

The combination of the above two, however, yields some interesting predicates. The class of nearest-neighbor iterative solutions can allow processors to check properties of their neighbor's intermediate results without resorting to explicit replication.

A processor that is faulty may exhibit two broad types of behavior. It may:

(1) deviate from the limits of acceptability and

(2) remain within the limits of acceptability.

Ideally, any deviation from the absolute correct calculation should be detected as an error, but this is not realistic in practice. However, if the solution remains correct even if some processors are allowed to 'wander' around, it may not matter. Furthermore, if it is acceptable for the final result to be very 'close' to the fault-free answer ($<$ some ϵ_0), then constraints may be gleaned from the theory of the solution.

The class of nearest-neighbor iterative solutions ranges from applicability to Partial Differential Equation (PDE) Relaxation solutions to relaxation labeling. In (McMillin and Ni, 1987) the authors gave a partial constraint predicate for PDE solutions. Here, we present a complete constraint predicate for relaxation labeling and prove its correctness and completeness.

14.5.2 Relaxation labeling predicate

The mathematical theory surrounding the application must be mature to facilitate development of an appropriate testing predicate. Such is the case with the relaxation labeling procedure given by Hummel and Zucker, which is essentially a constrained local maximization problem with the direction of updating solved by the method of feasible directions (Zoutendijk, 1976). Thus two properties are immediately determined from the boundary constraints:

(1) consistency of the solution and

(2) feasibility of the solution.

A third, more subtle, condition is that of:

(3) convergence

We prove a series of lemmas to show that at each iteration, the intermediate results must satisfy conditions 1–3.

Lemma 14.1
At each iteration, the following consistency conditions hold:

$$\sum_{\lambda=1}^{m} p_i(\lambda) = 1 \text{ and } 0 \leqslant p_i(\lambda) \leqslant 1,\ 1 \leqslant \lambda \leqslant m$$

Proof
Since step (5) of the algorithm RL_{NR} in Figure 14.1 chooses h such that $\vec{p}^{k+1}$ remains consistent, each $\vec{p}^{k+1}$ must satisfy the consistency conditions. Since the consistency constraints form a compact convex set over IR^m, then all intermediate solutions must remain within a convex cone in m-space (Zoutendijk, 1976). This 'funnels' the solution to the local attractor.

LEMMA 14.2
At each iteration the following feasibility conditions are maintained:

(1) $\sum_{\lambda=1}^{m} u_i(\lambda) = 0$

(2) $(\vec{s} - \vec{u}) \cdot \vec{u} = 0$

Proof

(1) At step 3, *projection-operator* performs an orthogonal projection of $\vec{s}$ onto the feasibility space $F_{\vec{p}}$. Thus $(\vec{s} - \vec{u}) \cdot \vec{u} = 0$.

(2) Since $\vec{u}$ lies in $T_{\vec{p}}$ <, $\sum_{\lambda=1}^{m} u_i(\lambda) = 0$ for all feasible $\vec{u}$.

LEMMA 14.3
Each iteration is subject to the following convergence conditions:

(1) If $\vec{u} \in F_{\vec{p}}$ and $//\vec{u}// = 1$, then $\vec{u}$ maximizes the gradient direction change.
(2) If $\vec{u}$ is a correct result of *projection-operator* and $\vec{u} \neq 0$, then $\vec{s}_i^{k+1} \cdot \vec{p}^{k+1} > \vec{s}_i^{k} \cdot \vec{p}^{k}$.
(3) Convergence occurs in a finite time within a suitable neighborhood of the solution under conditions of strict consistency.

Proof

(1) Immediate from the problem definition of *projection-operator*.
(2) If $\vec{s}_i^{k+1} \cdot \vec{p}^{k+1} < \vec{s}_i^{k} \cdot \vec{p}^{k}$ then for some $\vec{v} \in F_{\vec{p}}$, $\vec{v} \cdot \vec{s} > \vec{u} \cdot \vec{s}$. Thus $\vec{u}$ was not a correct result from *projection-operator*.
If $\vec{s}_i^{k+1} \cdot \vec{p}^{k+1} = \vec{s}_i^{k} \cdot \vec{p}^{k}$ then by step 5 of RL_{NR}, since $h > 0$, $\vec{u} = 0$.
(3) Immediate from Theorem 9.1 (Hummel and Zucker, 1984).

14.5.3 Predicate generation and proof

The correctness and completeness of the predicate is proven in the following theorem. The metric for correctness requires that if the algorithm RL_{NR}, under no faults, produces a correct solution, then the reliable algorithm RL_R, under a locally bounded number of faults t, also produces the same correct solution within some predetermined error tolerance ϵ_0.

It will be shown that the constraints given in Lemmas 14.1–3 are sufficient for the predicate correctness if one constraint is added. This constraint has nothing to do with the problem theory. It is possible for a Byzantine processor to arrange the vectors $\vec{u}$ and $\vec{p}$ as to erroneously signal early stopping. Thus, in the case of early stopping, the last calculation must be replicated. If the replication also produces a stopping point, then that solution is indeed the correct solution.

The method of proof is by considering all possible movements of the vector $\vec{p}$ during the iterations of the labeling algorithm.

THEOREM 14.3

A predicate D that embodies the features proven in Lemmas 14.1–3 plus the early stopping test will constrain Byzantine behavior such that if the unreliable solution computed by RL_{NR} is correct, the reliable solution with predicate D is also correct within the error tolerance ϵ_0.

Proof

Consider a point $\vec{p}^k$ that satisfies Lemma 14.1. A direction of movement by $\vec{u}$ may be to any point in m-space $\vec{p}^{k+1}$. Consider a movement by processor P_j (object j) that does not change $\vec{p}_j^k$ such that $\vec{s}_j^{k+1}$ is moved towards the local maximum and $\vec{p}_j$ has not already been found to be a solution. There are two cases:

(1) Lemma 14.3(2) is violated (Figure 14.5). If $\vec{u}_j^{k+1} \neq 0$, then processor P_j has made a 'nonconvergence error'. If $\vec{u}_j^{k+1} = 0$ then we must invoke the early stopping test. The members of the local fault group 're-run' the last iteration based on the values $\vec{p}_j^k$ and $\vec{u}_j^k$. If the replicated calculation is the same as the original $\vec{p}^{k+1}$, $\vec{u}^{k+1}$, then $\vec{p}_j^{k+1}$ is a solution and processor P_j stops.

(2) $\vec{p}_j$ satisfies Lemma 14.3 but does not satisfy Lemma 14.1. Thus $\vec{p}_j$ has moved 'outside' of the solution space (Figure 14.6) and has violated the consistency conditions.

If $\vec{p}_j^{k+1}$, $\vec{u}^{k+1}$ leads to a correct movement of $\vec{s}_j^k$ but does not make the maximal movement available, then Lemma 14.2 and Lemma 14.3(1) are violated.

Finally if Lemmas 14.1–2 are satisfied and conditions of Lemma 14.3(1) and (2) are satisfied and condition 14.3(3) is violated, then the Byzantine resource is attempting to delay convergence through zigzagging (Figure 14.7). However, zigzagging may occur as a result of errors even if the algorithm employs an anti-zigzagging procedure. Even though the solution is making progress by virtue of condition 14.3(1), for all practical purposes could be making progress as small as a 1-bit change in $\vec{s}_j$! Clearly, this would cause the solution to run for a very long time. However, we know that the convergence occurs within a finite amount of time, so the following test is utilized: if $\vec{s}_i^{k+1} \cdot \vec{p}^{k+1} - \vec{s}_i^k \cdot \vec{p}^k < \epsilon^{k+1}$ then a convergence

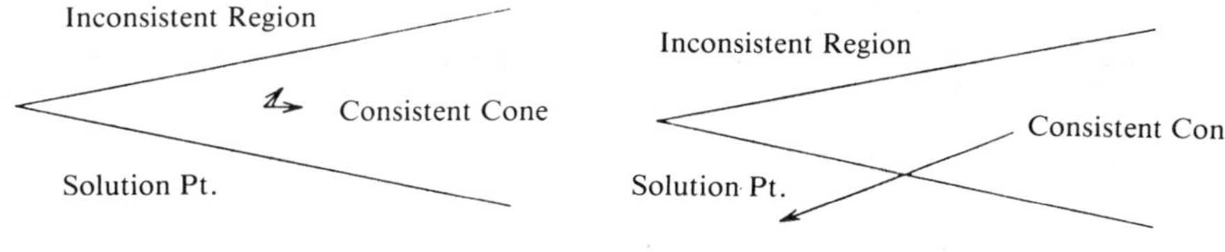

Figure 14.5
Non-maximizing movements.

Figure 14.6
Movement outside of consistency cone.

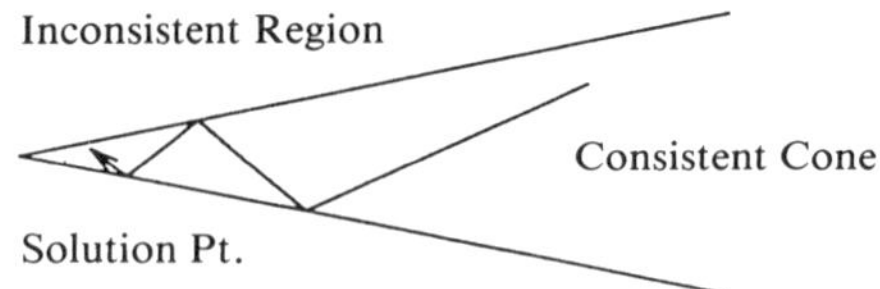

Figure 14.7
Zigzagging – convergence but no finiteness.

error is flagged. When $\epsilon^k < \epsilon_0$ for the predetermined error tolerance ϵ_0, the solution halts.

Thus the predicate D catches all movement errors that will lead to incorrect and slow solutions.

14.5.4 Reliable parallel algorithm for relaxation labeling

The reliable algorithm (Figure 14.8) is constructed from the proof of Theorem 14.3. At each iteration, *Agree* is called to exchange values among the members of the local fault group. The member's values are then checked according to the consistency, feasibility and convergence conditions. The additional stopping rule check is also employed to completely constrain Byzantine resource behavior.

14.6 Complexity analysis

In Section 14.3, it was demonstrated that an algorithm with no reliability could have an exponential expected run time. In this section, the reliable parallel algorithms developed are compared with the no-reliability solution in Section 14.2. While this chapter only covers the fault-detection aspects of this problem, it is understood that a reconfiguration will take place after the fault is detected (Garcia-Molina, 1982). This will enable the problem solution to continue in the presence of the detected errors.

The assumptions made concerning the implementation are detailed in Table 14.2.

14.6.1 Communication complexity analysis

If we assume communication time is the dominant factor, then the analysis considers only the communication setup latency S_L and the message transmission time. Setup latency is typically expensive. For example, the iPSC hypercube has $S_L = 1$ ms (Grunwald and Reed, 1986). This is large compared with a typical instruction time for most computers.

$$C_{cNR} = bV_B + 2S_L \tag{14.13}$$

$$C_{cR} = \sum_{i=0}^{t+1} (V_B bN^i + 2S_L) \tag{14.14}$$

$$C_{cR} \approx 2(t + 1)S_L + (V_b bN)^{t+1} \tag{14.15}$$

Figure 14.8
Reliable relaxation labeling algorithm RL_R for each processor P_i.

```
Initialize:
        Start with initial labeling assignment
                p⃗⁰ ∈ feasible labelings.
        k ← 0
        loop

        /* reliably send/receive neighbor's iteration values */
        p⃗_j^k, s⃗_j^k, u⃗_j^k ← agree(p⃗_i^k, s⃗_i^k, u⃗_i^k)

        /* Start of Predicate D */

                for each neighbor of P_i : P_j do begin
                        for λ = 1 to m do begin
                                if ( Σ_{λ=1}^{m} p_j^k(λ) ≠ 1 or p_j(λ) ∉ [0,1] )
                                then report error – inconsistent p_j^k(λ);
                        rof;
                        if ( Σ_λ u_j(λ) ≠ 0 ) then report error – infeasible
                          u_j^k(λ);
                        if ((s⃗_j^k – u⃗_j^k) · u⃗_j^k ≠ 0) then report error – infeasible
                          u⃗_j^k or s⃗_j^k;
                        if (//u⃗_j// then report error – nonconvergent u⃗_j^k;
                        if (ε^k < ε_0) then {declare P_j as stopped, result is p⃗^{k_j};
                          break;}
                        if (s⃗_j^k – s⃗_j^k – 1 < ε^k) then report error –
                          nonconvergent s⃗_j^k;
                rof;

/* End of Predicate D */

        /* nearest neighbor updating */
        s_i^k(λ) = Σ_j Σ_λ' r_ij(λ, λ') p_j^k(λ')

        */ Find a feasible gradient direction */
        u⃗^k = projection-operator (p⃗^k, s⃗^k)

        if (u⃗^k = 0) break;

        /* h is some small positive value */
        p⃗^{k+1} ← p⃗^k + h u⃗^k

        k ← k + 1

pool
```

Table 14.2 Implementation Assumptions.

Item	*Variable*	*Description*
Scientific word	b	60–80 bits per computation exchange
Data dominated message		Message header will not dominate the message length, that is, a single datum will dominate the message header/trailer (worst case assumption)
Message setup non-trivial	S_L	Communication setup latency (time either to send or receive a message taken by a processor)
Communication time	$C_{cNR\,(cr)}$	Communication time/iteration for algorithm $RL_{NR(R)}$
Computation time	$C_{pNR\,(pR)}$	Processing time/iteration for algorithm $RL_{NR}(R)$
Bus width	V_B	Communication velocity of the interprocessor interconnection

Now, if we assume the setup latency S_L is of order larger than the message transmission time $(V_b bN)^{t+1}$ Equations 14.13 and 14.15 reduce to:

$$\frac{C_{cR}}{C_{cNR}} \approx t + 1 \tag{14.16}$$

Thus the algorithm RL_R communication complexity is only a linear factor in $t + 1$ of the unreliable algorithm RL_{NR}.

14.6.2 Computation complexity analysis

Now assume that processing time is the bottleneck. The complexity components consist of the algorithm iterations, communication setup latency and reliability calculations. The algorithm *Agree*, as noted earlier, has $O(N^{t+1})$ computational complexity.

For the reliable algorithm RL_R:

$$C_{pR} = O\left[m^2 + Nm + 2(t + 1)S_L + N^{t+1}\right] \tag{14.17}$$

And the unreliable algorithm RL_{NR} has:

$$C_{pNR} = O\left[m^2 + Nm + 2S_L\right] \tag{14.18}$$

The ratio of the two computation times of RL_R to RL_{NR} is:

$$\frac{C_{pR}}{C_{pNR}} = O\left[\frac{m^2 + Nm + 2(t + 1)S_L + N^{t+1}}{m^2 + Nm + 2S_L}\right] \tag{14.19}$$

For reasonable small values of N and t, this ratio reduces to:

$$\frac{C_{pR}}{C_{pNR}} \approx t + 1 \tag{14.20}$$

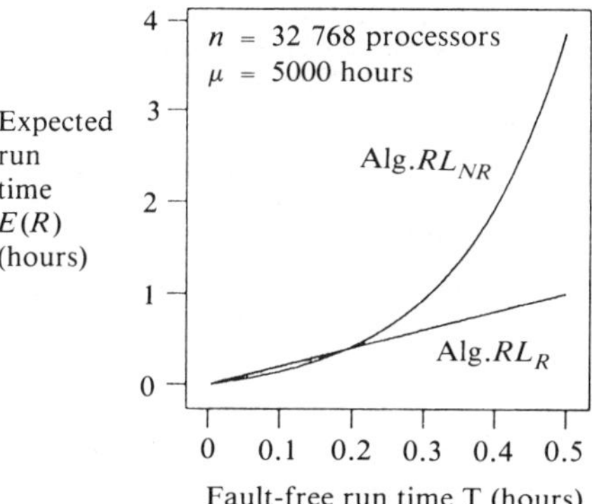

Figure 14.9 Expected run time comparison.

Thus for a small average N, small m, tolerant of one fault $t = 1$, both the computational and communication complexity hold the following relationship:

$$C_R \approx 2C_{NR} \tag{14.21}$$

The graph in Figure 14.9 shows the linear reliable solution compared with the exponential unreliable solution for a representative solution. The point of intersection is the crossover point. To the left of this point, it is better to run with no reliability (assuming that an error is somehow noticed). To the right of this point, in terms of run time, it is better to use the reliable solution. Additional tabulated data appears in Table 14.3 indicating crossover points for various values of n and μ.

Concluding remarks

The major contribution of this paper is the design, construction and proof of correctness and completeness of a constraint predicate for the relaxation labeling algorithm of Hummel and Zucker for a distributed multiprocessor environment. We not only proposed a parallel relaxation labeling algorithm but also provided a reliable parallel algorithm to guarantee a bound on the solution run time in the unreliable parallel environment, without which the expected run time grows exponentially. The reliable parallel algorithm developed couples the predicate with Byzantine agreement to locate faults reliably in this environment. The results of analysis show that large-scale multiprocessor systems running large-scale problems are particularly prone to frequent errors and will benefit most from this research. Smaller problems will endure an increased run time but with the added benefit of a very high degree of confidence in the solution's correctness.

The creation of an appropriate test is the most difficult problem facing implementors of reliable parallel processing. The constraint predicate, as a test, is a natural extension of the mathematical properties of the relaxation problem. The basic idea behind the predicate is that deviant behavior can be tolerated as long as it does not cause the problem solution to become incorrect. When this behavior exceeds predetermined problem dependent bounds, then the predicate signals an error. The vision predicate given satisfies these requirements and is easily implementable.

Table 14.3 Run time comparisons.

Failure Rate μ = 5000

n	*Crossover*	*E(R)*	*MTTF*
512	12.27	24.5	4.9
1 024	6.14	12.3	2.4
2 048	3.07	6.1	1.2
4 096	1.54	3.1	0.6
8 192	0.77	1.5	0.3
16 384	0.38	0.8	0.2
32 768	0.20	0.4	0.1
65 536	0.10	0.2	0.0

Failure Rate μ = 10 000

n	*Crossover*	*E(R)*	*MTTF*
512	24.54	49.1	9.8
1 024	12.27	24.5	4.9
2 048	6.14	12.3	2.4
4 096	3.07	6.1	1.2
8 192	1.54	3.1	0.6
16 384	0.77	1.5	0.3
32 768	0.38	0.8	0.2
65 536	0.20	0.4	0.1

Failure Rate μ = 50 000

n	*Crossover*	*E(R)*	*MTTF*
512	122.70	245.4	48.8
1 024	61.35	122.7	24.4
2 048	30.67	61.4	12.2
4 096	15.34	30.7	6.1
8 192	7.67	15.3	3.1
16 384	3.84	7.7	1.5
32 768	1.92	3.8	0.8
65 536	0.96	1.9	0.4

Failure Rate μ = 100 000

n	*Crossover*	*E(R)*	*MTTF*
512	245.40	490.8	97.7
1 024	122.70	245.4	48.8
2 048	61.35	122.7	24.4
4 096	30.67	61.4	12.2
8 192	15.34	30.7	6.1
16 384	7.67	15.3	3.1
32 768	3.84	7.7	1.5
65 536	1.92	3.8	0.8

Acknowledgment

This work was supported in part by the DARPA AMSP project and in part by the State of Michigan RE/ED project.

References

Fang Z., Li X. and Ni L. (1986). Parallel algorithms for 2D convolution. In *Proc. of the 1986 Int. Conf. on Parallel Processing*, pp. 262–9. Chicago IL, August 1986

Garcia-Molina H. (1982). Elections in a distributed computing system. *IEEE Trans. on Comp.*, **C-31**(1), 48–59

Grunwald D.C. and Reed D.A. (1986). *Benchmarking hypercube hardware and software.* Technical Report, UIUCDCS–R–86–1303, University of Illinois at Urbana-Champaign

Gustafson J.L., Hawkinson S. and Scott K. (1986). The architecture of a homogeneous vector supercomputer. In *Proc. of 1986 Int. Conf. on Parallel Processing*, pp. 649–52. Chicago IL, August 1986

Hayes J.P., Mudge T.N., Stout Q.F., Colley S. and Palmer J. (1986). Architecture of a hypercube supercomputer. In *Proc. of 1986 Int. Conf. on Parallel Processing*, pp. 653–60. Chicago IL, August 1986

Hillis D. (1985). *The Connection Machine.* Cambridge MA: MIT Press

Hills D. and Steele G. (1986). Data parallel algorithms. *CACM,* **29**(12), 1170–83

Hummel R. and Zucker S. (1984). On the foundations of relaxation labeling processes. *PAMI,* **PAMI-5**(3), 267–87

Hwang K. and Briggs F. (1984). *Computer Architecture and Parallel Processing.* New York: McGraw-Hill

Lamport L., Shostak R. and Pease M. (1982). The Byzantine Generals problem, *ACM Transactions on Programming Languages and Systems,* **4**(3), 382–401

McMillin B. and Ni L. (1987). Byzantine fault-tolerance through application oriented specification. In *Proceedings of COMPSAC 87*, pp. 347–53. Tokyo, October 1987

Mohammed J., Hummel R. and Zucker S. (1983). A gradient projection algorithm for relaxation methods. *PAMI,* **PAMI-5**(3), 330–2

Ni L., King C.T. and Prins P. (1987). Parallel algorithm design considerations for hypercube multiprocessors. In *Proceedings of the 1987 Intl. Conf. on Parallel Processing*, pp. 717–20. Chicago IL, August 1987

Schlichting R. and Schnieder F. (1983). Fail stop processors, an approach to designing fault-tolerant computing systems. *ACM Transactions on Computer Systems,* **1**(3), 222–38

Toy W. (1978). Fault-tolerant design of local ESS processors. *Proc. IEEE,* **66**(10), 1126–45

Zoutendijk G. (1976). *Mathematical Programming Methods.* Amsterdam: North-Holland

J. Viitanen
P. Hänninen
R. Saarela and
J. Saarinen

Tampere University
of Technology

15 · An efficient method for image pattern matching

Chamfer matching is a method for identifying and locating predetermined objects in 2D arrays. The method is reported to be very tolerant to noise due to the cumulative error calculation. This chapter will describe an efficient implementation of it for estimating rotational and translational parameters. It is suitable for use in vision systems where fast execution is essential, but where the scenes to be analyzed may be noisy and occluded. The algorithms can easily be vectorized for parallel execution.

15.1 Introduction

Template matching is one of the basic tools of pattern recognition. It is used for comparing objects of previously known shape with a scene, to find the closest match with the object. The results of such matching are the parameters of the geometric transformations of the best match of the applied model, and some measure of the fidelity of the match. It is a straightforward method, but its applicability in practice with 2D images is usually considered very costly in terms of processing time. This chapter will offer solutions for this problem in a three-parametric case with unknown rotation and *xy*-translation of the model in a scene.

Chamfer MAtching (CMA) is a proposed method for performing the template match. It uses a Distance Transform (DT) in order to generate a proper cost for the matching. A DT is an iterative method for calculating an approximation of a true Euclidean distance from a given reference point. It is used in order to speed up the calculation. The CMA is reported to be tolerant to both noise and occlusion, due to the cumulative method for error calculation. However, the basic CMA is quite unpractical in the original form. Therefore, Borgefors [1] has further developed it, using hierarchical resolution pyramids for stepwise execution: the matching process is first carried through in a lower resolution array with fewer starting points and positions, and fewer feature points for calculation. The calculation is then continued in higher resolution, until an exact match is reached. This HCMA method saves processing time and yields reliable results.

There are not many practical implementations of the HCMA: it is still too slow for real-time operations: [1] reports several tens of seconds of CPU time on a

DEC-10 mainframe for a three-parametric case. Our results show that, using efficient algorithms, the time can be lowered to a few seconds on a signal processor without the need for large tables or special arithmetic units; we also show how the algorithms can be vectorized for close to real-time video speed on a parallel processor.

15.2 The matching principle

The principle of the HCMA is described briefly: more details can be found in [1]. The scene to be analyzed is first processed with a proper way to detect relevant features. Then it is transformed to a **distance image**, an image where each pixel is replaced by a value which is proportional to the distance from the position of the pixel to the nearest feature point. In practice, various DTs are used, because the true Euclidean distance is very costly to compute. An example of such a distance image is in Figure 15.3, where a completely black pixel corresponds to a value 0, and completely white to 255.

The model to be compared against the scene, called also the **polygon**, is a list of coordinates of representative points of the original pattern of the model. The number of coordinates may be reasonably low, if they are selected well. The matching is performed by transforming the polygon to different translated, rotated, scaled or tilted locations, depending on the number of parameters in the recognition situations. We study the three-parametric problem of translation with respect to x- and y-axes and rotation. The transformed polygon point coordinates are used to address the distance image; the values of the selected pixels are accumulated (or squared and accumulated), and this single value is a measure of the closeness of the fit: with perfect fit it will be zero. This process is repeated with proper steps in the parameter values of the transform.

One can readily find that the problem is of an order n^x, where x is the number of parameters, and n the number of pixels in each dimension. Already, a three-parametric problem will be very costly in terms of computation time with the dimensions of real images. Therefore, in HCMA the process is first executed in images of reduced resolution. A number of the coordinates of the best candidates are then passed from the lower resolution (higher level) image pyramid stage to the next higher resolution stage, until the original distance image is reached. If the image pyramid is formed such that every four pixels in the lower level correspond to one pixel at the higher level, we have to examine the corresponding four neighbouring positions at the lower level for every candidate passed from the upper level.

15.3 Methods for fast calculation of the HCMA

Despite the hierarchical method of calculation, there are still some factors that slow down the execution of the matching: the geometric transformations of the model polygon are quite costly, and the dimensionality of a practical three-parametric problem is high. Therefore, we have developed a fast method for estimating the angle of rotation of the trial match positions that is especially suitable for parallel execution. Using this method we can virtually get rid of the third parameter, and reduce the problem to a two-parametric one. This method is described in the following. We have also developed a scanning method, which makes polar coordinate calculations faster.

In HCMA, the model image is scanned and transformed to a polygon approximation with coordinate pairs of each of (or a reduced number of) the featùre pixels. When the matching is done, distance image pixels are fetched and accumulated from the specified rotated and translated coordinate positions of the scene to be analyzed. The geometric transformations involved are very costly, if other than pure translation is used. To get rid of the rotational transforms, one can do the calculations in polar form, but then the polar coordinate transform must be provided and that is also costly. On the other hand, if we are able to order the calculation properly, so that only one of the parameters of the polar coordinate representation is varied while scanning, the calculation can be simplified. In this case, we found that we could utilize the properties of the 3–4 DT for developing a simple rule for approximately equal distance circular scanning of the scene. Thus only the angular variable has to be evaluated every step; these values can be stored in a reasonably small array for the whole model window. More about this subject is presented in [2].

The principle of recognizing objects by the ordering of their features in polar coordinate space has been proposed in several papers, for instance Gupta [3]; in this case, the use of this property with the distance image gives a very natural, single, cumulative cost figure.

The estimation is based on the following formulation: we denote by $F(x,y)$ the scene to be analyzed after the distance image calculation, and $G(v, w)$ the model to be matched, both in rectangular coordinates. Both are discrete 2D arrays. $G(v, w)$ is a binary image with 1s at the valid model feature points and 0s otherwise. The corresponding polar coordinate forms are: $F(\alpha, r, x, y)$ and $G(\beta, h)$, where α and β are the angles with respect to the x and y axis, and r and h are the distances from the origin of the window where the calculation is carried out; x and y are the rectangular coordinates of the origin of the window in the scene. The estimation involves a summation of the following form:

$$A(\alpha, x, y) = \frac{1}{NM(n)} \sum_{n=1}^{N} \sum_{m=1}^{M(n)} F(\alpha - \beta(n, m), h(n), x, y)\, G(\beta(n, m), h(n)) \qquad \textbf{(15.1)}$$

where N steps are taken over the valid (discrete) radial distance, and $M(n)$ is the number of feature pixels used in the calculation from the distance n. The angle α that corresponds to the minimum of A is taken as the best orientation of the model at position x, y.

In this form, the method does not offer much improvement over the straightforward one, but there are several simplifications to be done. G is a sampling function: only those values of n and m, which correspond to values of $G = 1$ are needed, and these can be arranged in a table at the beginning of the calculation for all the subsequent translational positions. Another simplification comes from the fact that usually we do not need all the model pixels for the matching, and we can take fixed $M(n) = M$ for the whole calculation. In our experiments, $M = 2$ was found to be sufficient. When both N and M are fixed, the calculation can be done effectively on an array processor.

Instead of the sampling-accumulation function (Equation 15.1) one could also accumulate the normal circular cross-correlation function:

$$A(\delta, x, y) = \frac{1}{NM} \sum_{n=1}^{N} \sum_{m=0}^{M-1} F\left(\frac{2\pi m}{M} - \delta, h(n), x, y\right) G\left(\frac{2\pi m}{M}, h(n)\right) \tag{15.2}$$

Now G should not be a sampling function, but a distance image similar to F to get good values for A. Therefore Equation 15.2 is much slower to calculate on a normal computer than Equation 15.1. However, there exist hardware convolution/correlation circuits that can calculate the function quickly. This possibility is analyzed later in the section on vectorization. Using Equation 15.2 there is no penalty in using several model points at each distance, so it could give better results in discriminating complicated objects with many feature points. However, in our experiments we used Equation 15.1, because we used one signal processor chip.

In practical calculations, there are several advantages of the method: only one scan through the neighbourhood is needed to find the best rotational fit. No calculation of sine or cosine terms of the rotational transforms of the model coordinates are needed; the table sizes are fixed, thus vector operations are possible. Also, the calculation of the distance from the origin of the window would be very costly, if other than circular scans were used, otherwise several largish tables would be needed: one for the distances of all the positions of the window, and another for the angle values. Also, for proper interpolation of the values in A, slow examination of the neighbouring angle and distance values would be needed.

15.4 The implementation

The pattern-matching method was implemented in a practical image-processing system. The system consisted of a PC AT computer, two Salora SVAM frame buffers with a capacity of 512 × 512 pixels, 8 bits/pel; a video image digitizer and a coprocessor board, that uses one TMS 320E15 signal processor for image processing. The programs were written in a C-type high-level language and compiled by the TAMC [4] compiler made for the TMS 320 family in our laboratory. The innermost loops were optimized by hand in machine language. The size of the complete image analysis program is less than 8 kwords of machine-loadable code.

The programs needed for the analysis can be grouped into four different parts: preprocessing and feature detection, distance image calculation and image pyramid creation, model parameter acquisition, and image scanning and hierarchical matching. Image preprocessing is dependent on the specific application; typical preprocessing could contain noise removal, contrast enhancement etc. Also, features could be detected with various methods; those that give sharp feature points give best results, otherwise several good matches may result. Edge thinning may be needed, if the contrast ratios of the objects vary extensively however, the method is not critical about continuation of the lines, or presence of specific points.

In distance image calculation, we use the sequential method for calculating the DT as described by Borgefors [1]. A 3–4 distance approximation is reasonably fast to calculate, although two passes are needed. The calculation involves sorting and scanning the image line by line. The execution time of this module, together with a four-level image pyramid creation, is 2.9 seconds for a 256 × 256 image, on one TMS 320E15 running at 20 MHz.

15.4.1 Model processing

The models need some preparation before they can be used as reference polygons. Because our method is intended for detection of objects of previously known shape, these operations are done offline, and are not time critical. The alignment of the model in the window is not critical in theory, but because in our program the maximum number of polygon points taken at each distance is two, we should first ensure that at least two points will fall to every usable circle, and that those points will represent the shape well. The scanning program uses simple logical statements to replace the current point by a new one. First a reference point is chosen on the polygon and then the program selects each point on the polygon. The current point is replaced by the next point if the radial distance from the reference point is below a certain threshold and the radial distance from the new point to the reference point is greater than this threshold. Once the good points are selected, they can be stored for use with the matching.

The model scanning module, besides scanning and model vector assembling, does other calculations, too. The model vector stores the information on the rotation angle and the distance between each selected polygon point and the window origin. The distance needs no calculation, because we do the scanning along the 3–4 DT equal distance contours. The angle calculation is based on a series approximation of arctan. Arctan is used rather than arcsin, which is faster to calculate, because the DT estimate is not exact. While scanning the window, the program also forms the angle difference values between successive positions. These values are passed to the matching module for use in the zeroth-order interpolation of the values stored to the vector A.

15.4.2 Matching

The practical implementation of the matching algorithm follows the outline of Section 15.3. We used only a three-level distance image pyramid, because the maximum model size was so small. An important part of the program is the selection of those local minima that are tracked through the levels of the pyramid. The most simple strategy is to select a number of the least minima, pass the coordinates of them to the next lower level, examine the corresponding pyramid neighbourhoods there, again select a number of best ones, etc. This simple strategy (denoted MIN1) has several disadvantages: all the positions at the starting level have to be examined, and there are usually several candidates around a local minimum. Thus, some good positions may have to be rejected due to memory and processing-time limitations. A better strategy is first to examine every nth position at the starting level, then select a number of best minima among them, do the minimization at their neighbourhood, and then proceed as above. This strategy is called MIN2.

The rejection of bad minima speeds up the computation; we use the rejection method developed by Borgefors [1]: the first non-zero minimum of a tracked minimum multiplied by a certain factor (called reject factor hereafter) is used as a reject threshold, against which we compare the difference between the minima of the successive levels. This is based on the observation that the edge distance of the correct position increases at most linearly, but others increase exponentially.

The operations in this program are simple. There are only two divisions with a variable in the program, and those are not in the innermost loops. No multiplications with a variable are used, also the constant multipliers are mostly twos powers; no trigonometric functions, square roots or other complicated functions are needed. The output of the program consists of the lists of the best candidates at each pyramid level, and the best-fitting rotation angle and translational coordinates from the last level.

The structure and parallelization of the matching program

The structure of the matching module is analyzed in this section. The simplified form is given below in C-like notation. The differences due to the minimization at the highest pyramid level are left out. The next-to-innermost loop of the program represents the accumulation of $A(\,)$. Its implementation on a SIMD vector processor would be easy without the innermost loop that is needed for performing a zeroth-order interpolation. This is because the angular difference of each step has a variable length at different distances, and also at different rotation angle positions, due to the discrete tessellation. The innermost loop has a variable length, so vectorization becomes a little more difficult. However, the angle difference values that define the interpolation loop can be tabulated and, with modern signal processors, the control structure of the type of the loop can be executed quickly. The result of the interpolation can be fed to an external vector processor that will do the accumulation.

The availability of fast hardware convolution/correlation ICs, like the INMOS A100, could make the angle estimation formula, Equation 15.2, more attractive than Equation 15.1 in a vectorized approach. That processor can calculate the cross-correlation function with a rate of 2.5 Msamples/second. It can also use feedback so that the interpolation needs to be done only once for a complete correlation function. Furthermore, the summation of Equation 15.2 for the correlation functions of the different distances could be done using a shift register of the length of the A vector. That could connect the output of the correlator to its cascade input, so we could always add the next value of the correlation function to the value from the previous distance.

The speedup in the vectorized form can be estimated. Our present program needs eight CPU cycles for doing the interpolation, and 36 cycles for the accumulation of two model samples. If we assume 16 candidates at the lowest pyramid level, 256/2PI values of angular resolution, and 24 distance steps in the model window, the interpolation + accumulation time is $16 \times 24 \times 256 \times 44 \times 200$ ns $= 0.87$ seconds with our present software version implementing Equation 15.1. Using eight A100s with the feedbacks and a fast host CPU chip, the time to complete Equation 15.2 would be $16 \times 24 \times 256 \times 400$ ns $= 0.04$ seconds without the interpolation; the interpolation can be done in parallel with the correlation calculation, because A100 can swap between its two coefficient registers in full speed. The zeroth-order interpolation time could be about 200–400 ns per sample with the new signal processors, so the total time would also be 0.04 seconds. Thus the speedup in the innermost loops would be of the order of 20. That could be approximately the total speedup factor, because that loop dominates the execution time. The results from Section 15.5 give a total execution time of close to 6 seconds for the matching program: with a speedup factor of 22, we could get that down to 273 ms.

```
main ( ){ /* PSEUDOCODE FOR THE MATCHING MODULE */
  read_the_model_vector ( );
  for (pyramid_level = 3; pyramid_level > 0; --pyramid_level) {
    for (candidate = 1; candidate < 17; ++candidate) {
      read_coordinates_of_candidate_from_higher_level ( );
      for (4_neighbor = 1; 4_neighbor < 5; ++4_neighbor) {
        clear_A( );
        for (distance = 31; distance > 7; --distance) {
          read_the_angle_difference_vector ( );
          set_image_read_address ( );
          for (angle = 0; angle < 2PI; angle += anglestep) {
            read_F[angle]; /* DATA PREFETCH! */
            modify_next_read_address_by_the_scan_rule ( );
            for (angledif = 0; angledif < anglestep; ++angledif) {
              A[angle + angledif - G[distance]] += F[angle];
            }
          }
        }
        search_for_minimum_of_A[ ] ( );
      }
      find_minimum_of_4_neighbor_minima ( );
      check_against_reject_criteria ( );
    }
    store_coordinates_of_minimum_for_next_pyramid_level ( );
  }
  find_minimum_of_the_16_candidates ( );
  output_MIN(A[ ]),_its_coordinates_and_angular_position ( );
}
```

Of course, the speedup using dedicated ICs for executing Equation 15.1 could be even higher, but so far we do not know of any such commercial hardware. The hardware that is able to calculate HCMA in the estimated time (the signal processor with the attached convolution processors) will be commercially available as a PC AT add-on board that is programmable in C language.

The algorithm also suits MIMD-like parallel processors like the TAMIPS [5] developed in our laboratory. On a MIMD multiprocessor, the most straightforward approach for dividing the matching process would be to assign each processor a vertical part of the distance image pyramid. The processors can then perform their own minimization tasks quite independently.

The parallelization of the DT algorithm may not be necessary for real-time operation, because in fact we only need a complete distance image at the lowest resolution level: at other levels only the windows corresponding to selected candidates need to be calculated. Thus, the most time-consuming part in the preprocessing is the sorting needed for the creation of the pyramid. This operation is difficult to vectorize (on a typical image processor), so a MIMD architecture would be needed.

15.5 Experimental results of detection with real scenes

Scenes with different objects have been analyzed with the hierarchical pattern-matching program package. Figure 15.1 shows one such scene after preprocessing and edge detection, as displayed on the frame store display. As we can see in the scene, the edge-detection algorithm was not at all optimal, the contrast ratios have been different with the different objects, giving very thick edges for some of them, while some of them have missing parts of the edges; the situation is thus very realistic. In practice, ideally thin and continuous edges are difficult to achieve. The rotation angle of the scene in this case, after two passes of the DT, was 180 degrees with respect to the model.

Figure 15.2 shows the model polygons. The maximum number of model points in the present program is 48 (not all the displayed points have to be used). In this case, the models were subsets of the scene, but this is not a limitation of the method. The reason for using model points that were extracted from the scene was that this way, we could get a controlled reference for comparisons with the cases where we have degraded the scene with additive or subtractive noise. The basic method and its tolerance to occlusion has been tested in previous work.

Figure 15.3 shows the scene after subsequent processing with the distance transform program. The same figure shows the four levels of the hierarchical image pyramid, too. In the following sections we first give the results of the measurements of the execution times of the matching program for one model, then we show the results of matching with the shown scene and models in various cases.

15.5.1 Execution speed

Execution speed of the matching program was measured using one TMS 320E15. The two different minimization strategies were tried: MIN1 scanned every translational position at the highest pyramid level of a three-level pyramid (the last case

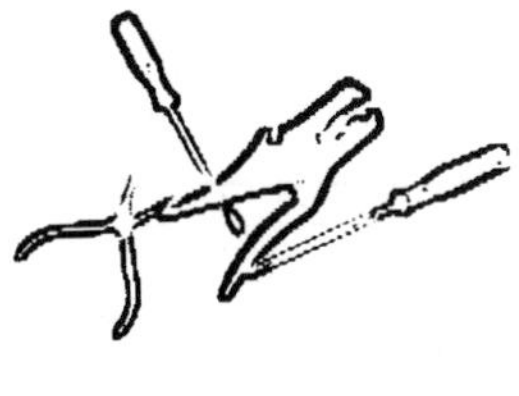

Figure 15.1
A scene after edge detection and thresholding.

Figure 15.2
The model polygons used in the matching: 'pliers', 'screwdriver1', 'stripax', and 'screwdriver2'. (All the points were not necessarily used; the maximum amount at each distance was 2.)

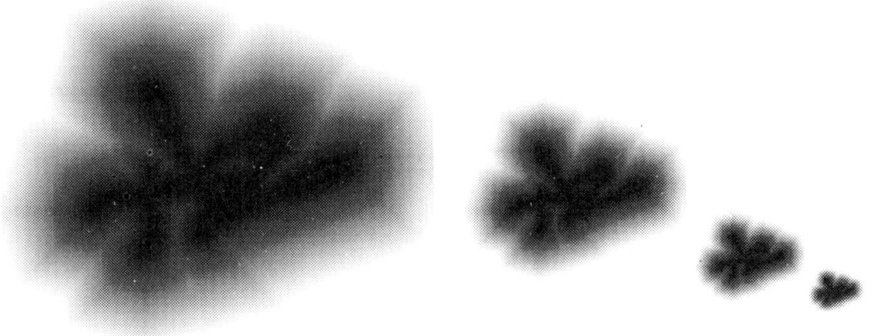

Figure 15.3
The distance image at different resolution levels of the pyramid.

used a four-level one), then the number of best candidates was indicated in each case at the lower levels. MIN2 first scanned one position of a 2-by-2 neighbourhood, selected 16 best candidates, then selected the best matching one of the neighbourhood positions of the candidates at the highest and subsequent lower levels. The rejection method described before was applied, so the number of candidates was reduced at lower levels of the pyramid, as indicated in each case. A three-level pyramid was used, too. The scene had four objects: a paper clip, a key, a machine screw and a coin. 30 points of the model were used, no noise was added to the scene, and it had no occluded objects. Scene dimensions were 256 × 256 pixels, 8 bits/pel. The measured execution times are shown in Table 15.1, assuming 20 MHz clock frequency.

The results show that MIN2 was much faster. The main reason was the lower number of scanned positions at the highest pyramid level. In MIN1, the time spent at the highest level was about 3/4 of the total time. If we could use a four-level pyramid, the execution time would be much lower. However, the four-level pyramid will be suitable only if larger model sizes are used. In some cases, MIN1 gave more accurate results than MIN2, because it could give several candidates around a local

Table 15.1 Execution times of the matching programs for one object.

MIN1 minimization

Number of candidates	*Execution time (s)*	*Notes*
18	19.3	
10	16.8	
6	15.6	
18	4.92	four-level pyramid; the detection failed

MIN2 minimization

Reject factor	*Execution time (s)*	*Number of candidates at each pyramid level*	*Notes*
2.5	7.95	16, 14, 2	
2.0	6.81	16, 10, 2	
2.5	6.25	16, 7, 5	noisy scene

minimum, and thus guarantee that the correct one was found at the lower levels. However, the maximum amount of candidates was so low that good ones could be rejected at the highest level; so generally MIN2 was found to be more reliable, and it was also used in the other tests in this chapter.

15.5.2 Recognition performance

Results of matching with the 'tools' scene are given in Table 15.2. MIN2 minimization was used. The scene consisted of four objects, 'pliers', 'stripax', 'screwdriver1' and 'screwdriver2' as shown in Figure 15.1. The cross-matching tables are given below for two cases: first, without noise, then in Table 15.3 with noise: 28% of all pixels were turned to false edge pixels, then filtered with a median filter. In each case the reject factor was 3.0, except for the screwdrivers in the noisy scene, when it was 2.5. Each figure of the first four columns gives the average distance of the MODEL from the object shown on the top of the column at the three pyramid stages. Note, that because the objects are located very close to each other, some overlapping, all except the correct match may be located somewhere in between the objects. So the others are merely spurious locations, which are selected to represent the closest object in the scene.

The other columns have the following meanings: the difference from the correct angular position is given in bits; the resolution was 256 bits/2PI. Next, the number of candidates at each level of the pyramid is shown (maximum = 16). This shows the effectiveness of the reject criterion with the given model shape. Next, the ranking of the final correct position among the 16 best ones selected at the highest level is given. This gives some estimate on the sensitivity of the method on how easily the correct shape is confused with others at the highest level: if the correct models frequently rank low, we should start at the lower level of the pyramid. The last column, showing if all the starting positions are zero, has a similar kind of meaning,

Table 15.2 The cross-matching table with four tools matched one at a time with a scene.

		Pliers	*Strip*	*Sdr1*	*Sdr2*	*Error of angle estimate (bits)*	*Number of candidates*	*Start rank among 16 best*	*All start minima = 0*
	level 3	0.17	0.00				16		
Pliers	2	0.18	0.36				7		
	1	0.44	0.59			2	7	12	no
	level 3		0.08				16		
Stripax	2		0.04				2		
	1		0.00			0	2	1	no
	level 3	0.00	0.00	0.00	0.00		16		
Sdriver1	2	0.19	0.58	0.20	0.27		7		
	1	0.48	0.72	0.24	0.41	0	6	1	no
	level 3	0.00	0.00	0.00	0.00		16		
Sdriver2	2	0.13	0.42	0.32	0.13		12		
	1	0.48	0.63	0.50	0.34	3	10	1	no

Table 15.3 The cross-matching table, with noise added to the scene.

		Pliers	*Strip*	*Sdr1*	*Sdr2*	*Error of angle estimate (bits)*	*Number of candidates*	*Start rank among 16 best*	*All start minima = 0*
	level 3	0.00	0.00	0.00	0.00		16		
Pliers	2	0.17	0.04	0.26	0.23		16		
	1	0.06	0.11	0.76	0.56	0	16	2	yes
	level 3	0.00	0.00	0.00	0.00		16		
Stripax	2	0.50	0.13	0.58	0.53		15		
	1	1.02	0.05	1.07	0.94	1	10	11	no
Sdriver1	level 3	0.00	0.00	0.00	0.00		16		
(reject	2	0.68	0.00	0.10	0.18		16		
factor = 2.5)	1	0.95	0.33	0.27	0.39	0	10	3	yes
Sdriver2	level 3		0.00	0.00			16		
(reject	2		0.21	0.17			16		
factor = 2.5)	1		0.61	0.28			4		yes

but it also hints if there are too many feature points in the scene to be analyzed, and if thinning or noise removal should be used prior to the distance image calculation.

Discussion of the results

From the match distances we note that, in the noiseless case, the method gave very good position and rotation angle estimates for all four models. It could always discriminate the correct object from the others, even in the case of the two screwdrivers, which are very similar. As could be expected, the margin of recognition was largest when matching the 'stripax' figure with the scene, because its shape was so different from the others: all the spurious positions were rejected already, when going to the second level of the pyramid (the other candidate listed was a close position to the correct one). Also, we could expect that the margins with the screwdrivers were small: they fit quite well, not only with each other, but also with several other positions in the scene.

Unexpectedly, the margin with the pliers was also quite small, especially with the stripax figure. The reason for this was found to be in the model point selection program: the simple logic in selecting the maximum of two points from each distance seemed to pick the model points mostly from the first two legs of the pliers in the scanning order. With some manual deletion of points from the legs of the model, we could achieve even that successful model as is shown in the table.

The noisy scene was generated in the following way: we added spurious (edge) feature pixels, an amount of 28% of the total pixel count to the scene at random positions (Figure 15.4). Then we used a median-type filter with a mask size of 3 × 3 pixels to filter out the noise. The filter type was 2LH+, using the notation of Nieminen *et al.* [6], who also give the filter characteristics. The edge image was filtered several times, until the root signal was achieved, that is, until no differences

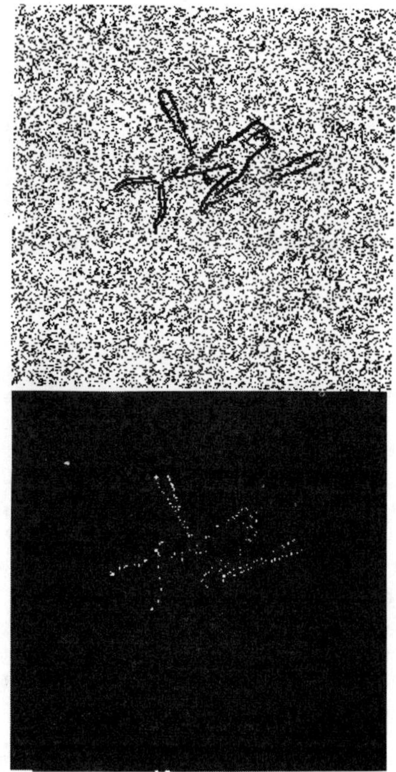

Figure 15.4
This sequence shows how the method can locate objects in a very noisy image: the first image (top left) shows a noisy scene: 28% of the pixels of the image have been randomly turned to false edge points. The next image shows the scene after processing with a 3 × 3 median-type filter and the last displays the models written on the distance image at the detected locations and orientations.

could be observed between successive filter outputs. Because the noise amount was so high, the root signal still contained many noise pixels, as can be seen in the next image in Figure 15.4. About 2% of the total pixel count of the frame were spurious edge pixels. Of course, the original edge image was also deteriorated by the filter: in some points, the edge has thickened, while in some parts, isolated or corner points have been removed. The resulting scene will be very difficult for any type of pattern recognition method.

The same models were applied as in the former case, and the cross-matching Table 15.3 is shown. In this case, all but the occluded screwdriver were located successfully. In that case, the result of the detection was the other screwdriver, so even then the method gave sensible, though incorrect results. The other screwdriver has also a very low margin: the stripax and the other screwdriver were also very close at the final stage. As could be expected, every case shows an increase in the number of spurious candidates.

The weak point of the detection has been at the highest pyramid level: most cases show that all the selected initial candidate positions have had an edge distance of zero, so we can expect that there were still several positions with zero distance that were rejected. So we should have had more initial candidates or we should have started at a lower level, which would have quadrupled the processing time. That was probably the reason for the negative result with the last object.

Otherwise, the performance of the method was practically unaffected by the noise: in the case of the pliers, the average distance was even lower than in the former case, and the angle estimate had no error. This may have been due to the fact that its otherwise small edge image has grown at the higher resolution thereby attracting more candidates, among which has been a better one than before. Although all the models could not be located, if matching was done one model at a time, we succeeded by first matching those models that had more distinct features and then removing their points from the distance image. The result of matching with the selected model points written on the distance image as white dots is shown in the last image of Figure 15.4.

15.5.3 The scene with randomly eroded features

The results of Table 15.4 are also quite interesting. In this case, we randomly deleted 60% of the points of the scene edge images, as is shown in Figure 15.5. As might be expected, all the achieved final edge distances are higher than in Table 15.2. However, for the easily detected objects, the pliers and strippers, the results were still quite good. With the screwdrivers the situation was much worse. Both cases were practically impossible to detect. The results with the first one show that the detection did not succeed, although we tried several different combinations of the model points. With the second one, we were able to find some combinations that were successful. One such position is shown in the table. It was interesting to see that when the same model points were tried in the original scene without the erosion, the

Table 15.4 The cross-matching table with scene features eroded by noise: 60% of the edge pixels were removed randomly.

		Pliers	*Strip*	*Sdr1*	*Sdr2*	*Error of angle estimate (bits)*	*Number of candidates*	*Start rank among 16 best*	*All start minima = 0*
	level 3	0.25	0.00				16		
Pliers	2	0.48	0.04				2		
	1	0.83	1.23			2	2	10	no
	level 3		0.17				16		
Stripax	2		0.57				3		
	1		0.67			1	2	1	no
	level 3	0.00	0.00	0.00	0.00		16		
Sdriver1	2	0.40	0.50	0.55	0.50		6		
	1	1.31	0.87	1.09	1.29		6	1	no
	level 3				0.00		16		
Sdriver2	2				0.30		2		
	1				0.77	0	1	2	no

NOTE: Sdriver1 and Sdriver2 used some different points of the model than in Tables 15.2 and 15.3, so the results are not completely comparable with the results of those tables.

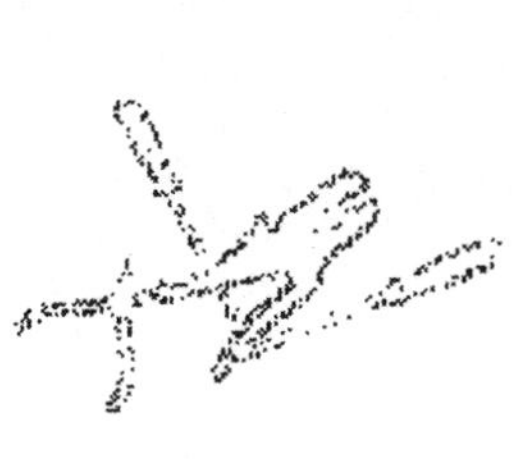

Figure 15.5
The scene and the corresponding distance image of Figure 15.1 after randomly deleting 60% of the scene edge pixels.

detection failed! Although this situation is quite a special one, it may give us a hint that in some cases this kind of 'random thinning', or erosion, may be even advantageous: if there are false objects with thick edges in the scene, the effect of these may be lowered in favour of the correct objects with thin edges at the higher pyramid levels using this kind of preprocessing. Naturally, the effect would be much better if the operation could be done by equalizing the number of edge pixels within a certain window.

Conclusion

The algorithms and the implementations described here have many good properties: they do not assume any special shape for the objects to be recognized, and are tolerant of occlusion, noise and discontinuities in the features. The implementation can be made fast, robust, and can utilize parallel hardware for applications requiring still faster operation.

Acknowledgement

This work was supported by the Academy of Finland.

References

1. Borgefors G. (1986). *On Hierarchical Edge Matching in Digital Images Using Distance Transformations*. Dissertation TRITA-NA-8602, The Royal Institute of Technology, Stockholm, Sweden
2. Viitanen J., Hänninen P., Saarela R. and Saarinen J. (1987). Hierarchical pattern matching with an efficient method for estimating rotations. In *Proc. 1987 IEEE Industrial Electronics Society Conference, IECON '87*, Cambridge MA, November 1987

3. Gupta L. and Srinath M.D. (1987). Invariant planar shape recognition using dynamic alignment. In *The 1987 International Conference on Acoustics, Speech, and Signal Processing*, Dallas TX, April 1987
4. Viitanen J., Salo J., Vanni P., Hänninen P. and Campbell G. Developing applications for the parallel TAMIPS image processor. In *The 8th International Conference on Pattern Recognition*, Paris, France, October 1986
5. Viitanen J. and Vanni P. (1985). The TAMIPS multiprocessor. In *International Conference on Parallel Processing*, Chicago IL, August 1985
6. Nieminen A., Heinonen P. and Neuvo Y. (1987). A new class of detail-preserving filters for image processing. *IEEE PAMI,* **PAMI-9**(1), 74–90

16. A parallel algorithm for object localization within the binocular visual field

D.H. House

Williams College, MA

The model described addresses the problem of simultaneously identifying and localizing a single object within the binocular visual field. As such, it treats a special case of the general depth-perception problem. The model was developed as part of a larger effort to understand the depth-perception abilities of frogs and toads, and is particularly suited to prey catching. It makes use of binocular disparity to determine depth, with lens accommodation providing information to disambiguate the binocular matching process. True to its biological roots, the model treats object identification and localization as two processes, implemented over parallel architectures, operating simultaneously within a feedback loop. Information derived from the object identification process defines points to be binocularly matched. Binocular matching provides a focal-length setpoint for accommodating the lenses. In turn, accommodation changes the visual input to the identification process. The natural feedback of this goal-seeking system heavily favors correct binocular matches and leads to the discarding of spurious matches.

Computer simulations are used to demonstrate the model's ability to handle various visual configurations correctly. Physiological, anatomical and behavioral support for the model's relevance to the original biological problem is also provided.

16.1 Introduction

The model described here had its beginnings in an attempt to understand the computational framework underlying the **depth-perception** abilities of anuran amphibians (frogs and toads). Early in the study, efforts were made to adapt mammalian depth-perception models to the task. Mammalian models all posit the presence of narrowly tuned disparity detectors in the visual system, whose purpose is to measure displacements between local features in right- and left-eyed images. These models also assume that the goal of depth perception is to build a depth map of the visual field (Dev, 1975; Hirai and Fukushima, 1978; Marr and Poggio, 1979), that can be interrogated by the brain to coordinate visuomotor tasks. This point of view is appropriate to the mammalian system, where pathways from the eyes to the visual cortex provide the brain with overlapping stimulus patterns from the right and left eyes.

However, frogs and toads do not have the anatomical and neurophysiological features necessary to support such a disparity-based, global, depth-mapping process. They have neither the ability to verge their eyes nor a distinct foveal region of the retina. Thus, there is no means by which a portion of a scene can be fixated and analyzed via sharply-tuned neural disparity detectors. Instead, their eyes are fixed (Grüsser and Grüsser-Cornehls, 1976) and receptors are comparatively evenly distributed over the retinal surface (Fite and Scalia, 1976). Figure 16.1 shows the main visual pathways of frogs and toads. Unlike mammals, the optic nerves cross completely at the optic chiasm, sending nearly all fibers to contralateral brain regions (Scalia and Fite, 1974). The main optic nerve projection site is the optic tectum, which thus lacks direct binocular input. The only ipsilateral input to a lobe of the tectum comes indirectly via a relay through the nucleus isthmi (NI in the figure) from the opposite tectal lobe (Grobstein and Comer, 1983). Since there is no direct binocular input, it is not surprising that the binocularly sensitive neuronal units that have been located in tectum (Raybourn, 1975) are not finely tuned for specific disparities. Instead, their firing rate appears to be controlled by total input across broad receptive fields. The tectum seems to be the main player in **prey acquisition** (Ingle, 1977), while the visual role of the thalamus appears to be mainly in barrier detection and navigation (Ingle, 1982). The thalamus is not considered further here.

Notwithstanding their lack of typical mammalian binocular machinery, frogs and toads are binocular animals and prefer binocular cues for depth perception, at least when localizing prey in the frontal visual field. This was shown conclusively by Collett (1977) in a series of experiments in which he mounted lenses and prisms in front of the eyes of the toad *Bufo marinus* to dissociate monocular and binocular depth cues. He was able to approximate observed prey-snapping errors with a linear formula that assigned a 94% weighting to binocular cues and only a 6% weighting to monocular cues.

However, a later study by Collett and Udin (1983) demonstrated that it is unlikely that toads use binocularity to build a global depth map for prey catching. Large lesions were made to the nucleus isthmi of toads (*Bufo marinus*), in order to sever the major source of binocular input to the optic tectum. Presumably, without

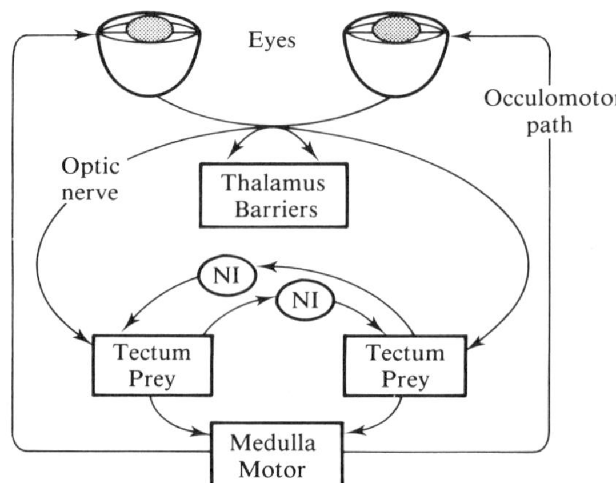

Figure 16.1
Frog/toad visual pathways.

these connections tectal binocular units would be deprived of their ipsilateral visual input, thus rendering them useless for any disparity-based depth-mapping process. Nevertheless, toads with these lesions are as accurate as controls in snapping at prey, and experiments with prisms showed that lesioned toads continue to use binocular depth-cues.

Further complicating the story is the considerable experimental evidence that monocular depth cues from lens **accommodation** play a more significant role in depth perception than Collett's linear analysis indicated. Apparently, these animals can infer depth from the amount of lens distortion needed to achieve a focused image. Although binocular depth cues are overwhelmingly preferred when available, both frogs and toads are able to utilize monocular cues to snap accurately at prey when deprived of binocularity. Monocular frogs (Ingle, 1976) and toads (Collett, 1977) show little reduction in accuracy when snapping at prey ipsilateral to their good eye. Experiments in which drugs were used to disrupt the normal action of the lens accommodation muscles demonstrated that lens accommodation is the most likely source of these monocular depth cues (Jordan *et al.*, 1980).

This preference for binocularity, together with the ability to rely upon monocularity, led us to explore various mechanisms by which these two sources of depth cues could be combined. An earlier model (House, 1982) addressed this goal by augmenting a disparity-based binocular model by Dev (1975) to include a second depth-mapping process driven by monocular depth cues from lens accommodation. The monocular process was coupled to the binocular process in such a way that depth estimates that were similar across the two processes would be reinforced, and those that were dissimilar would be suppressed. Although this model ignored the frog's apparent lack of anatomical and neurophysiological underpinnings for fine resolution of binocular disparity, it did succeed in mimicking the observed behavioral phenomena.

Experiments with this early model led us to conclude that the most powerful way to integrate depth cues from binocular disparity and monocular accommodation is to use the accommodation cues to help disambiguate the binocular correspondence problem (that is, the problem of matching local features between left- and right-eyed images). Lens accommodation provides depth cues that are unambiguous but inherently inaccurate. On the other hand, binocular matching suffers from well-known ambiguities in achieving correspondence but is capable of providing extremely accurate depth cues. Thus, if the coarse-grained accommodation cues are used only to assure correct binocular correspondence, and binocular matches are used to determine depth, full binocular accuracy is obtained but without the attendant uncertainty.

Our current model utilizes accommodation and disparity cues in this way, but departs from our earlier scheme in that it models a dynamic process for the localization of a single prey, rather than a passive process for producing a global depth map. In place of fine-grained local disparity matching, the model chooses and triangulates only a single target point. This process is similar to that observed in the praying mantis (Rossel, 1980). In this scheme, it is posited that each tectal lobe selects a particular visual object and passes its retinal position to a common downstream brain region. This region then uses these two retinal angles to determine the spatial location of that object only.

This system is, of course, subject to making binocular correspondence errors if the two brain sides select different objects. In the next section, we show that correspondence can be assured in all but the most pathological cases by tightly coupling the system in a feedback loop to control lens accommodation, and by the appropriate use of cross-tectal excitatory connections.

16.2 The model

16.2.1 Overview

The functional components of the model consist of a binocular imaging system, pattern recognizers, prey selectors and an accommodation controller. Figure 16.2 depicts these components and how they are interconnected. The lenses are assumed to be coupled so that they are both accommodated to the same depth. It is also assumed that the imagers produce visuotopically mapped output signals whose intensity is dependent upon the high spatial frequency content of the image at that position, and is thus directly affected by how clearly the image is in focus. The pattern recognizers take their input from the imagers and, in turn, provide visuotopically mapped output signals, modulated by the degree to which each region of the image matches recognition requirements. It is assumed that this pattern recognition process is also optimized when the image is in sharp focus. (Underlying these assumptions about both the imagers and the pattern recognizers is the notion that tuned detectors, highly sensitive to light–dark edge contrast, are to be found in both the retina and the optic tectum. This well-accepted notion was first discovered in frogs by Lettvin *et al.* (1959).) The outputs of the pattern recognizers project to the prey selectors. The prey selectors also receive input from cross-coupled connections with each other. The selectors are responsible for identifying the region of the original image that corresponds to the strongest signal from the pattern recognizers. The binocular cross-coupling assists the two selectors to agree upon the same visual object; since they take their input both from the pattern recognizers and from cross-coupling, they are biased in favor of points receiving strong stimulation on both sides of the binocular system. The outputs of the prey selectors are the image coordinates of the selected object. These coordinates project to the accommodation controller where they are used to compute depth from binocular disparity. This depth, in turn, is used to adjust the accommodative state of the lens.

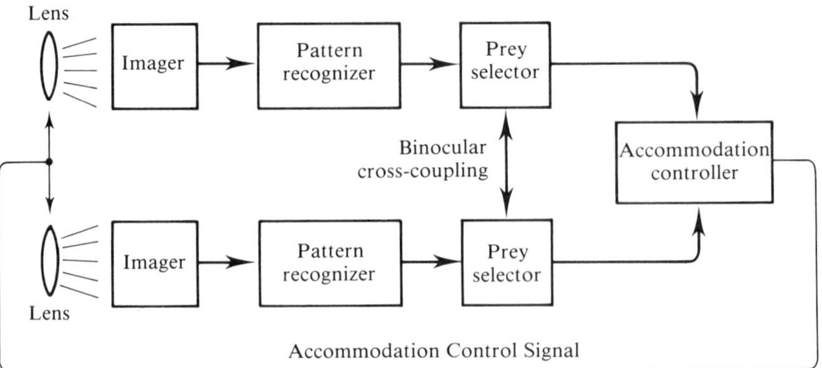

Figure 16.2
Functional diagram of the prey localization model.

Adjusting lens focus completes a feedback loop that, along with the binocular cross-coupling of the prey selectors, assists in the resolution of binocular ambiguity. If both prey selectors have chosen the same object in real space, then the resulting depth estimate will be correct, and the effect will be to adjust the focal length of the lenses to bring this object into sharper focus. The improvement of focus will increase the high spatial frequency content of the image, enhancing the pattern recognition process and improving both the confidence and angular resolution of the recognizer's output. However, if the prey selectors have chosen different objects, the depth estimate will be incorrect and the lens will be driven out of focus. This will affect activity in the pattern recognizers and their new outputs will alter the selection process.

If only a single object is present in the visual field, there will be no source of binocular ambiguity and the system will rapidly localize this object. If multiple objects are present, but at different depths, the action will be to bring one of these objects into clear focus, and again a correct depth estimation will be assured. The more difficult problem of multiple objects at the same depth will be resolved by the cross-coupling of the prey selectors. Thus, the only situations that will be ambiguous will be those in which the visual angle between two objects, at the same depth, is smaller than the resolution of the binocular cross-connections.

16.2.2 Simplifications

For the purposes of this initial study of the model, very simple test scenes were used. These consisted of only one or two elongated textureless stimuli presented in front of a featureless background. The use of such simple input was justified by the ample evidence that real frogs and toads in their normal environment actually 'see' their prey as sharply delineated targets that stand out in distinct relief from the background. For the same reasons, the simulation contains very little detail describing the imager and pattern-recognition stages of the model, while those components dealing with prey selection and binocular matching are addressed in detail. It is a well-known fact that substantial pattern recognition takes place within the retina of the frog. Although it is an overstatement to say that the frog retina is equipped with 'bug detectors', the type 2 net-convexity-detector units identified by Lettvin *et al.* (1959) are remarkably efficient at isolating small moving convex objects, even when they are presented before a complex natural background. Further, there is a less well-known but rather large body of evidence, summarized in House (1984), indicating at least a functional segregation of barrier avoidance to thalamic brain centers and prey catching to the optic tectum. Taken together, this evidence suggests that in frogs and toads, there is at least one information pathway in the brain providing visual information that is both highly selective for prey and relatively free from background confusion.

When designing the simulation program, a further simplification was made in the interests of computational efficiency; the simulation treats only 2D scenes projected onto 1D image planes.

16.2.3 Formal description

The functional elements of the model are represented as layered networks of interconnected cellular components (idealized neurons) that operate in parallel. This

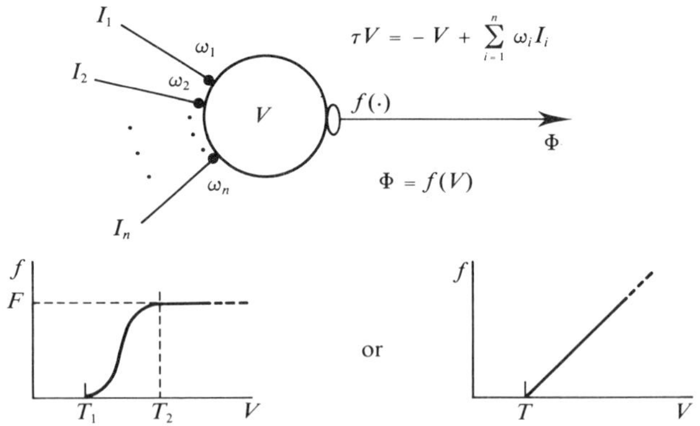

Figure 16.3
Idealized neuron as a computational unit.

representation was adopted so that computational algorithms would be suggestive of possible underlying neural mechanisms. Figure 16.3 depicts a single cellular component. It maintains an internal level of excitation V, that in steady state reaches the weighted (by weights ω_i) sum of its inputs I_i. The rate of change of this level is governed by the time constant τ. The output Φ of a unit is determined by applying a threshold function f to its level of internal excitation. f may take the form of a saturation threshold curve, as shown in the graph on the left, or a piecewise linear curve as shown on the right. In either case, the result is that the cell's output is held to zero until excitation reaches a threshold value. Above this level, output increases monotonically with excitation.

A particularly interesting circuit that can be formed from idealized neurons is the 'winner-take-all' circuit of Figure 16.4. Intercellular connections that end in filled circles are excitatory (positive weight), and those ending in Ts are inhibitory (negative weight). With weights chosen appropriately for the range of the inputs, this circuit will select the maximum of its inputs. It does this by reaching an equilibrium state where the cell receiving maximal input will be above threshold (producing an output), and all others will be below threshold (producing no output).

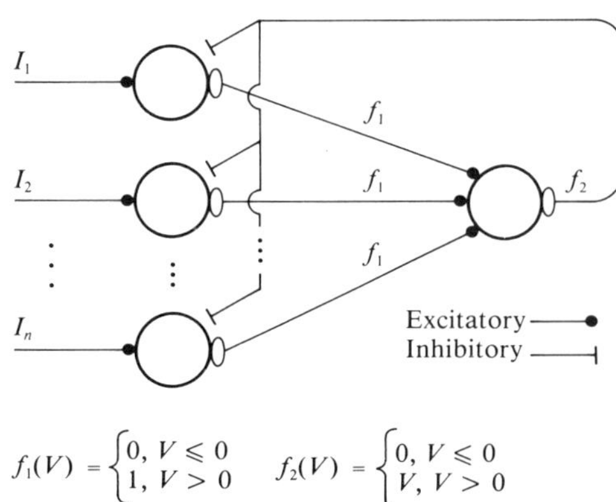

$$f_1(V) = \begin{cases} 0, & V \leq 0 \\ 1, & V > 0 \end{cases} \qquad f_2(V) = \begin{cases} 0, & V \leq 0 \\ V, & V > 0 \end{cases}$$

Figure 16.4
A winner-take-all circuit.

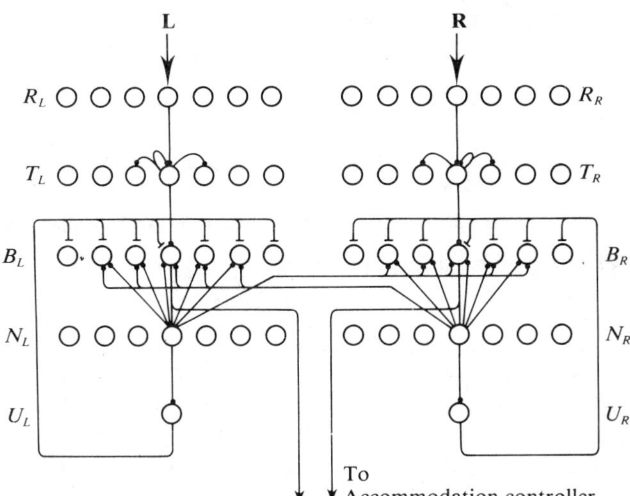

Figure 16.5
Implementation schematic of prey-localization model.

The cellular layers of the prey-localization model are shown in Figure 16.5 as rows of circles. Interconnections are shown as lines emanating from the circles. For simplicity, only output connections from the central cell of each layer are shown; similar connections are made for all other cells in the corresponding layers. Although this diagram shows only seven cells in each layer, the actual computer simulation used 41 cells per layer. The accommodation controller is not modeled as a network and is not shown on this diagram. L is the visual input to the left imager R_L, and R to the right imager R_R. The imagers supply input to the pattern recognizers, T_L and T_R. The prey selection function is performed by the interaction of the binocular layers, B_L and B_R, the relay layers, N_L and N_R and the inhibitory layers, U_L and U_R. These layers together form a winner-take-all network similar to that of Figure 16.4. This network will select the region of maximal excitation in the pattern recognizers but with a binocular bias so that both sides will tend to agree on the same visual object.

The mathematical description of the model approximates the layers of discrete cellular units by continuous analytical equations. However, the spatial integration scheme used to simulate the model restores spatial discretization. This convention was adopted for consistency with previous models (Amari and Arbib, 1977; House, 1984), and to facilitate later, purely analytical investigations. A fuller treatment of the mathematical description may be found in House (1988).

The cell layer representing the imagers simply relays image strength to the pattern recognition layer. The image strength is a function of both the intensity of the incident image and the state of lens accommodation. The effect of lens accommodation on the imagers is simulated by using a Gaussian function to modulate the intensity of the imager's output signal, according to the closeness of the projected point-in-space to accommodation depth. This function uses a non-linear disparity-based depth scale so that the acuity of accommodation cues decreases with depth in a realistic fashion, and nearby objects are more accurately located in depth than far objects. The modulating function representing accommodation in the left eye is given by:

$$A_L(q_L, d) = \exp\{-[(q_L - q_R - d)/(\sigma\, d_{max})]^2 / 2\} \quad \textbf{(16.1)}$$

where:

q_L and q_R are angular positions of the projected point on left and right hemispherical retinas,
d is the accommodation depth being considered (represented on a disparity scale), and
σ is a spread parameter measured per unit of maximum disparity, d_{max}.

An identical formula, modulo an interchange of subscripts L and R, represents accommodation in the right eye.

The pattern recognition mechanism is not modeled in any detail, since we were concerned only with its output. The need for pattern recognition was circumvented by limiting the visual input to a few selected points. The cellular elements of the pattern-recognition layer are modeled as making simple lateral-excitatory interconnections. Therefore, neighboring stimulated points tend to reinforce each other so that the intensity of the recognizer's output in response to an object is a function of both the strength of the signal from the imagers and the retinal angle subsumed by the object. A more realistic implementation of the model would require more sophistication in these layers. The level of excitation in the pattern recognition layers may be represented in analytical form by the integro-differential equations:

$$\begin{aligned}\tau_t \dot{T}_L(q, t) &= -T_L(q, t) + \int w_t(q - \zeta) f_t[T_L(\zeta, t)]d\zeta + K_{at} A_L[q, D_a(t)] \\ \tau_t \dot{T}_R(q, t) &= -T_R(q, t) + \int w_t(q - \zeta) f_t[T_R(\zeta, t)]d\zeta + K_{at} A_R[q, D_a(t)]\end{aligned} \quad \textbf{(16.2)}$$

Profiles of the internal potential in the pattern recognition layers are represented by continuous functions T_L and T_R, with spatial dimension q indicating retinal angle, and t representing time. Internal potential is converted to an external potential (or firing rate) by the saturation-threshold function f_t. The function w_t is a symmetric spread function that describes the extent and strength of the lateral excitatory connections between points in the pattern recognition layers. D_a is the current accommodative state of the lenses, represented on a disparity-based depth scale. It is used, along with retinal angle q, to index maps A_L and A_R of input from the imagers. The pattern recognizers take their input from the imagers through gain K_{at}. The rates of change of potential in layers T_L and T_R are governed by the time constant τ_t. Output from the pattern recognizers projects to a layer of binocular cells.

The binocular cell layer is the layer that actually accomplishes the prey selection. The output of this layer projects both to the accommodation controller and to a relay layer that, in turn, sends connections back to both the ipsilateral and contralateral binocular layers. Cells in the binocular layer sum both these ipsilateral and contralateral signals over broad receptive fields. The input to the binocular layers from the pattern-recognition layer is summed over a narrower receptive field. Thus, the binocular cells are excited by a combination of direct stimulation from the pattern recognizers and indirect binocular input. Stimulation from the pattern recognizers assures high angular acuity, and the binocular input biases the selectors so that they tend to select the same visual object. The binocular layer also receives a global inhibitory signal, proportional to the total excitation over the entire binocular layer.

The combination of excitatory receptive fields and global inhibition produces a network that will suppress activity except at that location receiving the maximum stimulation. This network is similar to one proposed by Didday (1970, 1976) for prey selection in frogs, and formalized by Amari and Arbib (1977). The binocular layers are described analytically by:

$$\begin{aligned}\tau_b \dot{B}_L(q, t) = & -B_L(q, t) + \int w_b(q - \zeta) f_b[B_L(\zeta, t)] d\zeta + I_L(q, t) + \\ & I_R(q, t) + K_{tb} f_t[T_L(q, t)] - K_{ub} g[U_L(t)] \\ \tau_b \dot{B}_R(q, t) = & -B_R(q, t) + \int w_b(q - \zeta) f_b[B_R(\zeta, t)] d\zeta + I_R(q, t) + \\ & I_L(q, t) + K_{tb} f_t[T_R(q, t)] - K_{ub} g[U_R(t)]\end{aligned} \qquad (16.3)$$

Here, B_L and B_R represent internal potential in the binocular layers, f_b is the saturation-threshold function converting internal potential to external potential, w_b is the binocular layer's spread function, and τ_b is its time constant. Inputs I_L and I_R are from the relay layers. The broad spread function associated with these inputs is lumped with the description of the relay layers (see below). The two other inputs are from the pattern recognition layers T_L and T_R through gain K_{tb}, and from the inhibitory layers U_L and U_R through gain K_{ub}.

The relay layer receives its input from the binocular cells and has two distinct outputs, one projecting to the inhibitory layer, and the other to both the ipsilateral and contralateral binocular cell layers. Projections to the inhibitory layer provide that layer with a signal modulated by total activity across the entire binocular layer. Projections to the binocular layers provide the cross-coupling pathways between these two layers. Since the function of the relay layers is simply to pass information to other layers, their transient characteristics can be lumped with those of the other layers. Thus, the equations used to describe the relay layers are equilibrium rather than differential equations, and are given by:

$$\begin{aligned}I_L(q, t) &= \int w_i(q - \zeta) f_b[B_L(\zeta, t)] d\zeta \\ I_R(q, t) &= \int w_i(q - \zeta) f_b[B_R(\zeta, t)] d\zeta\end{aligned} \qquad (16.4)$$

In these equations I_L and I_R represent the potential transmitted by the relay layers to the binocular and inhibitory layers. The function w_i provides the broad spread of relay potential as received by the binocular layers. In order to give the experimenter direct access to a potential representing the relay's inputs to the binocular layers, this spread function was applied directly to the relay layers and not to their inputs to the binocular layers.

The inhibitory layers are single units that simply integrate activity across the entire ipsilateral relay layer. Since the dynamics of the relay layers were not modeled in the simulation, this integration was actually performed over the ipsilateral binocular layer. Thus, the inhibitory layers are described by:

$$\begin{aligned}\tau_u \dot{U}_L(t) &= -U_L(t) + K_{bu} \int f_b[B_L(\zeta, t)] d\zeta \\ \tau_u \dot{U}_R(t) &= -U_R(t) + K_{bu} \int f_b[B_R(\zeta, t)] d\zeta\end{aligned} \qquad (16.5)$$

Here, U_L and U_R represent the internal potentials in the inhibitory layers, and τ_u is the layers' time constant. The gain K_{bu} is applied to the input from the binocular layers.

The mechanism for adjusting lens accommodative state, based on the output of the prey selectors, is depicted in Figure 16.6. The first process carried out in this

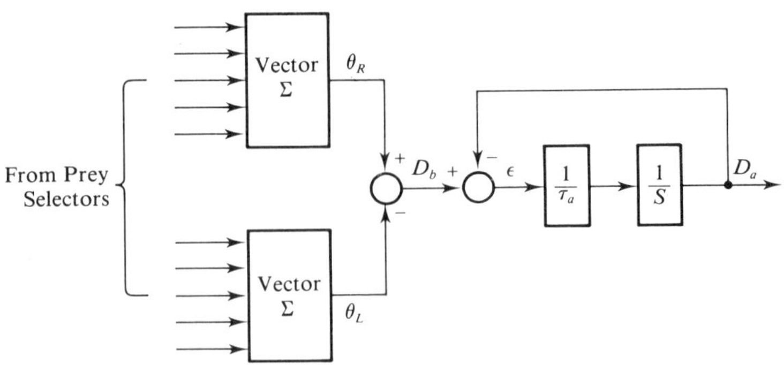

Figure 16.6
The accommodation controller.

mechanism is to identify a pair of image coordinates by determining the center of gravity of the activity pattern on each of the two prey selectors. In this process, the output from each point in the binocular cell layer is treated as a vector in a radial coordinate system, with its angular component representing retinal position and its radial component encoding the likelihood that there is a prey at that position. The vectors from each binocular layer are summed to produce a resultant whose angular component is the retinal position corresponding with the center of gravity, or locus of average excitation, on that side of the visual system. (The notion, employed here, of motor circuits computing a vector sum of their input in order to control output was originally advanced by Pitts and McCulloch (1947). Their hypothesis has found recent confirmation in studies of monkey arm movements by Georgopoulis *et al.* (1983), and cat superior colliculus by McIlwain (1982).) The loci of average excitation q_L and q_R in the binocular layers are determined by the formulae:

$$\theta_L(t) = \tan^{-1} \frac{\int f_b[B_L(\zeta, t)] \sin(\zeta / a) d\zeta}{\int f_b[B_L(\zeta, t)] \cos(\zeta / a) d\zeta}$$

$$\theta_R(t) = \tan^{-1} \frac{\int f_b[B_R(\zeta, t)] \sin(\zeta / a) d\zeta}{\int f_b[B_R(\zeta, t)] \cos(\zeta / a) d\zeta} \qquad \textbf{(16.6)}$$

where the scalar parameter a is simply a conversion factor between visual angle and retinal position. The two retinal angles q_L and q_R determined by this vector summation are subtracted to give disparity and thus a measure of depth, according to the formula:

$$D_d(t) = a[\theta_R(t) - \theta_L(t)] \qquad \textbf{(16.7)}$$

This depth estimate D_d is the setpoint for the controller. The controller's error signal ϵ is computed by subtracting an estimate of current lens accommodative state D_a from this setpoint. The controller's transfer function is simply a first-order lag with time constant τ_a that is meant to incorporate any delay in the controller and the lens-focusing mechanism. The controller is governed by the differential equation:

$$\tau_a \dot{D}_a(t) = -D_a(t) + D_d(t) \qquad \textbf{(16.8)}$$

The accommodation control algorithm will work perfectly in the case when both prey selectors have selected the same visual object. If this has occurred, then the only retinal position excited in each binocular layer will be the one corresponding with the position of the selected prey, and the retinal position from the vector summation will coincide with the position of the prey. Depth can be directly derived from two such retinal positions by triangulation.

However, before the prey selectors have produced such a refined output the pattern of excitation over the binocular layers is usually more complex. In this case, the desired depth, computed from the two centers of gravity, will probably not correspond with the actual depth of the true prey object. It will only be an approximation. This approximate depth will generally help to improve focus and, in turn, assist the prey selectors in converging on a single position.

The accommodation controller also contains a refinement that is not depicted in Figure 16.6. The magnitude of each vector sum is compared with a small threshold. If either magnitude is below this threshold, then the output of the corresponding prey selector is assumed to be too weak to be used to specify a retinal angle. In this case, the desired depth setting of the controller is set to a neutral or rest position.

16.3 Simulation results

16.3.1 Experiments with a single prey stimulus

When only a single prey is present in the visual field, there is no ambiguity in the binocular-matching process and prey localization should be accurate and rapid. Single prey experiments were done to verify that the model would function as expected, and to tune the model's parameters for optimal performance. Figure 16.7 shows typical results from these experiments. Each display shows both a schematic bird's-eye view of the scene and the resulting depth estimate. The square grid represents a 40 cm × 40 cm arena, with 10 cm grid elements. The simulated frog or toad is indicated by the cross-like icon below the arena, with circles indicating eye position. Prey stimuli are represented by solid rectangles within the arena. The lines emanating from the eyes and converging on the prey indicate the current attention-angles of the two eyes, and their point of intersection indicates the model's estimate of the spatial location of the prey. In all such cases, the model converged rapidly and accurately upon the prey stimulus wherever it was placed in the binocular field. The reduction in accuracy for the most distant prey (right-most figure) is within the bounds determined by the grain-size of the simulation.

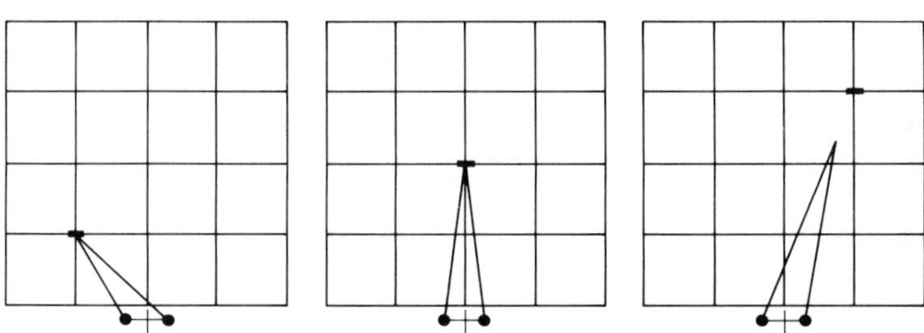

Figure 16.7
Sample results for a single prey.

16.3.2 Experiments with multiple prey stimuli

When multiple prey stimuli are present in the visual field, ambiguities in binocular correspondence arise. Since our model uses lens accommodation to provide additional information to assure correct correspondence, the system is most effective in disambiguating binocular matching when the stimuli are at different depths.

To confirm that our model is successful in correctly interpreting multiple prey configurations, we examined its response to several two-prey configurations where the prey were placed at different distances from the simulated frog. Figure 16.8 depicts typical results from a series of such experiments. The model converged upon a correct depth estimation in all but three of 120 trials.

A much more difficult problem for our model arises when two prey are placed symmetrically about the animal's midline. Since the prey are at the same depth, accommodation cues will not assist in disambiguating binocular matching. However, the crossed pathways between the prey selectors are usually effective in resolving the ambiguity. Even in these somewhat contrived situations, the model, when tuned for optimal performance, produced correct depth estimates for nearly 80% of symmetrical test cases in 120 trials. Further, of the 20% incorrect localizations, most could have been differentiated from correct ones by simple 'reasonability' checks; incorrect localizations often fell behind the eyes, or in locations where at least one eye was not directed towards a prey. The two model parameters that appear to have the greatest effect on response to symmetric presentations are the receptive field width in the binocular layer, and the net input gain in the binocular layer (House, 1984).

16.4 Discussion

Although the model's original intent was to explain biological phenomena, it is interesting in its own right and might be useful as a mechanism for depth perception in robots. Given a limited class of objects to localize and a controlled visual environment, the model could be used as the basis for a simple but powerful object localization scheme. Its internal structure would allow easy implementation in parallel hardware for real-time performance. Additionally, its layers could be programmed as separate modules running independently in separate computing units, and the modules could be individually tailored to suit a wide variety of applications. In particular, the pattern recognizers could be built for optimum performance with

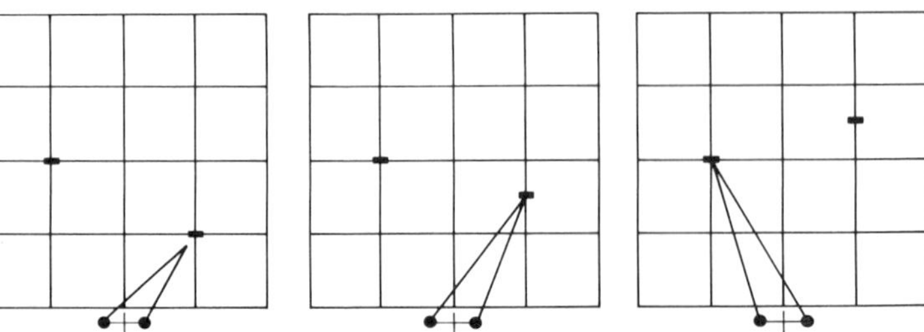

Figure 16.8
Results with two prey at different depths.

application-specific objects without modifying either the imagers, the selectors or the accommodation controller.

It is well known that motion plays a major role in facilitating the prey-catching process in both frogs and toads, but prey motion is ignored in the model as it currently stands. This is not an oversight, but is based on the fact that motion parallax alone cannot provide the absolute depth measurements required for prey catching. Systems that extract absolute depth from motion parallax depend upon known camera motion with respect to fixed targets (Lawton, 1984). This is certainly not the case with frogs, who typically catch prey from a stationary position.

However, it is very likely that motion plays an important role in pattern recognition for prey catching (Ewert, 1976). An interesting extension to the model involving motion would be to use relative motion cues as an additional aid in performing binocular matching. This would not only improve the performance of the model when faced with 'confusing' configurations, but would enhance its ability to deal with scenes involving several potential targets and complex natural backgrounds.

Acknowledgement

This research was support in part by NIH grant NS14971 03–05, M.A. Arbib, principal investigator.

References

Amari S. and Arbib M.A. (1977). Competition and cooperation in neural nets. In *Systems Neuroscience* (Metzler J., ed.), pp. 119–65. New York: Academic Press

Collett T. (1977). Stereopsis in toads. *Nature*, 267, 349–51

Collett T. and Udin S.B. (1983). The role of the toad's nucleus isthmi in prey-catching behavior. In *Proceedings of the Second Workshop on Visuomotor Coordination in Frog and Toad*, Technical Report 83-19, University of Massachusetts Amherst

Dev P. (1975). Perception of depth surfaces in random-dot stereograms: a neural model. *Int. J. Man-Machine Studies*, 7, 511–28

Didday R.L. (1970). The simulation and modelling of distributed information processing in the frog visual system. *Doctoral dissertation*, Stanford University CA

Didday R.L. (1976). A model of visuomotor mechanisms in the frog optic tectum. *Math. Biosci.* 30, 169–80

Ewert J.-P. (1976). The visual system of the toad: behavioral and physiological studies on a pattern recognition system. In *The Amphibian Visual System A Multidisciplinary Approach* (Fite K., ed.). New York: Academic Press

Fite K.V. and Scalia F. (1976). Central visual pathways in the frog. In *The Amphibian Visual System A Multidisciplinary Approach* (Fite K., ed.). New York: Academic Press

Georgopoulis A.P., Caminiti R., Kalaska J.F. and Massey J.T. (1983). Spatial coding of movement: a hypothesis concerning the coding of movement direction by motor cortical populations. In *Neural Coding of Motor Performance* (Masson W., Paillard J., Schultz W. and Wiesendanger M., eds). Berlin: Springer-Verlag

Grobstein P. and Comer C. (1983). The nucleus isthmi as an intertectal relay for the ipsilateral oculo-tectal projection in the frog, *Rana pipens*. *J. Comp. Neurol.*, 217, 54–74

Grüsser O.-J. and Grüsser-Cornehls U. (1976). Neurophysiology of the anuran visual system. In *Frog Neurobiology A Handbook* (Linás R. and Precht W., eds). Berlin: Springer-Verlag

Hirai Y. and Fukushima K. (1978). An inference on the neural network finding binocular correspondence. *Biol. Cybernetics*, 31, 209–17

House D.H. (1982). The frog/toad depth perception system – a cooperative/competitive model. In *Proceedings of the Workshop on Visuomotor Coordination in Frog and Toad*, Technical Report 82-16, University of Massachusetts Amherst

House D.H. (1984). Neural models of depth perception in frogs and toads. *Doctoral dissertation*, University of Massachusetts Amherst

House D.H. (1988). A model of the visual localization of prey by frog and toad. *Biol. Cybernetics*, 58, 173–92

Ingle D. (1976). Spatial visions in anurans. In *The Amphibian Visual System A Multidisciplinary Approach* (Fite K., ed.). New York: Academic Press

Ingle D. (1977). Detection of stationary objects by frogs (*Rana pipiens*) after ablation of the optic tectum. *J. Comp. Physiol. Physchol.*, 391, 1359–64

Ingle D. (1982). The organization of visuomotor behaviors in vertebrates. In *The Analysis of Visual Behavior* (Ingle D.J., Goodale M. and Mansfield R., eds). Cambridge: MIT Press

Jordan M., Luthardt G., Meyer-Naujoks Chr. and Roth G. (1980). The role of eye accommodation in the depth perception of common toads. *Z. Naturforsch.*, 35c, 851–2

Lawton D.T. (1984). Processing dynamic image sequences from a moving sensor. *Doctoral dissertation*, University of Massachusetts Amherst

Lettvin J.Y., Maturana H.R., McCulloch W.S. and Pitts W.H. (1959). What the frog's eye tells the frog's brain. *Proc. IEE*, 47, 1940–51

Marr D. and Poggio T. (1979). A computational theory of human stereo vision. *Proc. R. Soc. Lo. B*, 204, 301–28

McIlwain J.T. (1982). Lateral spread of neural excitation during microstimulation in intermediate gray layer of cat's superior colliculus. *J. Neurophysiol.*, 47, 167–78

Pitts W.H. and McCulloch W.S. (1947). How we know universals: the perception of auditory and visual forms. *Bull. Math. Biophys.*, 9, 127–47

Raybourn M.S. (1975). Spatial and temporal organization of the binocular input to frog optic tectum. *Brain. Behav. Evol.*, 11, 161–78

Rossel S. (1980). Foveal fixation and tracking in the praying mantis. *J. Comp. Physiol.*, 139, 307–31

Scalia F. and Fite K. (1974). A retinotopic analysis of the central connections of the optic nerve in the frog. *J. Comp. Neur.*, 158, 455–78

Section 4

High Performance Image Synthesis

17 · Coarse-grain and fine-grain parallelism in the next generation Pixel-planes graphics system

H. Fuchs
J. Poulton
J. Eyles
T. Greer

University of North Carolina

The current state of the graphics system, Pixel-planes 4 (Pxpl4), and the basic architecture planned for its successor, Pixel-planes 5 (Pxpl5) is described in this chapter. At the time of its introduction (at Siggraph'86 Conference in August 1986), Pxpl4 was one of the fastest machines for near real-time rendering of 3D scenes. In a year of constant use, it has opened new research possibilities, while also being frustrating with its limitations. This chapter introduces the preliminary design of its successor, Pxpl5, which is expected to: (1) be some 20 times faster, (2) overcome many of Pxpl4's limitations by having a much wider range of capabilities and applications, (3) be realized in a desk-height workstation pedestal, and (4) be reproducible in a variety of configurations from a few to a few dozen boards. Both coarse-grain and fine-grain parallelism will be used to realize its expected performance and generality.

17.1 Introduction

17.1.1 Goals for our experimental graphics systems

A primary goal with Pixel-planes has been to provide more effective, near real-time visual interaction for several difficult 3D applications:

(1) Radiation therapy planning for cancerous tumors.

(2) Molecular modeling of complex proteins.

(3) Comprehension of building designs by architects and their clients.

We work closely with colleagues specializing in these three applications to test the effectiveness of our graphics systems. Design decisions for our future systems are based on their specific needs. Thus, although we hope to have graphics systems that are widely useful, we concentrate on specific applications in the belief that more successful systems will result from first satisfying a few specific needs, rather than working in isolation, trying to meet vaguely perceived general needs and hoping that the resulting systems will somehow be useful for many applications.

The most challenging goal from these three applications has been to generate images from 3D scene descriptions in real time or as close to it as possible – certainly at several updates per second. We and our colleagues have found that the comprehension of complicated 3D structures (such as the relationship between a radiation isodose surface and the neighboring anatomy, or the shape of an active site in a protein) is drastically reduced whenever the update time for an object rotation or a cutting-plane move is reduced from, say 0.1 second to 1 second. We also find that comprehension is significantly increased whenever we can combine various 3D depth cues, for example, adding to dynamic object motion (kinetic depth effect) both stereo and head-motion parallax. Unfortunately, such capabilities require still greater graphics computation power. Thus, although the current system, Pxpl4, meets some of these needs more effectively than any other system available today, it is still insufficient for many of our applications' needs. It is largely these and other still unmet goals that inspire us to embark on the design and construction of another generation of Pixel-planes systems.

17.1.2 3D graphics fundamentals

Our systems, as well as most others, use a conventional graphics pipeline organization in which a display list of 3D objects is traversed by a graphics processor, each polygon (or other) primitive is transformed into the screen space, its parts outside the viewing frustum are clipped out, the proper colors as its vertices are calculated, and it is rendered into a frame buffer using a depth-buffer algorithm. (Pixel-planes is often programmed to perform other tasks, but the standard one sketched above is the most common.) Since it has been possible for many years to purchase systems that will generate, in real time, wire-frame versions of quite complex objects, we (and many others) have been concentrating on building systems that solve the back-end bottleneck, the image rendering. For a review of some of these related systems, see Fuchs (1987). A notable new system that had not appeared up to the time of that review and one that devotes dozens of custom processors to the back-end rendering is described in Silicon Graphics (1987) and in Jermoluk and Akeley (1988).

17.2 Current Pixel-planes system (Pxpl4)

17.2.1 System overview

This section presents a short overview of Pxpl4; see Eyles (1987) for a more complete description. The heart of the system, and its most unusual feature, is its frame buffer, which is composed of custom logic-enhanced memory chips that can be programmed to perform most of the time-consuming pixel-oriented tasks at every pixel in parallel (see Figure 17.1). The novel feature of this approach is a unified mathematical formulation for these tasks and an efficient tree-structured computation unit that calculates inside each chip the proper values for every pixel in parallel. The current system contains 512 × 512 pixels × 72 bits/pixel, implemented with 2048 custom 3-micron nMOS chips (63 000 transistors in each, operating at 8 million micro-instructions per second) (see Poulton, 1987). Algorithms for rendering spheres (for molecular modeling), adding shadows, enhancing medical images and rendering objects described by Constructive Solid Geometry (CSG)

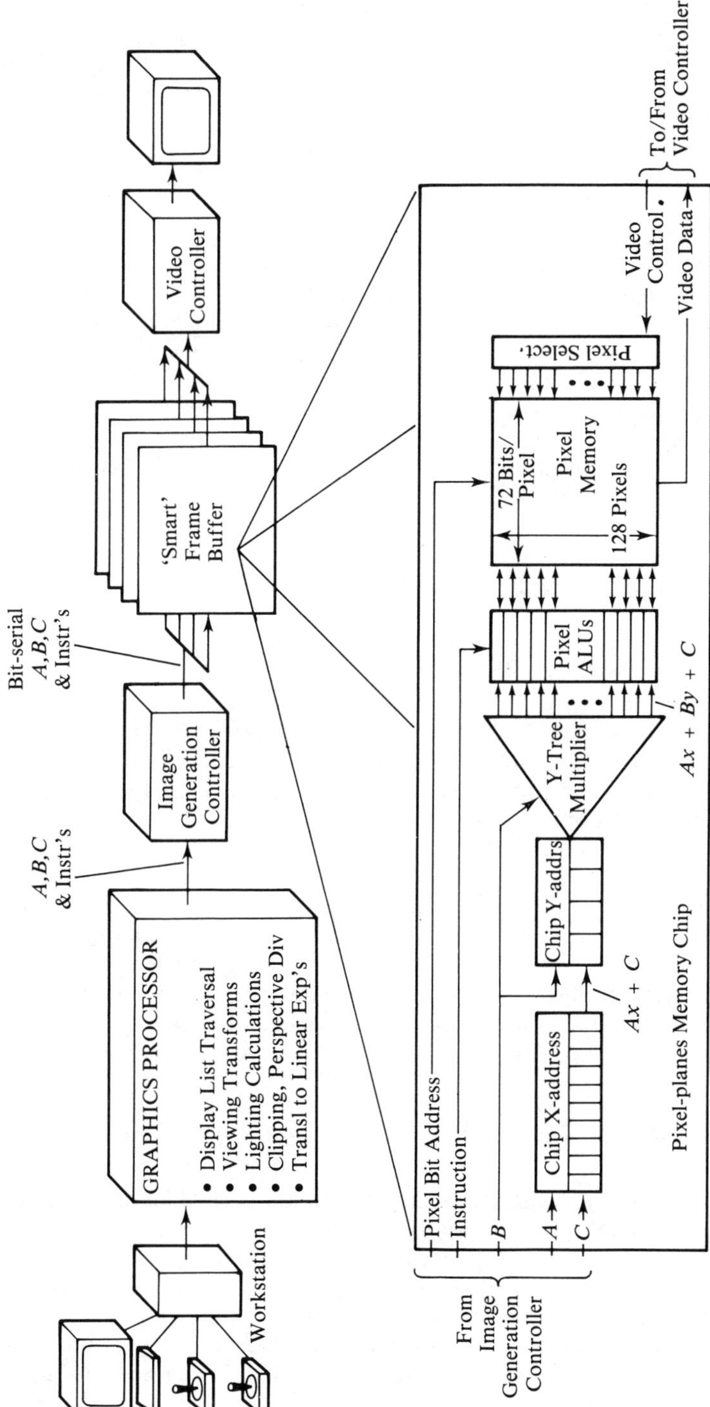

Figure 17.1
Pixel-planes 4 system overview.

directly from the CSG description have been devised by various individuals within and also outside our research group.

The Pxpl4 system is in daily use in our department's computer graphics laboratory, where applications in molecular modeling, medical imaging and architecture are being developed.

Concept

The front part of the system (the part that performs geometric transformations, clipping and lighting calculations) specifies the objects on the screen to the frame buffer in geometric, pixel-independent terms, and the frame-buffer memory chips themselves work from this description to generate the final image. Image primitives such as lines, polygons, and spheres are each described by expressions (and operations) that are 'linear in screen space', that is, by coefficients A, B, C such that the value desired at each pixel is $Ax + By + C$, where x, y is the pixel's location on the screen. Thus the information that is broadcast to the frame buffer is a sequence of sets (A, B, C, instruction), rather than the usual (pixel-address, RGB-data) pairs.

How it works

Pxpl4 contains a fairly conventional 'front end' graphics processor, implemented using the Weitek XL chip set, that traverses a segmented, hierarchical display list, computes viewing transformations, performs lighting calculations, clips polygons (or other primitives) that are not visible and performs perspective division. It then translates the description of each object into the (linear coefficients and op-codes) form of data for the 'smart' frame buffer. An image generation controller converts the word-parallel data and instructions into the bit-serial form required by the enhanced memory chips. A video controller scans out video data from the frame buffer and refreshes a standard raster display. The system is hosted by a conventional UNIX workstation that supports the system's user interface through various graphics input devices and that provides system programming tools (for example graphics libraries, microcode assemblers, language compilers). During system initialization, the host downloads microcode and setup information to Pxpl4 via a service bus not shown in Figure 17.1. (The fundamentals of the system are covered by US Patent No. 4 590 465, and another patent is pending.)

Smart memory chips

The heart of the system is the logic-enhanced frame buffer; an array of custom, VLSI, processor-enhanced memory chips. Each of these chips contains two identical 64-pixel modules. Each module has three main parts: a conventional memory array that stores all pixel data for a 64-pixel column on the screen, an array of 64 tiny one-bit ALUs, and a Linear Expression Evaluator (LEE) that generates $Ax + By + C$ simultaneously for all pixels. All ALUs in the system execute the same micro-instruction at the same time (in Single Instruction, Multiple Data fashion), and all memories receive the same address (each pixel ALU operates on its

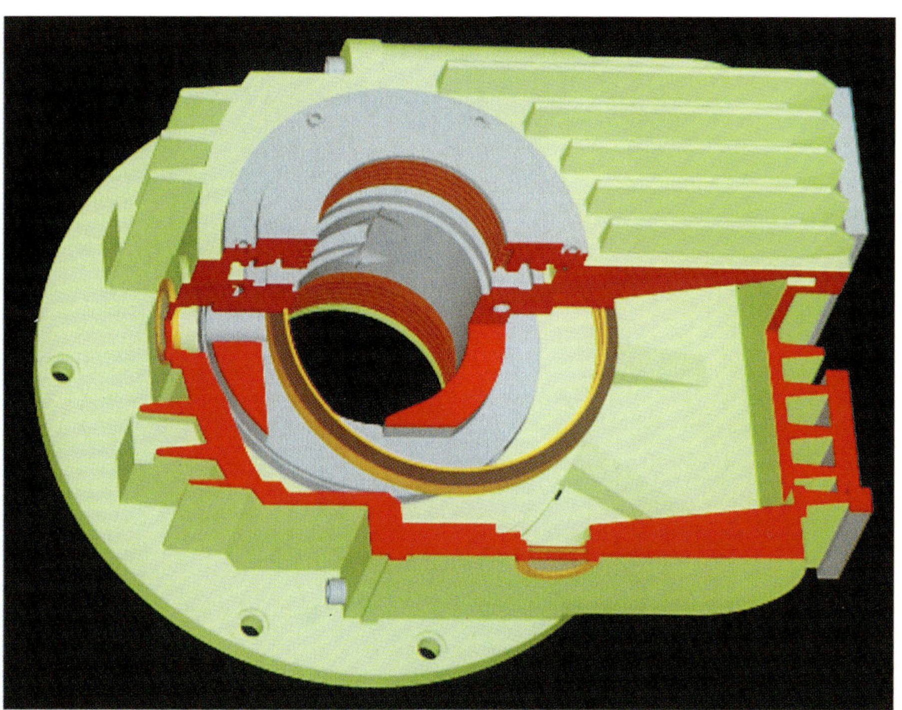

Plate 1
A Cover Plate modelled using Constructive Solid Geometry. This picture takes over 120 minutes on a VAX 8600. Picture by Gordon Oliver, Geometric Modelling Group, Leeds University.

Plate 2
A Representation of the Electric Potential surrounding the Molecule ENALAPRYL. This picture was produced by the image synthesis package WINSOM from Scientific Data provided by Dr. Graham Richards, Department of Physical Chemistry, University of Oxford. WINSOM was written by members of the IBM UK Scientific Centre in Winchester, England.

Plate 3
The effects on the level of detail due to undersampling the data. Each object has one fourth the number of grid cells as the one to its left. Shown here is a water cloud isosurface from a severe storm simulation (Wilhelmson and Klemp, 1978).

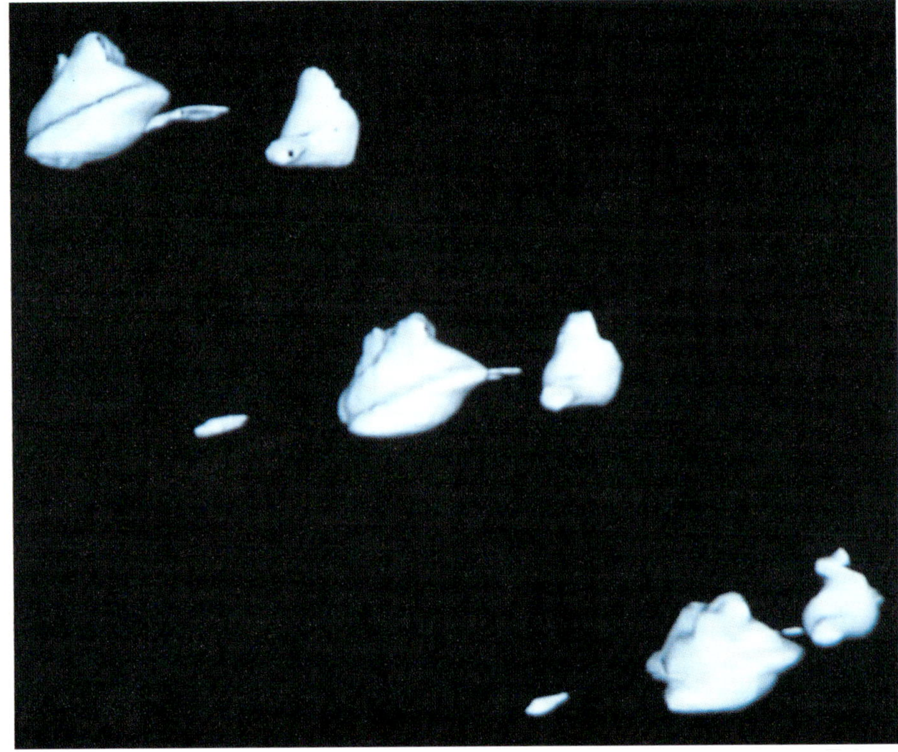

Plate 4
The density isosurface composed of 107 434 polygons consolidated from 293 585 triangles.

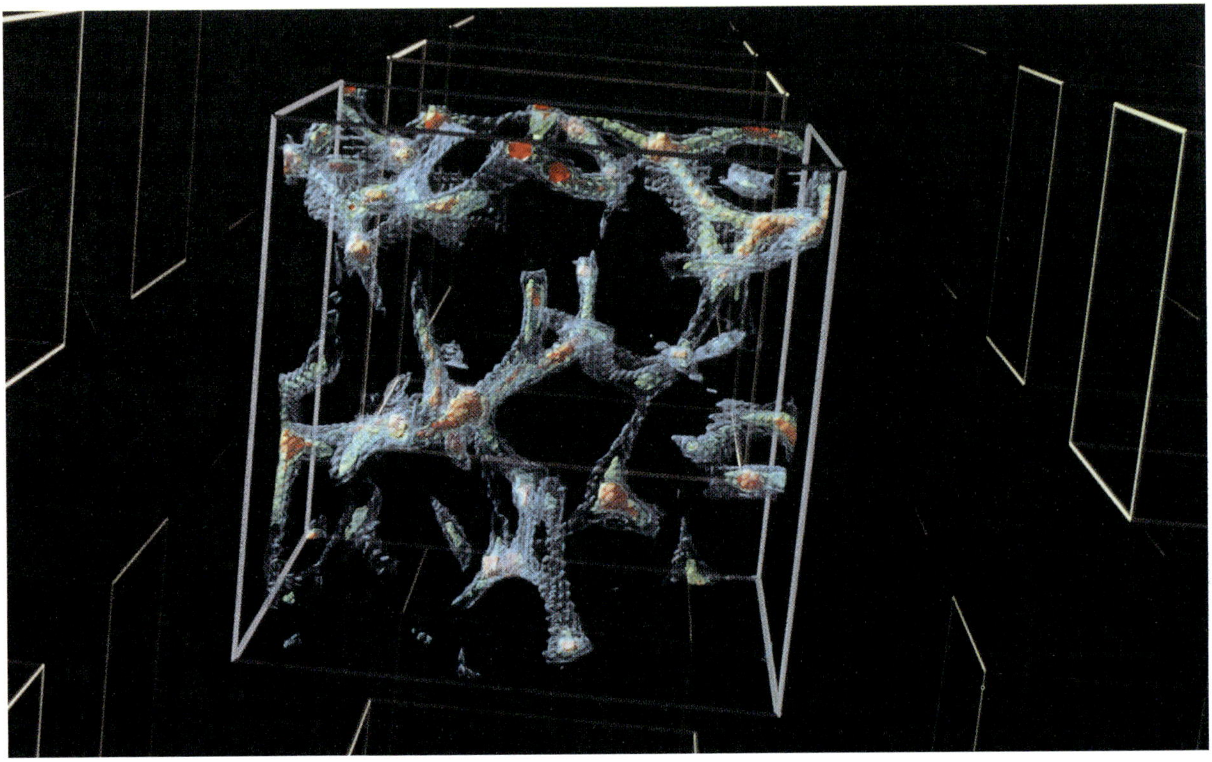

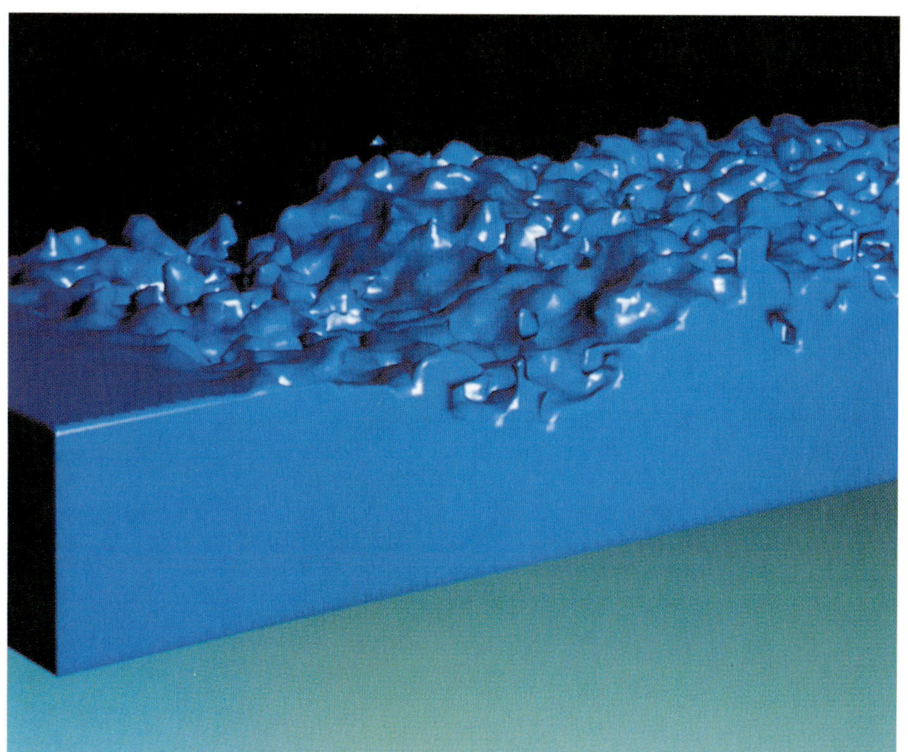

Plate 5
Three nested density isosurfaces of the aggregation of large-scale structure in the universe. The polygon count is 169 478 after consolidation.

Plate 6
The Tree image.

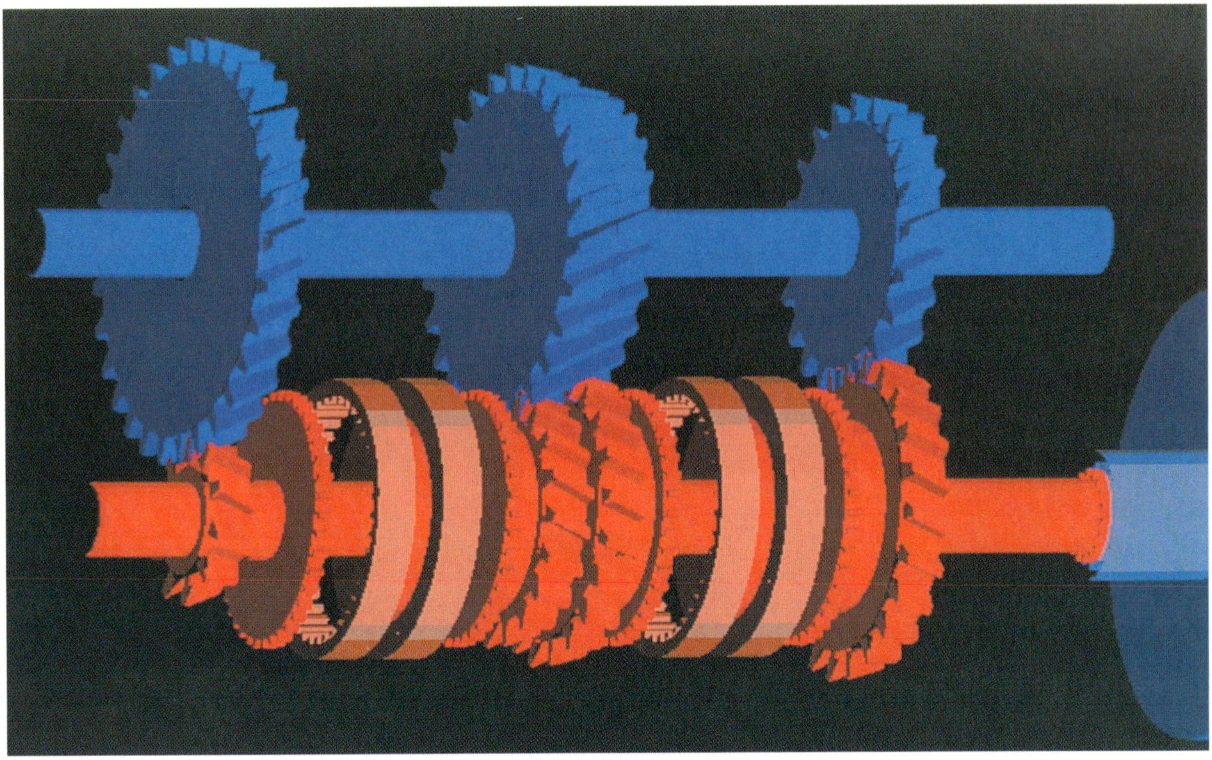

Plate 7
The Crankshaft image.

Plate 8
An organo-metallic molecular model.

Plate 9
A dining room scene..

Plate 10
A crystal lattice structure.

Plate 11
Cover plate model rendered at 256×256 pixels.

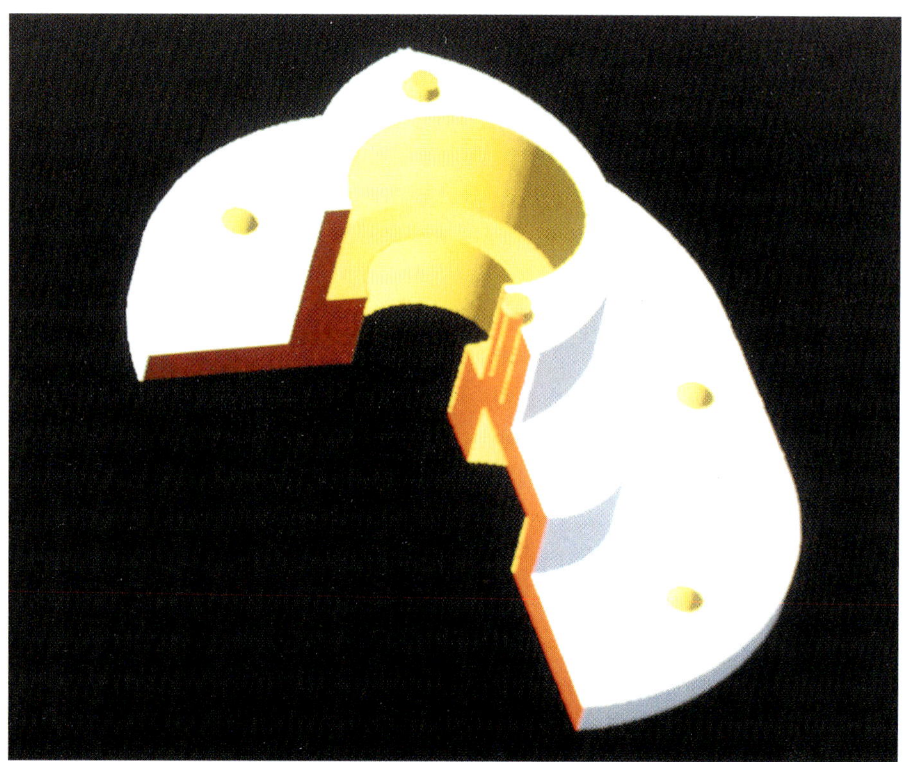

Plate 12
Molecule model rendered at 256×256 pixels.

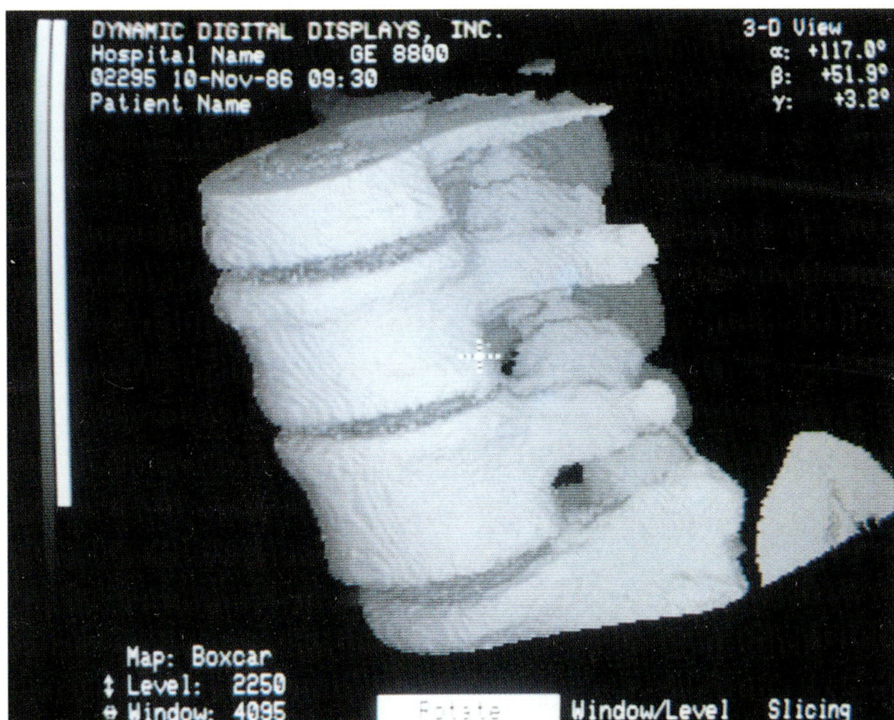

Plate 13
Shaded 3D view of a section of lumbar spine.

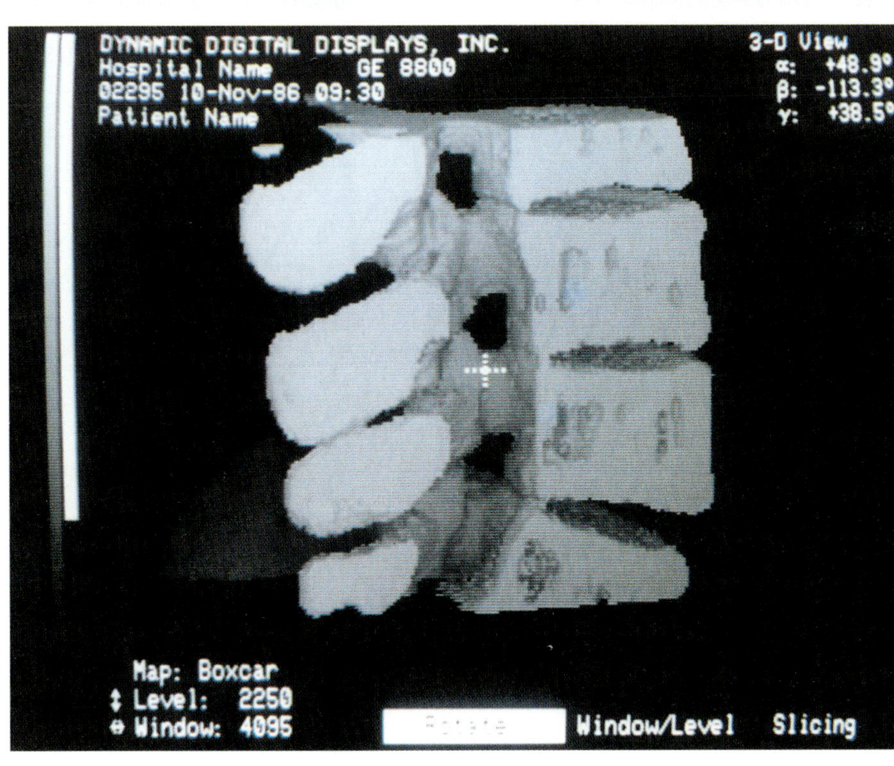

Plate 14
Shaded 3D view with slice plane revealing the spinal canal.

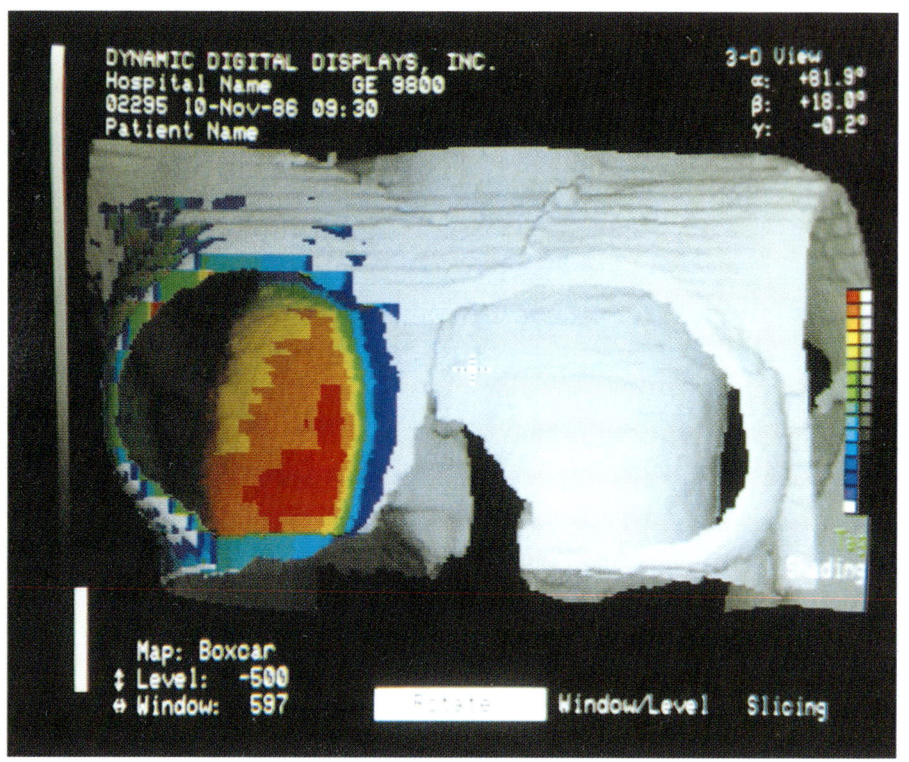

Plate 15

Computed dose superimposed on patient anatomy. Regions of high dose in red; low dose in blue.

corresponding bit of data) at the same time. The LEE provides the power of two 10-bit multiplier/accumulators at every pixel, but at much less expense in silicon area on the chip. The part of the LEE that is common to the pixels in a single column is factored out (10 stages of the X-multiplier and the first four stages of the *Y*-multiplier). The last six stages of the *Y*-multiplier can be built as a binary tree, since *Y*-products for a column are closely related, thereby reducing the cost in silicon area to about 1.2 bit-serial multiplier/accumulator stages per pixel for the entire LEE. Pxpl4 chips have 70% of their active area devoted to memory and 30% to processing circuitry.

Hardware configuration

The Pixel-planes 4 system consists of a Digital Equipment Corporation MicroVax II workstation, which acts as host, and a separate cabinet containing the prototype custom hardware. The prototype contains two card cages in a single rack: a multibus cage and a cage with a fully custom backplane. The custom cage contains the 512 × 512-pixel frame buffer on 32 15 inch × 15 inch boards, each with 64 logic-enhanced memory chips. The multibus cage contains all the other boards: a host interface board through which a DMA link to the host is realized, an analog input board to which joysticks and sliders are connected, the graphics processor (with 8 Mbytes of RAM), the image generation controller; and the video controller.

Performance

Pxpl4 can process about 35 000 smooth-shaded, *Z*-buffered triangles per second (quadrilaterals are about 20% slower). Shadows are cast at about 11 000 triangles per second, using true shadow volumes. About 13 000 smooth-shaded, *Z*-buffered, interpenetrating spheres can be rendered per second. Virtually any number of updates per second can be realized, since the entire *Z*-buffer and all the RBG buffers can be cleared in less than 10 microseconds.

17.2.2 Algorithms on Pixel-planes 4

New algorithms and applications have been appearing in a flurry since the system became operational in August 1986 and especially since the new, C-programmable graphics processor became operational in Spring 1987.

CSG system

Claire Durand, Steve Molnar and Greg Turk have implemented an interactive design system based on CSG and building on the methods described by Goldfeather, Hultquist, and Fuchs (1986) and by Jansen (1986). This is the first system, to our knowledge, that allows direct manipulation of the CSG tree via a Macintosh-style user interface and continuous rendering of the resulting solid object. Casual users have begun designing simple objects with the system: telephone sets and dining service and goblets. The design team has begun to interface their system with a CSG-to-polygons program (part of the BAGS package from Brown University developed by Professor Andries van Dam and students). The capability to deal with both CSG structure and polygons may allow the user–designer to enjoy both the ease of design within a CSG structure and the still much faster rendering of polygonal representation for objects that are no longer being changed.

Transparency

Two different algorithms have been implemented for transparency, one by David Ellsworth, the other by John Rhoades. Ellsworth's method displays transparent polygons as opaque polygons with randomly positioned single-pixel holes – the greater the polygon's transparency, the more holes. This method allows simple processing of polygons in an order, but results in distracting sparkling of holes as the polygon moves from frame to frame. Ellsworth is working on reducing this effect. Rhoades' method processes transparent polygons only after all the opaque ones. This involves partitioning the display list and, for the method to work properly, involves sorting the transparent polygons from, for instance, back to front. Rhoades' current implementation does not sort the transparent polygons but still gives results that are acceptable to our users. He is working on more advanced implementations, especially ones that will run efficiently on Pxpl5.

Textures

Two different algorithms for rendering textures are being explored, one by Vicki Interrante, the other by Brice Tebbs. Interrante's version displays a textured surface as one created by a cover of many tiny polygons, one between every consecutive texture sample. It works fine, although slowly. We plan to speed up this version by defining a hierarchy of textures, each with a different number of polygons, using progressive refinement techniques. When a texture is moved rapidly, only a rough (blurred) version will be displayed. When it is stopped, a more refined version will automatically appear.

Tebbs' version is an implementation of the techniques described by our team in Fuchs *et al.* (1985). Pixels within a textured surface are 'colored' with texture coordinates when they are originally rendered. After all the polygons have been rendered, the system broadcasts the texture(s) once; the pixels storing texture coordinates then replace these coordinates with the corresponding broadcast texture values. This method works well when there are only a few small textures used repeatedly throughout the image – like bricks and asphalt in a building scene. Still a problem is the situation in which a texture is compressed and multiple texture samples map onto the same pixel. The new partitioned parallelism of Pxpl5 and its graphics processor's ability to read back pixel values should help with both the speed of this processing and the handling of special cases like these, which occur only at a small percentage of the pixels.

Soft shadows and multiple light sources

Vicki Interrante is implementing a capability to specify multiple light sources. Already implemented is the ability to have an area, rather than point light source, so shadows can appear more naturally soft on the edges, with true penumbras. This is achieved by moving the light source slightly during each of the multiple passes that are normally done for anti-aliasing; just as area sampling within a pixel is approximated by random point sampling within that area, area sampling of the light source is approximated by random point sampling within the light's area. Interrante is now generalizing this method to allow multiple, arbitrarily positioned light sources.

Adaptive histogram equalization by progressive refinement

John Austin (a member of the project until recently joining Sun Microsystems in Raleigh, NC) implemented a version of Stephen Pizer's AHE algorithm for image enhancement that works by progressive refinement. This image enhancement technique, which takes more than one hour on a VAX 780, has been done in about 4 seconds on Pixel-planes 4. Austin adapted his method to calculate an approximate version of the enhanced image in a small fraction of a second and then refine it. This method works very well. Our medical colleagues are eager to use Pixel-planes for this and other applications.

Specular Phong shading studies

John Eyles has developed a fast new method of Phong shading for Pixel-planes. His method performs only part of the rendering of each polygon during that polygon's processing period and leaves the final calculations to be done after all the polygons have been processed. Then each pixel performs the final calculations with the already stored parameters for the surface that is visible at that pixel. Specifically, during each polygon's processing period, the linear coefficients for each component of the normal to the surface are broadcast. Then, after all the polygons have been processed, each pixel processor renormalizes the 'normal' that it is storing and performs the lighting calculations precisely for its visible surface. Although there are not enough bits per pixel in Pxpl4 to implement this method fully, it will provide in Pxpl5 the much more realistic specular shading (with multiple light sources) at almost the same speed as the cruder Gouraud shading we currently use.

Curved surfaces

Howard Good has started to render curved surfaces on Pxpl4, using recursive subdivision within the graphics processor followed by rendering of polygonal approximation in the enhanced memory chips. Good is now implementing adaptive subdivision methods. With Pxpl5, we hope to use the enhanced memory chips for a larger share of the computations. Both the quadratic expression evaluation and the memory readout capabilities of Pxpl5 will be used for this task.

Mandelbrot and Julia sets

Greg Turk has developed an algorithm for displaying Mandelbrot and Julia sets. It allows the user to explore the 2D plane of the set interactively, while the image is updated in real time. Since all pixel processors are enabled virtually all of the time, this algorithm gives far better utilization of the raw computational power of Pxpl4 than we have achieved with any other algorithm; to update these images on the 512 × 512 display at 25 Hz, the enhanced memories perform 1300 million 15-bit adds plus 655 million 15-bit multiplies per second.

PHIGS+ compatibility

David Ellsworth and Brice Tebbs have begun implementing a programmer's interface to Pxpl4 that is very close to a subset of PHIGS+, the latest version of the Programmer's Hierarchical Interactive Graphics Standard. This implementation is just beginning to run, with only polygons currently supported (other support is expected within weeks). The basic interface is expected to remain virtually the same for casual users of Pxpl5.

17.2.3 Applications on Pxpl4

Building walkthrough

As part of a project for exploring and modifying buildings in early design stages, John Airey, under the direction of Professor Fred Brooks, is developing a new visible surface algorithm optimized for dense, static environments in which the viewing position is inside that environment. Airey's method divides the environment automatically into convex regions and associates with each region the list of polygons possibly visible from any point in that region. In contrast to applications in which the rendered object, say, a mechanical part, covers only a part of the screen, in the building 'walkthrough' application, every pixel on the screen is covered by some part of the rendered object. Although Airey's method can use any display device, it is particularly well suited for Pxpl4 (and Pxpl5), on which rendering time is only a function of the number of polygons, not the size of each polygon on the screen.

Molecular modeling

Michael Pique (of Scripps Clinic, La Jolla, CA) and others on the GRIP molecular modeling team (led by Professor Fred Brooks) have programmed Pxpl4 to display molecular vibrations. They are eager to program Pxpl4 to help with molecular docking studies but await the enhancement that allows pixel memories to be read back by the graphics processor.

Medical imaging

Pxpl4 is used regularly and extensively for display of 3D anatomical structures and radiation therapy doses by the NIH-funded Med3D project led by Professors Henry Fuchs and Stephen Pizer. Kevin Novins, while employed by the UNC School of Medicine's Division of Radiation Oncology, developed a method of reducing the number of polygons in a reconstructed object with minimal degradation to its appearance. This work was motivated in part by the use of Pxpl4, on which the same surface represented by fewer polygons is displayed more rapidly. On other systems, which are more limited by the number of pixels on a surface than by the number of polygons, such polygon-reduction methods would not offer such great advantages.

17.3 Inadequacies of the current system and new opportunities

Although the Pxpl4 system's availability for more than a year has allowed us and others to explore new research, its limitations, both in performance and generality, leave us dissatisfied. We want not only to expand the present capacities of the system, but also to explore some new avenues that experience with it has suggested:

- **Polygon rendering rate.** For many situations, especially in medical imaging, we and our collaborators would like much higher rendering rate. Often, for instance, we would like to model a cancer patient's anatomy, radiation treatment beams and radiation isodensity surfaces with 50 000 or more polygons, and to manipulate the model on the screen smoothly to understand its structural subtleties. We need a 10 × speedup to achieve this kind of modeling. More advanced visualization mechanisms, such as stereo, head-motion parallax and head-mounted display, put still greater requirements on the polygon rendering rate.
- **Memory readback.** Many new applications we would like to pursue require the ability to process the results of computations in the frame buffer. Currently these results can only go to the video stream. In the near future we might enhance our video controller to put these results, under program control, on the multibus, for access by the graphics processor or the system host. For the long run, however, we would like this memory access to be more rapid and flexible than just coming through the video stream. Algorithms for collision detection in molecular modeling and for the calculation of radiosity 'form factors' could be sped up considerably with the pixel readback capability.
- **More memory.** As with virtually any computer, many applications run out of memory. Although 72 bits is a reasonable size for a frame buffer, it is very small for a memory system. Since additional memory comes at the expense of other silicon resources, a reasonable solution to the memory limitation problem is to implement a secondary memory mechanism.
- **Volumetric rendering.** For many medical situations (and for some molecular modeling situations), we expect that volumetric rendering will be the best imaging modality. Two separate investigations by PhD students Marc Levoy and Lee Westover are producing very exciting images. Mostly, however, these take a long time to generate, since they want to avoid voxel

artifacts in their images. Although at least one group of researchers has demonstrated a special-purpose machine for generating volumetric images rapidly (see Chapter 34), even they estimate that a full-size real-time version of their machine will cost about $250 000. (Even this machine's images would have obvious voxel artifacts!) We would like to render volumetric images, but within a more general-purpose graphics engine.

17.4 Pixel-planes 5 design

We expect Pxpl5 to be a dramatically more powerful machine than Pxpl4 for two reasons: (1) it will be much faster on currently run algorithms due to the higher clock rates, more parallelism throughout screen partitioning and more front-end graphics processor power, and (2) the architecture will be far less restricted than Pxpl4 with backing store and random access to pixels by the front-end graphics processor (and other parts of the system), which should allow whole new classes of algorithms to be implemented. In addition to its enhanced performance, Pixel-planes 5 will be configurable in a variety of ways that allow cost to be traded for performance. A system overview is given in Figure 17.2. The machine will also be much smaller physically than Pixel-planes 4 and will consume far less electrical power. The system's key features are:

- **Screen partitioning.** When rendering polygons, Pixel-planes 4 first disables all pixels on the outside of the first edge of the polygon. Subsequently, all pixels outside the polygon are disabled, and not until the beginning of the next polygon are any of these pixels' processors performing any useful computation. Since complex databases generally contain mostly very small polygons, the processors of the enhanced memories have a very low utilization. To remedy this, we plan to provide the means for processing simultaneously multiple polygons, lying in disjoint parts of the display screen. To implement this screen partitioning, the logic-enhanced frame buffer will be partitioned into a number of disjoint pieces, each controlled by

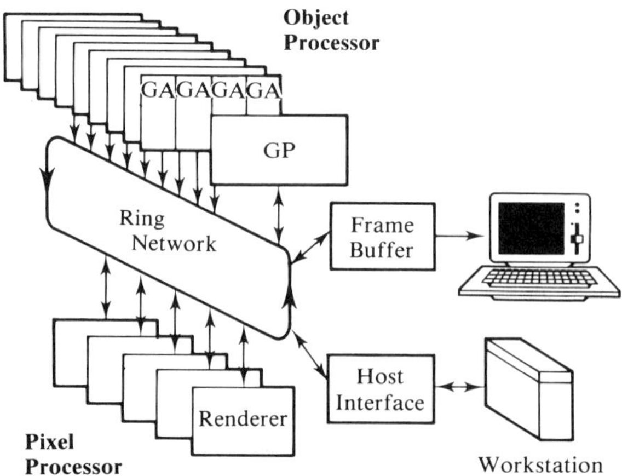

Figure 17.2
Pixel-planes 5 system overview.

a separate Image Generation Controller (IGC). Each IGC has a FIFO input buffer. The graphics processor (which computes the A, B, C coefficient sets and frame-buffer instructions) broadcasts each primitive only to those IGCs whose portion of the display is covered by that primitive. Since polygons will be quite small, the majority of polygons will be sent to only one IGC. Thus, if the IGC's FIFOs are deep enough, and if the order of the primitives is reasonably uncorrelated with their screen position, the multiple IGCs should be able to process several different primitives simultaneously. Simulations with even simple data sets and small FIFOs show speed-ups of 4 × or better for a system with 16 IGCs.

- **Backing store.** The new enhanced memory chips will communicate through a special I/O port with a large dynamic RAM 'backing store', thus forming a two-tiered pixel memory system. The backing store RAM will support direct addressing of pixel data and will allow rapid block transfers of pixel data to other system components, including a conventional frame buffer from which the display screen will be refreshed. Since pixels can also be moved rapidly to the elements of the MIMD front end, it can be used to carry out pixel-level calculations that cannot be readily done on the SIMD array of pixel processors. Rapid texturing will likely be supported in this way.
- **Separate refresh image buffer.** A separate frame buffer will allow a flexible mapping between the pixel processors in the Enhanced Memory Chips (EMC) and the pixels on the screen. This will permit much more effective utilization of these processors, since the EMCs can be dynamically assigned to those portions of the screen for which there is the most work. This feature will also allow much smaller configurations of Pxpl5 systems without sacrificing significant performance for many applications.
- **Fast communications network.** The building blocks of the system, called 'application boards,' will be linked together by a high-speed ring network, capable of moving data between the memory subsystems of the application boards at 160 mega-words per second.
- **MIMD graphics processor.** The 'front end' of Pxpl5 will consist of about 32 processors built with the Weitek XL chip set. One of these processors will have more memory resources than the others and will be the master of the system, although with no special privileges on the ring network.
- **Faster enhanced memory chips.** We are reimplementing our custom-enhanced memory chips in 1.2μ CMOS. We plan the new chips to have a 40 MHz instruction rate, 5 times that of the Pxpl4 chips, and to contain 256 pixels, with 256 bits per pixel. The new chips will also employ a quadratic expression evaluator (in place of the linear one in Pxpl4 chips); quadratic expressions are especially useful for rendering spheres for molecular modeling, for rendering objects described by CSG, and for rendering certain curves and surfaces. The quadratic expression evaluator and the additional memory will also speed up the calculation of higher-order polynomials.
- **Physical constraints.** Pxpl5 will occupy the volume of a workstation pedestal and should consume no more than 2 kW of power. The machine will be built entirely from multilevel printed circuit boards (since wirewrap is not useful in systems that must run at 40 MHz and faster) and will make considerable use of surface-mount packaging. Pixel-planes 5 will be a more modular system than its predecessor. The preprocessor and enhanced

memory array will each be implemented on multiple identical boards. The component boards can be combined in a variety of ways to form a range of configurations from small, inexpensive systems with modest performance to large systems with very high performance.

- **Current status.** We have finished the logic design for the Pxpl5 enhanced memory chips. The design includes a much more efficient quadratic expression evaluation tree than we had originally developed (Goldfeather and Fuchs, 1986). Detailed design of the communication network is well under way. We hope to have Pxpl5 operational by mid-1989.

Conclusions

We are encouraged that more graphics power is still opening up new opportunities for applications of interactive computer graphics. The widespread use of personal computers and workstations is making 2D graphics so much the norm that one can hardly imagine a workstation or an Apple Macintosh without a graphics display. In the future, there may also be such expectations for 3D graphics capabilities. We hope that we are contributing to the coming of that day.

Acknowledgments

The work we have reported was funded jointly by the US National Science Foundation (grant no. MIP–8601552) and the US Defense Advanced Research Projects Agency (order no. 6090).

We thank our team of graduate student research assistants, who developed much of the software environment and many of the algorithms described here: Clare Durand (now with the US Geological Service), David Ellsworth, Howard Good, Victoria Interrante, Roman Kuchkuda (now with Megatek, San Diego, CA), Steve Molnar, John Rhoades, Brice Tebbs and Greg Turk.

Our work in system building would have been impossible without our department's Microelectronic Systems Laboratory, its director Vernon Chi and staff members John Austin, Mark Monger, John Thomas and Brad Bennett. Austin and Monger has now joined Sun Microsystems in Raleigh, NC.

We thank Professor Jack Goldfeather of Carleton College for numerous ideas about a wide variety of topics, especially about curved surfaces and quadratic expression evaluation. We thank Mark Kellam and Wayne Dettloff of the Microelectronics Center of North Carolina for help with chip fabrication and system design and testing. We thank our colleague, Professor Frederick P. Brooks Jr., for years of advice and support and for the sphere-rendering algorithm. We thank our past graduate assistants, Greg Abram, John Comer, Amarie Helton, Justin Heinecke, Scott Hennes, Cheng-Hong Hsieh, Jeff Hultquist, Alex Melnick, Mary Ranade and Susan Spach, for years of dedicated, creative effort.

We thank Linda Houseman for patient editing of this chapter.

We also thank: the MOSIS Project for IC and circuit board fabrication; John Ousterhout, who has provided tools for the US university VLSI community; Chuck Seitz, whose ideas have greatly influenced our design style (Seitz, 1985); our colleagues at Xerox PARC, Alan Paeth (now at University of Waterloo), Lynn Conway (now at University of Michigan) and Alan Bell, who collaborated on early designs; Data General for gifts of cabinets and power supplies; and SCI, Inc., for wave soldering services.

References and Bibliography

Akeley K. and Jermaluk T. (1988). High-performance polygon rendering. *Computer Graphics,* **22**(4), 239–46

Austin J. and Pizer S. (1987). A Multiprocessor Histogram Equalization Machine. In *Proc. of the Xth Information Processing in Medical Imaging International Conference*, Utrecht, The Netherlands

Bishop T.G. and Weimer D. (1986). Fast Phong shading. *Computer Graphics,* **20**(4), 103–6

Eyles J., Austin J., Fuchs H., Gree T. and Poulton J. (1987). Pixel-planes 4: a summary. To appear in *Advances in Graphics Hardware 2: Proc. Eurographics '87 Second Workshop on Graphics Hardware.*

Fuchs H. (1988). An introduction to Pixel-planes and other VLSI-intensive graphics systems. In *Proc. NATO International Advanced Study Institute on Theoretical Foundations of Computer Graphics and CAD*, Lucca, Italy, July 1987. Berlin: Springer-Verlag

Fuchs H., Goldfeather J., Hultquist J.P. *et al.* (1985). Fast spheres, shadows, textures, transparencies, and image enhancements in Pixel-planes. *Computer Graphics,* **19**(3), 111–20

Fuchs H. and Poulton J. (1981). Pixel-planes: A VLSI-oriented design for a raster graphics engine. *VLSI Design,* **2**(3), 20–8

Fuchs H., Poulton J., Paeth A. and Bell A. (1982). Developing pixel planes, a smart memory-based raster graphics system. *Proc. 1982 MIT Conference on Advanced Research in VLSI*, pp. 137–46. Dedham MA: Artech House

Goldfeather J. and Fuchs H. (1986). Quadratic surface rendering on a logic-enhanced frame-buffer memory system. *IEEE Computer Graphics and Applications,* **6**(1), 48–59

Goldfeather J., Hultquist J.P.M. and Fuchs H. (1986). Fast constructive solid geometry display in the Pixel-Powers graphics system. *Computer Graphics,* **20**(4), 107–16

Jansen F.W. (1986). A pixel-parallel hidden surface algorithm for constructive solid geometry. In *Proc. Eurographics '86*, pp. 29–40. Amsterdam: Elsevier Science Publishers B.V. (North-Holland)

Pizer S.M., Zimmerman J.B. and Staab E.V. (1984). Adaptive grey level assignment in CT scan display. *J. of Computer Assisted Tomography,* **8**(2), 300–5

Poulton J., Fuchs H., Austin J.D., Eyles J.G. and Greer T. (1987). Building a 512 × 512 Pixel-planes system. In *Proc. 1987 Stanford Conference on Advanced Research in VLSI*, pp. 57–71. Cambridge MA: MIT Press

Poulton J., Fuchs H., Austin J.D. *et al.* (1985). Pixel-Planes: building a VLSI-based graphic system. In *Proc. 1985 Chapel Hill Conference on VLSI*, pp. 35–60. Rockville MD: Computer Science Press

Seitz C.L., Frey A.H., Mattisson S., Rabin S.D., Speck D.A. and van de Snepscheut J.L.A. (1985). Hot-clock nMOS. In *Proc. 1985 Chapel Hill Conference on VLSI*, pp. 1–17. Rockville MD: Computer Science Press

Silicon Graphics Computer Systems. (1987). *IRIS GT Graphics Architecture: A Technical Report*. Silicon Graphics Computer Systems CA

F.C. Crow

Xerox PARC

G. Demos
J. Hardy
J. McLaughlin
K. Sims

Whitney/Demos Productions

18 · 3D image synthesis on the Connection Machine

Supercomputers are coming into wider use for generating realistic imagery for commercial animation, special effects and scientific simulation. The Connection Machine requires a more radical rethinking of rendering algorithms than previous supercomputers since it is not intended to function as a scalar processor. A fascinating mix of changes from conventional approaches is emerging. Some procedures can run virtually unchanged while others must be turned completely inside out.

We have confidence, at this rather early point, in the viability of the Connection Machine as an architecture for high-end computer graphics. For complex scenes resulting in at least tens of thousands of polygons per frame, most steps of the rendering pipeline can make effective use of the massive number of processors available.

Early approaches to massively parallel graphics systems have focused on processor-per-pixel organizations. We show that a dynamic mix of organizations, including processor per pixel, processor per vertex and processor per polygon are necessary. Additionally, we note that an apparent consequence of the style of algorithm enforced by the Connection Machine is an enormously increased appetite for memory.

We are currently implementing a rendering system on a frequently upgraded Connection Machine installation at Whitney/Demos Productions. While the small memory of the first generation Connection Machine, CM-1, limited early experiments, the second generation Connection Machine, CM-2, has provided interesting experience toward understanding massively parallel computation applied to 3D image synthesis.

18.1 Introduction: the Connection Machine

For a long time, supercomputers were considered ridiculously cost-*in*effective for computer graphics. A specialized engine can always do a more efficient job of achieving a particular end as demonstrated by numerous systems designed for flight simulators over the years. However, in recent years, the demand for greater flexibility in high-end image synthesis systems, the explosion of suppliers of mini-supercomputers, and the wider variety of system architectures available has made supercomputers look more attractive.

When moving image synthesis algorithms to a conventional supercomputer, an immediate speedup can be expected due to the powerful scalar computation provided. Efforts in vectorizing the algorithms then yield incrementally greater performance. However, some newer entries in the supercomputer field, particularly the Connection Machine (Thinking Machines Corporation, 1987), depend strictly upon massive parallelism for their speed.

The scalar computational power of the Connection Machine is almost entirely dependent on its host processor. Since an individual Connection Machine processor is relatively slow, algorithms must be able to do thousands of operations at once to use the available power effectively. On the other hand, truly massive parallel computation is provided, currently 8K to 64K processors.

18.1.1 The Connection Machine in general

The Connection Machine processors are bit-serial devices, each executing several tens of thousands of instructions per second. All processors execute the same instruction stream. Therefore, any conditional expressions require some percentage of the processors to be idled while those processors whose data satisfies the condition execute the appropriate subsequent instructions. Then the idled processors, whose data failed the condition, are activated to execute the alternate instruction stream while the first set of processors is idled.

This encourages a different programming style. Wherever possible, data meeting similar or identical conditions must be gathered together for processing, so the minimum amount of effort is wasted in conditional instruction streams. The routing network joining the processors aids this by allowing data to be rearranged at different stages of an algorithm to fit different needs.

The Connection Machine uses an *n*-cube topology for its message routing network. Any processor may access data held by any other processor in essentially equal time. This frees the programmer from worrying about the arrangement of data in the machine (as long as excessive contention is avoided). The network also can do some logic/arithmetic on colliding messages, so that the sum of all data meeting some condition or enumeration of all processors active at a given state, is easily obtained.

Each processor may be set into an active or inactive state based on a test across all processors. For example, all processors in which the location, a, holds a non-zero value may be selected by idling the remaining processors. Only the active processors execute succeeding operations until the active/inactive state is reset. To override this protocol, a few operations are available which affect all processors, including inactive ones.

All standard arithmetic/logic functions can be applied to the same address in all active processor memories so that the operation, $a + b$, can be carried out simultaneously in all active processors, as one would expect. However, the routing network also implements fast operations *across* all active processors, treating the corresponding locations in each active processor memory as a vector. All the values, a, may be summed, for example.

Other operations in the routing network allow values simultaneously written to the same processor to be combined *en route*, using the full set of arithmetic/logic operations. If several processors send a value to the same location, requesting summing on collision, the sum of all colliding values will be stored at that location. Minimum and maximum functions are included in the applicable operations.

A pair of unique functions called **scan** and **rank** are also available. Scan does incremental operations across a set of active processors. For example, a running sum across corresponding locations may be performed, each processor ending up with the sum of all values held by earlier processors in the sequence. Other forms of scan allow the machine to be segmented so that a scan operates only across each segment. For example, a copy operation may be performed which distributes a value held by the first processor in each segment to all other processors within that segment. Thus unique values can be broadcast within each segment.

The rank operation provides a built-in sorting aid. The operation takes a corresponding value from each processor and returns the position of that value in a sorted ordering of the entire set of values. The position can be used in a subsequent operation to rearrange the data among the processors, putting them in a sorted sequence.

The routing network opens the Connection Machine to a much wider variety of applications than earlier massively parallel processors. Thinking Machines, the manufacturer of the Connection Machine, likes to call these **data parallel** applications (Hillis and Steele, 1986). On the other hand, if only nearest-neighbor communication is desired, the network can be restricted to such an organization with an attendant substantial increase in communication speed. It is really the implementation of this *n*-cube network which makes the Connection Machine useful. Earlier SIMD machines (Batcher, 1980; Slotnick, 1967, 1971) were applicable only to a very limited set of problems, chiefly those requiring only nearest-neighbor access.

Applications with more data items than processors may use a **virtual processor** capability. Each processor's memory may be divided into equal parts, each devoted to a different virtual processor. Each instruction is then repeatedly executed with a different base address until all virtual processors have been served.

The Connection Machine acts as an attached resource on a host computer (currently a DEC VAX or Symbolics Lisp Machine). Not being designed for a specific host, the interface is not always perfectly matched to the rate at which a given host can issue Connection Machine instructions. The virtual processor capability allows the Connection Machine to make use of a weaker host computer by trading longer instruction times for greater parallelism.

18.1.2 Two generations: the CM-1 and the CM-2

The first generation Connection Machine, the CM-1, provided 4K bits of memory per processor, or 8 to 32 megabytes per machine. The operating system took a certain amount of this, leaving around 3500 bits per processor. This rather severe memory limitation was a problem to early implementors of graphics algorithms.

Other difficulties with using the CM-1 for graphics included the lack of a display closely coupled to the processors, a relatively slow bit-serial floating-point implementation and inadequate I/O bandwidth for complicated scene descriptions. As a result, serious graphics applications of the Connection Machine have awaited the second generation CM-2.

Memory is expanded to 8K *bytes* per processor on the CM-2, or 128 to 512 megabytes per machine. A Weitek floating-point processor is provided for every 32 processors, or 512 to 2048 per machine. A full complement of 2048 floating-point processors provides an aggregate power of several gigaflops, on the order of a megaflop per $1000. This is certainly an economical way to acquire gigaflops if one's algorithms can be recast to get sustained utilization of a reasonable proportion of that capacity.

Each floating-point processor is time-multiplexed between 32 of the bit-serial processors. An interface chip translates between the bit-serial access patterns of the regular processors and the word-parallel mode of the floating-point chip. This chip also handles multiplexing the operations of the floating-point chip. The floating-point interface chip also allows some more flexibility in addressing. On the CM-2, a form of indirection is possible via **array-fetch** and **array-store** operations, which access an array of values local to a processor, using an index specific to the processor.

Two new options for the CM-2 provide increased I/O bandwidth: the DataVault and the high resolution graphics display. The DataVault attaches to an I/O controller. Each I/O controller transfers 256 bits in parallel into or out of the machine at a bandwidth of 40 megabytes per second. There can be up to eight controllers for a maximum aggregate bandwidth of 320 megabytes per second.

The DataVault is an array of 39 disk drives, providing 32 bits in parallel with single-bit error correction (the data can be reconstructed if one drive fails). The bandwidth matches that of the I/O port, 40 megabytes per second. A single DataVault can fill the entire memory of a 16K processor CM-2 in under 4 seconds. Up to eight DataVaults may be attached to a system.

The high resolution graphics display circumvents the I/O controller, attaching directly to the backplane where it can command up to 128 megabytes (1 gigabit) per second. This feeds a frame buffer memory with 28 planes of two megapixels each. The frame buffer refreshes a 1280 × 1024 pixel display at 60 Hz. The refresh processor also provides pan and zoom operations over the nearly two screensful of frame buffer memory.

With the advent of the CM-2, high-end image synthesis on the Connection Machine looks much more promising. In Section 18.2, some early attempts at using Connection Machines for graphics are explained. Section 18.3 explains the demands placed on a machine by attempts to render very complicated scenes. Section 18.4 discusses how the standard rendering pipeline can be recast for the Connection Machine. Finally, a short conclusion compares the options open to those who wish to produce animations of complicated scenes rapidly.

18.2 Early uses in computer graphics

Most concurrent computation in graphics has been based on pipelining. The prime examples come from the flight simulator systems. Here, a handful of operations are active simultaneously. By assembling a dedicated system from units with small levels of concurrency through forking, joining and parallel pipelines, substantial levels of concurrency can be obtained using the conventional graphics pipeline organization (Schachter, 1983; Watkins, 1970; Schumaker, 1980).

However, when asked to think about how one would use thousands or millions of processors, the first reaction is generally to try to map processors to pixels usefully. The Pixel-planes machine (Fuchs *et al.*, 1985) represents one successful venture in that direction. The first image synthesis programs for the Connection Machine were similar in approach.

Although a Connection Machine has nowhere near enough processors to devote a processor to each pixel of a high resolution image, it has the ability to simulate such a number through its virtual processor capability. Sixteen or twenty virtual processors per real processor, on a 16K processor machine, will provide a processor for every pixel of a standard television resolution image. Sixteen processors per pixel provide a 512 × 512 pixel image, 20 provide a 640 × 512 image.

Early graphics applications on the CM-1 focussed on similar mappings of processors to pixels. In the following sections, we describe an early effort by Karl Sims at one of the first Connection Machine installations, the Massachusetts Institute of Technology (MIT) Media Lab. We then sketch some early experience at Whitney/Demos Productions. Finally, we suggest some alternatives to using a processor per pixel, to be expanded upon in later sections.

18.2.1 Ray tracing at the MIT Media Lab

Karl Sims implemented a ray-tracing program at the MIT Media Lab which takes advantage of the Connection Machine's strong points. The program was aimed at images of a few simply defined objects. Therefore, it was practical to pass the objects in with the instruction stream, letting all processors operate on each object in turn.

Having implemented a ray tracer before, it took only a couple of days for Sims to implement the program and get the first images out. Debugging and improvements, of course, consumed considerable additional time. For this type of problem, programming the Connection Machine is quite straightforward. In effect, the usual computational loops over the array of pixels are merely unwound for calculation on all pixels at once.

The image was divided into 128 × 128 pixel subimages, thereby providing a pixel for each of the 16K processors in each subimage. The pixels in each subimage were contiguous. Each subimage was computed in turn, changing only the pixel locations between subimages. The process ran roughly as follows:

(1) All processors began with an initial value representing a pixel location. Each processor in the Connection Machine has a unique identification number ranging from zero to the number of processors minus one. Using this number, each processor computed its own pixel address using its identification number and the position of the first pixel in the current subimage.

(2) Given the pixel location, the direction of a ray through the eyepoint to the pixel was calculated for all pixels. The ensuing instruction stream consisted of a sequence of shape descriptions and instructions to determine whether the ray stored at a pixel would intersect each shape in turn.

(3) If a pixel's ray intersected a given shape, the intersection distance and surface normal were calculated. Only spheres and plane-filling functions were used as shapes to keep this computation straightforward. As each shape was processed, calculated intersections were compared to the previously stored intersection distances. Wherever the new distance was smaller, a new distance and surface normal were stored.

(4) After all shapes had been processed, pixels were left with a ray direction, the

closest ray intersection and the corresponding normal vector. Shading calculations then determined the color of the pixel using the normal vector, the direction of a light source and, for some surfaces, a texture map. The texture map was stored in memory, a pixel per processor, and the routing network was used to retrieve pixels from the texture map efficiently.

(5) To simulate surface reflections, a new ray direction was then calculated for each pixel. For shiny surfaces, the previous ray direction and the normal vector provided a reflected ray direction. For pixels with dull surfaces or no surface, a null vector would prevent reflection calculations. After updating the ray directions, the set of shapes in the image was processed again.

In theory, passes through the shape sequence should have been repeated until no pixel held an active ray. However, in the interests of practicality and efficiency, the computation was stopped after three passes.

How well does this kind of algorithm use the Connection Machine? Processor utilization was kept quite high by using simple scenes composed of large objects and computing subimages well matched to the number of processors available. For any given subimage, a shape covered half the pixels, on average, if it figured in the subimage at all.

Clearly, all processors were used for the first pass through the program. However, subsequent passes, activating only those pixels holding reflection rays, would use significantly fewer processors. It should be noted that dividing the picture into subimages adds the overhead of processing the description of the scene repeatedly. However, the description was kept very compact.

Much of the recent work in speeding up ray tracing has gone into techniques to avoid following unproductive rays. Sim's approach does not easily extend to such cleverness, although we believe it can be done. On the other hand, images were made at about 40 seconds per frame (on the CM-1), a quite respectable speed. This attests to the raw power of the machine. Respectable performance can be achieved without optimum utilization.

The most recent trend in ray tracing has been to subdivide the interesting region of space into small cells and tag each cell with those objects which intersect it. This avoids testing each ray against all objects in a scene, and therefore promises much improved performance in very complicated scenes. The time-consuming operation then becomes incrementing rays through the space structure. The Connection Machine can increment thousands of rays at once and thus may well prove to be a good match to this style of algorithm. This approach is currently being tried at MIT.

18.2.2 First efforts at Whitney/Demos

The first algorithm run on the Connection Machine at Whitney/Demos was similar to that used by Pixel-planes. Polygons were passed in, one at a time, each edge being tested against all pixels. After all edges for a polygon were evaluated, those pixels inside the polygon could be shaded. For very large polygons, this approach is reasonably effective. However, most of the machine is wasted while processing anything smaller.

As will be explained below, the limited memory of the CM-1 initially discouraged more aggressive algorithm development. However, this algorithm, though slow enough to be clearly useless in the long run, proved to be a useful basis for developing shading functions and other code needed on later systems. Since the CM-1 had no direct way of refreshing a display, pixels had to be read out and loaded into a frame buffer attached to the host computer, a Symbolics 3650. This took about 5 seconds for a 640 × 480 image or 20 seconds for 1280 × 1024.

At this writing (January 1988) the CM-2 has been available to Whitney/Demos for about 2 months. Not all Thinking Machines' software is yet able to take advantage of the improved hardware (for example, array addressing); however, updates arrive frequently. As an interim development environment, Whitney/Demos now runs two 8K processor CM-2s. Each machine is typically run as two separate 4K machines.

Currently, working programs generate moderately complex images. The basic algorithms are proven to that extent. However, there is a great deal of tuning and learning yet to be done. At this point, speedups by factors of two and four still occur frequently.

The programming crew includes some with substantial previous supercomputer experience. They have expressed pleasure at the compactness of the code being produced and the ease with which speedups are found at this early stage. Both a Lisp dialect (*Lisp) and a machine code assembler-equivalent (Paris) are being used, each having the traditional advantages.

Programmer discontent focuses on two major issues: (1) limits on memory size and the number of processors and (2) arcane coding style.

(1) Code would be vastly simpler in many cases if an unlimited number of processors each with an unlimited amount of memory could be assumed. We have become used to the relaxed constraints offered by virtual memory. There is, as yet, no way to page memory (or, somewhat equivalently, processors) in the Connection Machine.

(2) It is still a significant mental exercise for those with extensive experience in conventional programming to think in different terms (there are fewer complaints from the younger staff). Further, conventional modes of commentary in the code do not express the changing data organizations very well. Easily used graphical aids would be welcome. As has often been noted, there may be much better ways of expressing programs for massively parallel machines than by conventional languages born in a serially-oriented time.

18.2.3 Alternative approaches

High-end applications of realistic, synthesized images currently employ models including thousands or tens of thousands of patches, or hundreds of thousands or even millions of polygons. To do anything efficient with so many surface elements requires that they be treated in parallel. This indicates that algorithms based on a processor per polygon would be as compelling for complex scenes as those based on a processor per pixel.

In fact, several organizations will be necessary for effective use of the Connection Machine hardware.

(1) The pixels must be gathered up for delivery to the display and to determine which surfaces are visible, so the pixels must be stored one or more per processor (processor per pixel).

(2) To carry out transformations on vertices defining the surface efficiently, the vertices should be distributed over the processors (processor per vertex).

(3) Efficient polygon scan conversion requires that the polygons also be distributed over the processors (processor per polygon).

The routing network allows all these different data organizations to coexist and be referenced within the machine simultaneously. However, as we shall see in the following section, the size of the memory required quickly grows to a point where the hundreds of megabytes available in the CM-2 seem less impressive.

18.3 Typical memory requirements

How much memory is needed to carry out image synthesis algorithms? For example, consider organizing the memory as a processor per pixel in a 16K processor machine.

For simplicity, assume a 1K × 1K image to be computed. A 16K processor machine can only cover 128 × 128 pixels with a processor per pixel. So, each processor must hold 64 pixels, or 64 virtual processors must be used. If virtual processors are used, a processor's memory must be broken into 64 parts. In the CM-1, each pixel got 1/64 of the 3500 bits left by the operating system, or 54 bits per pixel.

A minimum application would call for full-color display with depth buffer and coverage buffer. This is a million pixels, each having 24 bits for RGB, 32 for depth, and 16 or more for coverage, at least 72 bits per pixel. The more elaborate shading techniques we intend to use will require considerably greater storage than that.

Next, we estimate the total memory load for a non-trivial scene. As seen from the above, just keeping the pixels stored will require 72 bits per pixel or 576 bytes per processor (9 bytes × 64). As mentioned above, an efficient algorithm will have to hold tens of thousands of surface elements in the machine, scan converting and shading them in parallel. A vertex may require considerable storage, largely depending on how complex the shading is to be. At minimum, the following are required:

(1) Floating-point world coordinates (3 × 32 bits),

(2) Three unsigned integer screen-space coordinates (10 + 10 + 24 bits),

(3) Surface color RGB (3 × 32 bits),

(4) Shaded surface color RGB (3 × 8 bits),

(5) Floating-point normal vector (3 × 32 bits),

(6) Floating-point texture coordinates (2 × 32 bits),

or roughly 53 bytes per vertex. For 64K vertices, we have four vertices per processor, or 212 bytes per processor.

Sixty-four thousand vertices would translate into 16K quadrilaterals stored directly. However, the usual polygon description allows vertices to be stored once only and shared among neighboring polygons. Therefore pointers to vertex descriptions are stored as polygon descriptions. A vertex pointer requires two bytes, and there are four of them, eight bytes, per quadrilateral. Using 64K vertices we can now store 64K polygons, 32 bytes per processor.

Texture mapping is considered a necessary part of modern commercial imagery. Some systems make use of multiple texture maps on the same surface

(Cook, 1984), and multiple texture maps within a scene are common. Texture maps can vary greatly in resolution, but are generally at least 256 × 256 pixels. Each texture map will then add at least four bytes per processor (four pixels times one byte per pixel). A full color 1K × 1K texture map adds 512 bytes per processor.

Adding up all the above, each processor will have to store 0.75 kbytes or more. This appears to fit handily in the 8 kbytes available in a CM-2. However, a word of caution is advisable. For the film industry, much higher resolution is often called for. Some use 4K × 4K pixels or more. Often, an order-of-magnitude-more shape description data is used to describe a more complicated scene. Furthermore, a number of calculations will require considerable temporary data. One eye must be kept on the storage limits at all times.

For complex images taking a long time to render, it may be practical to roll in data, such as texture maps, as needed. The DataVault could roll in a 1K × 1K RGB texture map (a million 24-bit pixels) in under a tenth of a second. At such speeds, it is probably practical to read in texture maps and other large sets of data as needed.

18.4 Adapting the conventional graphics pipeline

First, it should be noted that our intended use for the Connection Machine is to render scenes containing many more vertices and surfaces than there are processors. Typical scenes, in our experience, have run to hundreds of thousands of polygons. Few scenes require less than 30 or 40 thousand. Organizations of the machine in which each processor computes on a vertex and in which each processor computes on a polygon are both useful. Such uses will be intermixed within a task. A conventional graphics pipeline may call for:

(1) transforming vertices,

(2) clipping,

(3) scan conversion, and

(4) shading pixels.

The following sections show how such procedures could be adapted to the Connection Machine.

18.4.1 Transforms

Transforms can be done straightforwardly by allocating a number of vertices per processor. Typically, a complex scene can be expected to contain plenty of vertices to keep all of the processors occupied. However, there can be major changes in performance with incremental increases in the number of vertices. For example, 16 385 vertices will take twice as long to transform as 16 384 on a 16K processor machine.

The matrices defining the transforms must be built up from global transforms, representing the desired view of the scene, and local transforms, representing the positions and orientations of the shapes in the scene and the relative positions of subshapes to their parent shapes. Many of these matrices may not change from frame to frame, but a substantial number will.

At the time of writing, it appears that updating the matrices at each frame is done most efficiently in the host processor or another communicating processor. These calculations are generally different for each shape, making it unlikely that the parallel capability of the Connection Machine will be of much use. However, since there will generally be a similar number of transforms for each shape, the chain of transforms for all shapes can be concatenated in parallel.

The conventional method for concatenating and applying a sequence of matrices is first to concatenate the matrices and then to apply the resulting matrix to all appropriate vertices. However, we shall be applying the matrices in parallel to all vertices simultaneously. This turns the situation around. For less than four vertices per processor, it is more efficient to apply each matrix in turn to the vertex (16 multiplies, 12 adds for a 4×4 matrix), than to concatenate the matrices (64 multiplies, 48 adds). Additionally, since storage limits seem to be the main concern, it is probably preferable to pass changed matrices in anew with each frame than to try to operate on them in memory.

Generally, the number of distinct objects requiring a unique set of transforms can be expected to be much smaller than the number of processors. However, typical scenes may contain hundreds of independently moving shapes, and thousands have been used on occasion. Under such conditions, matrix updates may be better done in parallel.

18.4.2 Clipping

Clipping can use the vertex-per-processor organization and also the polygon-per-processor organization. Using a variant on the Cohen-Sutherland algorithm (Sproull, 1968), all vertices may be evaluated simultaneously for their relationship to each clipping plane in turn. This will yield a set of boolean values characterizing the clip state of each vertex.

Using a polygon-per-processor organization, each polygon can be trivially accepted if, by ORing together the clip states of all its vertices, it is discovered that all vertices lie inside. Similarly, ANDing all relevant clip states will indicate trivial rejection if all vertices lie outside the frame with respect to a given clipping plane. The *n*-cube interconnect of the Connection Machine makes it easy to access all corresponding vertices in parallel to perform these calculations. Those polygons which fail to be either rejected or accepted will then require further action. Generally, the polygons which actually need to have new vertices computed are a relatively small subset of the whole.

All such polygons can be clipped together. However, the processing will not be terribly efficient. Because of the architecture of the Connection Machine, the obvious algorithm would require that all steps in the clipping process must be executed for each clipping plane as long as any polygon needs to be clipped to that plane.

It may be possible to bunch clipping operations by setting up the parameters for a clip and waiting until all affected polygons have a clip operation ready before actually carrying it out. However, it is unlikely that this would net even a factor of two in increased performance. Happily, our experience has proven clipping to be an insignificant proportion of the total execution time for an image, making optimizations unnecessary.

18.4.3 Scan conversion algorithms

As seen above, massively parallel graphics fall most easily into the processor-per-pixel model. However, this is exceedingly inefficient for images containing a lot of little polygons. If polygons are passed to the machine in the instruction stream, then each processor must consider each polygon.

Consider a pair of example scenes. Figure 18.1 caused 666 polygons to be scan converted. The polygons averaged 127 pixels apiece. Figure 18.2 required 3248 polygons, averaging 14 pixels. These are very simple scenes by today's standards.

With a 16K processor machine, at best 0.7% of the processors will be effectively utilized in scan converting a 127 pixel polygon, or 0.085% for a 14 pixel polygon. This assumes optimal distribution of the processors, so that no processor handles more than one pixel from the polygon. Furthermore, all the techniques that have developed over the years for using coherence to reduce scan conversion to largely incremental operations are lost with this approach.

The Pixel-planes system (Fuchs *et al.*, 1985) has the same fundamental flaw, having a pixel-per-processor organization. However, the hardware in Pixel-planes is distributed over the processors in such a way that much of the calculation is shared. Thus the investment in each processor is considerably smaller.

Now, consider an alternative organization where each processor scan converts one or more polygons. For a thousand or fewer polygons, the first objection still holds. Not enough of the processors will be kept busy. However, incremental algorithms will make better use of those processors which have something to do. Furthermore, it is relatively straightforward to subdivide polygons in order to distribute the work over a larger number of processors.

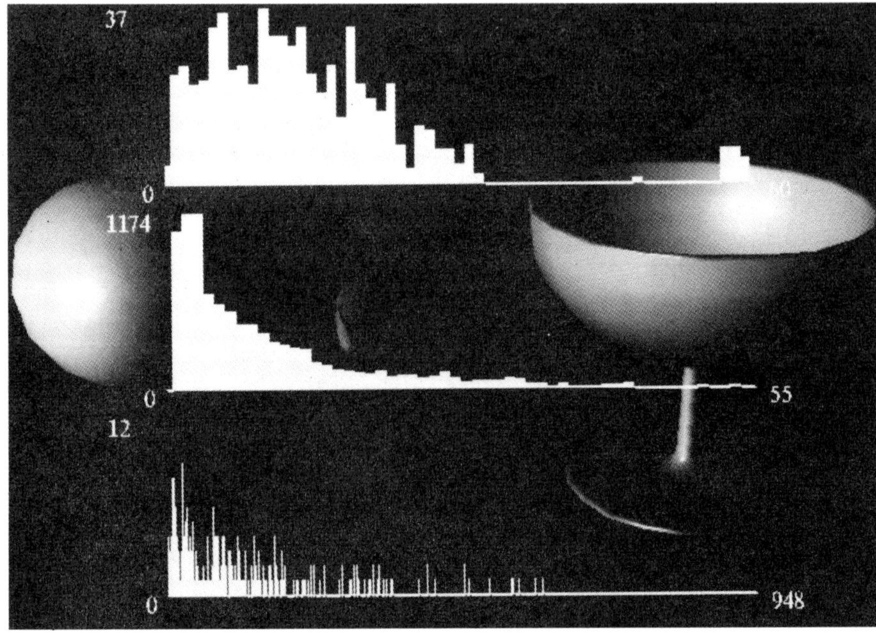

Figure 18.1
Glass, banana and egg with histograms showing the distribution of (top to bottom) polygon heights, scan segment lengths and pixels per polygon. 666 polygons were rendered for this scene (neglecting backfacing polygons), averaging 127 pixels apiece. The largest polygon contained 948 pixels. The average scan segment was 8 pixels, the largest 55. The average height for a polygon was 14 scanlines, the largest 60. Note that tall polygons in the stem of the glass cause a lump at the high end of the distribution of polygon heights. Numbers at the top left of each histogram show the maximum entry (for example, there were 1174 2-pixel scan segments).

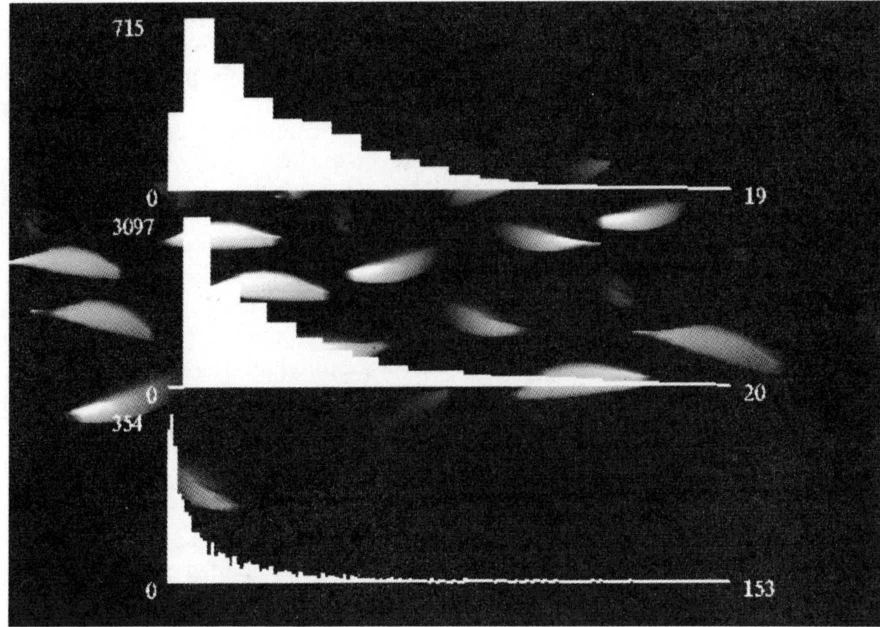

Figure 18.2
Bananas with histograms. 3248 polygons were rendered for this scene, averaging 14 pixels apiece. The largest polygon contained 153 pixels. The average scan segment was 4 pixels, the largest 20. The average height for a polygon was 3 scanlines, the largest 19.

Where larger numbers of polygons are involved, the polygon per processor approach looks better and better. We can examine a simplistic algorithm where all polygons are restricted to be triangles. To keep the efficiency up, we must try to keep the number of cases which must be enumerated to a minimum. Therefore, a restriction to triangles has advantages beyond simplicity. A scan conversion algorithm for triangles might proceed as follows:

(1) Visit all the vertices of the polygon, determining the uppermost.

(2) Determine the vertex defining the left edge and generate an incremental description.

(3) Determine the vertex defining the right edge and generate an incremental description.

(4) Generate an incremental description for the bottom edge.

(5) For each scanline spanned:
  (a) Generate an incremental description of the scan segment.
  (b) Write colors and depths to those pixels covered by the scan segment.
  (c) Update the left and right edge descriptions to the next scanline.
  (d) If either the left or right edge is exhausted, replace with the bottom edge.
  (e) If the bottom edge is already in use, quit.

This would run with little change on the Connection Machine. For example, take the process of generating the pixels from an incremental description of the scan segment. The loop which produces pixels must run until all processors have finished.

Therefore, each processor must drop out when its segment is completed and wait until all others have finished. The Connection Machine provides functions for quickly determining, via a global OR implemented in the *n*-cube network, whether all processors are finished.

There are many sources of inefficiency in using the above algorithm. Triangles may be of vastly differing sizes: all processors with shorter triangles will be idled for some part of the time while taller triangles run to completion. On each scanline, processors doing the narrower triangles will be idled while the wider ones run to completion. When updating to the next scanline, all processors not requiring that an edge be replaced will have to wait for those that do.

What could be done to mitigate some of these sources of inefficiency? One step has already been taken in the algorithm described above. It is considerably more efficient to calculate the incremental description of the bottom edge in advance, when all processors can do it together, than later when a large percentage of the processors would have to wait.

If triangles differ greatly in size, it is probably worthwhile to subdivide them to a narrower range of sizes. This could be done for the shape descriptions in advance or, more effectively, for the polygons after transformation. The Connection Machine provides functions for enumerating all processors in a given state. This can be used to find the unloaded or lightly loaded processors and distribute polygon fragments to them.

Even if triangles are similar in size, they may differ drastically in aspect ratio, some tall and thin, some short and fat. This disparity could be alleviated by the following method: first, determine, either by heuristic or measurement, a reasonable average scan segment length. Always run the scan segment loop for that predetermined length. Second, those processors whose scan segments were exhausted in the loop may increment their edges to the next scanline and generate a new scan segment. When the scan segment loop is run again, some processors will be resuming where they left off while others will be beginning a new scanline.

The above procedure will balance the behavior of tall and squat triangles to a degree. If the time to update to a new scanline is quite short, it could be better to reduce the standard scan loop to one third or one quarter of the expected average scan segment length. Some experience should tell us what the right balance is.

Another source of inefficiency arises in the process of writing out pixels. So far, the scan conversion process has used a processor-per-vertex organization to retrieve vertex information and a processor-per-polygon organization to drive the major loops. An organization using a processor per pixel(s) is needed to store the resulting pixels.

As each pixel is computed, it must be stored. A simple way to do this would be to use a depth buffer approach. Each scan conversion processor would send its address to the pixel processor where it wished to write. The pixel processors (the same set of processors, permuted) would then read the pixel depth from the scan conversion processor, compare their previously stored depths, then store the depth and read and store the color if the new depth were less.

There are significant possibilities for collisions as pixels are stored. More than one scan conversion processor may be trying to write to the same pixel. Moreover, since there are a million or more pixels in an image of reasonable resolution and only 16K to 64K processors, each processor may be handling as many as 64 pixels. Collisions are bound to occur frequently. The obvious solution is to repeat the pixel storage process until all pixels are successfully stored.

Note that the above algorithm requires considerable temporary storage for its execution. Incremental descriptions for all three sides of the triangle must be stored, as well as the incremental description for a scan segment. If many values, such as normal vectors and coordinates needed for texture calculations, are being carried along, attention must be paid to the storage limits.

18.4.4 Shading algorithms

Shading is straightforward for faceted or smooth (Gouraud, 1971) shading. In those cases, the shade may be calculated once per polygon or once per vertex, then propagated along through the scan conversion process, interpolating if smooth shading is used, and finally delivered to the pixel. For highlights, texture, shadows and other effects more calculation must be done at the pixel.

The most straightforward approach would be to do the more elaborate pixel shading whenever pixels were stored. However, this requires executing all pixel shading procedures at each pixel storage cycle. It would be more efficient to accumulate many pixels, then gather together those with similar shading requirements for calculation at some later point.

The notion of accumulating pixels raises two points. First, should a depth buffer scheme be used, preventing easy integration of transparent surfaces? Second, if pixels are accumulated without using a depth buffer, how can they be stored? The vast differences in depth complexity across the image would make it wasteful to allow space for the maximum depth complexity at every pixel, even if it could be known in advance.

Many of the fancier pixel shading techniques lend themselves very nicely to massively parallel computation. Consider, for example, environment mapping, in which a reflected ray from the surface is used to access an image representing the environment. The reflected rays can be calculated simultaneously for all participating surfaces, as can the calculation of a location in the environment image and retrieval of the color from that location.

Texture mapping is equally straightforward, as long as enough pixels are using the same texture map. The texture coordinates delivered to each pixel are used to calculate a texture address simultaneously. Then, texture pixels may be retrieved simultaneously using the *n*-cube network. If the texture (or environment map) is small enough to store one pixel per processor (128 × 128 for a 16K machine or 256 × 256 for a 64K machine), then the texture retrieval is simple.

Simple retrieval collisions (multiple processors accessing the same location) are supposed to be handled automatically by the routing network in the CM-2. However, retrieval collisions where more than one pixel is stored per processor require successive retries, messing up otherwise simple algorithms.

Calculating solid- or space-filling texture is, happily, almost ideally suited to the Connection Machine architecture. A space-filling texture amounts to an evaluation of an often complicated function which uses no input other than a set of three-space coordinates associated with the surface area represented by the pixel. As long as a sufficient number of pixels need the same function, the lock-step execution of the function by all processors is as efficient as any method. With sufficient surface area, solid texture should realize the full floating-point capability of the machine.

Conclusions

It is legitimate to ask whether the Connection Machine is a cost-effective solution to the task of a commercial animation production house. Alternative hardware bases include: (1) a fleet of workstation-class machines, each computing a single frame, as used by the Midnight Movie crew at Apollo, (2) another kind of supercomputer with greater scalar performance, such as the Cray used by Digital Productions, (3) specialized hardware, such as used by flight simulators, and (4) modern, semi-specialized 'image computers,' such as those provided by Pixar, Sun-Trancept, and AT&T Pixel Machines.

(1) Some arguments for using a centralized supercomputer rather than a decentralized scheme involving many workstation-class machines are:
   (a) It is easier to manage the facility. Shape data and scene descriptions do not have to be replicated in many locations with attendant problems in maintaining consistency.
   (b) Turnaround time on individual images and short animations is much better, making it easier to focus efforts during a deadline crunch.

(2) As mentioned above, the Connection Machine offers more raw power per dollar than conventional supercomputers. In our application, very high levels of parallel computation can be maintained, leading us to believe that the Connection Machine will prove to be the more cost-effective alternative.

(3) A modern animation house has to be light on its feet and able to incorporate new effects quickly. This tends to lessen the utility of dedicated, flight simulator style architectures for production purposes although they can be useful for 'pencil tests,' quick looks at the animation using restricted rendering styles.

(4) The image computers are still relatively new. Until very recently, such machines were restricted to fixed-point arithmetic. There is not enough experience with newer floating-point-based systems to be able to evaluate them, although they look very good. Such machines are relatively small, as yet, and therefore the objections under (1) above still hold, although to a lesser degree than for conventional workstations.

Although we have yet to demonstrate it, we believe that the Connection Machine provides a good match to our task. The combination of the massively parallel organization with the innovative use of the *n*-cube network opens new programming paradigms which we have barely begun to understand. Even as neophytes in this world, however, we have found reasonably efficient ways to do all tasks we have addressed.

References

Batcher K.E. (1980). Design of a massively parallel processor. *IEEE Trans. on Computers,* **C-29**(9), 836–40

Cook R.L. (1984). Shade trees. *Computer Graphics,* **18**(3), 223–31

Fuchs H. *et al.* (1985). Fast spheres, shadows, textures, transparencies and image enhancements in Pixel-planes. *Computer Graphics,* **19**(3), 111–20

Gouraud H. (1971). Computer display of curved surfaces. *IEEE Trans. on Computers,* **C-20**(6), 623–9

Hillis W.D. and Steele G.L., Jr. (1986). Data parallel algorithms. *Comm. ACM,* **29**(12), 1170–83

Sproull R.F. and Sutherland I.E. (1968). A clipping divider. In *Proc. FJCC 1968*, pp. 765–75. Washington DC: Thompson Books

Schachter B.J. (1983). *Computer Image Generation*. New York: John Wiley & Sons

Schumaker R.A. (1980). A new visual system architecture. In *Proc. 2nd Interservice/Industry Training Equipment Conference*, pp. 941–101. Salt Lake City UT

Slotnick D.L. (1967). Unconventional systems. In *1967 SJCC*, pp. 477–81. Reston VA: AFIPS Press

Slotnick D.L. (1971). The fastest computer. *Scientific American*, 2, 76–87

Thinking Machines Corporation (1987). *Connection Machine model CM-2 technical summary*. Technical report HA87-4

Watkins G.S. (1970). A real-time visible surface algorithm. *PhD Thesis*, University of Utah

R.L. Grimsdale

University of Sussex

19 · Techniques for real-time image generation

The production of good quality images in real time requires specialized computer architectures exploiting parallelism. In certain cases, coherence in object or image space may be used to reduce the processing load. Techniques and special architectures for performing the geometrical transformations from the 3D model representation to screen coordinates are described. Scan conversion methods which map the image on to the array of screen pixels are discussed with special reference to hidden surface removal, anti-aliasing and smooth shading. A high performance texturing system is described.

19.1 Introduction

There is now a considerable demand for systems which produce good quality images in real time. The most well-known application is the flight simulator visual system, but as costs fall, real-time image generation will be used increasingly in other forms of training simulators, and indeed wherever animated sequences are required.

A standard requirement for real-time image generation systems is the capability of producing images that change in time as a result of the movement of the viewpoint. The system latency, which is the time between a change in the viewpoint and the production of the resulting image, should be of the order of 0.1 s. A further requirement is the ability to display changes in the model. Raster scan colour CRT displays are normally employed and there are requirements for frame rates up to 60 per second. Typically, the display will comprise a 2D array of pixels with a resolution of between 512 × 512 and 1024 × 1024. Each pixel is defined by 256 levels in each of the red, green and blue components.

The images are produced by a set of transformations applied to a 3D stored representation of a model of a real object or of natural terrain. In order to achieve the high speed of image generation, it is desirable to use a simple representation for the model and it is normal to construct it as a set of polygon faces. The simplest case is when the model is composed of triangular faces.

The image generation process can be defined as a mapping of the faces of the model on to the pixel array. The model is defined in 3D in the **object space** and the image is produced in the **image space**. The mapping shows the faces which are visible from a particular viewpoint. Inherent in the process is the necessity to remove faces or parts of faces that are hidden by other faces. The discrete nature of digital processes gives rise to the possibility of quantization errors, and an important feature of the production of high quality real-time images is the elimination of these errors as far as possible.

The very high processing rate required to produce high quality images in real time introduces the necessity for some considerable degree of parallel processing. This chapter will discuss a number of possible arrangements whereby this parallelism may be introduced.

19.2 Model representation

A number of different forms of representation are used for the 3D model which constitutes a stored representation of the object or set of objects to be displayed. In the computational solid geometrical form, the model is represented as a set of solid objects defined by mathematical expressions. These include cubic patches, B-splines and Bezier curves. As an aid to the interactive construction of a complex model, Boolean operations may be performed on the components to produce a model of considerable complexity. Whilst this representation has many advantages, particularly during the construction stage, the representation is not amenable to the geometrical transformations necessary to create views of the model from any desired position within real-time constraints.

The standard technique for model representation to meet the real-time transformation requirements is, therefore, to define the model as a collection of linearly defined components. These components may take the form of intersecting halfplanes or planar-bounded surfaces in the form of polygons or facets (commonly known as B-Rep or boundary representation). A polygon face may be defined in terms of the coordinates of its apex points, each associated with number of parameters which define attributes of the surface including colour, translucency and texture. The process of transforming the facet from 3D to 2D may then be performed by transforming the coordinates.

It is often useful to structure the model, particularly during the original construction phase. Thus, a hierarchical model can simplify the understanding of the model and lead to the possibility of reuseable segments. In certain applications, a distance ordering is produced as an offline operation on the data structure forming the model. This can be used for a subsequent resolution of hidden surfaces, but the technique has limitations and can give rise to errors if the comparisons are based on a single priority value for each surface.

19.3 The image generation process

The overall task to be performed is the creation of a 2D image defined by the colour and luminance of the pixels in the image space formed by the CRT screen. There are two principal techniques whereby this may be achieved. In the **projective** method, the individual component faces are subjected to a geometrical transformation, with the parameters of the transformation being defined according to the relative positions of the model, the viewing screen and the eyepoint, together with the viewing direction. The alternative **ray-tracing** process operates by projecting rays from the viewpoint through each of the individual pixels and determining the points of intersection of the rays with the model. The direction of the rays reflected from the model may then be computed and the rays further traced through subsequent reflections with other surfaces until the source(s) of illumination is(are) reached.

Consideration will now be given to methods of realizing the projective technique in real time. Notable increases in speed of operation have been achieved in arithmetic units as a result of developments in VLSI technology. For example, fixed-point ALUs are currently available with throughputs of about 10 MIPs and floating-point ALUs can deliver 2 to 6 MFLOPs. However, a single processor is quite inadequate to provide the necessary computing power, as this can involve determination of the colour of as many as one million pixels in one tenth of a second. It is therefore necessary to exploit parallel processing.

A well-known problem of parallel processing is that of determining how to partition the task to allow concurrent processing. At a general level, parallelism may be introduced by partitioning in either object space or image space. An example of object-space parallelism is the provision of a processor for each polygon in the model. Each of the processors is given the task of determining the contribution, if any, of its associated polygon to each pixel in turn. In image partitioning, processors are assigned to regions of the image space, for example, individual scan lines or individual pixels. These processors are required to compute for each polygon in turn, the contribution of the polygon to the region of image space under consideration. Ideally, the parallel operations should be allowed to proceed independently of each other, but this is not possible because the ultimate colour of a pixel will be determined by resolving contention for that pixel from several polygon sources. Some form of depth sorting is thus necessary that inherently involves the interaction of the parallel processes. The problem is compounded when subpixel processing is introduced to overcome aliasing errors. A pixel at the boundary of several polygons will receive contributions from all those polygons.

A pure division into either object partitioning or image partitioning may not be ideal, and some sequential phases may profitably be introduced into the overall process. A particular example is the separation of the transformation processes, scan conversion and image rendering phases. These are described in the next sections.

19.3.1 Clipping, viewing transformation and perspective transformation

The transformation of the object from the 3D object frame of reference to the 2D image frame is achieved by the processes of clipping, viewing transformation and perspective transformation, the algorithms for which are well known. A clipping operation performed in 3D by clipping the surfaces of the model against the viewing cone will serve to eliminate surfaces and reduce the subsequent computing load. Following transformation to screen coordinates, a 2D clipping operation is performed against the screen boundaries. The clipping process involves arithmetic operations and decisions based on magnitude comparisons. As a result of clipping, it may be necessary to introduce additional edges into a polygon. The viewing transformation is normally performed by 3×3 matrix multiplication function applied to the 3D coordinates of the apex points of the polygons; this is followed by the perspective transformation which involves division operations. The two transformations require high-speed arithmetic processing.

19.3.2 Scan conversion and image rendering

The scan conversion operation performs the processing necessary to generate a raster image from the set of polygons that have already been transformed to screen coordinates. This process is responsible for removing hidden and invisible surfaces and performing at least part of the task of anti-aliasing to reduce staircase edge effects.

The image rendering operation computes the colour value of each pixel from the available data. The colour value specifies the luminance and chrominance. The pixels are rendered to produce surface shading and to perform anti-aliasing at the polygon boundaries. Additionally, texturing may be incorporated to enhance realism.

19.4 Architectures for geometry processing

Geometry processing, which includes clipping, viewing transformation and perspective transformation, involves an intensive amount of arithmetic operations being applied to a stream of data. This processing can be performed very effectively by a dedicated configuration of arithmetic processing elements. Two different schemes have been devised in the Multiple Application Graphics Integrated Circuit (MAGIC) I and MAGIC II systems (Agate *et al.*, 1987; Finch, 1987).

An architecture for MAGIC I has been developed with the aim of producing a VLSI geometry processor for a wide range of graphic applications, from personal computers through workstations to real-time flight simulator visual systems. The dominant requirements for this processor are therefore flexibility and performance.

Flexibility in MAGIC I is achieved through the use of a writeable control store, so that the precise functionality of MAGIC I may be defined by the user, rather than by the chip designer. MAGIC I uses the IEEE floating-point format to allow a large dynamic range in the object model to be accommodated. However, VLSI implementation of fast floating-point processors requires relatively large areas of silicon. This problem has been reconciled by designing MAGIC I to be a controller for geometry operations, and providing a floating-point coprocessor (Advanced Micro Devices, 1985; Analog Devices, 1985) to perform numerical computation.

Real-time applications are likely to require a higher performance from the geometry system than that attainable with a single instance of MAGIC I, even with the fast floating-point coprocessors currently available. The approach to parallelism adopted in the MAGIC I system is to arrange for each MAGIC I processor to handle a polygon at a time and to perform the entire transformation from world coordinates to screen coordinates. Whilst low-end performance systems may require only one MAGIC I processor, a flight simulator visual system might employ several instances of MAGIC I, transforming different areas of the active database concurrently, and passing their results on to the display processor.

19.4.1 MAGIC I operations

Transformation of objects from world coordinates to screen coordinates requires a sequence of geometric operations which are essentially vector computations. All these computations may be achieved using Cartesian (3-element) coordinates, and this approach generally leads to a lower processing requirement than the use of homogeneous (4-element) vectors. Vertex points have an associated intensity of illumination value for Gouraud (Gouraud, 1971) shading, which must be correctly interpreted during clipping, and may be modified for distance fade as part of the perspective projection.

The geometric operations performed in the geometry processor are:

- Backfacing surface removal which involves the computation of a dot product followed by comparison with a constant, to determine the orientation of the surface normal with respect to the vector to the surface from the viewpoint.
- Clipping in 3D against the viewing cone using the Sutherland-Hodgman clipping algorithm (Sutherland and Hodgman, 1974).
- Transformation from 3D to eye coordinates (or parallel projection). This is performed as a matrix operation implemented as three dot products with the addition of a constant.
- Perspective projection into 2D screen coordinates and the computation of the **proximity** which is the inverse of distance. These operations are described below.

Generation of proximity in the perspective projection

A point is transformed to eye coordinates (x, y, z) by a view matrix which incorporates scaling factors for the size of the viewing screen. The perspective projection to screen coordinates (x_s, y_s) may then be achieved by the following sequence:

$p := 1 / z$ where p denotes proximity

$$x_s := x_{cen} + (p * x)$$

$$y_s := y_{cen} + (p * y)$$

where (x_{cen}, y_{cen}) denote the coordinates of the centre of the viewing screen.

The proximity p is the inverse of the distance of the point on the object from the plane through the eye point parallel to the screen, as shown in Figure 19.1. It will be observed that although the intervals between the pixels on the viewing screen are constant, the corresponding visible points are non-linearly spaced across the planar surface in a perspective projection. Depth values at intermediate positions therefore cannot be linearly interpolated from endpoint values of z. This is a disadvantage since these values are required for the purposes of 2D clipping and z-buffer comparison for hidden surface removal.

Fortunately, it can be shown that the proximities $(1 / z)$ of the visible points across a perspective projection of a planar surface can be linearly interpolated. It is therefore much more convenient to implement a hidden surface algorithm in the display processor based on proximity comparisons, since the proximity at each pixel can be computed incrementally from its previous neighbour. This incremental computation is an example of the way in which coherence within the object may be

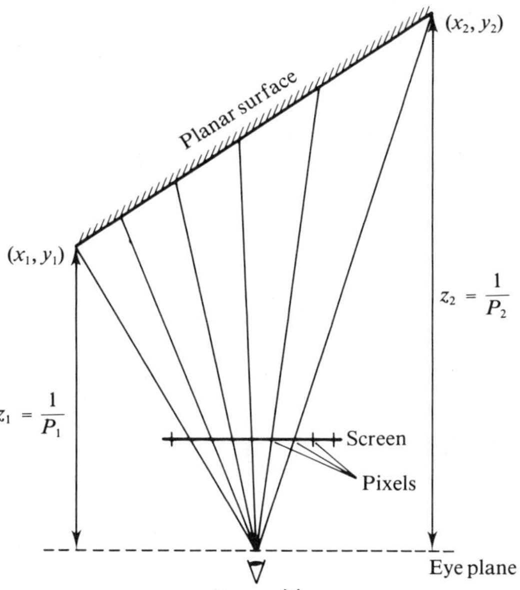

Figure 19.1
The incremental property of proximity.

exploited to reduce the computation load. Thus a proximity buffer (p-buffer) algorithm may be used instead of a z-buffer, in which case the surface with the greatest proximity value becomes the visible surface at each point. In the operation of 2D clipping to the screen boundaries, proximity values may be linearly interpolated to produce the new values at the clipped points and similarly the values for Gouraud shading may also be interpolated.

19.4.2 MAGIC I architecture

The proposed architecture for MAGIC I, with its associated memory and floating-point coprocessor, is shown in Figure 19.2. The principal components are the writeable microprogram store, the Operand Address Counters (OACs) and the pipeline registers. A 32-bit floating-point representation is used within the data registers. The memory is organized as three sections; one section contains the active database (or part thereof), the second section holds the screen and viewing parameters and is also used as workspace during transformations, and the third holds the transformed data for onward transmission to the display processor.

In a typical transformation sequence, MAGIC I tests each surface to determine if it is forward facing, and if so, performs the parallel projection on the untransformed data, storing the intermediate results in the workspace area until the resulting polygon is written into the transformed data section of the memory.

In each memory section, vector quantities are aligned to four-word boundaries, thereby allowing a simple technique for address generation to be employed. This uses the operand address counters, each of which comprises a Vertex Address Counter (VAC) and an Element Address Counter (EAC) as shown in Figure 19.3.

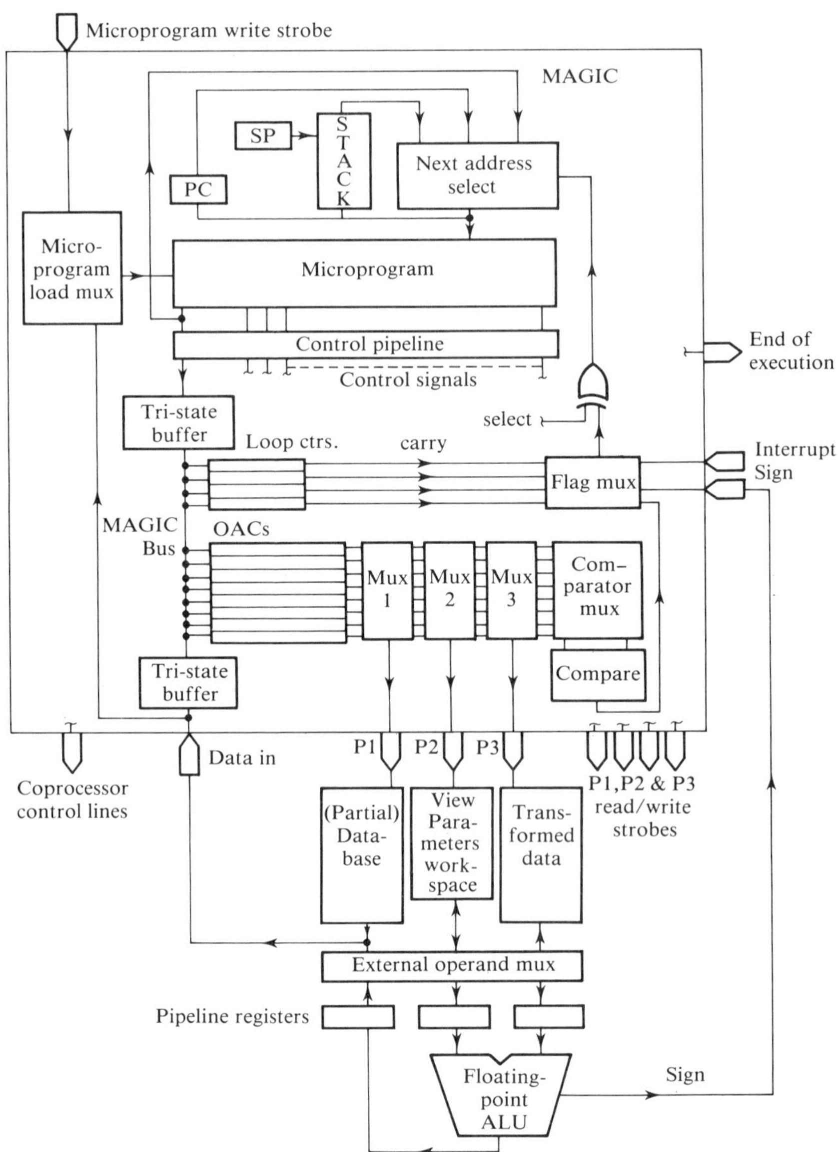

Figure 19.2
MAGIC I architecture.

In normal mode, the OAC is configured to operate as an 18-bit counter so that, on incrementation or decrementation, an overflow from the EAC will cause the VAC to increment or decrement. However, if this overflow is disabled, the EAC can be incremented to allow the addition of four. Decrementation modulo four and subtraction modulo four can be accomplished in a similar way.

With the vertex data being aligned to four-word boundaries, the VAC specifies which vertex is currently being accessed and the EAC points to the required

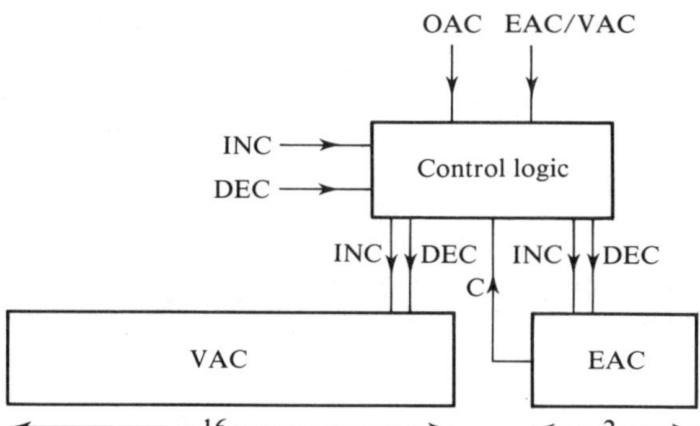

Figure 19.3
Operand address counter.

element within that vertex block. This provides a convenient and rapid generation of operand addresses without recourse to a generalized address computing unit. The OAC unit can be implemented as a regular hardware structure and, operating under microprogram control, allows address generation to be performed concurrently with other operations.

Ideally, the workspace RAM used by MAGIC I might be organized as a three-port structure, so that two operands can be fetched while the result of the previous calculation is being written back. However, as there is time for three memory accesses within one floating-point arithmetic unit cycle, the excessive interconnection problems of a three-port memory may be eliminated by the use of a high-speed RAM. The purpose of the pipeline registers, therefore, is to allow the two operands for the next floating-point computation to be prefetched and the previous result written back, all within the time of one arithmetic unit cycle.

The main functions of MAGIC I are to supply the three operand addresses and the control signals for the external mutliplexer and floating-point coprocessor. A **data in** port is required so that MAGIC I may read either the number of vertices or the address of the last vertex for the current polygon from the database; this port is also used to load the microprogram into the writeable store.

Once MAGIC I has completed its transformation sequence on all the data supplied, the **end of execution** signal is given, indicating that the memory may be accessed by other processors in the system. The architecture of MAGIC I incorporates a stack to allow the use of subroutines in the microprogram sequences. Loop counters are also provided to permit repetitive sequences.

19.4.3 MAGIC II architecture

In contrast to MAGIC I, a pipelined architecture has been adopted for MAGIC II. The fundamental principle underlying a pipelined system is that the processing time for each stage should be the same. This ensures that all stages produce and consume data at the same rate, resulting in a continuous, even flow of data throughout the pipeline from one end to the other. The rate at which a pipeline operates will depend on the number of stages employed and the processing time of one stage, but there will be a latency or delay between the input and output of the corresponding data. In general, the latency is neither important nor observable, and the performance is determined by the rate of processing. If any stage introduces an extra delay, it will add to the total processing time of the pipeline. Such pipelining is extremely well suited to the geometry processing task, owing to the repetitive nature of the task and the large quantities of data involved. Pipelining is also a favoured technique when designing VLSI devices, owing to the regularity of the individual processes and the opportunity to use local and regular connections.

Essentially, the architecture of MAGIC II is a pipeline of arithmetic and register file elements, with each element connected via several multiplexers to the next. The arithmetic elements are an array multiplier/divider and several adder/subtractors, while the register files are specially designed units suitable for general vector manipulation, as shown in Figure 19.4.

The design for the chip provides two input ports and one output port; if a second output port is required, and this is rarely necessary, an additional instance of MAGIC II may be used in parallel to provide this. A bus has been included that effectively bypasses all the functional units and register files. This is used to carry data that does not undergo processing at a particular stage; an example of its use is to carry the offset from the second input port past the multiplier stage to the adder in dot-product-plus-offset-type calculations.

Control of MAGIC II falls into two categories: setup operations which configure the elements of the pipeline to perform a given task, and run-time control which coordinates conditional, data-dependent operations. Setup control signals are multiplexed onto the data port lines; these are then decoded into a very long

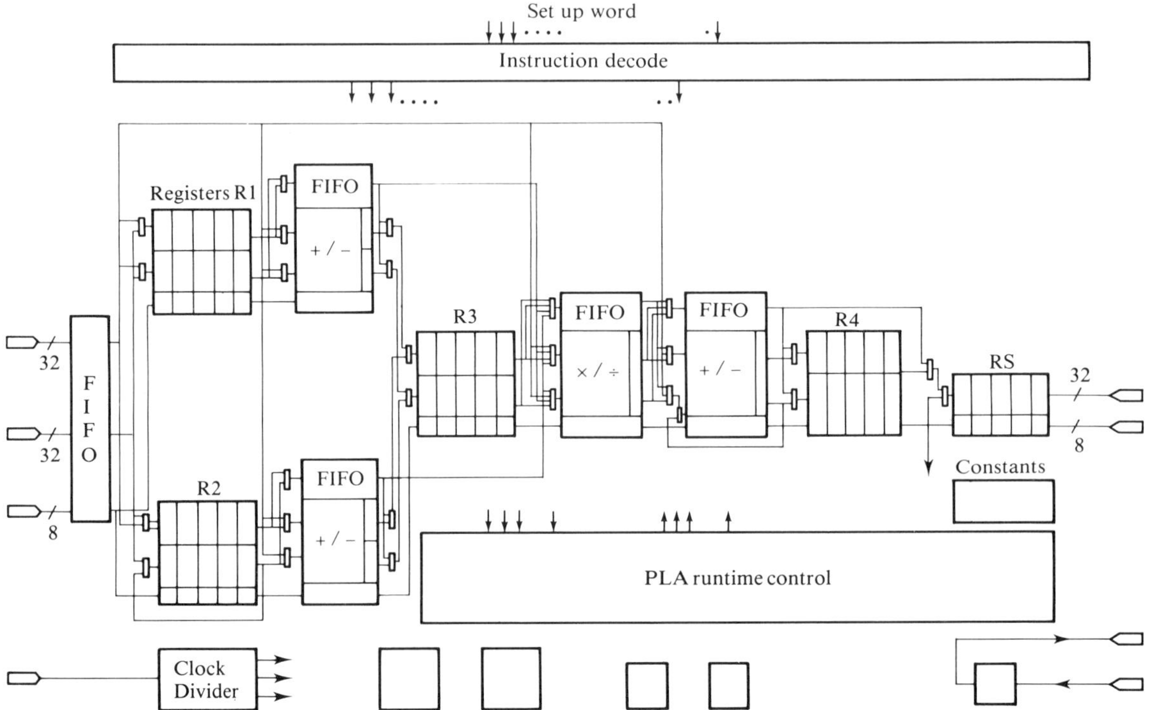

Figure 19.4
MAGIC II architecture.

instruction word (about 128 bits) which configures the register structures, arithmetic units and interconnections within the pipeline. The pipeline is then switched to operational mode with a static configuration of elements subject to run-time control.

Run-time control is effected by a PLA structure which takes flags (from the arithmetic units) and data tags as inputs and produces control signals (usually for data routeing) for all the elements in the pipeline. Each item of data in the pipeline has an encoded tag associated with it; the tags follow the data through the pipeline in parallel tag registers, so that the internal controller can identify the context of the data. For example, the *Last Vertex* in a polygon has a unique tag so that the controller can generate a closing edge using the saved *First Vertex* data.

19.4.4 MAGIC II system configurations

The MAGIC II processor provides direct support for three different levels of pipeline complexity, as typified in the following:

- A minimum geometry system, based on two instances of the MAGIC II processor.
- A fully pipelined system with a single numeric data stream, offering adequate performance for use in a flight simulator visual system.
- A pipelined system with three parallel streams of vector elements, giving a very high performance for use in future systems.

The first of these systems utilizes pipelining only at a numeric processing level (for example, a single chip can execute 32 simultaneous operations within the divider). The second level system operates at element rate, that is, it provides a pipeline of operations for performing all operations on a single stream of vector elements, and the third runs at vector rate, processing entire vectors at each clock cycle. A further option is to operate a number of parallel pipelines at element rate, offering greater potential for increased performance than the vector-rate system.

A minimum of two chips are required to implement all the geometry operations, since a clipping operation requires a parameter calculation and an intersection calculation working in parallel. These two processors must be configured for a single geometric operation prior to the passage of data, and buffering is required so that intermediate results are stored after each pass.

Figure 19.5 shows a fully pipelined geometry system. A single backfacing surface remover interacts with the controller to determine which surfaces are subsequently passed through the transformation pipeline. This pipeline comprises element-rate modules for parallel projection, perspective projection and clipping to a near plane and edges of the screen. A total of 16 instances of MAGIC II are required.

The vector rate pipeline is shown in Figure 19.6. For clarity, this does not show the separate instances of MAGIC II within each module. A bus width of 96 bits is required from the database (128 if homogeneous coordinates are used, or if intensity values are associated with each vertex). The system employs 36 MAGIC II processors.

An estimate of the performance of the minimum system is most easily derived from consideration of the fully pipelined systems, so this is deferred to the

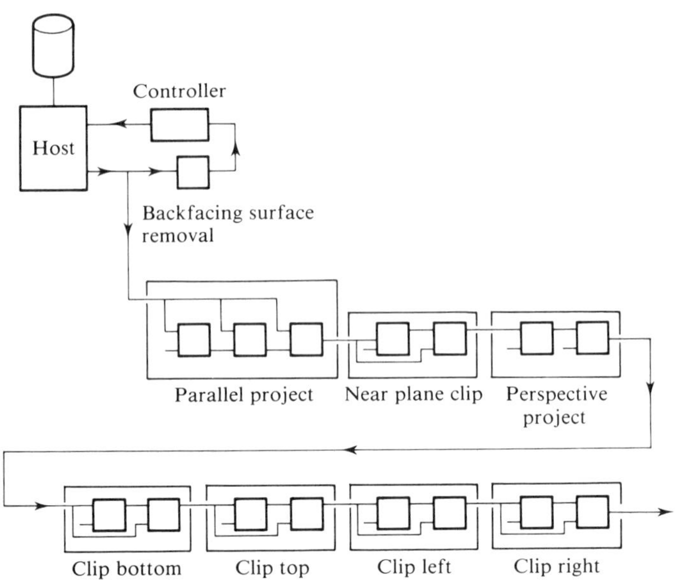

Figure 19.5
Pipelined geometry system using MAGIC II devices.

last. An average of four vertices per polygon are assumed with a real-time frame rate of 60 Hz. The pipeline is assumed to be clocked at 100 ns. Since it is difficult to quantify the number of surfaces which are backfacing or off-screen in any one frame, the number of polygons processed is discussed in preference to the number displayed. Polygons that are off-screen will introduce empty data slots into the pipeline at the clipping stages, whilst those detected as backfacing will yield only a few empty data slots between potentially visible surfaces.

An element-rate transformation pipeline is capable of reading a single cartesian coordinate vertex, with associated intensity values, every four clock periods. This corresponds to a rate of 2.5 million vertices per second, or approximately 10 000 polygons processed per frame. The vector-rate equivalent system runs at four times this speed, giving a processing rate of 40 000 polygons per frame.

The two-chip equivalent of the above pipeline has only a single module which is reconfigured for each operation. Thus, by comparison with the element-rate pipeline, the clipping phase will take five passes, perspective projection will take one pass, as will backfacing surface removal, and the parallel projection phase will run three times slower than the three-chip module. The whole projection phase therefore runs about 10 times slower than the element-rate pipeline, giving an overall rate of about 1000 polygons per frame.

The geometry processor serves to transform the model, comprising a set of polygons in 3D coordinates to a set of polygons in 2D screen coordinates. Because backfacing and off-screen surfaces have been eliminated, the two sets will not necessarily have the same membership. In addition, the clipping operation will have modified the shape of certain polygons by adding extra edges.

The display processor must now allocate the 2D polygons to the individual pixels on the screen, removing hidden surfaces and dealing with translucent surfaces. Also, subpixel operations are required to reduce aliasing errors at polygon

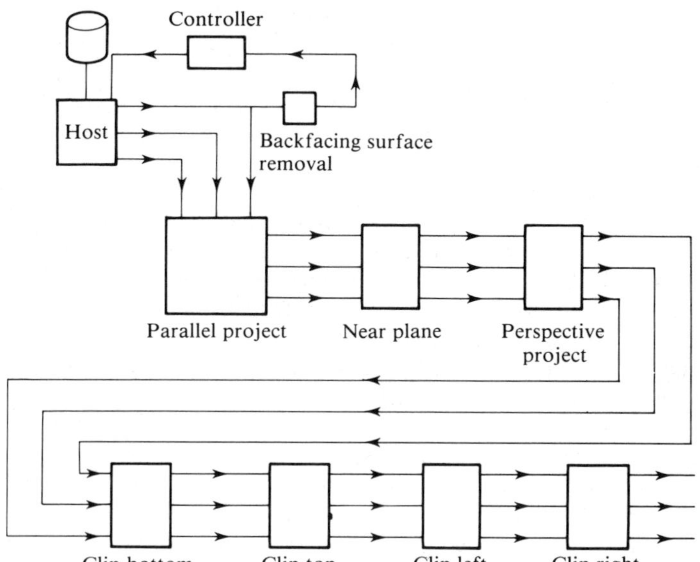

Figure 19.6
Vector rate pipeline.

edges. Finally, the polygons must be rendered to produce smooth shaded or textured surfaces.

The display process may exploit parallelism and coherence in either object space or image space or both.

Exploiting coherence

Parallelism implies that many similar operations are performed independently on data. For example, every pixel in an image may be computed separately. However, an analysis of typical images will reveal a considerable amount of regional coherence. This coherence is exhibited in both the object and image spaces. For example, there is coherence over the area of a polygon, and it is usually possible to identify coherence within individual scan lines.

The virtue of coherence is that the adjacent regions of a coherent area of an image are generally related by differences which may be computed incrementally. Such incremental operations involve perhaps one simple addition or subtraction operation in contrast to a complex algorithm, necessary if the pixel is computed from raw data. These complex algorithms can involve the lengthy operations of multiplication and division.

Another advantage of exploiting coherence within a surface, is that one set of data suffices for the entire surface and therefore the time spent in transferring data from the database to the processing elements can be minimized.

Parallelism in object space

The basic idea is to provide a processor for every polygon comprising the model as defined in object space. As noted above, the polygons have been transformed to 2D screen coordinates by the geometry processor, but depth information has been preserved, and the process has removed backfacing and off-screen surfaces. A collection of processors generate the image determining the colour intensity of each pixel. The Zone Management Processor (ZMP) system (Grimsdale *et al.*, 1979) uses this concept. A set of polygon processors, one for each polygon, operates in parallel at pixel rate in synchronism with the raster scan display.

For a given scanline, each processor computes the start and end points of each span and its distance (strictly, the proximity) at each pixel from the viewpoint. There is a common bus to which all processors are connected. Using a mechanism which is described below, a mutual resolution process is performed to determine the nearest polygon at each pixel and arrange for information about this polygon to be sent to the display (Price, 1984). This resolution process operates at pixel rate, but as it is pipelined, the result is delayed by a small number of pixel times.

The special advantage of this technique is the exploitation of area coherence. This is really object-space coherence, because it uses the property of the surface in object space, even though a transformation has occurred. Thus, using coherence, it is possible to perform computations for the parameters of the polygon at each pixel using incremental techniques. The start and end points of each span are computed from one scanline to the next, by the addition or subtraction of the edge gradient increment. Similarly, incremental calculations can be used to determine the proximity.

Further properties of the polygon are computed on an incremental basis. Smooth shading is also performed by incrementing the intensity from pixel to pixel. The availability of the proximity value at each pixel also allows distance fade to be computed accurately.

The problem of aliased edges can be minimized by computing the fractional contribution of the surface to the pixels on the edge. This technique, which effectively increases the resolution of the system, uses the information which is available within the ZMP about the whole polygon.

The priority or hidden-surface resolution has been demonstrated in a particular implementation of the system, in which the proximity values have been expressed as 16-bit integer quantities. The problem is to determine, for each pixel, which is the largest proximity value for all the polygons that are potentially visible at that pixel. The technique employed uses a sequential bit-wise comparison of the proximity values of all the contending polygons. The comparison starts with the most significant bit, and those processors for which the bit is not set remove themselves from the comparison process. The comparison operation is pipelined so that there is a short delay in obtaining the result. The technique is illustrated in the following example which is restricted to the case of 4-bit numbers.

	2^3	2^2	2^1	2^0
first value	1	1	0	1
second value	1	1	0	0
third value	1	0	1	1
fourth value	0	1	1	1

It will be observed that all the numbers except the fourth have the bit with the value 2^3 set. Therefore the fourth number is smaller than at least one of the other values and is thus eliminated.

	2^3	2^2	2^1	2^0
first value	1	1	0	1
second value	1	1	0	0
third value	1	0	1	1

The first, second and third numbers proceed to the comparison of the next most significant bit in which the third value is eliminated. The first and second values survive the next comparison and at the final comparison the first value becomes the winner.

The algorithm is implemented in hardware in order to achieve the necessary pixel-rate comparison. On each ZMP, there is a priority resolving circuit which asserts the proximity value on to an open collector bus. For each comparison at each stage in the pipeline, access is required to only one of the bus lines, so a 16-bit-wide bus suffices.

The number of ZMPs required in a system can be reduced to below the total number of polygons competing for the screen by a suitable allocation strategy. The conventional arrangement of horizontal scanning lines is assumed. To permit a ZMP to process more than one polygon per frame, an allocation strategy is adopted in which polygons are assigned to ZMPs in order of the highest of the topmost points. Immediately a ZMP completes the processing of a polygon, it is allocated to a further polygon. The number of ZMPs required therefore depends on the statistics of the number and distribution of polygons within the scene.

Image space partitioning

An alternative strategy is to distribute processing power over a number of regions of the image space. For example, the screen may be divided using a recursive quadtree structure. However, it is difficult to establish which polygons occupy a particular quad. Moreover, this will result in unnecessary subdivision of polygons between quads, thereby losing the advantages of coherence. The ultimate partitioning in image space is to assign a processor to each pixel (Fuchs *et al.*, 1982). All the pixel processors receive, in sequence, the specification of each polygon in the model and first test to determine if the pixel lies within the polygon. The depth of included polygons is computed at the pixel and a z-buffer technique is employed to resolve hidden surfaces.

Scanline processing

A preferable alternative is to use the **scanline** as the element into which to subdivide the image space. The scan conversion process is in two stages. Each polygon in image space will occupy several consecutive scanlines. The intersection of the polygon with a scanline is referred to as a span. First, it is necessary to generate the table of spans for the set of polygons that will constitute the image. The spans for each polygon are determined incrementally, exploiting the coherence within the polygon. The edges of the polygon are first determined from the apexes. The uppermost span is calculated and the start and finish positions of the spans on subsequent scanlines can be found from the values on the previous line by incrementing by the gradient. A set of processors operating in parallel can be used to generate the span table. Each polygon can be processed independently of the others with no restriction on the order of processing. A bucket sort is used to allocate the spans to the respective scanlines to produce the span table.

The second stage of the process employs a number of **line processors** operating in parallel to determine for each pixel the nearest span of the several that may occur at that position. The set of spans for the scanline have already been determined and allocated into a bucket for that line. The spans are processed by the line processor in any sequence. The line processor uses a modified z-buffer to eliminate the hidden surfaces. The line processor is presented with the starting point of the span, together with the colour intensity and proximity, as well as the values defining the incremental changes from pixel to pixel. The processor computes the proximity at each point and compares it with the value previously stored in the p-buffer. If the current span at the current pixel is nearer, then the colour intensity and proximity replaces the previously stored value. When all spans have been processed for every scanline, the visible surface at every pixel has been established.

A number of enhancements can be made to this system. In order to alleviate the staircase effect of aliasing, it is necessary, at pixels where two or more surfaces meet, to provide a record of data for all such surfaces. In addition, the system is arranged to operate at subpixel resolution, to enable the fractional occupancy of a pixel by several surfaces to be computed. In the case where translucent surfaces are permitted, it is also necessary to keep records of partially visible surfaces.

The nature of the contribution of the several surfaces to each pixel having been established, the final process is to render each pixel by computing the combination of these several contributions. It is appropriate to employ an associated **rendering processor** with each line processor.

The number of pairs of line and rendering processors can be selected to yield the desired performance. This can range from a single processor to up to one for every scanline, in which case a full frame time is available for the processing of a single line. Scanlines can be allocated to processors in such a way as to distribute the load. In the worst case, it is necessary to ensure that the scanline with the largest number of spans can be processed within the frame time. Under these circumstances, one processor will be solely occupied with processing this busy scanline and the remainder of the frame must be distributed amongst the rest of the processors.

19.5 The incorporation of texture

The incorporation of texture in an image can enhance realism and provide useful, additional, visual cues to aid the perception of distance. A pilot using a training simulator will derive distance cues from the appearance of objects, such as vehicles, buildings or runways, whose size can be estimated. The incorporation of texture, interpolated between known objects, provides a means of estimating distance in the regions between these objects. It also establishes the nature of the terrain, whether this be grassland, cornfields, water or tarmac.

It is essential that the texture should be accurately computed, if it is to provide visual cues. This will ensure that the visualization of the texture will be consistent at all times, independent of the position and orientation of the viewpoint.

A technique for incorporating texture in planar surfaces has been developed. This is based on a ray-tracing technique which incorporates a high-performance pipelined **surface scanner** coupled to an **image mapper**. The function of the surface scanner is to project rays originating at the eyepoint through each pixel, and to determine the points of intersection with the 3D surface defined in model coordinates. The surface scanner is preconditioned by setting up parameters based on information about the position of the viewpoint and viewing direction, together with the knowledge of the direction of the surface normal. The surface scanner executes the algorithm, exploiting pixel-to-pixel coherence to determine the points of intersection of the rays with the surface. The surface scanner generates a pair of coordinates in floating-point format at pixel rate and has an effective computing power of 171 MFLOPs.

The stream of coordinates output by the surface scanner are used by the image mapper to access a stored representation of a texture pattern. This representation can be constructed using a suitable algorithm, or be a digitization of a photograph of real terrain or an artist's impression thereof. The output of the surface scanner performs a spatial sampling of the stored representation. To avoid aliasing errors it is necessary to ensure that the data is sampled correctly. Consequently, the data is filtered to produce multiple copies at descending levels of detail. The appropriate level of detail is selected by determining the spatial separation between the ray intercepts in the plane of the surface.

The technique can be extended to portray large areas of terrain by using a two-stage representation in which areas on a large ground plane are designated to contain certain different texture types. The access to these two stages is performed by a pipelined process to ensure that data is generated at pixel rate to enable a raster scan display to be driven directly.

References

Agate M., Finch H.R., Garel A.A., Lister P.F. and Grimsdale R.L. (1987). A Multiple Application Graphics Integrated Circuit – MAGIC. In *Eurographics 86*. Netherlands: Elsevier Science Publishers B.V.

Advanced Micro Devices (1985). *Am29300 Family*. Advanced Micro Devices, Sunnyvale CA

Analog Devices (1985). *High-Speed 64-bit IEEE Floating Point Multiplier and ALU.* Technical Report ADSP–3210 and ADSP–3220, Analog Devices DSP Division, Norwood MA

Finch H.R., Agate M., Garel A.A., Lister P.F. and Grimsdale R.L. (1987). A Multiple Application Graphics Integrated Circuit – MAGIC II. In *Advances in Computer Graphics Hardware II* (Kuijk A.A.M. and Strasser W., eds). Berlin: Springer-Verlag

Fuchs H., Poulton J., Paeth A. and Bell A. (1982). Developing Pixel Planes, a smart memory-based raster graphic system. In *Proc. MIT Conf. on Adv. Res. in VLSI*, pp. 137–46. Cambridge MA

Grimsdale R.L., Hadjiaslanis A.A. and Willis P.J. (1979). Zone Management Processor; a module for generating surfaces in raster colour displays. *Computers and Digital Techniques,* **2**(1), 21–5

Gouraud H. (1971). Continuous shading of curved surfaces. *IEEE Transactions on Computers,* **20**(6), 623–8

Price S.M. (1984). A visual system for a flight simulator using computer generated images. *DPhil Thesis*, University of Sussex

Sutherland I.E. and Hodgman G.W. (1974). Reentrant Polygon Clipping. *Comm. ACM,* **17**(1), 32–42

C. Upson
S. Fangmeier

University of Illinois at Urbana-Champaign

20. The role of visualization and parallelism in a heterogeneous supercomputing environment

An approach to the tight coupling of a numerical approximation to a physical system is described with its visual representation. The goal of this work is the ability to guide the computation interactively as it progresses, just as a pilot steers a flight simulator. The near term objective is to compute an image of very high complexity in the time required to generate a simulation dataset, with a longer range goal of true interactivity, or the production of several images per dataset. The 3D simulation chosen as our case study is not feasible with current supercomputers, but will be typical within three to five years. A computational and visualization pipeline is defined, the required throughputs, capabilities and opportunities for parallelism are presented and the bottlenecks are detailed.

20.1 Introduction

John von Neumann's 1946 vision of an interactive numerical experiment, in which the digital computer would replace (or augment) the physical experiment in the study of natural phenomena, has yet to be realized. An integral part of this dream is that of an 'input/output organ', which today we call a highly interactive visual-based interface, tightly coupling the simulation machine and the human perceptual system. Von Neumann believed that this would revolutionize the way in which science was performed, and it is only now, due to technological advances in super-computers, high-speed graphics hardware and innovative algorithms, that we believe this vision can be realized. The advantages of a tight coupling of the simulation and analysis lie in the increased productivity of the scientist. This can permit an interactive modification of the simulation parameters to study the effect on the phenomena of interest, or even alteration of the equations to gain a better understanding of the numerical method.

The use of supercomputers as simulation machines has increased dramatically in the last ten years. Now, a computational scientist can numerically approximate natural phenomena ranging from thermal-induced atomic motions of DNA strands to the formation of large-scale structure in the universe. The current simulation scenario is to compute the solution in batch mode, save a subset of the derived data and post-process this information at a later time. There are several trends that affect this mode of computation and analysis:

(1) Simulations are rapidly growing in size. The current domain size in a large 3D fluid dynamics simulation is of the order of 10^6 computational grid cells. It is anticipated that this will grow by a factor of five to ten within the next three to five years.

(2) The disk capabilities at large supercomputer installations are not large enough to handle the volume of data resulting from such a large simulation. While disk densities are making incremental increases and the cost per Mbyte will probably decrease by a factor of two, the increase in data by an order of magnitude will more than compensate for these technological advances. At present, scientists can formulate and simulate more than they can afford to store.

(3) Currently, the analysis step takes much longer than the simulation, and as such is the rate-limiting step. As the simulation size continues to grow this gap will widen.

(4) The visual representation is frequently ten times more compute intensive than the simulation it depicts.

(5) A substantial fraction of supercomputer usage is wasted due to errors in the simulation definition and/or lack of sophisticated analysis tools.

Currently, the data from a large 3D simulation can swamp an entire supercomputer facility. Soon, insufficient storage capabilities coupled with the lack of analysis tools will make the full utilization of supercomputers prohibitively expensive. To prevent this from occurring, the simulation scenario of the future will include a tighter coupling between the simulation and analysis steps, a coupling that can be characterized by **interactive visualization**. Interactive visualization can minimize wasted computer cycles while at the same time decrease the amount of time required to comprehend a simulation's results. Post-processing of a large simulation in the future is not a possibility, thus ensuring that interactive visualization will be a certainty.

We will define the required capabilities of the simulation environment of the near future (three to five years from now) by extrapolating from our visualization experience with current large-scale numerical simulations. This environment is characterized as a computational and visualization pipeline composed of the **numerical simulation**, the extraction of key features in the resulting data, the conversion of that data into graphical primitives, and the image generation and display steps (Figure 20.1). In each step, we will describe the role of parallelism that is either inherent in the underlying algorithms or which must be exploited to allow a scientist to interact with his simulation as it computes.

20.2 The physical simulation

The simulation of an observed or hypothesized phenomena via numerical techniques has developed substantially in the past 30 years. Phenomena such as the formation of black holes, electron tunneling in protein molecules, heat dissipation in a mechanical part, crystallization of a fluid and the formation of a tornado are

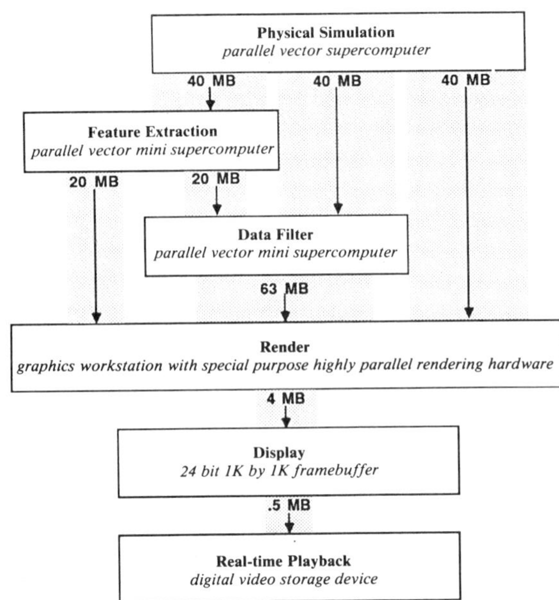

Figure 20.1
The interactive simulation environment. The data volume is per field variable.

typical examples of the current state of the art in this field. In each of these cases, the goal is to gain enough insight into the underlying physical mechanism of the phenomena to obtain a predictive capability of its workings.

The typical scenario in the computational sciences is a progression of steps from the formulation of the underlying equations to the analysis of the results. The first step is to approximate the known equations which determine the behavior of the material. For example, the development of a large-scale storm system is governed by the equations of motion of a fluid, the Navier-Stokes equations. As the full effects of turbulence cannot be simulated currently, these terms are approximated. This underlying set of continuum equations are again approximated to obtain discretized formulations that will be used in the simulation program. These discrete equations are generally based on a finite difference, finite element or Monte Carlo approach. After the equations are formulated, which generally takes between a month and six months to accomplish, the program is coded up, requiring a few months more. The program is then debugged (another few months) and the scientist is ready to test it out with a simulation. The development of a simulation scenario, or computational domain, can again require several months, as in the case of a large 3D simulation. This stage includes building the topology of the domain in three-space and setting the boundary conditions, initial conditions and all other parameters for a stable simulation – a highly iterative process.

The simulation is then run on a supercomputer such as a CRAY X-MP, where it will take from one to 1000 hours of CPU time. Currently the data, most commonly in the form of a series of scalar and vector fields defined on a grid in three-space, is archived onto a mass storage device. As the scientist cannot afford to save a complete solution set, a subset (frequently one-tenth or so) of the data is archived.

The analysis then begins. The typical tools available to the scientist for analysis can be generously characterized as archaic. There has been little progress in this area since the mid 1960s, and thus it is a fruitful area of research. The scientist will attempt to sort through billions of numbers to obtain some insight into the results of the simulation. In general, this is augmented with some 2D contour maps of select areas. When one is trying to simulate the development of a tornado, tools such as these are frequently the limiting factor in the comprehension of the results. In fact, it is this last stage of analysis in which the bulk of the effort is devoted: typically six months or more is required to understand fully a single, large, time-dependent, 3D simulation.

A general-purpose supercomputer is needed for the simulation machine due to the intense compute demands. For this task we have chosen a CRAY X-MP/48 with four processors (with a peak combined rating slightly less than 1 GFLOP), 64 Mbyte of central memory and 1 Gbyte of fast-access solid-state disk (with transfer rates of 1 Gbyte per second). These machines typically cost between 10 and 20 million dollars, and thus are considered a central resource for a relatively large number, usually hundreds, of users. Since the machine is a shared resource, the individual scientist must be fairly conservative in his computer usage – conservative to the point that he is reluctant to spend it on the generation of images. To date, the use of parallelism on machines such as these typically has a large-grain flavor, a situation that is slowing changing. It is anticipated that the next generation of supercomputers will be an order of magnitude faster than current machines and more conducive to parallelism.

20.2.1 The simulation case study

In order to define the system throughputs and computational capabilities required to accomplish interactive visualization in the next five years, we must first define the typical large-scale simulation of the future. This is a risky business, as there is a large variation in simulation techniques, so we will stick with the most common method from an area of large interest, a 3D gas dynamics simulation via a traditional explicit finite-difference technique.

To predict a complicated gas dynamics system accurately, one needs approximately 200 grid cells in each dimension, or roughly 10^7 cells for a 3D problem. At each node of this computational domain reside the approximated variables such as pressure, temperature, entropy, etc. A typical formulation has between five and ten variables per node and if it describes a phenomena that evolves over time, then several discrete timesteps, perhaps 500, are required to advance the solution forward in time. It has been estimated (Wincker *et al.*, 1986) that this simulation scenario will require a sustained 0.5 TFLOPs per second to accomplish real-time computations with real time being defined as nearly 30 timesteps per second (or about 15

GFLOPs per timestep). If we are willing to wait 5 to 10 seconds for each timestep then the required computational rate is a modest 1 to 3 GFLOPs per second sustained. This problem, infeasible with today's supercomputers but attainable within five years, is the problem that we will address in this chapter. The current simulation domain is generally restricted to less than 10^6 grid cells with a new time-step of data also produced every 5 to 10 seconds.

20.3 Feature extraction

Owing to the large amount of data resulting from the simulation and the relatively low transmission rates in a computer network, it is necessary to transmit only that data which is relevant to the visualization process. This step of feature extraction might be an undersampling or partitioning of the computational domain in which the uninteresting, insignificant, or unchanged portions are removed prior to transmission. In general, features on the resolution of an individual grid cell are beyond the accuracy of the numerical method; thus it is frequently meaningless to visualize to this level of detail (Plate 3). However, to detect numerical instabilities and round-off error one needs to see the variation from cell to cell, a function at which visualization clearly excels.

In addition to the partitioning of the domain, one might wish to calculate derived functions of the nodal variables. Examples of this are the calculation of the streamfunction from a velocity field, the heat flux from the temperature distribution, or flux lines from a magnetic field. In addition, there might be some pattern recognition processing that is necessary to extract the relevant data, such as the detection of vortex pairing, flow separation and the isolation of near-singularities in a field variable (Buning and Steger, 1985; Watson *et al.*, 1987).

Aside from the obvious parallelism in uncoupled calculations such as divided differences evaluated at nodal points, even the derivation of the streamfunction, an integral function of the velocity field, can run easily in a parallel manner. In this case, the streamfunction at a point is determined from an integration along a path from the previous known streamfunction evaluation. Each cell or block of cells can be integrated separately, deriving a relative streamfunction which can then be used to accumulate the absolute streamfunction at the nodes. Other examples of parallelism fall into the classical 'divide-and-conquer' approach of partitioning the computational domain into subdomains, each of which is searched for the required pattern or processed separately. We look to the computer vision and robotics fields for inspiration in the area of pattern recognition.

As the goal of this step is to minimize the amount of data to be transmitted, it is necessary for this to be accomplished on the compute server or any machine that is on a high bandwidth connection to the supercomputer. As the techniques for feature extraction are not well known (and thus a complexity expression is not meaningful yet) it is essential that this also be accomplished on a general-purpose computer. In general, we can expect the compute time required for this step to be much less than for the simulation, by one or two orders of magnitude, and the data reduction fraction to be between 0.125 and 0.5, given current techniques.

20.4 Data filter step

The data from the simulation is translated, on a timestep-by-timestep basis, from the simulation domain into a large set of graphical primitives. We generally choose to use a polygonal representation as it best preserves the underlying data, and because it is the most common 3D primitive used in hardware-rendering implementations. Currently a typical 3D simulation, such as the turbulent interface between two fluids travelling at vastly different speeds, requires approximately 10^5 polygons to model (Plate 4, simulation courtesy of Michael Norman). In this case, the density field is defined on a 3D (typically rectangular) domain, a threshold is chosen and a 3D contour is calculated by **tiling** the surface, computational cell by cell. While 10^5 polygons are sufficient to model this surface, we anticipate a ten-fold increase will be needed for future problems.

The tiling procedure is inherently parallel with a sequential step for some implementations. Each cell is queried for a possible intersection with the contour threshold; if there is a contribution to the surface (the extremum in the cell, defined by the eight corner nodes, straddles the threshold), then the intersections with the cell edges are calculated. As the surface formed by these intersections will not be planar, several polygons are created which satisfy the cell boundary conditions. This can be achieved either by subdividing the cell into several tetrahedra (Upson, 1986), on each of which the surface variation is guaranteed to be linear, or by enumerating the possible cases using a table lookup (Lorensen and Cline, 1987). In general, the subdivision method gives smoother surfaces, but also creates more polygons and is more computationally intensive.

If the rendering algorithm requires a single occurrence per vertex in the data structure (as most do in software), then the resulting data set of polygons must be searched for coincident point references. These are located by computing distances of points from adjacent cells or subcells (a localized *N*-Body problem). The smoothed surface normal is then calculated, now that all polygons which reference the vertex have been located, and the algorithm moves on to the next cell. Additionally, we consolidate contiguous polygons that are coplanar, further reducing the amount of data. A parallel implementation of the tiling is accomplished in two steps: first, the processors are allocated cells to test for surface intersection and polygon generation; and second, cell faces are partitioned among the processors to eliminate coincident points. The parallelism inherent in the divide-and-conquer method breaks down after the coincident vertices are eliminated from the list and a new, completely dense list is formed, a step which requires each subsequent point's reference number to be updated. This step is, however, vectorizable using conditional merge instructions. If a dense vertex list is produced, then the resulting volume of data is:

$$3 * n_p * f_v * (n_d * s_v + n_d * s^n + s_c) + n_p * f_t * n_v * s_p \qquad \textbf{(20.1)}$$

where n_p is the number of initial triangles (10^6), f_v is the compression fraction due to vertex consolidation (0.16), n_d is the number of spatial dimensions (3), s_v is the number of bytes of significance in the vertex location (4), s_n is the significance in bytes of the surface normal component (2), s_c is the significance in bytes of the vertex color (3), f_t is the compression fraction due to polygon consolidation (0.42), n_v is the average number of vertices per new polygon (4.9) and s_p is the significance in bytes of the polygon connectivities (3).

Using the typical values as shown in parentheses, the resulting amount of data varies between 12 Mbytes for a facet-shaded monochrome object to 16.3 Mbytes for a smooth-shaded polychrome object. If, on the other hand, the rendering algorithm requires a redundant point list (as hardware systems usually do) then the data volume is:

$$3 * n_p * (n_d * s_v + n_d * s_n + s_c) \tag{20.2}$$

where this varies between 36 Mbytes and 63 Mbytes (facet-shaded and monochrome to smooth-shaded and polychrome). The savings in data volume (between 66 and 75%) is at the expense of compute cycles. This is the amount of data to be transmitted per field variable. An approximate compute-complexity expression for the simpler algorithm is as follows:

$$t_{op} * n_c + p_{op} * n_p / n_{pc} + n_{op} * n_p + c_{op} * n_p \tag{20.3}$$

where t_{op} is the operation count to test a cell for possible intersections (50), n_c is the number of computational cells (10^7), p_{op} is the number of operations to construct polygons within an active cell (700), n_{pc} is the average number of polygons in an active cell (2.9), n_{op} is the surface normal operation count (300) and c_{op} is the vertex color operation count (150). For the problem of interest, this is approximately 1.2 GFLOPs.

Other data filters produce primitives such as points, lines, textures and sub-volumes. In each of these algorithms the parallelism is more straightforward than the vectorization. One example of this is the use of a velocity field to advect passive fluid particles that are then used to visualize the effect of the flowfield (Yaeger *et al.*, 1986; Buning and Steger, 1985). The particle list can be easily partitioned between the processors, but the inner loop which interpolates the velocity requires an indexed lookup, or a transmit index list operation, which does not vectorize on most vector machines (the Alliant FX-8 and the latest CRAY X-MP are exceptions).

As indicated above, this data filter step can be compute intensive; thus, it is essential to have a supercomputer or near-supercomputer for this task. For our current needs, we have chosen an Alliant FX-8 minisupercomputer with eight computational elements, each of which is a vector processor. Currently, the peak rating of the combined eight processors is approximately 94 MFLOPs. We anticipate that minisupercomputers will increase in compute power at a faster rate than supercomputers, thus this class of machine will be ideal for the data filter process. The ability to compute a task both concurrently and in vector mode is essential to the efficient translation of the data into primitives.

20.5 Image computation

The computational complexity of hidden-surface elimination and surface shading (the more compute-intensive of the two) required for rendering is about an order of magnitude more demanding than that required to advance the simulation forward in time. This, coupled with the fact that the simulation machine, a supercomputer, is the fastest general-purpose machine around, leads one to the conclusion that the rendering must be accomplished in special-purpose hardware. It is fortunate that rendering is the one step of the interactive visualization process that is probably the easiest to implement in hardware or firmware as the algorithms are very well defined for a restricted primitive set. Currently available hardware will not perform the 3D transformations, hidden-surface or shading calculations at the desired rate for interactive visualization. In addition, more advanced features such as anti-aliasing, transparency, texture and shadowing, while considered expensive luxuries now, will prove to be essential cues for comprehension as the complexity of the models increases, and thus must also be implemented in hardware.

Since geometric transformations, hidden-surface elimination and lighting models are common to the computer animation field in general, we can rely on the graphics industry for constant speedups in these areas. However, this reliance has proven to have one major downfall: the level of complexity present in the visualization of physical simulations generally surpasses that of 'entertainment-oriented' imagery by a substantial margin (very few television commercials have frames with up to 10^5 polygons). We have been observing a slow trend in this industry towards addressing requirements for scientific computer graphics both in the hardware and the software areas. However, it should be pointed out that rendering methods more specific to the nature of imaging scalar and vector fields in three-space may prove to be more effective and superior to common techniques (which is why the medical imaging field has developed its own volumetric algorithms), and that these more problem-specific solutions may prove to be the only valid approach for truly interactive visualization of simulation results.

The rendering at video resolution of a 10^5 polygon model from an astrophysical simulation (Centrella and Melott, 1983) (Plate 5) on a CRAY X-MP with optimized software (scanline method, single processor, vectorized and machine-coded kernels) takes approximately 40 seconds per frame for opaque objects and 60 seconds per frame for transparent objects. These times vary substantially with screen coverage, amount of transparency, depth complexity, etc. Assuming that a processing speed of 80 MFLOPs per second is sustained, the resulting computational burden is 4.8 GFLOPs. As a 'z-buffer' algorithm scales almost linearly with complexity (Foley and Van Dam, 1982), a model with 10^6 polygons will require about 50 GFLOPs to compute; thus we envision the rendering hardware as multiple streams of pipelined processors. While the transformation matrix computation for 10^6 triangles will take roughly 80 MFLOPs, we can expect the shading calculations to require several times more operations. Thus, it becomes obvious that each of these pipelined processors must be in the 100 to 200 MFLOPs per second range with tens of parallel streams, something that will soon be possible. As rendering is the most compute-intensive step in the interactive visualization process by an order of magnitude (two orders of magnitude when one uses shadows, textures and reflection mapping), it will require a complete rethink to move away from conventional methods into an area that holds more promise in delivering the necessary performance. Our current area of research includes direct volumetric rendering techniques that we hope will prove more fruitful from both computational and I/O standpoints. This approach would eliminate the need for a compute-intensive data filter step, thus allowing more time and resources for the rendering process. The main disadvantage of this approach is the difficulty of a hardware implementation.

20.6 Bandwidth issues

The goal of interactive visualization places a heavy strain on the I/O connections between computers, both between the supercomputer and the data filter machine, and between this machine and the rendering engine. Information in the first pipeline is the raw data. A simulation consisting of 10^7 nodes probably generates five to ten variables per node, only half of which are of interest. Assuming the worse case, in which there is no data reduction due to feature extraction, the resulting data volume is 40 Mbytes per field variable or 80 to 200 Mbytes per timestep (assuming four bytes per variable). There are few communication networks that can sustain rates of 40 Mbytes per second (200 Mbytes over a 5 second timestep) between heterogeneous machines. The VMEbus standard with its theoretical limit of 20 Mbytes per second will almost satisfy the lower ends of this constraint (one variable per node) but will not be able to handle the upper bound. Thus, one is forced to seek either a new bus architecture and/or protocol standards.

One possibility is to stripe parallel VMEbuses. Another possibility is to develop a new, very high-speed bus, as is currently under development by several companies, such as Ultra Corporation. This product, the UltraBus, is a 100 Mbyte per second communications bus between a CRAY X-MP or CRAY 2 computer and either another super- (or near-super) computer, or an output device, such as a frame buffer. The CRAY X-MP and CRAY 2 machines have 100 Mbyte per second I/O channels off their I/O processors, as do other large mainframes such as the ETA-10 (100 Mbytes/s), and SCS-40 (170 Mbytes/s). Others are actively investigating high-speed channels (Alliant and Convex). The ability to move data around at such rates is predicted on several restrictions, notably that the packet size is very large (0.5 Mbyte or so) and the protocol must not be chatty.

The ability to transfer and update a 1280 × 1024 × 24-bit image in real time (30 FPS) requires a sustained 118 Mbytes per second, which is not possible even with the proposed products, thus the framebuffer must be resident on the rendering engine bus. On the other hand, a general-purpose computer such as a CRAY cannot produce new images of even moderate complexity at that rate. In the 1990s, however, supercomputers, massively parallel machine architectures and hardware graphics pipelines will be able to generate images of the complexity shown in Plate 4 in real time. Thus, the need for a high-speed bus standard is essential now.

20.7 Display

The image display step should be as closely coupled to the rendering as possible to allow for sufficiently high update rates, that are achievable with current technology. Each image displayed should simultaneously be dumped to a digital video storage device for variable speed playback of the sequence computed thus far. We currently use an Abekas A-62 50 second digital video store for this purpose. Allowing for both static and dynamic displays is important, as both will reveal different types of information to the scientist and, as the wait between simulation timesteps increases, the availability of a real-time video playback capability will be of increased importance in the analysis process. It is only through the use of motion, that fine-scale features, both spatial and temporal, can be comprehended in a detailed three-dimensional simulation. This requires several hundred viewings.

20.8 Interactivity

The goal of this visualization system is an interactive analysis of simulation results which, in turn, will aid the interaction with and control of the physical simulation. To achieve this goal, we have to provide a high level of interactivity at every step in the pipeline between the simulation and the visual representation, in such a manner that the potential of this system can be fully realized. Available to the user during analysis should be multiple views, full positional object control, level of detail control and a complete range of image generation parameters. It must be made extremely easy to position light sources, assign object colors, surface characteristics, change 3D texture maps, etc. since the system will be expensive and in high demand. Scientists should not be expected to spend large amounts of their valuable time learning about computer graphics methods but rather concentrate on their fields of expertise.

It is also important to design the numerical simulation, feature extraction, data filter and image computation steps with high interactivity and flexibility in mind. A general menuing template that is easily tailored to a specific simulation will be essential to reduce the acclimation time required for a new scientist. Taken to its full potential, this interactive visualization system might even aid a researcher in the simulation code development and debugging phase, therefore becoming more than just an analytical tool.

In the overall interface design, we may very well envision a situation very similar to industrial flight simulators: several computer screens filled with various types of menus, a joystick or more advanced devices, a keypad for numerical input, a mouse for menu selection, etc. Considering the cost of this computational facility, it may not be unreasonable to train users on a mockup version to familiarize them with the interface to all the different control points linking the physical simulation to the visual analysis.

20.9 Discussion

A complete formulation of the compute and bandwidth requirements for this interactive visualization pipeline is not possible except for isolated case problems, thus our formulations are based on averages that we have tabulated from simulations in disciplines from computational fluid dynamics to astrophysics. The basic requirement is that the visualization process keeps up with the simulation, and that the pipeline length be sufficiently short to allow interactivity. Typical numerical methods require multiple, usually two, sequential datasets to advance the simulation forward in time. Thus, if the transit time in the pipeline is longer than a simulation timestep, the scientist cannot act upon what he has viewed as the data will have already been overwritten. The number of interruptions to the simulation must be minimized, as this requires the program space to be written to disk, an expensive process for a large program.

The pipeline length is the summation of the compute and transmission times for each segment. For a single field variable, the length is:

$$t_{sim} = x_{sim\text{-}fe} + t_{fe} + x_{fe\text{-}df} + t_{df} + x_{df\text{-}ic} + t_{ic} + x_{ic\text{-}d} + t_d \qquad \textbf{(20.4)}$$

where t stands for processing time for the simulation (*sim*), feature extraction (*fe*), data filter (*df*), image computation (*ic*), and display (*d*). The terms beginning with x denote the transfer time between processing elements. Obviously, there will be an overlap between the processing and transmission of a data packet and between processors that create and use the same data. Incorporating Equation 20.2, the combined data volume in bytes per field variable is a summation of the four transmission terms:

$$n_c * s_s + f_{fe} * n_c * s_s + 3 * n_p * (n_d * s_v + n_d * s_n + s_c) + s_c * n_{pix} \quad \textbf{(20.5)}$$

where s_s is the significance in bytes of the simulation data (4), f_{fe} is the fractional reduction of data due to feature extraction (say 0.5) and n_{pix} is the number of pixels in the display (1.3M). We can neglect the last term, image transmission, as it will almost completely overlap with the image computation. We can also safely assume that there will be at least a 25% overlap in computation and transmission. The combined computational time, however, is less easily defined:

$$c_{fe} / p_{fe} + c_{df} / p_{df} + c_{ic} / p_{ic} + c_d / p_d \quad \textbf{(20.6)}$$

Here c denotes the computational complexity and p represents the aggregate processing speed of the computer for each task. Again, the last term of image display is insignificant and will be ignored. If we similarly assume that the computational requirements for the feature extraction are small, the image computation requires about 50 GFLOPs, the I/O and processing overlap is 25% and the data filter requires 1.2 GFLOPs, then the requirements for the bandwidth along with data filter and rendering steps are:

$$0.75 * (123 / x_t + 1.2 * 10^3 / p_{df} + 5 * 10^4 / p_{ic}) \quad \textbf{(20.7)}$$

where x_t is the sustained bus bandwidth in Mbytes per second, and p_{df} and p_{ic} are both in MFLOPs per second sustained. To keep up with the simulation, this combined time will have to be approximately 10 seconds.

Conclusion

The requirements for an interactive simulation environment (Figure 20.1) have been presented. The constraints have been based on extrapolations from what is currently in use, to what will be needed in the near future. Visualization is a key feature of this environment and, in fact, it is the most demanding from a computational viewpoint. While all the computational aspects of this proposed visualization pipeline will be technologically feasible within the near future, the major bottlenecks will be the I/O throughput and the computational speed of the rendering machine. Clearly 100 Mbytes per second communication buses are needed, as are rendering machines which can sustain 1 to 5 GFLOPs per second. To ease the I/O problem, new high-speed communication standards, novel data compression and feature extraction schemes must be developed. To ease the rendering computational burden and thus permit a very interactive environment, new highly parallel, volumetric-rendering algorithms with hardware implementations must be produced. Once these two problems have been overcome, we can begin to explore John von Neumann's dream of an interactive numerical experiment.

References

Buning P. and Steger J. (1985). Graphics and Flow Visualization in Computational Fluid Dynamics. In *Proc. AIAA 7th Computational Fluid Dynamics Conference*, 1985

Centrella J. and Melott A. (1983). Three-dimensional Simulation of Large-Scale Structure in the Universe. *Nature*, 305, 196–8

Foley J. and van Dam, A. (1982). *Fundamentals of Interactive Computer Graphics.* Reading MA: Addison-Wesley

Goldstine H. and von Neumann J. (1963). On the principles of large-scale computing machines. In *John von Neumann, Collected Works*, Vol. 5. Oxford: Pergamon Press

Lorensen W. and Cline H. (1987). Marching cubes: a high resolution 3D surface construction algorithm. *Computer Graphics,* **21**(4), 163–9

Upson C. (1986). The visual simulation of amorphous phenomena. *The Visual Computer,* **2**, 321–6

Watson V., Buning P., Choi D., Bancroft G., Merritt F. and Rogers S. (1987). Use of computer graphics for visualization of flow fields. In *Proc. AIAA Aerospace Engineering Conference*, 1987.

Wilhelmson R. and Klemp J. (1978). A numerical study of storm splitting that leads to long-lived storms. *Journal of Atmospheric Sciences,* **35**(10)

Wincker K.H., Norman M. and Norton J. (1986). On the characteristics of a numerical fluid dynamics simulator. In *Supercomputers – Algorithms, Architectures, and Scientific Computation* (Matsen F. and Tajima T., eds). University of Texas Press

Yaeger L., Upson C. and Myers R. (1986). Combining physical and visual simulation-creation of the planet Jupiter for the film '2010'. *Computer Graphics,* **20**(4), 85–93

P.P. Tanner
B.M. Fowler
K.S. Booth

University of Waterloo

21 · Experience with graphics support for a multiprocessor workstation

A low-level graphics support package has been implemented for a multiprocessor – a package that exploits the parallel processing capabilities of the system in which it runs. The system provides multiple direct connections between the frame buffer and the distributed tasks responsible for graphics output. This contrasts with the traditional idea of a window server through which all frame buffer accesses must flow. The support package enables the system to take better advantage of the multiprocessing capabilities of the system, avoiding the bottleneck implicit in the window server model.

21.1 Introduction

Multiprocessing systems are becoming available for use in many applications. While graphics systems have made use of special-purpose processors for performing certain steps in the image-rendering function, there have not been many attempts to take advantage of the multiple, general-purpose processor systems that are currently available.

This chapter describes a graphics package implemented to provide graphics support on such a multiprocessor workstation. This package follows the multi-tasking paradigm of distributing duties over a number of tasks that execute on different processors. It avoids the traditional method of funnelling all frame buffer accesses through a single task or process, and thus avoids losing much of the benefit of the multiprocessor system. Instead, the system has achieved its goal of giving individual tasks, in a multitask application, direct access to that part of the frame buffer for which they are responsible. Tasks may output to the frame buffer simultaneously (within the constraints of the bus).

After presenting an overview of the hardware and Operating System (OS) support for this workstation and the applications for which it is being built, we will discuss various techniques that have traditionally been used for multiple access to frame buffers (usually window systems). This will be followed by a description of the Waterloo system, showing the use of the resource server model as applied to graphics. Finally, there will be a discussion of the difficulties of the current approach, and how they may be remedied.

21.2 Goals, hardware and programming methodology

The Computer Graphics Laboratory of the University of Waterloo has embarked on a project to build a multiprocessor workstation, which will be used for psychophysical, visual perception and interaction experiments, computer animation and ray tracing. The experiments have very strict requirements as to the timing of stimulus presentation, especially stimuli that are in response to subjects' actions. A real-time multiprocessor OS ensures that timing constraints can be met, by permitting tasks to be prioritized, with higher priority tasks being assigned to more lightly loaded processors, and by not seizing control of a processor for an unpredictable length of time. Both the animation and ray-tracing work require the processing power that can be provided by a multiprocessor. The workstation provides a basis for investigations into the use of parallel processing and multitasking in real-time computer graphics.

Physically, the system consists of a VMEbus backplane, several DY-4 68000 series processor boards with message-passing hardware support [1], a number of frame buffer boards grouped into one or more distinct frame buffers, and (eventually) an ethernet board and an A/D converter board.

The use of the Harmony OS influences greatly the programming style used to implement applications and system support on the workstations. Harmony [2] is a descendent of the Thoth OS [3] and a relative of the V-System [4] and Waterloo Port [5]. Harmony provides **lightweight processes** (called **tasks**) and inexpensive **synchronous message passing** through its send-receive-reply primitives.

Those who use Harmony, or any of its relations, write application programs as sets of tasks. The task plays a role similar to that of the function in traditional programming – the Send primitive taking the place of the function call. Critical resources are managed by administrators [6] or servers. Any task wishing to use such a resource must communicate with the resource server, requesting either that the server perform the requested operation, or that the server give permission for the task itself to perform the operation. Resource managers exist for peripheral devices, data structures, host communication, display lists, screen trackers and, as will be described below, frame buffer boards, display memory and the vertical retrace time interval.

Previous work by the authors, including multitask paint systems implemented in Thoth [7] and Harmony [8] and a Harmony-based workstation agent supporting parallel input [9], has shown that individual tasks that make up a graphics application are assigned roles such as menu management, rendering of 3D objects from a CAD data structure, or updating a colour box and sliders for use in colour selection, with the result that the tasks tend to restrict their interaction with the screen to a small, well-defined region.

These areas of the screen are, of course, windows – windows that do not make sense on their own, but which together form the graphics output required for a single application. Each window is associated with one or more tasks running at different priorities. The **echo handler** [10], which provides the lexical feedback, must run at a higher priority than a task that renders a complex image into a double-buffered display system.

The goal for the graphics support is to provide each of these tasks with the capability of performing its own graphics output as simply and directly as possible.

The graphics support must provide multiple connections to the physical frame buffer.

21.3 Window systems

There are two principal functions that must be performed by a graphics server to provide frame buffer access to multiple clients. The first is the **allocation** of frame buffer resources to client tasks. The second is the provision of a **channel** through which the client can communicate with the frame buffer. In many window systems, allocation of frame buffer resources is performed by a **window manager** with frame buffer access directed through a **window server**.

Common window servers act as **proprietors** or **administrators** for the graphics board. They are implemented with a simple FIFO queue in which display commands are sent from **window clients** and are processed in the order received by the window server. This means that a high-priority task will be blocked by one of lower priority if the lower priority task requests a time-consuming graphics update. This causes problems such as lexical feedback being delayed by lengthy low-priority screen updates. The window server approach also complicates distribution of the server functions across multiple processors.

A variation of this approach, used in SunWindows [11], is a **kernel-based** system. Access to the screen is via extensions to the OS kernel. Code, implementing graphics operations, is linked with each client. A disadvantage here is the great amount of application code that must be linked and stored with each client. More important is the problem of the possibility of a low-priority task blocking a high-priority task because of the screen-locking mechanism that is necessary to ensure synchronization of frame buffer access.

The window server model is inadequate for a tightly coupled multiprocessor environment for two reasons:

(1) All access to the frame buffer must be channelled through a single process, thus creating a bottleneck. While a necessary restriction in loosely coupled distributed systems, this problem is avoidable in tightly coupled systems.

(2) The server must finish one frame buffer request before processing the next, defeating any possibility of frame buffer access priority unless requests can be interrupted.

Previous Harmony-based graphics work has taken an approach different from that used by window servers. Both the Paint system [5] and Adagio [10] were implemented on an Adage-Ikonas 3000 system with the application code running under Harmony in the local 68000 processor. Some graphics operations involved manipulation of a display list, and were handled through a display list server. The display list was interpreted by a bit-slice microprocessor running in parallel with the 68000. Other graphics operations were handled by the graphics tasks themselves, which were assigned fixed areas of the screen.

These systems represented the first step in moving away from the single window server, but lacked the multiple-display-list support and window allocation scheme necessary for full multitask, multiprocess implementation.

21.4 Waterloo graphics server approach

The approach taken for the workstation graphics support is to provide a set of functions that allow each task to access the frame buffer independently and simultaneously. To support this approach, the graphics support includes three servers in addition to the graphics functions. The servers allocate resources and linearize, or make sequential, certain operations such as access to registers or modification of critical shared data. Tasks wishing to access resources under the control of a server establish a **connection** with the server. A record of the allocated resources is kept with this connection and, if the requesting task dies, the OS informs the server so that the task's resources may be deallocated.

21.4.1 Board server

The **board server** is called upon to allocate frame buffer boards to configure a frame buffer (Figure 21.1). A system may have any number of frame buffer boards (each having eight bits per pixel), with each frame buffer comprising one or three such boards. A system may support several frame buffers – in particular, we use two frame buffers to drive two displays which, using special optics, produce a binocular display.

21.4.2 Frame buffer server

The second server, the **frame buffer server**, is responsible for resources within the frame buffer. A frame buffer server exists for each frame buffer. Figure 21.1 shows an example where one frame buffer server has been created to manage a three-board frame buffer, and a second server to look after a one-board frame buffer.

The frame buffer server supports the definition of **bitbanks**. A bitbank is a contiguous set of bitplanes, where each bitplane in the frame buffer is allocated to exactly one bitbank. After the bitbank definition has been made, individual tasks may request allocation of a window. A window is defined as a rectangular region within a bitbank. For example, Figure 21.2 shows one task, responsible for a tablet echo, being allocated a one-pixel-deep window covering the whole screen, while a second task requests the remaining seven bits/pixel for a smaller screen window. In this situation, the entire frame buffer has been broken up into two bitbanks, one comprising one bitplane, the other with seven.

The division of the frame buffer into bitbanks is uniform across the frame buffer – one cannot divide the frame buffer into three-bit windows and five-bit windows in one area of the display while using the one-bit/seven-bit division from the example in another area. This would over-complicate the allocation of colour LookUp Table (LUT) entries.

The scheme for handling the LUT access for each window has some features in common with the X Window System [12], but respects the bitbank model of the window. When the frame buffer is initialized, and the bitbank definition is made, a mechanism for the use of the LUT is imposed. Two **colour lists** are defined for each bitbank. A bitbank n pixels deep will have a list of x **global colours**, and one of $2^n - x$ **local colours** where x is set by the routine that allocates the bitplanes

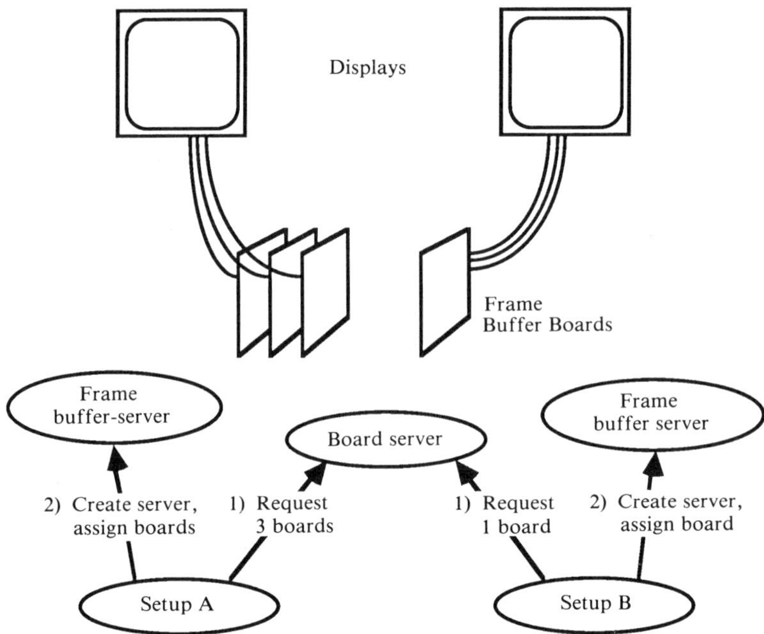

Figure 21.1
Board server.

to bitbanks. The global colours may be used by any task that has been allocated a window in the bitbank associated with that colour list. Local colours are allocated to individual windows in the bitbank, and may be used only by the tasks with a connection to that window.

The actual LUT entries associated with each of the entries in the colour lists are transparent to the application task. There may be more than one LUT entry for each colour depending on the definition of interbitbank priorities, but this complexity is handled by the graphics support routines.

While each display volume or window has a reserved area of the frame buffer memory, a set of colours in the LUT and the capability of defining viewports and window mappings anywhere within its boundaries, it cannot be treated as if it were an individual and separate frame buffer. The setting of CRT Controller (CRTC) registers falls outside this window model. Panning, scrolling and double buffering must be done on a screen-wide basis.

21.4.3 Vertical retrace server

Setting certain CRTC registers and manipulating LUT entries should be done during the vertical retrace interval to avoid observable artifacts flashing on the display. To accomplish this, the system considers that the vertical retrace interval is a scarce resource, and so a **vertical retrace server** has been written to manage it.

Any task which has been allocated screen resources may send the vertical retrace server a message requesting either that a register be changed during the next

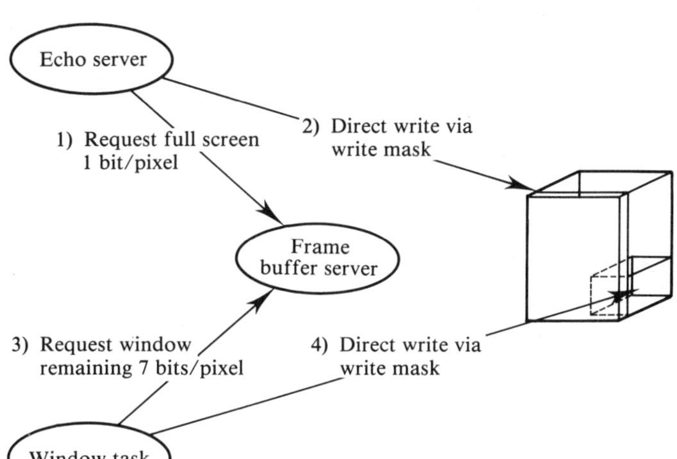

Figure 21.2
Frame buffer server.

vertical retrace interval, or that the change should occur at a specific interval in the future. The server puts these requests into a structure so that they can be carried out by the vertical retrace interrupt service routine. (Unfortunately, there is no vertical retrace interrupt available on the frame buffer boards (Matrox VIP-1024) in the system, so a timer is used that causes an interrupt just before the expected beginning of the vertical retrace interrupt. The interrupt routine then busy-waits on the vertical retrace status bit and performs the updates when the vertical retrace begins. Measurements indicate that less than 1% of the CPU cycles are 'wasted' on this busy-wait loop.) A task that sends a request to the vertical retrace server does not need to wait until the request is carried out, but may continue processing immediately.

21.4.4 Graphics support routines

Much of the graphics support takes the form of functions that are executed within the tasks that have been allocated window connections. These graphics support routines are used by the graphics tasks to write directly to the frame buffer. Each routine receives, as one of its calling parameters, a pointer to a **graphics context** which describes the resources on the screen allocated to the window by the frame buffer server. This context gives the routine the information it requires to restrict its output to lie within its assigned window. The graphics context also gives the routine the parameters necessary to perform the transformation from the task's coordinate system to the device coordinates. Tasks may remain unaware of the size, shape and position of the screen window. A graphics context may be shared among tasks if more than one task is to write to a single window. However, some mechanism must be used to ensure that only one function is accessing the graphics context at a time.

By using these three servers, with the corresponding graphics support routines, the Waterloo graphics server supports multiple simultaneous access to the frame buffer while providing support for those operations that must be linearized – particularly those that must occur during the vertical retrace interval. As Harmony permits tasks on a processor to share functions, multiple copies of the graphics functions are not required for the tasks on a single processor, but the functions must be replicated on each processor on which they are used.

The only major problem with this system is the unsuitability of the hardware as described in the next section.

21.5 Graphics server issues

21.5.1 Hardware registers

While providing rapid and parallel access to the frame buffer and assuring the real-time access necessary in some applications, this technique does prevent taking advantage of certain frame buffer capabilities. Registers, such as address or shade registers that speed up tiling operations, cannot be used by several tasks simultaneously. Such registers are designed to be used in a sequence of accesses to the frame buffer, and will become corrupted if they receive interleaved instructions from two separate tasks. An assumption that the screen areas being written do not overlap in x and y does not allow for standard bitmap techniques that allocate separate bitplanes for (multiple) trackers or chroma-key fields. Our bitbank model assumes disjoint regions in the frame buffer, but permits these regions to have overlapping pixels as long as different bitplanes are used. This requires the use of hardware write masks to make read-modify-write cycles atomic operations on the graphics board. Without this atomicity, collisions are possible where a read-modify-write from a low priority task is interrupted by that of a higher priority one, or interleaved with one on a different processor. In either case, the modification of the pixel by the task that finishes first will be undone.

The solution to this problem is best handled in two steps. As there is no bound on the number of tasks that may require frame buffer access, making the idea of a set of hardware registers per task infeasible, there should be:

- a set of registers for each processor, plus
- a mechanism for each processor to share these register sets among the processor's tasks.

For each processor, the critical hardware registers (address, shade and write masks) must be replicated, and the bus for frame buffer access extended to include an indication of the hardware register set to be used. The Adage Ikonas 3000, which allows simultaneous frame buffer access from its bitslice processor, an on-board M68000 and a host machine, puts the hardware register selection control in the bus address along with a function code. The address used for any frame buffer access then includes the actual pixel memory address plus bits to specify the function code and the register block – a technique specific to the Ikonas bus. An alternate approach, suitable for busses with a 32-bit address space such as the VMEbus, is to encode the register block selection in the frame buffer address. A pixel address would then contain 20 bits for a 1024×1024 display plus 3–4 more bits for the register block.

This solution breaks down when the number of tasks accessing the resources exceeds the number of register blocks available. However, in a multiprocessor, where the number of processors with such tasks is no greater than the number of register blocks, a block can be reserved for each processor. The context switch on each processor can then, when activating a task, load the contents of that task's register block into the block for that processor.

With neither the hardware support nor the OS support indicated, one must choose between an environment where collisions are impossible, or acceptance of the occasional pixel writing flaw. To make the collisions impossible, all tasks that talk directly to the frame buffer must be on the same processor, and run at the same priority. With the OS support only, the tasks must still be on the same processor, but may be run at different priorities. The Waterloo system, as currently implemented, has neither the hardware support nor the OS support (although the latter will be implemented shortly). As a result, software write masks must be used when needed, resulting in a slower pixel writing speed, and pixel writing collisions are possible although quite rare.

21.5.2 Movable windows

The current implementation of the multiprocessor graphics package supports only fixed windows. This is a design decision that reflects the applications that are to be carried out using the system. The fact that the windows are fixed has allowed a task structure that does not have a mechanism to change the graphics contexts when a window moves. This means that there is no way to signal a graphics function that the window to which it is writing has been moved. The system can be modified, however, to support movable windows when they are required.

To implement movable windows, a new task structure is required. The frame buffer server must inform all tasks whose resources have been modified, so that they may update their graphics contexts accordingly. A simple way of doing this is for the server to create a courier that would carry a message to each of these tasks. However, these tasks are dissimilar application tasks, and it would be unreasonable to expect them all to have been programmed to check for awaiting messages (a _Try_receive) within any given time limit.

A safer approach, and one that fits in well with the synchronous message-passing paradigm is to create individual **window servers**. These window servers would be unlike those used in current window systems which handle the full set of windows. In this case, there would be a window server for each window and it would be responsible for both performing all frame buffer accesses within its window, and updating the graphics context when the windows are moved (Figure 21.3). Tasks, that under the current scheme would send their output directly to the frame buffer, would now send a message to their window server which would perform the output.

Since Harmony messages take on the order of 0.35 to 1.5 ms, the overhead introduced to the frame buffer access could be substantial. This overhead can be limited, as it has been with window systems, by the use of higher-level graphics calls that are passed between the client and the window server.

To move a window, the frame buffer server would (using a set of couriers dedicated to this purpose) send details of the new window arrangement to each of the window servers. When the couriers report back that the messages have been received, a second message would be sent to all the window servers (again through

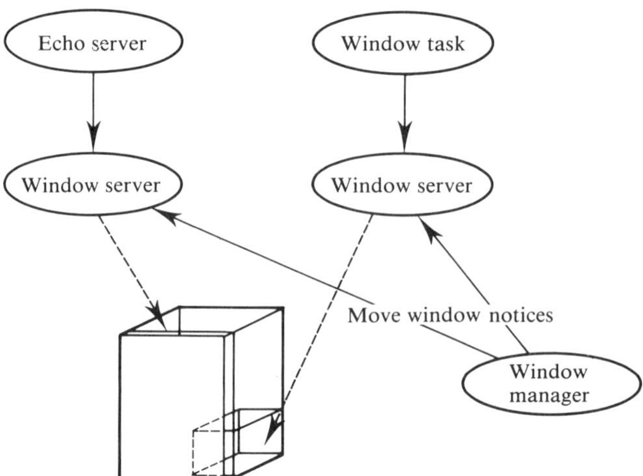

Figure 21.3
Task structure for movable windows.

the couriers) allowing them to restart frame buffer access – a window server cannot start writing into its new window until all the window servers have been notified of the new window arrangement. The overhead of this would be equal to two message passes per window plus the time necessary for the window servers to finish their current graphics output tasks.

Another advantage of this approach is that the window server is often a more appropriate place for image retention than is the task creating the output. Image retention capabilities vary from none at all, to retention of the bitmaps or simple structure such as text, to the full PHIGS graphics data structure (see [13] for a discussion of these issues). Different window servers, with different retention capabilities, could be created to suit the applications and reduce overhead caused by an inappropriate retention level.

Conclusion

Two problems with using standard window server approaches in a tightly coupled workstation environment are the loss of the ability to prioritize graphics operations, and the imposition of a bottleneck through which all graphics operations must flow. The graphics support environment described here avoids these problems, and gives direct simultaneous frame buffer access to all graphics tasks. An extension to the implemented model has been proposed to support movable windows.

The ability to take advantage of multiprocessor architectures in this way is compromised by the designs of present day graphics display hardware. Display boards should provide multiple write masks and other registers to avoid sharing critical resources. The frame buffer memory itself should be memory mapped and therefore be accessible by all processors. If these requirements are met, a general-purpose multiprocessor system may act as multiple display processors while achieving the flexibility and speedups that are possible with this architecture.

Acknowledgement

The authors would like to thank Joe Morrison for his design and implementation of the vertical retrace server.

References

1. DY-4 Systems Incorporated (1987). *DVME-134 Single Board Computer Operations Manual*. Ottawa, Ontario: DY-4 Systems Inc.
2. Gentleman W.M. (1983). *Using the Harmony Operating System*. Technical Report NRCC-ERB-966, Division of Electrical Engineering, National Research Council of Canada
3. Cheriton D., Malcolm M., Melen L. and Sager G. (1979). Thoth, a portable real-time operating system. *Comm ACM,* **22**(2), 105–15
4. Berglund E.J. (1986). An introduction to the V-System. *IEEE Micro,* **6**(4), 35–52
5. Waterloo Microsystems Incorporated (1984). *Waterloo Port*. Waterloo ON: Waterloo Microsystems Inc.
6. Gentleman W.M. (1981). Message passing between sequential processes: the reply primitive and the administrator concept. *Software Practice and Experience*, 11, 435–66
7. Beach R.J., Beatty, J.C., Booth K.S., Fiume E.L. and Plebon D.A. (1982). The message is the medium: Multiprocess structuring of an interactive paint program. *Computer Graphics,* **16**(3), 277–87
8. Booth K.S., Cowan W.B. and Forsey D.R. (1985). Multitasking support in a graphics workstation. In *Proc. 1st International Conference on Computer Workstations*, pp. 82–9. San Jose CA, November 1985
9. Tanner P.P., MacKay S.A., Stewart D.A. and Wein M. (1986). A multitasking switchboard approach to user interface management. *Computer Graphics,* **20**(4), 241–8
10. MacKay S.A. and Tanner P.P. (1986). Graphics tools in Adagio, a robotics multitasking multiprocessor workstation. In *Proc. Graphics Interface '86*, pp. 98–103, Vancouver BC, May 1986
11. *Programmer's Reference Manual for Sun Windows*. Mountain View CA: Sun Microsystems, Inc.
12. Scheifler R.W. and Gettys J. (1986). The X window system. *ACM Transactions on Graphics,* **5**(2), 89–109
13. Lantz K.A., Tanner P.P., Binding C., Huang K. and Dwelly A. (1987). Reference models, window systems, and concurrency. *Computer Graphics,* **21**(2), 87–97

W. Felger
M. Göbel
R. Ziegler
P. Zuppa

Fraunhofer
Gesellschaft

22·The realization of a multiprocessor GKS architecture

Implementers of graphical application systems hesitate to interface their applications to the GKS standard, because that usually means a loss of system performance.

This chapter describes a multiprocessor GKS that is based on functional distribution principles as well as on object-oriented distribution of a graphics system. The main concepts, using more than one processing unit with at least one output pipeline, are described.

22.1 Introduction

The Graphical Kernel System (GKS) (International Standards Organization, 1985a) covers a wide field of applications in interactive computer graphics. This involves a big system overhead and therefore often decreases the performance in single processor environments.

The approach described below is to distribute GKS on a number of parallel processors in order to improve the system efficiency. The applied multiprocessor system is a recently developed system providing a highly configurable hardware architecture, which is adaptable to a wide range of application requirements.

Two fundamental strategies are recognized for distributing graphical software, for example, GKS. The first is to decompose the system into its functional components and distribute them onto separate processing units. The second is to decompose a picture into its constructive elements and process them in parallel.

The combination of both strategies guarantees the most reasonable system response time during exceedingly interactive graphical applications. Our implementation of a multiprocessor GKS (mpGKS) basically consists of four different software modules, namely the GKS module, WISS module, OUTPUT module and INPUT module. Each module is associated with one processing unit. Most of the GKS functions are processed in a distributed manner. The logical interface for the communication between these modules is the workstation interface of GKS (International Standards Organization, 1985b).

22.2 Distribution policies and communication concepts for GKS

First we present a short outline of the GKS architecture and afterwards we discuss the issues of a distributed graphics system.

GKS became an international graphics standard (ISO/IS 7942) in 1985. This standard provides basic graphics functions to create and manipulate computer-generated pictures (Enderle *et al.*, 1987). The GKS functions are neither specific to application programs nor to devices. GKS defines an application interface and introduces the workstation concept, that is, an abstraction of graphics devices (Figure 22.1).

An application program calls GKS functions through the application interface. Graphical I/O devices are connected to GKS through the workstation interface. The GKS philosophy is based on the workstation concept. Each workstation belongs to one of six defined workstation categories (*output*, *input*, *outin*, *workstation independent segment storage*, *metafile output*, *metafile input*). All workstations are addressed in the same manner. The differences between the physical device capabilities are compensated by a device driver.

GKS itself is sequential, that is, a picture is defined by a stream of output primitive functions. To incorporate parallelism in GKS to get an mpGKS two fundamental distribution policies (Göbel and Krömker, 1986) are pursued:

(1) Decompose the system into its functions and distribute them onto different processors **(functional distribution)**.

(2) Decompose a picture into its logical elements (segments) and process them on different processors in parallel (**object distribution**).

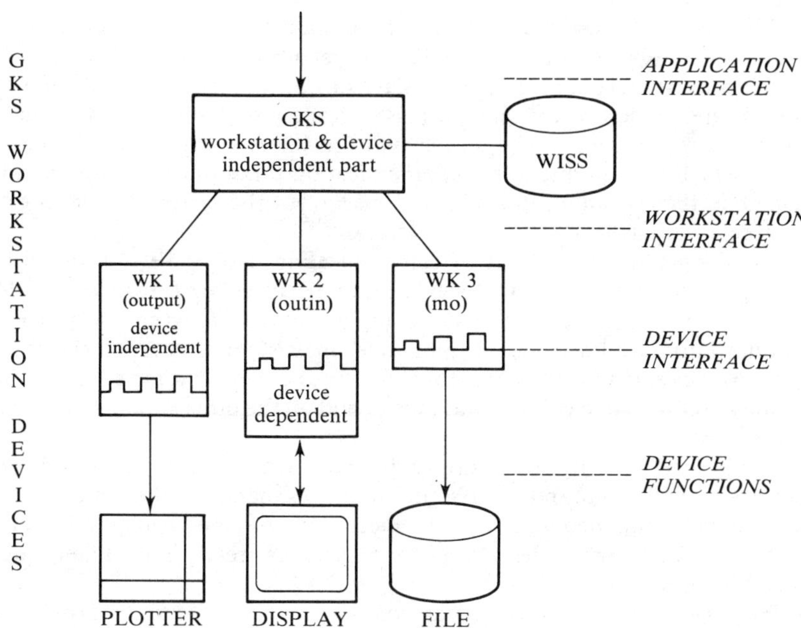

Figure 22.1
GKS interfaces and workstation concept.

Both concepts are supported by GKS. The functional distribution makes a logical division between output and input functionality, with the output pipelines and the measure and trigger process as results. Furthermore, the output pipelines for the six different output primitive functions can be separated. Also, special hardware, like clippers or text generators can be applied. Each output primitive could be processed by a specific processor.

Object distribution assumes that several processors provide the complete output facilities to process a graphical object (segment). These processors scan their segments into local caches in parallel. The final picture is obtained by collecting the separate pixel patterns via a pixel bus into a refresh buffer.

A combination of both concepts gives the most efficient solution for an interactive graphics system in terms of low system response time and real-time picture generation. The output and the input functionality is split according to the functional distribution, and within the output processing an object distribution is implemented. This allows asynchronous input and a fast picture regeneration when attributes change during an application.

mpGKS comprises several software modules that are executed on several processors (Felger *et al.*, 1987). The GKS module provides the application interface. The WISS module represents the Workstation Independent Segment Storage and the segment backup. Each OUTPUT module processes all output primitives and contains the distributed Workstation Dependent Segment Storage (WDSS). The INPUT module combines the measure and trigger processes for the logical input device modes of all input device classes.

Dividing GKS into several software modules that run as separate processes on different processors demands an interprocess communication within the system. A link between these processes is established by exchanging and interpreting data between disjoint memories. The logically transferred pieces of information are called **messages**.

Physically, we distinguish different communication modes relating to the roles and the number of the communication partners. During a communication cycle each processor has a role: **master**, **slave** or **outsider**. At any time there exists only one master in the system. Only the master is allowed to initiate the communication and address all slaves. The master and the slaves build up the master-slave group, in which the interprocessor communication takes place. **Outsiders** do not participate in the communication. Each processor of the system is able to get the master role.

Depending on the number of communication partners, we distinguish the addressing modes: **unicasting**, **multicasting** and **broadcasting** (Frank *et al.*, 1985).

Unicasting is the exclusive communication between two partners (1:1-connection). Multicasting defines one master and several slaves (1:*n*-connection). Broadcasting supposes that all connected processors participate in the communication with one processor as master and all the other modules as slaves or outsiders.

Additionally, a fourth addressing mode, the **multiple write** feature, is available (Gemballa and Lindner, 1982). This means that more than one sender can transmit data simultaneously. The data compete on the system bus and the information which wins the competition can be read immediately by all participating processors.

Messages can be interpreted as commands to a process or a delivery of results. Depending on whether or not the issuer of a command message expects results to be returned, we distinguish between two forms of interprocess communication in mpGKS: **synchronous communication** and **asynchronous communication.**

In synchronous communication, a producer waits until the receiver of a command message has completed the required task. A reply is returned which allows the producer to continue his task.

An asynchronous communication in mpGKS is based on the **no wait – send** communication principle. Within mpGKS, synchronous (for example, for input functions) and asynchronous (for example, for output primitive functions) communication is implemented. To handle the communication in mpGKS, a special communication layer is integrated (Figure 22.2). This layer organizes the different communication types in the four addressing modes, described above. In mpGKS, 23 different combinations of communication types and addressing modes, called communication **classes**, are realized to support the GKS functionality efficiently. Each GKS function is associated with a particular communication class.

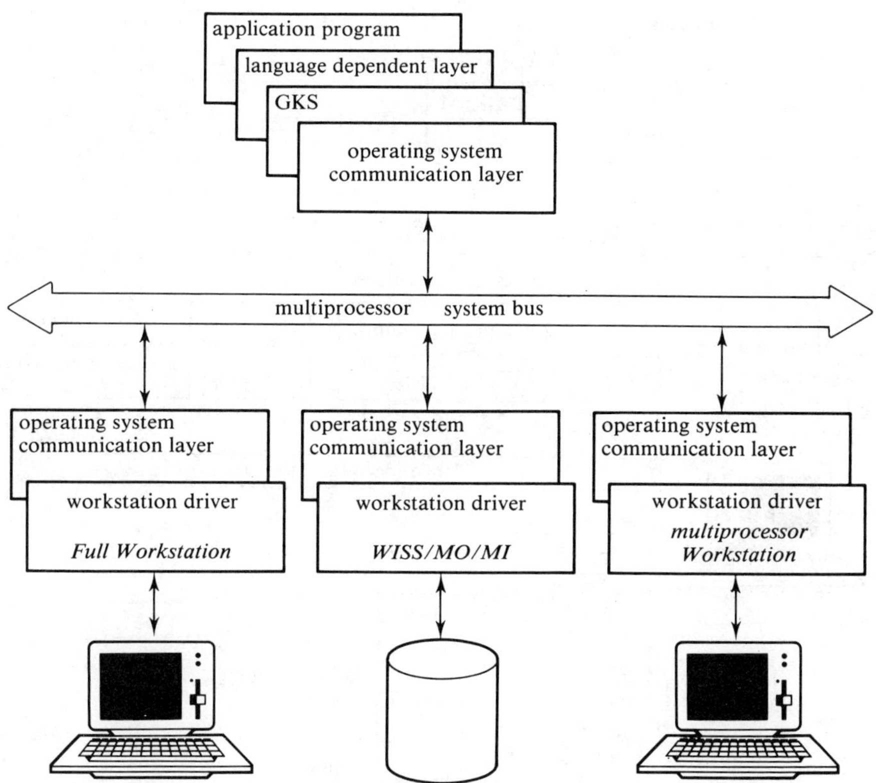

Figure 22.2
Embedding the communication layer in the GKS layer model (Felger *et al.*, 1987).

22.3 Conceptual design of mpGKS

The overall architecture of mpGKS is shown in Figure 22.3. The GKS module provides the application interface of GKS. The information describing the current configuration, that is, the number, type and capability of connected graphical workstations, is located on this module.

The WISS module realizes the workstation independent segment storage including a segment backup function. To support the backup functionality, the associated processor is equipped with a hard disk. This module can also handle output to and input from GKS metafiles.

The OUTPUT module realizes the graphical output pipelines for the various GKS output primitives within or outside of segments. Graphical output is generated in a local cache memory before it is transferred to the refresh buffer. Additionally, it represents the local part of the distributed workstation dependent segment storage. A very important aspect is the strategy of segment allocation, to achieve an optimal distribution, that is, a minimum of time requirement for picture regeneration. Moreover, this module provides echo generation facilities to support INPUT modules which have no graphical output capabilities.

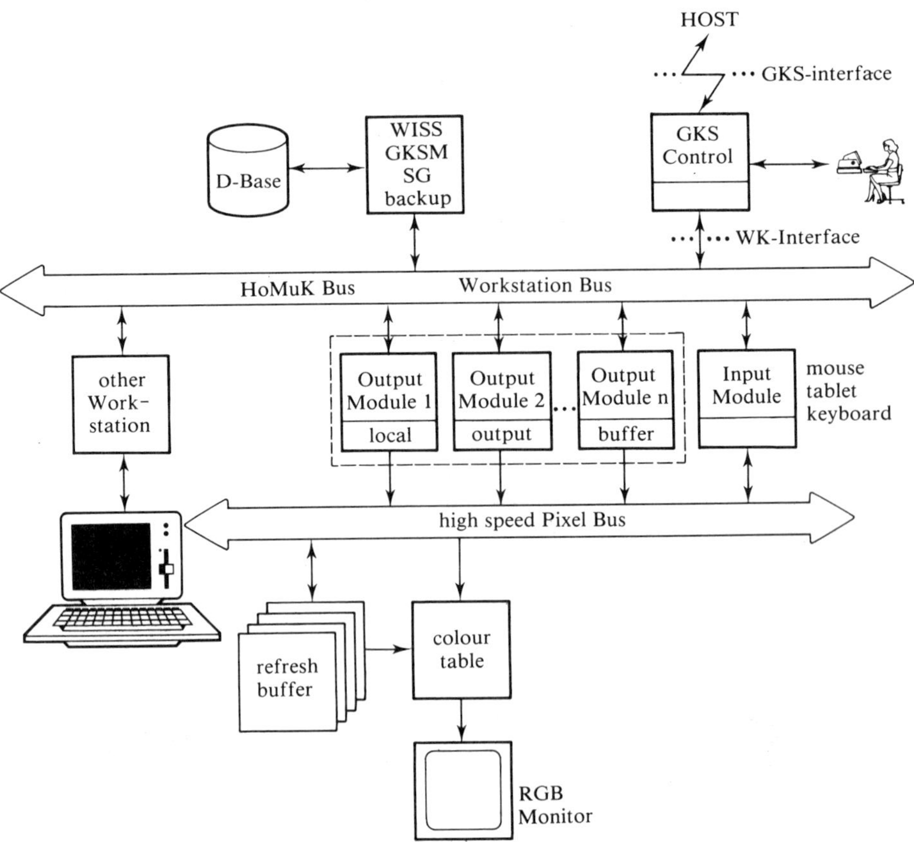

Figure 22.3
mpGKS architecture.

The INPUT module provides the functionality of graphical input in GKS. It maps logical input devices onto physical mouse, tablet or keyboard input. Furthermore, it represents the logical interaction process consisting of measure and trigger processes for the different input modes of the logical input devices, for example, REQUEST, SAMPLE and EVENT. This module is also responsible for echo generating and echo handling.

22.3.1 The GKS module

The application programs are executed on the GKS processor module. The GKS module, which provides the GKS application interface, is a link to all connected graphical devices. It has knowledge about the current configuration of the multiprocessor system. The GKS module also performs the handling of the INQUIRY functions and passing of a workstation's relevant information to the other modules. Furthermore, it controls the reorganization of the WDSS of connected workstations.

The mpGKS is implemented using a configurable hardware architecture that comprises at least four processor modules. The GKS module needs to have knowledge about the current configuration of the multiprocessor system to determine the physical access to all connected processor modules. An important feature of this procedure is the dynamic extension of the multiprocessor system. Connecting an additional processor module (and additional graphical devices) only requires a new entry in the configuration table of the multiprocessor system. A further task of the GKS module is to supply all processor modules with the corresponding GKS functions and data invoked by the application program.

The INQUIRY functions referring to GKS data structures, for example, the GKS state list, the segment state lists, the workstation state lists, etc. are of particular interest. In order to minimize interprocess communication, it is necessary to process all INQUIRY functions completely within the GKS module. All GKS data structures, that is, all state lists and description tables, are therefore implemented within the GKS module. The GKS module acquires the configuration information and the workstation description data during the initialization of mpGKS.

Most GKS functions are in two parts: one part executes the error handling and normalization transformation, the other is a function-specific component, for example, setting the attributes or picture regeneration. Although the first part mostly is realized within the GKS module, errors which occur at workstation level are returned to the GKS module.

One fundamental concept in mpGKS is the object distribution followed by the parallel processing of the segments by more than one OUTPUT module. The main aim is to achieve an optimal distribution of the segments on the OUTPUT modules. A high throughput performance will be obtained when segments are of approximately the same complexity and all OUTPUT modules need nearly the same scan time. The scan time during every picture regeneration activity is measured and compared to determine the performance of the mpGKS system. With the result of this function, the redistribution of the segments (see Section 22.3.2) can be decided. If necessary, the GKS module starts redistributing all segments stored in the segment backup onto the corresponding OUTPUT modules in a well-defined way. There are three ways of choosing the moment to start the redistribution process:

(1) Immediately when segment redistribution is necessary.
(2) Implicit segment redistribution, that is, this process is initiated by one module and can be started, for example, during processing a user interaction (REQUEST) with a logical input device.
(3) Explicit segment redistribution, that is, starting this process under control of the application program.

The software implemented on the GKS module contains:

- The GKS library (FORTRAN language binding to GKS, ISO DIS8651/1) (International Standards Organization, 1986).
- The subroutines for the management of the GKS state list, the segment state list, the error state list and the GKS description table.
- The subroutines for setting entries in the workstation description table.
- The new subroutines for processing segment redistribution.

The workstation interface supplies all connected workstations with the GKS function code and the corresponding parameters. Each GKS function has a definite code. In view of the communication direction from the connected modules to the GKS module, there exist additional return codes.

Within the realization of mpGKS, some functions concerning the GKS module have been supplied. These functions are as follows:

- The control functions OPEN GKS, OPEN WORKSTATION and ESCAPE.
- The output function CELL ARRAY.
- The INQUIRY functions.

The current state of the mpGKS configuration will be obvious in the configuration table. It comprises the workstation identifier, the workstation type, the workstation connection identifier and the physical address of each connected workstation. The entry of a mpGKS workstation has additional data, namely, the number of the OUTPUT modules, the physical addresses of the INPUT module and of all OUTPUT modules. After creating the configuration table, this table will be sent to all connected processor modules. Moreover, specific ESCAPE functions are implemented to have function codes concerning the INPUT and OUTPUT modules to adjust the input area of the tablet (precision) to the output part of the device driver or to adapt the parameters for complexity and the splitting size of the segments. Furthermore, there are function codes that start the segment redistribution process.

22.3.2 OUTPUT module and WISS module

The OUTPUT module and the WISS module are described together, because both categories deal with graphical output. The OUTPUT module realizes the graphical output pipelines and so performs the segment and workstation transformation, the clipping, the attribute binding and the primitive generation into a cache memory. More than one OUTPUT module can be associated with a workstation. Thus, a distributed WDSS is realized, that is suitable for fast picture regeneration and segment processing.

Output primitive processing

Each active workstation processes the current output primitive function (for example, POLYLINE). When a workstation comprises more than one OUTPUT module, mpGKS decides which OUTPUT module will process the output primitive function.

A simple algorithm controls the assignment of output primitives outside segments to OUTPUT modules. All modules have the same functionality, and thus an ordered list including all OUTPUT modules. The first module in this list accepts the first output primitive function, the second module the next output primitive function and so on. When the last module is reached, the first module accepts output primitive functions again. This algorithm is called **modulo distribution** and is most effective because it offers the highest parallelism and is easy to implement. All modules scan different output primitives simultaneously and the pixel output is sequenced according to the ordered OUTPUT module list.

Output primitives inside segments are assigned to all OUTPUT modules. They are stored in their local WDSS. The algorithm described above also determines one OUTPUT module, which finally scans the output primitive.

The OUTPUT and WISS modules accept, from the GKS module, unclipped Normalized Device Coordinates (NDC). All segments are stored in this coordinate system. The OUTPUT modules provide the segment transformation, mapping NDC to NDC, and the workstation transformation, mapping NDC to Device Coordinates (DC). When an application program changes the normalization transformation, the clipping rectangle and the geometric attributes are transferred to all OUTPUT modules and the WISS module for subsequent uses.

Distributed WDSS

A distributed WDSS is realized if a workstation comprises more than one OUTPUT module. The strategy of implicit segment assignment to the distributed WDSS is realized, as follows: at creation time, the segment is broadcast to all OUTPUT modules and the WISS module. When the segment is closed, each OUTPUT module performs a **best fit evaluation** and reports the evaluation to the other modules using the multiple write bus technique. The OUTPUT module with the best fit stores the segment in its local segment storage. All other OUTPUT modules lose the segment data. The aim of this best fit evaluation is to predetermine a good system performance, especially to minimize the picture regeneration time. The best fit takes into account the segment priority, the number of segments on the module with lower priorities and the capacity of the local segment storage.

The OUTPUT modules of one workstation are working at maximum capacity when all segments do not exceed a segment generation time limit. This is achieved by splitting a segment into fractions of approximately the same scanning time. The user is allowed to define this limit. When an open segment exceeds this limit, the mpGKS implicitly creates a sequence of subsegments with internal names, and performs the segment distribution on subsegment level. These system segment names are also used to find out the sequential order in the distributed segment state list, which is locally ordered by user segment priorities. Therefore, the system segment priority corresponds to the pair of user segment priority and system segment name. This relationship is unique in the entire system.

A segment redistribution is initiated by the GKS module any time when the regeneration time is 30% higher than estimated. The redistribution is performed by the WISS module. As a result of segment splitting, all segments have nearly the same complexity, therefore the redistribution is realized by modulo distribution, like the assignment of output primitive functions described before. The WISS module inspects the segment state list sequentially and assigns each segment to an OUTPUT module.

Each OUTPUT module contains local segment storage and cache memory that buffers one completely scanned segment. A picture regeneration causes a redrawing of all segments. Each OUTPUT module processes the segments which have been previously assigned to it. In each local segment state list, the segments are ordered by their priorities. In order to find the global sequential order, mpGKS has to merge all local segment state lists. Segments that are not stored locally in an OUTPUT module are made accessible by the WISS module before scanning. The pixel data of each segment is buffered in a local cache before it is written into the refresh buffer. The pixel data in these caches are merged by writing them sequentially into the refresh buffer. The sequential order again is determined by segment priorities. Segments with lower priorities are written first to guarantee overlapping effects. The lowest priority is found using the multiple write bus technique.

In addition, the OUTPUT modules and the WISS module support the INPUT module for input with logical input device **pick**. These modules receive the pick position and determine the picked segment by analytic calculations in the object space. Each OUTPUT module inspects its part of the distributed WDSS, while the WISS module inspects the segments which are not stored in the local storages. The module finding the segment with the highest priority aborts the search on the other modules and delivers the segment name and pick identifier to the INPUT module.

22.3.3 INPUT module

The INPUT module controls the interaction between operator and the application program and realizes the mapping of physical input to logical input. The logical input value is then returned to the application program on the GKS module. If the application program activates a logical input device, a separate process is initiated on the INPUT module. This process is called an **interaction process** and is running if there is at least one logical input device active. Embedded in this process are the measure and trigger processes of the active logical input devices. Operator action, manipulating physical input devices during an interaction, is controlled by this interaction process as well as the communication between the INPUT module and other mpGKS modules.

The GKS input functions are divided into two classes, depending on the communication type between INPUT module and the other modules. The first class consists of the GKS functions requiring synchronous communication between the GKS module and the INPUT module, because the application program is waiting for logical input data from the interaction process. The second class of GKS input functions is processed in an asynchronous pipelining mechanism. The functions are interpreted as tasks and processed on the INPUT module without returning parameters.

The GKS input functions REQUEST, SAMPLE and AWAIT EVENT require synchronous communication. These functions cause the application program to wait until the requested input values are returned. If the REQUEST function is invoked, a measure and a trigger process is initiated on the input processor module. These processes are active until the input is entered, or a break action is performed by the operator. The INPUT module evaluates the logical input value as return values for the GKS module. Analogously, the SAMPLE function is processed, but in this case the current logical input value of the specified logical input device is returned to the application program without waiting for any operator action. Furthermore, the INPUT module manages EVENT input. Therefore, it controls a workstation event queue containing temporally ordered event reports. Events from input devices are added to this queue asynchronously. The function AWAIT EVENT causes the application program to wait (if necessary) for an event to occur and transfers the oldest event report to the current event report in the GKS state list.

If the logical input device pick is active, additional communication and computation efforts are necessary to evaluate the logical input value. As the INPUT module has no access to the distributed WDSS, it transmits the pick position to the OUTPUT modules and requests the corresponding segment name and the pick identifier. The OUTPUT modules search in their local segment storage for the segment with the highest priority located at this position. The segment name and the pick identifier are returned to the INPUT module to determine the logical input value.

The following GKS functions belong to the asynchronous communication type, because no return parameters are expected by the application program. The function INITIALIZE transfers a data record containing default values for initial value, prompt/echo type and echo area to the INPUT module. This data is stored for the specified logical input device in the workstation state list. The functions SET MODE and FLUSH DEVICE EVENTS are processed in a similar way.

If an input queue overflow occurs during an interaction with logical input devices in EVENT mode, then an error message is sent to the GKS module and no more events are generated. This permits the application program to determine how many events were in the queue when the overflow occurred.

Echo generation

The interaction process controls the generation, update and deletion of echoes, prompts and acknowledgements. Two strategies are identified for echo handling. The first is to provide basic output facilities on the INPUT module, for example, point, line and text generation. The graphical output from the INPUT module then has to be synchronized with the graphical output produced from the OUTPUT modules. To avoid this, the INPUT module uses separate pixel planes in the refresh buffer. This allows the creation and deletion of echo symbols independently from the current picture. No picture regeneration is necessary if a menu is deleted, because graphical output is not damaged and will be regenerated during the next physical refresh. Furthermore, the pixel output for echoes need not be synchronized with the application output and will not be overwritten in case of asynchronous input.

The second strategy is to provide echo generation by the OUTPUT modules, if there are no output facilities available on the INPUT module. The part of the input devices data structure, which is relevant for echo generating, has to be realized on an OUTPUT module, that is, the current measure values, the entries for echo area, prompt/echo type, echo switch and the initial logical input values, for instance, the initial position of a locator device. This data structure is a part of the workstation state list, but it is held as a separate table, the echo description table. The process of generating an echo on a separate device is called **remote echoing**. The INPUT module controls the physical input devices, updates the current measure values of the logical input devices and sends them via messages to the OUTPUT modules to achieve the appropriate echo output.

22.4 Implementation of mpGKS

mpGKS was implemented using the functionality of a multiprocessor system called Homogeneous Multiprocessor Kernel (HoMuK) (Linder, 1983; Encarnacao *et al.*, 1984). HoMuK is a loosely coupled dynamic and configurable system that was designed specifically for use in graphics systems. The HoMuKbus interconnects the HoMuK modules. The hardware configuration of one HoMuK module is based on a Motorola MC680xx microprocessor with an on-board memory of at least 256 kbyte, a bus coupler and a local VMEbus. The bus coupler performs the HoMuKbus protocol and connects the global HoMuKbus with the local VMEbus.

The HoMuK system is a realization of the master-slave concept with the multiple write bus technique as its special feature. Uni-, multi-, and broadcasting communication are implemented as basic bus functions.

The GKS functions are grouped into definite classification groups, according to the communication requirements of the modules within an mpGKS.

Some application functions concern only one module (for example, INITIALIZE INPUT DEVICE), and are transmitted using unicasting communication. Functions concerning OUTPUT and WISS module (for example, UPDATE WORKSTATION) are transmitted by multicasting communication mode. Functions concerning all modules (for example, OPEN GKS) are transmitted by broadcasting. The multiple write bus feature is applied to decide high/low priorities for the fork and join operations of the picture later.

The implementation of mpGKS makes use of presumptively defined master-slave groups and cannot be changed during running time. Some GKS functions are transmitted to the OUTPUT modules (for example, POLYLINE), others to the WISS module only (for example, INSERT SEGMENT). Consequently, additional communication effort for setting-up and addressing varying master-slave groups has been avoided.

The overall performance of the mpGKS system is dependent on the pixelbus to handle fast data transfer from OUTPUT modules to the graphical output device. A high data transfer rate allows the connection of more OUTPUT modules and therefore a higher degree of parallelism.

In our prototype realization we have emulated the pixelbus. Each OUTPUT

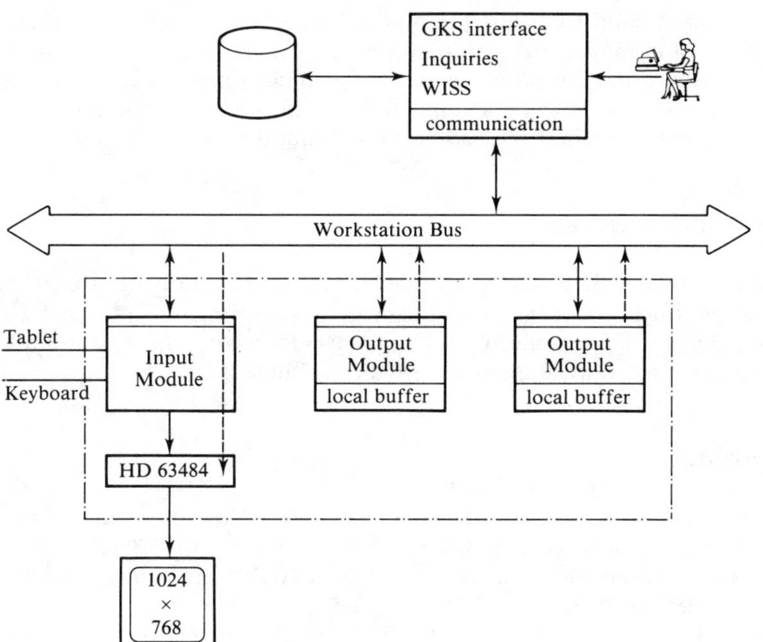

Figure 22.4
mpGKS prototype.

module transfers its graphical output data via the HoMuKbus to the processor module that is connected with the output device. The data transfer is implemented as basic fast block transfer.

A basic mpGKS configuration consists of one GKS module, one WISS module, one INPUT module and at least two OUTPUT modules, realizing GKS level 2c in all. The graphical output device is connected to the INPUT module. This allows the INPUT module to use the hardware capabilities of the Hitachi display controller (HD 63484) for echo generation (for example, hardware-crosshair). The data flow is shown by the dotted line in Figure 22.4. The OUTPUT modules scan the segments and transmit the pixel information to the INPUT module.

Summary

We have discussed conceptual strategies for using GKS in a multiprocessor environment. Furthermore, a realization of a prototype of a multiprocessor GKS architecture mpGKS was presented, which is highly configurable to application requirements such as low system response time in interactive sessions, or a high picture modification rate in real-time applications. However, the use of the mpGKS ranges from a basic structure consisting of four processor modules for basic application requirements, to an extremely sophisticated multiprocessor system consisting of several processor modules supplied with special software and hardware facilities for generating graphical output. Implicit reorganization of picture data is done any time mpGKS detects that the picture regeneration could be done much faster. The application is allowed to adjust the mpGKS architecture and the configuration parameters (for example, reorganization percentage, maximal segment complexity, etc.) to its needs. Future work will concentrate on identifying different application profiles and varying the mpGKS architecture and configuration parameters to determine optimal graphics systems for these applications.

Acknowledgements

We want to thank all those who helped in the preparation of this article. In particular, we thank D. Krömker, E. Klement, G.R. Hofmann, G. Englert, S. Haas and T. Tran for their insightful and valuable suggestions. Finally, we thank J. Encarnacao for his motivating assistance during our work.

References

Encarnacao J., Göbel M. and Lindner R. (1984). HoMuK – Ein Homogener Multiprozessor-Kern für verteilte graphische Systeme. In *Entwicklungsperspektiven mittlerer Rechnersysteme* (Proebster W.E. and Remshardt, R. eds). München: Oldenbourg Verlag

Enderle G., Kansy K., Pfaff G. (1987). *Computer Graphics Programming, GKS The Graphics Standard*, 2nd ed. Berlin: Springer-Verlag

Frank A.J., Wittie L.D. and Bernstein A.J. (1985). Multicast Communication on Network Computers. *IEEE Computer,* **18**(5), 49–61

Felger W., Ziegler R. and Zuppa, P. (1987). *Eine Multiprozessor-GKS-Workstation auf HoMuK.* Diplomarbeit, TH Darmstadt, FB Informatik, FG Graphisch-Interaktive Systeme (in German)

Gemballa R. and Lindner R. (1982). The Multiple-Write Bus Technique. *IEEE Computer Graphics and Application,* **2**(7), 33–41

Göbel M. and Krömker D. (1986). A Multi-Microprocessor GKS Workstation. *IEEE Computer Graphics and Application,* **6**(7), 54–60

International Standards Organization (1985a). *Graphical Kernel System (GKS); Functional Description* ISO/IS 7942. ISO

International Standards Organization (1985b). *A Workstation Interface for GKS* ISO/TC97/SC21/WG2–N238. ISO

International Standards Organization (1986). *FORTRAN Language Binding to GKS* ISO DIS8651/1. ISO

Lindner R. (1983). *Introduction to a Simple but Unconventional Multiprocessorsystem and Outline of an Application.* Berlin: Springer-Verlag

23 · Programming high performance graphics on the DAP

J. Smallbone

Intercept Systems Limited

The DAP is a massively parallel SIMD processor marketed by Active Memory Technology Limited. It is targeted at very high performance, general-purpose applications requiring a high degree of interaction. This chapter describes how the DAP may be programmed to render triangular polygons at video refresh rates and thus facilitate the real-time animated display of a computer-based terrain model as part of a flight simulation.

23.1 The requirement for visualization

When examining trends in supercomputing there is a common requirement for visualization of numeric results. Typical users of supercomputers access a shared central supercomputer either by networked local access or, remotely, by telephone links. A large computational task may run for just a few hours on the supercomputer, yet the results may take days, weeks or even months to interpret even with graphical postprocessing.

Ideally, what is needed is for the numerical supercomputer to be tightly coupled with a visualization engine. The total system should be interactive. There should be the flexibility to provide high-speed interaction by performing coarse visualization in the foreground, while still retaining the option to visualize selected areas of interest in more precision as a background task.

Special-purpose graphics devices exist, that may be configured very efficiently to meet specific production needs, but in the majority of cases there is a need for more flexibility than these special-purpose devices are able to provide. Furthermore, that flexibility is required to be easily programmable by the user, and the need to provide high performance visualization through software itself demands supercomputer processing power.

For user interaction, the graphical visualization capability must be local. The need for tight coupling dictates that either the users must come to the central computer facility or the numerical supercomputer power must be distributed to the users. Coupling a high performance graphical engine together with the supercomputer is a high budget solution and can only provide interactive supercomputing to a small fraction of the potential users. This leads us to examine the alternative solution of using one of the emerging generation of high performance, general-purpose, parallel computer systems to integrate general-purpose supercomputing with interactive visualization.

The two classes of systems which seem to offer most potential for exploitation in this way are the massively MIMD systems such as Hypercube, BBN Butterfly and Multi Transputer systems, and the SIMD systems such as the Connection Machine, MPP and DAP.

This chapter reports on Intercept work in this area using the DAP.

23.2 Background to the DAP

The DAP was developed by ICL [1] in the Seventies and the first product was delivered to Queen Mary College, London University in 1980. The original product was designed to share store with the early 2900 P-series mainframes and the typical price for a 2900/DAP system ranged from £1.5M to £2.5M.

ICL delivered about half a dozen systems in 1980/81 and the systems were used to investigate performance over a wide range of applications, mainly numerical. Performance comparisons achieved at the time [2] are shown in Table 23.1. In 1981, ICL introduced a new mainframe architecture and sales of the mainframe DAPs ceased.

Between 1981 and 1985, DAP development was targeted to exploit its potential in high performance signal- and image-processing applications for the defence industry. About a dozen MILDAPs were built and attached to the Perq workstation for development purposes. These machines embodied a very fast (40–50 Mbyte/s) data channel (FIO) and could be run quite independently from the hosts, allowing their use in embedded systems.

In 1986, Active Memory Technology (AMT) Limited was formed with an injection of venture capital funding, and in return for a minority shareholding in the new company, ICL vested in AMT all its rights in DAP.

AMT re-engineered the DAP into a commercial product, the DAP500 series,

Table 23.1 DAP performance comparison results.

Application	Comparison
Weather Modelling	5 * CDC 7600
3-D Magneto-Hydrodynamics	56 * ICL 2976
Monte-Carlo Simulations	30 * ICL 2900
Seismic Diffraction Migration	20 * IBM 3033
Ballistics Simulation	= CRAY 1
Estuary Simulation	139 * ICL 1904S
Plasma Physics	29 * ICL 2976
Molecular Dynamics	0.5 * CRAY 1
Special Poisson Solver	144 * IBM 3033
Econometric Modelling	31 * CDC 7600
Astronomical Image Processing – Geometric Correction	10–20 * IBM 360/195
Processing of Topographic Data – in raster form	orders of magnitude faster than IBM 370/168
Nuclear Reactor Turbulence Studies	7 * CDC 7600
Ising Model Calculation	5 * CRAY 1

Comparisons between achieved benchmark times on the ICL 2900/DAP with benchmark times on the stated machines.

and are committed to sell systems for attachment to a range of popular workstations and superminis, initially Sun and VAX. The DAP510 is currently being delivered to early customers.

The price range for host/DAP systems in the next two years is likely to be £50K to £250K (one tenth of the cost of the ICL mainframe host/DAP) and the first entry product the DAP510, when configured with a small Sun or microVAX falls in the middle of this price range.

23.3 Principles of the DAP

The architecture of the DAP is shown schematically in Figure 23.1. On the DAP510 there are 1024 Processing Elements (PEs) which all work under the control of a central Master Control Unit (MCU). The PEs have immediate access to their own store and may access the rest of store via nearest-neighbour routeing or via an MCU fetch and broadcast. The PEs are simple bit-serial processors and all operations are built up at the low level from a number of bit instructions.

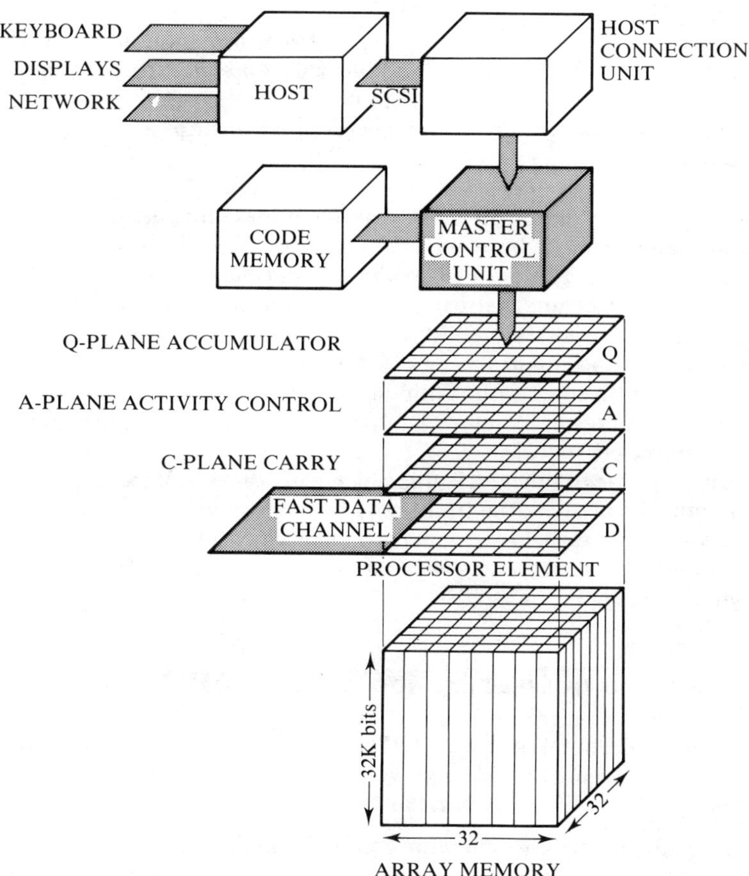

Figure 23.1
DAP 510-4 schematic.

The DAP may be programmed in the DAP assembly language APAL which is provided with a very powerful macro assembler, but applications programming is usually performed in FORTRAN PLUS [3] (originally DAP FORTRAN), which is an array extended FORTRAN forerunner of the emerging ANSI 8X standard FORTRAN. The FORTRAN PLUS would then be compiled into a sequence of calls to APAL macros. Parallel processing is programmed by statements of the form:

```
A = B + C
```

where A, B, C may be defined as arrays in statements of the form:

```
INTEGER*1 A(,),B(,),C(,)
```

The programs are developed and compiled on a host system, typically a Sun workstation or VAX, and then loaded into the DAP codestore for execution by the MCU.

In the above case of addition of two 8-bit integer arrays, the corresponding APAL macro (without overflow checking) will be as follows, where A, B, C represent the addresses of the least significant bits:

```
CF                        set carry register false
DO 8 TIMES
QS          B(-)          move bit from store into the PE accumulator
CQPCQS      C(-)          add bit from store into PE carry and
                            accumulator
SQ          A(-)          move result bit to store
LOOP
```

During program execution, the MCU will fetch these instructions from the code store and cause them to be executed in parallel over the array of PEs, hence computing the results for up to 1024 data items at the same time. The above loop would require 24 machine instructions to perform the inner kernel of 1024 8-bit additions from store to store. With a cycle time of 100 ns on the DAP510, this implies a performance approaching 400 MOPs for low precision (less than 8-bit) integer additions. In comparison with the 100 MOPs performance achievable from 32-bit integer arithmetic, we immediately see the benefit of utilizing variable word-lengths wherever possible.

All operations on the DAP are implemented store to store, and it is this same store that may be used for the framestore buffer of a video monitor. The DAP is equipped with a fast asynchronous data channel which allows 50–60 frame transfers per second from DAP store to a video monitor, with each frame holding up to a megabyte of data.

23.4 The role of visualization on the DAP

The DAP510 is being marketed by AMT as a general-purpose SIMD parallel processor system that may provide a powerful interactive supercomputer facility for specific applications. Visualization has two roles:

(1) The interaction possible with computational problems may be enhanced dramatically by providing a visual window into the heart of the executing

program. For example, at each iteration of a 3D thermodynamics simulation, a 2D section through the temperature field may be displayed in real time with the viewing parameters interactively specified by the user.

(2) There are specific graphical applications which require to be programmed flexibly but still require the very high performance associated with special-purpose devices. The DAP may be treated as a programmable graphics engine either for the computation and real-time display of animated imagery or for the cost-effective generation of high quality output.

Intercept Systems is a third-party software house specializing in tools that enable the exploitation of parallel processing. It provides both general-purpose software and specific solutions to customer requirements. Our recent work has been targeted to deliver software for the DAP that is capable of performing high performance visualization at video rates. By designing in flexibility, we intend to supply more general-purpose graphical software that may serve a range of potential applications.

23.5 Study of visualization at video rates on the DAP

The following work is extracted from a project where the DAP is used in data selection and display from a real-time terrain database. The application demands that 3D perspective views are generated from the data in real time and mixed with pixel data from other sources. The example, which we use here to illustrate visualization on DAP at video rates, is the foreground display of a surface represented by up to 1000 triangular polygons. The display task is completed by blending in the backdrop as a separate stage.

Each of the triangular polygons is described by the 3D world coordinates of its three vertices and a reference colour. The graphics task is to compute a 3D perspective view of the surface and draw the polygons, depth-cued with respect to the reference colour for the polygon. The view is to be redrawn 25 times per second from a viewpoint changing in time. The screen resolution is taken to be 768(H) × 576(V) pixels and each pixel is a 1-byte index to a colour table.

The triangular polygons are assumed to be held in an ordered sequence. In practice, the surface modelled in the sample application is that of a terrain with rectangular grid points. This surface offers several opportunities for further optimization, but in order to maintain the general nature of the resultant code, the only assumption is that the polygons are ordered to allow the use of the well-known 'painter's algorithm' [4] for the removal of hidden surfaces.

The approach taken is first to perform polygon processing in parallel using one processor per polygon. (Hence up to 1024 polygons in parallel.)

The polygon-processing task may be broken down into the following subtasks:

- Transform real world (x, y, z) coordinates into normalized screen coordinates (H, V, D).
- Derive line parameters for each pair of vertices using the line model:

  H = V * DHbyDV + HO where DH is less than DV
  V = H * DVbyDH + VO where DH is not less than DV

- Calculate the relative sheet address of the polygon within the screen.

- Using the depth of view, apply depth-cueing to calculate the colour for drawing the polygon.
- Identify and eliminate any backward-facing polygons to prevent unnecessary drawing.

Programming this is quite trivial in DAP FORTRAN. The scalar code for performing a perspective viewing transformation maps efficiently into the SIMD model of parallelism and indeed many of the techniques developed for pipeline processing of graphics are equally trivial. For instance:

```
REAL AH,AV,AD,AX,AY,AZ
AH = THX * AX + THY * AY + THZ * AZ + THW
AV = TVX * AX + TVY * AY + TVZ * AZ + TVW
AD = TDX * AX + TDY * AY + TDZ * AZ + TDW
```

is the FORTRAN scalar code to compute the perspective transform of one vertex whereas:

```
REAL AH(,),AV(,),AD(,),AX(,),AY(,),AZ(,)
AH = THX * AX + THY * AY + THZ * AZ + THW
AV = TVX * AX + TVY * AY + TVZ * AZ + TVW
AD = TDX * AX + TDY * AY + TDZ * AZ + TDW
```

is the corresponding FORTRAN PLUS code to perform the same function in parallel over 1024 vertices.

Conditional processing is performed efficiently by using the logical facilities of FORTRAN PLUS to perform conditional computation in parallel. For example, the line gradient and constant for:

H = V * DHbyDV + HO   if DH is less than DV
V = H * DVbyDH + VO   if DH is not less than DV

are calculated in the following code by merging data, subject to a logical array.

```
REAL AH(,),AV(,),BH(,),BV(,),DH(,),DV(,)
REAL GRADIENT(,),CONSTANT(,)
LOGICAL INVERT(,)

DH = AH - BH
DV = AV - BV
INVERT = ABS(DV). LT. ABS(DH)
GRADIENT = MERGE(DV,DH,INVERT) / MERGE(DH,DV,INVERT)
CONSTANT = MERGE(V,H,INVERT) - MERGE(H,V,INVERT) *
                                            GRADIENT
```

This style of programming may seem at first to be marginally more complex than performing conditional jumps to alternative code sections. However, the approach soon pays for itself in concise maintainable common code.

Each of the lines between vertices are processed serially over the three vertices and in parallel over the polygons. Then, having performed as much polygon processing as possible in parallel, we now draw the polygons serially using the data we have calculated for each polygon.

When we come to draw the polygons to the screen, we map a processor to each pixel of a 32 × 32 sheet of the screen. For clarity, the following example assumes that the triangular polygon to be drawn is contained within one sheet of the screen. In practice, our code builds up larger polygons sheet by sheet. This is left as an exercise for the reader!

The task of drawing individual triangles may be broken down into the following subtasks:

- Identify all pixels which lie in the halfspace delimited by the line between vertices 1 and 2.
- Identify all pixels which lie in the halfspace delimited by the line between vertices 2 and 3.
- Identify all pixels which lie in the halfspace delimited by the line between vertices 3 and 1.
- Identify the pixels which form the union of the above three halfspaces.
- Colour those pixels in the sheet which form the triangle.

Each of the three lines joining vertices of the Nth triangle are defined in terms of the numerical parameters GRADIENT and CONSTANT which are held to 16 bits of precision (2 bytes) and the logical parameter INVERT. The 8-bit colour shade for the triangle is held in COLOUR.

For each line we define a logical array whose bits are set 'TRUE' to the left of the line and 'FALSE' to the right of the line and then we find the union by ANDing these logical arrays. In FORTRAN PLUS this is:

```
LOGICAL MASK(,,3),TRIANGLE(,),INVERT(,,3)
EXTERNAL LOGICAL MATRIX FUNCTION LEFT__OF__LINE
INTEGER*2 GRADIENT(,,3),CONSTANT(,,3),
INTEGER*1 COLOUR(,)

MASK(,,1) = LEFT__OF__LINE(GRADIENT(N,,1),CONSTANT(N,,1),
                INVERT(N,,1))
MASK(,,2) = LEFT__OF__LINE(GRADIENT(N,,2),CONSTANT(N,,2),
                INVERT(N,,2))
MASK(,,3) = LEFT__OF__LINE(GRADIENT(N,,3),CONSTANT(N,,3),
                INVERT(N,,3))
TRIANGLE = MASK(,,1).AND.MASK(,,2).AND.MASK(,,3)
SHEET(TRIANGLE,,ROW,COL) = COLOUR(N)
```

We can create each of these logical 'left-of-line' arrays from the line parameters every time we need them but, in practice, there is a finite number of different 'left-of-line's. It turns out to be more efficient to compute the set of all logical arrays once and store them. If we use the line parameters as an index into the set we may then extract the required array with minimal computation. Thus, the above inner kernel processing simplifies to a sequence of bit operations and, when implemented in APAL, may be performed in a small number of machine cycles per polygon.

Performance

Our current implementation of the above polygon-rendering example allows an image of over 1000 visible polygons to be displayed at an update rate of 25 times a second, and the processing performed for each update not only covers the rendering of 25 000 polygons per second but also the full 3D perspective transformation on over 3000 3D vertices. This update rate provides us with smooth animation, and the capability to 'fly' over a foreground synthetic terrain. There is scope to further optimize the performance of the code and we intend to make available additional processing time which will allow us to create background detail, using pixel techniques to provide computer-generated imagery of a standard not possible at a similar budget level, or using equipment that is constrained to use a polygon approach.

References

1. Flanders P.M., Hunt D.J., Reddaway S.F. and Parkinson D. (1977). Efficient high speed computing with the Distributed Array Processor. In *Sym. on High Speed Computer and Algorithm Organisation*, University of Illinois, April 1977
2. Reddaway S.F. (1979). The DAP approach. In *Supercomputers*. Infotech State of the Art Report. Infotech Int. Ltd, Maidenhead
3. Active Memory Technology Ltd. (1987). *DAP500: FORTRAN-PLUS Language*. Technical Report man002
4. Newell M.E., Newell R.G. and Sancha T.L. (1972). A new approach to the shaded picture problem. In *Proc. ACM Nat. Conf.*, pp. 443

24 · Parallel incremental polygon rendering on a SIMD processor array

T. Theoharis
I. Page

University of Oxford

We demonstrate how a SIMD processor array can efficiently evaluate the linear function $f(x, y) = ax + by + c$ over a 2D grid of equidistant points, by taking advantage of the method of differences. Hence, a processor array can support rendering operations efficiently once such operations have been expressed in terms of linear function evaluations. For polygons of the order of size of the processor array or larger, the hardware utilization factor is high. A major attraction of the method we present is that it is based on a SIMD processor array; this style of parallel machine is now recognized as highly general purpose given the wide range of applications successfully implemented on it.

24.1 Introduction

Single Instruction, Multiple Data stream (SIMD) arrays of processors (or processor arrays) are the most widely used form of parallel processor (Hwang and Briggs, 1984), examples of which are the DAP, BSP, MPP and CLIP. The wide variety of existing algorithms make the processor array a general-purpose parallel processor. Although special-purpose parallel architectures can provide very efficient support for some restricted class of algorithms, the wider applicability of a general-purpose machine like a processor array often makes it more cost effective.

In what follows we make extensive use of a particular view of image space dictated by a mapping of image space onto a processor array. An $N \times N$ processor array may regard image space as consisting of $N \times N$ adjacent windows. Each $N \times N$ window contains N^2 ordinary pixels. Thus an $I \times I$-pixel image space is viewed by an $N \times N$ processor array as an $I / N \times I / N$-window space (Figure 24.1). Using this mapping and an appropriate algorithm, the array can compute an entire $N \times N$ window in constant time.

Incremental calculations are used where possible in raster graphics to improve the performance of algorithms. Some memory of the previous step in the calculation is maintained and is altered by the use of an increment in order to get the next step. Although it is definitely not possible to exploit coherence by incremental computation when adjacent pixels are processed in parallel, because incremental

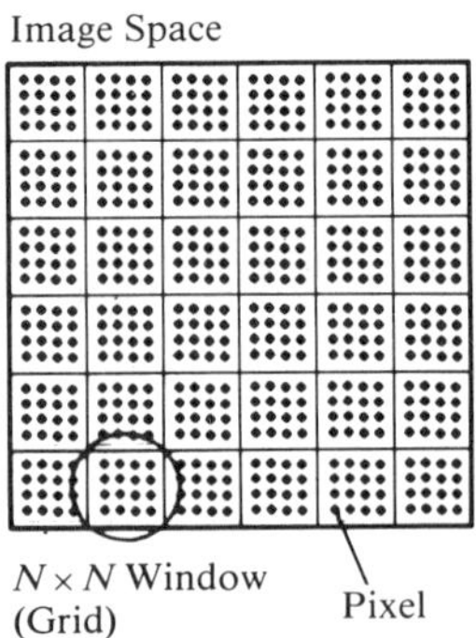

Figure 24.1
Image space, windows and pixels.

computation is based on sequential processing (memory of the previous step), it is still possible to take advantage of N-step coherence by N-step incremental calculations. This assumes that, in general, the area covered by a polygon spans several $N \times N$ windows (otherwise the polygon is not N-step coherent) and that the processor-per-pixel approach is too costly (which will be true for most applications in the foreseeable future).

The RasterOp graphics primitive (Newman and Sproull, 1979) can naturally be implemented on an $N \times N$ processor array and DisArray was originally built for the sole purpose of supporting RasterOp efficiently (Page, 1983). However, not all graphics output primitives can be implemented directly using RasterOp. Gupta (1981) has shown how to draw lines on a processor array using precomputed strokes of various slopes (a stroke is a line segment of length N) and here we show how polygons can be rendered on a processor array that supports planar arithmetic, that is, arithmetic operations on $N \times N$ matrices in parallel for all matrix elements. Planar arithmetic operations take on the name of their scalar counterpart prefixed by the word *planar*, for example, planar addition. The representation of an $N \times N$ numerical matrix on an $N \times N$ processor array under the mapping that places each matrix element in the memory of a single processing element is called a planar number. (For the rest of this chapter, matrix will refer to an $N \times N$ matrix and window will refer to an $N \times N$ window.) Planar arithmetic can be implemented both on bit-serial and bit-parallel processor arrays.

24.2 Using the evaluation of the linear function to implement rendering operations

Cohen and Demetrescu (1981) and Fuchs *et al.* (1985) describe how the evaluation of the bivariate linear function:

$$F(x,y) = ax + by + c$$

can be used in order to implement polygon rendering operations (filling, hidden surface elimination and smooth shading). They have both designed special-purpose architectures to evaluate the linear function. In this section, we shall summarize how the polygon rendering operations are implemented by means of linear function evaluations and in Section 24.3 we shall describe a method for the efficient evaluation of the linear function on a general-purpose processor array. The technique is restricted to convex polygons.

A convex polygon (which will be referred to simply as 'polygon') can be regarded as the intersection of n halfplanes defined by its n sides. Side i of the polygon lies on a line with equation:

$$F^i(x,y) = a_i x + b_i y + c_i = 0$$

Filling, the operation of identifying the pixels covered by the polygon, can be done as follows. Evaluate the n functions $F^i \mid i{:}0 \ldots n - 1$ for the coordinates of every pixel within the *extent* of the polygon, that is, the smallest possible rectangle that encloses the polygon. Now, if the coefficients of the F^i functions have been computed by considering successive pairs of polygon vertices in a consistent direction around the polygon (clockwise or anticlockwise), then the polygon will always lie on the same halfplane of the F^i (positive or negative). In other words, a pixel lies within a polygon if its coordinates give a positive (or, equivalently, negative) value to all of the n functions F^i. Thus the Boolean ANDing of the sign bits of the evaluations of the n F^i functions for the coordinates of a pixel (x,y) determines whether the pixel is covered by the polygon or not.

Hidden Surface Elimination (HSE), that is, the determination of the frontmost polygon at each pixel, can be handled by the familiar **z-buffer** algorithm. This algorithm maintains a depth buffer which is a memory that has one location devoted to the storage of the depth of the nearest polygon found so far, at each pixel. The depth of the polygon is determined at each pixel within it and is compared against the contents of the frame buffer for the same pixel. If the depth of the polygon is smaller than the previous contents of the depth buffer for the pixel, the depth buffer is updated with the new depth and the corresponding frame buffer pixel is assigned the colour of the polygon.

The evaluation of the polygon's depth at each of the pixels it covers is done by solving the image space plane equation $(ax + by + cz + d = 0)$ for z and expressing it as a function of x and y:

$$Z(x,y) = Ax + By + C$$

where $A = -a / c$, $B = -b / c$, $C = -d / c$.

Smooth shading (Gouraud, 1971) (in contrast to flat shading, that is, assigning a constant colour to all the pixels covered by a polygon) can be expressed in terms of the evaluation of three linear functions; one each for the red, green and blue colour components. The coefficients of each linear function are derived from the colour space coordinates of the vertices of the polygon. For example the $xyR(ed)$ coordinates of a vertex consist of its x, y coordinates and its *red* colour value. If the polygon is not a triangle, its colour space vertices may not be coplanar and in that case it will not be possible to derive a plane equation as we described for HSE (where the xyz coordinates of the polygon's vertices were assumed to be coplanar). There are two possible solutions; either we subdivide the polygon into triangles and determine their colour function coefficients separately, or we derive a plane equation by averaging the (non-coplanar) colour space coordinates of the polygon's vertices. Such an averaging technique has been suggested by Martin Newell and is reported in Sutherland *et al.* (1974).

24.3 Efficient evaluation of the linear function on a processor array

Evaluating a linear function $F(x,y) = ax + by + c$ for every pixel in the extent of a polygon is computationally expensive; it requires two multiplications and two additions per pixel. However, we can compute its values incrementally from window to window with only one planar addition per window (that is, N^2 pixels) since F is linear. Given the matrix R of the values of R at the current window we can evaluate R for the horizontal successor of the current window by adding to R the constant matrix H containing the **first forward differences** of F for an N-step change in x:

$$\begin{aligned}\Delta F_{k,*} &= F_{k+1,*} - F_{k,*} \\ &= F(x + (k + 1)N, y) - F(x + kN, y) \\ &= (a(x + (k + 1)N) + by + c) - (a(x + kN) + by + c) \\ &= aN\end{aligned}$$

where $F_{k,*} = F(x + kN, y)$. In a similar manner, we can compute the values of F for the vertical successor of the current window by adding to R the constant matrix V of the first forward differences of F for an N-step change in y:

$$\begin{aligned}\Delta F_{*,k} &= F_{*,k+1} - F_{*,k} \\ &= bN\end{aligned}$$

having defined $F_{*,k} = F(x, y + kN)$. Thus the pair of constant matrices:

$$H = [aN] \qquad \text{and} \qquad V = [bN]$$

can be used to compute incrementally (with one planar addition) the values of F from window to window as shown in Figure 24.2 (for a 2 × 2 array).

Each initial R matrix can be derived by evaluating the linear function:

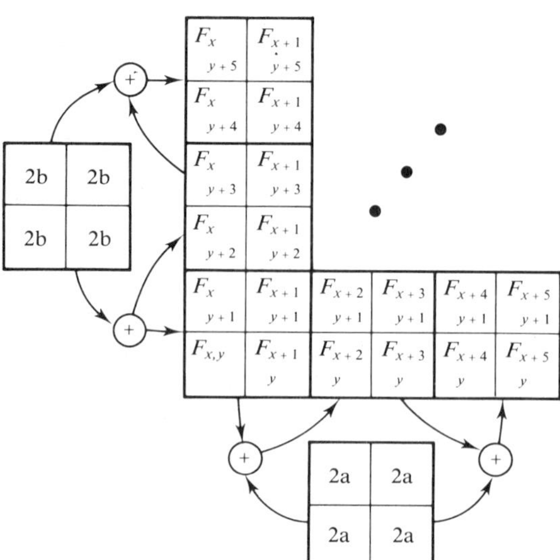

Figure 24.2
Incremental window calculations for $N = 2$.

$F(x,y) = ax + by + c$ within the first window using planar arithmetic. Take the (precomputed) matrices X and Y defined as:

$$X(i,j) = i \qquad\qquad Y(i,j) = j$$

Create constant matrices *XOFF* and *YOFF* (*OFF* for offset) containing the x and y coordinates of the initial window respectively. The coordinates of a window are the coordinates of its bottom-left pixel, that is, the pixel with the smallest x and y coordinates within the window. So, if the bottom-left pixel of the window has coordinates $(xmin, ymin)$ then *XOFF* and *YOFF* can be defined as:

$$XOFF(i,j) = xmin \qquad\qquad YOFF(i,j) = ymin$$

Adding *XOFF*(*YOFF*) to $X(Y)$ gives the matrices that contain the $x(y)$ coordinates of all pixels in the first window. Now create constant matrices A, B and C each containing the value of one of the coefficients of the linear function in every component. The initial R matrix can be computed as:

$$R = A \times (X + XOFF) + B \times (Y + YOFF) + C$$

The above computation requires two planar multiplications and four planar additions. If our planar numbers are M-bits deep and a bit-serial processor array is used, then the cost of a planar multiplication will be proportional to M^2, while a planar addition will have a cost proportional to M. That makes a total of $2M^2 + 4M$ steps for the calculation of the initial R matrix. The two multiplications involved in the calculation of the initial matrix mean that the initial matrix calculation will dominate the cost of rendering polygons that only span a few windows. We shall next describe a method of evaluating the initial R matrix that does not involve multiplications.

When the function $F(x,y) = ax + by + c$ is evaluated over a 2D discrete grid of points (for example, a window of pixels), its value at a particular point (x,y) is made up of the sum of three separate components; ax, by and c. Consider the evaluation of the ax component (x:0. . . $N - 1$). The multiplication of a by x can be replaced by a maximum of $[\log_2 x]$ additions of multiples of a and a power of 2. Such multiples of a can be obtained cheaply using shifts. For example, to get $a \times 13$ we have to add $a \times 2^3$, $a \times 2^2$ and a.

The value of the ax component will be the same for all points that belong to the same column of the grid. However, different columns will require the summation of different multiples of a and powers of 2. It is therefore necessary to be able to perform conditional planar additions, that is, planar additions that are only performed on the points of the grid indicated by a mask. Figure 24.3 shows the conditional planar addition of two 2×2 planar numbers A and B under a Boolean mask which only allows the top row of the result, S, to be updated.

For a grid of size $N \times N$, $\log_2 N$ conditional planar additions will be required for the evaluation of all the ax components (assuming N to be a power of 2). The kth

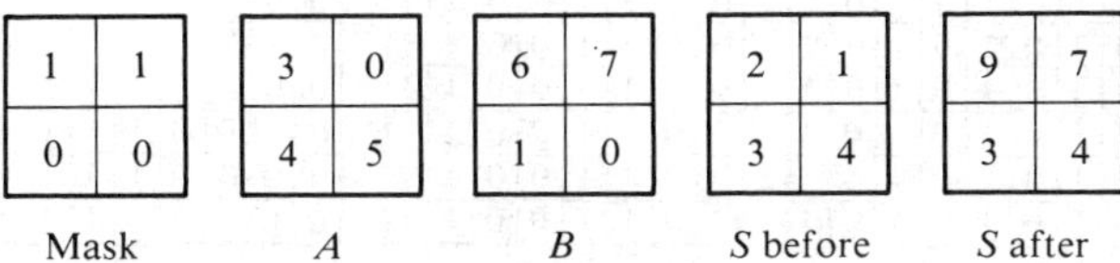

Figure 24.3 Conditional planar addition example (2×2 grid).

planar addition, k:0 . . . ($\log_2 N - 1$), will add the planar number $a \times 2^k$ under a mask which has $N / 2$ columns set and is organized as alternating groups of 2^k columns with the same value (0 / 1), the leftmost group of columns being 0 (not set). The masks for the evaluation of ax are shown in Figure 24.4 for $N = 8$. The planar number that is added to the sum under each mask is indicated underneath the mask. Three masks are required since three conditional planar additions are performed ($\log_2 8 = 3$).

The evaluation of by can be carried out in a similar manner. The masks required will be equivalent to the masks used for ax rotated by 90° anticlockwise.

The strategy for the evaluation of the function $F(x,y) = ax + by + c$ over an $N \times N$ discrete grid of points using a SIMD processor array is then the following: the controller (or a coprocessor) evaluates the function for the bottom-left point of the grid and broadcasts this value to the array forming a planar number S. The appropriate multiples of a and b by powers of 2 are then conditionally added to S as described above.

If we ignore the cost of the broadcasts and the evaluation performed in the controller (which can be done in a coprocessor), the cost of evaluating the function $F(x,y) = ax + by + c$ over an $N \times N$ grid of points is $2\log_2 N$ planar additions. The cost of each planar addition is proportional to the depth of the planar numbers, M, if the processor array is made up of bit-serial processors. The direct evaluation of the function (using multiplications) had a cost proportional to $2M^2 + 4M$. Thus the latter method (conditional planar additions) should outperform the former method (multiplications) provided:

$$2M\log_2 N < 2M^2 + 4M$$

or

$$\log_2 N - 2 < M$$

which holds true in the case of DisArray ($N = 16$) for $M > 2$ and in the case of the DAP ($N = 32$) for $M > 3$.

24.4 Architecture and performance

The architecture required to implement the rendering algorithms as described here, is a SIMD processor array with the features required in order to perform efficient planar arithmetic (such as the DAP (Reddaway, 1973)). The DAP processing elements possess the required registers and arithmetic logic that allow them to perform efficient planar arithmetic. Planar addition, for example, can be done at a

0	1	0	1	0	1	0	1
0	1	0	1	0	1	0	1
0	1	0	1	0	1	0	1
0	1	0	1	0	1	0	1
0	1	0	1	0	1	0	1
0	1	0	1	0	1	0	1
0	1	0	1	0	1	0	1
0	1	0	1	0	1	0	1

$a \times 2^0$

0	0	1	1	0	0	1	1
0	0	1	1	0	0	1	1
0	0	1	1	0	0	1	1
0	0	1	1	0	0	1	1
0	0	1	1	0	0	1	1
0	0	1	1	0	0	1	1
0	0	1	1	0	0	1	1
0	0	1	1	0	0	1	1

$a \times 2^1$

0	0	0	0	1	1	1	1
0	0	0	0	1	1	1	1
0	0	0	0	1	1	1	1
0	0	0	0	1	1	1	1
0	0	0	0	1	1	1	1
0	0	0	0	1	1	1	1
0	0	0	0	1	1	1	1
0	0	0	0	1	1	1	1

$a \times 2^2$

Figure 24.4
Masks for the evaluation of ax over an 8×8 grid.

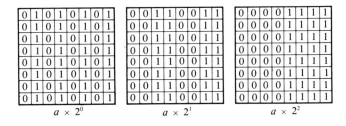

cost of only 2.5 cycles / bitplane when the result is one of the two operands (using a read/modify/write cycle), 3 cycles / bitplane otherwise. The DAP is a bit-serial processor, but a bit-parallel SIMD processor (a cubic architecture) would do even better if it could perform the planar arithmetic bit-parallel rather than bit-serial. Coloured objects would also be handled in parallel.

Define:

t_{ADD} to be the time required to perform an $N \times N$ planar addition using the $N \times N$ processor array.

t_{BROAD} to be the time needed to broadcast a scalar number to the processor array in order to create a constant planar number, that is, a planar number whose elements are all equal to the scalar.

$t_{EVAL} = 2\log_2 N \times t_{ADD} + 5 \times t_{BROAD}$ to be the time required for the evaluation of the first R matrix ($2\log_2 N$ planar additions plus three broadcasts of a, b and c as shown in Section 24.3) and the creation of the two increment matrices $[aN]$ and $[bN]$ (two broadcasts).

$t_{INC} = t_{ADD}$ to be the time needed to compute each subsequent R matrix incrementally, that is, the time to perform a planar addition.

The time required to evaluate a linear function over p windows is then:

$$T = t_{EVAL} + (p - 1)\, t_{INC}$$

The term t_{EVAL} represents the initialization time, that is, the time to compute the first R matrix and the increment matrices. $(p - 1)\, t_{INC}$ is the time taken to compute the rest of the R matrices incrementally.

To fill an n-sided polygon we must evaluate n linear functions. HSE requires the evaluation of one linear function, and smooth shading requires three linear functions to be evaluated (per polygon) provided the polygon is not split into triangles for the purpose of shading. One planar comparison and two planar assignments per window will also be required for the implementation of the z-buffer HSE algorithm.

To render a polygon, the linear functions are evaluated over the p windows enclosed by the extent of the polygon (see Figure 24.5) but it is possible to improve on that by only evaluating the linear function over the windows that actually intersect the polygon.

We shall now estimate the number of processor array cycles required to perform the planar arithmetic operations of t_{EVAL} and t_{INC}, on a processor array that can perform planar arithmetic with reasonable efficiency, such as the DAP. The sequential code overheads of planar arithmetic operations are negligible. Let us assume that the processor array is a 32×32 bit-serial DAP and that the planar numbers are 16 bits deep. A broadcast then takes 16 cycles, while a planar addition takes $2.5 \times 16 = 40$ cycles, provided the result is one of the operands which is our case.

The number of processor array cycles in t_{EVAL} and t_{INC} is then:

	Array Cycles	(32×32 architecture)
t_{EVAL}	480	$((2\log_2 32 \times 40) + 5 \times 16)$
t_{NC}	40	

for the evaluation of the linear function to 16 bits of accuracy over a 32×32 grid.

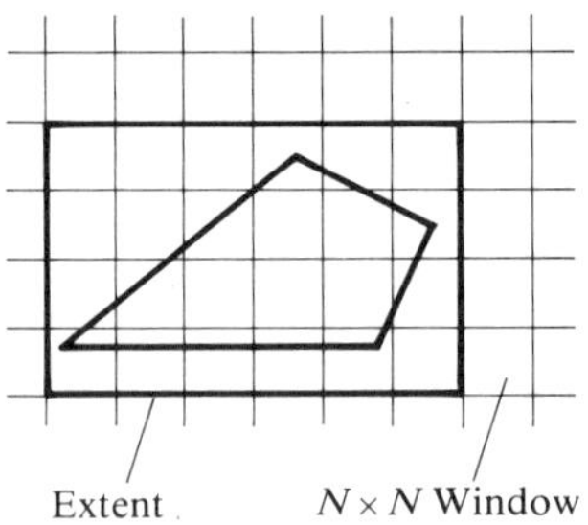

Figure 24.5
Extent of a polygon.

If a cubic architecture were available, say 8 × 8 × 16 (= 1024) for comparison with the 32 × 32 (= 1024) bit-serial approach, then planar arithmetic could be performed 16-bit parallel. It is reasonable to assume that the cost of a 16-bit-deep planar addition, the result of which is one of the operands, would be 2.5 cycles in analogy with the 2.5 cycles required by the bit-serial approach – assuming that carry propagation is negligible compared to the processor array cycle (by using carry-lookahead techniques). A broadcast would cost one cycle because all 16 bit-planes of the planar number would be created in parallel. The cost of t_{EVAL} and t_{INC} would then be:

	Array Cycles	(8 × 8 × 16 architecture)
t_{EVAL}	20	$((2\log_2 8 \times 2.5) + 5)$
t_{INC}	2.5	

for the evaluation of the linear function to 16 bits of accuracy over an 8 × 8 grid.

Evaluating the linear function over a 32 × 32 grid, that is, sixteen 8 × 8 grids, using the 8 × 8 × 16 architecture would therefore cost 20 + (15 × 2.5) = 57.5 cycles which is far shorter than the 480 cycles required by the 32 × 32 bit-serial architecture.

It is interesting to understand why the above difference arises between the performances of the above two architectures which use the same amount of silicon. Both architectures can perform the incremental evaluation of the linear function equally efficiently (the 32 × 32 architecture takes 40 cycles to evaluate incrementally the linear function over a 32 × 32 grid, and the 8 × 8 × 16 architecture also requires 16 × 2.5 = 40 cycles for the incremental evaluation of the linear function over the same grid). The difference between the performances of the two architectures in evaluating the linear function, must therefore result from differences in the cost of the initial evaluation, that is, the t_{EVAL} times. The ratio of the t_{EVAL} times of the two architectures, $r1 = 480 / 20$, is not equal to the ratio of their areas, $r2 = 32^2 / 8^2$. (In contrast, the ratio of the t_{INC} times, 40 / 2.5, is equal to the ratio of their areas.) The disparity between $r1$ and $r2$ arises because the amount of computation involved in t_{EVAL} is proportional to the area of the grid times the log of the grid's side. If we ignore the cost of the broadcasts involved in t_{EVAL}, then the amount of computation required for the initial evaluation of a linear function over an $N \times N$ grid is $2\log_2 N$ planar additions or $N^2 2\log_2 N$ additions. Thus, the computation cost per grid point is proportional to $N^2 2\log_2 N / N^2$ or $2\log_2 N$, that is, it is proportional to the logarithm of the side of the grid. Therefore the smaller the area of the grid, the more efficient the initial evaluation of the linear function will be. It is thus advantageous to use the available silicon in giving the processor array greater depth, rather than greater area, as far as the evaluation of the linear function is concerned. Of course, there is no point in having a processor array whose depth is greater than the depth of the planar arithmetic representation.

Conclusion

We have shown how a processor array can efficiently evaluate bivariate linear functions and thus implement rendering operations. Cheap, incremental computation is thus exploited in conjunction with N^2 parallelism on a parallel architecture that has come to be recognized as general purpose. Our algorithms map very naturally onto the processor array because they are based on the window which is the processor array's primitive graphical object.

Acknowledgements

The authors would like to express their gratitude to INMOS Ltd and Sigmex Ltd who have provided financial support for the doctoral studies of T. Theoharis.

References

Cohen D. and Demetrescu S. (1981). *A VLSI Approach to Computer Image Generation.* University of Southern California, Information Science Institute

Fuchs H. *et al.* (1985). Fast spheres, shadows, textures, transparencies and image enhancements in Pixel-Planes. *ACM Computer Graphics,* **19**(3), 111–20

Gouraud H. (1971). Continuous shading of curved surfaces. *IEEE Transactions on Computers,* **C-20**(6), 623–8

Gupta S. (1981). *Architectures and algorithms for parallel updates of raster-scan displays.* Technical Report CMU–CS–82–111, Computer Science Dept, Carnegie Mellon University PA

Hwang K. and Briggs F.A. (1984). *Computer Architecture and Parallel Processing.* Maidenhead: McGraw-Hill

Newman W.M. and Sproull R.F. (1979). *Principles of Interactive Computer Graphics.* Maidenhead: McGraw-Hill

Page I. (1983). DisArray: A 16 × 16 RasterOp processor. In *Eurographics 1983*, pp. 367–81. Zagreb

Reddaway S.F. (1973). DAP – a Distributed Array Processor. In *1st Annual Symposium on Computer Architecture*, Gainesville FA, 1973, pp. 61–5

Sutherland I.E., Sproull R.F. and Shumacker R.A. (1974). A characterisation of ten hidden surface algorithms. *Computing Surveys,* **6**(1), 1–55

F. Cheng

University of Kentucky

Y-K. Yen

Chung-Shang Institute of Science and Technology

25 · A parallel line clipping algorithm and its implementation

A parallel line clipping algorithm and its implementation on a parallel clipping hardware environment are presented. We first develop a simple theory to show that parallel clipping is possible for all types of line segments. We then present the architecture of a hardware environment, based on which parallel clipping is to be implemented. Based on our approach, only 141 cycles are required to clip a line segment. The corresponding figure for the famous J. Clark's Geometry Engine is 160 cycles.

25.1 Introduction

All display devices have limited display areas. It is impossible, in general, to display all the objects defined by the user in a single screen. The graphics system has to be informed explicitly which portion of the scene is to be viewed. This visible region, specified by the user, is called the window (view volume, in 3D graphics). Data not contained in the visible region should be discarded to avoid overflow of the internal registers of the display device. The process of removing the portions of an image that lie outside the visible region is called **clipping** [1].

Two kinds of clipping process have been frequently used in graphics, namely, line clipping and polygon clipping. For images composed of straight line segments, only line clipping is involved. Each line segment of the image is clipped against the window; only the **visible segment**, that is, the portion of the line segment that lies inside the window, is output for display. If an image comprises not only straight line segments but also polygons, then polygon clipping is required. In this case, not only the visible segment of each edge of a polygon has to be output, sometimes additional vertices have to be output also to make the output polygon correct.

Several well-known line clipping and polygon clipping algorithms have been proposed (see [1–5]). Some of them have been implemented in hardware (see [6, 7]). The basic idea used in [1], [4] and [5] ([6] and [7] as well) can be described as follows. If, say, 2D graphics is considered, then the given line segment or polygon is clipped against each boundary line of the window separately. For each boundary line of the window, we first divide the plane by the boundary line into two sides, **visible** and

invisible. The halfplane which contains the window is called the visible side. The given line segment or polygon is clipped against this boundary line by discarding the portions of the line segment or polygon that lie in the invisible side of the boundary line using techniques such as **outcodes, midpoint subdivision** or **in-out** relationship. The remaining portions (if there are any) are then clipped against the other boundary lines of the window using the same technique. After the given line segment or polygon has been clipped against all the boundary lines of the window, the remaining portions are the visible portions of the given line segment or polygon. They are then output for display. Since the clipping of a line segment or polygon against a boundary line has to be finished before they can be clipped against another boundary line, this approach can actually be considered as clipping of a line segment or polygon against several lines in sequential order.

(The original idea of Weiler and Atherton [5] was to trace around the border of the polygon only once with respect to all the boundary lines of the window. However, it can also be classified into this category if finding the intersections of the polygon with the window is done for each of the boundary lines of the window separately.)

The basic approach used in [2] and [3] is different from that of the above. The given line segment or each edge of the given polygon is expressed in parametric form first. Then parameters of the intersections of the straight line, defined by the parametric equation, with the boundary lines of the window are computed and compared together with 0 and 1 to determine if there is a visible segment. If there is a visible segment, then its endpoints are computed. If polygon clipping is considered, then sometimes turning vertices [3] also have to be found to make the output correct. Since the process of computing the parameters of the intersections does not depend on any particular order, they can be computed simultaneously. Therefore, this approach provides us with a possibility of clipping a line segment or polygon against several lines in parallel if the subsequent comparison process can be performed correctly.

In this chapter, we shall review the idea presented in [2], and develop a more general theory of line clipping for all types of line segments, such as vertical or horizontal line segments. We shall focus on 2D line clipping only. However, our approach can readily be extended to cover 3D line clipping too. We then present the architecture of a hardware environment based on which parallel line clipping is to be performed, and present a parallel line clipping algorithm for this hardware environment. According to our algorithm, only 141 cycles are required to clip a line segment. The corresponding figure for the famous J. Clark's Geometry Engine is 160 cycles. Therefore, our approach outperforms J. Clark's system by about 15%. Our algorithm can be extended to include parallel polygon clipping as well [8]. However, it is not within the scope of this chapter.

The remainder of this chapter is organized as follows. In Section 25.2, we will review some basic concepts and develop a general theory of line clipping. The architecture of a hardware environment based on which parallel line clipping is to be implemented is presented in Section 25.3. In Section 25.4, we will present a parallel line clipping algorithm for the hardware environment. The computational complexity of the algorithm is shown in Section 25.5. Finally, we will make some concluding remarks.

25.2 The basic idea

Let (x_{left}, y_{bottom}) and (x_{right}, y_{top}) be the lower-left and upper-right corners of a window (Figure 25.1). A line segment with endpoints (x_0, y_0) and (x_1, y_1) can be represented in parametric form as follows:

$$\begin{aligned} x &= x_0 + \Delta x * t \\ y &= y_0 + \Delta y * t \end{aligned} \tag{25.1}$$

where $\Delta x = x_1 - x_0$, $\Delta y = y_1 - y_0$ and $0 \leqslant t \leqslant 1$. Any point of the line segment which is inside the window must satisfy the following inequalities:

$$x_{left} \leqslant x_0 + \Delta x * t \leqslant x_{right}$$

$$y_{bottom} \leqslant y_0 + \Delta y * t \leqslant y_{top}$$

or, equivalently:

$$-\Delta x * t \leqslant x_0 - x_{left}, \qquad \Delta x * t \leqslant x_{right} - x_0$$

$$-\Delta y * t \leqslant y_0 - y_{bottom}, \qquad \Delta y * t \leqslant y_{top} - y_0$$

These inequalities can be written as:

$$P_i * t \leqslant Q_i, \qquad i = 1,2,3,4 \tag{25.2}$$

where:

$$\begin{aligned} P_1 &= -\Delta x; & Q_1 &= x_0 - x_{left} \\ P_2 &= \Delta x; & Q_2 &= x_{right} - x_0 \\ P_3 &= -\Delta y; & Q_3 &= y_0 - y_{bottom} \\ P_4 &= \Delta y; & Q_4 &= y_{top} - y_0. \end{aligned} \tag{25.3}$$

Now if $P_i \neq 0$ for all $1 \leqslant i \leqslant 4$ and if we define:

$$t_i = \frac{Q_i}{P_i}, \qquad i = 1,2,3,4 \tag{25.4}$$

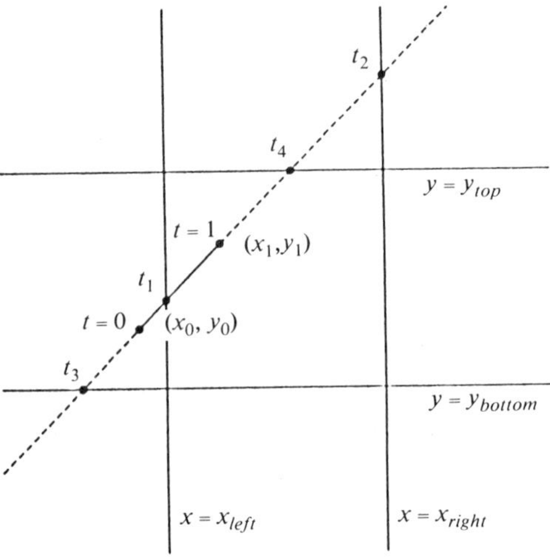

Figure 25.1
A window and a given line segment.

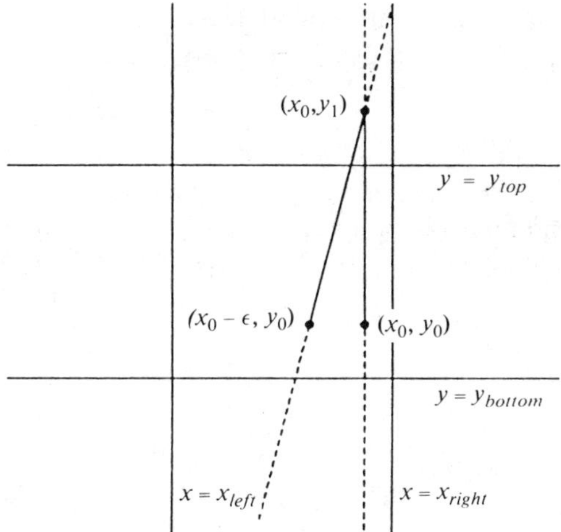

Figure 25.2
A vertical line segment and the oblique line segment generated from it.

then t_1 and t_2 represent the parameters of the intersections of the straight line defined by Equation 25.1 ($-\infty < t < +\infty$) with the left boundary line $x = x_{left}$ and the right boundary line $x = x_{right}$ of the window, respectively, and t_3 and t_4 represent the parameters of the intersections of the straight line defined by Equation 25.1 with the bottom boundary line $y = y_{bottom}$ and the top boundary line $y = y_{top}$ of the window, respectively (Figure 25.1). Since the value of each t_i is independent of the other t_js ($j \neq i$), the values of t_is can be computed in parallel. It was shown in [2] that if $P_i \neq 0$ for all i then the necessary and sufficient condition for the given line segment to have a visible segment is:

$$t_0' \leqslant t_1' \tag{25.5}$$

where:

$$\begin{aligned} t_0' &= \max\left(\left\{t_i = \frac{Q_i}{P_i} \mid 1 \leqslant i \leqslant 4, P_i < 0\right\} \cup \{0\}\right) \\ t_1' &= \min\left(\left\{t_i = \frac{Q_i}{P_i} \mid 1 \leqslant i \leqslant 4, P_i > 0\right\} \cup \{1\}\right) \end{aligned} \tag{25.6}$$

If Equation 25.5 is true, then the coordinates of the endpoints of the visible segment are:

$$\begin{aligned} x_0' &= x_0 + \Delta x * t_0'; \qquad & y_0' &= y_0 + \Delta y * t_0' \\ x_1' &= x_0 + \Delta x * t_1'; \qquad & y_1' &= y_0 + \Delta y * t_1' \end{aligned} \tag{25.7}$$

Again, t_0' and t_1', and then x_0', x_1', y_0', and y_1' can all be evaluated in parallel. However, if $P_i = 0$ for some i, that is, the given line segment is vertical or horizontal, then the above argument does not work any longer. In order to include vertical and horizontal line segments as well, we have to modify Equations 25.3, 25.4 and 25.6 in the following way.

First, observe that if we define P_i' the following way:

$$P_1' = P_2' = \Delta x; \qquad P_3' = P_4' = \Delta y$$

then t_i defined in Equation 25.4 can be written as:

$$t_i = \frac{(-1)^i Q_i}{P_i'}, \qquad i = 1,2,3,4 \tag{25.8}$$

if $P_i' \neq 0$. Where either $\Delta x = 0$ or $\Delta y = 0$, say $\Delta x = 0$, that is, the given line segment is vertical, we first think of it as an oblique line segment by replacing the x-coordinate of the endpoint (x_0, y_0) by $x_0 - \epsilon$, where ϵ is a small positive number (Figure 25.2). Since, in this case, $P_1' = P_2' = \epsilon$, it follows from Equation 25.8 that:

$$t_1 = \frac{-Q_1}{\epsilon}, \qquad t_2 = \frac{Q_2}{\epsilon} \tag{25.9}$$

and

$$t_3 = \frac{-Q_3}{P_3'}, \qquad t_4 = \frac{Q_4}{P_4'}$$

Then simply take the limits of Equation 25.9 when ϵ approaches 0 to get the corresponding t_1 and t_2 for the original line segment:

$$t_1 = \lim_{\epsilon \to 0} \frac{-Q_1}{\epsilon}, \qquad t_2 = \lim_{\epsilon \to 0} \frac{Q_2}{\epsilon}$$

This approach works when $\Delta y = 0$ also. In this case, we first replace the y-coordinate of the endpoint (x_0, y_0) by $y_0 - \epsilon$ $(\epsilon > 0)$ and then take the limits of $-Q_3 / \epsilon$ and Q_4 / ϵ when ϵ approaches 0 to get the corresponding t_3 and t_4 for the given horizontal line segment, that is:

$$t_3 = \lim_{\epsilon \to 0} \frac{-Q_3}{\epsilon}, \qquad t_4 = \lim_{\epsilon \to 0} \frac{Q_4}{\epsilon}$$

Therefore, if $P_i = 0$, t_i can simply be defined as:

$$t_i = \lim_{\epsilon \to 0} \frac{(-1)^i Q_i}{\epsilon} \tag{25.10}$$

where ϵ is a positive number. Its value is either $+\infty$ or $-\infty$, depending on the sign of $(-1)^i Q_i$. Consequently, by combining Equations 25.4 and 25.10, we get a general form for t_i as follows:

$$t_i = \begin{cases} Q_i / P_i, & P_i \neq 0 \\ -\infty, & P_i = 0 \text{ and } (-1)^i Q_i < 0 \\ +\infty, & P_i = 0 \text{ and } (-1)^i Q_i > 0 \end{cases} \tag{25.11}$$

Note that if the given line segment is vertical, that is, $\Delta x = 0$, then P_1 is always considered as having a negative sign and P_2 as having a positive sign; if the given line segment is horizontal, that is, $\Delta y = 0$, then P_3 is always considered as having a negative sign and P_4 as having a positive sign. Therefore, we can define a variable, *SIGN*(i), representing the sign of P_i for each i as follows:

$$SIGN(i) = \begin{cases} sign(P_i), & P_i \neq 0 \\ (-1)^i, & P_i = 0 \end{cases} \tag{25.12}$$

where:

$$sign(x) = \begin{cases} +1, & x > 0 \\ -1, & x < 0 \end{cases}$$

and define t_0' and t_1' in the following way:

$$\begin{aligned} t_0' &= \max(\{t_i \mid 1 \leqslant i \leqslant 4, SIGN(i) < 0\} \cup \{0\}) \\ t_1' &= \min(\{t_i \mid 1 \leqslant i \leqslant 4, SIGN(i) > 0\} \cup \{1\}) \end{aligned} \qquad \textbf{(25.13)}$$

where t_i is defined in Equation 25.11 and $SIGN(i)$ is defined in Equation 25.12. Then for any given line segment defined in Equation 25.1, simply use Equations 25.3, 25.11, 25.12 and 25.13 to find t_0' and t_1' and then use Equation 25.4 to determine if it has a visible segment. Note that in this case Equations 25.11, 25.12 and 25.13 can all be implemented in parallel too.

It should be pointed out that the above method can readily be extended to 3D line clipping if an orthogonal view volume is considered. This is done in the following way. If (x_0, y_0, z_0) and (x_1, y_1, z_1) are the endpoints of a 3D line segment and an orthogonal view volume is defined by the six boundary planes:

$$x = x_{left},\ x = x_{right},\ y = y_{bottom},\ y = y_{top},\ z = z_{front},\ z = z_{back}$$

then except those defined in Equation 25.3, we also need the following quantities:

$$\begin{aligned} P_5 &= -\Delta z, & Q_5 &= z_0 - z_{front} \\ P_6 &= \Delta z, & Q_6 &= z_{back} - z_0 \end{aligned}$$

where $\Delta z = z_1 - z_0$. But then everything else is similar to the 2D case.

25.3 The architecture of the hardware environment

The parallel clipping hardware environment which we are going to present here is actually a subsystem of a geometry system called PIPA [8]. PIPA is a PIpeline-architectured and PArallel-hardwired geometry system consisting of three pipelined subsystems: matrix subsystem, clipping subsystem and scaling subsystem. Each subsystem is composed of a certain number of Geometry Processors (GPs) [9] arranged in such a way that matrix multiplication, clipping and scaling can all be performed in parallel.

Basically, each GP is a four-component vector function unit implemented on a VLSI chip. It can be functionally divided into four subunits, as shown in Figure 25.3.

(1) Microprogrammed controller:
  (a) Sequencer
  (b) Microprogram control store

(2) Array processing unit:
  Four Arithmetic Logic Units (ALUs)

(3) I/O buffer

(4) Registers:
  (a) Four Local Registers (LRs)
  (b) Four Temporary Registers (TRs)
  (c) Four Curve Registers (CRs)

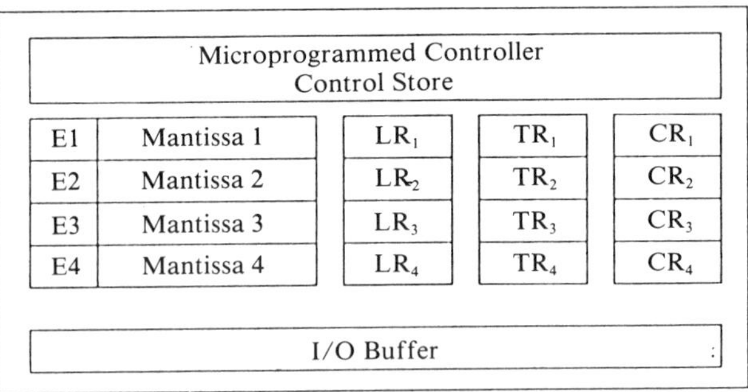

Figure 25.3
Layout of a geometry processor.

The array processing unit deserves special attention. It contains four parallel processing ALUs. Each ALU can operate on either 32-bit floating points or 24-bit integers [10]. In floating-point arithmetic, the processing is divided into two parts, namely, exponent and mantissa. These four microprogrammed ALUs can do parallel addition, subtraction and two-variable operations on either the mantissa or the exponents, that is, two-operand floating-point operations.

The 12 registers in each GP are grouped into three categories: local registers, temporary registers and curve registers. Local registers are used to store more sensitive values which will not be erased after each pipeline cycle. Curve registers are used to store scaling factors or coordinates of the window or the viewport. Temporary registers, as indicated by their name, are used to store temporary intermediate values in each operation.

The number of GPs required in each subsystem depends on the function of the subsystem. The matrix subsystem, performing parallel matrix multiplication and forward curve generation, requires four GPs. The clipping subsystem, performing parallel line clipping and polygon clipping, requires four GPs for 2D clipping and requires another two GPs if 3D clipping is needed also. The scaling subsystem, performing window-to-viewport mapping and generating monographic or stereographic views, requires only one GP. The operation within each subsystem is controlled by the preprocessor and controller. Pipelining between subsystems is controlled by the controller. Figure 25.4 shows the layout and data flow of a PIPA.

We shall use only four GPs here to illustrate the implementation of the parallel line clipping algorithm. The four GPs in the clipping subsystem are numbered GP5, GP6, GP7 and GP8. For each GPi, $5 \leqslant i \leqslant 8$, contained in the clipping subsystem, its local registers, temporary registers and curve registers will be named $LR_{i,j}$, $TR_{i,j}$ and $CR_{i,j}$ $(1 \leqslant j \leqslant 4)$, respectively. For instance, $LR_{5,3}$ represents the third local register of GP5. We shall assume that the contents of these registers within different GPs of the clipping subsystem can be exchanged during each pipeline cycle.

Data to be input from the matrix subsystem to the clipping subsystem are stored in the four I/O buffers $Buf_{i,1}$, $1 \leqslant i \leqslant 4$, of the matrix subsystem. Since the matrix multiplication executed in the matrix subsystem is performed in the homogeneous coordinate system, four coordinates are presumably to be output to the clipping subsystem. However, in order to fix the coordinates of the window or view volume and, consequently, simplify the work of the clipping subsystem, coordinates output from the matrix subsystem will be normalized by the matrix subsystem first,

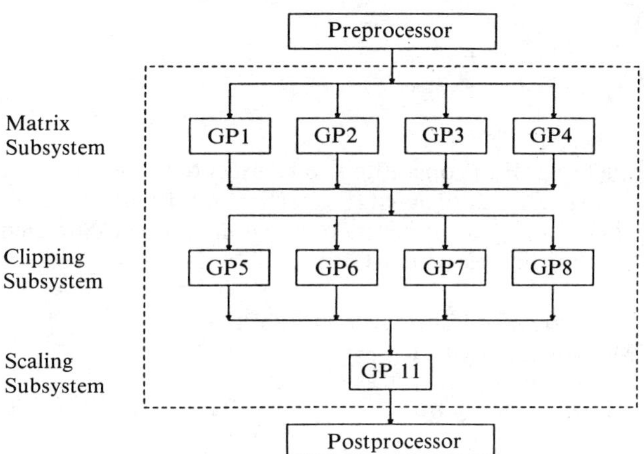

Figure 25.4
Layout and data flow of a PIPA.

before they are put into the I/O buffers. This means that coordinates in the Normalized Viewing Coordinate System (NVCS) are actually used in the clipping subsystem. Therefore, only the contents of $Buf_{i,1}$, $1 \leqslant i \leqslant 3$, will be needed for the clipping subsystem if 3D clipping is desired. In our case, since only 2D clipping is considered, only the contents of $Buf_{1,1}$ and $Buf_{2,1}$ will be needed for the clipping subsystem.

25.4 The algorithm

The parallel algorithm to be implemented on the above clipping subsystem will be presented in this section. In this algorithm, a block of instructions will be called a **parallel step** if it is bounded above by the key word **PARDO** and bounded below by the key word **DOPAR**. Any instructions contained in a parallel step are intended to be executed in parallel. A parallel step is said to be at the GP level if the instructions contained in this step are expected to be executed for each GP. It is said to be at the register level if the instructions within this step are designated to certain registers of a particular GP. If a parallel step is expected to be executed at the GP level then the statement 'for processor GP5,GP6,GP7,GP8' is usually attached to the key word **PARDO**. For instance, the following parallel step indicates: for each GP*i*, $5 \leqslant i \leqslant 8$, load register $LR_{i,2}$ with the contents of $LR_{i,1}$.

```
PARDO for processor GP5,GP6,GP7,GP8
      LR_{i,2} = LR_{i,1}
DOPAR
```

If it can be clearly inferred from the context that a parallel step is expected to be executed at the GP level, then the statement 'for processor GP5,GP6,GP7,GP8' is omitted. For instance, the following parallel step is at the GP level. It indicates: load registers $LR_{5,1}$ and $LR_{6,1}$ with the contents of $Buf_{1,1}$ and load registers $LR_{7,1}$ and $LR_{8,1}$ with the contents of $Buf_{2,1}$, simultaneously.

```
PARDO
        LR5,1, LR6,1 = Buf1,1
        LR7,1, LR8,1 = Buf2,1
DOPAR
```

In a parallel step, if the operations to be executed by each GP are different, then we list the instructions designated to a particular GPi under the statement 'for processor GP_i' as follows and any instructions within this block are then considered at the register level for this particular GP.

```
PARDO for processor GP5,GP6,GP7,GP8
        [for processor GP5]
                ...
        [for processor GP6]
                ...
        [for processor GP7]
                ...
        [for processor GP8]
                ...
DOPAR
```

Any instructions not enclosed by the key words **PARDO** and **DOPAR** are assumed to be executed in sequential order. The algorithm is given as follows.

Algorithm PLC: Parallel Line Clipping

```
1.      [Parallel loading of the x- and y-coordinates]
        PARDO
                LR5,1, LR6,1 = Buf1,1              {x-coordinate in NVCS}
                LR7,1, LR8,1 = Buf2,1              {y-coordinate in NVCS}
        DOPAR

2.      [Compute Δx and Δy and then t_i for each i]
        PARDO for processor GP5,GP6,GP7,GP8
2.1.    [for processor GP5]
2.1.1.  PARDO
                LR5,3 = LR5,1 - LR5,2              {Compute Δx}
                LR5,4 = LR5,2 - x_left             {Compute Q1}
        DOPAR
2.1.2.  if (LR5,3 = 0) then                        {Vertical line segment}
                begin
                if (LR5,4 > 0) then
                        TR5,1 = -∞
                else
                        TR5,1 = +∞
                sign(LR5,3) = +
                end
```

```
        else
                TR5,1 = -(LR5,4 / LR5,3)            {t1 = Q1 / Δx}
2.2.    [for processor GP6]
2.2.1.  PARDO
                LR6,3 = LR6,1 - LR6,2               {Compute Δx}
                LR6,4 = x_right - LR6,2             {Compute Q2}
        DOPAR
2.2.2.  if (LR6,3 = 0) then                         {Vertical line segment}
                if (LR6,4 > 0) then
                        TR6,1 = +∞
                else
                        TR6,1 = -∞
        else
                TR6,1 = -(LR6,4 / LR6,3)            {t2 = Q1 / Δx}
2.3.    [for processor GP7]
2.3.1.  PARDO
                LR7,3 = LR7,1 - LR7,2               {Compute Δy}
                LR7,4 = LR7,2 - y_bottom            {Compute Q3}
        DOPAR
2.3.2.  if (LR7,3 = 0) then                         {Horizontal line segment}
                begin
                if (LR7,4 > 0) then
                        TR7,1 = -∞
                else
                        TR7,1 = +∞
                sign(LR7,3) = +
                end
        else
                TR7,1 = -(LR7,4 / LR7,3)            {t3 = -Q3 / Δy}
2.4.    [for processor GP8]
2.4.1.  PARDO
                LR8,3 = LR8,1 - LR8,2               {Compute Δy}
                LR8,4 = y_top - LR8,2               {Compute Q4}
        DOPAR
2.4.2.  if (LR8,3 = 0) then                         {Horizontal line segment}
                if (LR8,4 > 0) then
                        TR8,1 = +∞
                else
                        TR8,1 = -∞
                else
                        TR8,1 = -(LR8,4 / LR8,3)    {t4 = Q4 / Δy}
        DOPAR

3.      [Rearrange Pis so that the signs of Pis appear in - + - + form]
        PARDO
                if (sign(LR5,3) = -) then
                        TR5,1 ←→ TR6,1              {Exchange TR5,1 and TR6,1}
```

```
        if (sign(LR_{7,3}) = − ) then
                TR_{7,1} ←→ TR_{8,1}                 {Exchange TR_{7,1} and TR_{8,1}}
    DOPAR

4.  [Find the values of t_0' and t_1']
4.1 PARDO
        TR_{5,2} = TR_{7,1}
        TR_{6,2} = TR_{8,1}
        TR_{7,2} = TR_{5,1}
        TR_{8,2} = TR_{6,1}
    DOPAR
4.2 PARDO
        TR_{5,4} = min(TR_{5,1}, TR_{5,2}, 0)        {Put t_0' in TR_{5,4}}
        TR_{7,4} = min(TR_{7,1}, TR_{7,2}, 0)        {Put t_0' in TR_{7,4}}
        TR_{6,4} = max(TR_{6,1}, TR_{6,2}, 1)        {Put t_1' in TR_{6,3}}
        TR_{8,4} = max(TR_{8,1}, TR_{8,2}, 1)        {Put t_1' in TR_{8,4}}
    DOPAR

5.  [If t_0' < t_1' then compute endpoints of the visible segment]
    if (TR_{5,4} < TR_{6,4}) then
        PARDO
            LR_{5,4} = LR_{5,2} + LR_{5,3} * TR_{5,4} {Compute x_0'}
            LR_{6,4} = LR_{6,2} + LR_{6,3} * TR_{6,4} {Compute x_1'}
            LR_{7,4} = LR_{7,2} + LR_{7,3} * TR_{7,4} {Compute y_0'}
            LR_{8,4} = LR_{8,2} + LR_{8,3} * TR_{8,4} {Compute y_1'}
        DOPAR

6.  [Shift operation]
    PARDO for processor GP5,GP6,GP7,GP8
        LR_{i,2} = LR_{i,1}
        output LR_{i,4}
    DOPAR
    {End of the algorithm}
```

25.5 Computational complexity of the algorithm

Since the six steps in the algorithm are all parallel steps at the GP level and the instructions involved in each parallel step are essentially the same, it is sufficient to evaluate the computational complexity of this algorithm simply by evaluating its computational complexity on GP5. Implementation of Algorithm PLC on GP5 is shown in Figure 25.5.

It is easy to see that scalar operations are required in Steps 2 and 5 only. In Step 2, we need one parallel subtraction for Step 2.1.1, one parallel division for Step 2.1.2 (the operations done in Step 2.1.2 are dominated by the division). Therefore, one subtraction and one division are required for Step 2. In Step 5, we need one multiplication and one addition to compute the coordinates of the end points of a visible segment. Therefore, in total, four scalar operations are required in our

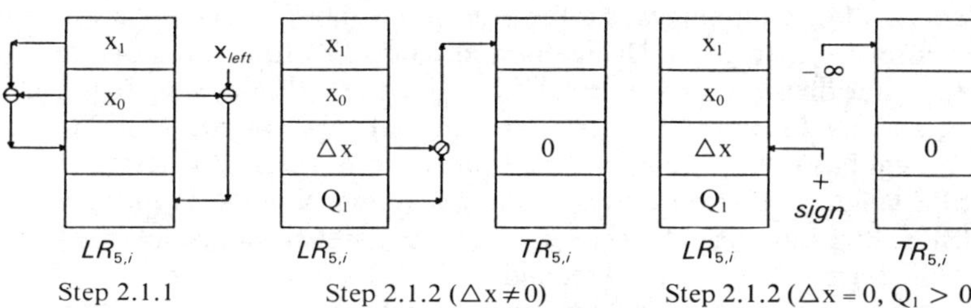

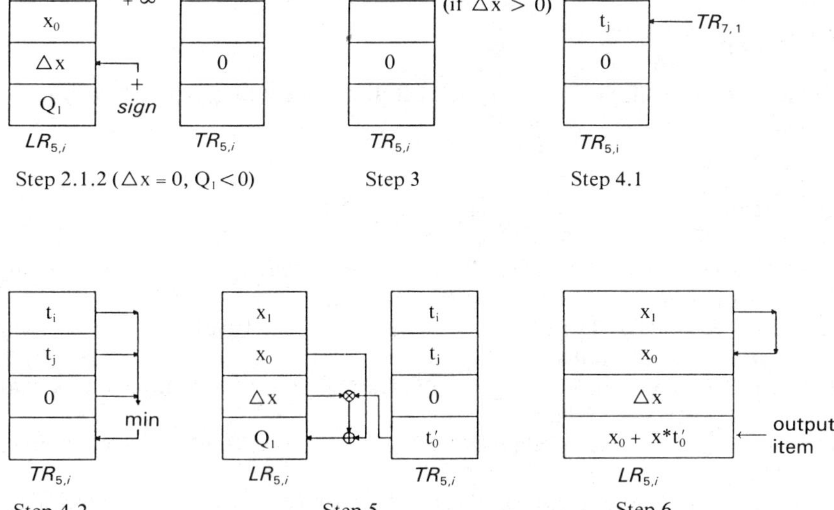

Figure 25.5 Implementation of algorithm PLC on GP5.

algorithm. Actually, by noticing that Step 1 and Step 6 can be performed in parallel, and the fact that a multiplication (division) needs 51 cycles, an addition (subtraction) needs 9 cycles, a data transfer (and I/O as well) needs 1 cycle, it can be shown that our clipping subsystem will require only 141 cycles to clip a line segment (1 cycle for Step 1, 65 cycles for Step 2, 4 cycles for Step 3, 7 cycles for Step 4 and 64 cycles for Step 5). Since J. Clark's system will require 160 cycles [10] to clip a line segment, our clipping process is indeed more efficient.

Conclusions

The architecture of a parallel clipping hardware environment and the associated algorithm have been presented. We first showed how a general theory of line clipping should be developed so that parallel line clipping can eventually become possible. We then presented the architecture of a hardware environment based on which the process of line clipping was to be performed. The associated parallel line clipping algorithm was then given. Using this approach, only four scalar operations: one subtraction, one division, one multiplication and one addition, were required to clip a line segment against a window or an orthogonal view volume.

Our system has been simulated. The simulation was done by describing the system in ISPS language [11], and then running a system simulation in Run Time Module in ISPS. By assuming a 4 mega clock rate, our system can process approximately 3800 line segments every 1/30 second.

Since, at most, two parallel arithmetic operations are required within each step of algorithm PLC, only two ALUs are actually needed within each GP. In fact, it should be relatively easy to implement the entire clipping subsystem on a single chip to make it more cost effective and more efficient.

Acknowledgement

We would like to thank H.C. Fu for helpful discussion during the preparation of this work.

References

1. Foley J.D. and van Dam A. (1982). *Fundamentals of Interactive Computer Graphics*. Reading MA: Addison-Wesley
2. Liang Y.D. and Barsky B.A. (1984). A new concept and method for line clipping. *ACM Trans. on Graphics,* **3**(1), 1–22
3. Liang Y.D. and Barsky B.A. (1983). An analysis and algorithm for polygon clipping. *CACM,* **26**(11), 868–77
4. Sutherland I.E. and Hodgman G.W. (1974). Reentrant polygon clipping. *CACM,* **17**(1), 32–43
5. Weiler K. and Atherton P. (1977). Hidden surface removal using polygon area sorting. *Computer Graphics,* **11**(2), 214
6. Clark J.H. (1982). The geometry engine: a VLSI geometry system for graphics. *Computer Graphics,* **16**(3), 127–33
7. Sproull R.F. and Sutherland I.E. (1968). A clipping divider. In *Fall Joint Computer Conference 1968*, pp. 765–75. Montvale NJ: AFIPS Press
8. Cheng F. and Yen Y-K., *PIPA: A pipeline-architectured and parallel-hardwired geometry system for graphics*, in preparation
9. Clark J.H. (1980). A VLSI geometry processor for graphics. *Computer,* **12**(7), 59–68
10. Fu H.C., Lee S.C. and Bao C.H. (1984). *The design of a real time geometry system for graphics*. Technical Report NCTU-ERSO Project Report RCGS-84-2, Institute of Computer Engineering, National Chiao Tung University
11. Barbacci M.R. (1979). *The ISPS computer description language*. Technical Report CMU-CS-79-137, Carnegie Mellon University

Section 5

Parallel Processing Techniques for the Visualization of 3D Models

26 · The design of a parallel processing system for computer graphics

T.L. Kunii
S. Nishimura
T. Noma

University of Tokyo

This chapter proposes a novel approach to designing an application-oriented parallel processing system for computer graphics. In our approach, we divide each problem into tasks, represent it with a directed acyclic graph (task graph) and determine the assignment of tasks to processors. To determine the task assignment, we introduce a newly developed task assignment algorithm, which considers both processing cost and communication cost. The designing of systems for ray tracing is described as an example of our approach.

26.1 Introduction

Parallel processing is one of the most powerful ways for improving the processing speed of computers. In the area of computer graphics in particular, many researchers have been trying to apply the techniques of parallel processing to various problems, and have succeeded to a considerable extent [1, 2]. There are three reasons for this research:

(1) Fast display is desirable for a better user interface.

(2) Some techniques, such as **ray tracing**, are too slow without parallel processing.

(3) Many problems in computer graphics potentially have parallelism.

The previous approaches to parallel processing in computer graphics have one characteristic in common: they are *ad hoc* for a specific problem. This chapter proposes an alternative approach direction to find the best parallel processing solution for a given problem.

In defining the best solution, we consider many things, namely, task schedule, hardware architecture, performance, etc. Our ultimate goal is to design a problem-oriented parallel processing system. The problems are not limited to those in computer graphics in essence. Our approach can also be applied to other topics.

In this chapter, we deal with **Multiple Instruction** stream **Multiple Data** stream **(MIMD)** systems because of their practical importance and theoretical interest. We divide each problem into tasks, represent it with a Directed Acyclic Graph (DAG) (task graph) and determine the assignment of tasks to processors.

This approach enables us to design and evaluate application-oriented systems, and it is in this respect that our approach differs most from previous approaches.

In Section 26.2, our approach is outlined and an introduction is given of some previous works on task assignment algorithms. In Section 26.3, we define our parallel processing model: an improved task graph and a newly developed task assignment algorithm. The main difference between our model and previous models lies in the integration of communication cost and task precedence. In Section 26.4, as an example, we apply the above approach to the generation of ray-traced images. Our conclusion includes some comments on future research directions.

26.2 The outline of our approach

26.2.1 Basic concepts

The basic concepts used in this chapter can be explained as follows. A **job** is a unit of execution which has a meaningful effect by itself. An example of a job is the generation of a ray-traced image. A job is composed of **tasks**, each of which is an identifiable and undividable unit of execution. A task (1) accepts its inputs, (2) performs its function, and (3) outputs the results. Each of the steps (1) through (3) are performed once. In our example, some tasks calculate an intersection point between a ray and a plane, and others select the intersection point nearest to the ray origin. Output of a task is passed to succeeding tasks. For example, the output of tasks calculating intersection points is input to a task selecting the nearest intersection point. This relation is called **task communication**. We assume a task communication to be one-way (simplex).

The above example is illustrated as a DAG (task graph) in Figure 26.1a. Each node represents a task, and each arc shows a one-way communication. Tasks 0 and 1 calculate intersection points and send their results to task 2, which selects the nearest intersection point. Obviously, there exist two relationships, namely, that task 0 is prior to 2 and that 1 is prior to 2. This we call **task precedence**.

A processor is a physical unit of data processing. A Central Processing Unit (CPU) with some memory units is an example of a processor. A task cannot be divided to execute on several processors, and each processor can only execute one task at a time. Of course, a processor can be shared by some tasks, if they are not executed concurrently. Next, we suppose that tasks 0 and 2 are assigned to processor A, and task 1 is assigned to processor B. Tasks 0 and 2 are assigned to the same processor, and consequently task communication between them can be ignored. However, task communication from 1 to 2 causes data transmission from processor B to A. To realize this data transmission, a communication link, a two-way data transmission path between two processors is necessary (Figure 26.1b).

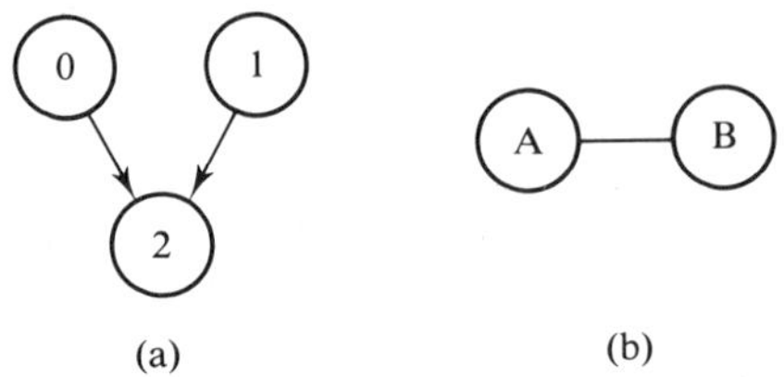

Figure 26.1
A task graph and the corresponding processor network.
(a) A task graph (without cost).
(b) The corresponding processor network.

26.2.2 Outline of designing parallel processing systems

This section describes how the output of our problem can be obtained. The design process consists of the following three stages.

Stage 1

We represent a job with a directed graph (task graph). Jobs are sometimes application problems, and sometimes part of an application problem. Figure 26.2 shows an example of a task graph. Each node of the graph stands for a task. The number inside the node shows the task number and the number next to the node shows the processing time of that task. The arcs from one node to another indicate communication between tasks and task precedence. For example, task 3 communicates with task 0, task 1 and task 5, and is not executable until both task 0 and task 1 have been completed. The number beside an arc shows the communication cost between the tasks. Since a loop structure in the job can be expanded to a set of tasks without any loop, we assume that the task graph has no (directed) cycle, and is, therefore, a DAG.

Stage 2

We assign tasks to processors and determine the execution order of the tasks, so that the total computation time is minimized and the assignment constraints are satisfied. The assignment of tasks implies a partition of tasks into subsets, where each subset contains the tasks assigned to a processor. For this stage, we propose an optimization/suboptimization algorithm, which is discussed in Section 26.3.

Stage 3

We repeat the second stage, varying the set of processors and assignment constraints. From the relation between the assignment constraints and the computation time, we can choose the appropriate architecture for the processor network. In some cases, with a given type of architecture, the relation between the number of processors and the total computation time shows whether the problem is appro-

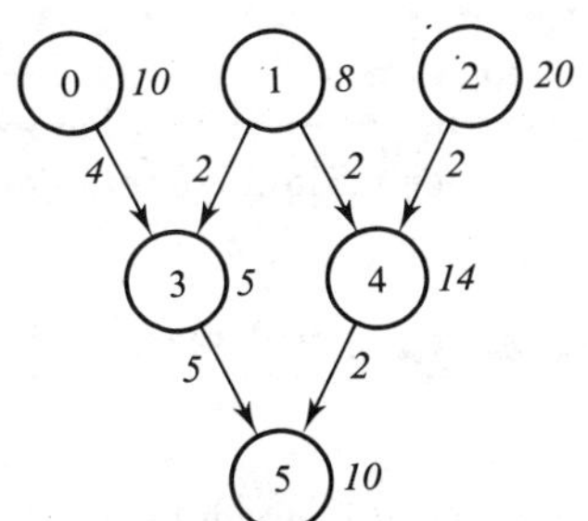

Figure 26.2
An example of a task graph.

priate for parallel processing with that type of architecture. If the computation time decreases in inverse proportion to the number of processors, parallel processing is a good solution for the problem. On the other hand, if the computation time is independent of the number of processors, as in the case of a simple linear task graph, parallel processing is not applicable to the problem.

26.2.3 Previous approaches to task assignment

For a given problem, the ideal is that the total computation time decreases in inverse proportion to the number of processors used. However, we cannot obtain this ideal because of the saturation effect, one of the most serious problems in parallel processing. This effect is caused by the following factors:

(1) Processor communication overhead.

(2) Unbalanced processor loads.

(3) Lack of parallelism due to task precedence.

Factor 1 can be avoided by allocating tasks, which communicate with one another, to the same processor. To minimize overall processor communication, all tasks would have to be allocated to a single processor. This is obviously the worst case with respect to factor 2. To balance loads, the tasks must be distributed evenly and thus processor communication increases. Therefore, we have a trade-off between factors 1 and 2. Factor 3 depends on the granularity of tasks. Thus, these three factors are complexly related.

To solve the above, task scheduling algorithms in multiprocessor or distributed processing environments have been studied by many researchers [3–6]. Shen and Tsai proposed an algorithm which is guaranteed to obtain the optimal solution when there exists little or no task precedence for distributed processing environments [6]. Another optimization/suboptimization algorithm called Depth-First/Implicit Heuristic Search (DF/IHS) is provided for multiprocessor environments by Kasahara and Narita [5]. The algorithm assumes that processors are tightly coupled and that the interprocessor communication overhead is negligible, and consequently it is efficient even for large-scale problems.

These approaches commonly take the relationships among tasks, the processors' specifications and the processor network as an input, and assign tasks to processors. One noticeable difference between the previous task scheduling methods and our method lies in the treatment of the network of processors. Some previous works take it as an input, and others do not consider it, while in our method, it is one of the outputs.

As we are going to design parallel processing systems, as opposed to scheduling tasks on existing hardware, we can afford to analyze the task graph in more detail, and thus propose an optimization/suboptimization algorithm which takes account of both task precedence and communication cost.

26.3 Parallel processing model and task assignment algorithm

In this section, we describe our task assignment algorithm. The inputs to this algorithm are the task graph of a job, a set of processors and the assignment constraints. The outputs are the assignment of tasks, the network of processors and the total computation time.

26.3.1 Parallel processing model

Task Graph

A task graph is a DAG which represents tasks and task communications in a job. Tasks and task communications are represented by the nodes and arcs of the graph, respectively. In our parallel processing model, communication from one task to another is unique, and thus an arc can be represented by a pair of tasks.

In general, the execution time of a single task depends on the processor to which the task has been allocated. In our model, however, the execution time of a task t is independent of the processor, and is denoted by $e(t)$.

Similarly, we assume that communication links are homogeneous, and interprocessor communication cost is independent of physical communication links. We also assume that tasks can only communicate with each other if they are allocated to the same processor or to different processors that are directly connected by a communication link. Therefore, interprocessor communication cost is a function of task communication. We consider two types of communication parameters as functions of a task communication c: communication overhead time $h(c)$ and communication delay time $d(c)$ (see Figure 26.3). $h(c)$ can be interpreted as the time for storing a packet to a sender buffer or restoring it from a receiver buffer. $d(c)$ is the time for actual data transmission. $h(c)$ and $d(c)$ depend heavily on the physical system architecture. For example, $d(c)$ should be almost zero in the case where the communication scheme consists of dual-port memory devices.

From the above discussion, we can formalize the definition of a task graph as follows:

Definition (Task graph)
A task graph G is given by:

$$G = (T, C, e, h, d)$$

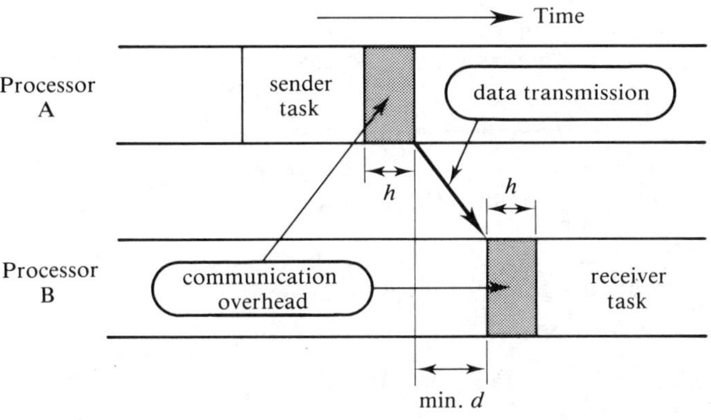

Figure 26.3
Our task communication model.

where:

(1) T: the set of tasks.

(2) C: the set of task communications:

$$C \subset T \times T$$

(3) e: a task execution time function:

$$e: T \rightarrow R^*$$

(4) h: a communication overhead time function:

$$h: C \rightarrow R^*$$

(5) d: a communication delay time function:

$$d: C \rightarrow R^*$$

(R^* is a set of non-negative real numbers. $R^* = \{x \mid x \in R, x \geqslant 0\}$.)

Since a task graph G is a DAG, it has no (directed) cycle. For later discussions, we define the set of predecessors and successors of a task t to be $Pred(t)$ and $Succ(t)$, respectively.

Definition (Predecessors and successors of a task)
The sets of predecessors and successors of a task t are given by:

(1) $Pred(t) = \{u \mid u \in T, (u,t) \in C\}$
(2) $Succ(t) = \{u \mid u \in T, (t,u) \in C\}$

Assignment, assigned task graph, and legal assignment

P is a set of processors. For the following discussions, we assume that P is a totally ordered set. (An alternative assumption is that processors are numbered 1 through $\#P$ ($\#X$ is the number of elements of a finite set X) and that each processor is identified with its number. Thus, $P = \{1,2, \ldots, \#P\}$.)

For each task, the task assignment determines both the processor where the task is executed and the number showing the position of execution in the processor. They are represented as functions of a task t: the assigned processor $pa(t)$ and the number showing the execution order $oa(t)$. In other words, task t is executed $oa(t)$th on processor $pa(t)$.

Definition (Task assignment)
A task assignment A of a task graph G is given by:

$$A = (pa, oa)$$

where:

(1) pa: a processor assignment function:

$$pa: T \rightarrow P$$

(2) oa: an order assignment function:

$$oa: T \rightarrow N$$

(N is a set of natural numbers.)

Needless to say, the following condition has to be satisfied:

$$\forall t \in T,\ oa(t) \geqslant 2 \Rightarrow \exists u \in T,\ pa(u) = pa(t),\ oa(u) = oa(t) - 1$$

A processor network, which realizes the execution of a job, is obtained by allocating communication links between processors if there is a task communication from a task assigned to one processor to a task assigned to another processor.

We suppose that communication links are two-way (duplex) and are represented as pairs of processors, where the first processor number is less than the second to eliminate duplicates. (This is why P is defined as a totally ordered set.) Therefore, a processor network is formalized as follows.

Definition (Processor network by assignment)
A processor network W resulting from a task graph G and its task assignment A can be defined as a pair of the set of processors P and the set of communication links L:

$$W = (P, L)$$

where:

$$L = \{(p_1,p_2) \mid p_1,p_2 \in P,\ p_1 < p_2,\ \exists t_1,t_2 \in T,\ pa(t_1) = p_1 \text{ and } pa(t_2) = p_2 \text{ and } ((t_1,t_2) \in C \text{ or } (t_2,t_1) \in C)\}$$

Next, we have to discuss the legality of a task assignment. There are two points to consider:

(1) The task assignment should be consistent with the task precedence represented in the task graph.

(2) The task assignment should fulfill the assignment constraints, described below.

On a task graph, there are task precedence relations between tasks. On the other hand, the order of execution in the same processor also means task precedence. To discuss the first point, we should add the task precedences due to a task assignment to the task graph, and examine whether there is a cycle on the graph. We call this new task graph an assigned task graph.

In an assigned task graph, the cost of task communications depends on a task assignment. If the tasks on both sides of task communication c are allocated to different processors, an assigned communication overhead function $h2(c)$ and an assigned communication delay function $d2(c)$ have the same value as $h(c)$ and $d(c)$, respectively. Otherwise, $h2(c)$ and $d2(c)$ are equal to 0, for the communication cost in the same processor can be ignored.

Definition (Assigned task graph)
An assigned task graph $G2$ is given by:

$$G2 = (T, C2, e, h2, d2)$$

where:

(1) T: the set of tasks.

(2) $C2$: the set of task precedences:

$$C2 = C \cup \{(t_1,t_2) \mid t_1,t_2 \in T,\ pa(t_1) = pa(t_2),\ oa(t_1) + 1 = oa(t_2)\}$$

(3) e: a task execution time function:

$$e: T \rightarrow R^*$$

(4) $h2$: an assigned communication overhead time function:

$$h2: C2 \rightarrow R^*$$

$$h2((t_1, t_2)) \equiv \begin{cases} h((t_1,t_2)) & : pa(t_1) \neq pa(t_2) \\ 0 & : pa(t_1) = pa(t_2) \end{cases}$$

(5) $d2$: an assigned communication delay time function:

$$d2: C2 \rightarrow R^*$$

$$d2((t_1, t_2)) \equiv \begin{cases} d((t_1,t_2)) & : pa(t_1) \neq pa(t_2) \\ 0 & ; pa(t_1) = pa(t_2) \end{cases}$$

We define the sets of predecessors and successors of a task t also on an assigned task graph.

Definition (Predecessors and successors of a task on an assigned task graph)
The sets of predecessors and successors of a task t on an assigned task graph are given by:

(1) $Pred2(t) = \{u \mid u \in T, (u,t) \in C2\}$

(2) $Succ2(t) = \{u \mid u \in T, (t,u) \in C2\}$

Before describing the conditions of a legal task assignment, we should define the assignment constraints. For a processor p, $ln(p)$ is the maximum number of processors with which p can be connected. For a task t, $tp(t)$ is the set of processors where t is executable. This kind of constraint is useful for tasks which request specified processors (for example, special function units, I/O devices such as disks, etc.). If the processors are homogeneous, $tp(t) = P$.

Definition (Assignment constraints)
The assignment constraints B are given as follows:

$$B = (ln, tp)$$

where:

(1) ln: a link number constraint function:

$$ln: P \rightarrow N \cup \{\infty\}$$

(2) tp: a task processor constraint function:

$$tp: T \rightarrow 2^P$$

From the above discussions, the condition for a task assignment to be legal can be defined as follows.

Definition (Legal assignment)
For a given task graph G, the set of processors P and the assignment constraints B, a task assignment A is called legal if, and only if, it satisfies the following conditions:

(1) An assigned task graph resulting from G, P, and A has no cycle.

(2) $\forall p \in P$,
$ln(p) \geqslant \#\{q \mid q \in P - \{p\},\ \exists t, u \in T,\ pa(t) = p$ and $pa(u) = q$ and $((t,u) \in C$ or $(u,t) \in C)\}$; ($\#X$ is the number of elements of a finite set X.)

(3) $\forall t \in T,\ pa(t) \in tp(t)$

Computation time

We evaluate the performance of a parallel processing system by its total computation time: the time from the start of the first task to the end of the final task. For its calculation, we have to determine the optimal scheduling for each task. This is defined by the task's starting time and completion time, as follows.

Definition (Starting time and completion time)
For a task t, the starting time $TM_s(t)$ and the completion time $TM_e(t)$ are given recursively by:

$$TM_s(t) \equiv \begin{cases} 0 & : Pred2(t) = \varnothing \\ \max\limits_{u \in Pred2(t)} (TM_e(u) + d2((u,t))) & : \text{otherwise} \end{cases} \tag{26.1}$$

$$TM_e(t) \equiv TM_s(t) + \sum_{u \in Pred(t)} h2((u,t)) + e(t) + \sum_{v \in Succ(t)} h2((t,v)) \tag{26.2}$$

The above starting time and completion time are optimally scheduled. (For the tasks which have no predecessors in an assigned task graph, $TM_s(t)$ is 0. Obviously, this is the earliest starting time. For a given starting time, the above definition of $TM_e(t)$ gives the earliest completion time. And if a task has predecessors, the maximum value of the sum of the completion time of predecessors and assigned communication delay time from them is obviously the earliest starting time of the task.) Therefore, the total computation time is defined as follows.

Definition (Total computation time)
For a given task graph G, the set of processors P, and a legal assignment A, the total computation time, that is, the total cost of computation, is given by:

$$TM(G, P, A) \equiv \max_{t \in T} (TM_e(t)) = \max_{t \in \{u \mid u \in T,\ Succ2(u) = \varnothing\}} (TM_e(t)) \tag{26.3}$$

26.3.2 Task assignment algorithm

The algorithm described in this section yields the task assignment with minimal total computation time from a given task graph, the set of processors and the assignment constraints.

Basically, we examine all the legal assignments by backtracking. We assign tasks to processors one by one, and check whether the intermediate state of assignment, called the task subassignment, is legal. To reduce the cost of the backtracking search, our algorithm evaluates the lower bound cost for all the legal subassignments, and searches task assignments by selecting the task subassignment with the smallest lower bound first. Therefore, if the minimal total computation time of task assignments found so far is less than the lower bound for a task subassignment, we need not proceed further [7] and, in addition, we can gain a suboptimal solution even if the search is aborted at an intermediate stage. Therefore, our algorithm is an optimization/suboptimization algorithm.

The algorithm consists of two phases: Phase I determines the order in which tasks are assigned during search. Phase II is the body of the backtracking search.

Phase I: determining task order by height

To determine the task assignment order, we calculate the height of each task in the task graph. The height is defined as the longest path length from the bottom nodes, the nodes without any successors. We can formulate the height of a task recursively.

Definition (Height)
The height of a task in a task graph G is given by:

$$ht: T \rightarrow R^*$$

$$ht(t) \equiv \begin{cases} 0 & : Succ(t) = \varnothing \\ \max\limits_{u \in Succ(t)} (ht(u) + e(u)) & : \text{otherwise} \end{cases} \qquad \textbf{(26.4)}$$

If task t_1 is one of the predecessors of task t_2, then $ht(t_1) > ht(t_2)$, because $e(t) > 0$ for any task t. If we assign tasks in descending order of their heights, for any task, every predecessor is assigned before the task itself. As described later, the height of each task is also used for cost evaluation during the backtracking search.

Phase II: backtracking search

In this phase, we perform the backtracking search in depth-first order, assigning tasks to processors by order of height as determined by Phase I. To clarify the description, we show the search tree of Figure 26.4 as an example. There the six tasks of Figure 26.2 are assigned to two processors, A and B. Each node of the search tree corresponds to a task subassignment, and the depth of the node in the search tree corresponds to the number of allocated tasks at the task subassignment, and is called level of search.

Task subassignment

A task subassignment S is the intermediate state of a task assignment in the backtracking search, and the set of tasks already assigned is represented by $U(S)$. A task subassignment is defined as follows.

Definition (Task subassignment)
A task subassignment S in a task graph G is given by:

$$S = (U(S), tpa_S, toa_S)$$

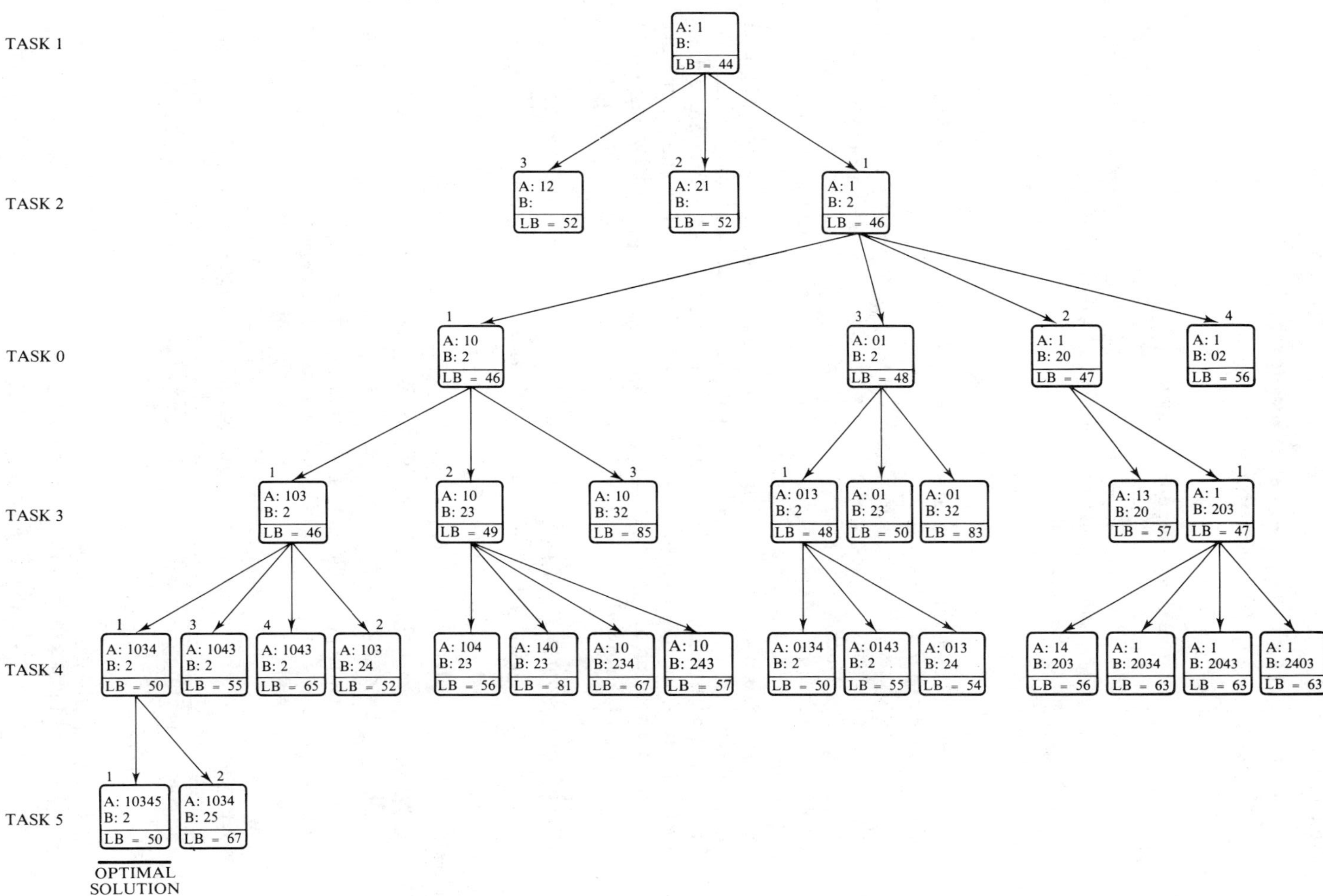

Figure 26.4
The search tree for the task graph in Figure 26.2.

where:

(1) $U(S)$ ($\subset T$): the set of tasks already assigned.

(2) tpa_S: a tentative processor assignment function:

$$tpa_S: U(S) \to P$$

(3) toa_S: a tentative order assignment function:

$$toa_S: U(S) \to N$$

A task subassignment is also represented with the sequences of task numbers for each processor. For example:

A: 1 0

B: 2

means that task 1 and 0 are allocated to processor A, task 1 being executed first, and task 2 is allocated to processor B.

The task subassignment where no task is assigned ($U(S) = \varnothing$), is called the initial subassignment, and is the start of search. The task subassignment where all tasks are assigned ($U(S) = T$), is called goal subassignment, and presents a solution (including not optimal solution) for a task assignment problem. A goal subassignment represents a task assignment.

As described above, we assign tasks one by one. To proceed to the next level of the search tree, we have to 'append a task to the current task subassignment'. To append a task t to a task subassignment S_1 and create a new task subassignment S_2, we need two parameters: the processor to which task t is assigned, p, and the number showing the position of execution in the processor, n. The procedure for appending a task, $append(S_1, S_2, t, p, n)$, is as follows.

Procedure $append(S_1, S_2, t, p, n)$

(1) $U(S_2) \leftarrow U(S_1) \cup \{t\}$

(2) $\forall u \in U(S_1)$, $tpa_{S_2}(u) \leftarrow tpa_{S_1}(u)$

(3) $\forall u \in U(S_1)$, $tpa_{S_1}(u) \neq p$ or $toa_{S_1}(u) < n \Rightarrow toa_{S_2}(u) \leftarrow toa_{S_1}(u)$

(4) $\forall u \in U(S_1)$, $tpa_{S_1}(u) = p$ and $toa_{S_1}(u) \geqslant n \Rightarrow toa_{S_2}(u) \leftarrow toa_{S_1}(u) + 1$

(5) $tpa_{S_2}(t) \leftarrow p$, $toa_{S_2}(t) \leftarrow n$

To be able to detect illegal task assignments as early as possible, we define a subassigned task graph and a legal subassignment in almost the same way as an assigned task graph and a legal assignment. The difference lies in treating only the tasks already assigned. In a subassigned task graph, $C3(S)$ includes the task precedences of the tasks that are already assigned and the original task communications. Unless both of the tasks of a task communication have been assigned, the communication overhead time and the communication delay time are treated as 0.

Definition (Subassigned task graph)
A subassigned task graph $G3(S)$ is given by:

$$G3(S) = (T, C3(S), e, h3_S, d3_S)$$

where:

(1) T: the set of tasks.

(2) $C3(S)$: the set of tentative task precedences:

$$C3(S) = C \cup \{(t_1, t_2) \mid t_1, t_2 \in U(S),\ tpa_S(t_1) = tpa_S(t_2),\ toa_S(t_1) + 1 = toa_S(t_2)\}$$

(3) e: a task execution time function:

$$e: T \rightarrow R^*$$

(4) $h3_S$: a tentative communication overhead time function:

$$h3_S: C3(S) \rightarrow R^*$$

$$h3_S((t_1, t_2)) \equiv \begin{cases} h((t_1, t_2)) & : t_1, t_2 \in U(S),\ tpa(t_1) \neq tpa(t_2) \\ 0 & : \text{otherwise} \end{cases}$$

(5) $d3_S$: a tentative communication delay time function:

$$d3_S: C3(S) \rightarrow R^*$$

$$d3_S((t_1, t_2)) \equiv \begin{cases} d((t_1, t_2)) & : t_1, t_2 \in U(S),\ tpa(t_1) \neq tpa(t_2) \\ 0 & : \text{otherwise} \end{cases}$$

Definition (Predecessors and successors of a task on a subassigned task graph) The set of predecessors of a task t on a subassigned task graph from a task subassignment S is given by:

(1) $Pred3_S(t) = \{u \mid u \in T, (u, t) \in C3(S)\}$

Similarly, in case of a legal subassignment, the conditions of legality consider only the tasks in $U(S)$.

Definition (Legal subassignment)
For a given task graph G, the set of processors P and the assignment constraints B, a task subassignment S is called legal if, and only if, it satisfies the following conditions:

(1) A subassigned task graph resulting from G, P and S has no cycle.

(2) $\forall p \in P$
$In(p) \geqslant \#\{q \mid q \in P - \{p\},\ \exists t, u \in U(S),\ tpa_S(t) = p$ and $tpa_S(u) = q$ and $((t, u) \in C$ or $(u, t) \in C)\}$

(3) $\forall t \in U(S),\ tpa_S(t) \in tp(t)$

Obviously, the condition of legality of a goal task subassignment is the same as that of a corresponding task assignment.

Branching rule

To append a task to a task subassignment and to proceed to the next task subassignment, the new task subassignment has to be legal. Otherwise, we need not proceed further, because of the following proposition.

PROPOSITION (Propagation of illegality: 1)
If a task subassignment S_1 is illegal, a task subassignment S_2 resulting from $append(S_1, S_2, t, p, n)$ is also illegal.

Obtaining all the legal task subassignments from the current task subassignment is performed in two steps. First, we pick out all the processors which realize legal subassignments (*select__processor*), and then select the order of legal subassignments (*select__order*). In the following discussions, S_0 is the current task subassignment, and t_0 is the task which is assigned next.

Procedure *select__processor*

(1) $X \leftarrow tp(t_0)$

(2) $\exists p_1, p_2 \in X, (\forall t \in U(S_0), tpa_{S_0}(t) \neq p_1, tpa_{S_0}(t) \neq p_2), ln(p_1) = ln(p2),$
$(\forall t \in U(S_0), p_1, p_2 \in tp(t) \text{ or } p_1, p_2 \notin tp(t))$
$\Rightarrow X \leftarrow X - \{p_2\}$

(3) $\exists p \in X$
$ln(p) < \#(\{q \mid q \in P - \{p\}, \exists t, u \in U(S_0), tpa_{S_0}(t) = p \text{ and } tpa_{S_0}(u) = q$
$\text{and } ((t, u) \in C \text{ or } (u, t) \in C)\} \cup \{q \mid q \in P - \{p\}, \exists t \in U(S_0), tpa_{S_0}(t) = q$
$\text{and } ((t, t_0) \in C \text{ or } (t_0, t) \in C)\})$
$\Rightarrow X \leftarrow X - \{p\}$

(4) $\exists p \in X, \exists q \in P - \{p\}$
$ln(q) < \#(\{r \mid r \in P - \{q\}, \exists t, u \in U(S_0), tpa_{S_0}(t) = q \text{ and } tpa_{S_0}(u) = r$
$\text{and } ((t, u) \in C \text{ or } (u, t) \in C)\} \cup Y(p, q, t_0))$
$\Rightarrow X \leftarrow X - \{p\}$

(5) $RESULT \leftarrow X$

where:

$$Y(p, q, t_0) \equiv \begin{cases} \{p\} : \exists t \in U(S_0), tpa_{S_0}(t) = q, ((t, t_0) \in C \text{ or } (t_0, t) \in C)) \\ \varnothing \quad : \text{otherwise} \end{cases}$$

In procedure *select__processor*, condition (3) of legal subassignment is considered in substep (1), and substep (2) is used for decreasing the computation cost by eliminating branches of the search tree without loss of generality. Substeps (3) and (4), which are very complicated, consider condition (2) of legal subassignment, and check whether the link number constraint is satisfied when task t_0 is assigned to processor p.

Next, for each processor p in *RESULT* of *select__processor*, we insert the new task into the task sequence of p in the current subassignment as shown in procedure *append*. Assuming the length of sequence is l, there are $l + 1$ positions to insert the new task. For example, suppose we assign task 3 to processor A, there are the three positions shown below:

(1) A: 3 1 0
B: 2

(2) A: 1 3 0
B: 2

(3) A: 1 0 3
B: 2

However, the task subassignments resulting from this procedure are not always legal, since their subassigned task graph may have a cycle. For example, the first two subassignments above are illegal, since in Figure 26.2, there exist arcs from task 0 to 3 and from 1 to 3.

To select legal subassignments, we utilize the following proposition.

PROPOSITION (Propagation of illegality: 2)
Suppose that tasks are appended in descending order of height, and S_0 is a legal subassignment. If the subassigned task graph of a task subassignment S_1 resulting from *append*$(S_0, S_1, t, p, n + 1)$ has a cycle, then the subassigned task graph of S_3 resulting from *append*(S_0, S_2, t, p, n) also has a cycle.

This means that if we examine whether the subassigned task graphs have cycles in descending order of assignment in a processor, and if one case is found to be illegal, the following cases are also illegal. Therefore procedure *select_order* is as follows:

Procedure *select_order*
For any processor p in *RESULT* of *select_processor* do the following substeps:

```
(1) L ← (the number of tasks assigned to processor p) + 1.
(2) while (L ≥ 1)
    begin
          if (the subassigned task graph of S resulting from
             append(S0, S1, t, p, L) has no cycle)
          then
                S is registered as a legal subassignment;
          else
                break;
          L ← L − 1;
    end
```

Selection rule

Our criterion for selecting a task subassignment for the next level is very simple: least lower bound cost first. When appending a task t_0 to a task subassignment S_0, we (1) obtain all the legal task subassignments at the next level, (2) calculate their lower bound costs as described in the next subsection, and (3) select the task subassignment in ascending order of lower bound costs.

Lower bound cost

The lower bound cost of a certain task subassignment is defined as being less than or equal to the total computation time of all its descendant goal subassignments. The better the evaluation of the lower bound cost, the more efficiently the search tree can be pruned.

We calculate the lower bound cost with the following stages. First, we define $V(S)$ as the set of tasks that have not yet been assigned, but have at least one immediate predecessor in $U(S)$, or that have no predecessor at all (start task):

$$V(S) \equiv \{t \mid t \in T - U(S),\ U(S) \cap Pred(t) \neq \emptyset \text{ or } Pred(t) = \emptyset\}$$

For task t in $U(S)$, we can determine the tentative starting time $tm_s(t)$ and the tentative completion time $tm_e(t)$ given recursively by:

$$tm_s(t) \equiv \begin{cases} 0 & : Pred3_S(t) = \emptyset \\ \max\limits_{u \in Pred3_s(t)} (tm_e(u) + d3_S((u,t))) & : \text{otherwise} \end{cases} \quad (26.5)$$

$$tm_e(t) \equiv tm_s(t) + \sum_{u \in Pred(t)} h3_S((u,t)) + e(t) + \sum_{v \in Succ(t)} h3_S((t,v)) \quad (26.6)$$

Although the assignment of a task t in $V(S)$ is unknown, we would like to determine $tm_e(t)$ in the same manner. First, by procedure *select__processor*, we obtain the set of all the possible processors to assign task t. Next, we take the minimal value of $t_e(t,p)$ for all of them. $t_e(t,p)$ represents the completion time assuming task t is assigned to processor p. In mathematical terms:

$$tm_e(t) \equiv \min_{p \in (RESULT \text{ of } select\_\_processor)} t_e(t,p) \quad (26.7)$$

$$t_e(t,p) \equiv \begin{cases} e(t) & : Pred(t) = \emptyset \\ \max\limits_{u \in Pred(t)} (tm_e(u) + X(u,p) \cdot d((u,t))) + \\ \sum\limits_{u \in Pred(t)} X(u,p) \cdot h((u,t)) + e(t) & : \text{otherwise} \end{cases} \quad (26.8)$$

$$X(u,p) \equiv \begin{cases} 1 : u \in U(S),\ tpa_S(u) \neq p \\ 0 : \text{otherwise} \end{cases}$$

If *RESULT* of procedure *select__processor* above is an empty set, we cannot proceed further down and have to backtrack on the search tree.

Now that we have the completion time for the tasks in $U(S)$ and $V(S)$, the lower bound cost is obtained as:

$$LB(S) \equiv \max_{t \in U(S) \cup V(S)} (tm_e(t) + ht(t)) \quad (26.9)$$

Note that the lower bound cost for a goal subassignment is identical with the cost defined by the Equation (26.3).

In actual computation of the lower bound, we utilize the information of the previous subassignment for calculating Equations 26.5 and 26.6, since almost all tm_ss and tm_es remain unchanged by adding a new task. Note that the starting time, the completion time and the lower bound cost never decrease by appending a new task. Therefore, to compute Equation 26.9, it is sufficient to consider the changed tm_es and the lower bound at the previous subassignment.

Pruning

Once a solution is found, task subassignments with lower bound cost greater than or equal to the best solution found so far can be pruned. This reduces the computing load remarkably.

26.4 A design example

In this section, we examine the validity of the method proposed in the previous sections through an example taken from computer graphics. We consider the intersection calculation in a ray-tracing algorithm as the example, because there is a high demand for fast ray tracing.

26.4.1 Ray tracing and its parallelization

Ray tracing is the method of choice for creating realistic images, since it can model the reflection/refraction phenomena on objects [8]. However, ray tracing is computationally very expensive because the ray–object intersection calculations increase in proportion to the complexity of the scene.

The outline of the ray-tracing algorithm is as follows. Rays are traced from the eye through each pixel of the picture plane in the opposite direction of the actual ray transmission. When a ray hits an object, new rays may be generated in the directions of reflection and/or refraction, as well as in the directions of light sources for shadowing. Then, these new rays are in turn traced. In the process of ray tracing, the main calculations for each ray are the intersection calculations and the intensity calculations. An intersection calculation determines whether a ray hits an object, and an intensity calculation computes the local intensity at the intersection point.

Since each pixel can be calculated independently, parallel processing greatly improves the algorithm's performance. In fact, several parallel processing system architectures for ray tracing have been proposed so far [1, 2, 9–11], some of which have actually been built for practical uses.

There are several ways to process the ray-tracing algorithm in parallel. Most existing systems adopt pixel-oriented parallel processing, where each processor generates a subimage of the picture [1, 2, 9]. Other researchers divide the object space into subspaces and allocate a set of subspaces to each processor [10, 11]. Whitted [8] suggests a system with one host processor and some processors dedicated to intersection calculations. Another way to parallel ray tracing is to utilize a fine-grain (instruction level) parallelism [9].

According to Whitted, in ray tracing most of the computation time is spent on intersection calculations between rays and objects. For complex scenes, the percentage of time required for the intersection calculation can increase to over 95%. Therefore, a dedicated parallel processing unit for intersection calculations will greatly improve the system performance.

Considering the above facts, we analyzed the intersection calculation using task graphs, and designed a dedicated parallel processing unit using the algorithm described in Section 26.3.

26.4.2 Task graphs

The purpose of the intersection calculation unit is to decide whether a ray intersects with an object, and if it does, to calculate the intersection points. The inputs to this unit are the point of the ray origin $\mathbf{o}$ and the normalized direction vector of the ray $\mathbf{v}$. The outputs are distances between the origin and the intersection points, which are infinite if the ray does not intersect the object. Component tasks of this unit are elementary operation tasks, which execute one floating-point operation each.

Here, we assume that objects are quadratic surfaces because the intersection calculations are simple, and many general shapes can be described. Therefore, with an appropriate transformation, the shape of an object is generally represented as:

$$\pm r_x'^2 \pm r_y'^2 \pm r_z'^2 = 1 \text{ or } 0 \tag{26.10}$$

while a transformation on the object is represented as:

$$\mathbf{r}' = M\mathbf{r} + \mathbf{r}_0 \tag{26.11}$$

where:

$$M = \begin{bmatrix} m_{11} & m_{12} & m_{13} \\ m_{21} & m_{22} & m_{23} \\ m_{31} & m_{32} & m_{33} \end{bmatrix} \tag{26.12}$$

By changing the signs of each term or the right side in Equation 26.10, or changing the transformation matrix M, we can represent general quadratic surfaces such as ellipsoids, hyperboloids, cylinders, cones, or planes.

On the other hand, rays in 3D space are represented with a parameter t as:

$$\mathbf{r} = \mathbf{v}t + \mathbf{o} \tag{26.13}$$

Hence, the intersection calculation is performed by solving the following quadratic equation:

$$(\pm y_x^2 \pm u_u^2 \pm u_z^2) \cdot t^2 + (\pm u_x w_x \pm u_y w_y \pm u_z w_z) \cdot 2t + (\pm w_x^2 \pm w_y^2 \pm w_z^2) = 1 \text{ or } 0 \tag{26.14}$$

where

$$\begin{aligned} \mathbf{u} &= M\mathbf{v} \\ \mathbf{w} &= M\mathbf{o} + r_0 \end{aligned} \tag{26.15}$$

To simplify the task assignment, we divide the intersection calculation into two stages, a transformation stage and an intersection solving stage, and develop a parallel processing unit for each stage independently. The transformation stage performs the transformations according to Equations 26.13–15 except the addition of $\mathbf{r}_0$ which appears in the second equation. The parallel processing unit for this stage is called the transformation unit. Actually, the transformation stage does only a 3×3 matrix multiplication. Consequently, the transformation unit can be used for other applications, which is another reason for isolating this stage from the intersection calculation. The intersection solving stage adds $\mathbf{r}_0$ to w and solves Equation 26.14. The unit for this stage is called intersection solving unit.

Now we show the task graphs for each stage. In our task graphs, we assume that the object informations, that is, M, $\mathbf{r}_0$ and the form of the Equation 26.10, are already resident in the appropriate processors prior to the intersection calculation, and we do not consider moving these informations.

The transformation stage can be divided into 15 floating-point operation tasks and three other tasks. Figure 26.5 shows the corresponding task graph. The 'copy' task receives a floating-point number as input and passes it through to the output. The purpose of this task is to distribute the input data to succeeding tasks.

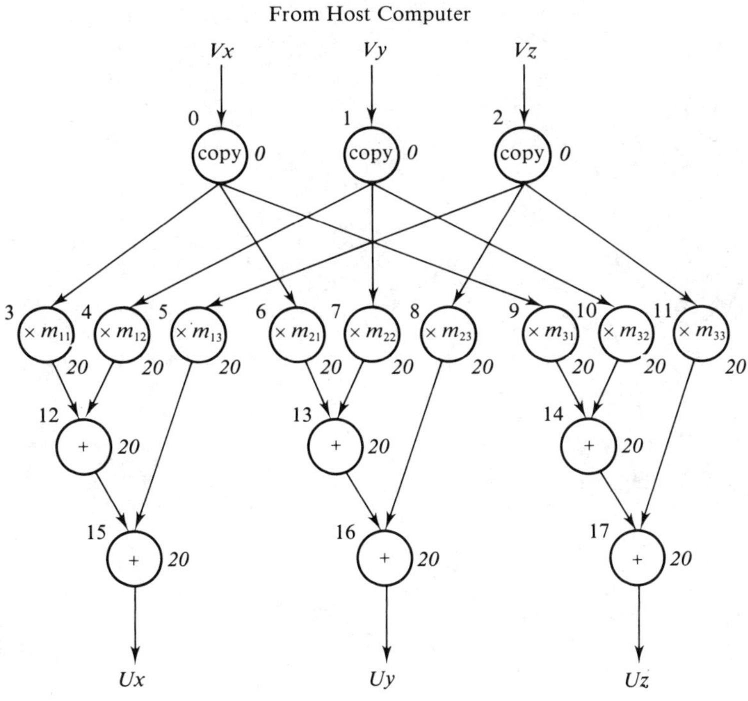

Figure 26.5
A task graph in the transformation stage.

Since the 'copy' task actually does nothing, its execution time of this task is zero. The '$\times m_{ij}$' task receives a floating-point number and multiplies it by m_{ij}, one of the components of the transformation matrix M. The '+' task adds two floating-point numbers.

The intersection solving stage can be divided into 28 floating-point operation tasks and three other tasks. Figure 26.6 shows the corresponding task graph. The '+', '−', '×', '÷', 'neg', 'x^2' and '$\sqrt{x}$' tasks correspond to addition, subtraction, multiplication, division, negation, square and square root operations, respectively. The '$\pm x^2$' and '$\pm\times$' tasks perform a square and a multiplication, respectively, and adjust their signs according to the object information.

The execution time of each task, which is shown beside each node of the task graphs in Figures 26.5 and 26.6, is determined as follows:

addition/subtraction/multiplication	20 μs
division/square root	40 μs

These values are approximately equal to the execution time on an INTEL Numeric Data Processor 8087(5 MHz). All the communication parameters have the same value, since all data items transmitted from one task to another consist of one floating-point number.

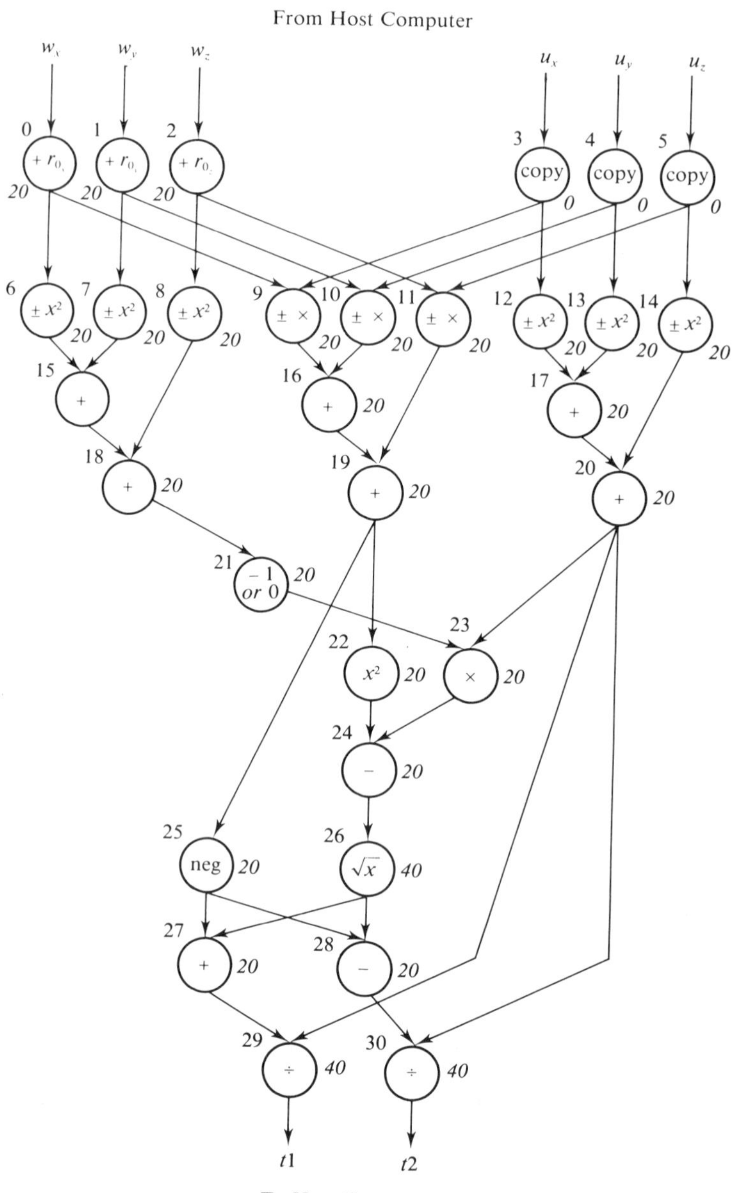

Figure 26.6
A task graph for the intersection solving stage.

26.4.3 Results

In this section, we describe the results of the proposed algorithm as applied to the task graphs of the intersection calculation. As an experiment, we tried the following four cases:

Case 1: $h = 5\ \mu s$, $d = 0\ \mu s$, assignment constraints: A
Case 2: $h = 0\ \mu s$, $d = 10\ \mu s$, assignment constraints: A
Case 3: $h = 0\ \mu s$, $d = 0\ \mu s$, assignment constraints: A
Case 4: $h = 0\ \mu s$, $d = 0\ \mu s$, assignment constraints: B

where h is the communication overhead time and d is the communication delay time. Assignment constraints A and B are as follows:

$$A = (ln, tp)$$

where:

$$\forall p \in P,\ ln(p) = \infty$$

$$\forall t \in T,\ tp(t) = P$$

and:

$$B = (ln, tp)$$

where:

P_e is a subset of P, and $\#P_e = 2$

$$ln(p) = \begin{cases} 1 & : \text{if } p \in P_e \\ 2 & : \text{otherwise} \end{cases}$$

$$tp(t) = \begin{cases} P_e & : \text{if task } t \text{ communicates with the host computer} \\ P & : \text{otherwise} \end{cases}$$

Under assignment constraints B, processors will be linearly connected, where both ends are connected to the host computer.

We implemented our algorithm on a DEC VAX8600, a HITAC M260D and a SONY NEWS NWS8000 in the C programming language under the UNIX operating system. The results for both task graphs with various numbers of processors are shown in Tables 26.1 and 26.2. Because of time limitations, we terminated our algorithm if the number of searched subassignments exceeded 5 000 000. In this case, we show a suboptimal solution. Figure 26.7 shows the relations between the number of processors and the speed-up factor defined as:

$$\textit{Speed-up factor} = \frac{\textit{total computation time with a multiprocessor}}{\textit{total computation time with a single processor}} \tag{26.16}$$

Figure 26.8 illustrates a time table of the transformation unit with three processors in Case 1. For this time table, we calculated the optimal solution (number of searched subassignments: 10 999 741), and found that it is the same as the corresponding suboptimal solution shown in Table 26.1. Therefore, we think that in most practical cases it will be sufficient to calculate only a suboptimal solution. In Figure 26.8, region i represents the execution of task i, and region $i \rightarrow j$ corresponds to the overhead due to the data transmission from task i to task j. The corresponding processor network is shown in Figure 26.9.

In the intersection calculation, the transformation stage is performed twice as often as the intersection solving stage. Therefore, we should choose the number of processors so that the total computation time of the transformation stage is nearly half that of the intersection solving stage. In Case 1, for example, the feasible

Table 26.1 Results for the transformation unit.

	Case 1					*Case 2*				
P	*Tc*	*Ns*	*Nf*	*T*1	*N*1	*Tc*	*Ns*	*Nf*	*T*1	*N*1
1	300					300				
2	185*	5 000 000	118	185	118	160*	5 000 000	115	160	115
3	120*	5 000 000	174 630	145	137	100	1 988 910	119 223	110	137
4	100	493 592	111 720	120	160	90	556 728	171	100	161
5	100	2 490 239	6 920	115	177	80	2 241	354	90	181
6	90	173 117	12 088	100	190	80	2 331	390	90	190
7	90	496 062	2 936	100	205	80	2 341	398	90	190
8	90	709 893	2 818	100	214	80	2 341	398	90	190
	Case 3					*Case 4*				
P	*Tc*	*Ns*	*Nf*	*T*1	*N*1	*Tc*	*Ns*	*Nf*	*T*1	*N*1
1	300					300				
2	160*	5 000 000	117	160	117	160*	5 000 000	117	160	117
3	100	2 908 930	134	100	134	120*	5 000 000	127 446	160	96
4	80	4 610	155	80	155	120*	5 000 000	135 480	160	6 656
5	80	10 728	172	80	172	120*	5 000 000	135 480	160	6 656
6	60	188	188	60	188	120*	5 000 000	135 480	160	6 656
7	60	207	207	60	207	120*	5 000 000	135 480	160	6 656
8	60	216	216	60	216	120*	5 000 000	135 480	160	6 656

Note

P Number of processors.
Tc Total computation time (μs) (* indicates a suboptimal solution).
Ns Number of searched subassignments until the search is terminated.
Nf Number of searched subassignments until the final solution is found.
*T*1 Total computation time of the first solution (μs).
*N*1 Number of searched subassignments until the first solution is found.

Table 26.2 Results for the intersection solving unit.

	Case 1					*Case 2*				
P	*Tc*	*Ns*	*Nf*	*T*1	*N*1	*Tc*	*Ns*	*Nf*	*T*1	*N*1
1	620					620				
2	410*	5 000 000	45 026	435	194	380*	5 000 000	197	390	193
3	345*	5 000 000	1 210 969	360	241	310*	5 000 000	520	340	245
4	315*	5 000 000	129 305	330	291	280*	5 000 000	5 444	300	292
5	300*	5 000 000	148 944	305	334	270*	5 000 000	1 255	300	340
6	295*	5 000 000	4 424	310	364	270*	5 000 000	1 851	300	365
7	295*	5 000 000	7 009	310	387	270*	5 000 000	2 683	300	388
8	295*	5 000 000	7 527	310	387	270*	5 000 000	2 811	300	388
	Case 3					*Case 4*				
P	*Tc*	*Ns*	*Nf*	*T*1	*N*1	*Tc*	*Ns*	*Nf*	*T*1	*N*1
1	620					620				
2	360*	5 000 000	190	360	190	360*	5 000 000	190	360	190
3	300*	5 000 000	240	300	240	300	3 517 490	202	360	163
4	260	308 493	2 160	280	282	300*	5 000 000	1 591 912	340	149
5	240	334	334	240	334	300*	5 000 000	1 591 912	340	149
6	240	356	356	240	356	300*	5 000 000	1 591 912	340	149
7	240	379	379	240	379	300*	5 000 000	1 591 912	340	149
8	240	379	379	240	379	300*	5 000 000	1 591 912	340	149

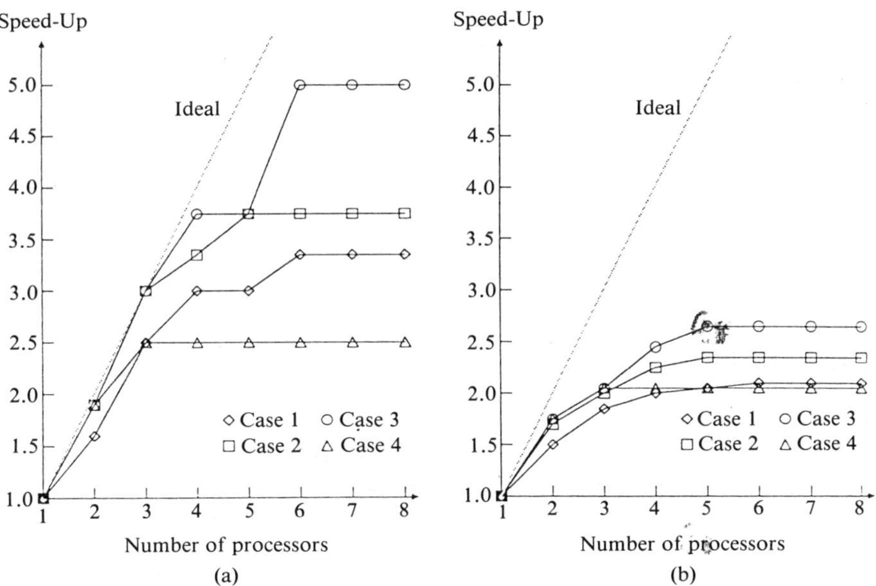

Figure 26.7
Speed-up factors as a function of the number of processors
(a) transformation unit
(b) intersection solving unit.

numbers of processors would be two for the transformation stage and three for the intersection solving stage.

From the results of our experiments, it was noted that the proposed algorithm finds the optimal solution very quickly if the number of processors is large and the communication overhead time or delay time is small; otherwise our algorithm may consume considerable time. This can be explained as follows: our lower bound in the algorithm is strong when the number of processors is large and the communication costs are small, but it is weak in other cases. One of the reasons for this lies in the difficulties in predicting whether the processor communication occurs or not. The improvement of the lower bound is a subject of future study.

If the communication overhead time and delay time are zero and the assignment constraints are *B* (Case 3), the first solution is optimal in most cases. This shows that a greedy algorithm, which terminates the search procedure as soon as the first solution is found, will work well here. It will require much less time than the backtracking algorithm, and can be used not only for system design but also for real-time scheduling.

→ Time

Time (μs)	proc. A	proc. B	proc. C
0–5	0 → 6	10	2 → 11
5–20	3	10	5
20–25	3	10 → 14	5
25–30	3 → 12	7	5 → 15
30–35	9	7	0 → 6
35–45	9	7	6
45–50	9	7 → 13	6
50–55	10 → 14	4	6
55–60	14	4	7 → 13
60–70	14	4	13
70–75	14	3 → 12	13
75–80	2 → 11	12	13
80–95	11	12	8
95–100	11	5 → 15	8
100–120	17	15	16

Figure 26.8
The time table for the transformation unit with three processors in Case 1.

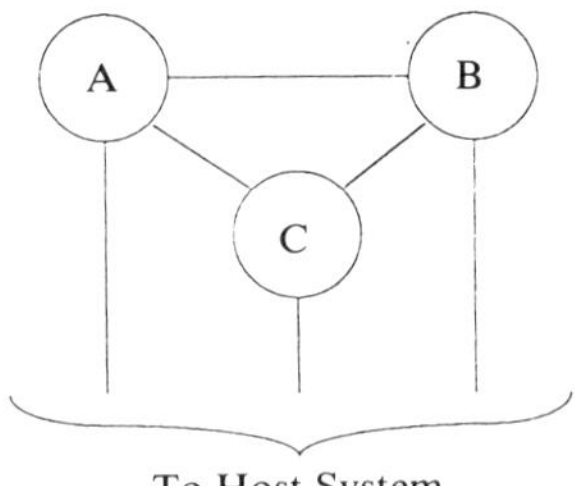

Figure 26.9
The processor network corresponding to Figure 26.8.

Concluding remarks

This chapter proposed a novel approach to the design of an application-oriented parallel processing system especially for computer graphics. The resulting system architecture is guaranteed to be optimal with respect to the total computation time; it is in this respect that our approach differs most from previous approaches. As an example to illustrate our approach, we designed a system for intersection calculation in ray tracing.

Many problems are still left unsolved. One of the most serious problems is how to adapt to applications with conditional branches. The task graphs of such applications change their form or the execution time of the tasks depending on conditions. For such applications, we have to consider the stochastic distribution of the total computation time.

In future, we would like to extend our approach to be applicable to VLSI design. To achieve this, we have to consider not only the computation time but also the area complexity. This extension will require much more work.

Acknowledgements

We are grateful to Professor Tadao Nakamura of Tohoku University and Mr Peter R.G. Bak of Imperial College, London, for their valuable suggestions. Our further gratitude goes to Mr Issei Fujishiro, Mr Naota Inamoto, Mr Yasuto Shirai and Mr Martin J. Dürst for their thoughtful comments. This work has been partially supported by Software Research Center (SRC) of Ricoh Co., Ltd.

References

1. Nishimura H., Ohno H., Kawara T., Shirakawa I. and Omura K. (1983). LINKS-1: a parallel pipelined multimicrocomputer system for image creation. In *Proceedings of the 10th Symposium on Computer Architecture*, pp. 387–94
2. Sato H., Ishii M., Sato K. *et al.* (1985). Fast image generation of constructive solid geometry using a cellular array processor. *ACM Computer Graphics,* **19**(3), 95–102
3. Chu W.W., Holloway L.J., Lan M-T. and Efe K. (1980). Task allocation in distributed data processing. *IEEE Computer,* **13**(11), 57–69

4. Efe K. (1982). Heuristic models of task assignment scheduling in distributed systems. *IEEE Computer,* **15**(6), 50–6
5. Kasahara H. and Narita S. (1984). Practical multiprocessor scheduling algorithms for efficient parallel processing. *IEEE Trans. on Comput.,* **C-33**(11), 1023–9
6. Shen C-C. and Tsai W-H. (1985). A graph matching approach to optimal task assignment in distributed computing systems using a minimax criterion. *IEEE Trans. on Comput.,* **C-34**(3), 197–203
7. Aho A.V., Hopcroft J.E. and Ullman J.D. (1983). *Data Structures and Algorithms.* Reading MA: Addison-Wesley
8. Whitted T. (1980). An improved illumination model for shaded display. *Comm. of ACM,* **23**(6), 343–9
9. Yoshida M., Naruse T., Takahashi T. and Naito S. (1985). *Design of a Graphics Computer - SIGHT.* Research Report 85–CA–60(60–4), Information Processing Society of Japan (in Japanese)
10. Dippe M. and Swensen J. (1984). Adaptive subdivision algorithm and parallel architecture and realistic image synthesis. *ACM Computer Graphics,* **18**(3), 149–58
11. Kobayashi H., Nakamura T. and Shigei Y. (1987). Parallel processing of an object space for image synthesis using ray tracing. *The Visual Computer,* **3**(1), 13–22

G. Kedem
J.L. Ellis

Duke University

27·The ray-casting machine

Geometric modeling is important in CAD/CAM, robotics, computer vision and other fields. Curve Solid Classification (CSC) is a computational utility central to many applications of geometric modeling; it effects segmentation of a curve into subsets that are inside, on the boundary and outside of a solid. CSC is the basis for ray casting (a technique for calculating shaded displays and mass properties of solids), boundary evaluation, collision detection and so forth.

CSC algorithms are dependent on the means used to represent solids. In this chapter we focus on solids represented in Constructive Solid Geometry (CSG) (loosely, as ordered 'additions' and 'subtractions' of simple primitive solids), and seek special computer structures that will allow CSC to be done 10 X – 1000 X faster than in conventional computers. Two types of modules are needed: domain dependent curve primitive classifiers, and domain independent classification combiners.

In this chapter, we describe the architecture of a machine that can classify curves against CSG solids in parallel at high speed. We concentrate, however, on the design of a ray-casting machine. The ray-casting machine described here is a parallel, pipelined, bit-serial machine that classifies a regular lattice of parallel lines. We describe the design of two-bit serial building blocks, the Classification Combine (CC) processor and the incremental, bit-serial, pipelined primitive classifier. These building blocks were designed from the outset for custom VLSI implementation. We describe how to use these building blocks to construct a highly parallel synchronous machine for ray casting. The building blocks are arranged in chips as bit-slice units. By adding more slices, larger and larger machines can be built. We also describe the implementation of a system prototype.

27.1 Introduction

Geometric modeling is an active research field in computer science and computer engineering, and the subfield dubbed 'solid modeling' has progressed especially rapidly in the 1970s. Solid modeling is now spawning a new generation of industrially oriented CAD/CAM systems [1] that is invading robotics for use in world modeling and trajectory planning [2], and has other important practical applications.

Most solid-modeling research systems and all of the emerging commercial solid-modeling systems are based internally on one or the other (or both) of the representation schemes shown in Figure 27.1. The Constructive Solid Geometry (CSG) scheme on the upper left (A) exploits the notion of 'adding' and 'subtracting' (via regularized set union and set difference operations [3]) simple solid building blocks or halfspaces. The Boundary (b-rep) scheme on the lower right (B) represents solids indirectly, via sets of faces that are represented by sets of bounding edges. Formally, CSG representations are binary trees whose interior nodes are regularized set operators and whose leaves are primitives; b-reps are unions of faces usually represented as 3- or 4-level graphs of solids, faces, edges and vertices [4, 5].

CSG and boundary representations are complete, that is, they contain enough information to permit, in principle, any well-defined geometric property of any represented object to be calculated automatically [4]. The b-rep scheme is familiar in computer graphics, and some commercial 'wire frame' CAD systems are evolving toward it. CSG representations, while less familiar, offer powerful set operators that are essential in CAD/CAM and robotics systems for testing interference via the intersection operator, for simulating machining via the difference operator, and so forth. CSG is the basis for several important modeling systems, for example, GMSOLID [6, 7], PADL-1 and PADL-2 [8–10], and SYNTHAVISION [11, 12], and henceforth we shall focus on it.

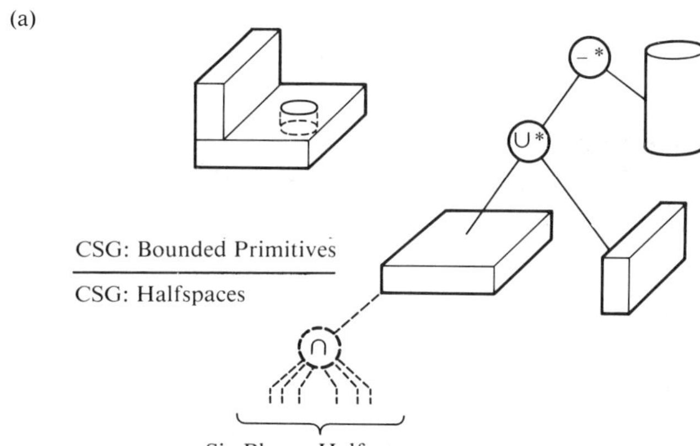

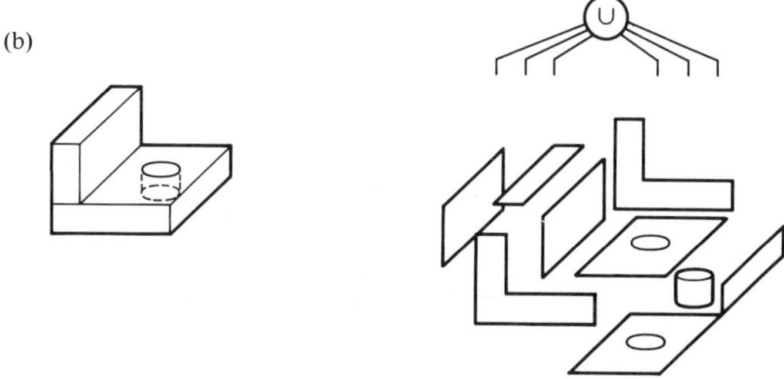

Figure 27.1
Solid representation schemes.
(a) Constructive Solid Geometry (CSG) schemes.
(b) Boundary (b-rep) scheme.

27.1.1 Curve Solid Classification (CSC)

CSC is a special case of the more general 'set membership classification function' defined by Tilove [13]. Figure 27.2 illustrates CSC using Tilove's $M(X, S)$ notation: X is a candidate set (a curve in our case), and S is a solid (a 2D solid in Figure 27.2) against which X is to be classified. The result is the subsets $XinS$, $XonS$, and $XoutS$ shown in Figure 27.2.

Tilove also defined a modified or extended classification function $M * (X, S) = (Xins, (XonS, N * [XonS, S]), XoutS)$ that contains the topological neighborhood $N*$ of $XonS$ relative to S [13]. In essence, $N*$ 'tells where the solid is' with respect to curve segments that lie in the boundary of the solid. We shall illustrate this extension in Section 27.1.4.

27.1.2 Applications of curve solid classification

CSC has a great variety of applications, and the intent here is to introduce briefly a few that are important in CAD/CAM. We begin by observing that CSC is a generalization of the notion of graphic 'clipping' [14], that is, segmenting a curve relative to a rectangular 'window', and hence is widely used in computer graphics.

Ray casting, another important technique in computer graphics [11, 12, 15] is another specialized version of CSC. As shown in Figure 27.3, the in-segment endpoint nearest to the viewing point on each ray is a visible point of the solid. Further, the set of all in-segments provides data from which the mass properties (volume, centroid, moment of inertia, etc.) of the solid may be computed with predictable accuracy [16].

'Wireframing' and 'boundary evaluation' from CSG representations provide still another application of CSC. To oversimplify somewhat, the goal is to compute the edges of faces in the boundary of a CSG-represented solid. The most widely used algorithms produce a set of candidate edges by intersecting all pairs of faces of primitives in the CSG representation; each candidate edge is then classified

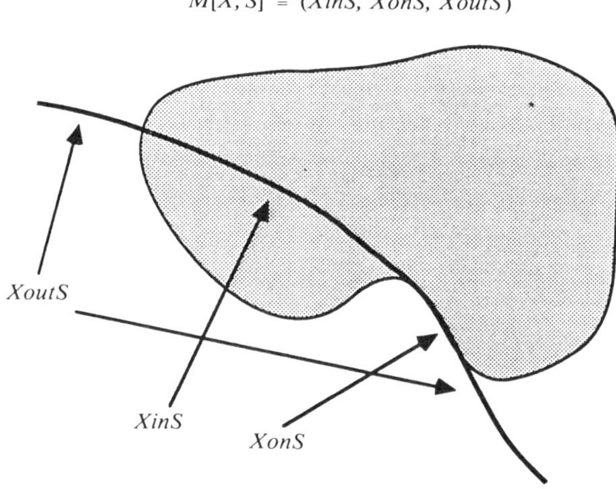

Figure 27.2
The membership classification function.

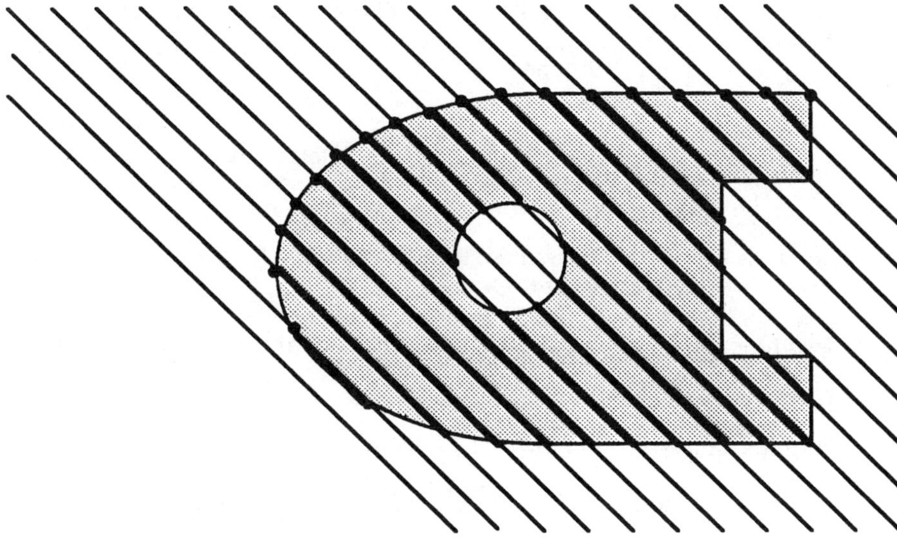

Figure 27.3
Ray casting.

with respect to the solid and the 'on' segment(s) added to the set of boundary edges. (See [17] for a more thorough discussion.)

Null-Object Detection (NOD) for constructively represented solids provides another example. The problem: given a solid S represented by a CSG tree T, determine whether $S = 0$ from computations on T. Tilove has produced an elegant new NOD algorithm wherein CSC is a central utility [18].

The final example is the production of very high resolution raster image of text and drawings. Internally, fonts are represented as 2D regions (2D objects) whose boundaries are piecewise polynomials (splines) [19]. These regions can be defined as unions, intersections and differences of 2D convex objects with spline boundaries. In order to produce a very high resolution raster image of these fonts, say more than 1000 dots per inch, one can find the intersecting segments of a horizontal line with the 2D objects. Only the line segments that are inside the objects should be painted black. This approach has the advantage of being resolution independent; it also gives a very compact representation of the raster data.

27.1.3 CSC algorithms

Thus far we have defined CSC and argued that it is useful, but we have not explained how it may be computed. CSC algorithms depend strongly on how reference sets (solids) are represented, as noted earlier. For CSG-represented solids, the best algorithms use the divide-and-conquer approach illustrated in the following recursive procedure.

The recursive CSC is illustrated by the following pseudo-Pascal procedure:

```
Classify (L : Curve, S : CSGSolid) : LineSegmentSet;
Begin
      if (IsPrimitive.S) then
      return (Prim(L,S))
else
      return (Combine(Classify(L, Left.S), Classify (L, Right.S),
              Operator.S))
end;

Combine (M1,M2 : LineSegmentSet, O : OPERATION) :
         LineSegmentSet;
{
This function computes the set operation O on the two line-segment
sets M1 and M2.
}

Prim (L : Curve, P : Primitive) : LineSegmentSet;
{
This function computes the classification of the curve L
against the primitive P.
}
```

In essence, one descends the CSG tree until the primitive level is reached, at which point special curve primitive classifiers are invoked; one then ascends the tree by combining classifications.

The foregoing procedure can be programmed recursively, more or less as shown, or it can be implemented by non-recursive stack operations on a tree represented in Polish notation; the latter approach is used in the PADL systems.

The procedure above shows that two types of calculations are needed for CSC on CSG representations; curve primitive classification and combination of classifications (henceforth 'combine' for brevity). We shall discuss these more fully below.

27.1.4 Curve primitive classification and classification combine

Curve primitive classification, namely, computing the curve segments that are outside, inside and on the boundary of the primitive solid, is domain dependent. That is, the computation depends on the primitives and on the curve. In the mechanical parts' domain (the domain we concentrate on), the primitives are blocks, cylinders, cones, etc. and the curves are either straight lines, conic curves, or piecewise polynomials.

The computation can be simplified by reducing it to classification of curves against infinite halfspaces with fixed orientation. This is done by first transferring the coordinate system so that the solid has fixed orientation. Then each solid is reduced to an intersection of halfspaces. For example: a block is made by the intersection of six infinite halfspaces. A cylinder is made by intersecting an infinite cylinder with two halfspaces. The classification of curves against halfspaces requires the solution of polynomial equations in one variable. With the exception of one computation that requires careful consideration of roundoff error, curve primitive classification is quite simple.

The classification combine step is simpler yet. First, the computation is domain independent. Each curve is given by a parametric representation ($x(t)$, $y(t)$, $z(t)$). Therefore, the combine operations are set operations on interval segments of the independent parameter t. Second, each combine operation only requires comparisons or alternatively min. and max. functions.

27.1.5 The hardware challenge

Since CSC is of central utility to many applications, it is natural to look for ways to compute this classification at high speed. Although better sequential algorithms might reduce the average computation time actually used [17], there is no hope of improving the computation speed by orders of magnitude. Therefore, a hardware solution is called for.

A simple approach, such as building a 'combine box' and a primitive 'classify box' out of MSI TTL parts, and attaching them to a general-purpose host computer, does not work. A careful analysis (Peck J., private communication) shows that such boxes will be too expensive and will not provide great speed-up compared to what can be achieved by assembly programming a VAX 11/780. The main problem is that most of the time is spent transferring data between the boxes and the host computer.

After studying the problem it became evident that the only way to speed up the computation by a large factor is to exploit the inherent parallelism in the problem.

Since CSC computation is made of two quite different parts, namely curve primitive classification and combine, it is natural to separate the two. Curve primitive classification can be done in parallel by computing the classification of a single curve against all the primitive solids at once. The combine computation, on the other hand, cannot all be done in parallel. The combine step at each node of the CSG tree depends on the results of the combine steps at the left and right subtrees. However, combine steps at the same level of the tree can be done in parallel. Moreover, the combine computation can be pipelined.

The task at hand is to develop an architecture that will exploit the parallel nature of the problem to the fullest extent. Care should be taken to avoid communication bottlenecks. An initial study by Brown [20] exposed several difficulties:

(1) The functional units of any special-purpose hardware must communicate at a high rate. Connecting processors to a bus almost certainly will result in large transmission delays.

(2) The intermediate results at each combine processor can vary in size. In the worst case there could be as many line segments as there are primitives. It will not be practical to provide each combine processor with enough buffer space to store all intermediate results.

(3) The combine processors must be connected as a binary tree that is isomorphic to the CSG tree. One needs somehow to load this tree into the processors.

(4) Since the CSG trees of different solids can be very different, one needs a scheme that will deal with all binary trees with no more than N leaves.

Our proposed architecture solves the above problems. The main idea is to construct a hardware binary tree of processors that mirrors the CSG tree

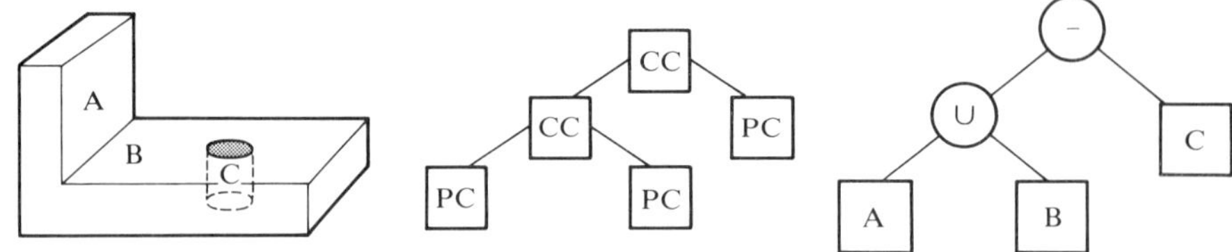

Figure 27.4
CSG solids and classification hardware.
(a) The object.
(b) The hardware.
(c) The CSG tree.

representing the solid. The leaves of the tree are primitive classifiers. The internal nodes of the tree are combine processors (see Figure 27.4). Each primitive classifier is loaded with the primitive and the curve (or curve family). Each combine processor is loaded with the appropriate set operator. All the primitive processors work in parallel, supplying line segments to the combine processors. The combine processors form a big pipeline shaped as a binary tree. Each processor receives a stream of line segments from its sons and passes a stream of line segments to its parent processor.

Each combine processor has a very small buffer (two words) for storing line segments. A simple handshake protocol (ready-to-send, send) is used between processors in order to coordinate the data transfer. If a processor cannot transmit its result to its parent or if its sons are not ready to produce a line segment for it, the processor will wait until the jam clears. The combine processors are arranged as a $\log_2 N \times N$ grid of processors. Each processor receives its inputs from below and from its right, and sends its output up and left. The array is used to embed any binary tree with N leaves (see Section 27.2.2). The primitive classifiers are connected to the bottom of the combine array. Each primitive classifier is connected to a single combine processor. In addition, all the primitive classifiers are connected to a system bus. More details about the architecture and the processors are given in Section 27.2.

27.2 The CSC machine

27.2.1 Restrictions and simplifications

When designing a special-purpose architecture, one needs to pay close attention to the simplifications one has to make, in order to achieve the desired goals. One requirement is a good balance between generality and utility on one hand, and performance, cost and design effort on the other. In the current case, we decided to make the following restrictions:

- No neighborhood information is going to be computed. All line segments are either inside or outside the solid. This simplification avoids some of the delicate issues in neighborhood computation and considerably simplifies the combine processors.
- While we discuss a more general system, we are going to concentrate only on straight line primitive classification.
- The classification machine uses fixed-point arithmetic rather than floating-point. This results in much simpler primitive classifiers and combine processors, with higher throughput.

- The constraints imposed by VLSI technology and cost considerations, such as the need of low chip count, the requirement of high degree of regularity, few custom chip types and limited number of pins per package led us to conclude that bit serial implementation is the only feasible route. While a full word-parallel CSC machine could be built, at the present time such a machine will be too expensive. Therefore we concentrate on a bit-serial design.

27.2.2 The main idea

The main idea behind the CSC machine is to build a tree of processors that mirrors the CSG tree representing the solid being classified. The binary tree has two types of processors: Primitive Classifiers (PCs) at the leaves of the tree, and Classification Combine processors (CCs) at the internal nodes of the tree. (See Figure 27.4.)

The PC's task is to compute the intersection of the curve (line) with the primitive solids. Each PC computes the intersection of a curve with a given solid. The computation of each PC is independent of the computation at other PCs, therefore they all work in parallel. More details about the PCs are given in Section 27.3.

The CCs compute the set operations (union, intersection or difference) on streams of interval segments. The CCs are arranged as a binary tree. Each CC receives, from its son processors, a stream of interval segments. It computes a set operation on the intervals, and sends a list of intervals to its parent processor. The CSC results come out of the root processor. More details about the CC are given in Section 27.4.

27.2.3 The embedding of binary trees

When designing a classification machine, one is immediately confronted with the question of how to interconnect the combine processors. One needs to interconnect the combine processors in such a way that it will be possible to embed in the network of processors any binary tree of processors with N leaves. Since each combine processor is small and many of them could be integrated on a single chip, one can afford to use more than N of them to embed a binary tree with N leaves. On the other hand, it is important to use all the primitive classifiers, since each of them is a large processor. Moreover, it is important to use a simple interconnection scheme in order to take the best advantage of VLSI technology.

Building a complete binary tree out of the processors is not very useful. Most CSG trees are not complete or even well balanced. Many of them tend to be highly unbalanced, almost linear. In the worst case, a complete tree with N leaves can only embed a linear tree (most unbalanced) of size $\log N$.

Unfortunately, it is impossible (in general) to balance CSG trees. This is due to the asymmetric nature of the difference operator. Therefore, what is needed is an interconnection scheme that will enable one to embed any given binary tree.

The problem of tree embedding in a grid has been studied before. A result due to Valiant [21] states that any binary tree with N leaves can be embedded in a rectangular grid with $O(N)$ processors in it. Valiant's result, however, is not very satisfactory since the leaves of the binary tree can be anywhere in the grid. If one requires all the leaves of the tree to be on the edge of the rectangular grid, O(N) processors are not enough.

It was shown by Brent and Kung [22] that if one insists that all the leaves of the binary tree will be on the boundary of the grid, it takes a grid of size O($N \log N$) to embed a binary tree with N leaves.

We have found that a $(1 + \log_2 N) \times N$ grid can be used to embed any binary tree with N leaves. Our solution is as follows: first the tree is made right heavy.

> *A binary tree is right heavy if the number of nodes in each right subtree is greater or equal to the number of nodes of the corresponding left subtree.*

Clearly each binary tree can be made to be right heavy by interchanging some of its left and right subtrees. In order to make a CSG tree right heavy, one introduces two difference operators: the regular difference operator, $-$, and the reversed difference operator, $*-$. $A *- B$ is defined to be $B - A$. If the left and right subtrees of a difference operator, $-$, are interchanged, the operator, $-$, is changed to $*-$. With the other operators $\cup$ and $\cap$ there is no difficulty since they are symmetric.

A right-heavy binary tree with N leaves can be embedded into a $(1 + \log_2 N) \times N$ grid as follows. The root is in the upper-left corner. The leaves are at the bottom edge. Left links of the tree point downward on the grid and the right links point to the right. The tree is embedded by traversing the tree in preorder. If a leaf is encountered before the bottom of the grid is reached, the last link is extended to the bottom. Each right link is extended according to the following rule: let K be the number of leaves that are before the current node (in prefix order). The right link is extended so that the node is in Column $K + 1$. (See Figure 27.5.)

It is easy to see that the above procedure is a constructive embedding for any binary tree with N leaves in a $(1 + \log_2 N) \times N$ grid.

The embedding is attractive for the following reasons:

- All leaves are at the bottom.
- All the internal processors are the same and therefore only two kinds of chips have to be designed.
- The interconnections to the outside grow slowly (like $\sqrt{M}$) as the number of processors per chip grow. Only the processors that are on the perimeter of the grid have to be connected to the outside. Therefore, as technology advances, the number of processors that could be integrated on a single chip can grow with only moderate increases in the number of pins required.
- It is easy to embed smaller trees. Moreover, it is simple to embed more than one tree at a time if the total number of leaves does not exceed N.

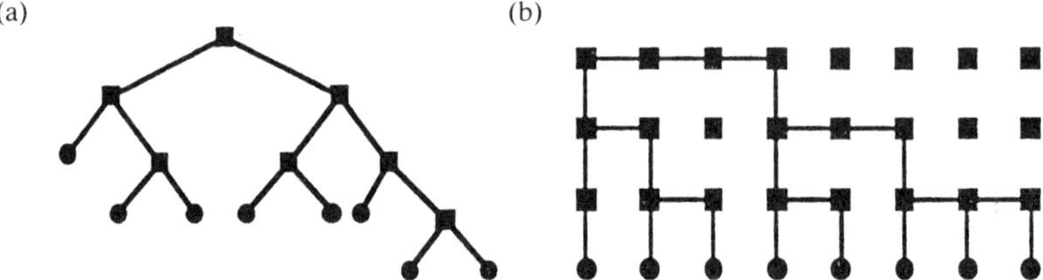

Figure 27.5
The embedding of a binary tree in a grid.
(a) Right-heavy tree.
(b) Embedding in a grid.

27.2.4 The ray-casting machine

The ray-casting machine is made of an array of $(1 + \log_2 N) \times N$ processors. There are two kinds of processors: PCs and CCs. The bottom row of the array is made of N PCs. Above it is a $\log_2 N \times N$ array of CCs. Each processor is a bit-serial special-purpose computer. The processors communicate bit-serially via three-bit-wide connections. Section 27.3 describes the PC, Section 27.4 describes the CC and Section 27.5 describes the whole system.

27.3 The primitive classifier

In order to compute line-primitive classification (that is, the intersections of lines with primitive objects), one needs to solve polynomial equations. The line is given by a parametric representation, that is, $P(t) = (X(t), Y(t), Z(t))$ is a vector-valued function of the parameter t. The primitives are given as a set of inequalities. For example, a cylinder is given by:

$$\begin{aligned} X^2 + Y^2 &\leqslant 1 \\ Z &\geqslant 0 \\ Z &\leqslant 1 \end{aligned} \tag{27.1}$$

One can simplify the computation by assuming that the primitives are linear or quadratic halfspaces. In that case, only a single quadratic inequality describes the primitive. Substituting the parametric representation of the line into the inequality results in an equation. The roots of this equation are the parametric values of the end points of the line intersecting the primitive.

In the mechanical CAD domain, all the primitives are described by polynomial inequalities. With the exception of the torus, all the polynomials are of degree two and one. Therefore the equations are either quadratic or linear (excluding the torus).

Line-primitive classification can be done at very high speed if it is done incrementally. The idea is not to compute the classification of one line but to classify an array of parallel lines. Most of the computation can be done once for the whole array as a preprocessing step. The incremental amount of computation needed for each line is small (four additions, one subtraction and one square root). The incremental algorithm is described in Section 27.3.2.

It is possible to design a pipelined bit-serial line classifier with a relatively small amount of hardware. There are two main restrictions. The first is that the computation will be done on a family of equally spaced parallel lines. The second restriction is that the primitive objects are restricted to be only linear halfspaces and quadratic halfspaces, that is, balls, cones, cylinders and so on, and any linear transformation of the above halfspaces. This does not mean that other primitives (say, torus) could not be used. However, the classification of lines against more complicated objects will have to be precomputed by the general-purpose host computer. This will result in reduced performance. Luckily, with the exception of the torus, the primitives usually used are all either linear or quadratic.

If one is willing to accept these limitations, a bit-serial classifier can be built with only one bit-serial square-root unit and some additional bit-serial adders. The algorithms used and the machine architecture are described in the following sections.

27.3.1 Incremental algorithms for classifying parallel lines

The main idea behind the incremental classification of a family of lines is as follows: one constructs a two-parameter family of straight lines $P(h, t)$. For each fixed value of h, say h_0, $P(h_0, t)$ is a straight line. By varying h one can construct a collection of lines. If:

$$P(h, t) = (a_0 t + a_1 h + x_0, b_0 t + b_1 h + y_0, c_0 t + c_1 h + z_0)$$

then we have a set of parallel lines. In order to classify the line against a primitive halfspace, say a unit cylinder, $x^2 + y^2 = 1$, one has to solve:

$$(a_0 t + a_1 h + x_0)^2 + (b_0 + b_1 h + y_0)^2 - 1 = 0$$

or:

$$A(h)t^2 + B(h)t + C(h) = 0$$

where $A(h)$, $B(h)$ and $C(h)$ are polynomials in the parameter h. It is not hard to show that for all quadratic halfspaces (balls, cones, cylinders and so on) the following is true:

(1) $A(h)$ is independent of h; that is, $A(t) \equiv$ constant.

(2) $B(h)$ is a polynomial of degree one in h.

(3) $C(h)$ is a polynomial of degree two in h.

The solutions of the quadratic equation are:

$$t_{1,2} = \frac{B}{2A} \pm \sqrt{\left(\frac{B}{2A}\right)^2 - \frac{C}{A}}$$

The discriminant:

$$D = \left(\frac{B}{2A}\right)^2 - \frac{C}{A}$$

is a second degree polynomial in h. To compute $t_{1,2}(h)$, one needs to compute the values of two polynomials $B(h) / 2A$ and $D(h)$, for a given value of h. It is well known [23–4] that if one needs to compute the value of an Nth-degree polynomial over a set of equally spaced points, one can use a difference table to compute the polynomial values using only N additions per value. For example, let $h_i = h_0 + i \times \delta h$ and let $P(h)$ be a second degree polynomial. Define:

$$P_i = P(h_i), \Delta P_i = P_i - P_{i-1} \text{ and } \Delta^2 P_i = \Delta P_{i+1} - \Delta P_i$$

Then:

(1) $\Delta^2 P_i$ is a constant independent of i.

(2) $\Delta P_{i+1} = \Delta P_i + \Delta^2 P_i$

(3) $P_{i+1} = P_i + \Delta P_{i+1}$

So if P_0, ΔP_0 and $\Delta^2 P_0$ are known, then P_i, $i = 1, 2, \ldots$ can be computed with only two additions per point using the recurrence relations shown above.

Therefore, $D(h_i)$ can be evaluated using two additions per point and $B(h_i) / 2A$ can be computed using only one addition per point. The set of parallel lines $P(h_i, t)$, $i = 0, 1, 2, \ldots$ can be classified against any quadratic halfspace using four additions, one subtraction and one square root operation per line.

The incremental algorithms for classifying parallel lines can be extended to work on a regular lattice of parallel lines, not only lines that lie in a single plane. Let $P(s, h; t)$ be defined as:

$$P(s, h; t) = (x_0 + a_2 s + a_1 h + a_0 t,\ y_0 + b_2 s + b_1 h + b_0 t,\\ z_0 + c_2 s + c_1 h + c_0 t)$$

and:

$$P_{i,j}(t) = P(s_i, h_j; t)$$

where $s_i = s_0 + i \times \Delta s$, $i = 0, 1, 2, \ldots$ and $h_j = h_0 + j \times \Delta h$, $j = 0, 1, 2, \ldots$

The collection of lines $P_{i,j}(t)$ form a regular lattice of parallel lines in space. For a fixed i, $P_{i,j}(t)$, $j = 0, \ldots N$, are classified by the incremental algorithm described above. The problem is how to start the computation for the next index i. As it turns out, this computation can be done incrementally as well. The discriminant:

$$D(s, h) = \left(\frac{B(h)}{2A}\right)^2 - \frac{C(h)}{A}$$

is a second degree polynomial in h where the coefficients are functions of s; $D(s, h) = a(s)h^2 + b(s)h + c(s)$. As before, it is not hard to show that $a(s)$ is a constant, $b(s)$ is a polynomial of degree one in s, and $c(s)$ is a polynomial of degree two.

Now, in order to be able to compute the values of the polynomial $D(s_{i+1}, h_j)$, $j = 0, 1, 2, \ldots$, one needs the zero, first and second differences of the polynomial $D(s_{i+1}, h)$ at h_0. The second difference is constant since $a(s)$ is a constant. The first difference as a function of s is a first degree polynomial and therefore can be computed incrementally from the previous first difference by one addition. The zero order difference, that is, the value of $D(s, h)$, is a second degree polynomial in s. Therefore the value of $D(s_{i+1}; h_0)$ can be computed from the difference table of $D(s_i, h_0)$ using only two additions. Therefore, in order to compute the coefficients of the difference table for $D(s_{i+1}; h)$ at h_0 from the difference table of $D(s_i; h)$ at h_0, one needs three additions. Similarly, one addition will be necessary for computing the difference table for $b(s_{i+1}; h)$ from the table for $b(s_i; h)$.

In conclusion, we have shown that four additions, one subtraction and one square root operation are needed for computing incrementally all parallel line classification against quadratic halfspaces. Four more additions are needed to make the incremental computation possible, not only for lines in a single plane, but for a regular lattice of parallel lines.

27.3.2 Primitive classifier architecture

The PC is a bit-serial pipelined processor, hard-wired to compute line-primitive intersections incrementally. The PC can compute the intersections of lines with linear and quadratic halfspaces. In addition, the PC can receive data from the host computer and pass it to the CC to which it is connected.

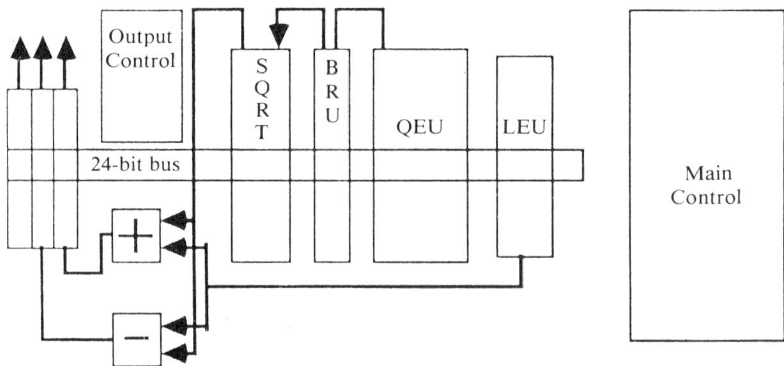

Figure 27.6
Primitive classifier block diagram.

The PC is made of a pipelined bit-serial data path, a main controller and an output section. The output section has an output buffer and an output controller. The data path is made of several units. A Quadratic polynomial Evaluation Unit (QEU), Linear polynomial Evaluation Unit (LEU), a bit-serial Square-Root unit (SQRT), a bit reverse unit, a bit-serial adder and a bit-serial subtractor (see Figure 27.6). The data flow is from the QEU to the bit reverse unit, then to the SQRT unit. From the SQRT unit it flows to the adder and subtractor. The LEU works in parallel with the QEU. The output from the LEU is also fed into the adder and subtractor.

The QEU is made of two parts. The main unit is made of two bit-serial adders adding two bits at a time and three registers. This unit is used to evaluate the quadratic polynomial $D(h)$. The second unit of the QEU is the coefficient update unit. This unit is used to update the values of the registers of the main unit when going from one row of lines to the next. See Section 27.3.2 for an explanation. Figure 27.7 illustrates the QEU. The LEU is similar to the QEU, only simpler. Its bit-serial adders add only one bit at a time.

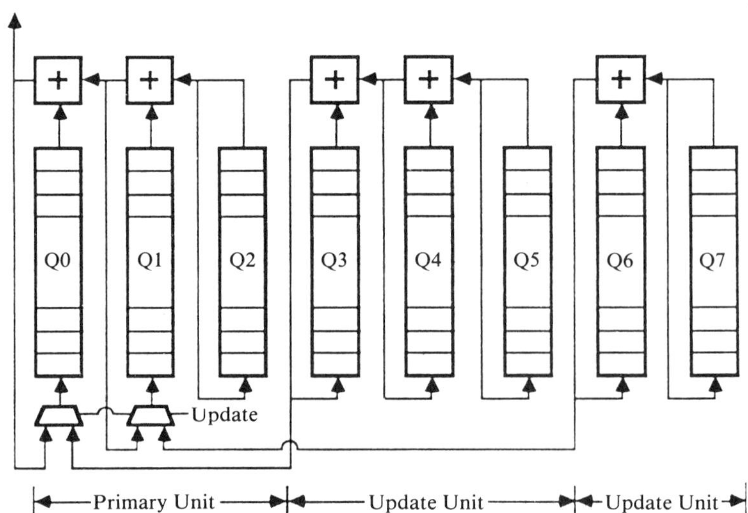

Figure 27.7
The quadratic polynomial evaluation unit.

The square root unit computes the integer square root of 48 bit numbers. The unit design is an adaptation of a well-known array square root design [25–6]. The unit is made of a controlled adder subtractor unit and two registers, the Q register and the R register. The Q register holds the current result and the R register holds the remainder. The controlled adder subtractor is implemented with a static Manchester chain adder with carry skip lookahead circuitry (see Figures 27.8 and 27.9).

All the PC registers, including the output buffer and mode register, are connected by a bus. Each register has a unique address and can be accessed from the outside by reading or writing into its address. The programming of the PC is done by the host computer. The host computer precomputes the divided differences and stores them in the PC registers. It also activates the PC by writing into a special address. The host can also send data directly to the CC array by loading it into the output buffer. This feature enables one to classify lines against primitives that the PC cannot do (say a torus) and also enables one to classify lines with CSG solids that cannot fit at once into the ray-casting machine. Larger solids could be broken down and classified using several passes. For testing purposes, the register content can be read by the host computer.

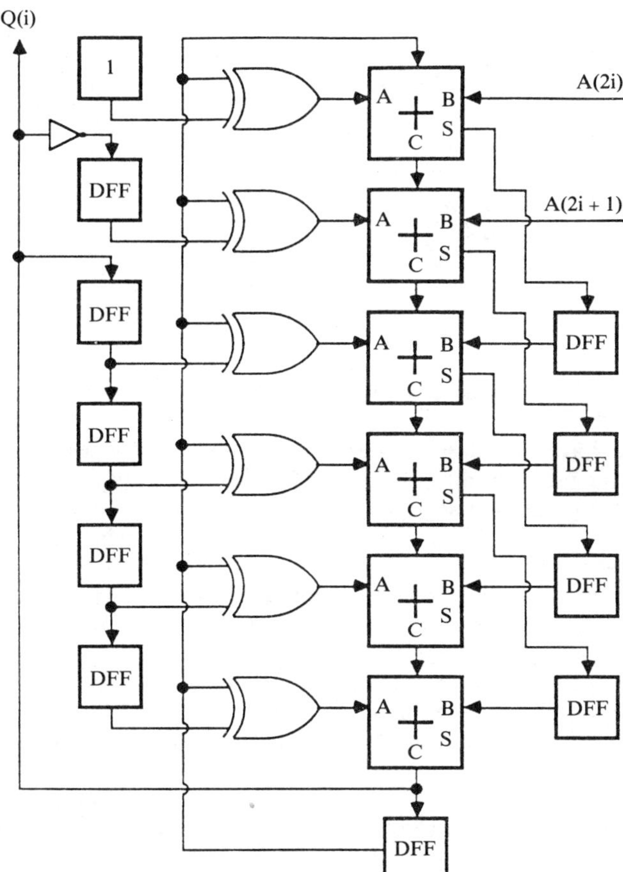

Figure 27.8
A bit-serial square root unit.

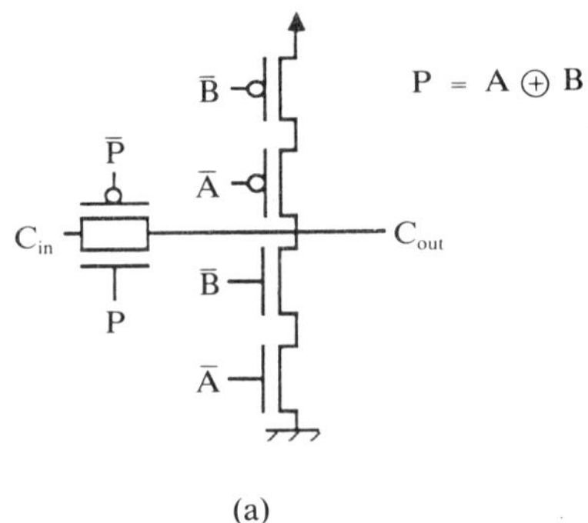

(a)

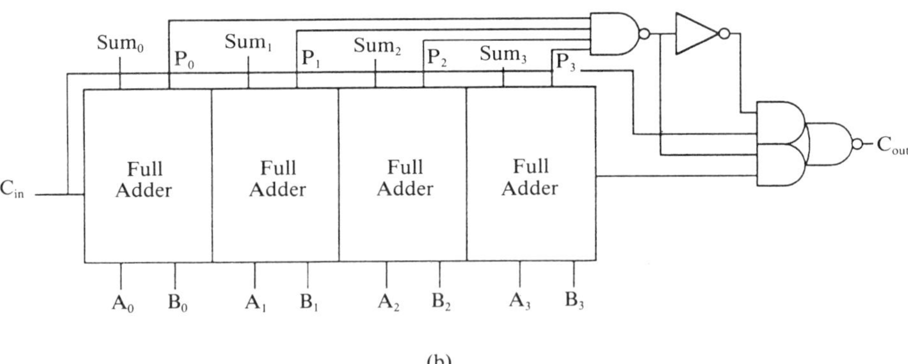

(b)

Figure 27.9
Static Manchester adder with carry skip.
(a) Static Manchester Carry.
(b) Carry Skip Adder.

27.4 The classification-combine processor

Once the lines have been classified against the primitives, the next step is to combine the resultant line segment sets as described in Section 27.1.3. Unlike line-primitive classification, the combine steps are quite simple and domain independent. As was pointed out in Section 27.1.4, the line segments can be given in terms of the parameter, t, used to parametrize the line. The combine steps are then set operations (union intersection or difference) on intervals of this independent parameter t.

The main idea behind the combine machine is to build a binary tree of combine processors. This binary tree will be exactly the same binary tree of operators describing the solid (see Figure 27.4). Each processor in the tree will correspond to a single set operator in the CSG tree. It will receive two streams of interval segments as input and it will compute the appropriate set operation on these segments. Each combine processor will accept streams of line segments from its sons and will send a stream of line segments to its parent processor. As indicated in Figure 27.5, links in the array of processors may need to be extended to the right or downward. Therefore each processor must not only do set operations on the incoming intervals, but also be able to pass the information, from the right or below, to its parent. In addition, each processor can load a new instruction. (See Section 27.5.3.)

As was explained in Section 27.2, the combine processors are arranged as a $\log_2 N \times N$ array. Each bit-serial combine processor receives its inputs from its neighbors at the right and from below. It passes its output to one of its neighbors above or to the left. The communication is bit-serial, three bits at a time; a bit stream for each end-point of the line segments, and a bit stream for tags. (See Section 27.4.2 for a discussion on tags.)

27.4.1 Classification combine architecture

The classification combiner (CC) is a very simple bit-serial pipelined processor. The CC must perform set operations on its input line segments. All of the necessary set operations can be performed in bit-serial fashion using only minimum and maximum functions.

In our current design, each CC processor consists of six parts (see Figure 27.10). There are three small finite state machines, two input controllers and one output controller. There is also a larger main controller. In addition, each CC has a small data path where the actual set operations are performed, and two registers. One register is used to store the intermediate results and one is used to buffer the possible output line segment. The main controller keeps the global state of the machine, controlling the combining section and the input/output controllers. The input and output controllers communicate with their neighbors, transferring data and instructions. The communication is fully synchronous using a full handshake protocol which will be described in Section 27.5. The handshake protocol is necessary because input may be needed from below only, from the right only, or from both and because a set of input may result in zero, one or two output line segments.

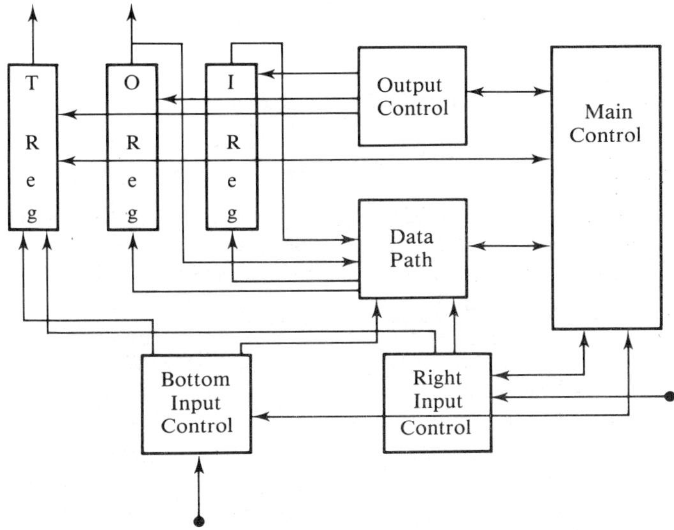

Figure 27.10
Combine processor block diagram.

The actual computation is done in the combine section by passing the data, in bit-serial fashion, through a network of five min-max function blocks. The computation is controlled by two multiplexors (MUX), one in front of the min-max network and one after it. The inputs to the input MUX come from the input controllers, the intermediate register and the output register. This MUX selects the two line segments to be input to the min-max network from among the three possible inputs. The output from the min-max network consists of the two input line segments, as well as the three minimum and maximum functions of their endpoints. These 10 bit streams then pass through a second MUX. This MUX selects the four endpoints to be used for the input to the two register pairs, the intermediate and the output registers.

27.4.2 Adding tags to rays

Discussions with potential users of the ray-casting machine showed the need for tagging the rays. Real objects quite often are made of many different materials. On many occasions it is important to be able to 'color' the ray by the type of material it passes through. Also, it is very useful to know at each point on the surface, which primitive determined the local shape of the surface.

In general, both requirements cannot be satisfied simultaneously by a simple tag calculation. However, after careful analysis, we were able to design a simple tag calculus that achieved the desired results. For objects that are made of a union of objects with different materials that do not intersect, the tag calculus will produce correct results. If one tags each primitive with a different tag, then the tag calculations will produce the correct tag for the entry point, that is, the first point of the first intersection segment. All that is done by a single tag algorithm.

Tags are implemented by adding one bit to each I/O port on the CC, and by adding four internal 16-bit registers. Two registers are used to hold the tags from the bottom and right ports, and two registers are used as shadow registers. In addition, a small amount of control circuitry was added to the main controller to decide which tag to output to the next stage of the pipeline.

27.5 The ray-casting system

27.5.1 System architecture

The ray-casting system is made of a host computer and the array. The machine is a $(1 + \log_2 N) \times N$ array of processors. The bottom row of the array is made of N PCs. Above it is a $\log_2 N \times N$ array of CC processors. Each CC has two input ports and one output port. The input ports are connected to the bottom and right neighbors. The output port is connected to both the top and left neighbors. Each input and output connection is three bits wide. See Figure 27.11.

Each PC has a three-bit-wide output port. That output port is connected to the bottom input port of the CC directly above. In addition, each PC is connected to a local system bus. All the registers of the PC are accessible from the local bus. Each register is given a unique bus address. The local bus is connected via an interface unit to the host main system bus. The interface unit between the local bus and the system

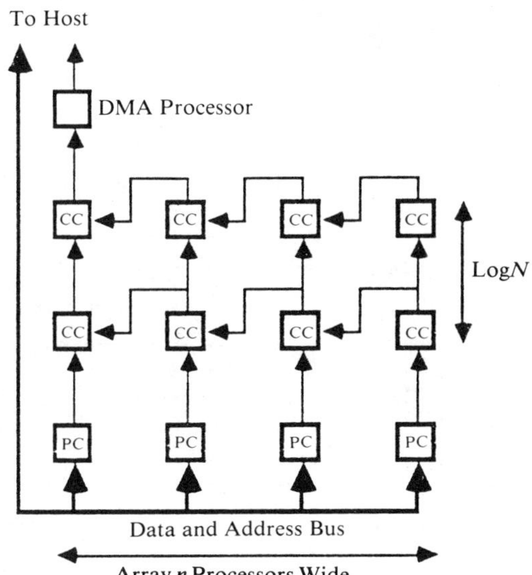

Figure 27.11 Array of combine machines.

bus enables the host computer to write directly into each PC register. Thus the host computer can directly control the operation of each PC.

The output of the array comes out of the output port of the top-left-most CC. The output from the ray-casting machine is transferred to the host memory by a DMA interface unit. Figure 27.12 is a block diagram of the ray-casting system.

27.5.2 System interface

The ray-casting machine interfaces with the host computer via two bus interface devices, the local bus interface unit and the DMA unit.

Local bus interface

The first interface is an interface between the host bus and the local ray-casting machine bus. The local bus (board-level bus) has 24-bit data and 10-bit address lines.

Each PC is driven by the host computer via the local bus. The PC is programmed by writing onto its registers. Each register is given a unique address and can be read and written to by the host computer. (Reading the registers is only used for testing.)

The DONE line is used to interrupt the host computer to signal that a PC has completed its computation.

The interface unit translates the system bus addresses into chip addresses and drives the ray-casting chips. It also generates host interrupts that tell the host which PC is idle. The host is then able to inquire as to the status of the idle PC. For the most part, the interface makes the ray-casting machine look like memory to the

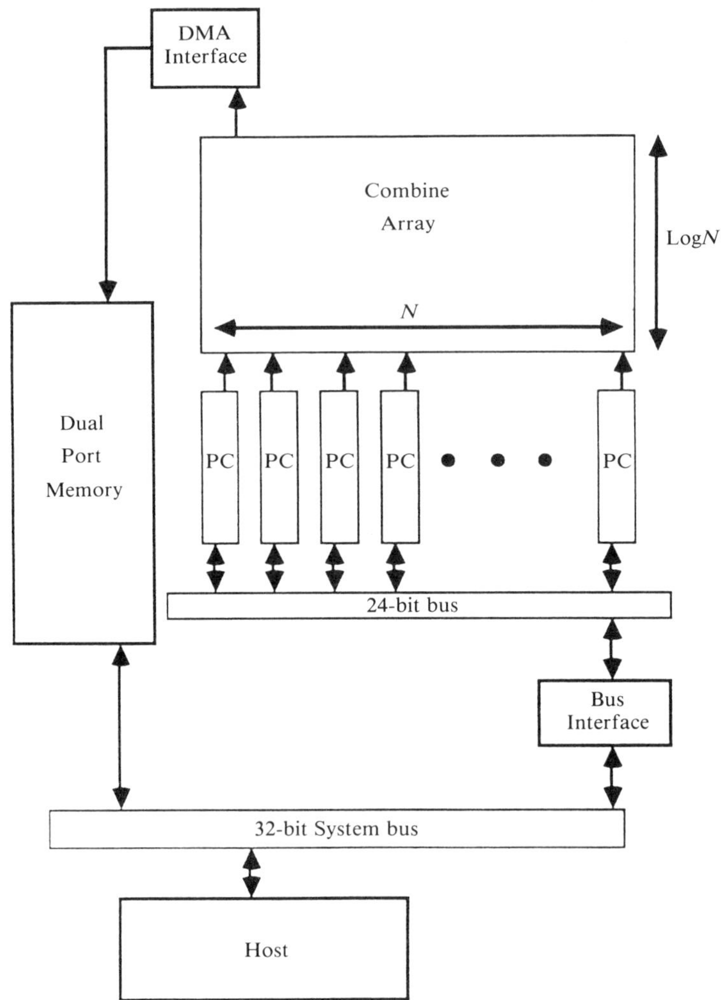

Figure 27.12
The ray-casting machine block diagram.

host. The only exception is that interrupts are generated to notify the host when a PC is idle.

The DMA interface unit

The output from the ray-casting machine comes out of the upper-left corner of the CC array. The output is bit-serial with three bits at a time. The same handshake protocol that is used internally between the CC machines is used between the CC array and the DMA interface device.

The DMA device task is to receive the data from the ray-casting machine and store that data in the host memory. The DMA device receives from the host an

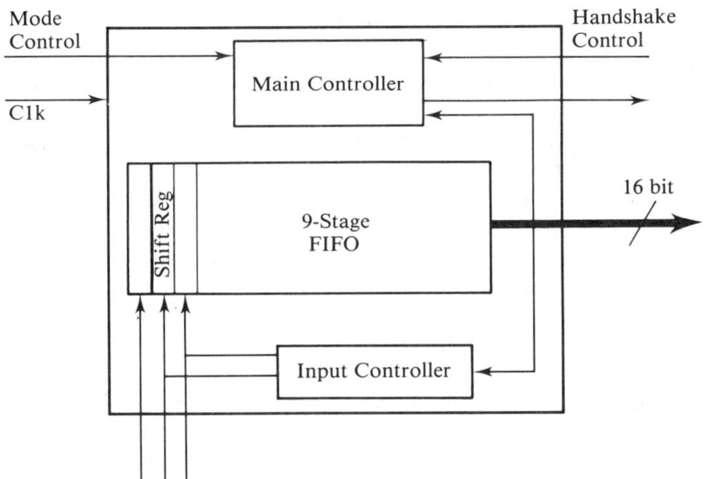

Figure 27.13
The DMA interface unit.

address, buffer size, the number of lines to classify and a start signal. It then proceeds to transfer the output of the ray-casting machine into the buffer. The DMA device interrupts the host when the buffer is full or if the transfer was complete. It then waits for a new address, buffer size and a start command to resume the transfer.

Each line classified against a solid can result in zero or more interval segments. Each interval segment is represented by two 16-bit integers (fixed-point numbers). The end of each line is represented by 16-bit words with all the bits on.

In addition to the normal mode, the DMA interface device will transfer only one 16-bit number per ray, corresponding to the first entry point of the ray to the solid. Figure 27.13 shows the DMA interface unit.

27.5.3 Programming the ray-casting machine

The ray-casting machine is programmed by the host computer. The host stores the recurrence coefficients in the data path registers of each PC. There is also a mode register that tells the PC which output of the data path to take, the leading edge, the trailing edge or both. In addition, the PC could be used to transfer data from the host to the CC array above intact. This is done by the host loading the output register of the PC and then loading the mode register by a transfer command.

The CC array is loaded with commands bit serially. An instruction packet is passed to the CC array. The command packet has instructions for all the CCs in the column. Each CC strips three bits out of the front of the command packet and passes the rest to its top neighbor. The command packet is loaded into the CC array from the PC, using the same protocol used to load data, only the header information differs.

27.5.4 Interprocessor communication

The ray-casting machine is made of synchronous machines. All the machines, the PCs and the CCs work with the same master clock. To synchronize data transfer, all the machines follow a full handshake protocol. Two of the wires that are used for data transfer between processors are used for the handshake protocol. As part of the protocol, two bits of header information are passed. The bits tell each CC if the coming data is an interval segment, a command packet, or if it is end-of-line (EOL) signal. When an EOL signal is passed no data is transferred.

27.6 Prototype implementation

We have designed and implemented a prototype ray-casting machine. The prototype machine is implemented as a printed circuit board set inside a commercial frame buffer (the ADAGE-3000 frame buffer). A MicroVAX is used to control the frame buffer and interface to the user. The frame buffer has a bit-slice bipolar processor that serves as the host to the ray-casting machine. The MicroVAX can also access the ray-casting machine registers. The ray-casting machine bus is part of the ADAGE-3000 system bus. All the PC registers can be accessed via the frame buffer bus. The output of the ray-casting machine is stored in a dual-ported memory

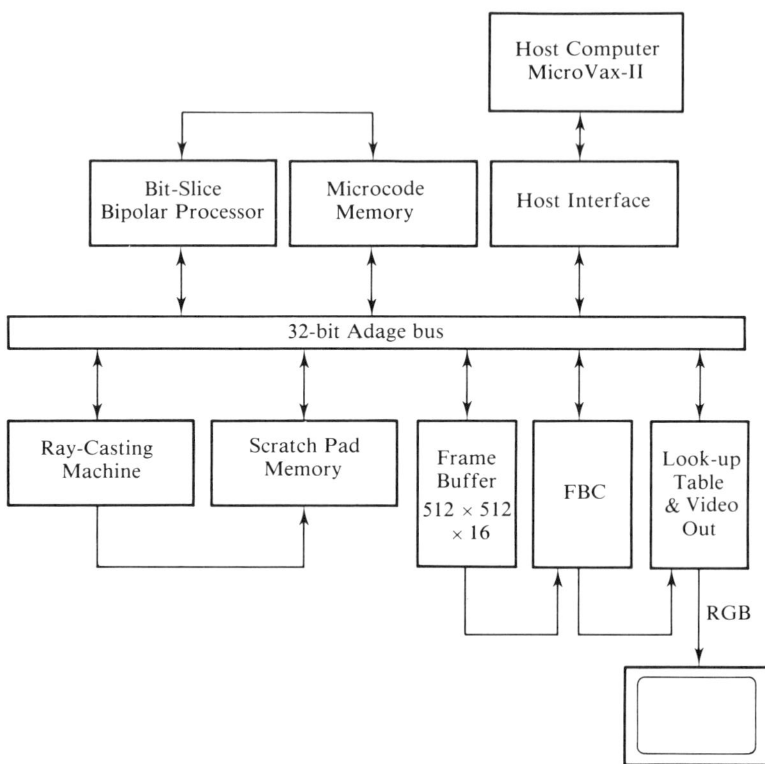

Figure 27.14
The Ray-Casting prototype system.

(a)
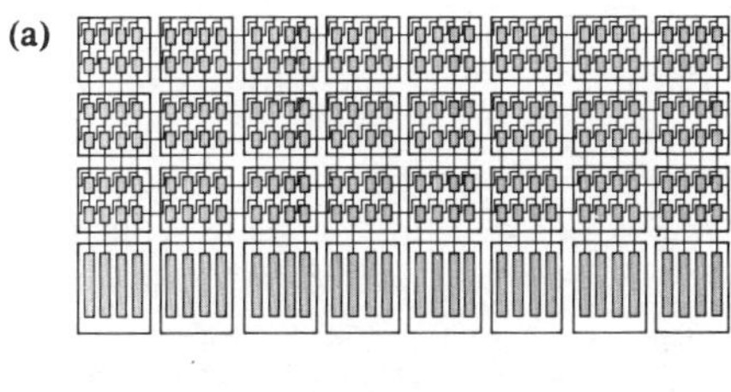

(b)
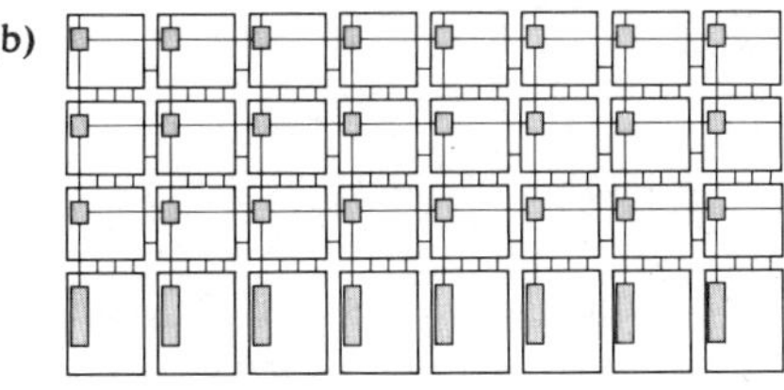

Figure 27.15
8 PCs and 32 PCs on a board.
(a) Ray-Casting system with 32 PCs.
(b) Ray-Casting system with 8 PCs.

module that is a standard option to the frame buffer system. The output of the DMA interface unit goes through the second port and does not interfere with the bus traffic. The output of the ray-casting machine is processed by the bipolar processor and then it is displayed by storing it in the frame buffer memory (see Figure 27.14).

The ray-casting machine is implemented as a single-card system that could be expanded up to an eight-card system. On each board there are eight PC chips and four rows of CC chips. The system is designed to accommodate up to four PCs inside each PC chip and up to 2 × 4 arrays of CCs inside each CC chip. Therefore, the smallest system has eight PCs and the largest has up to 256 PCs. Figure 27.15 shows how the system was designed to accommodate chips of different complexity.

We have designed three custom chip types: the PC, the CC and a DMA interface chip [27]. The CC chips were designed using our standard cell-based silicon compiler [28–9], only the registers were laid by hand. The PC data path was done with hand layout, and the control was done with standard cells. The DMA interface was done with standard cells. The PC and CC chips are housed in 84-pin grid array and the DMA interface chip is a 40-pin DIP. All chips were designed in 3μ CMOS. The chips are designed to run at 5 MHz, the speed of the frame buffer.

We have fabricated a 2 × 3 array of CCs and we are now in the process of designing four PCs on a chip and a 2 × 4 array of CCs. A 2μ CMOS technology is being used for these designs.

Work on a full-scale machine has started. We expect the full-scale machine to have 1024–4096 PCs and to run at 40 MHz. We plan to use 1μ CMOS technology for the custom ICs in the full-scale machine.

Acknowledgments

The ray-casting prototype is the product of many people. Kenneth Bartch designed the basic CC and the DMA interface unit. Jon Allingham added tags to the CC design. Mike H. Tate designed the PC. Tom Lyerley designed the printed circuit board. Many other people contributed to the work: Jack Briner, Wayne D. Dettloff, Tom Krakow, Kris Kozminski, Ricardo D. Pantazis, Ravi Subrahamian, Peter Suares, Dale Wimpler and Kathy E. Yount all contributed to the system design effort. The Ray-Casting prototype was developed in cooperation with The Microelectronics System Laboratory at UNC. The authors wish to thank H.B. Voelcker and A.A.G. Requicha for introducing them to this subject. This work would not have been possible without their help and encouragement. The authors thank Y. Golan for his help with the tree embedding problem. Discussions with Paul R. Stay and Charles M. Kennedy led us to add tags to the basic machine capabilities. This work has been supported in part by the National Science Foundation grant No. ECS–8306655, ECS–8412869 and MIP–8614740, and by the Microelectronics Center of North Carolina.

References

1. Requicha A.A.G. and Voelcker H.B. (1982). Solid Modeling: A Historical Summary and Contemporary Assessment. *IEEE Computer Graphics and Appl.,* **2**(2), 9–24
2. Wesley M.A. (1980). Construction and use of geometric models. In *Computer Aided Design* (Encarnacao J., ed.), pp. 79–136. New York: Springer-Verlag
3. Tilove R.B. and Requicha A.A.G. (1980). Closure of boolean operations on geometric entities. *Computer Aided Design,* **12**(5), 219–20
4. Requicha A.A.G. (1980). Representation for rigid solids: theory, methods, and systems. *ACM Computing Surveys,* **12**(4), 437–64
5. Requicha A.A.G. (1980). Representations of rigid solid objects. In *Computer Aided Design* (Encarnacao J., ed.), pp. 2–78. New York: Springer-Verlag
6. Boyse J.W. (1978). *Preliminary Design for a Geometric Modeller.* Research Pub. GMR–2768, Computer Science Department, General Motors Research Laboratories, Warren MI
7. Boyse J.W. and Gilchrist J.E. (1982). GMSolid: interactive modeling for design and analysis of solids. *IEEE Computer Graphics and Applications,* **2**(2), 27–40
8. Voelcker H.B., Requicha A.A.G., Hartquist E.E. *et al.* (1978). The PADL-1.0/2 System for Defining and Displaying Solid Objects. *Computer Graphics,* **12**(3), 257–63
9. Brown C.M. (1982). PADL-2: A Technical Summary. *IEEE Computer Graphics and Applications,* **2**(2), 69–84
10. Brown C.M. and Voelcker H.B. (1979). The PADL-2 Project. In *Proc. Seventh NSF Conf. Production Research and Technology*, F1–F6. Ithaca NY, September 1979
11. Goldstein R.A. and Nagel R. (1971). 3D visual simulation. *Simulation*, **16**(1), 25–31
12. Goldstein R. and Malin L. (1979). 3D modeling with the Synthavision system. In *Proc. First Ann. Conf. Computer Graphics, in CAD/CAM Systems*, pp. 244–7. Cambridge MA, April 1979
13. Tilove R.B. (1980). Set membership classification: a unified approach to geometric intersection problems. *IEEE Trans. Computers,* **C-29**(10), 874–83
14. Newman W.M. and Sproull R.F. (1979). *Principles of Interactive Computer Graphics* 2nd edn. New York: McGraw-Hill
15. Roth S.D. (1982). Ray casting for modeling solids. *Computer Graphics and Image Processing*, 18, 109–44

16. Lee Y.T. and Requicha A.A.G. (1982). Algorithms for computing the volume and other integral properties of solid objects. *Comm. ACM,* **25**(9), 635–50
17. Tilove R.B. (1981). *Exploiting Spatial and Structural Locality in Geometric Modeling*. Tech. Memo No. 38, Production Automation Project, University of Rochester
18. Tilove R.B. (1984). Null-object algorithms for use with CSG representations. *Comm. ACM,* **27**(7), 684–94
19. Knuth D.E. (1979). *TEX and METAFONT New Directions in Typesetting*. Digital Press
20. Brown C.M. (1981). Special purpose computer hardware for mechanical design systems. In *Proc. 1981 National Computer Graphics Assoc. Conf.*, Baltimore MD, June 1981
21. Valiant L.G. (1981). Universality Considerations in VLSI Circuits. *IEEE Trans. on Comp.,* **C-30**(2), 135–40
22. Brent R.P. and Kung H.T. (1980). On the Area of Binary Tree Layouts. *Information Processing Letters*, 11, 46–8
23. Atkinson K.E. (1978). *An Introduction to Numerical Analysis*. New York: John Wiley
24. Cohen D. (1969). *Incremental Methods for Computer Graphics*. Technical Report ESD-TR-69-193, Dept. of Eng. and Appl. Math., Harvard University
25. Hwang K. (1979). *Computer Arithmetic Principles, Architecture, and Design*. New York: Wiley
26. Tate M.H. (1986). *The Design and Engineering of a Custom Integrated Circuit for Primitive Classification*. MCNC Technical Report TR86-11, Department of Electrical Engineering, Duke University
27. Kedem G., Ellis J.L., Bartsch K.E. *et al.* (1986). Custom ICs for the Ray-Casting machine. In *Proc. CICC'86*, pp. 182–4. Rochester NY, May 1986
28. Kedem G., Rose J. and Krakow W. VPNR Users Guide. Unpublished.
29. Kedem G. and Kozminski K. (1986). A standard cell based silicon compiler. In *IEEE 1986 Custom Integrated Circuit Conference*, pp. 120–4
30. Kedem G. and Ellis J.L. (1984). The Ray-Casting machine. In *Proc. ICCD'84*, pp. 533–8. Ray NY, October 1984
31. Kedem G. and Hammond S. (1985). The Point-Classifier: A VLSI processor for displaying complex two dimensional objects. In *Proc. 1985 Chapel Hill Conf. on VLSI*, pp. 377–92. Chapel Hill NC, May 1985
32. Myers W. (1982). An Industrial Perspective on Solid Modeling. *IEEE Computer Graphics and Applications,* **2**(2), 86–97
33. Voelcker H.B. and Hunt W.A. (1981). The role of solid modelling in machining-process modelling and NC verification. In *Proc. 1981 SAE Int. Congress and Exposition*, pp. 1–8. Detroit MI, February 1981
34. Wesley M.A., Lozlano-Perez T., Lieberman L.T., Lavin M.A. and Grossman D.D. (1980). A geometric modelling system for automated mechanical assembly. *IBM J. Res. Dev.,* **24**(1), 64–74

E. Barton

Meiko Scientific Ltd

28 · Data concurrency on the Meiko Computing Surface

The problem of developing distributed graphics applications over a network of INMOS transputers is discussed. The Meiko Computing Surface is proposed as a solution to the problem.

28.1 Introduction

With the advent of devices like the INMOS transputer, the practical barriers to constructing systems with many cooperating processors have largely been eliminated. The founders of Meiko – who were all involved in significant positions at INMOS whilst the transputer was developed, and clearly are in a good position to create reliable, well-engineered equipment and systems software – have delivered almost 100 beta systems since transputers were first shipped in March 1986, demonstrated a 311 processor system at Siggraph in August 1986, and are currently installing a 1000 processor system. Systems software is still evolving. So we speak with some experience.

28.2 Graphics pipeline on the surface

One of our first customers was INMOS itself, who wanted a demonstration vehicle for launching the transputer. To show the power of the new device to a wide audience, it was clearly best to run a graphics program. The task was started in June 1985, by producing an implementation which mapped a conventional graphics pipeline over a large set of processors. This technique involved dividing the transformation, clipping and scanline conversion algorithms into computationally easy stages. The theory is, that if each processor can process its arguments in a very short time, then pipelining can allow all the stages of the algorithm to be overlapped, thus fully utilizing all the processors in the system to display single polygons with a latency equal to that of a single processor, but with a throughput proportional to the number of processors in the system. This technique can only go so far. Once each processor in the pipeline is only performing a single multiply, it becomes hard to see how the function can be further distributed. Secondly, when the time to perform the compute on a subproblem is less than the time taken to receive the operands or transmit the results, then the performance limit becomes the communications bandwidth, and adding extra processors to the system will not increase throughput. The solution was therefore to construct several pipelines in parallel, each targeting independent graphics devices.

Implementing this algorithm took longer to achieve than expected, because debugging a system composed of a large number of processors, in which the only communications medium is the set of point-to-point connections between the processors, is a very hard problem. When a processor in the interior of the system fouls up, it is very hard to detect what is happening if no failure messages can reach the outside world. The only solution was to include error message protocols along with the protocols for passing intermediate results between processors. This extra effort helped, however it did not solve the problem of ensuring that all processors in error could report their condition – a deadlocked processor nearer the periphery of the system could prevent the error messages from escaping. Neither did it address the problem of debugging the protocols themselves, the most common cause of deadlock in a transputer system. The net effects were, firstly, that a substantial period was required to get a first level implementation off the ground before system performance measurements could be taken. Secondly, a hardening resolve to include an orthogonal communications medium in future products resulted in the supervisor bus of the Computing Surface, which allows bi-directional communications between every processor in the system and the local host.

28.2.1 The results

Initial performance measurements were disappointing. Back-of-the-envelope performance estimates had indicated a potential throughput several times in excess of the measured figure, therefore processors in the system were either idle and doing nothing, or busy, but not performing useful compute. Idle processors could be explained by the fact that all of the processors in the pipeline were performing different operations. The throughput of a pipeline is limited by the throughput of the slowest element, therefore full utilization of all the processors may only be achieved when all of the processors are performing identical tasks.

When a pipeline has been formed out of processors doing the many and various tasks which compose graphical transformation and rendering, load balancing becomes nearly impossible. Even assuming a fully balanced pipeline, throughput measured on individual processors in the pipeline was still under par. This meant that the processor was being kept busy all the time, but not a high enough percentage of its activity was devoted to useful compute. Further examination of the organization of processes within each processor was therefore required.

28.3 Granularity and the cost of message passing

A processor operating in an environment of cooperating processors basically needs to perform only two functions: communication and compute. Compute is the function that contributes to solving problems, while communication is only a means to an end (allowing the compute to be distributed). Therefore, compute must be allowed to proceed at all times in order to fully utilize all processors in a system. The transputer gives direct support in the hardware for this function. Once an external communication has been initiated by the processor, it is completely free to continue execution of another process while the link DMA engines get along with the message passing, only stealing single memory cycles from the processor when a complete word of the message is passed between link and store. Given store cycle times of 50 nS (internal RAM) and achievable link bandwidths approaching 1/2 Mb/s, the only impact of message passing via a link once the communication has been initiated, is to steal one memory cycle in 160.

To exploit this feature, communication buffering processes running at high priority must be inserted between the process doing useful compute, and the links. The buffering processes run at high priority to allow them to initiate message passing eagerly in order to make continuous use of the links. Once the link communication is under way, they can only have a minimal impact on available memory bandwidth. Meanwhile, the compute process can continue to solve the task in hand. Provided that the time taken to solve a task exceeds the time taken to receive the operands or transmit the results, as soon as the compute process has finished the current task it can immediately offload its current result and get a new set of operands from the patiently waiting buffering processes.

This works fine in the steady state by ignoring all the startup costs, but what happens if one varies the size of messages? As message sizes approach zero, the linear costs associated with stealing memory bandwidth from the processor reduce correspondingly, however the startup costs remain fixed. Link communications must be initiated and processes must be scheduled as messages are passed between them, therefore these fixed costs begin to dominate as message sizes reduce. Coming back to the graphics pipeline, the messages being passed between processors were often single words. The impact on memory bandwidth for communicating these messages from link to input buffer, input buffer to compute process, compute process to output buffer and output buffer to link was negligible, however, all these processes were frequently being scheduled and rescheduled with its associated cost, so the processor was spending most of its time doing process administration.

What happens if the message size is increased to amortize the startup costs? The time to flow a message through a processor is increased correspondingly, therefore the compute process must be given a more lengthy, and therefore more difficult, task to perform to ensure that the processor spends all its spare time doing useful compute. In the case of the graphics pipeline, this suggested that it might be better to communicate whole polygons at a time between processors, rather than individual coordinates. This clumping up of the data meant that a single processor could now transform, clip and scan-convert a complete polygon, rather than splitting it up piecemeal between a set of hard to balance, but trivial, functions. In addition, all the intermediate working variables which came to hand during the course of a clumped calculation could be retained and used by all stages of the calculation, thereby reducing the need for redundant calculations in different processors.

The implementation was therefore changed so that each processor could perform a substantial step of the standard sequential algorithm. The ratio of compute to communications for an individual processor therefore swung heavily in favour of compute, and a single processor could not keep up with link bandwidth when transforming, clipping and rendering complete polygons. When a processor is compute bound by at least a factor of two, through routeing becomes appropriate. This has the effect of swinging the balance back in favour of communications. In a configuration of n processors, each processor only transforms $1/n$th of the world space polygons and passes the rest through to its neighbour, thus distributing the data, rather than the algorithm, between processors. The topology on the network remained the same. However, now that message sizes were reasonable, startup costs were amortized over relatively long communication and compute times.

28.4 The processor farm

This first attempt at mapping a graphics application over a large collection of processors gave the impression that the first thing that one should do, is try to decide how an algorithm can be replicated over many processors and how to distribute the data, rather than vice versa. Taken to its logical conclusion, this approach suggests that one makes best use of a Computing Surface when its processors engage in no communication at all. Full utilization is guaranteed, and as an added bonus, existing sequential implementations of algorithms do not have to be rewritten. This is not quite as far fetched as it sounds, and results in a style of usage of the system aptly called the **processor farm**.

Consider the case where a large number of batch jobs are queued up on an over-burdened mainframe computer. Jobs may be taken off the batch queue and farmed out to a single processor in the farm, where they run to completion. All the processors are performing independent tasks, therefore no interprocessor communication is required. All processors can be kept busy on individual tasks, therefore full utilization is maintained. An example of the direct relevance of this technique to the computer graphics industry can be found when rendering animation sequences. A typical animation may consist of hundreds of frames, and the task in hand is to render them all in the minimum possible time. The time taken to render a single frame may stay the same, however, as many frames can be rendered concurrently, the total rendering time may be divided by the number of processors in the system.

The interesting technical challenge still remains in rendering a single frame in a time inversely proportional to the number of processors in the system. Here, the computational complexity of the rendering algorithm must be taken into account. This is illustrated by two examples at opposite ends of the spectrum of image quality; ray tracing and flat shading with a z-buffer.

28.4.1 Ray tracing

Ray tracing is the simpler algorithm to implement because it is so computationally complex and therefore can probably deal with all the compute you wish, without ever stressing the communication bandwidths in a system. Each pixel in a scene is rendered by tracing rays from a point on the emulsion of a film in an imaginary camera, through the lens (pinhole is easy but real lenses give depth of field), and out into the world. More rays are traced to determine the appearance of any surfaces that the original ray may have hit. The fundamental property here is that it is quite difficult in the standard sequential ray-tracing algorithm to make use of pixel-to-pixel image coherence. Also, secondary rays always have to be traced independently. In other words, sequential ray-tracing algorithms do not usually care about the order in which pixels are calculated, as all ray–scene intersections have to be recomputed pixel by pixel. Also, any part of the world model may be visible in any portion of the frame when reflection and refraction are modelled. The natural implementation on a Computing Surface is therefore to replicate both a standard sequential ray-tracing algorithm and the world model it will be tracing over all the processors of the system. Each processor can now be assigned a subset of the pixels which make up a frame and can proceed with rendering them independently.

However, some processors may have been presented with more difficult regions of the frame than others, a situation which will be made worse if smart sorting algorithms have been used to limit the ray–scene intersection calculation. The solution is therefore to divide the scene into many more portions than there are processors, using a load-balancing task server to distribute rendering tasks to processors which have finished a previous task. This can be accomplished by a simple extension to an existing buffering and forwarding scheme by making the distribution of tasks dependent on which compute process input buffers are empty, therefore routeing tasks to the hungriest processors. This scheme has been implemented on a system with an excess of 300 processors. Communications were still understressed (30 second PAL frame generation times still fits into 1/2 Mb per second) therefore performance was still linear with the number of processors.

28.4.2 Flat shading

The second example, z-buffering with flat shading, is more computationally simple, therefore one could expect a corresponding increase in the ratio of communications activity. The basic task is to transform and clip a stream of world-space polygons into screen space, scan convert the polygons and finally render them into a z-buffer. Incremental methods for calculating the depth of a screen-space polygon at adjacent pixels means that a rendering processor naturally wants to be responsible for at least one scanline. This makes it difficult to distribute the transformation to screen space along with the rendering algorithm, as the ordering of polygons on scanlines cannot be done until after the transformation step, at which point a polygon may find itself in the wrong processor. The algorithm must therefore be divided between the transformation and rendering steps with possibly a sort step in between. A greater division of the algorithm is neither necessary nor desirable for the reasons noted above.

Division of the data between processors is accomplished by two different methods for the two major portions of the algorithm. The transformation processors utilize a load-balancing task server to assign polygons to processors in a way that keeps all the processors busy. The rendering processors must, however, divide their share of the screen-space polygons based on a division of the screen into a number of horizontal stripes, to allow the rendering algorithm to utilize scanline coherence.

Topology is the key to maintaining full utilization of a system in which communications will be stressed. Rendering polygons into rasters results in data expansion, therefore the total number of links into and out of the set of rendering processors must reflect this ratio. The MK015 graphics board can provide four links of bandwidth via its processor into the video RAMs which form the display, however, as more link bandwidth is required, these boards may be ganged together. Looking at the input side of the rendering array, it has to swallow data from a number of links coming from the transformation processors. This data is unordered, that is, each input link may carry screen-space polygons destined for any part of the scene, as the screen-space coordinates of a polygon are only known after the transformation step. A set of binning processors is therefore required to direct screen-space polygons from an arbitrary input link to a subset of the rendering array. This subset of the rendering array can then route the screen-space polygons through all its processors, each processor picking off the polygons which are of interest to it. Binning of the screen-space polygons can be implemented with a butterfly network as used in the evaluation of FFTs, and typically will require a relatively small number of processors compared with the total number in the system.

The compute performed within a rendering processor is just a standard scanline conversion and z-buffer algorithm. One point that should be raised however is the degree of buffering provided. On the input side, polygons of interest to this processor may not arrive at regular intervals, therefore enough buffering space needs to be provided potentially to store all the polygons for one frame while the previous frame is being rendered. Secondly, once all the polygons for a frame have been rendered into the z-buffer, the processor would ideally like to send off the corresponding rasters to the display device in a burst, so that it can proceed with the next frame. This can only happen if the output buffer can accept a complete frame's worth of rasters. The processor must therefore be able to double buffer a complete frame both for input and output.

Conclusions

To summarize, a Computing Surface can provide a system throughput proportional to the number of processors that compose it. The simplest means of both programming and guaranteeing full utilization is to replicate sequential programs over all processors, thus increasing throughput but keeping single task latency constant. However, with suitable attention to the ratio of compute to communications and the sizes of messages (and therefore processor topology), and by programming with the intention of minimizing the extent to which algorithms are divided between processors, single task latency can be reduced while still providing full utilization of all processors.

E. Caspary
I.D. Scherson

University of California

29 · A self-balanced parallel ray-tracing algorithm

A novel parallel processing algorithm for image synthesis using ray tracing is presented. The scene is first organized in hierarchical data structure which is cut at some level, and the object descriptions along with their bounding volumes are distributed accordingly among the processors of a MIMD system. There are two independent processes in each processor: the first one is demand driven and used for bounding volumes calculations, while the second one is data driven and used for intersection calculations. This scheme, where the first process can be executed by any processor, suggests an algorithm with an embedded load-balancing mechanism. It has an almost linear speedup and its storage requirements are small. Simulation results are presented to illustrate these features.

29.1 Introduction

The ray-tracing technique to generate computer synthesized images with improved shading, was first introduced by Whitted (1980). Since then, relevant research efforts have been directed in three main directions: to improve the realism of the images for various natural phenomena; to increase the range of geometric primitives that can make use of the method; and to improve the execution time of the computation.

The large amount of time required for intersection calculations is the main obstacle in making this method a standard tool in computer graphics. Several methods evolved in recent years to structure the scene description, in order to reduce the number of objects with which each ray must be checked for intersection. The most accepted division schemes are space division (octree or regular division) and hierarchical tree of extents. Still, traversal of the data structures is time consuming. Some representative traversal techniques can be found in Glassner (1984) and Fujimoto *et al.* (1986) for space traversal, and in Kay and Kajiya (1986) for tree search.

When Whitted introduced the implementation of a global illumination model by ray tracing, he realized that his program spent most of its time in computing intersections between rays and surfaces. He then suggested (Whitted, 1980) that a multiprocessing system might be useful to speed up intersection calculations, while the shading operations could be performed by the host computer. This challenge called for more detailed research.

The results of two studies were reported in 1983. The first one, by Cleary *et al.* (1983), suggested partitioning the space with a 2- or 3D uniform grid, and allocating each rectangular subvolume to each processor node of a mesh-connected array. Ray messages are then transferred in the mesh in the same way that light rays traverse the space. Each processor works in data-driven mode, calculates intersections with the objects residing in its associated subvolume, and then transmits ray messages, including reflection and refraction rays if necessary. The second study was done independently by Ullner (1983) in his PhD thesis. He suggested a similar scheme of processor arrays, as well as pipelined hardware for ray–polygon intersection calculations. Other parallel solutions for the ray–object intersection calculation were suggested later in Plunkett and Bailey (1985) and Pulleyblank and Kapenga (1987).

One of the main issues in parallel algorithms is the workload balance, because one heavily loaded processor may reduce drastically the speedup of the whole system. The number of penetrating rays and required intersection calculations in any part of the object space is not known before the ray-tracing algorithm is executed. The only acceptable solution is dynamic load balancing. This approach was first introduced by Dippe and Swensen (1984). In their adaptive subdivision algorithm, the size and shape of each subvolume is changed dynamically, in accordance with the workload of the associated processors. Objects are moved accordingly between neighboring processors, in order to keep their workload balanced. A similar adaptive algorithm was suggested in Nemoto and Omachi (1986). Here, the shape of the rectangular subvolumes is kept, but the boundary surfaces are permitted to slide.

The above algorithms assume a 2D or 3D mesh-connected architecture. In Kobayashi *et al.* (1987), the space is divided recursively into octree subvolumes, and each processor is made responsible for a cubical volume of different size. Thus a static load balance is achieved because all the processors have a similar number of objects. They chose a hypercube interconnection network because the subvolumes no longer correspond to a regular array.

A ring architecture is suggested by Dew *et al.* (1987). Their system is designed for solid modeling applications and is implemented using an array of INMOS transputers. Parallelism is achieved in two ways. Spatial parallelism is achieved by dividing the space recursively and letting the subvolumes be handled by different processors. Structural parallelism is achieved by dividing the processing of CSG construction trees among the processors.

The task allocation in all of these algorithms (except the last one) is data driven, in the sense that at any given time, only a small part of the database resides in any processor and all the tasks (intersection calculations) that need these data must be processed by that very processor. In the last system, any processor can execute any task and virtually can access the whole database. To achieve this, it has an LRU cache to store the most recently used objects.

This chapter proposes a novel algorithm with an embedded load balance mechanism for a MIMD environment. This is achieved without moving data between processors, and by using data-driven, as well as demand-driven, task allocation. In demand-driven task allocation, a new task can be requested by any free processor and need not be executed by a specific processor as in data-driven allocation. In addition to its excellent load balance, it has a linear speedup and minimal memory requirements for systems with 10–500 processors.

29.2 The sequential algorithm

The proposed parallel algorithm is based on the hierarchical extents method. The objects are first represented by a hierarchical data structure of bounding volumes. For each ray, its closest intersected object is found by traversing the hierarchical tree, starting at its root and moving towards its leaves. The method was first introduced by Rubin and Whitted (1980), it was improved by Weghorst *et al.* (1984), and made much faster by Kay and Kajiya (1986).

The first step in the algorithm is building the data structure. It can be done top down or bottom up. Each node in the hierarchical tree is associated with a bounding volume which contains all the bounding volumes of the node's children. Any object is associated with one bounding volume that contains it and resides at a leaf of the data structure.

The building of the data structure is not a trivial task. Rubin and Whitted (1980) designed an interactive program, and it took them about two days to build a hierarchical tree for a complex scene. In Kay and Kajiya (1986) the desired features of a 'good' hierarchy are described. They mention two methods: the median cut and the octree subdivision. We simulated these two methods and also a new multidimensional median cut, which yields better results. According to the new method, a volume is subdivided recursively into two, four, or eight subvolumes (according to the number of objects in the volume), such that the number of objects in each subvolume is similar. The results are reported in Scherson and Caspary (1988). This subject was studied independently by Goldsmith and Salmon (1987) who suggest a method to evaluate the cost of the hierarchical tree by estimating the number of intersection calculations.

After the hierarchical tree is constructed, the closest intersected object with any ray can be found by 'traversing' the tree. The traversal starts from the root: the ray is checked for intersection with each bounding volume at the root's children. Only those children intersected by the ray are further considered. The process continues recursively, such that all the children of the remaining nodes are checked for intersection.

Kay and Kajiya (1986) suggest arranging the bounding volumes according to their 'distance' from the ray's origin. A partially ordered heap structure is used to implement a priority queue, where the next closest bounding volume is always found on top of the heap. In this way, the various bounding volumes are considered in the order that they appear along the ray's path. The processing of each ray terminates when either no intersections with objects are found, or the closest bounding volume, on top of the heap, has a greater distance than that of the currently found intersected object.

29.3 The parallel algorithm

The algorithm is implemented in a general MIMD system where messages can virtually be sent between any two processors. A hypercube (Seits, 1985) interconnection network is a good example of such a system. There are three phases to the algorithm. The database is first preprocessed by the host computer which constructs the hierarchical tree in the usual way. See Scherson and Caspary (1988) or Kay and Kajiya (1986) for details. The second phase is to distribute the database (objects and bounding volumes) among the processors. A small part of it is duplicated in all the processors, and the rest is distributed randomly in a method that will be described immediately. The third phase is the intersection calculations and shading. This is executed by transmitting ray messages through the multiprocessing system.

The general idea of the algorithm is to divide the hierarchical data structure into two parts across some level of the tree, as illustrated in Figure 29.1. The first part is the upper tree, and it contains all the bounding volumes above (and including) the designated level. The second part is the set of lower subtrees which contain the bounding volumes below the designated level, together with the objects associated with the terminal nodes of the tree. This special level, across which the tree data structure is divided, will be named LEVEL in the following discussion. (Its choice will be discussed later.)

The database is divided among the processors in the following way. One duplicate of the upper tree is stored in each processor while each of the subtrees is randomly sent to only one of the processors. In this way, each processor contains two kinds of processes:

(1) A process to compute intersections between rays and bounding volumes in the upper tree.

(2) A process responsible for intersection calculations of rays with lower tree bounding volumes and objects stored in that processor.

For each ray, the first process can be executed by any processor because the necessary database exists in all the processors. The second process must be executed by a dedicated processor.

This division of all tasks into two kinds, one of which can be executed by any processor, is the key to the load-balancing feature of the algorithm. Those processors that have a heavy workload with the second process will perform the first

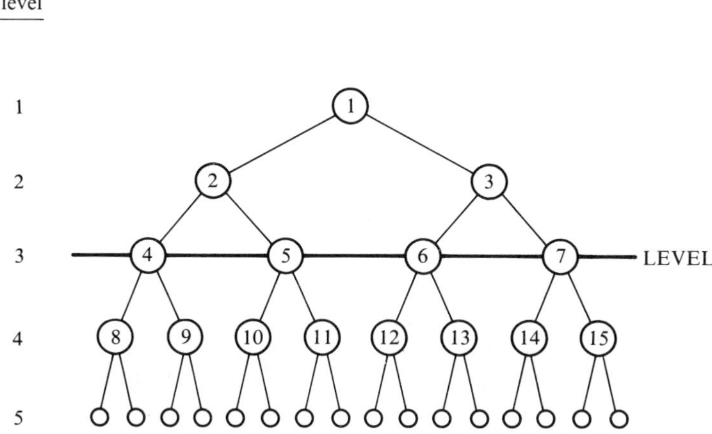

Figure 29.1
Hierarchy tree partition across LEVEL.

process only a small fraction of the time. On the other hand, the processors with low workload with the second process will perform the first process most of the time. In this way, the workload of all the processors will be almost even. This can be achieved only when LEVEL is low enough in the tree.

Traversal of the distributed data structure is done in the following way. Whenever the closest polygon that intersects a ray needs to be found, the responsibility for this task can be taken by any free processor. This 'parent' processor will request such a task from the host whenever its queue of ray messages is temporarily empty. The parent processor starts implementing the hierarchical tree search as usual. As a first step, it creates a heap of bounding volumes. Then it checks intersection of the ray with all the children of the root. Those childrens' bounding volumes intersected by the ray are inserted into the heap. The bounding volumes on top of the heap are processed similarly until an intersection is found with some bounding volume that resides in LEVEL. In this case, an inquiry message is sent to the processor responsible for the appropriate subtree. The parent processor does not continue processing the ray until it gets a return message that will either say that there is no intersection within that subtree, or provide the details of the closest intersection point found. In any case, the parent processor will continue to process the main heap until the termination conditions of the algorithm are satisfied.

Notice that during this whole process, there is one central heap of bounding volumes in the parent processor and many temporary heaps created by other processors which had to find an intersection point in their subtrees. The processing in the subtrees is done as in the original hierarchical extents algorithm and, as soon as the resulting ray message is returned to the parent processor, the temporary heap is deleted.

The specific algorithm to find intersection within each subtree could be any and need not be the same hierarchical algorithm as chosen here. One could choose any known, serial algorithm; several of them were mentioned in the introduction. There is always a trade-off between execution time and memory requirements, and we decided to choose an algorithm with minimal memory requirements, because it is more suitable to existing multiprocessing systems (Goldsmith and Salmon, 1987).

The organization of each processor is illustrated in Figure 29.2. The processors are connected by a hypercube-like interconnection network as mentioned before. There are two independent processes in each processor: the lower tree process (with two queues) and the upper tree process (with six queues). The lower tree process is responsible for only one function, namely, to calculate intersections of rays within the subtree (or several subtrees) for which it is responsible. This process will work in data-driven mode on inquiry messages coming from Q6, and will have the highest priority because the required data is available only here.

The upper tree process first gets some ray messages from the host. However, new ray messages will arrive on demand when the input queue length (Q3) decreases below some threshold value. During the processing of a new ray message, whenever a subtree must be checked, a subtree inquiry message will be sent via Q4 and the processing of the ray will be put to wait for a subtree return message. When a subtree return message arrives, the appropriate ray will be moved to Q8 to enable further processing. The priority of the queues will be first Q8, then Q5 and finally Q3.

When the desired intersection point is found, shading calculations are done. The relative color contribution of the intersection point is sent as a result message to the host via Q1. In addition, new ray messages might be generated (Q2) due to reflec-

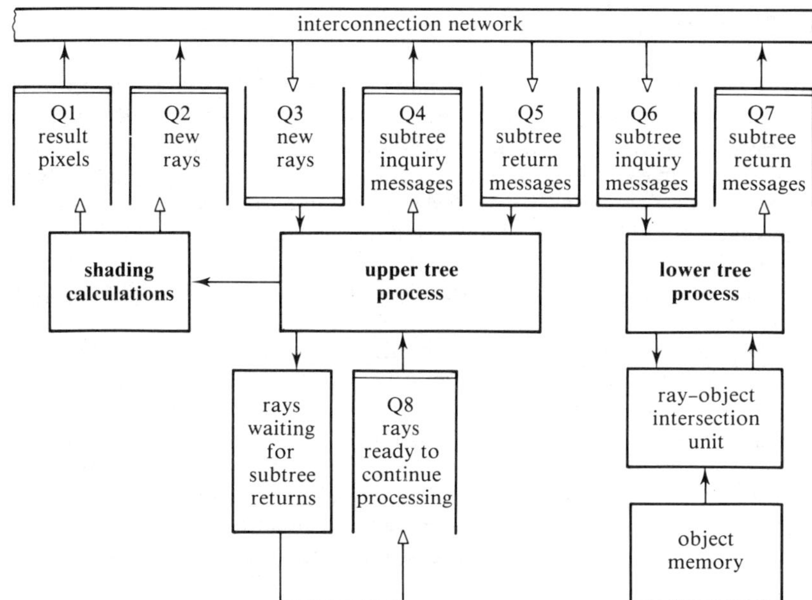

Figure 29.2
Processor organization.

tions and refractions. If there are free locations in the new messages input queue (Q3), the generated rays are stored there. Otherwise, the host is signalled to remove these messages and let another processor take care of them. The upper tree process works in data-driven as well as demand-driven allocation modes. It will have to complete processing of all the rays for which it took responsibility, and will demand new rays only if it is not loaded.

The choice of the LEVEL parameter is not obvious. If it is chosen too high in the hierarchical tree, the number of subtrees might be very small and even less than the number of processors. If LEVEL is too low, the size of the upper tree, which is duplicated in all the processors, will be very large. The choice of LEVEL affects many parameters of the algorithm as listed below:

- the number of subtree hierarchies that are distributed,
- the total number of polygons checked for intersection for each ray,
- the number of messages in the system,
- the number of intersection calculations with bounding volumes,
- the load balance in the system, and
- the execution time of the algorithm.

The appropriate relations will be discussed along with the simulation results in Section 29.4.2.

The key factor to the success of this parallel algorithm is that a large portion of the work is done in the upper part of the hierarchical tree while the amount of database required for this processing is very small. This fact enables us to duplicate this database among all the processors (without paying too much in storage requirements) while achieving a simple mechanism for load balance.

29.4 Simulation results

The algorithm was programmed and simulated on a UNIX-based uniprocessor system. The interconnection network was assumed to be similar to the hypercube with a message transmission time proportional to $\log_2 N$, where N is the number of processors. This type of interconnection complexity is more cost effective for our application. Several test images were used to evaluate the algorithm, two of them appear in Plates 6 and 7. The Tree image contains 3878 polygons and is a subset of the tree introduced in Kay and Kajiya (1986). The database was generously given to us by the authors. The second image is a Crankshaft designed at UCSB and contains 5788 polygons.

A typical breakdown of the algorithm average execution time (average among all the processors) is shown in Figure 29.3. Notice that almost half of the time is spent to traverse the upper tree. This diagram does not include the preprocessing time which amounts to less than four per cent. Building the hierarchical data structure is done by the host itself, and the preparation of polygon parameters for intersection calculations is done independently by the appropriate processors. Let us now look at the performance of the algorithm as a function of the LEVEL chosen and as a function of the number of processors in the system.

29.4.1 Choosing LEVEL

The performance of the algorithm as a function of the chosen LEVEL is illustrated in Figure 29.4. These simulation results are from rendering the Crankshaft with 20 processors. The average number of polygons checked for intersection in each processor is shown in Figure 29.4a.

The number of polygons is the same in the two extreme cases, namely:

(1) LEVEL is chosen at the root: there is only one subtree and all the work is done in one processor. This processor has all the information and therefore checks only the necessary number of polygons.

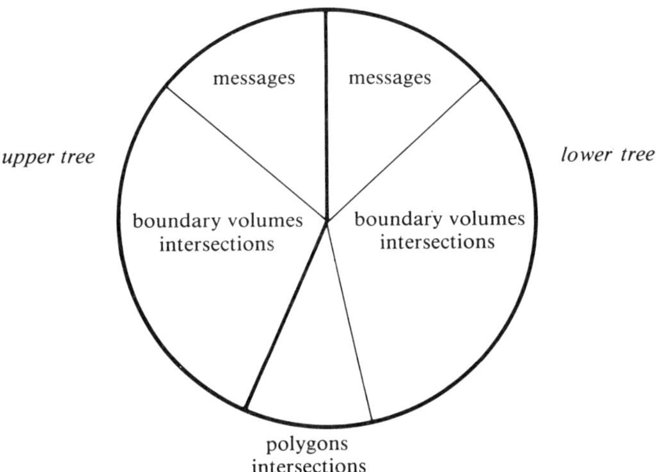

Figure 29.3
Breakdown of the execution time.

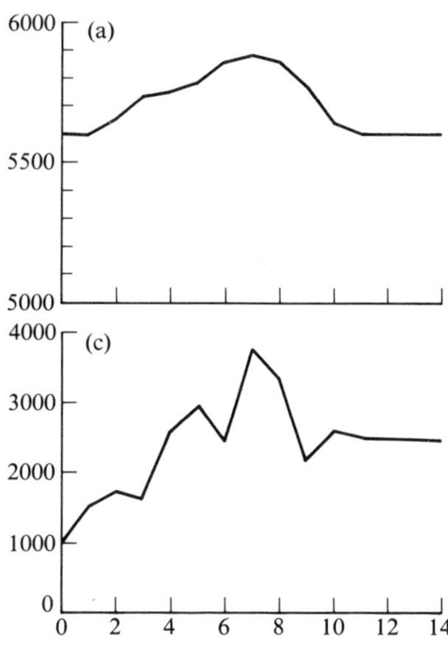

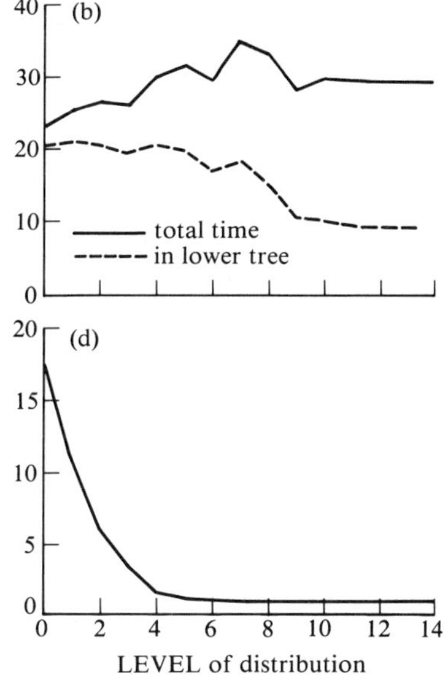

Figure 29.4
Performance as a function of LEVEL.
(a) Number of polygons.
(b) Number of messages.
(c) Execution time.
(d) Load balance.

(2) LEVEL is chosen at the lowest leaf node: all the bounding volumes belong to the upper tree and nothing is left to the subtrees. Now, the upper tree process has all the information and the polygons chosen for intersection calculation are the same as in the uniprocessor case.

In any intermediate LEVEL, the number of intersected polygons is higher than in the above extreme cases because the information is not available in one place: the parent processor has some information and the processors responsible for the relevant subtrees have the rest. In the uniprocessor case, when the processor has access to all the information needed, there is one heap and the bounding volumes are processed in order. Now, the heap is divided into one main heap in the parent processor and several temporary heaps in the other processors. A temporary heap must be exhausted before a ray message is sent back to the parent processor. If this temporary heap had been combined with the parent main heap, it would not have been necessary to process some of its bounding volumes. Nevertheless, the degradation of the algorithm by this effect is only five per cent.

The average number of messages transmitted by each processor is shown in Figure 29.4b. The curve is not monotonic but we may observe an average increase until LEVEL equals 8. The graph decreases for a while and stays constant for values of LEVEL beyond 12. In order to understand the behavior of the number of messages as a function of the LEVEL chosen, let us concentrate for a while on the structure of the hierarchy.

A typical hierarchical tree is shown in Figure 29.5. Terminal nodes (that is, bounding volumes with polygon) may appear at any level. In the process of building this tree, whenever the number of polygons is smaller than some predefined value, the bounding volume is not subdivided any more. The dashed lines in the diagram denote one instance of traversing the tree for some ray. The traversal along each

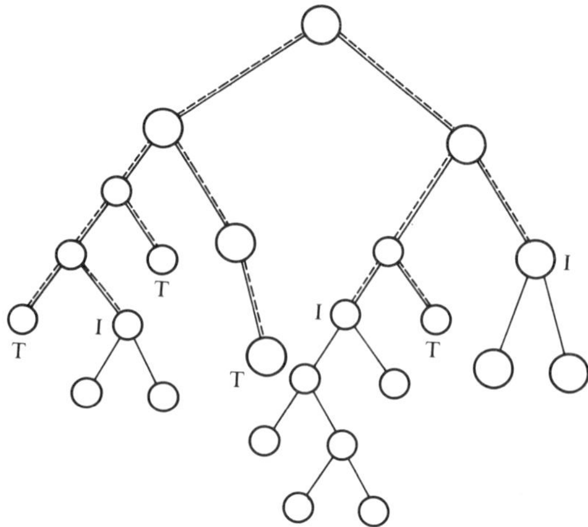

Figure 29.5
An example of hierarchy traversal.

branch may terminate either in a terminal node (designated by T in the diagram), or in an internal node (designated by I) if the ray does not intersect the bounding volume associated with that internal node.

Let us consider the number of edges traversed in each level of the hierarchical tree. As the distance from the root is increased, two contradicting factors affect this number:

(1) The total number of edges is increased for every level, and therefore the number of edges traversed is increased.

(2) Many routes down the tree terminate before a leaf is encountered (as explained above), and this decreases the number of edges traversed.

The net effect of these two factors is that the number of edges traversed is first increased (by Factor 1), and then decreased (by Factor 2). The number of edges traversed in LEVEL is *exactly the number of messages between parent processors and their subtrees*. This explains the behavior of the number of messages in Figure 29.4b. The graph is not monotonic because the effects of (1) and (2) above are not the same for each level.

The third component in the execution time of the algorithm is calculating intersections with bounding volumes. When LEVEL is increased, the number of bounding volumes in the upper tree is increased, and therefore also the number of intersection calculations for the upper tree process. The specific processes associated with the subtrees get fewer bounding volumes and perform less intersection calculations with objects. It happens that the sum of these two parts of the number of bounding volumes is almost constant.

The total average execution time as a function of LEVEL is shown in Figure 29.4c. The pattern of the number of messages is recognized in the total execution time. The effect of the decreasing number of intersected volumes in the subtrees is recognized in the lower tree part of the figure (the dashed line). Notice that the amount of time spent in processing the upper tree is equal, on the average, to the time spent in processing the subtrees. As long as the time in the upper tree is large enough, it is easier to achieve a uniform load balance.

Although Figure 29.4c suggests choosing LEVEL equal to 0 or 1 when the total execution time is minimal, it is not guaranteed then that the small amount of work in the upper tree will be sufficient to make the workload in all the processors even. And, in fact, it is not sufficient, as shown in Figure 29.4d. This figure illustrates the dynamic load balance factor (the ratio of maximum to average load) in the system, after the upper tree workload was distributed among the less busy processors. It is obvious that, in this case, the algorithm will function properly only if a LEVEL of 4 or more is chosen. For LEVEL equal to 3 there are only eight subtrees and this number is too small for distribution among 20 processors. It is recommended to keep the value of LEVEL as low as possible (4 or 5 in this case) in order to keep the size of the upper tree database small. However, about two subtrees should be assigned to each processor to enable the balancing mechanism.

29.4.2 Performance as a function of the number of processors

Consider now the behavior of the algorithm when the number of processors is changed. The simulation results in Figure 29.6 are from rendering the Tree image. The speedup of the algorithm is illustrated in Figure 29.6a and the achieved load balance in Figure 29.6c.

Notice that the load balance is 'ideal' up to 200 processors. For more processors the load is not balanced, because the number of subtrees becomes smaller relative to the number of processors. When more complex scenes are rendered, this breakpoint appears for a larger number of processors. To achieve dynamic balance in systems with more processors, subtrees together with their polygons can be moved between processors in the usual way. In generating Figure 29.6a, the latter data transferring was assumed (only for 500 processors or more), with a cost of 20% from the excess load of the busiest processor.

The performance of the algorithm cannot be evaluated without considering the amount of memory required to implement it. The total amount of memory in each processor, as a function of the number of processors, is shown in Figure 29.6b. This memory, as already mentioned, has three components:

(1) bounding volumes in the upper tree (duplicated in all the processors),

(2) bounding volumes in subtrees (specific to each processor),

(3) polygons.

It is obvious that the number of polygons in each processor, as well as the number of subtree bounding volumes, is decreased as the number of processors is increased, because the same size of database is distributed now among more processors. But Figure 29.6b shows a small increase in the memory requirements from a 200 processor system to 500 processors due to the increase of LEVEL (in 500 processors) to obtain more subtrees and therefore an improved load balance.

Figure 29.6d demonstrates the cost performance of the algorithm, assuming that the processor cost is four times lower than that of the memory required to store the whole database. The algorithm achieves best cost performance ratio for less than 100 processors, where the load balance is still perfect.

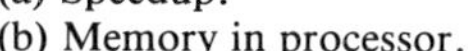

Figure 29.6
Performance as a function of the number of processors.
(a) Speedup.
(b) Memory in processor.
(c) Load balance factor.
(d) Cost/performance.

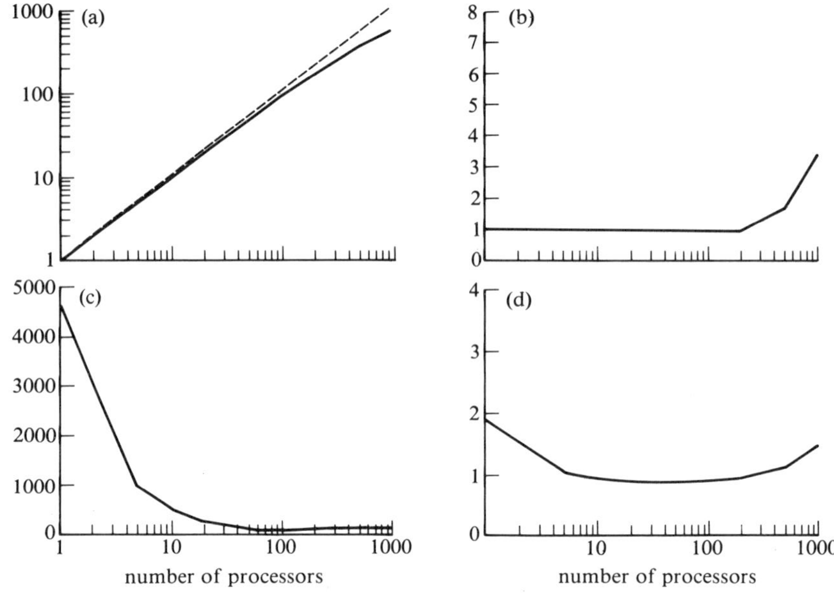

Conclusions

We proposed here a self-balanced parallel algorithm that is suitable for a moderate size multiprocessing system, similar to the hypercube. For this number of processors the workload balance is nearly 'ideal' and the speedup is almost linear. A demand-driven process and a data-driven process share the resources of each processor. The load balance is achieved by processors demanding new work only when they are free from the work they have to do anyway.

References

Cleary J.G., Wyvill B., Birtwistle G.M. and Vatti R. (1983). *Multiprocessor Ray Tracing*. Research report No. 83/128/17, University of Calgary

Dew P.M., de Pennington A. and Morris D.T. (1987). Programmable VLSI Array Architecture for Solid Modelling, CG Tokyo 87, April 1987

Dippe M. and Swensen J. (1984). An adaptive subdivision algorithm and parallel architecture for realistic image synthesis. *Computer Graphics,* **18**(3), 149–58

Fujimoto A., Takayuki T. and Iwata K. (1986). ARTS: Accelerated Ray-Tracing System. *IEEE Computer Graphics and Applications*, **6**(4), 16–26

Glassner A.S. (1984). Space subdivision for fast ray tracing. *IEEE Computer Graphics and Applications,* **4**(10), 15–22

Goldsmith J. and Salmon J. (1987). Automatic creation of object hierarchies for ray tracing. *IEEE Computer Graphics and Applications*, **7**(5), 14–20

Kay T.L. and Kajiya J.T. (1986). Ray Tracing Complex Scenes. *Computer Graphics,* **20**(4), 269–78

Kobayashi H., Nakamura T. and Shigei Y. (1987). Parallel processing of an object space for image synthesis using ray tracing. *The Visual Computer*, 3, 13–22

Nemoto K. and Omachi T. (1986). An adaptive subdivision by sliding boundary surfaces for fast ray tracing. In *Proceeding on Graphic Interface 1986*, pp. 43–8

Plunkett D.J. and Bailey M.J. (1985). The vectorization of ray-tracing algorithm for improved execution speed. *IEEE Computer Graphics and Applications,* **5**(8), 52–60

Pulleyblank R. and Kapenga J. (1987). The feasibility of a VLSI chip for ray tracing bicubic patches. *IEEE Computer Graphics and Applications,* **7**(3), 33–44

Rubin S. and Whitted T. (1980). A 3-dimensional representation for fast rendering of complex scenes. *Computer Graphics*, **14**(3), 110–16

Scherson I.D. and Caspary E. (1983). Data structures and the time complexity of ray tracing. *The Visual Computer*, **3**(4), 201–13

Seits C. (1985). The cosmic cube. *Comm. ACM*, **28**(1), 22–33

Ullner M.K. (1983). Parallel machines for computer graphics. *PhD Thesis*, CalTech

Weghost H., Hooper G. and Greenberg D. (1984). Improved computational methods for ray tracing. *ACM Transactions on Graphics*, **3**(1), 52–69

Whitted T. (1980). An improved illumination model for shaded display. *Comm. ACM,* **23**(6), 343–9

M. Chalmers

University of East Anglia

30 · On the design and implementation of a multiprocessor ray tracer

A ray tracer has been developed on a multiprocessor machine at the University of East Anglia, as a vehicle for research into realistic image synthesis. Various components of the tracer are distributed across processing elements. The development of the tracer was hampered by a lack of flexibility of configuration, and a low level of data abstraction.

Consideration of these problems led to the construction of an occam programming style based on object-oriented and actor languages. The specification and implementation of processes are described, along with the inheritance of functionality, the communication infrastructure, pseudo-dynamic process creation and facilities for monitoring and debugging.

30.1 Introduction

It is well known that ray tracing is a computationally expensive method of image synthesis. In order to ease experimentation [1] with reflection models in distributed ray tracing, a multiprocessor machine was chosen for use. A ray tracer was developed on a Meiko Computing Surface with fourteen T414 transputers, using **occam** [2]. An example configuration is shown in Figure 30.1. One processor is used for monitoring and controlling the program's execution, for managing file access, and feeding the first processor in each of three **farms** – four linearly connected processors – with blocks of pixels. The last processor in each farm is connected to a processor which has a frame buffer.

As the capabilities of the first version of the tracer grew, the process which was central to the program became increasingly unwieldy. This process, traceRay, calculated the intensity for a pixel by tracing rays through the modelled environment. The method of software development used was much the same as that used for sequential languages: subprocess 'stubs', initially small, grew as they were worked upon and refined. Each instance of traceRay had a copy of the scene's shape and reflectance data, making traceRay a large, inflexible code module.

The 12 processors in the farms each have 256 kb of memory. The graphics processor has 128 kb, and the 'system' processor has 8 Mb. There are many ways in which one might consider placing the set of processes and interconnecting the

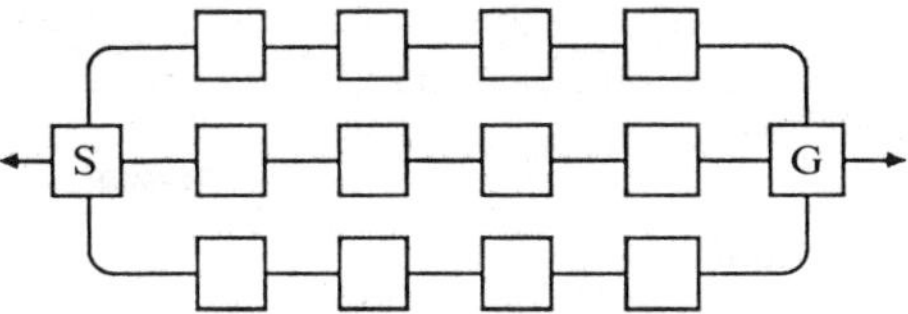

Figure 30.1
An example configuration of the tracer. A system node (S) connects through to the file system of the host. Node G, the graphics node, provides graphical output. Between the two are three farms of processors which perform the intersection and shading calculations.

processors involved in tracing rays. Such configurations could be compared in order to maximize the system's efficiency. Each configuration could be considered as a view of the structure of the ray-tracing algorithm – no one area of activity in the program is necessarily the 'right' one to choose when deciding how to partition the subprocesses which constitute a ray tracer. One might plan to allocate a processor to each shape in the scene, a processor to each voxel, a processor to each of a number of screen areas, or one might employ a combination of these arrangements.

The future plans for the tracer included changes and additions to many areas of activity within the program. Gains in image quality and execution speed would be achieved at the cost of a considerable rise in program size and complexity. Given the structure of the program, assessing the benefits of different approaches to partitioning code and data would require significant remodelling of the program at each stage. Greater modularity would allow the design of components with little or no regard to their configuration. By reducing the interdependence of code sections and increasing the level of data abstraction, changing and adding code would become quicker and more reliable.

Modularity can be gained by partitioning data amongst parallel processes, each of which supervises access to its private data. By comparison with many other languages, however, occam's facilities for data abstraction are poor. Speed of execution and compatibility with the transputer were paramount criteria in the language's design. Consequently, the management of modularity and data abstraction is, to a large extent, in the hands of the programmer. In order to make software development both more effective and more elegant, features from other more 'ornate' languages can be used to build upon the austere but efficient foundation of occam.

The expressiveness and modelling power of **object-oriented languages** [3] have become more widely known and used in recent years. In such languages, objects provide a basic unit of abstraction for data and associated procedures. Classes of objects are related by a hierarchy of inheritance: an instance of a class can handle the messages of its superclass, and may also handle other messages which define the more specialized nature of the class. Objects communicate by sending messages to one another. By using the basic units of processes and channels, hierarchies of independent object worlds can be created to combine the process and object paradigms [4]. Some of the notions of objects, classes and methods, inheritance, protocol and implementation descriptions, and the dynamic creation of object instances can be applied to an occam context.

Semi-synchronous message passing, as in [5], is combined with selectivity in message acceptance, as used in [6] and [7]. Debugging and monitoring are facilitated by the adoption of a simple message priority scheme. Some features of module structure are drawn from the actor model of computation [8] which is derived from object-oriented languages and the lambda calculus. The actor model provides a foundation for a more flexible and dynamic treatment of parallelism than that provided by CSP [9], the formal model which is the progenitor of occam.

30.2 Designing a class

> 'A class describes the implementation of a set of objects that all represent the same kind of system component. The individual objects described by a class are called its instances. A class describes the form of its instances' private memories and it describes how they carry out their operations.'

The definition of a class, above, is that used in Smalltalk [10]. A means of constructing classes of objects according to a methodology based on Smalltalk is presented in this section. Section 30.2.1 describes the informal specification of the protocol of a class, and its use in the construction of a 'blueprint' for the final implementation. Section 30.2.2 describes a means of using this blueprint to write occam code to implement the class.

30.2.1 Protocol and implementation descriptions

A protocol description lists the messages handled by a class. Each message pattern in this list contains a message selector and a number of argument names and their classes, together with a brief description of what will happen on receipt and the format of the reply, if any. Message selectors are drawn from a vocabulary shared by all classes in the object world, forming a basis for operator overloading. Messages may be activation messages, which initiate activity within the object, or data messages, which are responses to activations and are described only briefly in the protocol description of the receiver. Recursive and mutually recursive control structures can be built up using message passing.

As an example, the following is the protocol for class Shape, which is the template for all 3D shape classes (for example, Sphere) in the tracer. Most of the messages were defined (as data messages) when writing the Ray implementation description, but others were only included after the first draft of the Shape implementation description. By having subclasses of Shape conform to this protocol, a Ray class has been created which is independent of the range of Shape subclasses in the program, with consequent gains in clarity and ease of maintenance.

Shape protocol

setShape coeff:[]real32	Set up the shape surface using coeffs.
setMaterial m:Material	Set the material of the shape to be m.
setEmittance e:Emittance	Set the emittance of the shape to be e.
hit O:vector V:vector minSoFar:real32	Test the shape for a hit with the ray O + tV within the range t = (0, minSoFar). Reply noHit or hit point: distance:.

normal point:vector	Reply normal N: at point on surface
emittance lambda:real32	Reply intensity i: of wavelength lambda at shape surface, and replyDest used.
reflectance point: vector N:vector V:vector R:vector lambda:real32	Reply with the reflectance rho: of the shape when hit at point with normal N, view and reflection vectors V and R, and wavelength lambda.
reflectance rho:real32	Data message returned by a material.

Unlike Smalltalk, the implementation description is 'pseudocode' – an intermediate blueprint made prior to code construction. It is used to describe how an object moves from one state (or behaviour, in the actor terminology) to another in response to input messages. Within each state the 'methods' that the object uses to handle each message are defined, giving the acceptable messages and senders, and the responses to them. The 'superclass' statement specifies the inherited functionality of the class.

```
class name:          Shape
superclass:          Object
states:              setup,serve      --initially 'setup'
variables:           materialID, emittanceID :id
methods:
    setup
        msgsIn : int -- initially zero
    anyone ? setShape coeffs              -- only firstsetShape is
        subClassResponsibility            valid
    anyone ? setMaterial materialID       -- only first setMaterial
        msgsIn := msgsIn + 1              is valid
    anyone ? setEmittance emittanceID     -- only first setEmittance
        msgsIn := msgsIn + 1              is valid

    → serve if msgsIn = 2

serve
    anyone ? hit O V minSoFar
        subclassResponsibility
    anyone ? normal point
        subclassResponsibility
    anyone ? emittance lambda
        emittanceID ! emittance lambda/replyDest = anyone
    anyone ? reflectance point N V R lambda
        calc H
        materialID ! reflectance (N·R) (N·H) lambda
        materialID ? reflectance rho
        ... calculate rho, the final reflectance
        anyone ! reflectance rho
```

The use of the name of the sender before '?' (and receiver before '!') is a convenient shorthand, reminiscent of the original CSP format. As Hoare points out, this brings the advantage of not having to introduce any concept of channels or their use. Notes can be included in the implementation description to comment, for example, on what to do if the message fails to be delivered (see Section 30.3.1). Usually, the communication subsystem can be treated as a feature of the environment which need not complicate the implementation description.

A Shape instance is in setup until all initialization messages have been received. On receiving setMaterial, the object sends for data on its material, to be used later. Once set up, a Shape stays in serve until it dies. When no constraint on the sender exists, then 'anyone' can be the sender. Information on the sender and the internal state of the receiver may affect the action on delivery, even if the message has a recognized message selector and arguments. For example, a Shape will reject a duplicate setMaterial message.

Each subclass of Shape need not be concerned with reflectance and emittance messages, and can leave them to be handled in Shape. Emittance spectra may be shared between shapes, so messages are referred to the object which manages this data. The replyDest specification informs this object that it should send its result directly to the sender of emittance. The sender must allow for this.

Messages like setShape, hit and normal are examples of messages which are expected by the object but are the responsibility of a class which is a specialization of Shape. If such a message reaches Shape, then an error will be called. A similar message classification (which does not occur in the example above) is shouldNotImplement. This means that although some superclass has specified that subclasses should handle this message, its usage is inappropriate for this class.

Implicit in every protocol description are the standard messages that are accepted by every object – die, vocabulary, and new. When die arrives, the object ceases execution. In response to vocabulary, the object returns the message selectors it handles. Potentially, any object may send new class: to create a new class instance. In return, the object receives new id: with the new object's name. The message free id: releases an object. The classManager, which handles free and new, and sends die, is described in Section 30.4.

By breaking down the overall pattern of activity into a number of states, and defining the acceptable messages in each state, the structure of the class instance can be decomposed into easily manageable code sections. The range of possibilities which have to be catered for at any stage in an object's execution is reduced, and the complexity arising from the many possible sequences of queued messages can be brought under more effective control. Also, mechanisms to break off useless computations can be introduced more cleanly.

When a subclass takes over the functionality defined for a method from its superclass, it also must take on some responsibility for the superclass' subsequent behaviour. In the best case, all other methods in the superclass are unaffected by the exclusion of the overridden method, both in terms of variables used and the pattern of subsequent behaviour transitions. If this convenient situation does not arise, then achieving a useful pattern of behaviour for the object may involve overriding other associated messages – a likely situation anyway – or sending messages to super that move the superclass on into a behaviour that allows the unassociated parts of the superclass' functionality to be available. In the Shape example, a subclass which takes on setShape must also take on all the messages that are associated with it –

hit, normal, etc. If a subclass was to override reflectance and setMaterial, it would have to send a message to the Shape instance to move it on into serve.

30.2.2 Producing code from an implementation description

Every class of object except the fundamental 'Object' class is built according to a standard format as shown in Figure 30.2. Messages taken from the queue handler (Q) are forwarded by the msgDirector process (mD) to either the priority message handler (P), the normal message handler (N) or the superclass (S). Messages from N go through msgDirector either to the 3:1 muxer, or to S when the receiver id is the pseudovariable super. The class Object has no superclass, and so is constructed with no S or associated channels and has, accordingly, a 2:1 muxer.

Q supervises message I/O, buffering input until the object specifies the next message it is prepared to accept. Specification can be made using the sender of the message and/or the message selector. This prevents incorrect interleaving of accesses to the object. Q processes behave in a way similar to the 'receptionists' of actor systems [11].

By keeping the superclass' process as a separate but internal process, the object inherits the attributes of S while keeping its internal structure hidden. If the implementation of S changes, the code for the class will not have to be changed unless it affects the protocol of the class. Initially, the use of several S processes for a class was considered. This would provide multiple inheritance, but the complications in message handling made the author settle, for the meantime, for simple inheritance. Multiple inheritance would allow greater potential modelling power, but the initial development of the tracer did not suggest an immediate demand for it. Similarly, an alternative implementation of simple inheritance would be to have all superclasses at the same level. The visibility of superclasses and the increased complexity of the msgDirector were felt to outweigh the speedups arising from reduced numbers of message transfers.

Each message buffered at Q is passed to the first msgDirector. If it conforms to the 'vocabulary' of the class, then N receives the message. This check greatly simplifies the design of N. Alternatively, if a 'priority' message (Section 30.3.2) is fed in, it will be passed to P and S. If the message is for neither N nor P, then it is passed to S. This checking of inherited message tables continues up the class hierarchy until either the message is accepted or the Object class calls an error procedure, doesNotUnderstand.

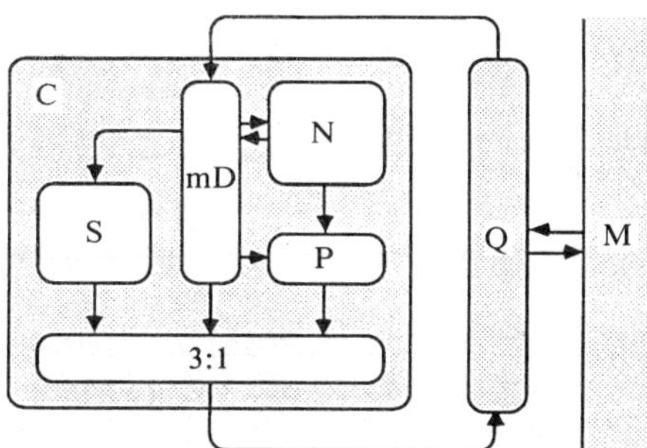

Figure 30.2
The structure of an instance of class C with superclass S. A message queue handler, Q, connects the instance to the messenger (M). Nesting of superclasses continues until the class Object, which has no superclass, is reached.

An accepted message and the current state of the object are used in N to branch to the section of code indicated in the implementation description. At the end of the activation, the state variable can be reset to change the set of input tests and branches used in the next pass through the main loop.

A standard set of facilities for objects allows the sending and receiving of messages, instance creation and termination, class and vocabulary testing, error handling, status reports and temporary suspension of communication. Most of these methods are based on the Smalltalk protocol for class Object, with the exceptions of status reports and communication suspension (discussed in Section 30.3.2).

30.3 On communication between processes

In occam, communication between processes is done on a one-to-one, synchronized basis. In order to send to more than one process, some intermediary process must be used to direct and buffer messages. The 'messenger' is such an intermediary, although buffering is primarily done by the Q processes attached to each object. The basic features of message transfer are described in Section 30.3.1. The messenger is at the core of all activity in the system. Every object's behaviour is dependent on its input, and this behaviour can only be reported using objects which have channels which lead out of the object world. The object which passes all status and debugging information out of the object world is the monitor. The relationship of the monitor to the P processes inside objects is described in Section 30.3.2.

30.3.1 Messages and the messenger

Every message passed between objects is a variable-length array of integers, making channel types simple and uniform. Arguments are retyped into a slice of the array. The first four array elements store the id of the receiver, the message selector, the id of the sender and the id for replies, respectively. The reply destination field may be used by an object to nominate replacement objects during a dialogue, so spreading the workload, or it may be used to access facilities unavailable in the current object.

Messages are sent in a semi-synchronous manner, as in the SR language [5]. An acknowledgement of receipt is returned when a message is queued by its receiver. A failure message is returned if the queue is full, the message selector is not in the vocabulary of the receiver, or the receiver is dead or undefined. A sender may retry several times, using exponentially increasing wait periods, before reporting a failure to the monitor object and calling the local failure procedure. This type of message protocol can be used to avoid delays for the sender while the receiver is serving someone else, and delays while the receiver is waiting for another server to serve it. After receiving an 'ack', the sender can get on with other work before looking in its queue for any expected replies.

A class should guarantee to handle eventually every message in its queue, otherwise the queue may fill up with 'ignored' messages. The subprocess which accepts an activation message is responsible for the specification and handling of data messages and for returning the object to a state in which it can accept another activation. An essential feature of objects is that they should not make the messenger wait for longer than is absolutely necessary, as their delay could affect the entire system. This is the main reason for the queue handler's acceptance of messages, even when its queue is full.

A number of ids, or mail addresses, are known to all objects. These are the pseudovariables Q, self and super – the queue handler, the object itself and the superclass of the sender respectively – and the fixed ids of the monitor, the classManager, and the fileManager.

One messenger on each processor controls message transfer in an object world. The messengers can trace subsets of the messages in the system. Traces are requested and filed via the monitor, and can be used for later analysis.

30.3.2 Monitoring, debugging and the use of priority messages

Inside an object, each N has a channel to inform P of its state. P tallies the states of N to build a simple profile. An object's P processes can be sent into a debug mode by the monitor, so that a report is sent whenever a state change message arrives from N. If not in debug mode, each P will only send a report when asked to by the monitor. The monitor has channels which lead out of the object world, and these are used to create log and trace files, and to connect through to the screen and keyboard. Messages to P processes have priority over normal messages and are passed into an object by Q on arrival.

The monitor can send a message which makes every msgDirector in an object refuse to communicate with its N, thus 'freezing' normal communication. The P processes can still respond to messages from the monitor and from N. The queue handler will buffer messages until another privileged message arrives from the monitor to thaw the object. Since semi-synchronous message passing is used, at most one message from any one sender can be in mid-journey to a frozen object. Therefore at most one acknowledgement message need be returned to that sender. If the sender is not frozen by the time the acknowledgement returns, then the ack will be accepted by the object in the normal way. If it is frozen, then the queue handler can store one ack message. If the queue of a frozen receiver is full then noSpace is returned, even if the message is one for which it is waiting. A freeze can be used to hold a system state while taking its 'snapshot', or to observe output.

The monitor can send messages with a false 'from' tag, circumventing the normal 'send' procedure which uses the id of the sender. Thus the monitor can be used by another object or by the user to break deadlock. Usually this feature is used with who, which is a request for a Q's current message specification.

30.4 The topology of an object world

An object world is a process like any other, and so can be replicated or built into hierarchies of independently developed occam modules. Processes which have channels unconnected to the messenger, such as the monitor and file objects, form the interface between an object world and its environment. The simple protocol between object and messenger simplifies the formation of such an interface. These features facilitate the development of systems by groups of programmers.

In occam, all processes have to be placed explicitly on processors. If an object world is to be located on one processor alone, then placement is trivial.

Otherwise, each processor has a subset of objects and a messenger to manage the transfer of messages along the hard links. Since the details of the communication subsystem and the configuration are hidden from objects, an object world can be considered as having a very simple topology, with each object connected to one network-spanning messenger. An object can be designed without reference to the placement of its acquaintances, which may equally well be running on the same processor, another processor in the same machine, or even another machine altogether.

Each object world has one monitor, fileManager and classManager. Having more than one of each would increase speed and reliability, but problems such as data consistency seemed an unnecessary burden given the scale of the current application. The freezing of objects may help with such problems, and allow features such as object migration. If a system was frozen, then an object could be made to transfer state information to an object on another processor. When unfrozen, the system would redirect messages to the latter object, whose behaviour would be equivalent to the continuation of the former. Migration allows automatic load distribution, and the clustering of objects that frequently communicate with each other.

Initially, only the messenger, monitor and classManager need be 'alive'. All objects required by a program could be designed to be active when the program begins execution. A more flexible approach is to create object processes dynamically, but this is not a standard feature of occam. This is not a restriction enforced by the transputer instruction set, but is present to allow occam's static memory allocation. In certain occam environments, true dynamic process creation appears to be possible [12]. On the Meiko, this approach did not seem easily practicable, and a method of pseudo-dynamic object creation was used.

A pool of processes, each with a Q process, is connected to the messenger, but each lies dormant until activated by the classManager with isA class:. When Q passes in the isA to the 'protoObject', a simple branch on the class name leads to an invocation of the process for the class. When die arrives from the classManager, the process terminates and the object reverts to its primordial state, to wait for the next isA. When an object sends new class:, it is making a request to the classManager to send an isA to a protoObject. The argument in the reply to new is the protoObject's id. Note that an object can live on after the object which asked for its creation has died.

Since code is shared, the vector of words in memory that forms the workspace of a protoObject is only enough for the local variables and temporary values manipulated by the process [13]. When space is tight, one can use protoObjects that may call a subset of class procedures, each of which uses a roughly similar amount of space. The space required for a protoObject is the space required for the largest in the subset. Further space savings may be traded off against speed if each state in an N process is represented by a different procedure, so that variables local to each state are overlaid.

The space required for a member of the class hierarchy may be excessive for simple, common structures (for example, stacks and queues), especially if used by only one other object. It has been found useful in this case to have a 'toolkit' of processes, for use inside objects, which do not have the general facilities of objects but use the standard message format.

30.5 On the behaviour of objects

The causal ordering of behaviour transitions and the use of data during behaviours define the sequentiality in the code needed to implement a class. If a behaviour is such that once started it requires no more input messages, and it relies on no variables which may be written to in some subsequent behaviour, then its replacement behaviour can commence and execute concurrently with the current behaviour. At the simplest level, this pipelining effect can take the form of asking Q for the first message that will start the replacement behaviour. More complex would be the use of concurrent processes inside N. This would incur the cost of extra mux/demuxers, channels and workspaces.

Formal axiomatic methods could be used to specify and validate the relationships between behaviours by making the postcondition statement for each one match the preconditions of all possible immediate successors.

CSP is the obvious candidate for use in analyzing occam processes. A number of authors have reported on systems for analyzing networks of processes [14–16]. Recent work [17] suggests that an alternative style of proof system based on temporal logic might be more applicable for networks of processes, especially networks which use asynchronous message passing. Also, the specification and proof for a process are formed naturally from the specifications and proofs of its components. The authors note that trace-based systems such as CSP can cause difficulty when specifying liveness properties such as progress and termination.

One problem area which is not adequately served by formal proof systems is that of the use of real number representations in computers. The work of producing proofs of satisfaction may seem exasperatingly futile when real number inaccuracies and flop errors show the disparity of the mathematics used in theory and in practice [18].

Conclusion

A ray tracer has been constructed according to an occam programming style presented, based on the modularity offered by processes. Drawing upon paradigms such as object-oriented languages and the actor model has aided data abstraction, the development and reuse of modules, and modelling power.

An obvious extension of the work presented would be to develop a system to support a language whose program modules were similar to the implementation descriptions of Section 30.2. A first step would be a program to translate such descriptions down to occam. It would, of course, be preferable to have a full language which compiled down to assembler, offered more detailed monitoring and debugging information, had facilities for compound data structures, and provided true dynamic object creation. A worthy research goal would be to develop an analogue of the much-admired Smalltalk programming environment, where the languages for commands, programming and debugging are essentially the same. Greater exploitation of highly concurrent machines such as the Meiko should be possible if languages – and environments to support them – are available which are more expressive than occam, and are founded on a less restricting model of concurrency.

Acknowledgements

This work was carried out as part of a PhD research project sponsored by the Science and Engineering Research Council. I am also grateful to my supervisor, Professor Robin Forrest, who 'got me into all this'. Lang may yer lum reek. One name considered for the tracer was Obsidian, taken from a letter from Dick Lister to the *Guardian* (8th April 1987) 'Obsidian: *ob*sessive *s*yntactically *i*ngenious *d*ev*i*sing or *a*cronymical *n*onsense'. Connoisseurs may particularly appreciate the initial double and, in the classic style, the plucking out of the right 'i'.

References

1. Chalmers M. (1989). Realism and design techniques in multiprocessor graphics systems. *PhD Thesis*, University of East Anglia
2. Jones G. (1987). *Programming in occam*. London: Prentice-Hall International
3. Rentsch T. (1981). Object-oriented programming. *SIGPLAN Notices,* **17**(9), 51–7
4. Strom R. (1986). A comparison of the object-oriented and process paradigms. *SIGPLAN Notices,* **21**(10), 88–97
5. Andrews G. and Olsson R. (1986). The evolution of the SR language. *Distributed Computing,* **1**(3), 133–49
6. Nguyen V. and Hailpern B. (1986). A generalised object model. *SIGPLAN Notices,* **21**(10), 78–87
7. Yonezewa A., Briot J-P. and Shibayama E. (1986). Object-oriented programming in ABCL/1. *SIGPLAN Notices,* **21**(11), 258–68
8. Agha G. (1986). *Actors*. Cambridge MA: MIT Press
9. Hoare C.A.R. (1985). *Communicating Sequential Processes*. London: Prentice-Hall International
10. Goldberg A. and Robson J. (1983). *Smalltalk-80: The Language and its Implementation*. Reading MA: Addison-Wesley
11. Hewitt C., Reinhard T., Agha G. and Attardi G. (1985). Linguistic support of receptionists for shared resources. In *Seminar on Concurrency* (Brookes S.D., Roscoe A.W. and Winskel G., eds), pp. 330–59. Berlin: Springer-Verlag
12. Thomas I. (1987). Object orientated programming on transputers. In *BCS Workshop on Parallel and Distributed Object Orientated Programming*, London, October 1987
13. INMOS Ltd (1986). *The Transputer Instruction Set – a Compiler Writer's Guide*. London: Prentice-Hall
14. Apt K., Francez N. and de Roever W. (1980). A proof system for communicating sequential processes. *ACM TOPLAS,* **2**(3), 359–85
15. Levin G. and Gries.D. (1981). A proof technique for communicating sequential processes. *Acta Informatica*, 15, 281–302
16. Misra J. and Chandy K. (1981). Proofs of networks of processes. *IEEE Trans. Soft. Eng.* **SE-7**(4), 417–26
17. Nguyen V., Demos A., Gries D. and Owicki S. (1986). A model and temporal proof system for networks of processes. *Distributed Computing,* **1**(1), 7–25
18. Forrest A.R. (1987). Computational geometry and software engineering. In *Techniques for Computer Graphics* (Rogers D.F. and Earnshaw R.E., eds), pp. 23–38. Berlin: Springer-Verlag

31 · A parallel algorithm and tree-based computer architecture for ray-traced computer graphics

S.A. Green
D.J. Paddon
E. Lewis

University of Bristol

The ray-tracing algorithm is well known for its high computational complexity and this has motivated research into exploiting the inherent parallelism of the algorithm by using multiprocessor systems. However, an object model to describe a scene of realistic complexity requires a very large database, which restricts the scope for designing an effective concurrent architecture. In this chapter, we describe and evaluate research which has led to a multiprocessor system that supports a database of arbitrary size. The results of the system show an optimal speedup for small databases while still maintaining a good performance for larger problems.

31.1 Introduction

Currently, the most popular method for the generation of realistic computer images is by **ray tracing** [1]. The ray-tracing algorithm has the dual advantage of being simple yet sufficiently powerful to model many natural phenomena such as reflection, refraction, transparency and shadows. However, it has the disadvantage that to generate the image requires a great deal of computer processing, mostly due to the ray–object intersection calculations which give rise to large numbers of floating-point operations.

Many aspects of the ray-tracing method are attracting research attention, in particular, finding and improving intersection tests for a variety of objects [2–6], extending the range of optical effects to be simulated [1, 7, 8], antialiasing [1, 7, 9–11] and reducing the number of intersection tests [1, 12–16]. However, on conventional uniprocessors of average power, the generation of an image is slow and tedious, and in many cases, impractical, particularly when the object space to be modelled consists of many thousands of primitives.

One of the advantages of the ray-tracing algorithm is that the illumination at each pixel can be computed independently. This pixel independence allows the ray-tracing method to be used concurrently and the algorithm to be implemented on a suitable network of processors. Parallel computer architectures fall into three major classes: vector processors, array processors and multiprocessor systems. Although the computation for 3D image creation consists mainly of vector and matrix arithmetic, the dimensions of the operands are too low to take advantage of the first two computer types. A number of special-purpose, parallel computer architectures have been proposed and designed and these are all multiprocessor systems. For example, the LINKS-1 [17, 18] is a parallel-pipelined multiprocessor consisting of a root (controller) computer and 64 unit computers, which was designed for image creation. In this system, the root computer allocates a subset of the rays to be rendered to each unit computer, and in order to perform the ray-tracing tasks, each processor requires the description of each object in space to be available locally. Thus, this scheme is not suitable for large databases of objects which may require more memory for storage than there is available on each unit computer.

Other schemes use tightly coupled multiprocessor systems, usually consisting of 2- or 3D arrays of processors for which an object space partition has been pre-computed [19–21]. Allocated to each processor is a section of the object space, and therefore only the descriptions of those objects contained within that section are required. As rays propagate through the environment, they are passed between adjacent processors as they cross subspace boundaries. While these schemes reduce the execution time as more processors are added to the systems, in general an unbalanced load distribution among the processors results. Dippé and Swensen [20] have proposed a means of performing load balancing at run time by using dynamically adaptable subregions so that busy processors can reduce their work load by dividing their section of space amongst their neighbours. Although effective to some extent, dynamic scheduling inevitably causes overhead at run time, thus degrading the performance of the system.

In general, special-purpose hardware is expensive, and often restricts the scope for research on the ray-tracing algorithm by the nature of the predetermined system implementation. There is still much scope to investigate software issues before developing extensive special-purpose parallel systems. What is required is a general-purpose parallel architecture that permits the researcher to investigate the ray-tracing algorithm independently of the hardware configuration. Here, we present a system testbed that consists of an infinitely extendable network of processors. The ray-tracing code is written within a harness which is duplicated on each processor, together with a local database manager. The architecture supports a database of arbitrary magnitude; distribution of data items and tasks are demand driven, and this mechanism is transparent to the user, which allows flexibility in developing different aspects of the ray-tracing algorithm.

31.2 System architecture

We assume that a large number of processors are available, each with a relatively small amount of local memory. Additionally, there exists a controller process which is given the responsibility of generating the tasks associated with a particular ray-tracing application, and allocating these tasks to processors on demand. A schematic model of this arrangement is shown in Figure 31.1, where **Work Processors** ($WP_1 \ldots WP_n$) perform ray-tracing operations in parallel, a **Distribution Processor** (DP) partitions the tasks, and the results are collected by a **Collection Processor** (CP) which is associated with the display hardware. This type of computational model is known as a **processor farm**, and was originally proposed by May and Shepherd [22].

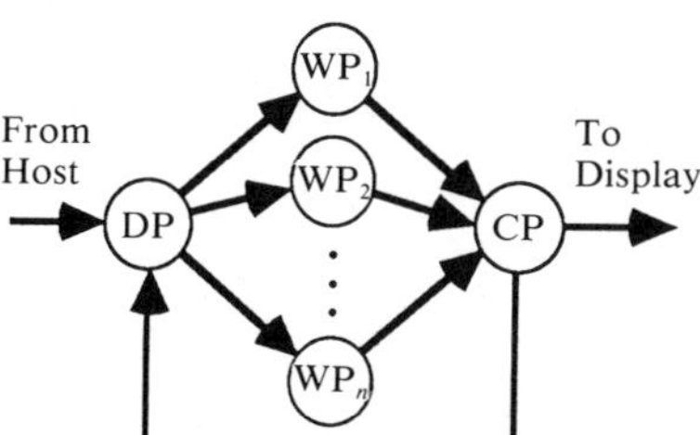

Figure 31.1
Conceptual architecture.

This arrangement is similar to the one adopted for the LINKS-1 system, however, the fanout introduces a bottleneck which, for more than a small number of processors, makes the arrangement prohibitive, as communication time exceeds processing time. What is required is a configuration that is conceptually equivalent to Figure 31.1, but that does not incur the same degradation due to the communications bottleneck. In the general case, the problem domain consists of a very large object space (say, several megabytes) relative to the size of local memory available to each processor (typically several kilobytes). This assumption implies that we must communicate portions of the database between processors, thus degrading the performance of the system by introducing additional communications overhead.

The strategy we employ here is to arrange the processor system into a tree structure with the controller processor placed at its root. In this case, for an N processor system with k subtrees per node, interprocessor communication is $O(\log_k N)$. An advantage of this configuration over, say, a square array, is that communications are much simplified: when a processor becomes idle, a request is made for work. Since all work originates at the root, this is propagated *up* the tree. Similarly, if a particular data item is required which is not available locally, it is requested by passing a message *up* the tree. Tasks and data items are satisfied by passing the relevant message *down* towards the requesting node. Adopting this mechanism of issuing requests up, and satisfying them down the tree makes communication simple, thereby reducing the overhead of message processing.

We are left to determine the means by which results are to be extracted from the network. One technique would be to use a separate collector processor as shown in Figure 31.1 to multiplex the results from the leaf nodes of the tree. To keep the architecture general and impose as few restrictions on the configuration of processors as possible, a collector network is not suitable, since it does not make efficient use of processors, nor does the resulting network conform to the requirements which keep the control structure simple. Thus, it is preferable to pass the results of the ray-tracing tasks back up the tree to the root, which then forwards them to the display hardware. The overall system architecture is illustrated in Figure 31.2.

31.3 Node process model

The architecture is represented by two processes which run concurrently on the tree structure. Firstly, the root process acts as the controller for the whole network and

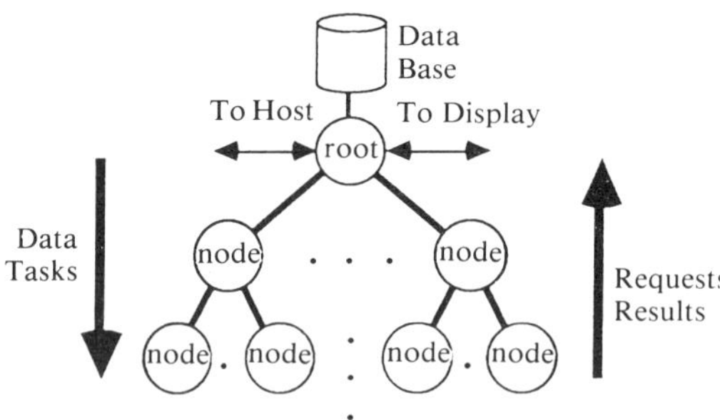

Figure 31.2
System architecture.

also as an interface to the host computer and the display hardware. It is this process that is responsible for generating all of the primary rays to be traced, corresponding to the screen pixels that are required by the rendering processes. In addition, the root process has available locally a copy of the total database, describing the object model, which is distributed to the network as required.

The second type of process, called a **node process**, is replicated as many times as there are renderers in the tree. The requirements of a node process are threefold: first and foremost, to perform the ray-tracing operations as they are passed down the tree and to return the completed tasks to the root. Secondly, the node process must receive messages from its parent, and in the case of a non-leaf node process, from its child/children, and relay them as appropriate. Finally, the node processor itself must maintain a local database of objects which, in general, will be much smaller than the description of the whole object space. In particular, the node processor must maintain copies of the most frequently used objects.

These three functions are entirely independent and, therefore, can be represented by three communicating subprocesses operating concurrently within a node. A process model representing this configuration is shown in Figure 31.3, where the processes are named the **Work Processor** (WP), **Work Distribution Manager** (WDM) and **Database Manager** (DBM) respectively.

31.4 Task management

One of the reasons for the computational complexity of the ray-tracing algorithm can be attributed to the way in which natural phenomena are modelled. The hidden-surface elimination effected by ray–object intersections may give rise to secondary rays spawned in the directions towards each light source: in the case of **shadow rays,** in the mirror direction with respect to the surface normal for specular reflection, and in the direction given by Snell's Law for coherent refraction [1].

Two separate stages in the recursive implementation can be identified. They are:

(1) Performing the hidden surface elimination (closest ray–object intersection).

(2) Calculating the intensity of the ray based on an illumination model.

Stage (2) can only be performed when all secondary rays spawned at the current intersection have been rendered, and since these secondary rays are independent of one another, then they may be rendered concurrently on a number of processors.

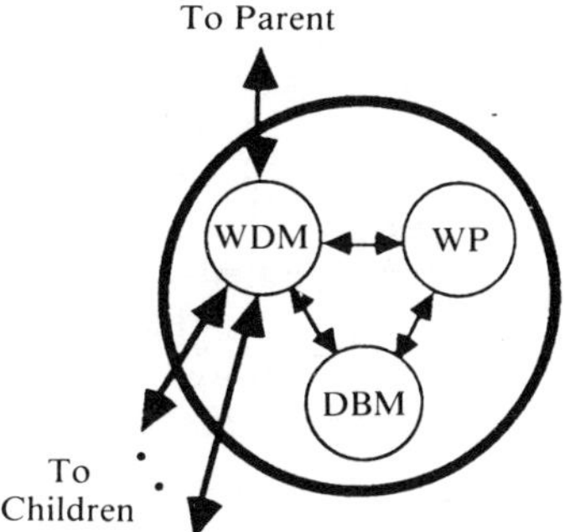

Figure 31.3
Node process model.

For each new ray spawned there may or may not be an idle processor ready to receive and begin processing the task. Thus, at each node we maintain a **ready work stack** of tasks waiting to be performed. When a WP becomes idle, it makes a **request for work** to its WDM. If the ready work stack is non-empty, then a task is popped and given to the WP to perform. New tasks which are spawned as a result of the current task are passed back to the WDM and pushed onto the stack. In the case where a request for work cannot be satisfied locally, because the ready work stack is empty, a global request for work is issued by the WDM to its parent. Thus, each WDM must monitor not only its WP for requests but also its children.

One of the features which will determine the efficiency of the system is the redundancy of the WP at each node. Requests for work which can be satisfied locally ensure a minimal idle time of the WP. Thus, in maintaining the ready work stack, the WDM initiates a request for work of its own when the stack becomes empty. If a task arrives at a node while its WP and children are busy, then it is pushed onto the stack to be taken up at a later time. In this way, availability of tasks at each node is improved, thus reducing idle time of WPs, and this will reflect in the performance of the system as a whole.

Any bottleneck in the system will be caused by internode communications, therefore it is essential that this communication is minimized whenever possible. The use of distributed ready work stacks ensures that, in general, requests can be satisfied locally without the need for each request to propagate to the root of the tree. Another feature of the WDM which helps to reduce global communication is the way in which requests are multiplexed. We maintain a list of which of a node's WP and children require work, and only a single request is passed to the parent node. When a task arrives to satisfy the request, it is given to the local WP, or if this is busy to one of the child nodes. A further request for work is then made if necessary.

A second data structure is maintained by the WDM for task management. This is the **delayed work list** and is necessary since the illumination contribution of each ray in the ray tree cannot be determined until each of its subrays is known. Such rays are said to be **delayed** and are placed on the delayed work list until all of the subrays have been rendered, when the ray can be made **ready** and placed on the ready work stack to have its illumination contribution calculated. Secondary rays are labelled with the identifier of the node from which they originated, and are returned to this node when they have been rendered where their corresponding parent ray will be resident in the delayed work list.

An efficient way to distribute ray-tracing tasks and to minimize communication overhead is to subdivide the image space into patches of pixels. For example, a patch may be a 16 × 16 area of the screen, and this can be passed to the network as a message consisting of an identifier only, which is derived from the (x, y) coordinates of one corner of the patch in screen space.

The anti-aliasing scheme incorporated is a straightforward supersample of rays through pixels on the screen. Figure 31.4 illustrates the way in which the hierarchy of image space subdivisions is built for a screen of $n.m \times n.m$ pixels divided into $n \times n$ patches of $m \times m$ pixels and supersampled by 16 rays per pixel.

31.5 Data management

Thus far, the way in which the task management algorithm is implemented on the system has been described. Since some tasks may be more computationally complex than others, a demand-driven technique is adopted so that an even work load can be achieved throughout. If it is assumed that a copy of the entire database which describes the object space resides locally to each node, then this can be considered to be a **task-oriented** system, since tasks are handed to nodes for processing as they become idle, and there is little or no overhead associated with obtaining objects from the database. However, such systems may be implemented more efficiently and effectively using a simpler scheme such as the one of Packer [23] in which a process model runs on a linear arrangement of processors performing ray-tracing operations. Unfortunately, each processor requires a copy of the entire database, and thus the scheme does not support databases of arbitrary size and complexity, since no facility is provided to communicate data items between processors.

The other type of multiprocessor system in which each processor has associated with it a fixed portion of the database, and a task is passed to the processor with the relevant objects to perform the ray-tracing operation, is termed **data oriented**. For example, Cleary *et al.* [19] describe a system using a 2- or 3D array of closely coupled processors with four and six nearest-neighbour connections respectively, where each processor is associated with the objects contained within a cubic subregion of the object space. As rays propagate through the environment, so they are passed from one processor to the next along the path of the ray. However, schemes of this kind have a flaw which has serious implications for even distribution of tasks across the network, and thus with speedup as more processors are added to the system. This arises since processors associated with 'busy' regions of the scene containing many objects and through which pass many rays, will be overloaded with work, while others with few objects and few rays may be idle.

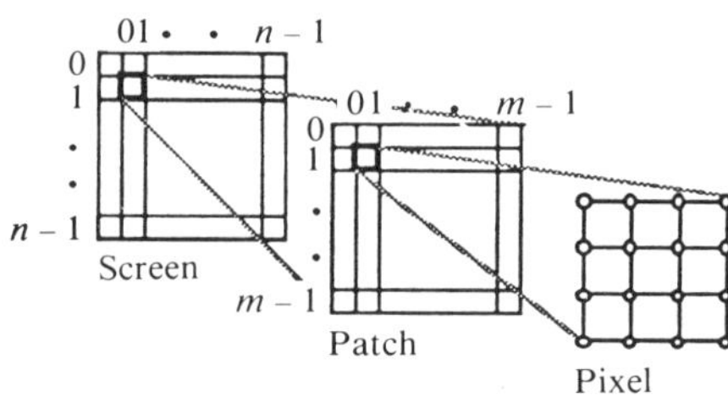

Figure 31.4
Image space subdivision.

What is needed for a general-purpose testbed is a sensible compromise between the task- and data-oriented approaches. Essential to this compromise is the way in which the database is distributed and managed by the network. If we assume that the space available for the storage of data at each node is small relative to the size of the whole database, then some object-space partitioning must be performed in order that the description of the scene can be subdivided in a sensible way. For this partitioning to be effective, it must tie in well with the ray-tracing algorithm itself. Fortunately, a number of such schemes have been proposed and, moreover, these schemes show an improvement over the standard algorithm. One possibility is the method of hierarchical bounding volumes [1, 14–16] where objects are nested in a hierarchy of simple enclosing volumes such as spheres or parallelepipeds, for which an intersection test is relatively simple. Another possibility, and the one adopted in this implementation, is the use of an octree structure for object space subdivision [12, 13]. Space is subdivided adaptively into cubic subvolumes, **voxels**, each containing a small number of objects. When a ray is traced, the voxel in which it starts must first be determined, and then the ray is intersected with each of the objects contained therein. If an intersection is not found, then the next voxel along the path of the ray is considered. This procedure is repeated until an intersection is found or until the ray exits the object space. The octree subdivision consists of a number of independent tasks which can themselves be performed concurrently on the network of processors as a preprocessing stage before image generation commences.

We can identify a storage overhead associated with any of the schemes which form an object space subdivision. In the case of the hierarchy of bounding volumes, the description of each volume must be stored, together with a list of all bounding volumes and/or object primitives that it contains. For the octree structure, a list of all voxels/object primitives contained within each voxel must be recorded; no information describing the voxel bounding planes need be stored however, since this is encoded implicitly in the identifier [13]. Thus, the database consists of two parts: an octree description and object descriptions.

A static allocation of data items to processors is inappropriate in view of the considerations already given, and a dynamic technique is favoured. The distributed database is managed at each node by its DBM in a manner similar to a cache memory. When a local request for data fails, the WDM polls its parent for the data item. On receipt of a request for data from a child node, a WDM relays the request to its DBM which replies with a 'not found' if the item is not resident, or with the item itself if it can be found, which is then passed to the child node.

When a data item is received by a WDM, which is required by the corresponding WP, it is sent to the DBM which stores it in the cache. A least-recently-used algorithm is employed to overwrite the least popular, currently stored data item. In general, if an image is generated by rendering adjacent pixels of the screen sequentially (for example, from top to bottom), then the object coherency present in the scene will minimize the amount of global data communication between processors, so that degradation of the performance of the system will be graceful as the complexity of the scene is increased.

In many cases, it is not necessary that a WP halts processing when a request for data fails locally. For example, when performing ray–object intersections within a voxel, a list of all the objects contained is initialized, and as each object is tested, it is removed from the list. Processing of the voxel continues until the list is empty. If one of the objects is not available locally, then a global request is made, and the WP resumes processing with the next object in the list, returning to the previous object when it becomes available.

31.6 Implementation

All aspects of the processor architecture which have been described are provided by the INMOS transputer. The transputer is a VLSI component, integrating a microcomputer with its own local memory and with a number of serial links to enable closely coupled networks of these devices to be assembled. The transputers used in this implementation are T414-15 devices, comprising a 32-bit microprocessor operating at 15 MHz with 2 kbytes of on-chip RAM, and four serial links operating at the standard speed of 10 Mbits per second.

In this implementation, the root process was executed on a board comprising a T414 transputer with 2 Mbytes of external RAM. One of the links of this processor was connected to the host, an IBM PC with a similar board to interface to the network. A second link connected to a transputer on a board which controlled the display hardware. Thus, two links of the root processor were available for connecting to the tree of processors. Each node process was executed on a transputer with 256 kbytes of external memory.

The parallel algorithm and the ray-tracing code were written entirely in occam, [24], a high-level programming language based upon a model of concurrency where all communication is synchronized and unbuffered, and takes place through the use of a data structure called a **channel**. Processes communicate by passing messages along channels. The implementation described here requires that a number of distinct messages of varying sizes are to be passed down channels at different times.

The message itself consists of an array of elements. The first of these elements is a unique identifier which indicates the type of the message. Subsequent elements correspond to the data fields for the particular message.

The principal messages to perform the ray tracing are Render (a task item: ray to be rendered), Illuminate (a task item: illumination contribution to calculate), DoneRender (a completed task), Object and Voxel (data items for distribution).

31.7 Results

Ten transputers were used to test the system architecture previously described. The processors were allocated as follows: one processor to the root process, one processor to the display handling and the remaining eight processors to define the tree structure. The configurations shown in Figure 31.5 (designated T1 . . . T8) were chosen to use a balanced topology so that characteristics of the systems were comparable.

It is important when observing speedup of any multiprocessor system to ensure that like subsystems are being compared, since spurious results ensue if processor speed and memory access times are not consistent.

Three different object databases of varying complexity were defined to evaluate the performance of the system. The databases represented the following images:

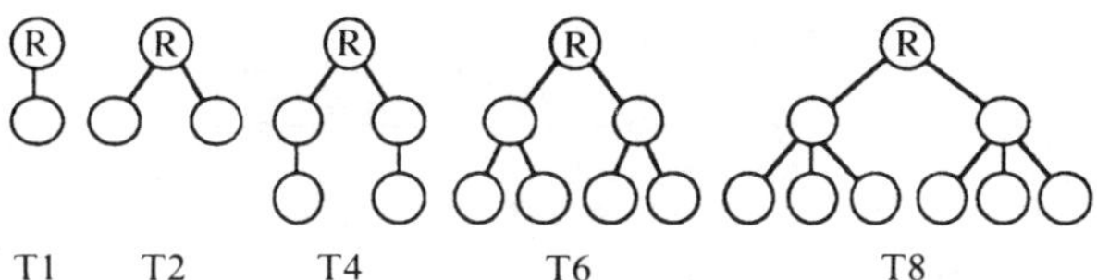

Figure 31.5
Tree topologies.

(1) an organo-metallic molecular model
(2) a dining room scene
(3) a crystal lattice structure

These are illustrated in Plates 8, 9 and 10 respectively, for which a 1024 × 1024 image was generated, anti-aliased by a 16-point supersample per pixel.

(1) The database representing the molecule consists of 64 reflecting spheres, and is sufficiently small that a complete copy can reside locally in the cache of each node process. This is a special case which reduces to the problems addressed by previous systems [17–19, 23], and for the new scheme to be viable this case must be well supported and demonstrate a near linear speedup with the number of processors in the system. The results indicate that this is achieved, and are shown in Table 31.1. As an indication of the relative performance of each node in the network, the table also shows the average number of rays traced by each node processor per second of rendering time. In the ideal case, this figure is constant for all topologies of processors.

(2) An order-of-magnitude increase in the number of objects is shown in the image of Plate 9 which is represented by a database consisting of 633 polygons. This model is used to test and evaluate the performance of the DBM when a small local cache is used. A maximum of 50% of the database could reside locally, so the DBM was employed to distribute objects as required. The tests with this system did not give significantly different results to those of section (1), so the DBM was forced into higher activity by artificially restricting the size of the local cache. Results are presented for a cache size equivalent to 10% and 5% of the full database, and given in Table 31.2.

A degradation of performance is indicated as the caching activity is increased, but even with a cache size of 5% of the database, the system is still better than 78% efficient with eight node processors.

Table 31.1 Results for the molecule shown in Plate 8.

Tree	*Rays Node^{-1}s^{-1}*	*Speedup*
T1	44.43	1.00
T2	44.39	2.00
T4	44.26	3.98
T6	44.17	5.96
T8	44.25	7.97

Table 31.2 Results for the room shown in Plate 9.

Tree	*% local cache*			
	10%		*5%*	
	Rays Node^{-1}s^{-1}	*Speedup*	*Rays Node^{-1}s^{-1}*	*Speedup*
T1	22.96	1.00	21.98	1.00
T2	22.80	1.99	21.85	1.99
T4	21.64	3.77	19.84	3.61
T6	21.06	5.50	18.73	5.11
T8	20.55	7.16	17.68	6.44

Table 31.3 Results for the lattice shown in Plate 10.

Tree	*% local cache*							
	10%		*5%*		*1%*		*0.5%*	
	*R**	*S**	*R*	*S*	*R*	*S*	*R*	*S*
T1	29.00	1.00	30.14	1.00	29.10	1.00	28.83	1.00
T2	28.62	1.97	29.75	1.97	28.73	1.98	28.42	1.97
T4	25.59	3.53	25.67	3.41	22.71	3.12	21.76	3.02
T6	24.08	4.98	23.59	4.70	19.15	3.95	17.78	3.70
T8	22.88	6.31	21.83	5.79	16.22	4.46	14.57	4.04

* R = Rays per Node per Second; S = Speedup

(3) The complex database of the crystal lattice shown in Plate 10, consisting of 2000 spheres, allowed us to evaluate the system performance with local caches containing a maximum of 10% of the database to the extreme case of when only 0.5% of the database can be resident at any time. In these cases, the amount of communication of data items between processors increases proportionally with their number, giving rise to a degradation in performance as can be seen from the results in Table 31.3.

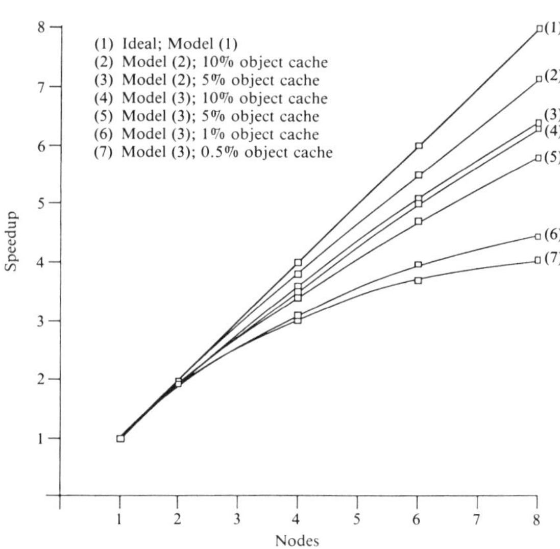

Figure 31.6
Summary of results.

In models (2) and (3), the size of the voxel cache was held constant while that of the object cache was changed. Thus, performance of model (2) was better than that of model (3) since the local voxel cache had capacity for proportionally more of the voxels in the octree structure. The results given for the three models are summarized graphically in Figure 31.6.

Conclusions

We have established and tested a tree architecture system for a distributed database, that has been evaluated using a ray-tracing algorithm. We have shown that the system exhibits near linear speedup when a world model can reside in its entirety at each processor node. However, a degradation of performance is shown when a data distribution is required due to small local caches (relative to the database size).

The processors used, T414 transputers, implement floating-point operations in software. Therefore, the processing time relative to communication time is high. Faster processors such as the new T800 floating-point transputer will radically change the ratio of computation to communication time for floating-point intensive problems. Further research needs to be carried out to determine if the power of these new processors will be eroded by relatively high communication times.

There is much scope for further research into aspects of the parallel algorithm itself. Many requests for data items are made to the DBM during each execution, and an investigation of caching strategies and optimum cache sizes should bring to light obvious areas for improvement.

The current implementation is intended to be general purpose, thus all messages and object descriptions contain data fields where each component is one or more 32-bit word. In a realistic implementation, this degree of generality will not be required, and so messages and object descriptions may be shortened to improve communications and storage requirements significantly.

The optimum configuration for a given number of processors is not fully understood, and research in this area is essential for a better understanding of the characteristics of the tree architecture.

Acknowledgements

We have benefited from discussions with Neil Davies and Paul Chapman. Thanks to Guy Orpen for the data for the molecule, Dave Rogers for invaluable help in converting images into transparencies, and to Nick Holliman for helpful comments on the paper.

References

1. Whitted T. (1980). An improved illumination model for shaded display. *Communications of the ACM,* **23**(6), 343–9
2. Barr A.H. (1986). Ray tracing deformed surfaces. *ACM Computer Graphics,* **20**(4), 287–96

3. Kajiya J.T. (1982). Ray tracing parametric patches. *ACM Computer Graphics,* **16**(3), 245–54
4. Kajiya J.T. (1983). New techniques for ray tracing procedurally defined objects. *ACM Transactions on Graphics,* **2**(3), 161–81
5. Kajiya J.T. and Von Herzen B.P. (1984). Ray tracing volume densities. *ACM Computer Graphics,* **18**(3), 165–74
6. Van Wijk J.J. (1984). Ray tracing objects defined by sweeping planar cubic splines. *ACM Transactions on Graphics,* **3**(3), 223–37
7. Cook R.L. (1986). Stochastic sampling in computer graphics. *ACM Transactions on Graphics,* **5**(1), 51–72
8. Hall R.A. and Greenberg D.P. (1983). A testbed for realistic image synthesis. *IEEE Computer Graphics and Applications,* **3**(8), 10–20
9. Amanatides J. (1984). Ray tracing with cones. *ACM Computer Graphics,* **18**(3), 129–35
10. Cook R.L., Porter T., Carpenter L. (1984). Distributed ray tracing. *ACM Computer Graphics,* **18**(3), 137–45
11. Heckbert P.S. and Hanrahan P. (1984). Beam tracing polygonal objects. *ACM Computer Graphics,* **18**(3), 119–27
12. Fujimoto A., Tanaka T. and Iwata K. (1986). ARTS: Accelerated Ray-Tracing System. *IEEE Computer Graphics and Applications,* **6**(4), 16–26
13. Glassner A.S. (1984). Space subdivision for fast ray tracing. *IEEE Computer Graphics and Applications,* **4**(10), 15–22
14. Goldsmith J. and Salmon J. (1987). Automatic creation of object hierarchies for ray tracing. *IEEE Computer Graphics and Applications,* **7**(5), 14–20
15. Kay T.L. and Kajiya J.T. (1986). Ray tracing complex scenes. *ACM Computer Graphics,* **20**(4), 269–78
16. Weghorst H., Hooper G. and Greenberg D.P. (1984). Improved computational methods for ray tracing. *ACM Transactions on Graphics,* **3**(1), 52–69
17. Deguchi H. *et al.* (1984). A parallel processing scheme for three-dimensional image generation. In *Proceedings of IEEE 1984 International Symposium on Circuits and Systems*, 1285–8.
18. Nishimura H. *et al.* (1983). LINKS-1: A parallel pipelined multimicrocomputer system for image creation. In *Proceedings of the 10th Annual International Symposium on Computer Architecture*, 387–94
19. Cleary J.G. *et al.* (1983). *Multiprocessor Ray Tracing*. Technical Report No. 83/128/17, University of Calgary
20. Dippé M. and Swensen J. (1984). An adaptive subdivision algorithm and parallel architecture for realistic image synthesis. *ACM Computer Graphics,* **18**(3), 149–58
21. Kobayashi H., Nakamura T. and Shigei Y. (1987). Parallel processing of an object space for image synthesis using ray tracing. *The Visual Computer,* **3**(1), 13–22
22. May D. and Shepherd R. (1987). *Communicating Process Computers.* INMOS Technical Note 22. Bristol: INMOS Ltd
23. Packer J. (n.d.) *Exploiting Concurrency: A Ray Tracing Example.* INMOS Technical Note 7, Bristol: INMOS Ltd
24. INMOS Ltd (1984). *Occam Programming Manual.* London: Prentice-Hall

32 · An evaluation of the processor farm model for visualizing constructive solid geometry

N.S. Holliman
D.T. Morris
P.M. Dew
A. de Pennington

University of Leeds

The real-time visualization of constructive solid geometry is an essential requirement for the development of interactive workstations to support mechanical engineering design. The identification of computational models is important if new hardware is to be exploited to speed up existing algorithms. An experimental parallel solid modeller is described that uses spatial parallelism to produce tasks to be executed on a processor farm. Four rendering algorithms have been implemented using this computational model and results are given from an implementation on an array of transputers.

32.1 Background

Computational descriptions of the 3D geometry of solid objects play a fundamental role in many scientific and engineering fields including computer graphics. Set theoretic solid modelling or Constructive Solid Geometry (CSG) is now a well-established field of computational geometry. At Leeds, a solid modeller, using CSG as its primary representation scheme, forms a major component of an information support system being developed to aid the mechanical designer in the design, analysis, manufacture and inspection of discrete goods.

Unfortunately, industry has been slow to exploit CSG-based systems for interactive design work. Part of the reason for this is the computational complexity of the geometric queries required by the rendering algorithms. One research project is studying the design of a parallel computational geometry engine in order to answer geometric queries on CSG models quickly and efficiently. It is expected that this will enable the development of an interactive graphical system for creating and editing CSG models of solid objects.

To help understand the problems of mapping geometric computations onto parallel architectures, a collaborative project is underway with the IBM UK Scientific Centre, to investigate the real-time visualization of CSG models. As part of this project, an experimental parallel solid modeller called MISTRAL has been implemented to evaluate ways of exploiting parallelism in a variety of CSG rendering algorithms. In particular **spatial parallelism** has been used to generate tasks that are executed on a **processor farm**.

This chapter reports on the development of MISTRAL, including a discussion of the processor farm model, the support software needed and some of the problems encountered when exploiting simple spatial parallelism. MISTRAL has been implemented on a Meiko Computing Service [1] which is a general-purpose parallel computer, based on the INMOS transputer [2], providing a useful environment for prototyping parallel algorithms.

32.2 Computational models

A computational model provides a level of abstraction between applications and systems. It allows applications to be targeted at a virtual machine which may be supported on several physical machines. An example of this approach is provided in Leonard *et al.* [3] who implement a specific application, namely, an image processing language called Apply, on several serial and parallel machines.

Kung [4] describes eight computational models for the CMU Warp and states that the range of computational models a machine supports defines its usage patterns, that is, the type and diversity of algorithms the machine can usefully compute. May and Shepard [5] describe two models for communicating process computers, the pipeline and the processor farm. They give no definition of these terms, and simply observe that a number of applications correspond to one of the two descriptions. These models are equivalent to the pipeline and task queue models proposed by Kung.

Sound and consistent definitions of models are needed if they are to be supported successfully on real machines. The following is the working definition of the processor farm used in the implementation of MISTRAL.

32.2.1 The processor farm

The processor farm is made up of three independent modules (Figure 32.1):

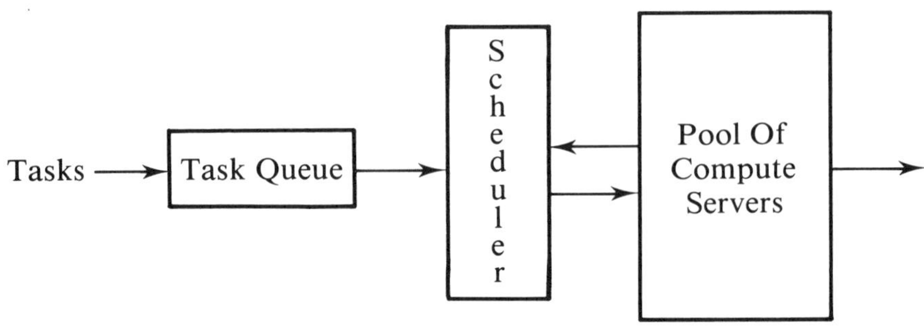

Figure 32.1
Overview of the processor farm.

- A **task queue** of independent tasks awaiting execution. Executing tasks do not communicate with each other.
- A pool of identical **compute servers** capable of executing any task from the task queue.
- A **scheduling algorithm** that assigns tasks to compute servers, this may be centralized or distributed.

The processor farm allows applications to be implemented independently of the topology of the network; it is easily extensible and performance degrades gracefully if compute servers fail, providing sufficient communications bandwidth is available. However, the processor farm does not abstract away from parallelism; it is still the application programmer's responsibility to produce a set of independent tasks and a compute server to execute them.

At a higher level of abstraction, it may be appropriate to remove all details of how an algorithm is executed. This approach has been adopted by the Alvey Flagship project [6]. The Flagship machine will be programmed in a functional language, which means the user has no way of specifying explicit control information. When the program is executed, graph reduction is used to produce a set of independent tasks automatically. Tasks are executed on a processor farm of close-coupled processor store elements which are connected to a high bandwidth communications system. Flagship is a fine-grain machine and is likely to incur large communications and load-balancing overheads; to help overcome these problems, items of specialized hardware are being designed.

Jesshope [7] proposes an active-data model for implementing vision algorithms. The model separates the activation of processors from the methods applied to the data; only those processors that are activated apply the current method to the data they hold. This could easily be implemented as a processor farm on a communicating process machine or a systolic machine such as the Warp. What makes the paper interesting is the description of how the active data model could be implemented on a SIMD machine, in particular the RPA processor.

The last two examples suggest that an algorithm designed around the processor farm model can be implemented on a wide variety of machine architectures. The authors believe that it is important to identify computational models underlying classes of algorithms. Then, in a field where there is constant change, it should be possible to map algorithms onto physical devices, whether that device is a general-purpose serial or parallel machine, or a special-purpose VLSI chip set designed specifically to support one computational model. Jesshope [7] notes that a computational model should describe attributes of a computation rather than attributes of a particular computer system.

The next section discusses the four rendering algorithms used in MISTRAL and how they can be implemented using the processor farm model.

32.3 The CSG representation scheme and rendering algorithms

Any scheme for representing solid objects must satisfy the formal properties presented in Requicha [8]. Of the six schemes identified as satisfying these properties, one of the most widely used is CSG. This is used as the primary representation scheme in the systems being developed at Leeds since it is concise, valid (due to the closure of regularized set operators on regular sets) and can be expressed as a procedural language.

There is a wide variety of techniques for rendering images of CSG models; see Rossignac and Requicha [9] for a brief survey. The four rendering algorithms used in MISTRAL are:

(1) Ray casting: this casts one ray per pixel and has no optimizations. See Roth [10] or Whitted [11] for detailed descriptions of the ray-casting algorithm.

(2) The Woodwark algorithm, which creates a partial Spatially Divided Solid Model (SDSM) using octree subdivision and renders the cells on the fly. The serial algorithm used in MISTRAL was developed by Woodwark and Quinlan in [12].

(3) A modification of the previous algorithm so that an efficient prescriptive shader is used to render cells containing only one halfspace.

(4) Parallel adaptive refinement: this is a parallel version of the algorithm developed by Broonsvort *et al.* [13]. Initially, a low resolution image is raycast and a simple image processing technique is applied to decide which areas to refine by ray casting at higher resolutions. The effect is to refine the quality of the image incrementally; this is similar to the techniques used by Bergman *et al.* [14] to render polygons and Forrest [15] to render vectors.

The obvious way to find parallelism in the rendering algorithms is to subdivide image space into a set of disjoint regions. This is possible since the computation for each ray can be performed independently, as is noted by Morris and Dew in [16], who call this technique for exploiting parallelism in rendering algorithms **spatial parallelism**. This approach allows the rendering algorithms to be mapped onto the processor farm model; each subdivision of the image forms an independent task and no task need communicate with any other task while it is being executed. The rendering algorithms have been matched to the computational model independently of a specific implementation; the next section describes how MISTRAL has been implemented.

32.4 Implementing MISTRAL

The implementation of MISTRAL required the development of system software to support the processor farm on a transputer array and the conversion of existing application code from Ada to occam. The support software needed fell into three categories: communications, system services and task scheduling. These were developed as reusable, application-independent libraries. The diagram (Figure 32.2) gives the logical structure of MISTRAL.

Occam provides local communications between two adjacent processes via explicitly defined channels. Implementation of the processor farm requires global communications, allowing messages to be routed to any processor in the network via intermediate processors. A packet switching protocol was developed, that provides source-to-destination data transfer; the protocol makes no provision for feedback to the sender confirming the arrival of a message. A set of processes that run concurrently with the application program, route packets to their destination by

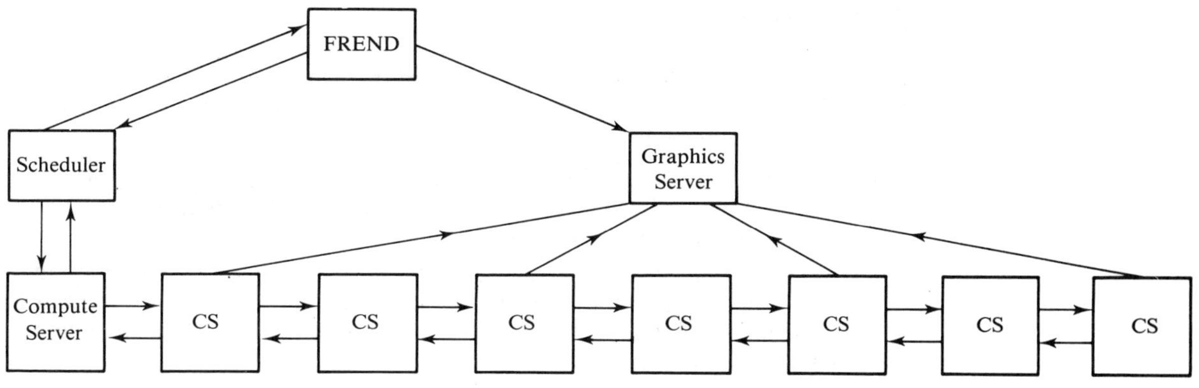

Figure 32.2
The logical structure of MISTRAL.

comparing routeing information attached to each packet with fixed routeing tables. These include a multiplexor, a demultiplexor and a buffer process, which can be connected together to provide the required infrastructure.

It was also necessary to provide some system support software. This was developed as a set of servers that accept packets from the communications processes. The packet contents are interpreted and the required function invoked. Two levels of graphics support are provided as servers, and a load-monitoring server receives packets of statistics from probes in the application code and displays these on the graphics device.

Two scheduling algorithms were implemented: one that assigns tasks statically to compute servers, and one that schedules tasks dynamically on a demand-driven basis. Both algorithms are implemented as one central process, as opposed to being distributed (as is the case in the Flagship machine). The dynamic algorithm gives more efficient processor utilization for the data-dependent rendering algorithms.

The application code was converted to occam and placed in a communications harness. This forms the compute server which, like the system servers, accepts packets from the network to invoke application functions. Each compute server contains a copy of all the rendering software and a copy of the CSG tree, hence it is capable of rendering any subset of the image. Creating tasks is trivial, as each task can be uniquely specified with two pairs of coordinates defining a rectangular sub-image. Currently, a regular grid is used that produces square subimages. The number of squares along each side of the grid can be altered, and this provides a crude throttle mechanism for controlling the granularity and number of tasks. The pixels that are generated are routed to the graphics server and placed on the graphics card. All four links into the transputer controlling the video memory are used for pixel transport.

FREND is an interactive front end which interprets a simple command language, allowing the user to read in model definitions created by existing modellers, alter lighting parameters or redisplay the image using one of the four rendering algorithms.

32.5 Results

To establish whether using spatial parallelism to drive a processor farm is an effective way of implementing the rendering algorithms, the behaviour of MISTRAL was studied in two ways.

(1) Vary the number of compute servers available, while keeping all other variables constant. Ideally, there should be a linear relationship between the number of compute servers used and the rendering times.

(2) Vary the number of tasks available, keeping all other variables constant, including the number of processors. This should establish whether it is more efficient to use a large number of finer-grain tasks, or a smaller number of coarser-grain tasks.

The results were measured using T414B transputers, each processor having 256K of local memory. Plate 11 shows a simple component rendered using the Woodwark algorithm again at 256 × 256 pixels. The results given are for rendering the molecule image in Plate 12 at a resolution of 256 × 256 pixels. This model is the set theoretic union of 23 spherical halfspaces.

Figure 32.3 shows the relative speedup obtained as the number of compute servers used is increased. For the ray-casting algorithm, there is a linear speedup up to 152 compute servers. For the Woodwark algorithm, the linear relationship holds up to 128 processors but then the graph flattens out. This is due to the pixels being generated at a greater rate than they can be transmitted to the graphics server and displayed. This can be inferred from the line showing the Woodwark algorithm with graphic output switched off (no I/O), when the linear relationship is re-established. This is not apparent in the ray-casting algorithm since it is significantly slower than Woodwark's algorithm and does not saturate the pixel transport and display systems.

Figure 32.4 shows how the performance varies if the number of compute servers is held constant, at 152, and the subdivision of the image into tasks varied. The ray-casting algorithm shows an initial decrease in rendering times as the end effect is reduced, but then levels out with no further performance benefits to be gained by producing smaller tasks. The Woodwark algorithm shows a small initial decrease in runtime but as the tasks become smaller it becomes increasingly

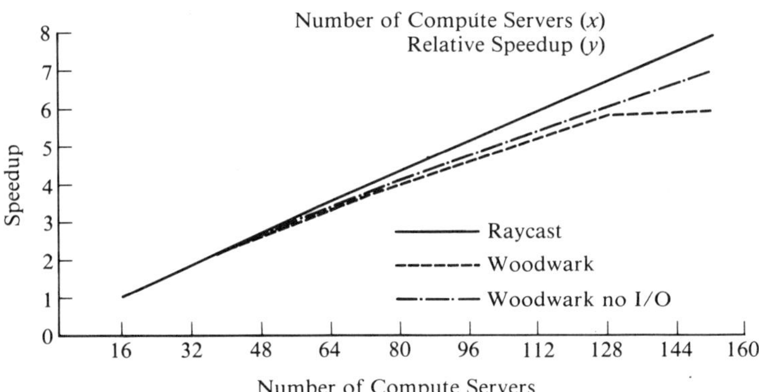

Figure 32.3
Relative speedup as number of compute servers is increased.

inefficient. This, as predicted by Woodwark [17], is due to the loss of the benefits of spatial coherence and the need to classify large trees repeatedly against many small volumes of space.

Conclusions

Using spatial parallelism to subdivide the application algorithm, and mapping this onto a transputer array using the processor farm model has proved to be a successful approach when using moderate numbers of processors. A linear speedup has been obtained when using up to 128 compute servers. This is then limited by the rate at which pixels can be transported to and displayed by the graphics device. The problem could be removed by using more than one transputer to access video memory; this would increase both the communications bandwidth into video memory and the rate at which pixels could be displayed, allowing more compute servers to be utilized.

A throttle mechanism has been provided to allow the amount of parallelism to be varied to match the properties of the machine in use. Although no results are presented to show that this is useful in all cases, Figure 32.4 shows that most efficient use of the machine can be found by varying the number and granularity of tasks being executed. Practical experience indicates that the best throttle setting is different for configurations with different numbers of compute servers rendering the same image.

There are two drawbacks to using the approach adopted in MISTRAL.

(1) Each processor must have enough memory to store the entire CSG tree, primitive definitions, quadtrees, lighting models, pixel buffers and code. This may affect the number of processors that can sensibly be afforded.

(2) If a large number of processors is used, the image is divided into many small subimages to be rendered. As can be seen in Figure 32.4, the Woodwark algorithm becomes very inefficient for small subimages. This is because the Woodwark algorithm exploits coherence to achieve better performance; unfortunately, this is lost when rendering small areas of an image.

These drawbacks are due to the use of spatial parallelism and not to the

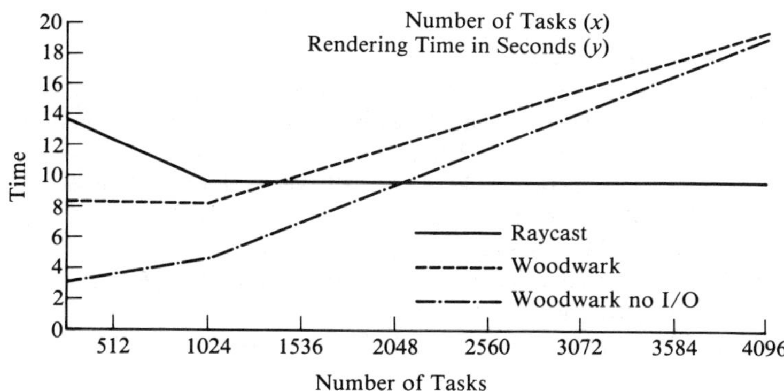

Figure 32.4
Performance variation with subdivision of image into tasks.

processor farm model. This suggests that a different problem subdivision may give better results; the next section introduces future work in this area.

Future work

To overcome the problems of exploiting spatial parallelism for efficient rendering algorithms Morris and Quarendon [18, 19] have examined the Woodwark algorithm in more detail. The approach taken is to exploit both spatial and structural parallelism in a hybrid parallelism using dynamic dataflow techniques. The algorithm is still based on the processor farm and tasks (CSG tree against voxel classifications) are scheduled to compute servers as before. The algorithm was designed to have a set of variables that can be used as a throttle to match the tasks to the capabilities of the machine in use. It avoids the need to store the entire CSG tree at each node and still exploits coherence. This algorithm is currently being prototyped on a Computing Surface.

As computational models are identified and shown to be of practical use they can be described formally in a language such as CSP [20]. This would allow proof of lack of deadlock and a better understanding of their properties.

Acknowledgements

The authors would like to thank all those at the IBM United Kingdom Scientific Centre who have contributed to this work. In particular, Peter Quarendon and Steven Todd for many helpful discussions, Bill Ricketts and Norman Winterbottom for their invaluable help implementing the support software and Tom Heywood for having the foresight to support the work at Leeds and loan us a Meiko Computing Surface.

Thanks also to Meiko Ltd for the use of a larger Computing Surface to collect some of the results presented in this paper.

Nick Holliman is a research student supported by an SERC CASE award sponsored by the IBM UK Scientific Centre and David Morris is a research fellow sponsored by the IBM UK Scientific Centre.

References

1. Meiko Ltd (1987). *The Computing Surface.*
2. INMOS Ltd (1987). *The Transputer Family.* Product Information
3. Leonard G.C., Webb J.A. and I-Chen W. (1987). Low level vision on Warp and the apply programming model. *Parallel Computation and Computers for Artificial Intelligence* (Kowalik J., ed.). Kluwer Academic Publishers
4. Kung H.T. (1988). Computational models for Warp-like machines. *Phil. Trans. Royal Society,* **A326**, 357–71
5. May D. and Shepard R. (1987). *Communicating Process Computers.* INMOS Technical Note 22. Bristol: INMOS Ltd
6. Watson I., Sargeant J., Watson P. and Woods V. (1987). Flagship

computational models and machine architecture. *ICL Technical Journal,* **5**(3), 555–74

7. Jesshope C. (1987). A dynamic load balanced, active-data model of parallel processing for vision. In *Parallel Architectures and Computer Vision* (Page I., ed.). Oxford: Clarendon Press
8. Requicha A.A.G. (1980). *Representations for rigid solids: theory, methods and systems. ACM Computing Surveys,* **12**(4), 437–64
9. Rossignac J.R. and Requicha A.A.G. (1986). Depth buffering display techniques for constructive solid geometry. *IEEE Computer Graphics and Applications,* **6**(9), 29–38
10. Roth S.D. (1982). *Ray casting for modelling solids. Computer Graphics and Image Processing,* **18**(2), 109–44
11. Whitted T. (1980). An improved illumination model for shaded display. *Communications of the ACM,* **23**(6), 343–9
12. Woodwark J.R. (1982). Reducing the effect of complexity on volume model evaluation. *CAD Journal,* **14**(2), 88–95
13. Bronsvoort W.F., van Wijk J.J. and Jansen F.W. (1984). Two methods for improving the efficiency of ray casting in solid modelling. *Computer Aided Design*, **1**(1), 51–5
14. Bergman L., Fuchs H., Grant E. and Spach S. (1986). Image rendering by adaptive refinement. *Computer Graphics,* **20**(4), 29–37
15. Forrest A.R. (1985). Antialiasing in practice. *NATO ASI Fundamental Algorithms for Computer Graphics,* **F17**, 113–34
16. Morris D.T., de Pennington A. and Dew P.M. (1987). Programmable VLSI array architectures for solid modelling. *Parallel Processing for Displays; BCS Displays Group Day Conference Proceedings*, May 1987
17. Woodwark J.R. (1984). A multiprocessor display architecture for viewing solid models. *Displays Technology and Applications,* **5**(2), 97–103
18. Morris D.T. and Quarendon P. (1985). An algorithm for direct display of CSG objects by spatial subdivision. *Proc. NATO ASI on Fundamental Algorithms for Computer Graphics*, 725–37. Ilkley, Yorkshire, March 1985
19. Morris D.T. (1987). Parallel architectures and algorithms for the display of constructive solid geometry. *PhD Thesis*, Leeds University
20. Hoare C.A.R. (1985). *Communicating Sequential Processes.* London: Prentice-Hall International

D.T. Morris
P.M. Dew

University of Leeds

33 · Dynamic dataflow algorithms for ray tracing CSG objects

This chapter describes how solid objects may be rendered by the use of dynamic dataflow techniques. Particular emphasis is given to the ray-tracing algorithm. The objects are described by constructive solid geometry. The algorithms are designed to be executed on a processor farm coupled with a data-driven dataflow machine. Many of the limitations of previous approaches, such as the Kedem-Ellis ray-casting machine are overcome. For example, the size of the objects that can be drawn directly is increased, the shading computations are made more efficient and there is better hardware utilization.

33.1 Introduction

With the advent of modern CAD/CAM systems based around solid modelling techniques, there is a need for extremely high performance workstations to allow the engineer to manipulate and display solid models at interactive speeds. Conventional von Neumann architectures need minutes and even hours to produce an image of a complex solid model, hence the need for parallelism. The solid representation to be used in this chapter is Constructive Solid Geometry (CSG), as described by Requicha and Voelker (1977).

One technique for rendering CSG objects is the ray-tracing algorithm described by Roth (1982). An image of a CSG object is computed by determining which part of it lies nearest the front of the screen at every pixel. This can be done by casting a **visibility ray** through each pixel on the screen and classifying it against the CSG tree to find the points of intersection. The visible surface is the one passing through the intersection point nearest to the eye. For the purposes of this chapter, this will be referred to as **ray casting** to find visible surfaces. A more sophisticated extension of ray casting is **ray tracing** which allows reflections, refraction and shadows to be modelled. Once the visibility ray has been cast, and the visible point has been determined, additional rays can be fired from this point in different directions. For instance, a further ray can be cast in the direction of the light source to see if the point is in shadow. If the ray encounters any objects along the way, then the light is hidden from view, and the point is in shadow. Reflections can be modelled by casting rays from the surface in the direction of the reflected light.

The first part of the object encountered along this ray is the one reflected in the surface.

33.2 Parallelism for the ray-tracing algorithm

The ray–CSG intersection algorithm is an example of the standard line classification algorithm discussed by Tilove (1980). This section describes techniques for exploiting the parallelism inherent in this algorithm.

From inspection of the serial algorithm, it is evident that the two operands of any operator node in the CSG tree can be classified independently of each other. This implies that the classify-combine algorithms at any given level in the tree may all be classified in parallel. In particular, all of the primitive classifications may be executed concurrently. This kind of parallelism will be called **structural parallelism** because it exploits the inherent structure of the CSG tree. Parallelism is exploited by attaching processors to individual nodes (or subtrees) in the CSG tree in order to execute classifications in parallel. This is equivalent to the **functional parallelism** or **and-parallelism** exploited in dataflow and reduction machines. Two factors determine how much parallelism may be exploited in this way. Firstly, the number of primitives in the tree controls how many primitive classifications may be executed concurrently. Secondly, the degree to which the tree is balanced determines parallelism for the Merge-Classification operation. A perfectly balanced CSG tree will yield maximum potential parallelism, with 2^D concurrent classifications to be executed, where D is the tree depth. A completely left- or right-heavy CSG tree (one in which every right or left operand is a primitive) results in every combine classification being executed serially. There are several approaches that can be used when mapping the nodes in the CSG tree onto a processor array. The first, and simplest, is to build a **tree machine** whose structure mirrors that of the CSG tree. In practice, the trees are not balanced, and do not necessarily match the size of the processor array being used.

33.2.1 The Kedem-Ellis Ray-casting Machine

Kedem and Ellis (see Chapter 27) propose an architecture that exploits structural parallelism by embedding the binary CSG tree into a rectangular processor array, in order to allow unbalanced trees to be processed.

There are several points to note about this architecture: firstly, an array of processors of fixed size must have some mechanism for matching the size of the problem being solved to the processor resources available. This is not the case for the Kedem-Ellis machine. Either the number of primitives in the tree will be small, in which case many processors will be unused, or as is more likely, the number of primitives will be large in comparison with the array size. In this case, the combine-classify array will have to be loaded and unloaded repeatedly in order to process all of the primitives.

Secondly, even *with* an efficient embedding algorithm, many processors are idle or passing data from child to parent without processing it. The Kedem-Ellis technique requires a $\log N_{prim} \times N_{prim}$ array of processors to embed a tree with N

leaf nodes, where N_{prim} is the number of primitives in the tree. Unfortunately, a tree with N_{prim} leaf nodes has $N_{prim} - 1$ operator nodes, which implies that only $(N_{prim} - 1) \times 100 / (N_{prim} \times \log N_{prim})$ percent of the nodes will be used to perform combine classification. If the goal is to utilize silicon area efficiently, this is unacceptable.

Finally, this architecture processes CSG trees in parallel, but each ray is executed serially. Also, there are no mechanisms to map trees of arbitrary shape and size onto such an architecture efficiently. It also dedicates a lot of hardware to the classify-combine process, which only needs a small amount of the computational power needed for the algorithms. As pointed out by Tilove (1981) virtually all of the work done in the ray-casting algorithm is in the primitive classification calculations. This accounts for the success of so-called spatially divided solid models which reduce the number of ray–primitive intersections to be calculated.

33.3 An improved ray-casting machine

We will now discuss requirements for an improved ray-casting machine. The first version of the Kedem and Ellis Ray-casting Machine output a stream of fixed-point parameters of intersection with the solid, with no information on which surfaces lay at each intersection point. This makes shading difficult, as the surface normal at the point of intersection cannot be computed easily. Also, it is possible to assign different surface attributes such as colour and texture to each visible point. Therefore, the first requirement is to support explicit identification of the parameters of intersection output from the machine, in order to make shading algorithms as easy as possible. (This has been implemented in later designs for the Ray-casting Machine.) From an examination of the serial ray-tracing algorithm, the following information is needed:

- *An initial classification* This is a boolean flag to indicate whether the ray originated inside the object.
- *A stream of sorted ray–primitive intersections* Each intersection must contain three items of information:
- *Parameter t* This is the ray distance parameter as described by Kedem and Ellis. It must be a 32-bit floating-point number for sufficient accuracy in ray casting complex models.
- *Primitive surface* A surface identifier that uniquely determines on which primitive surface the intersection point lies. This makes it possible to determine the surface normal for shading purposes.
- *Primitive sign* If the intersection point was generated as a result of an odd number of difference operations in the CSG tree, the surface at the intersection is implicitly 'inside out', that is, the surface normal must be reversed in any further calculations. Therefore a 1-bit Boolean flag is needed for every intersection point. The sign bit of the primitive surface tag may be used for this purpose.

We will now discuss the design of algorithms and architectures that can supply such information.

33.4 Dataflow techniques for ray tracing

The Kedem-Ellis machine is a special case of a parallel, data-driven *static* dataflow machine. Details of such machines are described by Gurd and Watson (1980). In this case, the dataflow graph consists of the nodes in the CSG tree, while the terminal nodes are the primitives at the leaves. This is shown in Figure 33.1. Each active processor in the classify-combine array holds a *single* dataflow node which is executed when both operands are available (hence it is a static dataflow machine). The terminal nodes in the graph are held in the primitive classification processors.

An alternative form of parallelism is now discussed for the ray-tracing algorithm. Instead of classifying nodes in the CSG tree in parallel, entire ray–tree classifications are executed concurrently, by partitioning the screen into disjoint regions and allocating each region to a processor. For a 512 × 512 image, up to 256K visibility rays may be processed in parallel. Details of this approach are given by Holliman *et al.* (1988).

There are now two ways of exploiting parallelism: structural parallelism and spatial parallelism obtained from partitioning space. The Kedem-Ellis machine can only exploit spatial parallelism if replicated entirely. This is equivalent to copying the dataflow graph. An alternative is to use a dynamic dataflow algorithm as described in the next section.

33.5 Dynamic dataflow techniques

This chapter proposes that **dynamic dataflow machines** are more suited to the task of rendering **large CSG trees**. These machines allow a dataflow graph (in this case the CSG tree) to be used in more than one context, therefore allowing many operations on the graph to be executed in parallel. Instead of allowing a single data value (**token**) to pass along an arc in the dataflow graph at a given time, every token is given a unique label to indicate its context. For the ray-tracing algorithm, this means that each ray–tree intersection list is given an identifier which states the CSG tree node from which it comes, and which ray was being processed. (As described in Section 33.3, this information is required anyway if the results are to be useful generally.) A substantial benefit of this technique is that it allows ray–tree

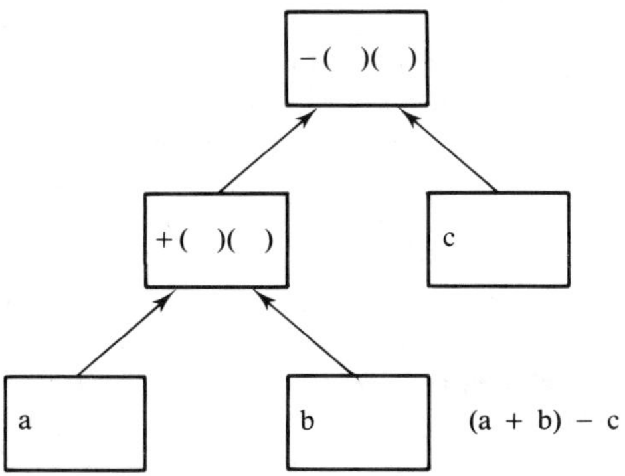

Figure 33.1
Dataflow graph for CSG tree.

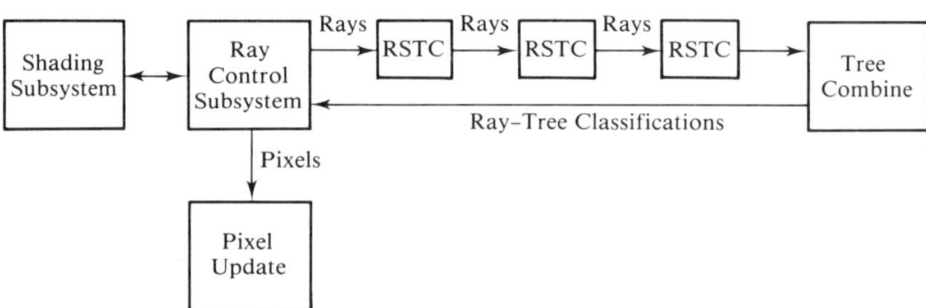

Figure 33.2
Structure of Ray-tracing Machine.

intersections from *many* rays to be processed in parallel. This makes it possible to combine structural and spatial parallelism.

A dynamic dataflow machine also allows us to break the one-to-one mapping between the primitive classifier processors and the network of processors implementing the CSG combine array. An alternative structure is shown in Figure 33.2.

The machine consists of four basic sections:

(1) A ray controller which is responsible for deciding which rays need to be cast, and for scheduling them into the CSG combine classifier. This uses a demand-driven dataflow control algorithm.

(2) A shading subsystem which is used for computing pixel intensities.

(3) A primitive classifier which executes a set of ray–primitive classifications in parallel.

(4) A CSG combine classifier which combines the results from the primitive classifier array and returns complete ray–tree intersection lists to the ray controller. A dynamic data-driven algorithm is used for this purpose.

Together, the primitive and CSG combine classifiers form a CSG classifier system which takes trees and rays as input and returns ray–tree classifications. Each separate section will be described briefly.

33.5.1 Ray-control subsystem

In order to implement a non-recursive version of the ray-tracing algorithm, each recursive invocation of the ray-tracing function must be represented by an explicit data structure. This replaces the implicit information stored in the procedure activation record on a conventional machine.

The initial input to the ray-control algorithm is a rectangular region to be drawn. A visibility ray is cast through every pixel in the region using the non-recursive version of the ray-tracing algorithm. This works as follows. Multiple invocations of the ray-casting algorithm are represented as Ray-Control Blocks (RCBs), which are created on demand when needed, and deleted when the final intensity value has been computed. Each RCB is given a unique tag (Ray-id) by which it can be referenced, allowing multiple RCBs to be chained together into a dataflow graph. The dataflow graph (actually a tree) for the computation is given in Figure 33.3. The downward arrows represent requests to cast one ray into the CSG solid and compute an intensity value. One RCB is created for each of these. The

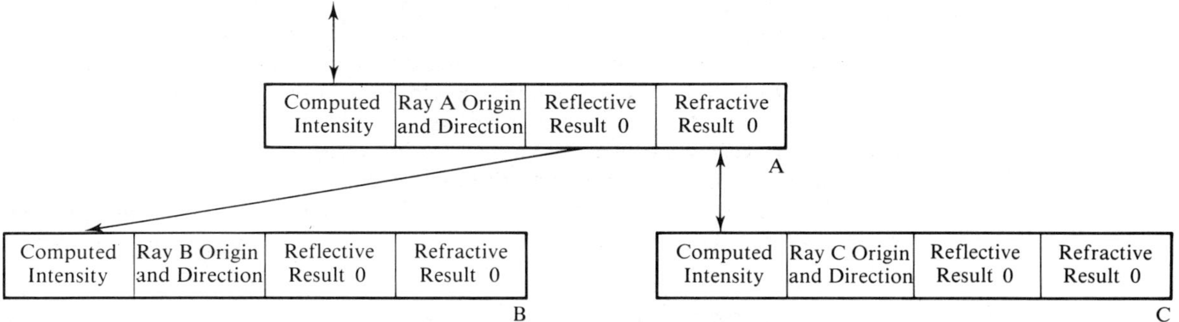

Figure 33.3
Dataflow graph for ray tracer.

upward arrows are the resulting intensities of the surfaces intersected by the rays. These must be stored in the RCB that requested the intensity calculation (the **parent** RCB). For example, in Figure 33.3 the visibility ray A intersects a reflective surface which is also transparent. Before the final pixel intensity can be calculated, it is necessary to compute the reflected intensity at the point by firing reflective ray B and refractive ray C. Once the intensities have been computed they are stored in the RCB for ray A, which may then complete execution. This implies that each RCB must store the identity of its parent RCB, to allow the resulting intensity to be returned before it terminates. The resulting structure is a backward-chained tree of RCBs that implement the dataflow graph. All of the dataflow trees for every pixel on the screen form a forest of trees that may be executed in parallel. In addition, all tree nodes at the same recursion depth may be executed concurrently. The overall structure of the ray controller is given in Figure 33.4. It consists of three parallel processes, the **ray analyser**, the **pending ray stack** and the **ray scheduler**. The pending ray stack is used to buffer those rays that are waiting to be classified against the CSG Tree. The ray scheduler is responsible for communicating with the CSG combine subsystem, in order to start the parallel execution of the rays on the pending ray stack.

33.5.2 The ray analyzer process

This process reads and analyzes the ray–tree intersection results from the CSG combine subsystem. Each result contains an initial classification, an intersection list

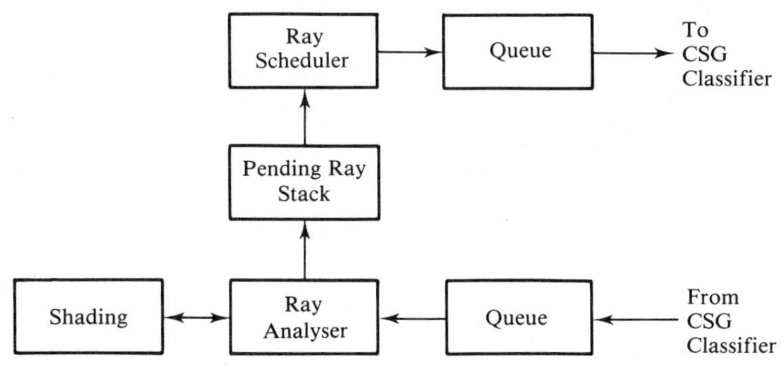

Figure 33.4
Structure of ray controller.

as described above and an RCB tag that identifies the ray to which the result belongs. The algorithm for the ray analyzer consists of two main parts. A main analyzer loop repeatedly reads ray–tree intersection lists, and extracts the Ray-id to determine the RCB for the ray being processed. If the list is empty, then the resulting intensity for the ray is the background colour, otherwise the first intersection is taken as the visible surface. The actual position and normal of the surface are then computed. If required, a reflective ray direction is computed and a new RCB created so that the reflective intensity can be found. This is put on the pending ray stack.

33.6 The CSG combine subsystem

This section will describe the CSG combine subsystem that computes complete ray–tree intersection lists from the ray–primitive intersections generated by the primitive classifier.

The structure of a single PE in the combine classify array will be similar to that of the ARVIND dataflow machine at MIT (Hwang and Briggs, 1984), with additional support for variable length operands. Figure 33.5 shows this structure.

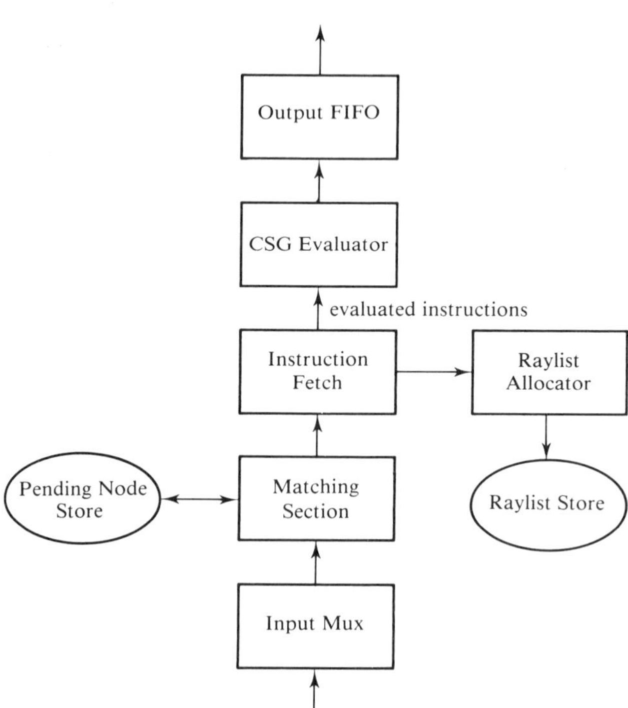

Figure 33.5
Combine classify subsystem.

33.6.1 Result and instruction formats

A ray–tree classification result which forms the input to the combine-classify subsystem contains the following information:

(1) A parent destination node id which is used to identify the tree node to which the result is to be attached,

(2) A Ray-id that identifies *which* ray was intersected with the tree, and

(3) A ray intersection list.

Note that the outputs from the primitive classifier are in this format so that they can be used directly. Also, outputs from the combine classifier are similar, with the difference that the root node of the CSG tree, by definition, has no parent node. Therefore, a special value is reserved to indicate that a result is the classification of the root node. All results containing this value are sent to the ray control subsystem which uses the Ray-id to identify the ray to be processed.

33.6.2 Parallel primitive classification

A completely general parallel primitive classifier must be able to input N_{ray} rays, classify these against the N_{prim} primitives in the tree, and output $N_{ray} \times N_{prim}$ ray–primitive intersections. In order to make these results useful, they must contain enough information to be input directly to the combine-classify processors described above. Therefore, the rays input to the primitive classifier must contain a unique Ray-id, together with the ray direction and origin vectors. Primitive classification results must also contain the Ray-id, and a ray intersection list containing the points where the ray enters and exits the solid. A processor farm can be used to perform these classifications because they are independent, self-contained computations that may be executed in any order. Details of rendering CSG objects using a processor farm may be found in a paper by Holliman *et al.* (see Chapter 32).

33.6.3 Adaptive granularity of computation

It is possible to relax the separation of the ray–tree intersection processor into two logical subsystems: primitive classification and combine classify. If we use CSG *subtrees* as the atomic unit of computation for the 'primitive' classifier, we have a system with a similar structure but whose problem granularity can be controlled. This is an advantage because it allows us to trade-off the overheads of creating, scheduling and combining classifications against the amount of parallelism available.

If we define the size of any CSG tree as the number of primitives it contains, then maximum parallelism is gained when the size of the subtrees to be processed is one, so that primitives are processed in parallel. As the subtree size increases, fewer trees may be processed in parallel, but fewer nodes need to be created and recombined by the combine-classifier array. If the size increases beyond the actual size of the CSG tree, then we have the spatial parallelism technique described earlier.

This allows us to balance the computation speed of the combine classifier with that of the primitive classifier array.

Conclusion

We have presented a method of executing the ray-tracing algorithm in parallel, with special emphasis on improving the Kedem-Ellis ray-tracing machine. A novel architecture was proposed, which combines the benefits of structural parallelism and spatial parallelism by the use of dynamic dataflow machines, coupled to a processor farm that executes the costly ray–primitive intersections. Finally, the concept of small tree classification was introduced, as a technique for varying computational granularity to match the hardware available.

Acknowledgements

The authors would like to thank the staff of the IBM UK Scientific Centre for their financial support and encouragement.

References

Gurd J. and Watson I. (1980). Data driven system for high speed parallel computing. *Computer design*, Parts I–II, June–July 1980

Hwang K. and Briggs F.A. (1984). *Computer Architecture and Parallel Processing*. Maidenhead: McGraw-Hill

Requicha A.A.G. and Voelker H.B. (1977). *Constructive Solid Geometry*. Technical Memorandum 25, Production Automation Project, University of Rochester NY

Roth S.D. (1982). Ray casting for modelling solids. *Computer Graphics and Image Processing,* **18**(2), 109–44

Tilove R.B. (1980). Set membership classification: a unified approach to geometric intersection problems. *IEEE Trans. on Computers,* **C-29**(10), 874–83

Tilove R.B. (1981). *Exploiting spatial and structural locality in geometric modelling*. Technical Memorandum 38, Production Automation Project, University of Rochester NY

34·High performance graphics processors for medical imaging applications

S.M. Goldwasser
R.A. Reynolds
D.A. Talton
E.S. Walsh

Dynamic Digital Displays, Inc.

A family of high-performance graphics processors with special hardware for interactive visualization of 3D human anatomy is described. The basic architecture expands to multiple parallel processors, each processor using pipelined arithmetic and logical units for high-speed rendering of Computed Tomography (CT), Magnetic Resonance (MR) and Positron Emission Tomography (PET) data. User-selectable display alternatives include multiple 2D axial slices, reformatted images in sagittal or coronal planes and shaded 3D views. Special facilities support applications requiring color-coded display of multiple datasets (such as radiation therapy planning), or dynamic replay of time-varying volumetric data (such as cine-CT or gated MR studies of the beating heart). The current implementation is a single processor system which generates reformatted images in true real time (30 frames per second), and shaded 3D views in a few seconds per frame. It accepts full scale medical datasets in their native formats, so that minimal preprocessing delay exists between data acquisition and display.

34.1 Introduction

Computerized medical imaging devices such as Computed Tomography (CT), Magnetic Resonance (MR) and Positron Emission Tomography (PET) scanners have the ability to acquire vast quantities of data about the human body, usually in the form of cross-sectional images or 'slices' containing anatomical, physiological or biochemical information. Although each slice is a 2D entity, when stacked together enough information is available to make a 3D representation of a volume of interest. Recently developed computer techniques permit this information to be presented to the physician in a number of ways including:

- Display of the original 2D cross-sectional slices.
- Display of additional 2D slices generated at new orientations via MultiPlanar Reformatting (MPR) [1].
- Display of individual 3D objects, with realistic surface shading [2].
- Animated replay of time-varying datasets, such as a beating heart [3].

The imaging scientist is faced with the problem of making these alternative display strategies available to the physician in the manner best suited to the application at hand – which may be diagnosis of disease, evaluation of trauma, detection and localization of tumors, or a number of specialized applications such as surgical planning [4], or evaluation of radiation therapy alternatives [5].

This chapter describes a family of high-performance graphics processors which provide the above display facilities and have been designed specifically with medical imaging applications in mind. Based on the Voxel Processor architecture [6, 7], these systems implement an important capability currently lacking in most medical image display workstations: true interaction with the 3D dataset, with real-time or near real-time update rates. Standard features include: storage of multi-dimensional datasets at full spatial and density resolution; rapid display of 2D slices; instantaneous reslicing of the original data via MPR; rapid selection and rotation of shaded 3D objects; volume of interest extraction via subregioning; and interactive segmentation via thresholding or windowing, based on tissue densities.

The Voxel Processor system provides 3D presentations on a 2D video monitor using computer graphics techniques such as **hidden surface removal**, **realistic shading**, and **motion parallax** to enhance the perception of depth. Objects are depicted as solids, not as wire-frame outlines; and special viewing facilities such as vibrating mirrors or stereo glasses are not required. Object memory can be organized as 2D, 3D, or 4D arrays of sample points or **voxels** – datasets are loaded essentially in the form they were acquired, with little preprocessing and no loss of image quality. All display modes (2D slices, MPR, 3D views etc.) are active simultaneously, permitting instantaneous selection of whichever presentation is most appropriate to the task at hand. The Voxel Processor may be thought of as an instrument for the exploration and analysis of medical imaging data in much the same way that a microscope is an instrument for examining biological specimens.

This chapter concentrates on medical applications of the Voxel Processor, however, similar display techniques can be applied to any objects whose internal structure can be measured or computed. Non-medical applications include: industrial simulation; non-destructive testing; visualization of machine perception algorithms in robotics; spatial mechanism design; topographic analysis; and the display of rock formations (seismic tomography).

The remainder of the chapter is organized into three sections. Section 34.2 describes a single processor implementation, known as the Physician's Workstation Prototype (PWP); Section 34.3 shows how the architecture encompasses multiple parallel processors for improved performance on very large datasets. Section 34.4 illustrates some specialized features for applications in general diagnosis, surgical and radiation therapy planning.

34.2 The Voxel Processor Physician's Workstation Prototype

The PWP consists of a high-performance graphics processor connected to a host computer and controlled via interactive devices such as a keyboard, trackball and pushbuttons. The graphics subsystem might be described as a 3D frame buffer – with the ability to interact in real time (or near real time) with the stored data.

The PWP has a nominal display capacity of 8 million 16-bit voxels, but can be expanded through additional memory boards to 16 million 16-bit voxels (or more). A system with 16 million voxels of object memory will hold 256 separate 256 × 256 2D slices, that is, a 256-cube 3D dataset. However, the memory can be organized into any arbitrary shape, such as 512 × 512 × 64. Data are stored at full spatial and density resolution, essentially in the format provided by the scanner, with minimal preprocessing. For example, on-the-fly interpolation between slices is provided so that the original slices can be stored at the spacing at which they were acquired – unlike previous systems, pre-interpolation to form cubic voxels is not needed [8].

The PWP provides the following display capabilities:

- Display of 2D slices with full spatial and grey-scale resolution.
- Instantaneous reformatting into axial, sagittal, or coronal slices.
- Subregioning, windowing and thresholding of 3D datasets.
- Rapid display of 3D objects with full hidden surface removal and realistic visible surface shading.
- Rotation of 3D objects to arbitrary orientations.
- Positionable slice planes for viewing object interiors.
- Tag-bit facilities for simultaneous display of multiple datasets.
- Full color output.

All 2D slice and multiplanar functions are provided in true real time (30 frames per second). Surface-shaded images of 3D objects are generated at 10 million voxels per second – 0.1–10 seconds per frame depending upon the object size involved.

The PWP incorporates several additional architectural features which have been developed specifically to support the display of multimodal datasets – such as the combined anatomy/radiation dose presentations required for radiation therapy planning. These features include:

(1) A **data formatter** which permits the selection of separate bit fields within each 16-bit voxel. For example, 12 bits may be assigned to CT density while the remaining 4 bits are used to label user-entered structures, or radiation beams. Another possibility would be to assign 8 bits to CT, and the remaining 8 bits to the computed dose distribution.

(2) A set of loadable **Look-Up Tables** (LUTs) which provide tone scale mappings to be performed on the 3D data during image generation. These include basic segmentation functions based on thresholding or windowing of the CT numbers, or the selective display of groups of voxels based on the tag field value or slice plane position.

(3) A **color-mapping system** which enables up to 65 536 shades (8 bits of color and 8 bits of intensity) to be displayed simultaneously from a palette of over 16 million colors. This facilitates the display of multimodal datasets since tagged voxels can be displayed in different colors.

The high-level organization of the PWP is shown in Figure 34.1. The major system components are described in the remainder of this section.

34.2.1 Host computer (CPU)

The PWP consists of a custom, programmable 3D graphics subsystem connected to a general-purpose CPU (for example, a Digital Equipment Corporation MicroVAX II). Interactive commands are generated by the user through a trackball or input via the keyboard on a control terminal. These requests are serviced by the host

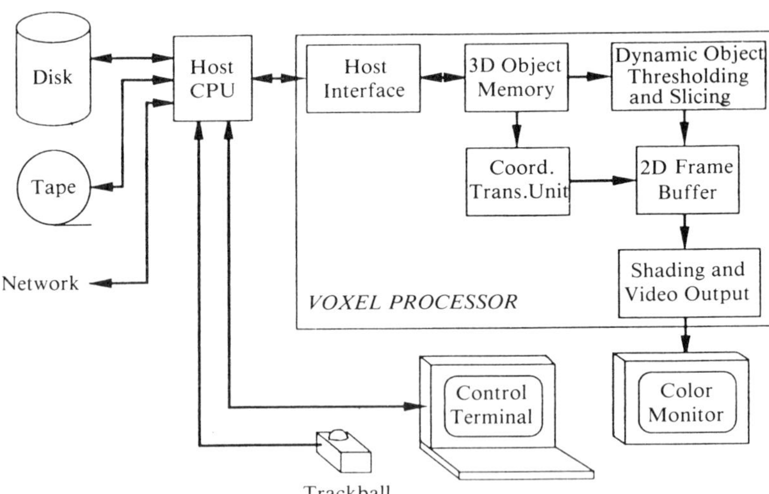

Figure 34.1
Voxel Processor Physician's Workstation Prototype.

computer and display commands are transmitted to the graphics subsystem. Connected to the host computer are peripherals for data storage and communication, such as a disk drive and magnetic tape drive or Ethernet controller.

34.2.2 Host Interface (HI)

The 3D graphics subsystem is connected to the host computer via the HI which provides for the loading of datasets and the transmission of display commands. The HI provides the communication protocols to receive data and commands from a standard DMA interface (typically, a DRV11-W). The HI additionally contains a bit-slice microprocessor (AMD 29116) to perform format conversions on datasets on the fly as they are loaded. For example, the complex bit manipulations needed to merge multimodal datasets (such as anatomy and dose) can be accomplished using the HI.

34.2.3 3D Object Memory (OM)

A 3D OM of 8 or 16 million 16-bit voxel capacity stores the objects to be displayed. We use off-the-shelf memory boards in the interests of economy. Object memory can be expanded to accommodate multiple datasets, or for situations where more than 16 bits per voxel would be appropriate (for example, multiparameter MR datasets). This approach also permits dynamic (4D) display of time-varying data, such as a beating heart. Rapid switching between memory banks permits entire 3D datasets to be displayed in 'cine' mode, without any loss of interactive facilities such as rotation, windowing or slicing.

34.2.4 Coordinate Transform Unit (CTU)

The programmable CTU performs sequenced linear transformations at 100 ns per point (10 million coordinate transformations per second). This unit transforms the voxel coordinates from object space to image space, producing the appropriate Back-To-Front (BTF) voxel sequences [9] in accordance with the display parameters for each view (object orientation, slice plane location, etc.). From these coordinates, the object space (OM) and image space (FB) memory addresses are derived.

34.2.5 Dynamic Object Thresholding and Slicing (DOTS)

The DOTS unit is a pipelined display processor which selectively renders the voxels and stores the image in the 2D Frame Buffer (FB). The unit contains the special hardware designed for processing multimodal or merged datasets, as illustrated in Figure 34.2. DOTS also contains the LUTs necessary for grey-scale segmentation (thresholding and windowing), tag-bit selection and slice-plane implementation. A pipeline structure ensures full use of OM bandwidth.

Data from the OM are passed through a data formatter, a hardware interpolator and several LUTs. The hardware interpolator operates on the density portion of each voxel only – not on the tag field, which typically contains labels that would not be meaningful to interpolate. This hardware interpolator greatly expands the dataset capacity of the system since only the acquired slices need be stored – additional data points along the z-direction are generated on the fly, not in a pre-processing step.

34.2.6 Frame buffer

The 2D FB is basically a fast memory to hold the images as they are created for display. A double buffer system is used to provide maximum throughput. The frame buffer hardware supports overlays for graphics and text, and 2D pan, scroll and zoom capabilities. The images stored in the frame buffer are passed through a Shading and Video Output (SVO) processor before display.

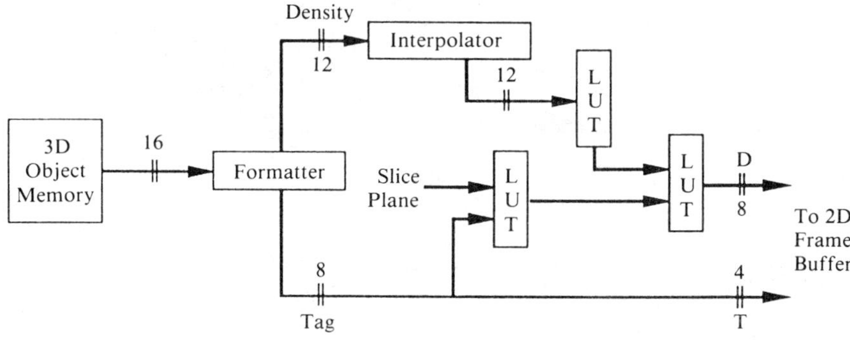

Figure 34.2 Dynamic Object Thresholding and Slicing (DOTS).

34.2.7 Shading and video output

The SVO module is used to combine density, tag, depth and overlay information into a final video image, as shown in Figure 34.3. Industry standard, analog, RGB signals are prepared and the images are displayed on a standard color video monitor. A separate monochrome channel (W) is also available. LUTs are provided for color display. A depth mapping table (ZMAP) and multipliers are provided to generate density-shaded, depth-shaded and/or gradient-shaded images.

A unique feature of the Voxel Processor is that the density values (for example, CT numbers) are available at all stages of the computation, and can be used to implement complex shading schemes on the final image. The data stored in the frame buffer consist of several components. These include the density and tag of each active point in the object – those which have not been removed through thresholding or slicing, for example. Another component is the depth or Z' coordinate – the distance of the visible voxel from the screen. The Z' coordinate is used for depth- and/or gradient-shading functions [10].

34.3 Multiple processor systems

The Voxel Processor performs volume rendering by mapping 3D object space into 2D image space using a BTF time-ordered sequence. This procedure guarantees that any point that should be obscured by something in front of it will, in fact, be invisible in the final image.

In order to reduce the problem of real-time display of very large 3D datasets to manageable proportions, it is necessary to partition either the input (object) space or output (image) space – or some combination of these – and distribute the computations to multiple processors. Partitioning input space and assigning each partition to a separate Processing Element (PE) will avoid input memory access

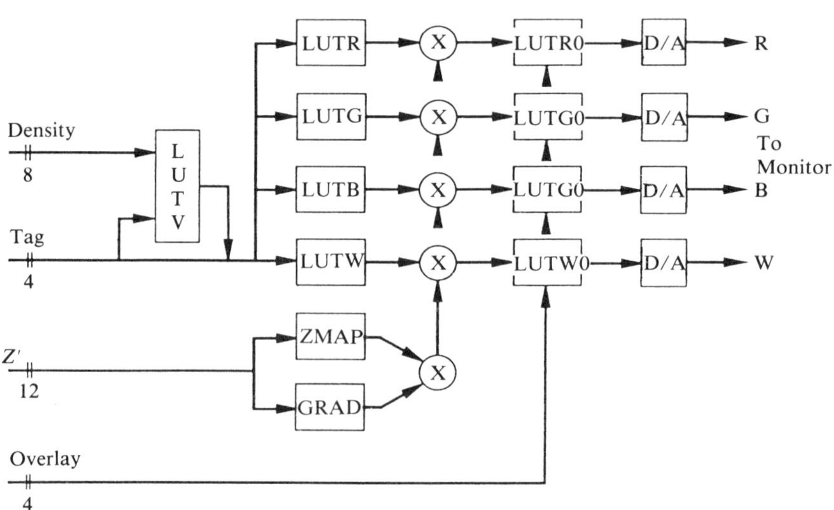

Figure 34.3
Shading and Video Output (SVO).

conflicts, whereas partitioning output space will avoid output memory access conflicts. The former scheme is preferred because there is a substantial amount of data reduction (on the order of N where N^3 is the size of object space) in the projection from 3D to 2D space. The problem of outputting to a common memory is handled hierarchically to minimize the access conflicts involved.

The processing strategy consists of the following steps. Each PE accesses its own object memory module exclusively and computes the 'mini-picture' that would be seen from the same orientation if all other PEs were absent. Each PE contains a double buffer, each half of which is sufficient to hold the largest image that can be created from the object module. For convenience, we assume the object modules are $64 \times 64 \times 64$ and the double buffers are 128×128 (Figure 34.4a) – although any convenient partitions can be used. The halves of the buffers are used alternately; one half is filled by the PE while the other is emptied by the Intermediate Processor (IP).

Each of the eight IPs (Figure 34.4b) merges the minipictures generated by its set of eight PEs into the appropriate position in the eight intermediate 256×256 double buffers, following priority rules based on which PEs can obscure others. The Output Processor (OP) merges the eight intermediate buffers into the final 512×512 double frame buffer, following the same priority rules.

The BTF readout sequences are identical for all PEs in the display system. This means that the arithmetic processing can be performed by a single CTU and distributed throughout the system, accessing all the memory modules in lock-step (SIMD) mode. Alternatively, the display of independently configurable objects can be achieved by maintaining separate CTUs controlling individual PEs (or groups of PEs) and modifying the merge strategies. This would permit complete control for objects within their own subcubes [11].

34.4 Applications

In this section, we illustrate some special features of the Voxel Processor system. All images were photographed from the screen of the PWP.

34.4.1 General diagnosis and surgical planning

Applications in general diagnostic radiology center around the ability to display the original 2D slices and generate new reformatted slices rapidly. In surgical planning applications, 3D display of bony structures is becoming increasingly important.

The PWP has the ability to display the original 2D slices in full detail and, additionally, can advance instantaneously from one slice to the next. This feature is useful in replaying multiple slices rapidly, in 'cine' mode.

MPR can be performed interactively in true real time. Positioning a cursor at a desired location on an axial slice (Figure 34.5a), the user can instantaneously generate the corresponding coronal slice (Figure 34.5b) or sagittal slice (Figure 34.5c). Using the trackball, he can then instantaneously advance from the current slice to the next or previous slice in either axial, coronal, or sagittal mode.

Shaded-surface display of 3D objects can be accomplished interactively on the PWP, requiring 0.1–10 seconds per view depending on the dataset involved

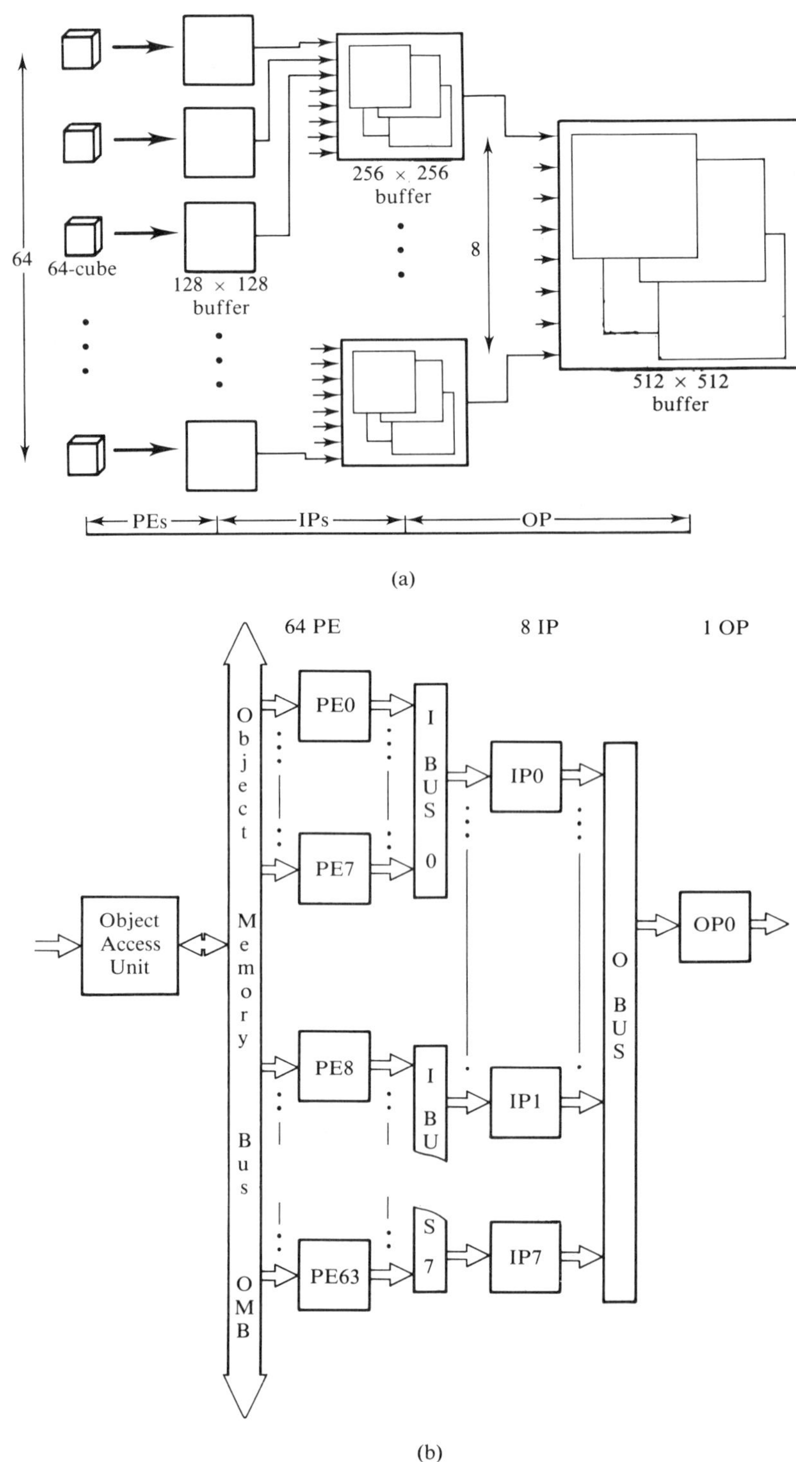

Figure 34.4
Multiprocessor system
(a) Hierarchical merge scheme.
(b) Implementation.

(a)

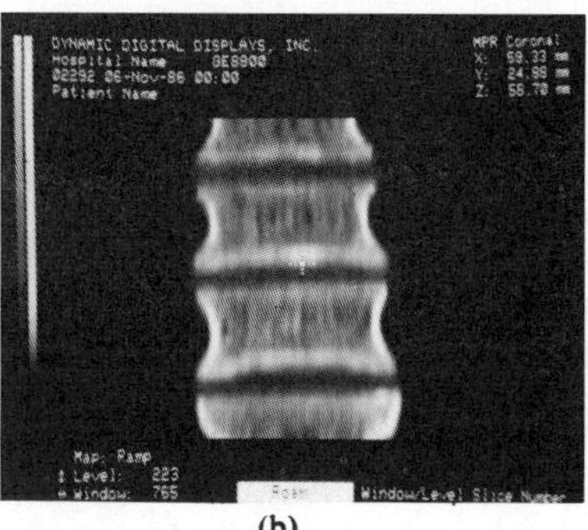

(b)

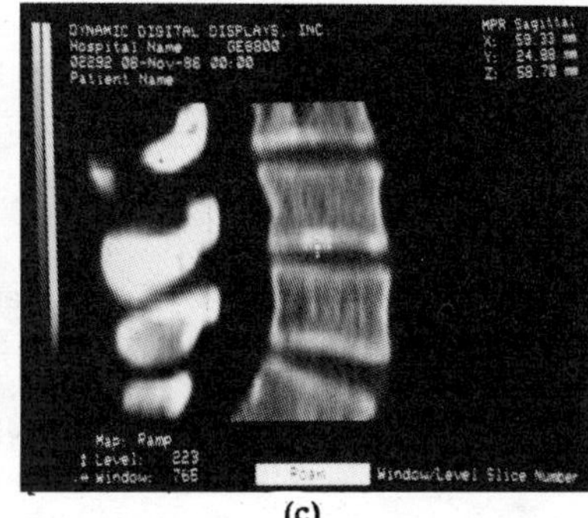

(c)

Figure 34.5
Real-time MPR
(a) Axial slice.
(b) Coronal slice.
(c) Sagittal slice.

(3 seconds per view is typical). Plate 13 shows a gradient shaded 3D view of a section of lumbar spine. Plate 14 shows the effect of introducing a slice plane (which can be positioned interactively) to generate a cutaway view, revealing the spinal canal.

34.4.2 Radiation therapy planning

The goal of radiation therapy is to deliver a lethal dose of ionizing radiation (x-rays, gamma rays, or electrons) to cancer cells, while sparing surrounding healthy tissue from permanent damage. 'Treatment Planning' refers to the individualized design of a course of radiation therapy for the cancer patient [12]. Treatment planning includes not only the determination of tumor extent, delineation of target volume and identification of adjacent sensitive structures, but also the computation of dose distributions based on the patient outline and radiation beam parameters. A state-of-the-art treatment planning facility should be capable of displaying both the CT and MR data from which diagnostic and treatment decisions will be made, and the dose distribution resulting from a detailed computation.

Plate 15 shows an image rendered from a CT dataset merged with a 3D dose distribution. The patient was a 36-year-old female being treated for a right breast malignancy. Within each voxel, 12 bits were used to represent the CT values and 4 bits were assigned to dose. Regions of high dose were coded in red, whereas low dose regions appear in blue. Plate 15 is a cutaway view of the anterior chest, revealing lung and showing the proposed dose distribution. Such images give an immediate indication of the amount of lung within the treatment field, suggesting that repositioning the radiation beams may be necessary.

Summary

A family of high-performance graphics systems for medical imaging applications has been developed. A single processor system has been constructed, and a generalized architecture supporting multiple parallel processors for future systems has been devised. The current PWP can accommodate full-size datasets from many different imaging modalities – including CT, MR and PET scanners – and features instantaneously selectable 2D, MPR and 3D display modes. Special capabilities support color-coded display of multimodal datasets, for applications such as radiation therapy planning.

Acknowledgements

The radiation therapy applications were developed in association with Dr Marc Sontag, Department of Radiation Therapy, Hospital of the University of Pennsylvania. This work was supported in part by NIH grants R01–NS23636 and R43–CA42615, and in part by the Commonwealth of Pennsylvania's Ben Franklin Partnership, through the Advanced Technology Center of Southeastern Pennsylvania (the ATC is a program of the University City Science Center in Philadelphia).

References

1. Rhodes M.L., Glenn W.V. and Azzawi Y.M. (1980). Extracting oblique planes from serial CT sections. *J. Comput. Assist. Tomogr.,* **4**, 649–57
2. Reynolds R.A., Gordon D. and Chen L.S. (1987). A dynamic screen technique for shaded graphics display of slice-represented objects. *Computer Vision, Graphics, and Image Processing,* **38**(3), 275–98
3. Barrett W.A. and Eisenberg H. (1987). Dynamic three- and four-dimensional display of skeletal and cardiac anatomy. In *NCGA'87 Technical Sessions Proceedings,* **III**, 35–44. Philadelphia PA, March 1987
4. Vannier M.W., Marsh J.L. and Warren J.O. (1984). Three-dimensional CT reconstruction images for craniofacial surgical planning and evaluation. *Radiology,* **150**, 179–84
5. McShan D.L., Silverman A., Lanza D.M., Reinstein L.E. and Glicksman A.S. (1979). A computerized three-dimensional treatment planning system utilizing interactive color graphics. *British J. Radiology,* **52**, 478–81
6. Goldwasser S.M. and Reynolds R.A. (1983). An architecture for the real-time display and manipulation of three-dimensional objects. In *Proc. Int. Conf. on Parallel Processing*, pp. 269–74. Bellaire, MI, August 1983
7. Goldwasser S.M. and Reynolds R.A. (1987). Real-time display and manipulation of 3-D medical objects: The Voxel Processor architecture. *Computer Vision, Graphics, and Image Processing,* **39**(4), 1–27
8. Goldwasser S.M., Reynolds R.A., Bapty T. *et al.* (1985). Physician's workstation with real-time performance. *IEEE Computer Graphics and Applications,* **5**(12), 44–57
9. Frieder G., Gordon D. and Reynolds R.A. (1985). Back-to-front display of voxel-based objects. *IEEE Computer Graphics and Applications*, **5**(1), 52–60
10. Gordon D. and Reynolds R.A. (1985). Image space shading of 3-dimensional objects. *Computer Vision, Graphics, and Image Processing,* **29**, 361–76
11. Goldwasser S.M. (1984). A generalized object display processor architecture. *IEEE Computer Graphics and Applications,* **4**(10), 43–55
12. Goitein M.G. and Abrams M. (1983). Multi-dimensional treatment planning. *Int. J. Rad. Onc. Biol. Phys.*, (6), 777–87

35 · Parallel processing for 3D voxel-based graphics

A. Kaufman
R. Bakalash

State University of New York
Ben-Gurion University

The CUBE architecture for 3D graphics and its associated algorithms have been designed as three autonomous processors that input, manipulate and project 3D images stored in a huge Cubic Frame Buffer (CFB) of voxels (unit volume elements). The CFB represents a discretized model of the 3D inherently continuous scene (for example, medical, solid modeling). The huge throughput that has to be handled in order to synthesize, input, manipulate, project and render the 3D images in real time, requires special parallel memory, parallel architecture and parallel processing. Fortunately, the discrete topology and repetitive nature of the voxel data representation lend themselves to parallel organization and parallel computation at various levels.

The majority of the algorithms associated with the three processors have been parallelized for implementation on a parallel machine. Of special interest is the projection procedure which requires a throughput in the order of gigabits per projection. In order to handle this huge throughput in real time, both a massively parallel machine and a special parallel bus have been explored. The latter has been designed to select from a beam of voxels the opaque voxel closest to the observer in log n time using n processing units. In addition, a unique skewed-memory organization for parallel storage and retrieval of beams has been developed.

35.1 Introduction

The **CUBE architecture** [1, 2] is a general-purpose 3D voxel-based graphics system, which is based upon discretizing, sampling and storing the 3D inherently continuous scene in a large 3D **Cubic Frame Buffer** (CFB) of unit cubic cells called volume elements or **voxels**. Three-dimensional objects are digitized and a regularly spaced array of values is obtained and stored in the CFB, which is accessed by three autonomous processors. The digitization is performed either by a 3D geometry processor synthesizing (scan-converting) a 3D geometric model, or by a 3D frame-buffer processor which loads the CFB with experimental voxel data obtained, for example, by a 3D medical scanner. The images within the CFB are directly manipulated by the 3D frame-buffer processor, and are projected onto a 2D display and rendered by a 3D viewing processor.

A CFB with $1024 \times 1024 \times 1024$ resolution and 8 bits per voxel, for example, is a huge memory buffer of size 1 Gbytes. The extremely large throughput that has to be handled requires a special parallel architecture and processing attention. Fortunately, the discrete and repetitive nature of the CFB representation lends itself to parallel organization and parallel computation at different levels. To support this, a unique 3D memory organization, which enables fetching/storing an entire beam of voxels in parallel, and a special common bus, which processes a full beam of voxels simultaneously, have been designed for the CUBE architecture. The memory and the bus are the two primary components of CUBE that have enabled it to handle a beam of voxels in parallel rather than single voxels one at a time. Consequently, the complexity of the solution has been reduced from n^3 voxels to n^2 beams of voxels, allowing CUBE to operate in real time.

The other voxel-based architectures reported in the literature employ one of two approaches. One approach, adopted by GODPA [3], Voxel [4] and 3DP[4] [5], is a hierarchical, pipelined, hardware organization, in which the 256-cube voxel memory is divided into 64 symmetric equal subcubes, each processed by a separate concurrent processing element. The result is processed by eight intermediate processors which feed one output processor.

The second approach, developed for the PARCUM system [6], divides the memory cube into $4 \times 4 \times 4$ macro voxels each of which is $4 \times 4 \times 4$ voxels, one bit each. A read access fetches a macro voxel which is sorted in an output dataword. Two hardware implementations for the projection have been proposed: a surface detection technique which is a ray-following method using a binary rate multiplier, and an analytical approach using matrix multiplication.

35.2 The CUBE architecture

The layout of the CUBE architecture is depicted in Figure 35.1. A CFB, which is a large 3D cubic memory, is at the center of the architecture. The atomic memory entity is a voxel with a numerical value which represents the colour, material and translucency ratio of a small unit cube of the real scene. There are three autonomous processors, the 3D Geometry Processor (GP3), the 3D Frame-Buffer Processor (FBP3) and the 3D Viewing Processor (VP3), which access the CFB in order to synthesize, input and manipulate, and view and render the CFB images, respectively.

The GP3 synthesizes (scan-converts) 3D geometric objects into their 3D discrete representation within the CFB. The GP3 generates voxel-based versions of 3D geometric objects or compositions thereof. These objects are 3D lines, polygons

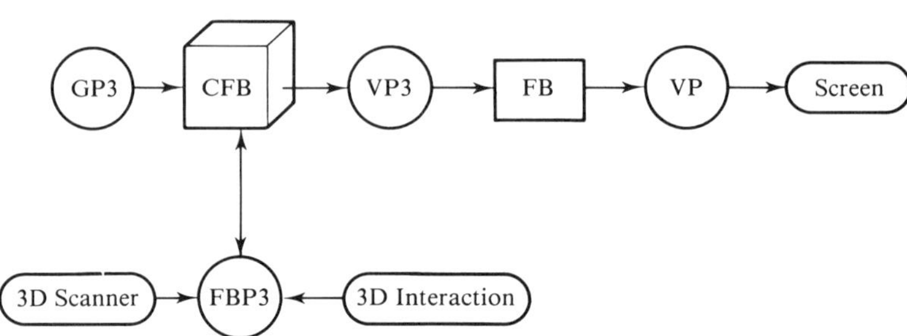

Figure 35.1
General overview of the CUBE architecture.

(optionally filled), polyhedra (optionally filled), parametric curves, surfaces and volumes (possibly bounded by planes), circles (optionally filled) and quadratic objects, such as spheres, cylinders and cones (optionally filled). The GP3 is basically a write-only algorithmic-oriented processor, where for each geometric object a 3D scan-conversion algorithm is applied [7]. Most of the GP3 algorithms have been implemented in parallel, in incremental steps and/or in integer arithmetic. For linear objects (lines, polygons [8], polyhedra) either a 3D variation of the run-length Bresenham algorithm [9], a 3D variation of the multiprocessing Sproull algorithm [10], a 3D first-order DDA, or a modified scanline algorithm, is utilized. For cubic polynomial objects (curves, surfaces), a third-order DDA is used [11]. For quadratic objects, adaptations of the 2D circle and ellipse algorithms are used. The GP3 interfaces the CFB by a simple protocol, passing information about the colour and the address of either a voxel, or a run (sequence) of voxels, parallel to a principal axis. The algorithms for scan-converting polyhedra, spheres and volumes write a whole run of voxels in parallel into the CFB, exploiting the special organization of the CFB (see Section 35.3).

The FBP3 is the 3D extension of the 2D Frame-Buffer Processor [12], which in turn is a variation of a **bitblt** engine [13] with a richer repertoire. The FBP3 as a voxel-map engine may thus be termed as a **voxblt** engine. It manipulates and processes 3D discrete images stored in the CFB. It also channels in 3D scanned data and acts as an interface for 3D input devices. The primitives of the FBP3 are 3D subarrays of the CFB of three types: rectangular **boxes** (3D windows), **jacks** (3D cursors) and **figurines** (3D icons). A box (also called **room**) is a cuboid defined by two opposite corners and a priority value which is a unique value for each box facilitating the support of overlapping boxes. Jacks provide a flexible feedback mechanism and enable the user to tour the 3D scene. Figurines are small application-oriented, constant, 3D images, that are either anchored to a box or may float independently.

The instruction set of the FBP3 includes register operations (for example, set, get), control instructions (for example, jump, jump on error, call, return, pop, push, activate, halt, reset, attach/disattach device) and box, jack and figurine operations (for example, define, delete, write, read, erase, swap, translate, rotate, scale, spin, copy, filter, change priority). Special care has been taken to provide simple and fast operations, especially for the large box operands. Furtunately, the discrete topology and repetitive nature of voxels and beams of voxels lend themselves to parallel computation. All operations, and more specifically transformations, including shifting, scaling (using non-integral factors) and rotation (through any angle) are performed using a parallel-incremental transformation technique, in which each beam is transformed, based on the new position assumed by its immediate previous beam neighbour, with a maximum of three additions. For each beam, all its voxels are moved to their new location in parallel, employing the parallel access CFB (Section 35.3) and the barrel shifting of beams across memory modules.

Two-dimensional projections of the CFB images onto the graphics display are performed by the VP3. The VP3 generates from the CFB parallel orthographic projections. Arbitrary parallel projections and perspective projections can be generated by several techniques which are outside the scope of this chapter. The VP3 also renders the 2D image during the projection process, implementing semi-transparency, lighting and shading (using the local gradient field).

In order to generate an orthographic projection, the following algorithm might first be attempted. Assume, for example, a 'front' projection in the direction of the positive z-axis. For each (x, y) the VP3 should scan inwards, examining each voxel at a time, skipping over the transparent voxels until an opaque voxel is encountered, the value of which is assigned to the (x, y) pixel of the FB. A full projection frame would require, on average, the processing of half of the voxels in the CFB. Consequently, the throughput required of the VP3 is enormous. For a resolution of $1024 \times 1024 \times 1024 \times 8$, the required rate is in the order of 4 giga bits/second when the VP3 generates, for example, a new FB frame only once every second. Since this rate is far beyond the capabilities of existing or forthcoming single processors, parallel processing is imperative. Hence, the VP3 employs a sequence of processing units which simultaneously process a full beam of voxels and select the first opaque voxel in a time that is dependent only on the log of the length of the beam. To support this concept a special common bus, the Voxel Multiple-Write Bus (VMWB), has been designed. The VMWB is described in Section 35.4.

35.3 Parallel access to the CFB

Assume a CFB of n^3 voxels. It is constructed in such a way as to enable a simultaneous access to a full beam of n voxels, regardless of the view direction. The physical memory is divided into n modules, each of which has exactly n^2 voxels, each with its own independent access and its own independent addressing unit, so that no two voxels of a beam reside in the same module. Therefore, all the voxels of a beam can be fetched simultaneously in one memory cycle. This division, however, should occur for all the three principal viewing directions.

These restrictions have suggested a modular memory construction which consists of diagonal parallel sections having a 45 degree angle with the main axes planes (see diagram [1, 14]). The diagonal sections are sequentially numbered and grouped modulo n into n modules indexed 0 through $n - 1$. This skewed organization is formalized as follows. A voxel with space coordinates (x, y, z) is being mapped onto the kth module $(0 \leqslant k \leqslant n - 1)$ by:

$$k = (x + y + z) \bmod n \qquad \textbf{(35.1)}$$

Since two coordinates are always constant along any beam, the third coordinate guarantees that one, and only one, voxel from the beam resides in any one of the modules. The internal mapping (i, j) within the memory module is given by:

$$i = x, \qquad j = y \qquad \textbf{(35.2)}$$

In the case of a linear internal address a $(0 \leqslant a \leqslant n^2 - 1)$, the mapping is simply:

$$a = x + ny \qquad \textbf{(35.3)}$$

Thus the kth memory module can be regarded as a 2D projection of all the diagonal sections in that module (those that are indexed k) onto the $x - y$ plane.

In the case of a memory cube of $1024 \times 1024 \times 1024$ there are 1024 memory modules, each one containing 1024×1024 voxels or 1 Mbytes, assuming one byte per voxel. The time needed to retrieve a full beam of 1024 voxels is a single cycle time, for example, 100 nanoseconds. Scanning the whole CFB beam by beam will take only about 100 milliseconds instead of about 2 minutes in a conventional sequential voxel retrieval.

When scanning the CFB beam after beam for viewing, the internal order of the modules along the beams of voxels is changing. This means that the module sequential index, which is the distance of a voxel along a beam from the view position, is not constant when moving from one beam to the next. Actually, the module index is either incremented or decremented by one when moving to the next beam (usually stepping to the right), and this change is controlled locally by the local address unit of the module. The initial assignment of the module indices depends only upon the viewing direction. Consequently, even the simple arithmetic involved in Equation 35.1 is avoided during the time-consuming viewing process and only a trivial incremental procedure is used instead. Nevertheless, the VP3 has the highest priority in accessing the CFB for the bulky viewing process, and the CFB access is being arbitrated between the GP3 and the FBP3 when not in use by the VP3.

35.4 The voxel multiple-write bus

A full beam of n voxels, fetched from the CFB along the view direction in one memory cycle, is placed into the VMWB processing logic, for the selection of the opaque voxel closest to the assumed observer. The VMWB logic is composed of n identical processing units as shown in Figure 35.2. Each of the n memory modules is associated with, and physically connected to, one of the processing units in the VMWB logic, and the voxel originated in the module will be placed and processed by its processing unit.

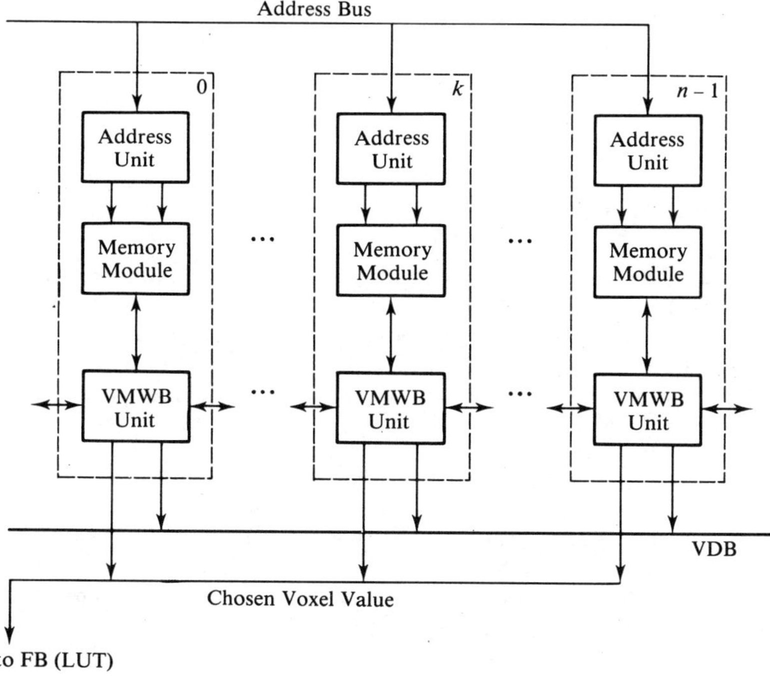

Figure 35.2
Modular structure of the CFB and the VMWB.

All the processing units are identical in nature, and are different only in their sequential index which is stored locally in the processing unit itself. All the units access the Voxel Depth Bus (VDB) simultaneously, each attempting to place its index onto the VDB. All the processing units holding voxels defined as transparent or residing in a clipped (invisible) plane are disqualifying themselves. All the other units which are enabled and holding opaque voxels are racing for the bus and the one closest to the observer (for example, with the largest/smallest index) succeeds.

The VDB competition is based on the Multiple-Write Bus technique [15] that has been developed for solving the hidden-surface problem on the pixel level. All the processing units which are qualified, simultaneously attempt to write one bit at a time on the VDB. Starting with the most significant bit of their index, they attempt to write it on the current most significant bit of the VDB. If the index bit is greater than or equal to the VDB bit, then the index bit is written on the bus and permission is granted to compare the next bit. If a unit loses the competition for that bit, an internal signal disables the next and all the following less significant bits. After a small settling time, the remaining units are ready for the next competition with the next less significant bit.

Only one unit survives all the comparisons: it is the one with the largest (smallest) index. This unit then grants permission to its voxel value to pass to the FB. The selection time is proportional to the size in bits of the index, which is equivalent to the log of the length of the beam. For a beam of 1024 voxels, for example, the selection time takes 10 steps, where a step is the delay time for three gates.

The bidirectional connection between the VMWB processing units (see Figure 35.2) enables the barrel shifting of the voxel beam across the modules by a given offset, and writing it back into the CFB at a different rotated order at a different position. This is actually a fast memory-to-memory move-beam mechanism. This mechanism is employed, for example, by the FBP3 to parallelize box transformations. More specifically, the FBP3 using this mechanism can rotate the entire CFB in real time, assisting in viewing the image from an arbitrary direction. For example, this mechanism enables the CUBE system to rotate through an arbitrary angle a 256^3 cube in about 45 milliseconds.

35.5 Implementation

The CUBE architecture has been developed and simulated at both the State University of New York at Stony Brook and the Center of Computer Graphics of the Ben-Gurion University. The simulations of the three processors and the CFB have been carried out on VAX 11/780 and 11/750 machines and SUN-3 workstations, all running UNIX. The 2D graphics systems used for displaying the projections include a RAMTEK 9400 and SUN-3/160C. A Sequent B8K 12 processor parallel machine has been utilized to examine closely the underlying parallel concepts of the CUBE architecture and its algorithms.

A reduced-resolution hardware prototype system of 16 × 16 × 16 voxels, 8 bits each, has been realized in hardware and has been integrated at the Ben-Gurion University under an IBM-AT with a GALAXY graphics display controller and a mouse. This prototype has been running successfully in real time. The hardware realization consists of 16 modules, each of which is implemented as a custom-built wirewrap board, containing a CFB module with its addressing mechanism, its

VMWB processing unit, viewing, translucency control, depth sectioning, etc. Currently, a larger and more complete hardware system is being developed as a direct expansion of the 16^3 prototype.

Concluding remarks

We have described in this chapter a 3D architecture with a novel parallel memory organization, three special-purpose autonomous processors and a powerful parallel bus, which team up to achieve real-time performance in voxel environment. Handling in parallel a beam of voxels instead of a single voxel at a time, provides a spectacular gain in performance of the CUBE system, which is improved from n^3 complexity to $n^2 \log n$ complexity. Consequently, the CUBE architecture, realized in hardware, has the potential of operating faster than any other known hardware or software system of the same category.

Acknowledgements

This work was supported by the National Science Foundation under grant DCR-86-03603, and partially by the Fraenkel Center for Computer Science of the Ben-Gurion University. We would like to thank the many dedicated individuals at both SUNY at Stony Brook and Ben-Gurion University who have worked on the CUBE project.

References

1. Kaufman A. and Bakalash R. (1988). Memory and processing architecture for 3-D voxel-based imagery. *IEEE Computer Graphics & Applications,* **8**(11), 10–23
2. Kaufman A. and Bakalash R. (1987). CUBE – an architecture based on a 3-D voxel map. In *Theoretical Foundations of Computer Graphics and CAD* (Earnshaw R.A., ed.), pp. 689–701. Berlin: Springer-Verlag
3. Goldwasser S.M. (1984). A generalized object display processor architecture. *IEEE Computer Graphics & Applications,* **4**(10), 43–55
4. Goldwasser S.M. and Reynolds R.A. (1983). An architecture for the real-time display and manipulation of three-dimensional objects. In *Proceedings International Conference on Parallel Processing*, pp. 269–74. Bellaire MI, August 1983
5. Ohashi T., Uchiki T. and Tokoro M. (1985). A three-dimensional shaded display method for voxel-based representation. In *Proceedings EUROGRAPHICS '85*, pp. 221–32. Nice, France, September 1985
6. Jackel D. (1985). The graphics PARCUM system: a 3D memory based computer architecture for processing and display of solid models. *Computer Graphics Forum,* **4**, 21–32
7. Kaufman A. and Shimony E. (1986). 3D scan-conversion algorithms for voxel-based graphics. In *Proceedings ACM Workshop on Interactive 3D Graphics*, pp. 45–76. Chapel Hill NC, October 1986

8. Kaufman A. (1987). An algorithm for 3D scan-conversion of polygons. In *Proc. EUROGRAPHICS'87*, pp. 197–208. Amsterdam, August 1987
9. Bresenham J.E. (1985). Run length slice algorithm for incremental lines. In *Fundamental Algorithms for Computer Graphics* (Earnshaw R.A., ed.), pp. 59–104. Berlin: Springer-Verlag
10. Sproull R.F. (1982). Using program transformations to derive line-drawing algorithms. *ACM Transactions on Graphics,* **1**(4), 257–73
11. Kaufman A. (1987). Efficient algorithms for 3D scan-conversion of parametric curves, surfaces, and volumes. *Computer Graphics,* **21**(4), 171–9
12. Kaufman A. (1988). A Two-Dimensional Frame Buffer Processor. In *Advances in Computer Graphics Hardware II* (Kuijk F. and Strasser W., eds), pp. 93–109. Berlin: Springer-Verlag
13. Guibas L.J. and Stolfi J. (1982). A language for bitmap manipulation. *ACM Transactions on Graphics,* **1**(3), 191–214
14. Kaufman A. (1986). Memory organization for a cubic frame buffer. In *Proceedings EUROGRAPHICS '86*, pp. 93–100. Lisbon, Portugal, August 1986
15. Gemballa R. and Lindner R. (1982). The multiple-write bus technique. *IEEE Computer Graphics & Applications,* **2**(7), 33–41

36 · Parallel image reconstruction by using a dedicated asynchronous cellular array

D. Lattard
G. Mazare

Laboratoire de
Génie Informatique

The large amount of information to be dealt with is the critical problem in all image processing. We show how it is possible to reconstruct an image, in a very parallel way, using an asynchronous cellular array, with real-time performance. We present the architecture of this network, and the system performing the whole reconstruction.

36.1 Introduction

Image reconstruction is a way to visualize the internal structure of an object or a living body. The process is used in many fields such as radiology, radio astronomy, electron microscopy, optics, etc. As part of radiology, this allows us to analyze the structure of human organs, detect eventual tumours and then help medical diagnosis (tomography, scanners). All these applications have created a particular interest in the image reconstruction problem; many studies have been made and different systems built.

Measurements of radiation passing through an object at a certain level, make it possible to calculate the internal distribution of density : section image of the object. We will first detail how we can reconstruct an image with the measurements, then show how to parallelize this technique, its interest and its implementation on an asynchronous cellular array.

36.2 Reconstruction method

36.2.1 Measuring principle

We X-ray the object being studied, following the plane in which we want to realize the image section; the rays are collected after their passage through the object. The ray intensity decreases with the quantity of material passed through (length and density); this ray attenuation is the line integral on its path of the object density:

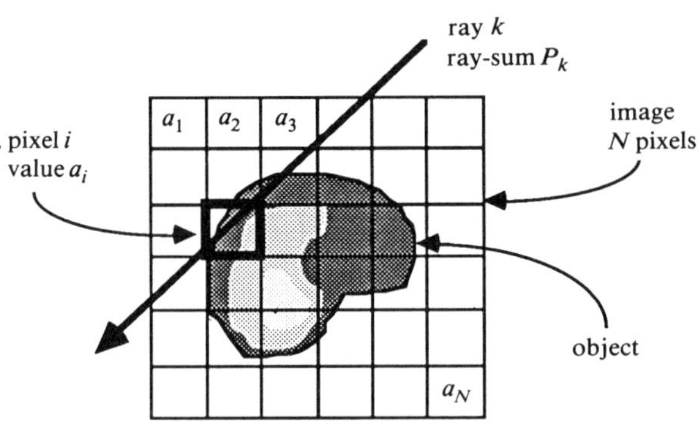

Figure 36.1
Dividing the image into pixels.

$$\text{attenuation} = \int_{\text{path}} \text{density}$$

The image is divided into N pixels (see Figure 36.1); a_i is the value of the ith pixel, P_k the ray-sum of the kth ray (attenuation). We can write $P_k = \Sigma_{(i=1 \text{ to } N)} (w_{ik} * a_i)$, where w_{ik} is a geometric factor (effect of the kth ray on the ith pixel, w_{ik} is null if the kth ray does not pass through the ith pixel) (Kingswood, *et al.*, 1986).

The image reconstruction problem is to determine the pixel values $a_1, a_2, \ldots, a_N$ from the set of ray-sums P_k obtained by radiating around the object. We have to resolve a linear system of K equations (number of radiation measurements P_k) with N unknowns (number of image pixels).

36.2.2 Reconstruction principle

A solution for the previous system is to use an algebraic method such as the usual Gaussian or Cholewski triangulation; but considering the large amount of information to be processed, this approach is not realistic.

There are two ways to perform the reconstruction: analytic and algebraic methods. Radon worked on this subject, and has shown that it is analytically possible to solve the problem.

The best-known analytic method is the back-projection of the filtered measurements (Herman, 1980; Herman and Natterer, 1980).

Another efficient solution is to use an 'Algebraic Reconstruction Technique' (ART); this iterative process comes from the Kaczmarz's algorithm (linear system resolution, in numeric analysis) (Gordon *et al.*, 1970; Gordon, 1974; Gordon *et al.*, 1975; Censor, 1983).

36.2.3 The back-projection of the filtered measurements

This method includes two parts:

(0) The projection filtering.

(1) The distribution of the filtered projections to the pixels crossed by the ray.

The filtering is a 1D computation, and can be performed by convolution or multiplication in the Fourier domain.

The algorithm is:

```
                  SEQ
initialization  a_i := 0 for all pixels
Phase (0)           projection filtering
Phase (1)           distribution of P_k on the ray path to modify the a_i
                    values
```

36.2.4 The algebraic reconstruction technique

The principle is very easy; each iteration includes two phases:

(1) For each ray, we distribute uniformly the ray-sum P_k to the pixels crossed by the ray.

(2) From the new pixel values (given by Phase (1)), we calculate a set of pseudo ray-sums P'_k.

We repeat the process with the distribution of the differences $(P_k - P'_k)$ until the calculated ray-sums (P'_k) are not very different from the measured ray-sums (P_k). At each step, the image improves; the final image is a reliable representation of the object density distribution in the studied plane ($P_k \approx P'_k$ for all rays).

More precisely, the algorithm is as follows:

```
                    SEQ
initialization        a_i := 0 for all pixels
                      P'_k := 0 for all rays
                    REPEAT
iteration step          SEQ
      Phase (1)               Distribution of (P_k - P'_k) on the ray path
                                to modify the a_i values.
      Phase (2)               Evaluation of a set of pseudo ray-sums
                                P'_k using the previous a_i values.
      test                    For each ray, do the difference between
                                the measured P_k value and the
                                calculated P'_k value.
                    UNTIL error sufficiently small (P_k ≈ P'_k)
```

36.3 Parallel algorithm and asynchronous cellular array

36.3.1 The parallelism

We are interested only in Phases (1) and (2) because they are 2D.

If we consider the large amount of computation involved in Phases (1) and (2) of the algorithms, we can easily see that a monoprocessor architecture cannot perform in real-time (that is, obtain an image a few seconds after acquiring the radiation measurements).

An easy way to compute these algorithms in a very parallel manner is to use an array of processors, each one dealing with one pixel (see Figure 36.2). The information about each ray forms a message, moving into the network. A host computer manages the network I/O and the synchronizations between the different computation phases.

36.3.2 The network

The main specifications of the network (Figure 36.3) are:

- Each cell is a processor able to realize simple operations.
- Each cell is surrounded with eight unidirectional buffers (four input buffers and four output buffers).
- Each cell communicates with its four neighbours using a message routeing mechanism.
- The cells are asynchronous; they compute independently and only when they have messages to process (Cornu-Emieux *et al.*, 1987).

A message contains many information fields:

- Its type (distinction between the two phases).
- A ray-sum field, that differs with the type:
  - Phase (1): ray-sum distributed to the crossed cells.
  - Phase (2): pseudo ray-sum calculated by the crossed cells.
- Geometric information: ray entry position in the cell, and ray angle (cosine, sine).

The messages move between cells through the buffers; each of them has a flag that indicates its state to the neighbouring cells: full (there is a message in the buffer) or empty (no message).

The network allows us to parallelize the two computation phases of the algorithms; the host processor realizes message send and receive and the repeated process of the second algorithm.

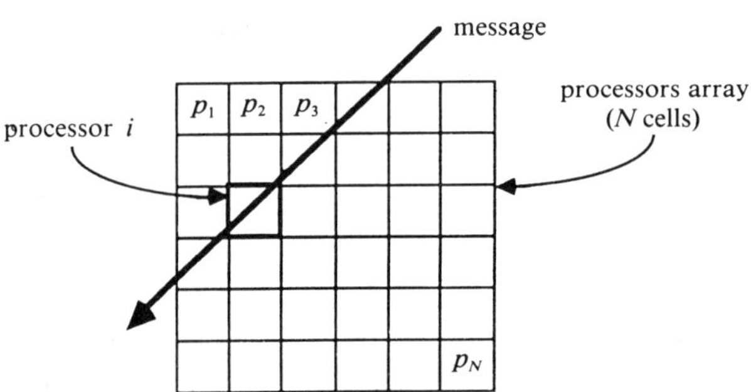

Figure 36.2
Processor array.

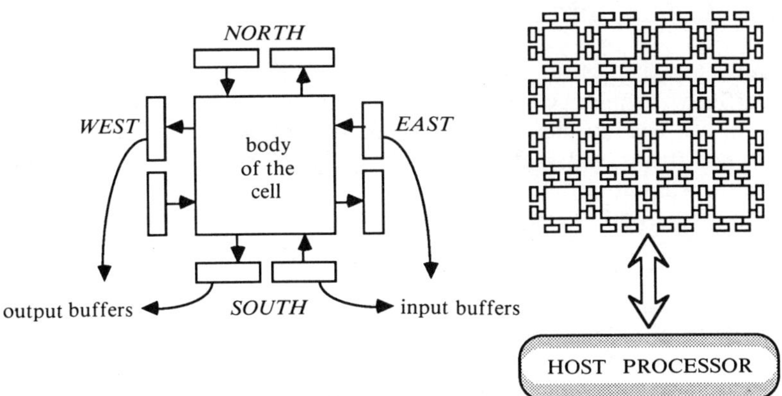

Figure 36.3
A cell and a 4 × 4 network.

Host computer algorithm

Back-projection of the filtering measurements

```
SEQ
   initialize the network
   send the Phase (1) messages
   receive the issued messages from the network
   receive the results (final image)
```

The Phase (1) can start as soon as the acquisition of the radiation measurements begins.

Algebraic Reconstruction Technique

```
SEQ
   initialize the network
   REPEAT
      SEQ
         PAR
            send the Phase (1) messages
            receive the issued messages from the network
         PAR
            send the Phase (2) messages
            receive the issued messages from the network
         compare the calculated P'k values to the measured Pk
            values
   UNTIL (Pk − P'k) sufficiently small
   receive the results (final image)
```

36.3.3 Cell algorithm

The principle of the algorithm performed by a cell is simple. After inspection of the input buffers to acquire an eventual message, the cell determines the neighbouring cell to which it has to transmit the message. If the transmission can be performed (addressee buffer is empty), then it processes the message, otherwise it keeps the message in the input buffer.

The cell algorithm is:

```
SEQ
  select an input buffer
  WHILE TRUE
        SEQ
          test the flag of the selected input buffer
          IF the selected input buffer is full
            SEQ
              read the message in the input buffer
              generate the next address
              test the flag of the addressee output buffer
              IF the addressee output buffer is empty
                SEQ
                  write the message to the output
                      buffer
                  fill the output buffer
                  empty the input buffer
                  process the message
          select the next input buffer
```

36.3.4 Details of the algorithm

The most complex parts to implement are the computation of the next address and processing of the message. Before detailing these parts, we define the geometric information of the message (Figure 36.4).

The computation of the next address has several objectives:

- Determine the addressee cell (it is necessary to know what cell the message will pass before processing it, because the cell processes the message only if it can be routed).

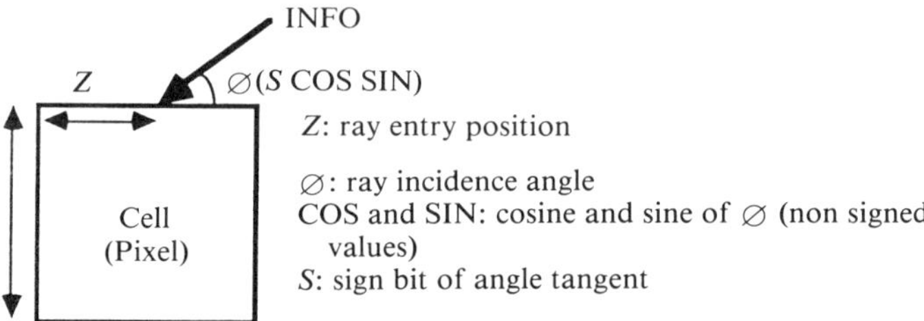

Figure 36.4
Geometric information of the message.

- Compute the new geometric information of the message that eventually will pass after the process.
- Compute the length of the ray path across the pixel (this result will be used in the process of the message; it is the previously mentioned geometric factor w_{ik}).

The process of the message depends on its type; for Phase (1), the cell adds the product (ray-sum value * length of the path across the pixel) to the previously evaluated pixel value. For Phase (2), the cell adds the product (pixel value * length of the path) to the received ray-sum value.

Message structure

For the computation of the next address, we have to determine the geometric information of the next message COSS, SINS, SS, ZS (Figure 36.5), the output side of the ray OUTPUT and the length of the path LEN. All these calculations are functions of the geometric information of the received message, and of the input side of the ray INPUT (see Figure 36.6).

We can detail the equations and illustrate them in the case S = 0 (tangent TG = SIN/COS < 0):

LEN = Z/COS	LEN = DIM/SIN
ZS = DIM − (Z*TG)	ZS = Z − (DIM/TG)
COSS = SIN	COSS = COS
SINS = COS	SINS = SIN
SS = S	SS = 1 − S (binary complement)

We can also pass the angle tangent instead of cosine and sine, then do an approximate computing for the length, and the message is shorter. This is possible because we do not need a good precision for the length computing.

36.4 Validation and perpectives

36.4.1 Simulations

Functional simulations of the whole 32 × 32 network and host processor have been done to validate the algorithmic studies. A simple language, occam, based on CSP, allows the description of such concurrent processes; the synchronization and communication between processes are realized by a channel communication mechanism (Hoare, 1978; INMOS Ltd, 1984). A microprocessor, the transputer, was specially developed for this language by INMOS, to obtain excellent execution performance for this kind of parallel processes (INMOS Ltd, 1986). The PC-board B004, including a transputer and 2 megabytes of memory, and the transputer Development System software (INMOS Ltd, 1986) allow access to the microprocessor in an easy and efficient way to study such parallel architectures.

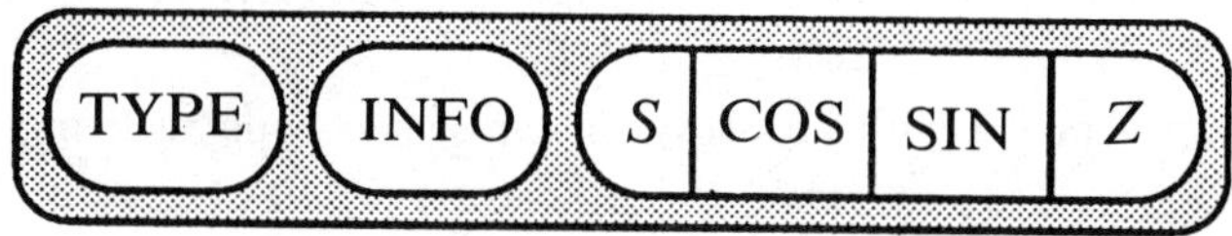

Figure 36.5
Message structure.

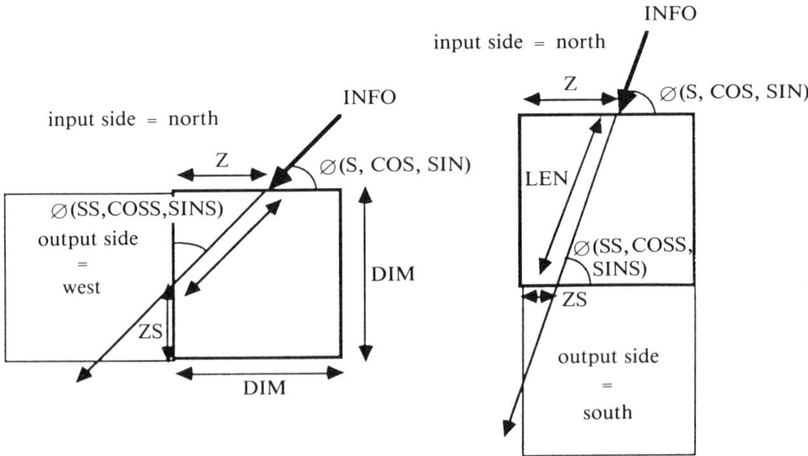

Figure 36.6
Geometric information of received message.

As for the radiation measurements we needed to do the reconstruction, they have been provided by Jean-Louis Amans (Amans *et al.*, 1985).

We now study more precisely the architecture on which we will implement the algorithm, and the realization of a VLSI chip, integrating the cellular array.

36.4.2 Performances

The efficiency of the parallel method with respect to the sequential method is evident. All the pixels are processed simultaneously, and the cost saved is in the order of N^2 (N: size of the reconstructed image, number of pixels). The global amount of computation of the sum of all cells is in the order of N^3 by projection (there are approximately N points by projection); as for the cellular array, that processes in a parallel manner, the total cost is in the order of N by projection (the number of projections necessary to obtain an image good enough is in the order of N).

36.4.3 Integration

When we know the performance of such a technique of parallel image reconstruction, the goal is to integrate a maximum number of elementary cells on a single chip; with the perspective of working with a high resolution image. The existing systems use images that have a maximum of 1024 × 1024 points, almost the definition of the television image.

Of course, we could not think of integrating such a network on a chip today, though future advances may make this possible. We can follow two possible routes to oppose this limitation:

- Develop a board with an array of chips, each one realizing a small size network.

- Take interest in the Wafer Scale Integration aspect (WSI), that is today more and more important. Studies about this problem are led in our laboratory; but this second proposition involves a modification of the algorithm because the messages must be correctly routed and they have to avoid the defective cells; these are the results of the technological defaults (Leighton and Leiserson, 1985; Ansade *et al.*, 1986a).

36.4.4 Perspectives

After a first study of the architecture and its timing, and taking account of the real-time constraints (acquisition speed of radiation measurements), we can say that the cell process is too fast, and the network use is not optimized. Therefore, we associate an array of pixels to a processor. The messages have the same structure, and each cell performs an iterative process to deal with its pixels array.

The goal is to realize a chip of 4 × 4 cells, each one dealing with a 16 × 16 pixels array. A chip also processes a 64 × 64 image.

Conclusion

Why this particular interest in parallel architectures? There are two possibilities for increasing classical architecture performances; first, with a monoprocessor that is faster and more advanced, and can realize complex operations; second, with a multiprocessor architecture as a cellular network, where the job is distributed on each cell.

We chose the second class of architecture because a monoprocessor will always stay a monoprocessor though it is faster and faster, and it will never use the algorithm parallelism (the jobs are processed sequentially). A particular application does not use all the monoprocessor possibilities; on the other hand the cellular array is specially conceived and designed, and consequently optimum.

In the case of image processing, it is very easy to parallelize such algorithms, immediately the pixel-processor association comes to mind.

Many other applications have been studied for the presented asynchronous cellular array, in particular, logical simulations, placement and neural network (Ansade *et al.*, 1986b).

Acknowledgements

This work is supported in part by the 'Pôle Architecture' of the group 'Coopération, Concurrence et Communication' (C3) of the Centre National de la Recherche Scientifique (CNRS).

We thank Jean-Louis Amans for his help and his competence in the field of image reconstruction techniques.

References

Amans J.L., Campagnolo R. and Garderet P. (1985). *Imagerie médicale: méthodes de reconstruction et techniques instrumentales*. Note technique LETI/MCTE No. 1511, Laboratoire d'Electronique et Technologie de l'Informatique / Centre d'Etudes Nucléaires de Grenoble

Ansade Y., Cornu-Emieux R., Faure B. and Mazare G. (1986). WSI asynchronous cell network. In *Wafer Scale Integration* (Saucier G. and Trihle L., eds). Amsterdam: North Holland

Ansade Y., Cornu-Emieux R., Faure B., Mazare B. and Objois P. (1986). Algorithms dedicated to a network of asynchronous cells. In *Parallel Algorithms and Architectures* (Cosnard M. and Robert Y., eds). Amsterdam: North Holland

Censor Y. (1983). Finite series-expansion reconstruction methods. *IEEE Proceedings,* **71**(3), 409–19

Cornu-Emieux R. Mazare G. and Objois P. (1987). An integrated highly parallel architecture to accelerate logicial simulation. In *ISELDECS 87*, Kharagpur, India

Gordon R. (1974). A tutorial on ART (Algebraic Reconstruction Techniques). *IEEE Trans. Nucl. Sci.,* **NS-21**, 78–93, 95

Gordon R., Bender R., Herman G.T. (1970). Algebraic reconstruction techniques (ART) for three-dimensional electron microscopy and X-ray photography. *Journal of Theoretical Biology,* **29**, 471–81

Gordon R., Herman G.T. and Johnson S.A. (1975). Image reconstruction from projections. *Sci. Amer.,* **233**(4), 56–68

Herman G.T. (1980). *Image reconstruction from projections: the fundamentals of computerized tomography*. New York: Academic Press

Herman G.T. and Natterer F. (1980). *Mathematical aspects of computerized tomography*. Berlin: Springer-Verlag

Hoare C.A.R. (1978). Communicating sequential processes. *Communication ACM,* **21**(8), 666–77

INMOS Ltd. (1984). *Occam Programming Manual*. London: Prentice-Hall

INMOS Ltd. (1986a). *Transputer Development System v.2.0, user manual.*

INMOS Ltd. (1986b). *Transputer, reference manual.*

Kingswood N., Dagless E.L., Belchamber R.M., Betteridge D., Lilley T. and Roberts J.D.M. (1986). Image reconstruction using the transputer. *Proceedings IEEE, PT. E,* **133**, 139–44

Leighton T. and Leiserson C.E. (1985). Wafer Scale Integration of systolic arrays. *IEEE Transactions on Computers,* **C34**(5)

Radon J. (1917). Uber die Bestimmung von Funktionen durch ihre Integralwerte langs gewisser Mannigfaltigheiten. *Berl. Verh. Sachs. Akad. Wiss. Leipzip, Math-Nature Kl. 69*

37 · A multimicroprocessor architecture for image reconstruction in CT

A.R. Borges
A.M.B. Ferrari de Almeida

Universidadė de Aveiro

A microcomputer-based pipelined multiprocessing system for image reconstruction in computed tomography is described. Filtered backprojection algorithms are shown to map efficiently onto the architecture. The system has been designed to be used in applications where the reconstruction time constraints are not very severe (allowing for values in the 30–60 s range) and/or spatial resolution is not critical and 2D image displays of 128 × 128 are acceptable.

37.1 Introduction

Image reconstruction from projections is being employed currently in many different fields. A good survey of what has been achieved and what can be expected in the future is presented in [1]. Medical imaging, however, remains the major application area: this technique is routinely used in radiology (X-ray transmission tomography [2]), nuclear medicine (single photon and proton emission tomography [3]), magnetic resonance [4] and ultrasound imaging [5].

The reconstruction problem can be stated, in general, as a process of evaluating either the 2D (cross-section) or the 3D (volume) distribution of a physical property of an object from measured estimates of its line integrals along a finite number of paths taken through different directions.

Each line integral is normally referred to as a **ray integral** and the collection of ray integrals taken through a given direction is called a **projection**. Figure 37.1 shows one of these projections for a parallel scanning geometry in a 2D situation.

An important characteristic of tomographic reconstruction is the large amount of data that has to be processed. In a typical CT scanner, a minimum of 512 samples (ray integrals) are taken per projection and as many as 700 or more projections are obtained around the patient. The reconstructed body section is then displayed with 256 × 256 or 512 × 512 picture elements. The reconstruction time is normally of the order of magnitude of the scanning time which goes up to 12 seconds. In this way, during a clinical examination, several slices can be viewed in sequence without reducing significantly the patients' throughput.

Very powerful computational resources are obviously required to

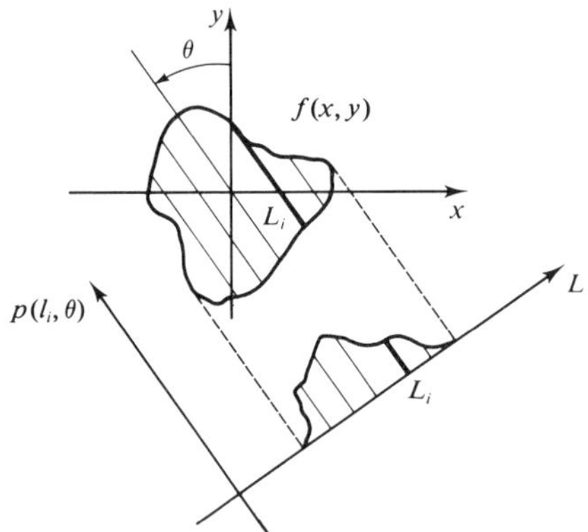

Figure 37.1
Projection at angle θ.

$f(x, y)$ – 2D distribution of the physical property of the object
$p(l_i, \theta) = \int_{L_i} f(x, y)\, dL_i$ – ray integral

accomplish this. A typical setup consists of a minicomputer which controls the gantry, handles the data acquisition and store of information and interfaces with the operator, and of an associated array processor to perform the computations [6].

In cases where requirements are still more stringent, solutions using special-purpose processors, mapping the reconstruction algorithms directly, have been proposed [7]. Gains of about two to three orders of magnitude in the reconstruction time were reported.

This chapter describes a multimicroprocessor-based architecture which, as in [7], takes advantage of the parallelism present in the algorithms and partitions the computational task among several processors by assigning to them specific processing parts of the reconstruction procedure. A trade-off between cost and speed is achieved through the replacement of expensive dedicated hardware by inexpensive general-purpose LSI/VLSI chips.

Applications expected for it are those where reconstruction time constraints are not very severe (30–60 s range), as in nuclear medicine, and/or where spatial resolution is not critical, allowing 128 × 128 image displays, as in radiotherapy planning.

A previous general assessment of the architecture may be found in [8].

37.2 Image reconstruction algorithms

Many different reconstruction algorithms are reported in the literature [9, 10]. However, the most popular in medical imaging is, undoubtedly, the filtered back-projection method. The reason for this is related to its efficiency: the back-projection method transforms the reconstruction problem into a pipeline of operations performed on successive projections. This means that processing can start right after the first projection data is collected, thus enabling an overlapping with data acquisition.

It is obtained from the discretization of the Radon inversion formula. Derivation procedures for different scanning geometries are presented in [11, 12]. Besides the parallel geometry, described in Figure 37.1, other common scanning geometries are the fan beam ones whose basic types are shown in Figure 37.2 for the 2D case.

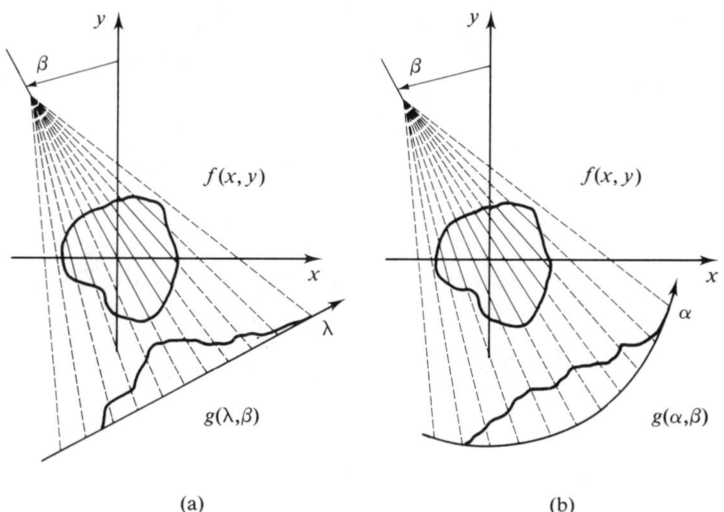

Figure 37.2
Fan beam geometries.
Projection at angle β.
(a) Linear detector strip.
(b) Circular detector strip.

The filtered backprojection algorithm for data collected by a fan beam circular detector strip geometry is given by the equations:

$$f(I,J) = \sum_{j=0}^{M-1} g_j(\alpha' / \Delta\alpha) \,.\, K_p(j,I,J)$$

$$g_{i'j} = \sum_{i=0}^{N-1} F_{i'-i} \,.\, K \,.\, D \cos(i\,\Delta\alpha) \,.\, p_{ij}$$

where:

$$K_P(j, I, J) = \frac{1}{D^2 / \Delta p^2 + I^2 + J^2 + 2(D / \Delta p)[I \sin(j\,\Delta\beta) - J \cos(j\,\Delta\beta)]}$$

$$\alpha' / \Delta\alpha = \left[\tan^{-1} \frac{I \cos(j\,\Delta\beta) + J \sin(j\,\Delta\beta)}{D / \Delta p + I \sin(j\,\Delta\beta) - J \cos(j\,\Delta\beta)}\right] / \Delta\alpha$$

I, J = reconstructed image pixel center coordinates

$$-P / 2 \leqslant I, J \leqslant P / 2$$

Δp = pixel side length
D = distance from the fan beam focus to the centre of rotation
$\Delta\alpha$ = detector cell angular length in the circular strip
N = number of detector cells
$\Delta\beta$ = projection angular increment
M = number of projections taken around the object
p_{ij} = measured estimate of raysum i in projection j
$g_{i'j}$ = element i' in projection j after multiplication by a predefined factor and filtering
$g_j(\alpha' / \Delta\alpha)$ = interpolated value corresponding to a path that goes through the centre of pixel (I, J) in projection j

$f(I, J)$ = reconstructed image
K = constant with value $(\Delta\alpha \,.\, \Delta\beta) \,/\, (4\pi^2 \,.\, \Delta p^2)$
F_m = filter coefficients

$$F_m = w_m \,.\, \text{sinc}^{-2}\,(m\Delta\alpha)$$

the weights w_m are determined through the sampling in the spatial domain of the function

$$F(X) = \text{abs}(X) \,.\, W(X)$$

where $W(X)$ is a filter dependent window function [13].

The pipeline of operations performed on each projection data now becomes apparent and can be easily identified:

- PREMULTIPLICATION

$$p^*_{ij} = \sum_{i=0}^{N-1} p_{ij} \,.\, K\,D \cos\,(i\,\Delta\alpha)$$

- FILTERING

$$g_{i'j} = \sum_{i=0}^{N-1} F_{i'-i} \,.\, p^*_{ij}$$

- INTERPOLATION The values of the filtered projection $g_{i'j}$ are linearly interpolated to the middle point s successive times, yielding a much denser collection of projection values $g_{i''j}$.
- BACKPROJECTION For every pixel (I, J) of the digitized image, three additional steps can be considered:
  Determination of $g_j(\alpha' \,/\, \Delta\alpha)$
  This is obtained through nearest-neighbour approximation of $g_{i''j}$ after the evaluation of $\alpha' \,/\, \Delta\alpha$.
  Post-multiplication

$$g^*_j(\alpha' \,/\, \Delta\alpha) = g_j(\alpha' \,/\, \Delta\alpha) \,.\, K_P(j, I, J)$$

  Updating the pixel value

$$f(I, J) = f(I, J) + g^*_j(\alpha' \,/\, \Delta\alpha)$$

Direct calculation of the expressions for $\alpha' \,/\, \Delta\alpha$ and K_P is rather time consuming due to their complexity. This is especially critical because they have to be obtained for every pixel in the digitized image $(P + 1)^2$ times. An approach similar to [7] was adopted, and an iterative procedure, based on a polynomial approximation to the Taylor series expansion of the expressions and table look-up or direct calculation of specific values, was developed.

37.3 System description

The drastic reduction in prices and the increasing sophistication of general-purpose LSI/VLSI chips are making possible the design of powerful microprocessor-based functional units.

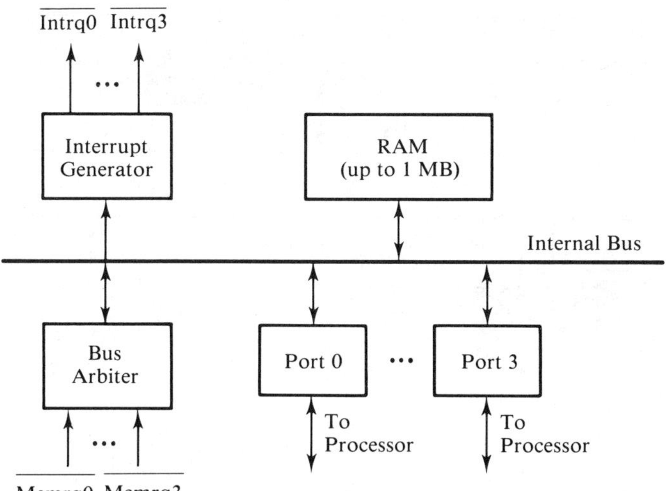

Figure 37.3
4-port memory.

To take advantage of these cheap yet powerful units in applications whose processing requirements far exceed the capabilities of a single microprocessor, systems must be designed in a regular way through a suitable interconnection of those modules [14]. Two aspects have to be borne in mind:

(1) A compromise must be made on the number of interconnections per functional unit because their cost and board area occupation can easily become a dominant factor.

(2) The balance between the loads of intermodule communication and internal processing has to be carefully considered [15]; good performances are only to be expected in cases where the algorithms can be partitioned into tasks requiring a high amount of internal processing when compared to intertask communication [16].

A 2D grid topology was adopted. It is based on two different modules: a 4-port common memory and a processor module, each to be built on a single double-eurocard. It is meant to be efficient for tomographic reconstruction but also flexible enough to be applied in other situations.

System interconnection was established such that all interprocessor communication is performed through common memory using a mailbox interrupt driven scheme. Figure 37.3 shows a block diagram description of the 4-port memory module.

Round-robin arbitration for access to common memory was selected to enable equal access probability through any port, limiting any processor's waiting time to a maximum, well-defined value.

The interrupt generator is used to implement a simple mailbox interrupt driven rule. Writing in any of the last four 16-bit memory locations activates one of the interrupt lines. The line is only reset when data is read from it. Figure 37.4 shows a block diagram of the processor module.

The external memory addressing unit is actually not more than the decoding of four linear 1 Mb segments of the microprocessor's addressing space together with

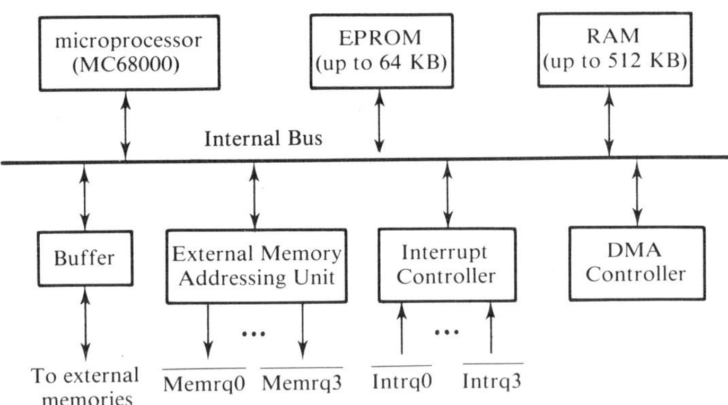

Figure 37.4
Processor module.

a time-out timer to prevent deadlock because of memory malfunction or when accessing a not-connected memory.

The DMA controller works for data transfer between internal and external memory and between any two external memories, providing, in the latter case, a fast link between two non-adjacent processors.

No dedicated arithmetic hardware (neither an arithmetic coprocessor nor a multiplier unit) is included in the design of the processor module. It has been intentional to keep the unit's price and simplicity as low as possible. We felt that, at the present stage, it was more important to test the qualities of this architecture in terms of distributed processing rather than speed. A significant gain in performance can be obtained by using special processor units designed around digital signal processing chips.

A small monitor was developed for the processor units. Besides having debugging facilities, it implements a set of primitives enabling loading and running of specific tasks in addressed processors and performing interprocessor communication [17].

Single processors are identified by two numbers representing its coordinates in the 2D grid. The outgoing connections in the processor modules and the ports in the 4-port common memories are generally designated by the cardinal points: North, West, South and East. A rule has been established for the regular system set up by imposing as the only legal connections between processors unit and memories, the ones corresponding to opposite directions, that is, North-South and West-East.

Figure 37.5 presents a general block diagram of the system for tomographic reconstruction based on four processor modules and four 4-port memories. It maps directly the filtered backprojection algorithm described above. It may be thought of as a three-stage pipelining beginning at the top-left corner with the preprocessing unit. Backprojection, which is the most computation requiring stage, is assigned to the two lower units.

The module boards have been inserted in a rack for compactness, the back panel being used to maintain the interconnection maze among the units through flat cable connections.

The preprocessing unit takes care of the premultiplication of projection data and of several other operations performed on it because of mechanical and electrical misalignments on the scanning system and of physical problems associated with data collection.

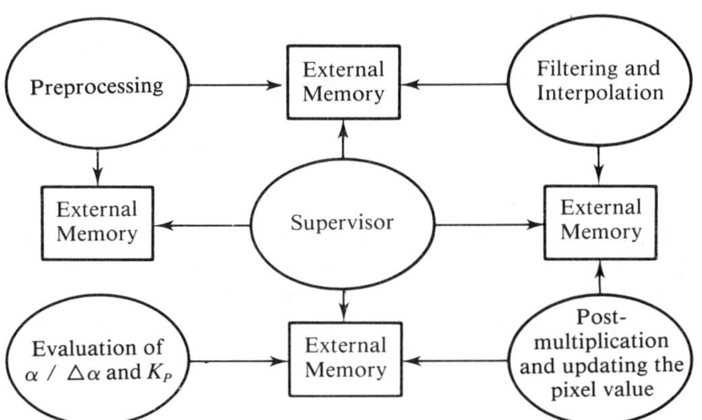

Figure 37.5
General system block diagram.

Filtering is carried out through the use of fast digital convolution algorithms using a combination of multidimensional techniques and number theoretic transforms [18]. Algorithms based on the mappings introduced by Agarwal and Burrus, and Agarwal and Cooley and using modular arithmetic (modulo the Fermat number 5, that is, $2^{32} + 1$) to perform the computations, were developed [19].

They make possible, when required, the splitting of the processing among several processors in a straightforward way, with an increase of performance approximately equal to the number of processors assigned to the task.

The backprojection stage is also highly parallel. First, evaluation of $(\alpha' / \Delta\alpha)$ and K_P can be done in different processors. Next, the reconstructed image can be segmented and several processor groups put to work on different segments. The only data they share is the filtered and interpolated projection. If this is made available to all the groups at the beginning of the stage, no further interaction is necessary among them.

The supervisor acts as a front-end processor, assigning the tasks to the different processors, sending the required raw data and saving the reconstructed image which is then displayed. It is, at the moment, a VME-based 68000 microcomputer running a CP/M 68K operating system. It is intended to be replaced in the future by an engineering workstation.

Conclusion

A multimicroprocessor-based architecture for image reconstruction in computed tomography was described. It maps the filtered backprojection algorithms and consists of inexpensive modules designed with general-purpose LSI/VLSI chips connected in a 2D grid topology.

The whole reconstruction process was simulated in a general-purpose computer and performed well. A system prototype, similar to the one described in Figure 37.5, is being built. Its test with real data from X-ray transmission tomography and emission tomography is expected to start presently.

Acknowledgement

This work was sponsored by INIC – Instituto Nacional de Investigação Científica.

References

1. Bates R.H.T., Garden K.L. and Peters T.M. (1983). Overview of computerized tomography with emphasis on future developments. *Proc. IEEE,* **71**, 356–72
2. Robb R.A. (1982). X-ray computed tomography: an engineering synthesis of multiscientific principles. *CRC Crit. Reviews in Biomed. Eng.,* **7**, 265–333
3. Budinger T.F., Gullberg G.T. and Huesman R.H. (1979). Emission computed tomography. In *Image Reconstruction from Projections: Implementation and Applications* (Herman G.T., ed.). Berlin: Springer-Verlag
4. Hinshaw W.S. and Lent A.H. (1983). An introduction to NMR imaging: from the Bloch Equation to the Imaging Equation. *Proc. IEEE,* **71**, 338–50
5. Greenleaf J.F. (1983). Computerized tomography with ultrasound. *Proc. IEEE,* **71**, 338–50
6. Alexander P. (1983). Array processors in medical imaging. *Computer*, 17–30
7. Gilbert B.K. *et al.* (1981). Rapid execution of fan beam image reconstruction algorithms using efficient computational techniques and special-purpose processors. *IEEE Trans. on Biomed. Eng.,* **BME28**, 98–116
8. Borges A.R.O.S. and Ferrari de Almeida A.M.B., Computed tomography: a multi-microprocessor approach. In *Proc. of 1984 Moroccan Workshop on Signal Processing and its Applications*, pp. A3/1.1–1.16. Morocco
9. Lewitt R.M. (1983). Reconstruction algorithms: transform methods. *Proc. IEEE,* **71**, 390–408
10. Censor Y. (1983). Finite series expansion reconstruction methods. *Proc. IEEE,* **71**, 409–19
11. Horn B.K.P. (1978). Density reconstruction using arbitrary ray-sampling schemes. *Proc. IEEE,* **66**, 551–62
12. Horn B.K.P. (1979). Fan-beam reconstruction methods. *Proc. IEEE,* **67**, 1616–23
13. Rowland S.W. (1979). Computer implementation of image reconstruction formulas. In *Image Reconstruction from Projections: Implementation and Applications* (Herman G.T., ed.). Berlin: Springer-Verlag
14. Feng T. (1981). A survey of interconnection networks. *Computer*, 12–27
15. Weitzman C. (1980). *Distributed Micro/Minicomputer Systems: Structure, Implementation and Application*. Prentice-Hall
16. Wiley P. (1987). A parallel architecture comes of age at last. *IEEE Spectrum*. 46–50
17. Bowen B.A. and Buhr R.J.A. (1980). *The Logical Design of Multiple-Microprocessor Systems*. Prentice-Hall
18. McClellan J.H. and Rader C.M. (1979). *Number Theory in Digital Signal Processing*. Prentice-Hall
19. Borges A.R.O.S. and Ferrari de Almeida A.M.B. (1987). Comparative Performance Analysis of Fast Digital Convolution Algorithms. To appear in *Proc. of the Ninth Annual Conference of the IEEE/Eng. in Medicine and Biology Society*, November 1987

38 · Hardware architecture with transputers for fast manipulation of volume data

E.G. Hiltebrand

Eidgenössiche
Technische
Hochschule ETH

For interactive display and manipulation of volume data as used in medical diagnosis (CT, MR) there is a strong need for powerful computing systems. Even with the fastest known single processors, the time to display a cube with a 128 voxels edge length is over ten seconds. The algorithm we use for shaded-surface display can easily be formulated in parallel, and for that reason the task can be done with a multiprocessing system. A 9-transputer system for direct display of medical data is under construction. To improve the system performance, a supporting hardware is connected to the data path of each transputer.

38.1 Introduction

Several methods, including CT and MR imaging, are capable of providing 3D information about a human body in the form of volume images. The visual evaluation of the image content necessitates both a fast presentation of the measured densities of an oblique 2D cross-section of the data volume, and fast oblique projections of surfaces of extracted objects onto a 2D plane such as a CRT display. Recent developments in MR imaging have reduced the recording time for data volumes consisting of 256^3 elements from several hours to a few minutes. Therefore, it is easy to predict that fundamental 3D image operations such as shaded-surface display, segmentation and cutting operations with good user interaction will be of great clinical interest in the near future.

38.2 Display and manipulation

For the shaded-surface display of volume images, various methods are in use. One type of these first requires an explicit determination of the object surface. Thereafter, standard computer graphics algorithms such as hidden-surface removal, clipping, surface shading and transparency can be applied to display the extracted surface [1, 2]. Considerable data reduction is achieved by the surface extraction but, on the other hand, an additional preprocessing step is introduced which is very time consuming due to the complex nature of biological and anatomical objects.

Manipulation of the volume data such as removing of unwanted parts requires this preprocessing step once again.

Another method treats the data throughout as volume elements (voxels). A shaded-surface view is generated either by a ray-casting [3] or by a back-to-front technique [4]. Using the back-to-front method all slices, rows and columns of the volume array are checked in the order of decreasing distance to the observer. All opaque voxels are projected onto the screen overwriting any previous projections, thereby resulting in hidden-surface removal. The ray-casting technique progresses from the screen to the object. Projection rays are cast into the volume and the first opaque voxel is determined for each ray. Current implementations of both methods are handicapped by the huge amount of computation required for the generation of the projection.

In a recent prebuffer method, the generation of a view is decomposed into two parts for time efficiency [5–7]. First, an intermediate projection parallel to that of the three main axes, which is within an angle of less than 45 degrees, is generated. The final distance buffer is obtained by applying a 2D coordinate transform. The principal advantage of the decomposition resides in the size invariance property of the prebuffer, owing to the parallelism of the projection plane and the planar sections of the volume perpendicular to the determined main axis. In every section, the sampling raster resulting from the intersections of the rays is identical with the original raster except for a fractional offset. This results in a time-saving way of generating the voxel addresses.

The shading is usually accomplished by mapping the distance from the projection plane to grey values, or combining the distance information with the surface gradient determined at each surface location [8].

Depending on the raw data, some preprocessing steps are of advantage before segmentation or display operations are carried out. The data matrix is generally interpolated to obtain an isotropic resolution. Standard filtering techniques may be applied for noise suppression and surface enhancement. For segmentation, either thresholding or a more refined method based on difference of Gaussian is used.

Investigation of anatomical malformations and surgical planning are some of the most promising medical application fields for volume imaging. Therefore, it is essential to have functions to manipulate the data interactively by cutting away obscuring parts and by setting different levels of transparency.

38.3 Performance evaluation

With the transputer from INMOS [9], one can realize a powerful multiprocessor system with little expense, because there are functions on this chip which support message passing, task switching and management in hardware. The Pascal-like, high-level programming language occam includes constructs for parallel execution of operations and for the configuration of programs corresponding to the chosen topology of the interprocessor communication network.

To get an idea of the performance of this new processing element, we built a single processor system with 4 Mbytes of RAM and a frame grabber on a PC slot card. Several image transform and processing algorithms were implemented and compared to assembly language routines on a digital signal processor. We observed a small superiority of the signal processor on multiplication intensive tasks. For the treatment of high resolution images and of computerized tomography data sets, there is a great advantage in the 32-bit architecture of the transputer owing to the greater precision and addressing range.

The back-to-front algorithm using the prebuffer technique has been implemented on the above single transputer system. The memory capacity allows us to operate with volume data up to 128^3 elements. The prebuffer from an oblique direction is generated in less than 8 seconds for a 128 cube. Let n be the edge length of the cube, then the amount of computation is proportional to $n^3 + a \times n^2 + b \times n$ which can be approximated to n^3 for large ns with small errors. The distance coding and the 2D transformation requires 0.6 to 1.5 seconds using a non-aliasing, two step interpolation technique [10]. The variation results from the viewing direction, dependent size of the prebuffer and of the final buffer.

38.4 The voxel-based display processor

The voxel-based display processor permits an interactive, near real-time display and manipulation of objects represented by a grey-scale voxel database. The architecture is highly modular and contains a lot of regularity making it suitable for VSLI implementation. Thanks to the prebuffer algorithm no computational operation more complex than add and compare is required to generate the prebuffer from the 3D data set. The operation is controlled by two tables containing the coordinate offsets of each slice in the prebuffer.

The design goals of the voxel-based display processor are the following:

- An interactive display of segmented 3D objects on a 2D screen with a near real-time update rate.
- Interactive removal of obscuring parts by planes or free form surfaces to allow surgical planning and reveal the internal structure.
- A minimum amount of preprocessing to display 3D objects using segmentation by threshold.
- Mixed generation of shaded-surface display and measured properties coded in colour and selectable grey scale.
- Planar or curved 2D cross-sections with arbitrary orientation showing the measured properties.
- Modular expansion of the system.

38.5 System design considerations

Owing to the limited access bandwidth of large-size dynamic RAM, there is no way around parallel operation of multiple subunits with local volume data memory. The partition of the image memory will avoid access conflicts of the different processing elements and ease the hidden-surface removal using back-to-front projection.

To improve the performance of the display operation these are the most promising possibilities:

- modularization of the algorithm
- use of dedicated hardware
- use of parallel processors

- use of pipelining
- use of faster technology

Our first idea was to use the combination of dedicated hardware, algorithmic modularization and pipelining. This would have led to a very fast implementation of the display operation but, on the other hand, would be limited in operations like segmentation and would not be flexible enough to suit future demands. However, we are going to discuss this approach more in detail in the next section.

38.6 Dedicated hardware

For an extremely fast display realization, the algorithm is modularized by subdividing the data volume into eight cubes with half the edge length. The partial prebuffers are calculated in parallel by specialized hardware and merged in the sequence determined by the components of the viewing direction vector.

The system (Figure 38.1) consists of eight identical modules to generate the partial prebuffers, and is controlled by the host computer which receives the information about the viewing direction, thresholds and clipping planes by user interaction. After transforming, this information is distributed to all modules, where it is used to control the loading of the registers of the address generators and the data manipulators. The subvolume is accessed row by row, and for opaque voxels the true distance from the observer is determined by the data manipulator, and written into the local prebuffer.

The prebuffers are combined in a back-to-front order by the merger to form the sum prebuffer. A separate fast processor is used to warp the sum prebuffer and a further one to generate the gradient shading. The time to carry out the operations in 2D is not limiting, owing to the data reduction from 3D to 2D, which is above 64 : 1 for a 256^3 data matrix.

All 2D buffers are realized as double buffers to obtain a pipelined operation of all stages without collisions and loss of data integrity. Such a system is estimated to generate a surface view of objects in a 256 cube from an oblique orientation with an update rate of four views per second. A similar system using 64 subsystems and a two-level merging process is described in [4], but only a very limited prototype of a submodule was realized [11].

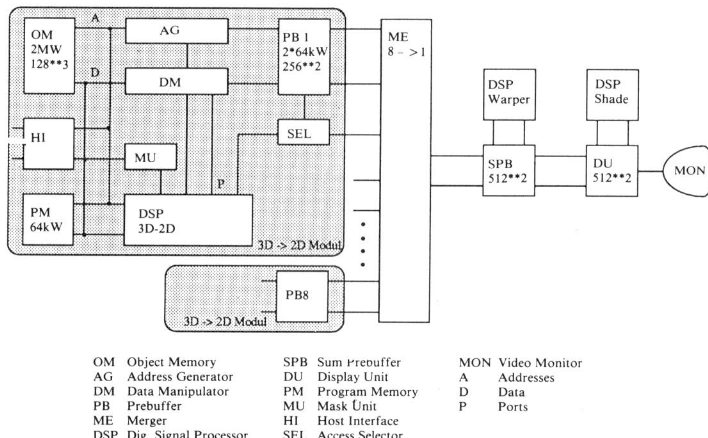

Figure 38.1
Overview of the dedicated hardware for fast generation of shaded surface views from volume data.

38.7 Multitransputer display engine

Encouraged by the good results the implementation of the prebuffer algorithm showed on a single transputer, we examined the use of a multitransputer for this task, applying a parallel version of the algorithm.

Now we are developing the concept for a 9-processor system for direct display of medical data in a 256 cube with the prebuffer algorithm. Eight processors calculate the partial views of the subcubes with edge lengths of 128 voxels. The prebuffers are transmitted over the links and combined in the order given by the components of the viewing direction by the ninth transputer. This transputer controls the system, calculates the coordinate lookup tables and puts the results into the frame buffer.

The processing nodes should be connected in such a way that the partial prebuffers can be merged efficiently for all possible viewing directions. The merging operation can be done either by a single processor sequentially or by multiple processors in different steps working partially in parallel. If a single transputer is collecting the prebuffers, it is necessary to transmit most of them across another node because of the limited number of links. If a multiple-step merging scheme is applied, many different sequences of combining the prebuffers have to be distinguished.

Tests showed that the transmission of the prebuffers over the serial operating links is quite slow, so the idea of using a conventional bus system for moving large data blocks proposed in [12] was considered valuable. To reduce the number of connection lines between the processing nodes, we consider an 8-bit-wide data bus providing 10 Mbytes/s peak rate adequate. The synchronization of the transfer can be achieved using the links. The arbitration of the global bus is done once for a packet and is supervised by the system controller. The destination addresses are generated by the global bus interface and the data is stored in one page of a double buffer disconnected from the memory bus of the destination processor. After completion of the data transfer, the pages are swapped and the buffer contents can be accessed by the destination transputer in the usual way. Such a system would also be of great use for 2D high-speed image processing like filtering, labelling, feature extraction or tracking.

To obtain a projection from an oblique direction in less than one second, it is necessary to improve the innermost loop of the display algorithm by adding supplementary hardware to the data path of the eight volume processors. Two different topologies are shown in Figure 38.2. We use the ability of the transputer to move data with the maximum speed of the connected memory. The supplementary hardware determines the visibility of each voxel by thresholding its density and testing the cutting information. If a voxel is opaque, its distance from the projection plane is written into the prebuffer. This method results in a voxel processing rate of at least 4 million voxels per second at each processor and requires only a few MSI circuits like registers, comparators and counters plus a small static RAM to build the prebuffer. Compared to the software solution, an improvement factor of at least 15 is gained for the data reduction from 3D to 2D.

The operation carried out by supplementary hardware is quite similar to the additional raster graphics operation draw2d of the T800 transputer [13]. The organization of the system is shown in Figure 38.3. This instruction copies a byte of a 2D block (slice of volume data) to the destination block (prebuffer) if it is not

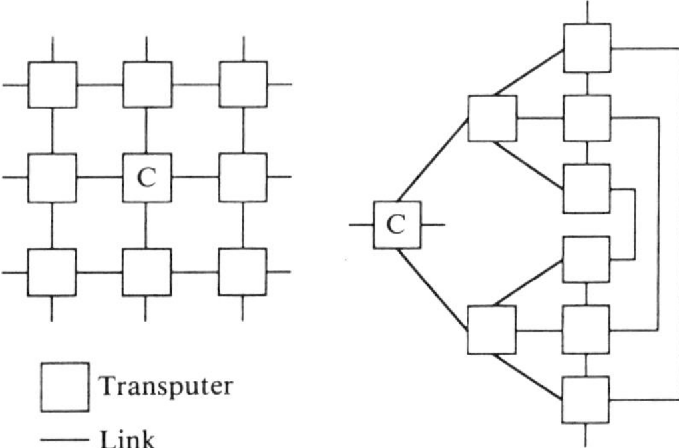

Figure 38.2
Different topologies of the interconnection network.

equal to zero. If this instruction could have been microcoded a little more generally and could allow thresholding, an even more simple and efficient implementation of the prebuffer algorithm would be possible.

Conclusions

Different solutions of the shaded-surface display on a 2D screen with various degrees of specialization and performance have been presented. The general-purpose approach of the multitransputer display engine is favoured, because of the minimum of hardware requirements compared to the performance and because of the ease of programming in a high-level language. The use of available VLSI circuits featuring a fast and power saving CMOS technology results in a reliable, compact and affordable desktop display station for the physician.

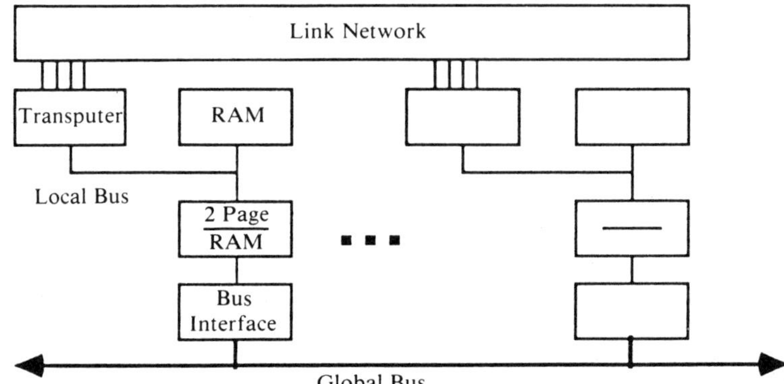

Figure 38.3
Overall architecture of the multitransputer display engine.

Future work

The realization of the multitransputer system described above is in progress. Parallel to the building of the hardware, the prebuffer display algorithm is being adopted and new features are being integrated. In the next phase of the project, we plan to implement automatic segmentation in 3D. The proposed architecture seems to be quite well-suited because for each voxel being tested only a local neighbourhood has to be taken into account.

Acknowledgements

The author wishes to thank J. Yla-Jaaski for the valuable contributions and S. Mathis for the implementation of the image transform operations on a digital signal processor. The work is supported by Schweizerischer Nationalfonds grant 2.931-0.85.

References

1. Herman G.T. and Liu H.K. (1979). Three-dimensional display of human organs from computed tomograms. *Computer Graphics and Image Processing*, 9, 1–21
2. Udupa J.K. (1983). Display of 3D information in discrete 3D scenes produced by computerized tomography. *Proc. IEEE,* **71**, 420–31
3. Tuy H.K. and Tuy L.T. (1984). Direct 2-D display of 3-D objects. *IEEE Computer Graphics and Applications,* **4**, 29–34
4. Frieder G., Gordon D. and Reynolds R.A. (1985). Back to front display of voxel-based objects. *IEEE Computer Graphics and Applications,* **5**, 52–60
5. Klein F. and Kübler O. (1986). Fast direct display of discrete volume data. In *Proc. 8th ICPR*, pp. 633–5. Paris, 1986
6. Klein F. and Kübler O. (1986). A prebuffer algorithm for instant display of volume data, *Proc. SPIE*, 596, 1986
7. Kübler O., Yla-Jaaski J. and Hiltebrand E. (1987). 3D segmentation and real time display of medical volume images. In *Proceedings of the International Symposium CAR 87*, pp. 637–41. In Berlin
8. Gordon D. and Reynolds R.A. (1985). Image space shading of 3-dimensional objects. *Computer Vision, Graphics and Image Processing,* **29**, 361–76
9. INMOS Limited (1986). Transputer Reference Manual. Bristol
10. Fant K.M. (1986). A nonaliasing, real-time transform technique. *IEEE Computer Graphics and Applications*, 71–80
11. Goldwasser S.M. and Reynolds R.A. (1987). Real time display and manipulation of 3-D medical objects: The voxel processor architecture. *Computer Vision, Graphics and Image Processing,* **39**, 1–27
12. Gaudiot J.-L., Dubois M., Lee L.-T. and Thome N.G. (1986). The TX16: a highly programmable multi-microprocessor architecture. *IEEE Micro*, 18–31
13. INMOS Limited (1986). *IMS T800 Architecture*, Technical Note 6. Bristol